THE BICENTENNIAL EDITION
OF THE
WORKS OF JOHN WESLEY

General Editor RICHARD P. HEITZENRATER

Textual Editor FRANK BAKER

THE WORKS OF
JOHN WESLEY

VOLUME 12

DOCTRINAL AND CONTROVERSIAL TREATISES

I

EDITED BY

RANDY L. MADDOX

ABINGDON PRESS
NASHVILLE
2012

THE WORKS OF JOHN WESLEY, VOLUME 12
DOCTRINAL AND CONTROVERSIAL TREATISES I

This book is printed on acid-free paper.

Cataloging-in-Publication Data has been requested from the Library of Congress.

ISBN 978-1-4267-4430-3

The Graeca® font used to print this work is available from Linguist's Software, Inc., P.O. Box 580, Edmonds, WA 98020-0580; telephone (206)775-1130.

12 13 14 15 16 17 18 19 20 21—10 9 8 7 6 5 4 3 2 1

MANUFACTURED IN THE UNITED STATES OF AMERICA

THE BICENTENNIAL EDITION OF THE WORKS OF JOHN WESLEY

THIS edition of the works of John Wesley reflects the quickened interest in the heritage of Christian thought that has become evident during the last half century. A fully critical presentation of Wesley's writings had long been a desideratum in order to furnish documentary sources illustrating his contribution to both catholic and evangelical Christianity.

Several scholars, notably Professor Albert C. Outler, Professor Franz Hildebrandt, Dean Merrimon Cuninggim, and Dean Robert E. Cushman, discussed the possibility of such an edition. Under the leadership of Dean Cushman, a Board of Directors was formed in 1960 comprising the deans of four sponsoring theological schools of Methodist-related universities in the United States: Drew, Duke, Emory, and Southern Methodist. They appointed an Editorial Committee to formulate plans and enlisted an international and interdenominational team of scholars for the Wesley Works Editorial Project.

The works were divided into units of cognate material, with a separate editor (or joint editors) responsible for each unit. Dr. Frank Baker was appointed textual editor for the whole project, with responsibility for supplying each unit editor with a critically developed, accurate Wesley text. The text seeks to represent Wesley's thought in its fullest and most deliberate expression insofar as this can be determined from the available evidence. Substantive variant readings in any British edition published during Wesley's lifetime are shown in appendices to the units, preceded by a summary of the problems faced and the solutions reached in the complex task of securing and presenting Wesley's text. The aim throughout is to enable Wesley to be read with maximum ease and understanding, and with minimal intrusion by the editors.

This edition includes all Wesley's original or mainly original prose works, together with one volume devoted to his *Collection of Hymns* (1780) and another to his extensive work as editor and publisher of extracts from the writings of others. An essential feature of the project is a Bibliography outlining the historical settings of the works published by Wesley and his brother Charles, sometimes jointly, sometimes separately. The Bibliography also offers full analytical data for identifying each of the two thousand editions of these 450 items that were published during the lifetime of John Wesley, and notes the location of copies. An index is supplied for each unit and a General Index for the whole edition.

The Delegates of the Oxford University Press agreed to undertake publication, but announced in June 1982 that because of severe economic problems, they would regretfully be compelled to withdraw from the enterprise with the completion in 1983 of volume 7, the *Collection of Hymns*. Abingdon Press offered its services, beginning with the publication of the first volume of the *Sermons* in 1984, the bicentennial year of the formation of American Methodism as an autonomous church. The new title now assumed, however, refers in general to the bicentennial of Wesley's total activities as author, editor, and publisher, from 1733 to 1791, especially as summarized in the first edition of his collected works in thirty-two volumes, 1771–74.

Dean Robert E. Cushman of Duke University undertook general administration and promotion of the project until 1971, when he was succeeded as President by Dean Joseph D. Quillian Jr. of Southern Methodist University, these two universities having furnished the major support and guidance for the enterprise. During the decade 1961–70, the Editorial Committee supervised the task of setting editorial principles and procedures, and general editorship was shared by Dr. Eric W. Baker, Dean William R. Cannon, and Dean Cushman. In 1969 the Directors appointed Dr. Frank Baker, early attached to the project as bibliographer and textual editor for Wesley's text, as Editor-in-Chief also. Upon Dean Quillian's retirement in 1981, he was succeeded as President of the project by Dean James E. Kirby Jr., also of Southern Methodist University. In 1986 the Directors appointed Richard P. Heitzenrater as General Editor to begin the chief editorship of the project with the *Journal and Diaries* unit, with Dr. Baker continuing as textual editor. Dean Dennis M. Campbell of Duke University was elected President of the project in 1990. Dean Russell E. Richey of Emory University succeeded Dr. Campbell in 2003. At that same point the directors named Randy L. Maddox as Associate General Editor, to work alongside Dr. Heitzenrater in completing the project. Most recently, Dean William B. Lawrence of Southern Methodist University assumed the role of President in 2006.

Other sponsoring bodies have been successively added to the original four: Boston University School of Theology, the Conference of the Methodist Church of Great Britain, the General Commission on Archives and History of The United Methodist Church, The United Methodist General Board of Higher Education and Ministry, and the World Methodist Council. For the continuing support of the sponsoring institutions, the Directors express their profound thanks. They also gratefully acknowledge the encouragement and financial support that have come from the Historical Societies and Commissions on Archives and History of many Annual Conferences, as well as the donations of private individuals and foundations.

On June 9, 1976, The Wesley Works Editorial Project was incorporated in the state of North Carolina as a nonprofit corporation. In 1977, by-laws were approved governing the appointment and duties of the Directors, their Officers, and their Executive Committee.

The Board of Directors

EDITOR'S PREFACE

THIS volume has been in process—off and on—for many years. As I send it to press, I am deeply aware of how much it owes to the contributions of predecessors and colleagues.

As he did with the other volumes that have appeared to date in this edition of Wesley's *Works*, the late Frank Baker undertook the initial collation and preparation of the critical text for the items included. This is demanding work, which he carried out with great care.

Robert E. Cushman was the original unit editor teamed with Paul Chilcote to handle the collection of Wesley's doctrinal and controversial treatises. While Dr. Cushman was central to initial decisions about the contents and structure of this project, the press of other obligations and his untimely death limited much further contribution. His role passed to Thomas A. Langford, who needed some time to clear his table of other tasks, and just as he was preparing to turn to this project, he was also taken from us unexpectedly. The present volume, and the two following in the series, are offered in tribute to Drs. Cushman and Langford for their role as mentors and models to many of us in Wesley Studies—and particularly their contributions to Paul Chilcote, who worked with them closely.

Paul Chilcote has been the constant presence in this project, helping shape its overall structure, which grew over time to comprise three volumes. He also took primary responsibility for the section of the collection devoted to debates over Christian perfection (to appear in volume 13). I was asked to team with Paul a few years ago. As we divided up the work, I took primary responsibility for the material appearing in this volume. I want to offer special thanks to Paul for his expertise and encouragement that have made my work much easier. I also want to express gratitude to Seattle Pacific University and Duke Divinity School for supporting my work on this project over the past decade.

Randy L. Maddox
William Kellon Quick Professor of Wesleyan and Methodist Studies
Duke Divinity School

CONTENTS

SIGNS, SPECIAL USAGES, ABBREVIATIONS xiii

INTRODUCTION TO WESLEY'S DOCTRINAL AND CONTROVERSIAL TREATISES 1

SECTION I: FOUNDATIONAL TREATISES ON SOTERIOLOGY 23

Introduction to Foundational Treatises on Soteriology 25

The Doctrine of Salvation, Faith, and Good Works (1738) 27
- An Introductory Comment 27
- Text 31

An Extract of Mr. Richard Baxter's Aphorisms of Justification (1745) 45
- An Introductory Comment 45
- Text 53

An Extract from the *Shorter Catechism* of the Westminster Assembly (1753) 89
- An Introductory Comment 89
- Text 92

The Doctrine of Original Sin: According to Scripture, Reason, and *Experience* (1757) 117
- An Introduction 117
- Text 155
  - The Preface 156
  - Part I: The Past and Present State of Mankind 160
  - Part II: The Scriptural Method of Accounting for This Defended 212
  - Part III: An Answer to Mr. Taylor's Supplement 306
  - Part IV: Extracts from Dr. Watts and Mr. Hebden 352
  - Part V: The Doctrine of Original Sin, etc. 402
  - Part VI: The Doctrine of Original Sin Explained and Vindicated 424
  - Part VII: The Doctrine of Original Sin, etc. 448

Appendix
Wesley's Text: Editions, Transmission, Presentation, and Variant Readings 483

SIGNS, SPECIAL USAGES, ABBREVIATIONS

[ ]	Indicates editorial insertions or substitutions in the original text, or (with a query) doubtful readings.
. . .	Indicates a passage omitted by the writer from the original and so noted by Wesley, usually by a dash.
[. . .]	Indicates a passage omitted silently by Wesley from a text he was quoting, to which the present editor is drawing attention; the brackets are not used in editorial annotations and introductions.
a, b, c	Small superscript letters indicate footnotes supplied by Wesley.
1, 2, 3	Small superscript figures indicate footnotes supplied by the editor.
Cf.	Before a scriptural or other citation by Wesley, indicates that he was quoting with more than minimal inexactness, yet nevertheless displaying the passage as a quotation.
See	Before a scriptural citation, indicates an undoubted allusion or a quotation that was not displayed as such by Wesley, and that is more than minimally inexact.

Wesley's publications. Where a work by Wesley was first published separately, its title is italicized; where it first appeared within a different work, such as a collected volume, the title appears within quotation marks. References such as '*Bibliography*, No. 3' are to the forthcoming bibliography in this edition (vols. 33–34), which has a different numbering system from Richard Green's *Wesley Bibliography*.

Book titles in Wesley's text are italicized if accurate and given in roman type with capitals if inaccurate. If a title consists of only one generic word that forms a major part of the original title, it is italicized; but if it is inaccurate (such as 'Sermons' for a volume titled *Discourses*), it is printed in lowercase roman.

Abbreviations.

Works frequently cited are abbreviated thus:

AV	Authorized Version of the Bible, 1611.
BCP	The Book of Common Prayer, London, 1662.
Bibliography	Frank Baker, *A Descriptive and Analytical Bibliography of the Publications of John and Charles Wesley* (in preparation), vols. 33–34 in this edn.
CW	Charles Wesley.
Homilies (1683)	*Certain Sermons or Homilies Appointed to be Read in Churches in the Time of the late Queen Elizabeth of Famous Memory; and now Thought fit to*

	be Reprinted by Authority from the King's Most Excellent Majesty, Oxford: Thomas Guy, 1683.
JW	John Wesley, 1703–91.
Migne, *Patrologia Graeca*	J.-P. Migne, *Patrologiae cursus completus . . . Series Graeca*, 161 vols., Paris, 1857–66.
Migne, *Patrologia Latina*	J.-P. Migne, *Patrologiae cursus completus . . . Series Latina*, 221 vols., Paris, 1844–91.
NT Notes	John Wesley, *Explanatory Notes Upon the New Testament*, 3rd corrected edn., Bristol: Graham and Pine, 1760–62.
OED (2nd edn.)	*The Oxford English Dictionary*, 2nd edn., New York: Oxford University Press, 1989.
Works (1771–74)	John Wesley, *The Works of the Rev. John Wesley*, M.A., 32 vols., Bristol: Pine, 1771–74.

INTRODUCTION TO WESLEY'S DOCTRINAL AND CONTROVERSIAL TREATISES

Volumes 12–14 of this edition of John Wesley's *Works* are devoted to his doctrinal and controversial treatises. In approaching these materials, it is helpful to recognize their distinctive place within the larger body of Wesley's theological writings and the larger background against which Wesley undertook this genre of theological engagement.

I. Wesley the 'Practical Theologian' and the Range of His Theological Activity

From shortly after his death, through much of the twentieth century, it was common for scholars to dismiss characterizations of Wesley as a 'theologian'. This was as true among his Methodist heirs as it was among the critics of Methodism. Over the last few decades it has become clear that this dismissal resulted in large part from judging Wesley by an anachronistic (and increasingly challenged) standard—the model of theology that now dominates the Western academy.[1] The more appropriate standard for evaluating Wesley's theological activity is a long-standing earlier conception and practice of theology.

This earlier approach, tracing back to the beginnings of the Church, identified theology as ultimately a practical discipline (*scientia practica*) and reflected an awareness of several dimensions to this enterprise. The foundational dimension was the basic orientation of believers to their lives in the world. As Paul put it,

[1] For more on this point, see Randy L. Maddox, 'Reclaiming an Inheritance: Wesley as Theologian in the History of Methodist Theology', in Maddox, ed., *Rethinking Wesley's Theology for Contemporary Methodism* (Nashville: Kingswood Books, 1998), 213-26.

Christians perceive things rightly and act appropriately only when they have the 'mind of Christ' (1 Cor. 2:16; see Phil. 2). That this involves holistic dispositions, not merely intellectual convictions, is evident from Paul's parallel emphasis on Christians nurturing the 'fruit of the Spirit' (Gal. 5:22-23). The mind of Christ fosters and is reciprocally strengthened by, for example, loving service to and with others.

Paul's passionate appeal for Christians to emulate the mind of Christ reflects the reality that this orienting disposition is not unilaterally infused by God at one's conversion. Neither does it emerge spontaneously over time. It must be cultivated as part of the intentional process of growing in Christlikeness. This need defined the second dimension of the earliest Christian model of theology—the pastoral task of nurturing and (re)shaping the self-understanding or worldview of believers. In keeping with its holistic goal, this task involved a variety of first-order activities aimed at invoking and shaping beliefs, affections, and character dispositions. As such, early Christians came to prize most highly as 'theologians' those who crafted formative practical-theological materials like hymns, liturgies, catechetical orations, and spiritual discipline manuals.

These activities in turn frequently spawned second-order normative activities (a third dimension of the overall theological enterprise). That is, they sparked debates and writings focusing not only on the adequacy of particular practices for forming a Christian worldview but also on alternative conceptions of this basic worldview and alternative proposed implications of the worldview for concrete action in the world. But even at this second-order level, theology remained a practical discipline, ultimately basing the most metaphysical reflections about God on the life of faith and drawing from these reflections ethical and soteriological implications.

Moving beyond these dimensions that focused primarily on those who had embraced (to some degree) the Christian worldview, the fourth dimension evident in this earlier approach to theological activity was the apologetic/evangelistic concern to engage those who are questioning or rejecting central Christian beliefs and practices.

One further perennial dimension of the overall theological enterprise is the concern to train new generations to carry out the formative, normative, and apologetic dimensions. Through the first millennium, this took place largely by mentoring. As such, it generated few distinctive forms of theological expression. One learned how to engage in first-order, second-order, and apologetic activities under the guidance of a practicing pastor, abbot, catechist, and so on. By contrast, as specialized academic institutions increasingly subsumed this training task in Western Christianity in the second millennium, it became common to privilege the curricular forms developed within this new setting (compendiums, *summae*, systematic theologies, and the like) as serious theology, and to consider the instructors in these institutions the real theologians.

Significantly, Wesley's context stood in some contrast to this trend. Early leaders in the Church of England assigned special authority to the beliefs and practices of the early Church. Among precedents that they imbibed from this focus was the model of theology as a practical discipline. This is evidenced partly by the forms chosen for articulating official doctrine. Like the early Church, theological energy was devoted particularly to expositing creeds, constructing liturgies (the Book of Common Prayer), and providing catechetical sermons (the *Homilies*). Further evidence would be the typical insistence in a manual for clergy candidates that Wesley read shortly before his own ordination that 'theology is doubtless a *practical science*, [there is] nothing in it but aims at this end'.[2]

Thus, as Wesley understood and engaged in theological activity (or, as they called it at that time, 'divinity'), the defining task was not to develop an elaborate system of Christian truth-claims; it was to nurture and shape the worldview or disposition that orients believers' lives in the world. Pastor-theologians (divines) may well engage in apologetic dialogues or in debates over doctrinal issues, but ideally because—and to the extent that—these are in service to their more central task.

This means that Wesley would have considered the first-order literary forms of liturgy, catechism, hymn, sermon, and the like to be central to the work of theologians. But they would not have been the exclusive forms. Eighteenth-century English authors typically identified three types of theology: (1) practical divinity, focused on helping individuals practice the Christian life, (2) doctrinal or speculative divinity, concerned with articulating and defending specific doctrines, and (3) controversial divinity, aimed at criticizing on rational,

[2] George Bull, *A Companion for the Candidates of Holy Orders* (London: Richard Smith, 1714), 18. Wesley records reading this work in his Oxford diary on Sept. 18, 1725.

historical, or scriptural grounds the beliefs and practices of rival groups.[3] Most first-order literary forms fit naturally within practical divinity. The other two types of eighteenth-century divinity, which each intertwined the second-order dimensions of normative reflection and apologetic engagement, were more likely to take the form of monographs, essays, and tracts.

Much of Wesley's published work gathered in this edition clearly fits in the first-order category of practical divinity—beginning with his collections of *Sermons*[4] and moving through his comments on Scripture, the 1780 *Collection of Hymns*,[5] his careful recrafting of the liturgy in the Book of Common Prayer, his devotional and catechetical materials, and his fifty-volume abridgment of similar work by others in the *Christian Library*. Isabel Rivers has even argued that his *Journal* may be the most important work of practical divinity in the eighteenth century.[6] The dominance of this genre is no accident; it reflects Wesley's conscious privileging of the formative dimension of theological activity, which he often defended by a quotation from the early Church: 'God made practical divinity necessary; the devil, controversial.'[7]

Despite his preference, Wesley recognized that the other dimensions of theological activity can play a critical role in service to the formative dimension, and he engaged them as occasion demanded. The works gathered in these three volumes are the fruit of that engagement, comprising his major output in (second-order) doctrinal and controversial divinity.[8] They touch on a wide spectrum of doctrinal topics and stake out Wesley's position in a range of debates in his day. Some are book length, with one being the longest monograph he ever published; others were circulated

[3] See Isabel Rivers, 'Dissenting and Methodist Books of Practical Divinity', in I. Rivers, ed., *Books and Their Readers in Eighteenth-Century England* (New York: St. Martin's, 1982), 127-64.

[4] JW was following here a standard Anglican model, echoed in his father's advice, of preparing a set of sermons that offers, as much as possible, 'the whole body of divinity'. See Samuel Wesley, *Advice to a Young Clergyman* (London: Rivington, 1735), 56.

[5] The Preface, §4, 7:74 in this edn., designates the collection a 'little body of experimental and practical divinity'.

[6] Rivers, 'Practical Divinity', 152.

[7] E.g., *Journal*, Nov. 19, 1751, 20:407 in this edn.; and letter to Joseph Benson, July 31, 1773.

[8] The *Appeals* and open letters gathered in vol. 11 of this edn. fit broadly in these categories as well.

as tracts in the midst of debates and as essays in the *Arminian Magazine*.

II. The Theological Spectrum within which Wesley Engaged Doctrinal Issues

Doctrinal reflection and debate are inherently dialogical. Insights emerge, emphases are maintained, and counterarguments are framed in response to alternative views on the issues at hand. As such, Wesley's doctrinal and controversial treatises are best read with some awareness of the theological spectrum within which they were composed. This spectrum was quite broad, due to the distinctive history that lay behind it.

The original split of the Church of England from Rome was more over jurisdictional matters than theological concerns. Henry VIII was no champion of Protestant agendas. Through his reign, there were mixed influences of moderate Lutheranism and currents of the Reformed tradition with strong continuing Catholic sympathies. When Edward VI was enthroned (1547), the Reformed influences grew stronger, but this was abruptly halted by Edward's death and the ascension of Mary Tudor (1553), who attempted to restore Roman Catholic primacy in England. While Mary's short rule produced several hundred martyrs, it did not accomplish her broader goal. Elizabeth I quickly renewed the autonomy of the Church of England from Rome and provided stability for this status through her extended tenure on the throne (1558–1603).

The Elizabethan church is often described as a *via media* (middle way) between Rome and Geneva (as the eventual center of the Reformed tradition). This description may fit when considering issues of church organization and liturgical practice, but not the larger theological tone of the period. It suggests that the mainstream of the Church held to moderating views on central issues like predestination and justification, similar to the stance of Philip Melanchthon. Recent studies have built a strong case that the majority of church leaders and educated laity in the Elizabethan church were instead solidly Reformed in their theological commitments and stress how this identity carried over through the reign of James I (1603–25).[9] If this majority stance considered itself a theological *via media*, it was as a broadly Reformed church (drawing as heavily from Strasbourg and Zürich as from Geneva) that spurned the antipodal dangers of the Roman church and the Radical Reformation (Anabaptists, spiritualists, and so on). Another way to put this is that it was a blending of Reformed faith with Catholic order.

To be sure, this general identity was not uniform. There were moderate voices in the Elizabethan and Jacobian eras like Lancelot Andrewes, Richard Hooker, and John Overall, who challenged (at least by tone and emphasis) some aspects of standard Reformed teaching.[10] There were also continuing traces of Anabaptist and Erasmian 'freewill' traditions on the fringes of the Church.[11] Thus, the overall spectrum within the Church of England in 1625 stretched from the few Laudians on one pole to the nonconforming Puritans on the other (who differed from the mainstream not by being Reformed but by resisting the use in worship of ritual and ornate furnishings that they considered non-scriptural).[12]

When Charles I took the throne in 1625, William Laud and some associates were given key leadership roles in the Church. They emphasized episcopal authority, sacramental piety, and the use of liturgy and symbolism in worship, while downplaying or rejecting

[9] This case was staked out by Patrick Collinson, *The Religion of Protestants: The Church in English Society, 1559–1625* (Oxford: Clarendon, 1982); and Dewey D. Wallace Jr., *Puritans and Predestination: Grace in English Protestant Theology, 1525–1695* (Chapel Hill: University of North Carolina Press, 1982). It has come under some attack, most notably by Peter White, *Predestination, Policy, and Polemic: Conflict and Consensus in the English Church from the Reformation to the Civil War* (New York: Cambridge University Press, 1992). A good survey of the debate is Dewey D. Wallace Jr., '*Via Media*? A Paradigm Shift', *Anglican and Episcopal History* 72 (2003): 2-21.

[10] Good introductions include Nigel Voak, *Richard Hooker and Reformed Theology: A Study of Reason, Will, and Grace* (New York: Oxford University Press, 2003); and Anthony Milton, '"Anglicanism" by Stealth: The Career and Influence of John Overall', in K. Fincham and P. Lake, eds., *Religious Politics in Post-Reformation England* (Woodbridge: Boydell, 2006), 159-76.

[11] D. Andrew Penny, *Freewill or Predestination: The Battle over Saving Grace in Mid-Tudor England* (Rochester, N.Y.: Boydell Press, 1990).

[12] See the discussion in Daniel W. Doerksen, *Conforming to the Word: Herbert, Donne, and the English Church before Laud* (Lewisburg, Pa.: Bucknell University Press, 1997), 13-24, and his chart on p. 22. Also helpful is Kenneth Hylson-Smith, *The Churches in England from Elizabeth I to Elizabeth II*, 3 vols. (London: SCM Press, 1996–98), vol. 1 covering 1558–1688.

the Reformed stance on predestination. They justified these emphases by appeal to a model of the *via media* that now cast Geneva as the equally undesirable antipode of Rome. This provocative framing struck many of their fellow clergy and English laity as a reversion to 'popery'. The concern this generated played a significant role in the outbreak of civil war in 1642 and the subsequent martyrdoms of Laud (1645) and Charles I (1649).[13]

The Commonwealth government that displaced Charles I was dominated by Puritans. They set about transforming the Church of England towards a presbyterian polity, replacing the Book of Common Prayer with a Reformed Directory of Public Worship, and crafting the Westminster Confession of Faith as an alternative to the Articles of Religion. These were heady times for Puritans, but short-lived. Continuing political chaos led to the recall of Charles II to the throne in 1660, and soon after to the restoration of the Church to its pre-war standards of doctrine and practice. This was capped by the Act of Uniformity of 1662, which forced some two thousand Puritan clergy out of the established Church, effectively ending the hegemony that Reformed theological emphases had held within the Church of England for more than a century.[14]

This dramatic change left the stream of seventeenth-century theologians who shared the High Church emphases of Laud and supported Charles (hence, known as the 'Caroline divines') as the new centrist position within the Church of England. Since those who remained loyal to prayer-book religion and episcopacy during the interregnum had laid special claim to the title 'Anglican', this term has come to be reserved by most scholars to designate those *from this period forward* who stand in the stream flowing from the Caroline divines.[15]

[13] Reading the Puritan revolution as a reaction to the provocation of Laud and others was advanced by Nicholas Tyacke in 'Puritanism, Arminianism, and Counter-Revolution', in Conrad Russell, ed., *The Origins of the English Civil War* (London: Macmillan, 1973), 119-43. Cf. Peter Lake, 'Puritanism, Arminianism, and Nicholas Tyacke', in Fincham and Lake, *Religious Politics*, 1-15.

[14] For a survey of these changes, see John Spurr, *English Puritanism, 1603–1689* (New York: St. Martin's, 1998).

[15] See John W. Packer, *The Transformation of Anglicanism, 1643–1660* (Manchester: Manchester University Press, 1969); and Kenneth Fincham, 'Introduction', in *The Early Stuart Church, 1603–1642* (Stanford: Stanford University Press, 1993), 3-4.

One of the deep concerns of the Caroline divines was to demonstrate continuity of their church with the broad Christian tradition, particularly in its primitive form. This led to a distinct flowering of patristics studies and a particular interest in reintroducing many of the Eastern (Greek-writing) Christian theologians who had been relatively neglected in the (Latin) West.[16] Lest this be seen as a turn to antiquarianism, these divines often invoked the example of the early Christian apologists as warrant for equally engaging the emerging Enlightenment emphases on reason and scientific explanation in British culture. Indeed, the most characteristic feature of emerging Anglican theology was its methodological emphasis on the importance of *integrating* consideration of Scripture, tradition, and reason—as opposed to the one-sided alternatives of biblicism, traditionalism, or rationalism.[17]

The Caroline divines generally shared Laud's view that the doctrine of unconditional reprobation makes 'the God of all mercies to be the most fierce and unreasonable tyrant in the world'.[18] This placed them in the Arminian camp of the current debates within the Reformed arena, even if their rejection of the model of God's unilateral action in salvation drew more from alternative voices in the early Church than from Jacob Arminius and other Remonstrants in the Netherlands.[19]

[16] See esp. Leslie W. Barnard, 'The Use of the Patristic Tradition in the Late Seventeenth and Early Eighteenth Century', in R. Bauckham and B. Drewery, eds., *Scripture, Tradition and Reason* (Edinburgh: T & T Clark, 1988), 174-203; Robert D. Cornwall, 'The Search for the Primitive Church: The Use of Early Church Fathers in the High Church Anglican Tradition, 1680–1745', *Anglican and Episcopal History* 59 (1990): 303-29; and Jean-Louis Quantin, *The Church of England and Christian Antiquity: The Construction of a Confessional Identity in the 17th Century* (New York: Oxford University Press, 2009), 155-202.

[17] See Henry R. McAdoo, *The Spirit of Anglicanism: A Survey of Anglican Theological Method in the Seventeenth Century* (New York: Charles Scribner's Sons, 1965). Concerning their approach to Scripture, see Gerard Reedy, *The Bible and Reason: Anglicans and Scripture in Late Seventeenth-Century England* (Philadelphia: University of Pennsylvania Press, 1985). For their emphasis on reason, see Frederick C. Beiser, *The Sovereignty of Reason: The Defense of Rationality in the Early English Enlightenment* (Princeton: Princeton University Press, 1996).

[18] William Laud, 'Answer to the Lord Say's Speech Touching the Liturgy', in *The History of the Troubles and Trial of the most Reverend Father in God, and blessed martyr, William Laud*, 2 vols. (London: Richard Chiswell, 1695–1700), 1:503.

[19] See the discussion of Richard Montagu's sources in White, *Predestination*, 215-17; and John Spurr, *The Restoration Church of England, 1649–89* (New Haven: Yale University Press, 1991), 311-30.

The Caroline divines also shared a deep uneasiness with antinomian themes developed by some Reformed writers defending justification by faith *alone*.[20] Jeremy Taylor was particularly prominent in developing an alternative conception of justifying faith, which emphasized the vital connection of true faith with obedience and love. Drawing on the title of his most influential book (*The Rule and Exercises of Holy Living*), those contemporaries who shared Taylor's stress are often designated 'holy living divines'. For some scholars they epitomize the regrettable turn from authentic Reformation theology towards moralism; for others, they represent a long-needed recovery of broad Christian emphases in spirituality into the Augustinian West.[21]

Hesitancies about predestination and antinomian models of justification were not limited to the emergent Anglicans in the second half of the seventeenth century. Indeed, fractures had begun to emerge in the Puritan camp during the reign of Charles I, as they interacted with the opposing Laudians. While most defended Reformed orthodoxy, some proposed moderating alternatives to limited atonement, unconditional reprobation, and justification by faith alone. Over time a few of these moderates (most notably John Goodwin and John Milton) shifted to an explicit Arminian stance on these issues, sparking the expected rebuttals. Others like Richard Baxter sought to be peacemakers, while modifying rigorous Calvinism in many aspects.[22]

One other issue that dominated the second half of the seventeenth century was whether the Church of England should define itself broadly enough in terms of doctrinal commitments and liturgical practices to include (or 'comprehend') both the Puritan and the Anglican parties. This debate emerged during the Commonwealth period with Puritans as the default establishment and eventually

[20] The main such 'antinomians' were Tobias Crisp (1600–1643), John Eaton (1574/5–1641), and John Saltmarsh (d. 1647). Saltmarsh is mentioned in Wesley's extract of Baxter's *Aphorisms*, Prop. XVII (below, pp. 69-70).

[21] Cf. the strongly negative evaluation of Taylor in C. FitzSimons Allison, *The Rise of Moralism: The Proclamation of the Gospel from Hooker to Baxter* (Wilton, Conn.: Morehouse-Barlow, 1966), with that in Rowan A. Greer, *Christian Hope and Christian Life* (New York: Herder, 2001).

[22] See David Como, 'Puritans, Predestination, and the Construction of Orthodoxy in Early Seventeenth-Century England', in P. Lake and M. Questier, eds., *Conformity and Orthodoxy in the English Church, c. 1560–1660* (Rochester, N.Y.: Boydell, 2000), 64-87; and Ellen More, 'John Goodwin and the Origins of the New Arminianism', *Journal of British Studies* 22 (1982): 50-70.

reappeared under Charles II with the Anglicans now in this role.[23] The (minority) 'broad church' stance on this issue argued for limiting required conformity on doctrine and practice to only the 'essentials', allowing as large a range as possible for varying opinions on non-essential items.[24]

Towards the end of the reign of Charles II, there was mounting support to broaden the definition of the Church of England, with a goal of reincorporating the Puritans who had been pushed into (minimally tolerated) Dissenting churches in the 1660s. This support crumbled when James II succeeded to the throne in 1685. James had converted to the Roman church and pushed to include Roman Catholics in the circle to be comprehended—or at least tolerated. For the vast majority of his citizens, including the Anglican bishops, this was too much. The staunchly Reformed William of Orange, who was married to James's daughter Mary (also Protestant), was encouraged to invade, and he soon drove James into exile. William was then put on the throne, with support for this move gathered in part by issuing the Act of Toleration in 1689, which granted freedom of worship to all Dissenting churches that were trinitarian except Roman Catholics.

In opting for toleration of the Dissenters (rather than their comprehension), the Anglican stance of the Church of England was generally solidified, even if a sprinkling of Reformed theologians and clergy remained in the Established Church.[25] But the Anglican stance was also modified by a side effect of William's replacement of James II. A group of nine bishops and more than three hundred clergy refused to take the Oath of Allegiance to William and Mary on the grounds that they had taken a previous oath to James II—who was still alive—and could not break it. These Nonjurors[26] were generally the Anglicans who put the most stress on conformity to the teaching and practice of the early Church, and part of their hesitation was the lack of precedent in the early Church for supporting a revolution against a reigning sovereign. They were deprived of their

[23] See the survey of these debates in Norman Sykes, *From Sheldon to Secker: Aspects of English Church History, 1660–1768* (Cambridge: Cambridge University Press, 1959), 68-104.

[24] A good overview of those making this case can be found in Paul Avis, *Anglicanism and the Christian Church* (Minneapolis: Fortress, 1989), 117-54.

[25] See Stephen Hampton, *Anti-Arminians: The Anglican Reformed Tradition from Charles II to George I* (New York: Oxford University Press, 2008).

[26] 'Jurare' in Latin means to 'take an oath'.

positions in 1689, becoming a splinter tradition that dwindled over the coming century. While they continued to have some influence, their departure left the theological stance of the Established Church less primitivist in emphasis and somewhat less High Church.

In contrast with its predecessor, the eighteenth century was void of major political changes that directly shifted theological stances in the Church of England. From the end of the Stuart reign under Queen Anne (1702–14) through the successive Hanovers (Georges I, II, and III) the general Anglican commitments of the church remained in place. There was a relative tone of peace and unity within the Church. The differences are best understood as a spectrum of *tendencies* rather than as aggressively competing parties.[27]

The Anglican commitments that were most broadly shared across this spectrum through the century were the Arminian rejection of unconditional predestination and the holy living discomfort with emphasis on justification by faith *alone*. While the departure of the Nonjurors left the Church with fewer stalwart defenders of the High Church commitments inherited from Laud, some prominent voices kept them as part of the mix through the century.[28] The most significant theological tensions within Anglicanism during this time emerged around the dynamics of theological method—converging forces challenged the Caroline ideal of seeking the consensus of early Christian tradition, Scripture, and reason.[29]

One stream of the challenge was the growing awareness that early Christian tradition was neither as unified nor as developed as the Caroline divines had assumed. There were variations in belief and practice within the Church from the beginning. Some central teachings, like the doctrine of the Trinity, reached full formulation only in the fourth century—and then with some continuing differences of emphasis between the (Greek-speaking) Eastern and

[27] See John Walsh and Stephen Taylor, 'Introduction: The Church and Anglicanism in the "Long" Eighteenth Century', in Walsh et al., eds., *The Church of England, c. 1689–c. 1833* (New York: Cambridge University Press, 1993), 1-64; and William Gibson, *The Church of England, 1688–1832: Unity and Accord* (London: Routledge, 2001).

[28] See F. C. Mather, *High Church Prophet: Bishop Samuel Horsley (1733–1806) and the Caroline Tradition in the Later Georgian Church* (Oxford: Clarendon, 1992), esp. 1-23; and Peter B. Nockles, *The Oxford Movement in Context: Anglican High Churchmanship, 1760–1857* (New York: Cambridge University Press, 1994).

[29] For details on the following summary see Sykes, *Sheldon to Secker*, 140-87; and Gordon Rupp, *Religion in England, 1688–1791* (Oxford: Clarendon, 1986), 243-77.

(Latin-speaking) Western churches. Recognition of this reality opened the door to arguments that these later formulations were not organic developments from Scripture but ill-fitting metaphysical impositions upon it. Samuel Clarke's *Scripture Doctrine of the Trinity* (1712) exemplified this strategy. Many of Clarke's peers read him as equating the teaching of the New Testament (and some of the earliest church fathers) with an Arian model of the Godhead, fueling a debate that spanned the century.[30]

The instinctive Anglican response to a proposal like that of Clarke was to defend the authority of conciliar tradition. Several such defenses were published. But the growing embrace of Enlightenment assumptions in eighteenth-century British culture eroded the persuasiveness of these defenses for many readers. To be sure, the dominant British appropriation of Enlightenment emphases was distinctly more religious in tone and conservative in politics than, for example, in France.[31] But it still included the tendency to question *merely traditional* authority, calling for truth-claims to be based on criteria that are available to any person at any time—with reason and empirical experience being the most broadly accepted examples. The impact of Clarke's *Scripture Doctrine* reflects how he conformed to these criteria, asking readers to investigate Scripture anew (as did the earliest church fathers) and decide for themselves which model of the Godhead was most supported by the evidence. Several of Clarke's respondents chose to restrict their focus as well to the biblical text, providing alternative arguments about which interpretation of this evidence was most reasonable. In the process they quietly left the question of tradition on the side or, more radically, suggested that only the non-technical teachings of Scripture should be considered essential to affirm, placing traditional doctrinal elaborations in the category of non-essential opinions. The tendency to move in

[30] The developments leading up to Clarke are well described in Philip Dixon, *Nice and Hot Disputes: The Doctrine of the Trinity in the Seventeenth Century* (London: T & T Clark, 2003). Clarke and similar 18th-century British voices are well surveyed in Maurice Wiles, *Archetypal Heresy: Arianism through the Ages* (Oxford: Clarendon, 1996), 62-164. But note as well the argument that Clarke was actually endorsing the more Eastern model of the Trinity in Thomas Pfizenmaier, *The Trinitarian Theology of Dr. Samuel Clarke* (New York: Brill, 1997).

[31] This thesis has been argued particularly by J. G. A. Pocock. See the helpful summary and reflections in Knud Haakonssen, 'Enlightened Dissent: An Introduction', in *Enlightenment and Religion: Rational Dissent in Eighteenth-Century Britain* (New York: Cambridge University Press, 1996), 1-11.

this direction, which began in the mid-seventeenth century, is usually called 'latitudinarianism'.[32] It became fairly widespread among Church of England clergy during Wesley's era.

Those moving in this direction inevitably confronted another stream of the challenge to the Caroline ideal, the stream focused on the special status assigned to the Bible. In this case, the growing awareness was of other religions that affirmed some of the same truths as the Bible. The traditional account assigned the similarities to God's somewhat ambiguous 'general revelation' and affirmed the distinctive claims of Christianity as fruits of God's clearer 'special revelation'. But a few freethinkers like John Toland and Matthew Tindal vied to reverse this valuation. Invoking the Enlightenment standard of universality as a criterion of truth, they proposed that those places where Christian teaching was shared by broader humanity were most central and reliable, while distinctive elements should be considered non-essential or recognized as only allegories of universal truths. Some other provocateurs offered related suggestions for elements in Scripture like predictive prophecy and miracles, which they took to be in conflict with the universal laws of nature being discovered by modern science.[33] The overall result (which only the most liberal latitudinarians embraced) was to replace Christian revelation with natural religion as the normative basis for belief and practice.

Toland and his compatriots are typically called 'deists', which reflects that they still believed in a God who upholds order in the universe and moral accountability. Overt deists remained a small group in England through the eighteenth century. Explicit atheism was even rarer, particularly in contrast with the contemporary situation in France.[34]

[32] See John Spurr, '"Latitudinarianism" and the Restoration Church', *Historical Journal* 31 (1988): 61-82; and W. M. Spellman, *The Latitudinarians and the Church of England, 1660–1700* (Athens: University of Georgia Press, 1993).

[33] These challenges are highlighted (and a bit overplayed) in John Redwood, *Reason, Ridicule, and Religion: The Age of Enlightenment in England, 1660–1750* (Cambridge, Mass.: Harvard University Press, 1976); and Roy Porter, *The Creation of the Modern World* (New York: Norton, 2000), 96-129.

[34] See B. W. Young, *Religion and Enlightenment in Eighteenth-Century England* (Oxford: Clarendon, 1998); in some comparison with Gerald R. Cragg, *Reason and Authority in the Eighteenth Century* (Cambridge: Cambridge University Press, 1964).

Dissenting churches could no more escape the impact of the Enlightenment currents in eighteenth-century British culture than could the Established Church.[35] Since most of these traditions shared Puritan roots, surveys of their differences often focus on polity—distinguishing Presbyterians, Congregationalists, and Baptists. But the more significant divergence through this century was their response to the Enlightenment trend in broader culture and the Established Church. Many (particularly in Presbyterian circles) embraced the rejection of creedal traditions and the positive estimate of human ability to pursue virtue. Appealing to rational interpretation of Scripture as their norm, they shifted towards Arminian (and eventually Socinian) conclusions about soteriology, while adopting Arian (and eventually Unitarian) conclusions about the nature of Christ.[36] In sharp rebuttal, other Dissenters (more often Independents or Congregationalists) vigorously defended Reformed orthodoxy. The Baptists, who came into the eighteenth century already divided into Arminian and Calvinist branches, had these divisions reinforced by the pressures of the century.[37]

While the Quakers (or Society of Friends) were included among the tolerated Dissenters, their emphasis on the inner light of the Spirit over all external authorities continued through the eighteenth century to raise fears of enthusiasm from the range of other churches. By contrast, the continuing fear about Roman Catholics focused not just on their perceived superstitious practices and theological errors, but on the political danger of renewed submission to the pope.

One other dynamic in eighteenth-century British religious life became central to Wesley's spiritual journey and to his doctrinal and controversial writings—the evangelical revival that bubbled up in

[35] Good surveys of these traditions can be found in Hylson-Smith, *Churches in England*, vol. 2, 1689–1833; Isabel Rivers, *Reason, Grace and Sentiment: A Study of the Language of Religion and Ethics in England, 1660–1780*, 2 vols. (New York: Cambridge University Press, 1991–2000), 1:90-204; Rupp, *Religion in England*, 108-79; and Michael Watts, *The Dissenters* (Oxford: Clarendon, 1978), 394-490.

[36] See particularly Jeremy Goring, 'The Break-Up of the Old Dissent', in C. G. Bolam et al., eds., *The English Presbyterians* (London: Allen & Unwin, 1968), 175-218; and David Steers, 'Arminianism Amongst Protestant Dissenters in England and Ireland in the Eighteenth Century,' in T. M. Van Leeuwen et al., eds., *Arminius, Arminianism, and Europe* (Leiden: Brill, 2009), 159-200. These developments are elaborated below in the introduction to JW's *Doctrine of Original Sin*.

[37] Raymond Brown, *The English Baptists of the Eighteenth Century* (London: Baptist Historical Society, 1986).

continental European Pietism, spilled over to Britain, and spread to North America.[38] At the heart of this 'religion of the heart' was the concern that Christian identity not be equated with mere church affiliation or mere intellectual affirmation of Christian doctrine. In reaction to this tendency that they perceived around them, Pietists emphasized the importance of a *personal* faith in Christ's atoning work that is evidenced by a specific *experience* of assurance (the witness of the Holy Spirit). They also developed innovative structures and practices to nurture this personal experience of faith.

As Pietist currents began to spread in England in the early eighteenth century, two negative evaluations were common, particularly in the Established Church: (1) their emphasis on personal assurance was judged to be an inappropriate elevation of emotions over reason; and (2) they were often accused of being antinomians. Behind this second charge was the tendency of Pietists, who emerged in strongly Protestant settings, to frame their emphasis on vital personal faith in terms of reliance on *faith alone* for justification. This ran directly counter to the holy living sensibilities of most Anglicans and many Dissenters. On the other hand, it provided a point of contact for the small contingent of Reformed clergy that had remained in the Established Church after 1662. This wing, which had dwindled to near extinction by 1730, was rejuvenated through this contact and began to grow slowly as the evangelical wing of the church.[39]

The items collected in these three volumes reflect that John Wesley had connections with most of the currents that have been highlighted in this historical review. His grandfathers on both sides—John Westley (*c.* 1636–70) and Samuel Annesley (*c.* 1620–96)—were Puritan clergy expelled from the Established Church when Charles II was recalled. Yet both of John's parents opted as young adults to return to the Established Church. Samuel and Susanna clearly shared the Anglican commitments concerning predestination, holy living, primitivism, and High Church spirituality. Their most famous disagreement was over William of Orange replacing James II, which Samuel supported while Susanna joined

[38] Good overviews are Ted Campbell, *The Religion of the Heart* (Columbia: University of South Carolina Press, 1991); and W. R. Ward, *The Protestant Evangelical Awakening* (New York: Cambridge University Press, 1992). See also Rupp, *Religion in England*, 325-490.

[39] See Kenneth Hylson-Smith, *Evangelicals in the Church of England, 1734–1984* (Edinburgh: T & T Clark, 1988).

in the Nonjuror dissent. Thus John imbibed classic Anglican sensibilities in his youth, including the deep appreciation for early Church doctrine and practice championed by the Nonjurors. These commitments were reinforced by his Oxford training, which privileged the writings of the Caroline divines. But Wesley was also exposed to the currents of Enlightenment thought in his academic work. And on his trip to Georgia he made contact with the emerging evangelical movement in its Moravian form. This contact led to Wesley's spiritual renewal in 1738 and the beginnings of the Methodist Revival.

With the revival came the inevitable questions and criticisms of onlookers, which were the stimulus for the earliest doctrinal and controversial treatises gathered below. While Wesley reluctantly undertook this form of theological publication, there were few in his day who were as well prepared to engage the range of debates that ensued.

III. The Situational Nature of Wesley's Doctrinal and Controversial Treatises

Given the spectrum of eighteenth-century British religion, Wesley found it necessary to define and defend the emerging Methodist movement on a variety of theological fronts—often alternating from one to another. For example, in the summer of 1739, at the outset of the revival, some in Bristol accused Wesley of being 'a Papist, if not a Jesuit' because he was preaching outside the channels of the Established Church. Wesley rebutted them by stressing how his preaching emphasized 'justification by faith alone'.[40] But this response led Josiah Tucker, a local Anglican priest, to then ascribe to Wesley the potential antinomian imbalance of 'faith alone', requiring Wesley to turn and defend his preaching as conforming to the Anglican standards of doctrine.[41]

[40] *Journal*, Aug. 27, 1739, 19:89 in this edn.

[41] See *Principles of a Methodist*, §§2-10, 9:50-53 in this edn.

Within such multifront dynamics, it is not too surprising that Wesley was accused of inconsistencies in his various publications.[42] He typically rejected such charges, often arguing that the supposed inconsistencies reflected simply the accuser's failure to recognize variations in the situations or audiences being addressed. For example, if he had preached mainly about forgiveness of sins early in the revival, and later shifted his emphasis more to the need for growing in holiness, it was because his early audience was heavily comprised of unbelievers while his later audience was predominantly followers who had begun the Christian life.[43]

This appeal to the contextual and occasional dynamics of doctrinal and controversial writings is in keeping with the nature of theology as a practical discipline. At the same time, Wesley's description of these dynamics is too idealized. The pastoral realities of a growing movement are often more fluid and multivalent than his description suggests. This is particularly clear in considering Wesley's various publications concerning predestination. They reflect how deeply torn he was in addressing the topic. On the one hand, Wesley was personally convinced not only that God's offer of saving grace was universal and resistible but also that the practical effects of preaching the alternative were usually negative. On the other hand, he recognized that open debate on the topic was likely to alienate some of his closest associates and to split the Methodist movement. As a result of this tension, Wesley's comments on predestination reveal more contextual variations than perhaps any other doctrine.[44] At times when he was most concerned about the damaging impact of the doctrine on his followers, he issued impassioned defenses of unlimited atonement such as his sermon *Free Grace*.[45] At times when he was more troubled by the damage being done within the Methodist movement by the debate over the doctrine, he searched for any possible common ground he shared with his opponents and the most conciliatory ways that he could express his central concerns.[46] Through all of these variations, however, his affirmation of God's universal resistible grace remained consistent.

[42] For one of the first instances see ibid., §§14-31, 9:56-66 in this edn.

[43] See Minutes, Aug. 2, 1745, *Q.* 15, 10:152 in this edn.

[44] These variations are traced in detail in Allan Coppedge, *John Wesley in Theological Debate* (Wilmore, Ky.: Wesley Heritage Press, 1987); and Albert Brown-Larson, *John Wesley and the Anglican Evangelicals of the Eighteenth Century* (Edinburgh: Pentland, 1994).

[45] Sermon 110, *Free Grace*, 3:544-59 in this edn.

[46] E.g., the conciliatory statement in *Journal*, Aug. 24, 1743, 19:332-33 in this edn.

Given their situational nature, it is important to identify the context and occasion of each of Wesley's doctrinal and controversial treatises. But it is also important to recognize that the convictions articulated in such treatises can have application beyond their immediate context and occasion. Although Wesley apparently judged a few treatises to be so narrowly situational (or so ill-considered) that he never republished them, he reissued the majority throughout his life.[47] More to the point, he issued a collected set of these treatises in 1758, titled *A Preservative against Unsettled Notions in Religion*, with the goal of reinforcing the convictions of his Methodist people on a wide spectrum of controverted issues of the time.[48]

IV. Development within Wesley's Doctrinal Convictions and Concerns

When he responded to accusations of inconsistency in his views, Wesley occasionally admitted that there had been a significant alteration in his doctrinal convictions between his early publications (beginning in 1733) and the beginning of the Methodist Revival (1738); namely, he had acquired a deeper appreciation for the doctrine of justification by grace and for the experience of faith as a conscious pardon from sin. However, Wesley typically insisted that he had remained thoroughly consistent in his doctrinal convictions since this earlier alteration. As he put it in 1789, 'I defy any man living to prove that I have contradicted myself at all in any of the writings which I have published from the year 1738 to the year 1788.'[49] To be sure, there were a few times when he quietly admitted changes on issues even after 1738 (such as whether one must have a sense of

[47] Note in particular that JW did not republish, or include in his collected *Works* (1771–74), either the *Queries proposed to . . . Zinzendorf* (1755; see *Bibliography*, No. 208, and vol. 14 in this edn.) or his parodied extract of Augustus Toplady's *Doctrine of Absolute Predestination Stated and Asserted* (1770; see *Bibliography*, No. 322, and vol. 13 in this edn.).

[48] The preface of this vol., as well as most of the treatises, can be found in vol. 14 of this edn. See also *Bibliography*, No. 226.

[49] JW's letter to William Green, Oct. 25, 1789 (vol. 31 in this edn.).

pardon to be justified).[50] But as Albert Outler noted, Wesley was typically more willing to qualify overstatements later than to acknowledge them as being overstatements in the first place, or to admit any inconsistency between the earlier and later remarks.[51]

Later scholars have had to deal more forthrightly with both discontinuities and developments in Wesley's thought.[52] As they have studied his convictions on a range of topics, it has become increasingly common to distinguish between the convictions of the early Wesley (1725–38),[53] the middle Wesley (1738–65), and the late Wesley (1765–91). While emphases differ, these designations are typically correlated to transitions in Wesley's general view of the Christian life from (1) a dominant holy living emphasis on the importance of moral rectitude or conformity to the likeness of God (or, at least, sincere *attempts* at obedience),[54] to (2) a deeper appropriation of Protestant emphases concerning salvation by grace, creating some initial tensions within his thought, and eventually climaxing in (3) a mature integration of the primacy of grace into his enduring concern for Christian holiness.

In considering this three-fold model of Wesley's theological transitions, it is important to recognize that the early Wesley did not have a total lack of appreciation for the role of grace and faith in the Christian life. After all, the doctrine of justification by faith was present in the Thirty-nine Articles of his Church.[55] While Wesley undeniably gave this doctrine more orienting influence following 1738, this transition was neither *de novo* nor a total reversal of his concern for Christian holiness.

It is equally important to recognize that, for all of his continuing emphasis on the primacy of God's grace in salvation, the middle

[50] JW's letter to CW, July 31, 1747, 26:254-55 in this edn.

[51] Introduction to Sermon 41, 'Wandering Thoughts', 2:125 in this edn.

[52] For a survey of historical tendencies and debates on these issues, see Randy L. Maddox, 'Reading Wesley as Theologian', *Wesleyan Theological Journal* 30, no. 1 (1995): 7-54.

[53] The initial date marks when JW began to keep a spiritual journal and his letters home began to reflect theological debates.

[54] See the section of JW's 1732 MS extract of Robert Nelson's *The Great Duty of Frequenting the Christian Sacrifice* (1707) that is reproduced in 4:527 of this edn.

[55] See Jeffrey S. Chamberlain, 'Moralism, Justification, and the Controversy over Methodism', *Journal of Ecclesiastical History* 44 (1993): 652-77, esp. 659-71.

Wesley was soon rethinking and progressively revising several assumptions about salvation by grace that shaped the initial 'great-expectations' of his transition in 1738.[56] These revisions connected the emphasis on grace more integrally with the hope and expectation of holy living, contributing towards the broad integration of these themes that characterized the late Wesley.

Finally, it must be recognized that there is no decisive demarcation of the transition to the late Wesley. His mature integration emerges on some topics in the early 1740s.[57] He is still debating others into the 1780s. But a general stability is present by the 1760s. The year 1765 has been chosen as a conventional marker because the sermon *The Scripture Way of Salvation*, which was published that year, is the classic articulation of his mature conviction that salvation is thoroughly grounded in grace and thoroughly oriented towards holiness of heart and life.

All of the treatises gathered in these three volumes were published after 1738, so none represent the early Wesley directly. Some, like *The Doctrine of Salvation, Faith, and Good Works* and the Preface to the 1739 *Hymns and Sacred Poems*, are manifestos of the transition to the middle Wesley. Many others reflect the revising of some initial expectations of this transition and the move towards the late Wesley.

Readers are encouraged to pay particular attention to how transitions in Wesley's convictions are reflected in his revision of some early works when they are republished. These are particularly evident in the collected *Works* that Wesley published in 1771–74. In the Preface to this collection Wesley noted that his goal was to 'present to serious and candid men my last and maturest thoughts; agreeable, I hope, to Scripture, reason, and Christian antiquity'.[58] Honoring his wish, we will draw attention in introductions and footnotes to Wesley's editorial revisions that have theological relevance.

[56] See Richard P. Heitzenrater, 'Great Expectations: Aldersgate and the Evidences of Genuine Christianity', in *Mirror and Memory: Reflections on Early Methodism* (Nashville: Kingswood Books, 1989), 106-49.

[57] Note, e.g., the change JW introduced in 1740 to his 1738 manifesto *The Doctrine of Salvation, Faith, and Good Works*, II.3 (below, p. 39, n. 35).

[58] Preface, §4, *Works* (1771), 1:vii.

V. Grouping of the Treatises in This Edition

Finally, a word about the organization of these volumes that collect Wesley's doctrinal and controversial treatises. When Wesley did his own collection in 1771–74, he chose to gather treatises by topic rather than just by date of publication, and we have done the same.

Volume 12 is devoted to the first subset, gathering four key works where Wesley stakes out his central convictions about human fallenness, God's universal saving intent, and the dynamics of salvation.

Volume 13 contains Wesley's writings defending his emphasis on the doctrine of Christian perfection, and another subset of controversial treatises devoted to debate with (both Methodist and non-Methodist) Calvinists over predestination and the imputed righteousness of Christ.

Volume 14 includes a fourth subset of publications arising in debate with the English Moravians; a fifth subset focused on Roman Catholic belief and practice; and a final subset that is more diverse, reflecting the range of materials that Wesley included in *A Preservative against Unsettled Notions in Religion*.

SECTION I

Foundational Treatises on Soteriology

INTRODUCTION

THIS first subset of Wesley's doctrinal and controversial writings gathers four treatises that deal with some of the most debated issues of soteriology in his day. Significantly, none of the works are strictly original to Wesley. Three are entirely abridgments of works by others, while in the fourth Wesley engages in an extended dialogue with another publication and then appends extracts from yet three more writers. Wesley chose to publish such derivative pieces on these issues because he was trying to demonstrate his concurrence with official standards and prominent theological figures—or, at times, to show their agreement with stances for which he was being attacked.

Wesley's primary purpose in issuing the extract of the *Homilies*, for example, was to convince his fellow Anglican clergy that the evangelical emphasis on believers experiencing a conscious assurance of God's pardoning love was consistent with this standard of Anglican doctrine. The extract of Richard Baxter's *Aphorisms of Justification* was aimed more at those who shared his evangelical emphasis, invoking this honored moderate Puritan to challenge antinomian conceptions of the doctrine of justification by faith. By including the extract of the *Shorter Catechism* issued by the Westminster Assembly in his *Christian Library*, Wesley was affirming broad areas of agreement with this standard of Reformed doctrine—while quietly removing items with which he (as an Arminian) disagreed. Finally, Wesley's extended response to the Dissenter John Taylor on the doctrine of original sin highlighted differences within the broad Arminian camp, with Wesley resisting a drift towards naively optimistic views of human nature and the rationalist moral psychology that he discerned in Taylor.

While these works were largely appropriated from other authors, Wesley consistently treated them as part of his works. When he advertised the first collected set of his writings in 1746, the extracts of the *Homilies* and of Baxter's *Aphorisms* were included.[1] *The*

[1] This collection was first advertised at the end of the 3rd edn. of the *Farther Appeal to Men of Reason and Religion* (Bristol: Felix Farley, 1746). It did not involve new printings of the various items but the binding together of the most recent edns. into fifteen vols. The *Homilies* extract was included in vol. 9; Baxter in vol. 15.

Doctrine of Original Sin joined these two in his formal collected *Works* (1771–74). As Wesley noted in the preface to this latter collection, it did not include items from the *Christian Library* (like his extract from the *Shorter Catechism*) because they remained available as a set.[2] It is in keeping with this precedent that we have gathered these four treatises as expressions of Wesley's foundational convictions in soteriology.

[2] For more details on these various collections see Richard P. Heitzenrater, 'John Wesley's *Christian Library*, Then and Now', *Summary of Proceedings, 55th Annual Conference of the American Theological Library Association* (Chicago: ATLA, 2001), 133-46.

THE DOCTRINE OF SALVATION, FAITH, AND GOOD WORKS (1738)

An Introductory Comment

ONE of the many problems facing the newly independent Church of England was how to ensure proper preaching in churches throughout the land in light of the number of disaffected and unlearned clergy. The plan emerged to issue a set of standard homilies that these clergy could read aloud from the pulpits and use as models for their sermon preparation. An initial set of twelve homilies was collected under the guidance of Thomas Cranmer in 1543. Henry VIII apparently refused to authorize this collection, resisting its stress on justification by faith alone, so it was not formally issued until 1547, early in Edward VI's reign. A second set of twenty-one additional homilies was published in 1571. These collections soon acquired status alongside the Book of Common Prayer and the Thirty-nine Articles as a repository of doctrine for the Church of England.

Scholars generally agree that the first five homilies came from the pen of Thomas Cranmer (1489–1556). They exemplify Cranmer's twin concerns: (1) to establish the nature of salvation as God's free gift of grace while (2) demonstrating that this did not result in the collapse of morality, so good works remain an essential part of the Christian life.[1] These entwined goals frame the third homily 'Of Salvation', which begins by describing justification in terms of forensic imputation of an alien righteousness (being careful not to make pardon dependent on prior internal change), then insists that the emphasis on faith alone is opposed not to good works per se but to

[1] See the fine study of Cranmer's soteriology in Ashley Null, *Thomas Cranmer's Doctrine of Repentance: Renewing the Power to Love* (New York: Oxford University Press, 2000). Null deals with the four homilies JW extracted on pp. 213-53.

their merit, and closes with a section stressing the believer's role of having a faith that bears good works. The subsequent homilies 'Of Faith' and 'Of Good Works' elaborate on the connection of faith and works—the first stressing the necessity of good works in the life of the justified, while the second insists that no work is good unless it flows from saving faith.

The dynamic tension in these homilies reflects how integrally Cranmer connected justification with regeneration. In addition to imputing Christ's righteousness, Cranmer insisted that God sends the Holy Spirit to indwell the new believer, stirring up a 'true and lively faith' that issues in loving obedience to God. Significantly, while he personally affirmed the irresistible nature of this indwelling (and unconditional predestination) as following logically from the notion of justification by grace, Cranmer was careful to exclude these emphases from the *Homilies* because they would not comfort congregations. The result was that these initial homilies could be read as consistent with a synergistic model of human cooperation in salvation.[2]

This made these homilies an ideal vehicle for Wesley when he found it necessary in 1738 to defend his new evangelical emphasis to his fellow Anglican clergy. The initial focus of debate was primarily on the emphasis that Wesley was now placing on an experiential *assurance* of one's saving relationship to Christ. He was confronted in print by Arthur Bedford almost immediately after this theme entered his preaching and was soon also debating the emphasis privately with his older brother.[3] Pondering the Anglican standards for doctrine in light of the questions being raised, Wesley became convinced that Cranmer's early homilies presented his 'new' teaching as the old and official teaching of the Church of England.[4] He promptly published an extract of them, placing specific emphasis

[2] See ibid., 222, 252-53.

[3] See Arthur Bedford, *The Doctrine of Assurance; or, The Case of a Weak and Doubting Conscience* (London: C. Ackers, 1738); JW's letter to Bedford, Sept. 28, 1738, 25:562-66 in this edn.; and the letter to JW from Samuel Wesley Jr., Nov. 15, 1738, 25:578-79 in this edn.

[4] See *Journal*, Nov. 12-18, 1738, 19:21 in this edn. Note also the older Wesley's memory that 'the book which, next to the Holy Scripture, was of the greatest use to them in settling their judgment as to the grand point of justification by faith was the *Book of Homilies*'. Sermon 107, 'On God's Vineyard', I.4, 3:505 in this edn.

on Cranmer's insistence that authentic faith includes a *sure trust and confidence* in God's mercy.[5]

While his primary goal was to convince his fellow Anglican clergy about the importance of assurance, it is clear that Wesley also appreciated Cranmer's stress on the necessity of good works. This aspect of Wesley's early holy living convictions remained firmly in place; in fact, the only reservation he displayed in his initial editing of Cranmer was with any suggestion that our obedience will always be imperfect.[6]

The value Wesley placed on this pamphlet extract from the *Homilies* can hardly be overemphasized. When the revival started in Bristol in 1739, he gave it away by the hundreds, remarking to a colleague that it was 'better than all our sermons put together'.[7] He reprinted it twenty times during his life and included excerpts in several of his other writings defending the revival.[8] It can rightly be considered—along with the sermon *Salvation by Faith* issued the same year—as the theological manifesto of Wesley's evangelical reframing of his holy living Anglican heritage.

It is most likely that Wesley prepared his extract working from the Oxford edition of the last reprint of the *Homilies* authorized by Charles II, issued in 1683, and this edition is used for comparison purposes below.[9] There is little noteworthy in most of Wesley's small alterations in the text of *Homilies* within his extract. But we will mark transitions, note major omissions, and highlight any elisions that may be of theological importance. We will also indicate some changes the late Wesley made when including this extract in his *Works* (1771–74).

[5] See sections I.9, I.13-15, II.2, and II.3 below, noting in each case the sentences that JW chose to italicize. There are no italics for these passages in any prior edn. of the *Homilies*. It could be argued that JW was reclaiming Cranmer's intended emphasis on assurance; see Ashley Null, 'Thomas Cranmer and Tudor Evangelicalism', in M. A. G. Haykin and K. J. Stewart, eds., *The Emergence of Evangelicalism* (Nottingham: Apollos, 2008), 221-51.

[6] See below, sections I.7 (n. 9), I.10 (n. 18), and I.12 (n. 22).

[7] Letter to James Hutton, May 8, 1739, 25:645 in this edn.

[8] See *Principles of a Methodist*, §§3-9, 9:51-53 in this edn.; *Earnest Appeal*, §59, 11:68-69 in this edn.; and *Farther Appeal*, Pt. I, §II.7, 11:114-15 in this edn.

[9] *Certain Sermons or Homilies Appointed to be Read in Churches in the Time of the late Queen Elizabeth of Famous Memory; and now Thought fit to be Reprinted by Authority from the King's Most Excellent Majesty* (Oxford: Thomas Guy, 1683). The Bridwell Library at Southern Methodist University holds a copy of this edn. that is purported to have belonged to JW, but there are no internal markings or collaborating evidence to confirm this claim.

Wesley was quite conservative in this abridgment. While he digested thirty-six quarto pages down to twelve duodecimo pages, omitting some whole sections, he rarely changed words or inserted his own content. The end result is a relatively seamless document that fairly represents the material being abridged (with Wesley's particular emphases being added by use of *italics*).

The text presented here is based on the first edition of 1738. For a stemma illustrating the transmission of the text through the nineteen extant editions issued during Wesley's lifetime, together with the substantive variant readings from those editions, see the appendix, pp. 484-85. For further details see *Bibliography*, No. 11.

THE

DOCTRINE

OF

Salvation, Faith,

AND

Good Works.

Extracted from the *Homilies*
Of the Church of *England.*

OXFORD:

Printed in the YEAR 1738.

THE DOCTRINE OF SALVATION, FAITH, AND GOOD WORKS

To the Reader

He that desireth more perfectly to understand these great doctrines of Christianity ought diligently to read the Holy Scriptures, especially St. Paul's Epistles to the Romans and the Galatians.[1] And 'Whosoever giveth his mind to Holy Scriptures, with diligent study and burning desire, it cannot be that he should be left without help. For either God will send him some godly doctor to teach him, or God himself from above will give light unto his mind and teach him those things which are necessary for him. Man's human and worldly wisdom or science is not needful to the understanding of Scripture, but the revelation of the Holy Ghost, who inspireth the true meaning unto them that with humility and diligence search for it.'[a]

[I.] Of the Salvation of Mankind[2]

1. Because all men are sinners against God and breakers of his law, therefore can no man by his works be justified and made righteous before God. But every man is constrained to seek for another righteousness or justification, to be received at God's own hands. And this justification or righteousness, which we receive of God's mercy and Christ's merits embraced by faith, is taken, accepted, and allowed of God for our perfect and full justification. For the more clear and full understanding hereof it is our part ever to remember how that all the world being wrapped in sin, God sent his only Son into the world to fulfil the law for us, and by shedding his blood to make satisfaction to his Father for our sins, to assuage his indignation conceived against us.

2. Insomuch that infants, being baptized and dying in their infancy, are by this sacrifice washed from their sins. And they who in act or deed sin after their baptism, when they turn again to God unfeignedly, are likewise washed by this sacrifice from their sins, in

[a] 'Homily of Reading the Holy Scripture' [Wesley excerpts—and digests—a short section from Pt. II of the homily; cf. *Homilies* (1683), 5. This excerpt is actually Cranmer's translation of two quotations from John Chrysostom's homilies on Gen. The first two sentences are from Homily 35, §2, Migne, *Patrologia Graeca*, 53:321; the last sentence is from Homily 21, §1, ibid., 53:175.].

---

[1] This prefatory sentence is original to Wesley.

[2] I.e., 'A Sermon of the Salvation of Mankind, by only Christ our Saviour, from Sin and Death Everlasting', *Homilies* (1683), 12-19.

such sort that there remaineth not any spot of sin that shall be imputed to their damnation. This is that justification or righteousness which St. Paul speaketh of when he saith, 'No man is justified by the works of the law, but by faith in Jesus Christ.' And again, 'We are justified by the faith of Christ, and not by the works of the law; for by the works of the law shall no flesh be justified.'[b]

3. The great wisdom of God in this mystery of our redemption has tempered his justice and mercy together. His mercy he showed in delivering us from our captivity without requiring any ransom to be paid or amends to be made upon our parts; which thing by us had been impossible to be done. And whereas it lay not in us to do that, he provided a ransom for us; that was the precious body and blood of his own Son, who, besides this ransom, fulfilled the law for us perfectly.[3] And so the justice of God and his mercy embraced together, and fulfilled the great mystery of our redemption.

4. Of this justice and mercy of God knit together speaketh St. Paul in the third chapter to the Romans: 'All have sinned and come short of the glory of God', but are justified 'freely by his grace, through the redemption that is in Jesus Christ, whom God hath set forth to be a propitiation, through faith in his blood.'[4] And in the tenth, 'Christ is the end of the law, for righteousness to everyone that believeth.'[5]

[b] Gal. 2[:16]. [Cranmer provided his own English translations for scripture quotations. In almost every case (exceptions will be noted) JW substitutes the AV.]

---

[3] *Works* (1772) omits 'who . . . perfectly'. This is the first of three omissions that reflect the concern JW developed in the years following his original abridgment about the emphasis in the Reformed model of the atonement (assumed by Cranmer) on the imputation of Christ's *active* righteousness or obedience to believers. See his initial articulation of this concern in letter to Rev. James Hervey, Oct. 15, 1756, vol. 13 in this edn.; and his more developed reflections in the 1762 *Thoughts on the Imputed Righteousness of Christ*, vol. 13 in this edn., and Sermon 20 (1765), *The Lord Our Righteousness*, 1:449-65 in this edn.

[4] Rom. 3:23-25.

[5] Rom. 10:4. In the errata to his *Works* (1772) JW calls for the omission of the following passage, which is struck through in his personal copy of the vol., though it is in fact retained in all edns. through his life:

> 'And in the eighth chapter, "That which was impossible by the law, inasmuch as it was weak through the flesh, God sending his own Son in the likeness of sinful flesh, and for sin, condemned sin in the flesh; that the righteousness of the law might be fulfilled in us, who walk not after the flesh, but after the Spirit." ' (Rom. 8:3-4)

In the printed errata he adds the explanatory note: 'the latter part of which manifestly relates not to justification, but sanctification'.

5. In these places the Apostle toucheth specially three things which must go together in our justification: upon God's part, his great mercy and grace; upon Christ's part, the satisfaction of God's justice by the offering his body and shedding his blood, with fulfilling of the law perfectly and throughly;[6] and upon our part, true and lively faith in the merits of Jesus Christ.[7] So that in our justification there is not only God's mercy and grace, but his justice also. And so the grace of God doth not shut out the righteousness[8] of God in our justification, but only shutteth out the righteousness of man—that is to say, the righteousness of our works.

6. And therefore St. Paul declareth nothing on the behalf of man concerning his justification, but only a true and lively faith, which itself is the gift of God. And yet that faith doth not shut out repentance, hope, love, and the fear of God, to be joined with faith in every man that is justified. But it shutteth them out from the office of justifying. So that although they be all present together in him that is justified, yet they justify not all together.

7. Neither doth faith shut out good works, necessarily to be done afterwards of duty towards God (for we are most bounden to serve God in doing good works, commanded in Scripture, all the days of our life). But we may not do them to this intent, to be justified by doing them. For all the good works we can do are not able to deserve our justification,[9] but our justification cometh freely of the mere mercy of God. And of so great and free mercy that whereas all the world was not able to pay any part towards their ransom it pleased him, without any of our deserving, to prepare for us the most precious jewels of Christ's body and blood, whereby our ransom might be paid, the law fulfilled, and his justice satisfied. So that Christ is now the righteousness of all them that truly believe in him. *He for them paid their ransom by his death. He for them fulfilled the law in his life;*[10] so that now in him and by him every Christian may be called

[6] *Works* (1772) omits 'with fulfilling . . . throughly'. JW had already made this deletion in his excerpt of this section in Sermon 20, *The Lord Our Righteousness*, II.6, 1:456 in this edn. See n. 3 above.

[7] Note how JW repeats this summary in defining what he means by 'justification by faith alone' in *The Principles of a Methodist*, §3, 9:51 in this edn.

[8] JW consistently substitutes 'righteousness' for Cranmer's term 'justice'.

[9] JW omits Cranmer's explanation: 'all the good works that we can do *be imperfect, and therefore* not able'. *Homilies* (1683), 13. JW's contrary assumption is discussed in the the treatises on Christian perfection in volume 13.

[10] JW adds the italics; cf. *Homilies* (1683), 14.

a fulfiller of the law, forasmuch as that which their infirmity lacked Christ's righteousness has supplied.[11]

8.[12] You have heard that no man can be justified by his own works, inasmuch as no man fulfilleth the law. And St. Paul in his Epistle to the Galatians proveth the same, saying, 'If there had been a law given which could have justified, verily righteousness should have been by the law.'[13] And again, 'If righteousness come by the law, then is Christ dead in vain.'[14] And to the Ephesians he saith, 'By grace are ye saved through faith and that not of yourselves, it is the gift of God; not of works, lest any man should boast.'[c] And to be short, the sum of all Paul's disputation is this: 'If righteousness come of works, then it cometh not of grace; and if it come of grace, then it cometh not of works.'[15] And to this end tend all the prophets, as St. Peter saith: 'To him give all the prophets witness, that through his name whosoever believeth in him shall receive remission of sins.'[d]

9. And that we are justified only by this true and lively faith in Christ speak all the ancient authors, specially Origen, St. Cyprian, St. Chrysostom, Hilary, Basil, St. Ambrose, and St. Augustine.[16] By which they take away clearly all merit of our works and wholly ascribe our justification unto Christ only. *This faith, the Holy Scripture teacheth us, is the strong rock and foundation of the Christian religion. This doctrine all ancient authors of Christ's church do approve. This doctrine setteth forth the true glory of Christ and beateth down the vainglory of man. This whosoever denieth is not to be accounted for a Christian man, nor for a setter forth of Christ's glory, but for an adversary to Christ and his gospel, and for a setter forth of men's vainglory.*[17]

10. But that this true doctrine of justification by faith may be truly understood, observe that justification is the office of God only, and is not a thing which we render unto him, but which we receive of

[c] Eph. 2[:8-9].
[d] Acts 10:43.

---

[11] *Works* (1772) omits 'He for them paid . . . has supplied.' See n. 3 above.
[12] Pt. II of the homily 'Of Salvation' begins here; *Homilies* (1683), 14.
[13] Gal. 3:21.
[14] Gal. 2:21.
[15] Cf. Rom. 11:6.
[16] JW combines names from two lists that Cranmer gives, limiting his selection to authors from the first four centuries, while Cranmer includes later figures like Anselm and Bernard; cf. *Homilies* (1683), 14-15.
[17] JW's italics; cf. *Homilies* (1683), 15.

him by his free mercy, through the only merits of his beloved Son. And the true sense of this doctrine—'we are justified freely by faith without works' or 'we are justified by faith in Christ only'—is not that this our own act 'to believe in Christ', or this our faith in Christ which is within us, doth justify us (for that were to account ourselves to be justified by some act or virtue that is within ourselves). But that although we have faith, hope, and charity within us, and do never so many works thereunto, yet we must renounce the merit of all—of faith, hope, charity, and all other virtues and good works which we either have done, shall do, or can do—as far too weak[18] to deserve our justification, for which therefore we must trust only in God's mercy and the sacrifice which Christ offered for us on the cross.

11. As then John [the] Baptist, as great and godly a man as he was, yet in this matter of forgiving sin put the people from him and pointed them to Christ, saying, 'Behold the Lamb of God, which taketh away the sins of the world'[19]; even so, as great and godly a virtue as faith is, it putteth us from itself and pointeth us to Christ, to have only by him remission of sins or justification. So that our faith (as it were) saith unto us thus, 'It is not I that taketh away your sins. It is Christ only, and to him alone I send you for that purpose, forsaking all your good virtues, words, thoughts, and works, and putting your trust in Christ only.'

12.[20] And in truth neither our faith nor our works do justify us, that is, deserve remission of our sins. But God himself doth justify us, of his own mercy, through the merits of his Son only. Nevertheless because by faith given us of God we embrace the promise of God's mercy and of the remission of our sins, therefore the Scripture saith that 'faith doth justify', yea, 'faith without works'. And as it is all one to say 'faith without works' and 'only faith doth justify us', therefore the ancient Fathers from time to time speak thus, 'only faith justifieth us', meaning no other than St. Paul meant when he said, 'faith without works justifieth us'.[21] And because this is wrought through the only merits of Christ, and not through our merits, or through the merit of any virtue we have within us, or of any work that cometh from us, therefore in that respect we renounce, as it were, again faith, works, and all other virtues. For our

[18] Wesley omits 'and insufficient and imperfect'; cf. *Homilies* (1683), 16.
[19] John 1:29.
[20] Pt. III of the homily 'Of Salvation' begins here; *Homilies* (1683), 16.
[21] Gal. 2:16.

corruption through original sin is so great that *all our faith, charity, words, and works cannot merit or deserve any part of our justification for us.*[22] And therefore we thus speak, humbling ourselves to God, and giving to our Saviour Christ all the glory of our justification.

13. To justify, then, is the office of God to man. Our office and duty to God is not to pass our time sinfully or unfruitfully, for this were to serve the devil and not God. For that faith which bringeth not forth repentance, but either evil works or no good works, is not a right, pure, and living faith but a dead and devilish one, as St. Paul and St. James call it. For even the devils believe that 'Christ was born of a virgin; that he wrought all kind of miracles, declaring himself very God; that for our sakes he suffered a most painful death, to redeem us from death everlasting; that he rose again the third day; that he ascended into heaven, and sitteth at the right hand of the Father, and at the end of the world shall come again to judge both the quick and the dead.'[23] These articles of our faith the devils believe, and so they believe all that is written in the Old and New Testament. *And yet for all this faith they be but devils. They remain still in their damnable estate,*[24] lacking the very true Christian faith.

14. *The right and true Christian faith is, not only to believe that Holy Scripture and the articles of our faith are true, but also to have a sure trust and confidence to be saved from everlasting damnation by Christ; whereof doth follow a loving heart to obey his commandments.*[25]

15. And this true Christian faith neither any devil has, nor yet any man who in outward profession, in his receiving the sacraments, in coming to church, and in all other outward appearances, seemeth to be a Christian and yet in his life showeth the contrary. For how can a man have this *true faith, sure trust, and confidence in God that by the merits of Christ his sins are forgiven and he reconciled to the favour of God,*[26] *when*

[22] JW adds italics, while deleting Cranmer's insistence that 'all is imperfect within us, faith, charity, . . . '; cf. *Homilies* (1683), 17.

[23] Cf. the Nicene Creed as contained in the Communion service of the BCP. The homily does not cite this source, but JW indicates that it is a quotation.

[24] JW's italics; cf. *Homilies* (1683), 18.

[25] Ibid.

[26] Ibid. The early Wesley had stressed the nature of faith as 'assent on rational grounds' (letter to Susanna Wesley, July 29, 1725, 25:175 in this edn.) and then as 'assent to what God has revealed, because God has revealed it' (letter to Susanna Wesley, Nov. 22, 1725, 25:188 in this edn.). In the transitions of 1738–39 this definition from the *Homilies* emerged as his new standard—see letter to Dr. Henry Stebbing, July 25, 1739, 25:671 in this edn.; Sermon 2, 'The Almost Christian', II.5, 1:139 in this edn.; *Principles of a Methodist*, §9, 9:53 in this edn.; *An Earnest Appeal*, §78, 11:78 in this edn.; and Sermon 18, 'The Marks of the New Birth', I.3, 1:418-19 in this edn.

he denieth Christ in his works? Surely no ungodly man can have this faith and trust in God!

16. If we do truly believe that whereas we were condemned to hell and death everlasting, God has given his own Son to take our nature upon him and to suffer death for our offences, to justify us and to restore us to life everlasting; if we truly believe that he has made us his dear children, brethren unto his only Son, and inheritors with him of his eternal kingdom of heaven; these great and merciful benefits of God will move us to render ourselves unto God wholly, with all our hearts, might, and power, to serve him in all good works, to seek in all things his glory, evermore dreading to offend in word, thought, or deed such a merciful God and loving Redeemer. They will also move us to be ever ready for his sake to give ourselves to our neighbours, and as much as lieth in us to study with all our endeavours to do good to every man. These are the fruits of true faith: to do good, as much as lieth in us, to every man; and above all things, and in all things, to advance the glory of God; to whom be praise and honour, world without end!

[II.] Of True Christian Faith [27]

1. The first coming unto God is through faith, whereby we are justified before God. But lest any man should be deceived for want of right understanding thereof, it is diligently to be noted that faith is taken in Scripture two ways. There is one faith which the Scripture calleth a dead faith, and this by St. James is compared to the faith of devils, who 'believe and tremble'[28] and yet do nothing well. And such a faith as this have wicked Christians, who 'profess they know God, but in works deny him'.[29]

2. *This faith is a persuasion that there is a God, and a belief of all the truths contained in his Word. So that it consisteth only in believing that the Word of God is true. And this is not properly called faith.*[30] But as he that readeth Caesar's *Commentary*,[31] though he believeth it to be

[27] JW combines under this heading 'A Short Declaration of the True, Lively, and Christian Faith', *Homilies* (1683), 19-27; and 'A Sermon of Good Works Annexed unto Faith', ibid., 27-36.

[28] Jas. 2:19.

[29] Titus 1:16.

[30] JW's italics; cf. *Homilies* (1683), 19.

[31] I.e., Julius Caesar's account of his wars in Gaul and the civil war with Pompey.

true yet is not properly said to believe in Caesar, of whom he looketh for no benefit, even so he that believeth all the Bible to be true and yet liveth ungodly is not properly said to believe in God. For he has not such a faith and trust in God whereby he surely looketh for grace, mercy, and everlasting life at God's hand.[32] For, inasmuch as faith without works is dead, it is not faith, as a dead man is not a man.[33]

3. Another faith there is in Scripture which is not idle or unfruitful, but (as St. Paul declares) 'working by love'.[34] And as that is called a dead faith, so this may be called a quick or living faith. *This is not only a belief of the articles of our faith, but also a true trust and confidence of the mercy of God through our Lord Jesus Christ, and a steadfast hope of all good things at God's hand,*[e] called by St. Paul 'the full assurance of faith'![35] A confidence that though we should fall from him by sin, yet if we return to him by true repentance he will forgive our offences for his Son's sake, and make us inheritors of his everlasting kingdom. That in the meantime he will be our protector and defender, and not withdraw his mercy finally from us if we commit ourselves wholly unto him, hang only upon him, and call upon him, ready to obey and serve him. This is the true, living, Christian faith, which is not in the mouth and outward profession only, but it liveth and stirreth inwardly in the heart. And this faith is not without hope and trust in God, nor without the love of God and of our

[e] It is the doctrine of the Church of England, to which every minister of our Church has subscribed in subscribing the Thirty-fifth Article, that 'without or before this can no good work be done'. [The article cited, 'Of Homilies', asserts that they 'contain a godly and wholesome doctrine, necessary for these times'. JW then quotes from the homily 'Of Good Works', Pt. I (see below, section II.9). Note also that JW has added the italics for the sentence in the main text; cf. *Homilies* (1683), 20.]

---

[32] *Works* (1772) omits this sentence.

[33] This sentence is a quotation from Didymus Alexandrinus, *Enarratio in Epistolam Beati Jacobi*. Migne, *Patrologia Graeca*, 39:1752.

[34] Gal. 5:6. Here we have one of Wesley's rare switches of the AV text from 'worketh' to 'working'. This phrase became one of JW's favorite texts from preaching on faith and good works; see Albert Outler's list of examples in 1:139n58 in this edn.

[35] JW inserted this reference to Heb. 10:22 into Cranmer's text in his original 1738 extract; cf. *Homilies* (1683), 20. He removed it from the 3rd (1740) and all subsequent edns. This removal reflects the fact that JW had come to question the claim of the English Moravians that every true believer has from the beginning a 'full assurance of faith'. See in particular his summary of this point in his *Journal*, Dec. 31, 1739, 19:131-32 in this edn.

neighbour, nor without the fear of God, nor without the desire to hear God's Word and to follow the same in avoiding evil and gladly doing all good works.

4. Of this faith three things are specially to be noted. First, that it is fruitful in bringing forth good works; secondly, that without it can no good works be done; thirdly, what good works this faith doth bring forth.

5. For the first, as light cannot be hid, but will show itself at one place or other, so true faith cannot be hid, but will break out and show itself by good works. And as the living body of a man ever exerciseth such things as belong to a living body, for nourishment and preservation of the same, even so the soul that has a living faith will be always doing some good work, which shall declare that it is living. Therefore if any man fancy he is set at liberty from doing good works, it is a manifest token he has no true faith. Yea, he knoweth not what true faith meaneth. For true Christian faith is not only a belief of all the things of God which are contained in Holy Scripture, but also an earnest trust and confidence in God that he is careful over us as the father is over the child whom he loveth, and that he will be merciful to us for his Son's sake. And this true faith, when we consider what God has done for us, is also moved through continual assistance of the Spirit of God to serve and please him, to keep his favour, to fear his displeasure, to continue his obedient children; showing thankfulness by observing his commandments, and that freely, for true love chiefly, and not for dread of punishment or love of temporal reward;[36] considering how clearly without our deservings we have freely received his mercy and pardon.

6.[37] Therefore if it do not appear in our conversation,[38] the faith we pretend to have is but feigned, because true faith is manifestly shown by good living and not by words only. As St. Augustine saith, 'Good living cannot be separated from true faith, which worketh by

[36] *Works* (1772) omits 'and that freely . . . reward'. This omission likely reflects JW's rejection of the assumption that love of God is pure or proper only when one loves in recognition of God's inherent perfections rather than in gratitude for God's gracious pardon. JW once shared this assumption, but became convinced that our love for God is actually only possible in *response* to our awareness of God's love for us. Cf. letter to John Robertson, Sept. 24, 1753, 26:518 in this edn.

[37] Pt. II of the homily 'Of Faith' begins here; *Homilies* (1683), 22.

[38] In Cranmer's 16th century, 'conversation' referred to all of our ways of dealing with other persons, not just verbal interchange; see *OED* (2nd edn.), first two definitions.

love';[39] and St. Chrysostom, 'Faith is full of good works; as soon as a man believeth, he shall be adorned with them.'[40] How plentiful it is of good works St. Paul teacheth at large in the eleventh chapter to the Hebrews,[41] evidently declaring that true faith is no unfruitful thing but a thing of perfect virtue, of wonderful operation and strength, bringing forth all good motions and good works.

7. Every man therefore must diligently examine himself, whether he has this faith in his heart or not.[42] He that feeleth his heart set to seek God's honour, and leadeth not his life after his own desire but setteth his mind to serve God for his own sake,[43] and for his sake to love all his neighbours, whether they be friends or adversaries, doing good to every man (as opportunity serveth) and willingly hurting no man; such a man may well rejoice in God, perceiving by his life that he has a living faith. But he that doeth not live according to God's Word deceiveth himself if he think he believeth in him.

8. Let us then by our works declare our faith to be the living, Christian faith, and by such virtues as ought to spring out of faith. 'Let us add to (or in) our faith, virtue; in our virtue, knowledge; in our knowledge, temperance; in our temperance, patience; in our patience, godliness; in our godliness, brotherly kindness; and in brotherly kindness, charity.'[44] So shall we both certify our conscience that we are in the right faith, and also confirm other men. If you feel and perceive such a faith in you, rejoice in it, and be diligent to maintain it. Let it be daily increasing more and more by good works. So shall you be sure that you shall please God and, when his will is, 'receive the end of your faith, even the salvation of your souls'.[45]

9.[46] The second thing that was noted of true faith was that without it can no good works be done. For 'as the branch cannot bear

[39] *Of Faith and Works*, chap. xiv. Migne, *Patrologia Latina*, 40:211.

[40] *On Faith and Natural Law*, §1. Migne, *Patrologia Graeca*, 48:1081.

[41] JW omits here Cranmer's summary of Heb. 11 and a parallel summary of how the faith of early Christian martyrs and teachers was expressed in their lives; cf. *Homilies* (1683), 22-23.

[42] JW omits another long section where Cranmer argues that the test of lively faith is good works, appealing particularly to the writings of St. John. JW resumes with Pt. III of the homily 'Of Faith'; *Homilies* (1683), 25.

[43] *Works* (1772) omits 'for his own sake'. On the likely reason for this omission, see n. 36 above.

[44] 2 Pet. 1:5-7. In this citation JW follows Cranmer, using the preposition 'in' rather than the AV's 'to'; cf. *Homilies* (1683), 26.

[45] 1 Pet. 1:9.

[46] Here JW moves to Pt. I of the homily 'Of Good Works'; *Homilies* (1683), 27.

fruit of itself' (saith our Saviour Christ) 'except it abide in the vine, no more can ye, except ye abide in me. I am the vine; ye are the branches. He that abideth in me, and I in him, he bringeth forth much fruit, for without me ye can do nothing.'[47] And St. Paul proveth that Enoch had faith, because 'he pleased God. For without faith' (saith he) 'it is impossible to please him'.[48]

10. Faith giveth life to the soul, and they are as much dead to God who want faith as they are to the world whose bodies want souls. Without faith all we do is but dead before God, be it ever so glorious before man. Even as a picture is but a dead representation of the thing itself, so are the works of those who have not faith before God. They are but shadows of good and living things, and not good and living things indeed. For without faith no work is good before God. We must set no good works before faith. 'Let no man' (saith St. Augustine) 'reckon upon his good works before his faith, for where faith was not, good works were not. There is one work in which are all good works, that is, faith which worketh by love. If you have this you have the ground of all good works. Without this you have only the shadows of them.'[49]

11. To the same purpose saith St. Chrysostom, 'Many who have not the true faith, yet flourish in works of mercy. But the chief work is lacking, to believe in him whom God has sent. So soon as a man has faith he shall flourish in good works. For faith is full of good works, and nothing is good without faith. They that shine in good works without faith are like dead men, who have goodly and precious tombs. Faith cannot be naked, without good works, for then it is no true faith. And when it is adjoined to works, yet it is above the works. For as men first have life and after are nourished, so must our faith in Christ go before and after be nourished with good works. And life may be without nourishment, but nourishment cannot be without life. A man must needs be nourished by good works, but first he must have faith. He that doeth good works, yet without faith, he has no life. I can show a man that by faith without works lived and came to heaven, but without faith never man had life. The thief that was hanged when Christ suffered did believe only, and the most merciful God justified him. Faith by itself saved him, but works by themselves never justified any man.'[50]

[47] John 15:4-5.

[48] Heb. 11:5-6.

[49] Cf. Augustine, *Psalms*, XXXI.ii.4-8. Migne, *Patrologia Latina*, 36:259-63.

[50] Chrysostom, *On Faith and Natural Law*, §1. Migne, *Patrologia Graeca*, 48:1081.

12.[51] The third thing to be noted of true faith is what good works it doeth bring forth. And this Christ himself has plainly declared: 'If thou wilt enter into life, keep the commandments.'[52] So that we are taught by Christ's own mouth that the works of the commandments of God are the true works of faith, the very way that doeth lead to everlasting life.

13.[53] Wherefore, as you have any regard for everlasting life, apply yourselves above all things to read and hear God's Word, mark diligently what his commandments are, and with all your endeavour follow the same. First, you must have an assured faith in God and give yourselves wholly unto him. Love him in prosperity and adversity, and dread to offend him evermore. Then for his sake love all men, friends and foes, because they are his creatures and image, and redeemed by Christ as ye are. Cast in your minds how you may do good unto all men, unto your powers, and hurt none. Obey all your superiors and governors. Serve your masters faithfully and diligently. Disobey not your fathers and mothers, but honour, help, and please them to your power. Oppress not, kill not, beat not, neither slander nor hate any man. But love all men, speak well of all men, help and succour every man as you may, yea even your enemies that hate you, that speak evil of you, and hurt you. Take no man's goods, nor covet your neighbour's goods, but be content with your own, and bestow them charitably as need requireth. Flee all idolatry, witchcraft, perjury. Commit no manner of adultery, fornication, or other unchastity in will or deed. And labouring continually in thus keeping the commandments—which, wrought in faith, God has ordained to be the pathway unto heaven—you shall not fail to come to that everlasting life where you shall live in glory and joy with God for ever.

[51] Pt. II of the homily 'Of Good Works' begins here; *Homilies* (1683), 29.

[52] Matt. 19:17.

[53] JW omits a long section where Cranmer first comments on how humans have continually resisted good works and then tries to distinguish authentic religious duties from mere human traditions; *Homilies* (1683), 30-35. JW then uses the conclusion of the homily 'Of Good Works' (ibid., 35-36) to conclude his extract.

AN EXTRACT OF MR. RICHARD BAXTER'S APHORISMS OF JUSTIFICATION (1745)

An Introductory Comment

WHILE Wesley's initial apologetic focus after Aldersgate was on convincing his fellow Anglicans that his evangelical emphasis was in keeping with the standards of the Church of England, he soon found it necessary to address the opposite front as well—defending his Anglican convictions against evangelical critiques. The topic of predestination was an immediate flashpoint, sparked by Wesley's provocative sermon *Free Grace* published in May 1739.[1] A section of volume 13 is devoted to this continuing debate. The focus of the present piece is on the other issue that drew Wesley's early apologetic attention on the evangelical front: debates over differing models of atonement and justification.[2]

The question of how Christ's holy life and sacrificial death resolve the problem of human sinfulness stands at the core of Christianity. The juridical dimension of this question—how the work of Christ *atones for the guilt* of sin or *justifies* sinners—became a particular focus of the Western stream of the Christian tradition. In the early medieval period Anselm crafted an influential model of the atonement emphasizing how Christ's death satisfied divine honor, so that God could honorably restore right relationship with the creation.

[1] Sermon 110, *Free Grace*, 3:544-59 in this edn.

[2] For more details on the following summary, see particularly Paul S. Fiddes, *Past Event and Present Salvation* (Louisville: Westminster/John Knox, 1989); Randy L. Maddox, *Responsible Grace: John Wesley's Practical Theology* (Nashville: Kingswood Books, 1994), 101-6; and Peter Schmiechen, *Saving Power: Theories of Atonement and Forms of the Church* (Grand Rapids: Eerdmans, 2005).

At the height of the medieval period Thomas Aquinas drew on Aristotle's recovered political and ethical writings to frame an account of the atonement that focused more on expressing divine righteousness and mercy (by satisfying the penalty due to sin) than on satisfying divine honor. While it never totally obscured the earlier 'divine satisfaction' emphases, this 'penalty satisfaction' model of the atonement was dominant in Western Christianity by the Reformation and remains influential in many circles to the present. But a significant variant increasingly challenged it in Protestant circles.

Many Reformers were bothered by two features of the earlier models: (1) they focus more on God's provision for restoring the fallen order *as a whole* than on the issue of individual justification; and (2) they deal almost exclusively with our *forgiveness* for sin, providing little sense of how we achieve the positive righteousness that merits eternal blessing. While the earlier models are clear that humans cannot merit salvation itself, they appear to leave open a role for humans to make a praiseworthy contribution to receiving the benefits of Christ's atonement and expressing positive righteousness.

Luther, in particular, emphatically rejected any such role for human merit in salvation. This concern led to the development in central strands of Protestant scholasticism of a model of atonement that might be called 'substitutionary justification'. The model focuses on imputation of Christ's passive *and* active righteousness. Christ's passive righteousness is his suffering of the ultimate punishment for sin in death. Active righteousness is Christ's full conformity with God's moral law during his life. The developed model argues that the act of justification involves God making Christ the legal substitute for individual sinners—such that the sinner's guilt is imputed to Christ (who suffers its penalty in his passion), while Christ's active righteousness is imputed to the justified sinner (who now is not merely pardoned but deemed worthy of salvation as righteous). Through this dual emphasis, the substitutionary justification model rests one's entire salvation on the merits of Christ alone.

The doctrinal standards of the Church of England in Wesley's day reflected the reigning seventeenth-century Western emphases concerning atonement and justification. The topic was broached briefly in the Articles of Religion, with Article XI affirming: 'We are accounted righteous before God, only for the merit of our Lord and Saviour Jesus Christ, by faith.' But the article also referred the reader to the Homily on Justification, where one reads (in a section that Wesley retained in his extract):

> The Apostle toucheth specially three things which must go together in our justification: upon God's part, his great mercy and grace; upon Christ's part, the satisfaction of God's justice by the offering his body and shedding his blood, with fulfilling of the law perfectly and throughly; and upon our part, true and lively faith in the merits of Jesus Christ. So that in our justification there is not only God's mercy and grace, but his justice also.[3]

The emphases of the penalty satisfaction model of atonement resound in this passage. But the distinction between Christ's active and passive righteousness is also present, providing warrant for those who would champion the specific claims of the substitutionary justification model.

Wesley's deeper appropriation of the importance of justification by grace in 1738 was fostered by his contact with Moravians and other evangelicals who strongly championed the substitutionary justification understanding of atonement. His retention of the quotation in the extract of the *Homilies* that year might suggest Wesley's full embrace of the model. But his continuing Anglican emphasis on holy living almost immediately led to questions about the specific claim of the imputation of Christ's *active* righteousness to believers. Interactions with the Moravians, in particular, convinced Wesley by 1741 that this claim could easily lead to antinomianism.[4] But he also recognized that this emphasis was standard in most earlier Puritan and contemporary evangelical accounts of justification. This made him hesitant to contest it—at least publicly.[5]

By June 1744, when Wesley held the first annual Conference with his growing group of preachers, his concern about this issue had grown to the point that he placed on the agenda for debate the question: 'In what sense is the righteousness of Christ imputed to

[3] See *The Doctrine of Salvation, Faith, and Good Works*, I.5, p. 34 above.

[4] John Cennick's shift from alliance with Wesley towards affiliation with the Moravians in early 1741 was marked by his doubts that JW was content to base salvation solely on imputed righteousness. See *Journal*, Feb. 22, 1741, 19:182-83 in this edn. JW's dialogue with Zinzendorf later that year focused on the theme of imputed righteousness and culminated in JW's warning about the antinomian potential of a one-sided emphasis on this theme. See *Journal*, Sept. 3, 1741, 19:211-23 in this edn.

[5] E.g., he waited to publish the fourth extract of his *Journal*, which contained the Cennick debate and the Zinzendorf dialogue, until July 1744 (*after* the first annual Conference).

believers, or to all mankind?' The reply recorded in the Minutes reads: 'We do not find it affirmed expressly in Scripture that God imputes the righteousness of Christ to any, although we do find that faith is imputed unto us for righteousness.'[6] The Conference went on to suggest that they had perhaps unawares leaned too much towards Calvinism and antinomianism.[7] Recognition of this danger made it vital for Wesley to provide clarifying teaching on justification for his preachers and people. In early 1745, as part of his research towards this goal, Wesley was sent a copy of Richard Baxter's *Aphorismes of Justification* when he had requested another tract on the subject.[8] He found Baxter's reflections so agreeable that he soon decided to publish an abridgment for the benefit of his Methodist movement.

Wesley had inherited a general appreciation for the writings of Richard Baxter (1615–91) from his parents.[9] Although Baxter was a Dissenter and moderate Calvinist, Samuel and Susanna Wesley resonated with his hope of articulating the fundamentals of Christianity in a way that could reconcile Calvinists and Arminians.[10] John Wesley later praised the pastoral tone of Baxter's mature writings.[11] But what drew him to *Aphorismes of Justification*, Baxter's first publication, was its more polemical nature. Its specific goal was to identify and reject antinomian strains in some Calvinist accounts of justification.[12] This made an abridged republication a fitting means for Wesley to address his evangelical critics and instruct his Methodist followers.

[6] Minutes (June 25, 1744), *Q.* 16, 10:129 in this edn.

[7] Ibid., *QQ.* 17-18, 10:130 in this edn.

[8] Wesley describes this event in 'To the Reader' below. He appears to have received the original edn.: Richard Baxter, *Aphorismes of Justification* (London: Francis Tyton, 1649). This edn. will be used below for comparative purposes, as the only other release was a reissue of the unchanged text set on larger (and fewer) pages.

[9] See Samuel Wesley, *Advice to a Young Clergyman* (London: Rivington, 1735), 50; and letter from Susanna Wesley to JW, Oct. 25, 1732, 25:345 in this edn.

[10] This is particularly the goal of Baxter's *Catholic Theology* (London: Simmons, 1675).

[11] See his description of Baxter as a 'loving, serious Christian' who writes 'dipping, as it were, his pen in tears'. *Journal*, May 1, 1755, 21:10 in this edn.

[12] Baxter highlights this as the background for *Aphorismes* in his biographical reflections *Reliquiae Baxterianae; or, Mr. Richard Baxter's narrative of the most memorable passages of his life and times* (London: T. Parkhurst, 1696), 107.

The bedrock for antinomian versions of Calvinism, in Baxter's view, was denial of any conditionality in God's dealing with the elect in the covenant of grace.[13] The foundation of this denial was the posing of the covenant of works established with Adam and the covenant of grace instituted through Christ in opposition with each other.[14] It was accentuated by affirming 'justification from eternity', where justification is construed as a single eternal act of pardoning both past and future sins. Another frequent claim was strict correlation between the merit of Christ's death (passive righteousness) and the total debt of the sins of the elect—leaving no room to increase or decrease the debt covered. Then there was emphasis on the imputation of Christ's active righteousness to the justified. Wesley's abridgment retained the major points that Baxter made in response:

1. The covenant of grace supplements and reframes the covenant of works, but does not set it aside totally for the justified (§§I–VII).
2. Christ's death should be understood as offering 'sufficient satisfaction' for pardoning all sin, rather than payment of the 'proper debt' (§IV.7-8, §XI).
3. The notion of the imputation of Christ's active righteousness is unwarranted and should be rejected; active righteousness is instead *imparted* (§IV.8, §XIII, §XVII).
4. Justification is best defined simply as 'acquitting upon consideration of merits' (§§XXIV–XXV).
5. There is no scriptural support for 'justification from eternity' (§XII, §XXXII).
6. Grace is resistible; salvation is remissible (§XII, §§XXVII–XXVIII).
7. Justification/salvation *is conditional* upon faith (§XII, §XVII, §XX, §XXVI, §XLIII).

[13] The best critical analysis of Baxter on this point is Hans Boersma, *A Hot Pepper Corn: Richard Baxter's Doctrine of Justification in Its Seventeenth-Century Context of Controversy* (Zoetermeer: Uitgeverij Boekencentrum, 1993).

[14] For analysis of the emergence of this strong contrast between the covenant of works and the covenant of grace in the federal theology of English Puritanism, see David A. Weir, *The Origins of the Federal Theology in Sixteenth-Century Reformation Thought* (Oxford: Clarendon Press, 1990); and Michael McGiffert, 'The Perkinsian Moment of Federal Theology', *Calvin Theological Journal* 29 (1994): 117-48.

8. Not faith *alone*, but as expressed in works/love (§XXXV, cf. §§VII–XI).

Wesley's abridgment also retained Baxter's succinct articulation of his understanding of justification:

> God the Father doth accept the sufferings and merits of his Son as a full satisfaction to his violated law, and as a valuable consideration upon which he will wholly forgive the offenders themselves, and receive them again into his favour, and give them the addition of a more excellent happiness also, so that they will but receive his Son upon the terms expressed in the gospel.[15]

This is a classic expression of the penalty satisfaction model of atonement, without the additional claims of substitutionary justification. It resonates with and elaborates the definition of justification that Wesley and his preachers adopted at their first Conference: 'to be pardoned and received into God's favour and into such a state that, if we continue therein, we shall be finally saved'.[16]

Wesley published his abridgment of Baxter's *Aphorisms*[17] prior to the 1745 Conference with his preachers. When they gathered, Wesley read the abridgment in public session and instructed the group to 'consult the Scriptures cited therein, and bring what objections might occur the next morning'.[18] The discussion on the following day reflected Baxter's concern to exalt 'the merits and love of Christ' while avoiding antinomianism. While no specific objections were raised to the abridged *Aphorisms*, Wesley was encouraged to 'write one or two more dialogues', perhaps reflecting concern about the technical nature of Baxter's treatise.[19]

As requested, Wesley issued two dialogues 'between an antinomian and his friend' before the end of 1745.[20] He also released early the next year the sermon 'Justification by Faith' in the first volume of *Sermons on Several Occasions*. Each of these works reflects the position that Baxter defended in *Aphorisms*. To highlight one example, while Wesley freely speaks about God remitting our punishment in 'Justification by Faith', he avoids any suggestion of the

[15] See section IV.8.9 (p. 58 below).

[16] Minutes (June 25, 1744), *Q.* 1, 10:126 in this edn.

[17] Wesley changed the spelling from *Aphorismes* in his abridgment.

[18] Minutes (Aug. 1, 1745), *Q.* 4, 10:149 in this edn.

[19] Minutes (Aug. 2, 1745), *QQ.* 24-25, 10:153 in this edn.

[20] See *Bibliography*, Nos. 102 & 106, vol. 14 in this edn.

imputation of Christ's active righteousness to believers.[21] Continuing influence of Baxter's treatise can be discerned in materials contained in volumes 13 and 14, which Wesley produced during debates with the Calvinists and the Moravians.

While Wesley supplemented his extract of *Aphorisms* with more accessible presentations, he did not set it aside. For example, he worked through the volume with his preachers in Ireland during a Conference in 1752, carefully comparing each claim to the scripture verses cited and weighing all objections. The recorded conclusion was full consensus with the position taken there. It was specifically queried why so many (including some Methodists) were prejudiced against the book, to which the response was that they did not understand it.[22] Wesley led a similar study of *Aphorisms* in Leeds the following year and likely on several other occasions.[23]

Wesley's abridgment of *Aphorisms* was both radical and conservative. On the one hand, he eliminated thirty-five of the original eighty aphorisms and reduced the treatise by three-fourths in length. On the other hand, the aphorisms removed were generally subsidiary in nature, and much of the text removed came from Baxter's tracing of scholastic debates related to his topics.[24] Wesley retained all of Baxter's major points and largely reproduced Baxter's very words. The general flow of his abridgment will be traced in annotations, while specific exclusions will be noted only when they may reflect theological disagreement.

Wesley published his abridgment of *Aphorisms* in April 1745, and a slightly revised reprint appeared in London in July of that year. The volume was not reprinted often, likely reflecting the limited audience for its technical discussion. But Wesley continued to value the work, placing it in his collected *Works* (1773), 22:141-94, and republishing it separately in 1784. The appearance in his *Works* is of

[21] See Sermon 5, 'Justification by Faith', 1:182-99 in this edn., esp. I.8-9, II.4-5, IV.5.

[22] Minutes (Limerick Conference, Aug. 14, 1752), *QQ*. 3-7, 10:251-52 in this edn.

[23] Minutes (Leeds, May 22, 1753), *QQ*. 8-9, 10:262 in this edn.

[24] E.g., JW deleted a section of the original *Aphorismes* surveying debates whether Christ provided the 'solution' for our debts or instead the 'satisfaction' for these debts (pp. 25-35). He similarly omitted an extended survey of those who insisted that Christ's passive righteousness is strictly imputed to us, versus those who contended that it only serves (along with Christ's active righteousness) as a 'satisfaction' of our 'debt' (pp. 52-61).

particular interest because Wesley made several editorial changes (noted below as appropriate) that reflect his mature concerns and positions on related issues. These changes do not appear in the 1784 edition because (as was his typical practice) Wesley sent the printer one of the last copies of the independent publication to reprint.

The text presented here is based on the first edition of 1745. For a stemma illustrating the transmission of the text through its four appearances during Wesley's lifetime, together with the substantive variant readings from those editions, see the appendix, pp. 485-88. For further details see *Bibliography*, No. 99.

AN

EXTRACT

OF

Mr *Richard Baxter's*

APHORISMS

OF

JUSTIFICATION.

PUBLISH'D

By *JOHN WESLEY*, M. A.
FELLOW of *Lincoln* College, OXFORD.

NEWCASTLE UPON TYNE:
Printed by JOHN GOODING, on the *Side*:
Sold by R. AKENHEAD, on *Tyne Bridge*, *Newcastle*; by T. TRYE, at *Gray's Inn Gate*, *Holbourn*, at the *Foundery*, near *Upper-Moorfields*, *London*; and at the *New-School* in the *Horse-Fair*, *Bristol*. 1745.
[Price THREE-PENCE.]

AN EXTRACT OF MR. RICHARD BAXTER'S *APHORISMS OF JUSTIFICATION*

To the Reader

I had not heard that there was such a book in the world as Mr. Baxter's *Aphorisms of Justification* when it was sent me by a bookseller, to whom I had sent for another tract on the same subject.[1] But before I had read many pages therein, I saw the wise providence of God and soon determined (notwithstanding a few expressions, which I do not altogether approve of) to reprint the substance thereof in as small a compass and at as low a price as possible.

O may he, who hath so solemnly declared, 'Think not that I am come to destroy the law or the prophets, [. . .] verily I say unto you, not one jot or one tittle shall pass from the law, till heaven and earth pass away,'[2] give the same blessing to this little treatise now as he did near an hundred years ago. May he once again make it a powerful antidote against the spreading poison of antinomianism, and thereby save many simple unwary souls from seeking death in the error of their life.

Newcastle upon Tyne,
March 25, 1745. John Wesley

[1] This claim is a little surprising. Wesley records reading *Reliquiae Baxterianae; or, Mr. Richard Baxter's Narrative . . . of his Life and Times* (London: T. Parkhurst, 1696) in his diary on July 3, 1741 (see 19:466 in this edn.). Baxter describes the debates over *Aphorismes* on pp. 107-11 of this vol.

[2] Matt. 5:17-18.

Proposition I [4][3]

The first covenant made by God with Adam did promise life, upon condition of perfect obedience, and threaten death upon the least disobedience.[4]

Prop. II [5]

This covenant being soon by man violated, the threatening must be fulfilled, and so the penalty suffered.

The word of his threatening being once past, he cannot absolutely pardon without the apparent violation of his truth or wisdom. Some think that it proceeded from his wisdom, rather than his justice, that man must suffer. But why should we separate what God hath joined? However, whether wisdom or justice or truth—or rather all these—were the ground of it, yet certain it is that a necessity there was the penalty should be inflicted, or else the Son of God should not have made satisfaction, nor sinners bear so much themselves.

Prop. III [6]

This penalty the offender himself could not bear without his everlasting undoing.

That is, not the full penalty. For part of it he did bear, and the earth for his sake, and all mankind to this day. But the full penalty would have been an everlasting suffering.

Prop. IV [7]

Jesus Christ, at the will of his Father, and upon his own will, being perfectly furnished for this work with a divine power and personal

[3] The number in brackets is the corresponding thesis in Baxter's original. JW omits the first three theses, in which Baxter allows that God's will in the broadest sense includes God's unilateral predestination of both the elect and the reprobate. Baxter then emphasizes that his focus in this treatise will be on God's 'legislative will', which calls for obedience within the Christian life (for the elect).

[4] For the origins of this typical English Puritan definition of the 'covenant of works', see Weir, *Origins of Federal Theology*; and McGiffert, 'Perkinsian Moment'.

righteousness, first undertook and afterwards discharged this debt by suffering what the law did threaten and the offender himself was unable to bear.

1. The love of God to the world was the first womb where the work of redemption was conceived (John 3:16, as it is taken conjunct with his own glory). The eternal wisdom and love found out and resolved on this way of recovery when it never entered into the thoughts of man to contrive or desire it.

2. The will of the Father and the Son are one. The Son is a voluntary undertaker of this task. It was not imposed upon him by constraint. When he is said to come to do his Father's will (Heb. 10:7-9) it doth also include his own will. And where he is said to do it in obedience to the Father, as it is spoken of a voluntary obedience, so is it spoken of the execution of our redemption, and in regard to the human nature especially, and not the undertaking by the divine nature alone. Not only the consent of Christ did make it lawful that he should be punished, being innocent, but also that special power which, as he was God, he had over his own life more than any creature hath (John 10:18, 'I have power,' saith Christ, 'to lay down my life.').

3. No mere creature was qualified for this work. Even the angels, that are righteous, do but their duty and therefore cannot merit for us, neither were they able to bear and overcome the penalty.

4. It must therefore be God that must satisfy God, both for the perfection of the obedience, for to be capable of meriting, for the bearing of the curse, and for the overcoming of it, and doing the rest of the works of the mediatorship which were to be done after the resurrection. Yet mere God it must not be, but man also, or else it would have been forgiveness without satisfaction, seeing God cannot be said to make satisfaction to himself.

5. Had not Christ been perfectly righteous himself, he had not been capable of satisfying for others.

6. The undertaking of the Son of God to satisfy was effectual before his actual satisfying, as a man that maketh a purchase may possess and enjoy the thing purchased upon the mere bargain made, or earnest paid, before he have fully paid the sum.

7. I know man's guilt and obligation to suffer is but metaphorically called his debt, yet because it is a Scripture phrase, expressing our obligation to bear the penalty of the violated law, I use it in that sense.

Christ did suffer a pain and misery of the same sort and of equal weight with that threatened, but yet because it was not in all respects the same, it was rather satisfaction than the payment of the proper debt.

8. Many say that Christ did as properly obey in our stead as he did suffer in our stead,[5] and that in God's esteem we were in Christ obeying and suffering, and so in him we did both perfectly fulfill the commands of the law by obedience and the threatenings of it by bearing the penalty. And thus, say they, is Christ's righteousness imputed to us—*viz.* his passive righteousness for the pardon of our sins, and delivering us from the penalty; his active righteousness for the making of us righteous, and giving us title to the Kingdom.

This opinion, in my judgment, containeth a great many mistakes.

1) It supposeth us to have been in Christ before we did believe, or were born, and that not only in a general sense, as all men, but in a special, as justified.

2) It teacheth imputation of Christ's righteousness in so strict a sense as will neither stand with reason nor the doctrine of Scripture, much less with the phrase of Scripture, which mentioneth no imputation of Christ or his righteousness to us at all, and hath given great advantage to the Papists against us in this doctrine of justification.

3) It seemeth to ascribe to God a mistaken judgment, as to esteem us to have been in Christ when we were not, and to have done and suffered in him what we did not.

4) It maketh Christ to have paid the same that was due and not the value, and so to justify us by payment of the proper debt and not by strict satisfaction. And indeed this is the very core of the mistake, to think that we have by delegation paid the proper debt of *obedience* to the whole law, or that in Christ we have perfectly obeyed; whereas (1) it cannot be said that *we* did it, [and] (2) that which Christ did was to satisfy for *our* non-payment and disobedience.

5) It supposeth the law to require both obedience and suffering in respect of the same time and actions, which it doth not. And whereas they say that the law requireth suffering for what is past and obedience for the future, this is to deny that Christ hath satisfied for future sins. The time is near when those future sins will be also past; what doth the law require then? If we do not obey for the future, then we sin; if we sin, the law requires nothing but suffering.

[5] Reflecting the Puritan establishment at the time of his writing, Baxter had said, 'Most of our ordinary divines say . . .'.

6) It fondly supposeth a difference betwixt one that is just and one that is no sinner, one that hath his sin or guilt taken away and one that hath his unrighteousness taken away. Whereas, as there is no middle betwixt straight and crooked, so neither between conformity to the law (which is righteousness) and deviation from it (which is unrighteousness).

7) It maketh our righteousness to consist of two parts—*viz.* the putting away of our guilt, and the imputation of righteousness; *i.e.*, (1) removing our crookedness, (2) making us straight.

8) It ascribeth these two supposed parts to two distinct supposed causes—the one to Christ's fulfilling the precept by his active righteousness, the latter to his fulfilling the threatening by his passive righteousness—as if there must be one cause of introducing light and another of expelling darkness, or one cause to take away the crookedness of a line and another to make it straight.

9) The like vain distinction it maketh between delivering from death and giving title to life, or freeing us from the penalty and giving us the reward. For as when all sin of omission and commission is absent, there is no unrighteousness; so when all the penalty is taken away, both that of pain and that of loss, the party is restored to his former happiness. Indeed there is a greater superadded degree of life and glory procured by Christ, more than we lost in Adam. But as that life is not opposed to the death or penalty of the first covenant, but to that of the second; so is it the effect of Christ's passive, as well as of his active righteousness.

The other opinion about our participation of Christ's righteousness is this: that God the Father doth accept the sufferings and merits of his Son as a full satisfaction to his violated law, and as a valuable consideration upon which he will wholly forgive the offenders themselves, and receive them again into his favour, and give them the addition of a more excellent happiness also, so that they will but receive his Son upon the terms expressed in the gospel. This opinion, as it is more simple and plain, so it avoideth all the forementioned inconveniences.

Prop. V [8]

Wherefore the Father hath delivered all things into the hands of the Son, and given him all power in heaven and earth, and made him Lord both of the dead and living (John 13:3; Matt. 28:18; John 5:21-27; Rom. 14:9).

Prop. VI [9]

It was not the intent either of the Father or the Son that by this satisfaction the offenders should be immediately delivered from the whole curse of the law, and freed from the evil which they had brought upon themselves; but some part must be executed on soul and body, and the creatures themselves, and remain upon them at the pleasure of Christ (Rev. 1:18; 1 Cor. 15:26).

The common judgment is that Christ hath taken away the whole curse from believers (though not the suffering) by bearing it himself, and now they are only afflictions of love and not punishments. I do not contradict this doctrine through affectation of singularity, the Lord knoweth, but through constraint of judgment, and that upon these grounds following.

1. It is undeniable that Christ's taking the curse upon himself did not wholly prevent the execution upon the offender (Gen. 3:7-19).

2. It is evident from the event, seeing we feel part of the curse fulfilled on us. We eat in labour and sweat. The earth doth bring forth thorns and briars. Women bring forth their children in sorrow. Our native depravity is the curse upon our souls. We are sick and weary, and full of fears and sorrows and shame, and at last we die and turn to dust.

3. The Scripture tells us plainly that we all die in Adam (even that death from which we must at the resurrection be raised in Christ; 1 Cor. 15:21-22), and that death is the wages of sin (Rom. 6:23), and that the sickness and weakness and death of the godly is caused by their sins (1 Cor. 11:30-31). And if so, then doubtless they are in execution of the threatening of the law, though not in full rigour.

4. It is manifest that our sufferings are in their own nature evils to us, and the sanctifying of them to us taketh not away their natural evil, but only produceth by it, as by an occasion, a greater good. Doubtless so far as it is the effect of sin it is evil, and the effect also of the law.

5. They are ascribed to God's anger, as the moderating of them is ascribed to his love (Ps. 30:5, and a thousand places more).

6. They are called punishments in Scripture, and therefore we may call them so (Lev. 26:41-43; Lam. 3:39 and 4:6, 22; Ezra 9:13; Hos. 4:9 and 12:2; Lev. 26:18-24).

7. The very nature of affliction is to be a loving punishment, a natural evil sanctified, and so to be mixed of evil and good, as it

proceedeth from mixed causes. Therefore, to say that Christ hath taken away the curse and evil but not the suffering is a contradiction, because so far as it is a suffering it is to us evil and the execution of the curse.[6] What reason can be given why God should not do us all that good without our sufferings, which now he doth by them, if there were not sin and wrath and law in them? Sure he could better us by easier means.

8. All those scriptures and reasons that are brought to the contrary do prove no more but this, that our afflictions are not the rigorous execution of the threatening of the law, that they are not wholly or chiefly in wrath.

9. The Scripture saith plainly that death is one of the enemies that is not yet overcome, but shall be last conquered (1 Cor. 15:26), and of our corruption the case is plain.

10. The whole stream of Scripture maketh Christ to have now the sole disposing of us and our sufferings, to have prevented the full execution of the curse, and to manage that which lieth on us for our advantage and good, but no where doth it affirm that he suddenly delivereth us.

Prop. VII [10]

Man having not only broken his first covenant, but disabled himself to perform its conditions for the future; and so being out of all hope of attaining righteousness and life thereby, it pleased the Father and the Mediator to prescribe to him a new law, and tender him a new covenant; the conditions whereof should be more easy to the sinner and yet more abasing, and should more clearly manifest and more highly honour the inconceivable love of the Father and Redeemer.

1. If Christ should have pardoned all that was past, and renewed the first violated covenant, and set man in the same estate that he fell from, in point of guilt, yet would he have fallen as desperately the next temptation. Yea, though he had restored to him his primitive strength, yet experience hath showed on how slippery a ground his happiness would have stood.

2. God the Father, and Christ the Mediator, who have one will, did therefore resolve upon a more suitable way of happiness.

[6] *Works* (1773) omits these first two sentences of this paragraph.

3. This way, as the former, is by both a law and covenant. As it is a law, it is by Christ enjoined, and either obedience or the penalty shall be exacted. As it is a covenant, it is only tendered, and not enforced.

4. Though without grace we can no more believe than perfectly obey, as a dead man can no more remove a straw than a mountain, yet the conditions of the gospel, considered in themselves or in reference to the strength which God will bestow,[7] are far more easy than the old conditions (Matt. 11:29-30; 1 John 5:3). And more abasing they are to the sinner, in that he hath far less to do in the work of his salvation, and also in that they contain the acknowledgment of his lost estate through his own former self-destroying folly.

Prop. VIII [11]

Not that Christ doth absolutely null or repeal the old covenant hereby, but he superaddeth this as the only possible way of life. The former still continueth to command, prohibit, promise, and threaten; so that the sins even of the justified are still breaches of that law, and are threatened and cursed thereby.

I know it is the judgment of many that the law, as it is a covenant of works, is quite null and repealed in regard to the sins of believers. Yea, many do believe that the covenant of works is repealed to all the world, and only the covenant of grace in force. Against both these I maintain this assertion, by the arguments which you find under the following position, and I hope, notwithstanding that, I extol free grace as much, and preach the law as little, in a forbidden sense, as though I held the contrary opinion.

Prop. IX [12]

Therefore we must not plead the repeal of the law for our justification, but must refer it to our surety, who, by the value and efficacy of his one offering and merits,[8] doth continually satisfy.

[7] *Works* (1773) omits 'or in reference . . . will bestow'; likely to reflect more clearly that no one has to wait for the strength given to all in *prevenient grace*.

[8] *Works* (1773) replaces 'the value and efficacy of his one offering and merits' with 'his works'. JW was likely seeking to avoid any suggestion of the distinction between Christ's passive righteousness (his 'offering') and his active righteousness (his 'merit').

I shall here explain to you in what sense and how far the law is in force, and how far not, and then prove it under the next head.

You must here distinguish betwixt (1) the repealing of the law and the relaxing of it; (2) between a dispensation, absolute and respective; (3) between the alteration of the law and the alteration of the subject's relation to it; (4) between a discharge conditional, with a suspension of execution, and a discharge absolute; and so I resolve the question thus:

1. The law of works is not abrogated or repealed, but dispensed with or relaxed. A dispensation is (as Grotius defineth it)[9] an act of a superior whereby the obligation of a law in force is taken away, as to certain persons and things.

2. This dispensation therefore is not total or absolute, but respective. For (1) though it dispense with the rigorous execution, yet not with every degree of execution. (2) Though the law be dispensed with, as it containeth the proper subjects of the penalty—*viz.* the parties offending, and also the circumstances of duration, etc.—yet in regard of the mere punishment, abstracted from person and circumstances, it is not dispensed with. For to Christ it was not dispensed with, his satisfaction was by paying the full value.

3. Though by this dispensation our freedom may be as full as upon a repeal, yet the alteration is not made in the law, but in our relation to the law.

4. So far is the law dispensed with to all as to suspend the rigorous execution for a time, and a discharge conditional procured and granted them, but an absolute discharge is granted to none in this life. For even when we do perform the condition, yet still the discharge remains conditional, till we have quite finished our performance. For it is not one instantaneous act of believing which shall quite discharge us, but a continued faith. No longer are we discharged than we are believers. And where the condition is not performed, the law is still in force, and shall be executed upon the offender himself.

I speak nothing in all this of the directive use of the moral law to believers, but how far the law is yet in force even as it is a covenant of works, because an utter repeal of it in this sense is so commonly but inconsiderately asserted. That it is no further overthrown, no not to believers, than is here explained, I now come to prove.

[9] See Hugo Grotius (1583–1645), *Defensio fidei Catholicae, de satisfactione Christi* (Leiden: Patius, 1617), chap. 3.

Prop. X [13]

If this were not so, but that Christ had abrogated the first covenant, then it would follow (1) that no sin but that of Adam, and final unbelief, is so much as threatened with death, or that death is deserved by it; for what the law in force doth not threaten, that is not deserved, or due by law. It would follow (2) that Christ died not to prevent or remove the wrath and curse so deserved, or due to us for any but Adam's sin, nor to pardon our sins at all, but only to prevent our desert of wrath and curse, and consequently, to prevent our need of pardon. It would follow (3) that against the eternal wrath at the day of judgment we must not plead the pardon of any sin but the first, but our own not deserving wrath because of the repeal of that law before the sin was committed. All which consequences seem to me unsufferable, which cannot be avoided if the law be repealed.

Scripture plainly teacheth that all men—even the elect—are under the law till they believe and enter into the covenant of the gospel. Therefore it is said, 'He that believeth not is condemned already' (John 3:18) and 'the wrath of God abideth on him' (ver. 36). And we are said to believe for remission of sins [in] Acts 2:38, Mark 1:4, Luke 24:47, Acts 10:43, and [Acts] 3:19; which show that sin is not before remitted, and consequently the law not repealed, else how could the redeemed be by nature the children of wrath (Eph. 2:3)? The circumcised are debtors to the whole law (Gal. 5:3-4), and Christ is become of no effect to them. But they that are led by the Spirit are not under the law, and against such there is no law (Gal. 5:18, 23).[10] The Scripture hath concluded all under sin (and so under the law no doubt) that the promise by faith in Jesus Christ might be given to them that believe (Gal. 3:22). We are under the law when Christ doth redeem us (Gal. 4:5; see also James 2:9-10; 1 Tim. 1:8, 1 Cor. 15:56; Gal. 3:19-21). Therefore our deliverance is conditionally from the curse of the law—*viz.* if we will obey the gospel. And

[10] *Works* (1773) omits the prior two sentences. JW became even more sensitive after the release of this tract to the importance of emphasizing the legitimate continuing role of the law in Christian life. See particularly three sermons published in 1750—No. 34, 'The Original, Nature, Properties, and Use of the Law', 2:4-19 in this edn.; No. 35, 'The Law Established by Faith, I', 2:20-32 in this edn.; and No. 36, 'The Law Established by Faith, II', 2:33-43 in this edn. Cf. his letter to an 'Evangelical Layman', Dec. 20, 1751, 26:482-89 in this edn.

this deliverance, together with the abrogation of the ceremonial law, is it which is so often mentioned as a privilege of believers and an effect of the blood of Christ, which deliverance from the curse is yet more full when we perform the conditions of our freedom. And then we are said to be dead to the law (Rom. 7:4) and the obligation to punishment dead as to us (ver. 6), but not the law void or dead in itself.

Again, all the scriptures and arguments (pages 60-61)[11] which prove that afflictions are punishments do prove also that the law is not repealed. For no man can suffer for breaking a repealed law, nor by the threats of a repealed law. Yet I know that this covenant of works continueth not to the same ends and uses as before, nor is it so to be preached or used. We must neither take that covenant as a way of life, as if now we must get salvation by our fulfilling its condition, nor must we look on its curse as lying on us remedilessly.[12]

Prop. XI [14]

The tenor of the new covenant is this: that Christ, having made sufficient satisfaction to the law,[13] *whosoever will repent and believe in him to the end shall be justified, through that satisfaction, from all that the law did charge upon them, and be moreover advanced to far greater privileges and glory than they fell from. But whosoever fulfilleth not these conditions shall have no more benefit from the blood of Christ than what they here received and abused, but must answer the charge of the law themselves; and for their neglect of Christ must also suffer a far greater condemnation. Or briefly, whosoever believeth in Christ shall not perish, but have everlasting life; but he that believeth not shall not see life, but the wrath of God abideth on him* (Mark 16:16; John 3:15-18, 3:36, 5:24, 6:35-47, 7:38, 11:25-26, 12:46; Acts 10:43; Rom. 3:26, 4:5, 5:1, 10:4, 10:10; 1 John 5:10; Mark 1:15, 6:12; Luke 13:3-5, 24:47; Acts 5:31, 11:18, 20:21, 2:38, 3:19, 8:22, 26:20; Rev. 2:5, 16; Heb. 6:1, 2; 2 Pet. 3:9).

[11] This refers to pages in Baxter's book that are digested in Prop. VI above.

[12] *Works* (1773) omits the last two sentences in this paragraph. On the likely reason, see n. 10 above.

[13] *Works* (1773) replaces 'to the law' with 'for us'. This may reflect the discomfort that JW developed in later debates over the imputation of Christ's active righteousness about speaking of the law as a 'person injured and to be satisfied'. Cf. letter to James Hervey, Oct. 15, 1756, JW's comment on Hervey's p. 54, vol. 13 in this edn.

1. Christ's satisfaction to the law goes before the new covenant, though not in regard to its payment (which was in the fullness of time) yet in regard of the undertaking, acceptance, and efficacy. There could be no treating on new terms till the old obligations were satisfied and suspended.

I account them not worth the confuting who tell us that Christ is the only party conditioned with, and that the new covenant, as to us, hath no conditions. The place they allege for this assertion is that Jer. 31:31-33, cited in Heb. 8:8-10, which place containeth not the full tenor of the whole new covenant. But it is called the new covenant because it expresseth the nature of the benefits of the new covenant as it is offered on God's part, without mentioning man's conditions, that being not pertinent to the business the prophet had in hand.[14]

But those men erroneously think that nothing is a condition but what is to be performed by our own strength. But if they will believe Scripture, the places before alleged will prove that the new covenant hath conditions on our part as well as the old.

2. Some benefit from Christ the condemned did here receive, as the delay of their condemnation and many more mercies, though they turn them all into greater judgments.

Prop. XII [15]

Though Christ hath satisfied the law, yet is it not his will that any man should be justified or saved thereby who hath not some ground in himself of personal and particular right and claim thereto, nor that any should be justified by the blood only as shed or offered except it be also received and applied. So that no man, by the mere satisfaction made, is freed from the law or curse of the first violated covenant absolutely, but conditionally only.

I have showed before that Christ intended not to remove all our misery as soon as he died, nor as soon as we believed. I am now to show that he doth not justify by the shedding of his blood immediately, without somewhat of man intervening to give him a legal title thereto. We are therefore said to be justified by faith. Let all the

[14] Wesley omits Baxter's suggested alternative explanation: 'or else it speaks only of what God will do for his elect in giving them the first grace and enabling them to perform the conditions of the new covenant' (p. 91).

antinomians show but one scripture which speaks of justification from eternity.

There are several other necessaries to justify and save, which being supposed, the blood of Christ will be effectual. Not that it receiveth its efficacy from these, nor that these do add anything at all to its worth or value—no more than the cabinet to the jewel, or the applying hand to the medicine, or the offender's acceptation to the pardon of his prince. Yet without this acceptation and application this blood will not be effectual to justify us. So that, as Austin saith, 'He that made us without us, will not save us without us.'[15] A legal title we must have before we can be justified, and there must be somewhat in ourselves to prove that title, or else all men should have equal right.

Prop. XIII [16]

The obeying of a law and performing the conditions of a covenant, or satisfying for disobedience or non-performance, is our righteousness in reference to that law and covenant.

If we understand not what righteousness is, we may dispute long enough about justification to little purpose.

There is a two-fold righteousness, or fulfilling of God's law. The primary and most proper righteousness lieth in the conformity of our actions to the precept. The secondary is, when, though we have broke the precepts, yet we have satisfied for our breach, either by our own suffering or some other way.

The first hath reference to the commands, when none can accuse us to have broke the law. The second hath reference to the penalty, when, though we have broke the law, yet it hath nothing against us for so doing because it is satisfied. These two kinds of righteousness cannot stand together in the same person in regard of the same law and actions. He that hath one, hath not the other. He that hath the first, needs not the second. There must be a fault, or no satisfaction. This fault must be confessed, and so the first kind of righteousness

[15] Baxter cites here St. Augustine's sermon on Phil. 3:3-16 (Sermon 169, xi, Migne, *Patrologia Latina*, 38:923). This use may have brought the quotation to JW's attention. In any case, he cites it with favor in two of his own later sermons emphasizing the co-operant nature of God's saving work: Sermon 63, 'The General Spread of the Gospel,' §12, 2:490 in this edn.; and Sermon 85, 'On Working Out Our Own Salvation,' III.7, 3:208 in this edn.

disclaimed, before satisfaction can be pleaded; and satisfaction must be pleaded before a delinquent can be justified. This, well understood, would give a clearer insight into the nature of our righteousness and justification than many have yet attained. The great question is: Of what sort is our righteousness whereby we are justified? I answer: of the second sort, which, though it be not a righteousness so honouring ourselves, yet it is honourable to Christ. The first kind of righteousness, as it is in Christ, cannot, retaining its own form, be made ours. And to that the Papists' arguments will hold good.[16] The law commanded our own personal obedience and not another's for us. We did not so personally obey, we did not really *obey in Christ*,[17] and God doth not judge us to do what we did not. If we had, yet it would not have made us just, for one sin will make us unjust though we were never so obedient before and after. Therefore, if we had *obeyed in Christ*, and yet sinned *in ourselves*, we are breakers of the law still, and so our righteousness cannot be of the first sort. This breach therefore must be satisfied for, and consequently our righteousness must be of the second sort, seeing both cannot stand in one person. Christ only had both these kinds of righteousness—*viz.* the righteousness of perfect obedience, and the righteousness of satisfaction for disobedience.

Prop. XIV [17]

Therefore, as there are two covenants with their distinct conditions, so is there a two-fold righteousness and both of them absolutely necessary to salvation.

Prop. XV [18]

Our legal righteousness, or righteousness of the first covenant, is not personal, or consisteth not in any qualifications of our own persons or actions performed by us (for we never fulfilled, nor personally satisfied the law) but it is wholly without us in Christ. And in this sense it is that the apostle (and every Christian) disclaimeth his own righteousness, or his own works.

[16] *Works* (1773) omits this sentence.

[17] JW adds emphasis, not present in Baxter, in this and the following two instances.

Objection 1: Doth not the apostle say that as 'touching the righteousness which is in the law' he was 'blameless' (Phil. 3:6)? *Answer:* That is, he so exactly observed the ceremonial law, and the external part of the moral law, that no man could blame him for the breach of them. But this is nothing to such a keeping of the whole covenant as might render him blameless in the sight of God.

Objection 2: Then Christ's righteousness and our own works do concur to the composing of our perfect righteousness. *Answer:* Though this objection doth puzzle some, yet the vanity of it may be easily discovered thus: (1) An action is not righteous which is not conformable to the law. If in some respects it be conformable, and in some not, it cannot be called a righteous action. So that we, having no actions perfectly conformed to the law, have therefore no one righteous action. (2) If we had yet many righteous actions, if but one were unrighteous, will not serve to denominate the person righteous according to the law of works. And that these, joined with Christ's righteousness, do not make up one righteousness for us is plain thus: The righteousness which we have *in Christ* is not of the same sort with his, for his is a righteousness of the first kind—*viz.* consisting in conformity to the precept. But Christ's righteousness, imputed to us, is only that of the second sort—*viz.* by satisfaction for our disobedience—and cannot therefore possibly be joined with our imperfect[18] obedience to make up one righteousness for us.

Prop. XVI [19]

Those only shall have part in Christ's satisfaction, and so in him be legally righteous, who believe and obey the gospel and so are in themselves evangelically righteous.

Prop. XVII [20]

Though Christ performed the conditions of the law, and satisfied for our non-performance, yet it is ourselves that must perform the conditions of the gospel.

[18] In the 2nd edn. (1745) JW changes Baxter's 'imperfect' (*Aphorismes*, 106) to 'perfect', apparently trying to remove the suggestion that Christian obedience will always be imperfect. This change remains in *Works* (1773) and the 1784 edn.

These two positions seem to me so plain and clear that they need not much explication. Yet because some antinomians oppose them I shall say something thereto, though, for my part, I do so much wonder that any able divines should deny them that methinks they should be articles in our creed and a part of children's catechisms.

The righteousness of the new covenant being the performance of its conditions, and its conditions being our obeying the gospel, or believing, it must needs be plain that on no other terms do we partake of the righteousness of Christ. To affirm, therefore, that our evangelical or new covenant righteousness is *in Christ* and not *in ourselves*, or performed by Christ and not by ourselves, is such a monstrous piece of antinomian doctrine as no man who knoweth the nature and difference of the covenant can possibly entertain, and as every Christian should abhor as unsufferable.

For 1. it implieth blasphemy against Christ, as if he had sin to repent of, or pardon to accept, and a Lord that redeemed him to receive and submit to, for these are the conditions of the new covenant.

2. It implieth that Jews and pagans, and every man, shall be saved. Do not say that I odiously wring out these consequences, for they are plain. For if any be damned, it must be either for breaking the first covenant or the second. If the former be charged upon him, he may escape by pleading the second fulfilled; if the latter, the same plea will serve. So that if Christ hath fulfilled both covenants for all men, then none can perish.

3. And [it implies] that believing is needless, not only as to our justification but to any other use. For what need one thing be twice done? If Christ hath fulfilled the new covenant for us, as well as the old, what need we do it again? Shall we come after him, to do the work he hath perfected?

4. It confoundeth law and gospel. It overthroweth all the laws and precepts of Christ. It contradicteth the whole scope of the Scripture, which tells us that Christ was made under the law (and not under the gospel), fulfilled the law (but not the gospel covenant), bore the curse of the law (but not the gospel), and which imposeth a necessity of fulfilling the conditions of the gospel themselves upon all that will be justified and saved. To quote the scriptures that assert this would be to transcribe almost all the doctrinal part of the New Testament. What unsavoury stuff then is that of Mr. Saltmarsh,

of *Free Grace*[19] (pages 83-84) who directeth those that doubt of their gospel sincerity to see it *in Christ* because Christ hath believed perfectly, he hath sorrowed for sin perfectly, he hath repented perfectly, he hath obeyed perfectly, he hath mortified sin perfectly, and all is ours, etc. If this be meant of gospel believing, repenting, sorrowing, obeying, and mortifying, then it is blasphemy—as if Christ had a saviour to believe in for pardon and life, or sin to repent of, and sorrow for, and mortify. But if he meant it of legal believing in God, or repenting, sorrowing for, mortifying of sin *in us*, and not *in himself*, then is it no more to the business in hand than a harp to a harrow, as they say. It is not legal believing which is the evidence doubted of, and sure Christ's repenting and sorrowing for our sin is no clearing to us that we repent of our own, nor any acquitting of us for not doing it. And for his mortifying sin in us, that is the doubt: whether it be done in the doubting soul or not? But I let go this sort of men, as being fitter first to learn the grounds of religion in a catechism than to manage those disputes wherewith they trouble the world.

Prop. XVIII [21]

Not that we can perform these conditions without grace (for without Christ we can do nothing), but that he enableth us to perform them ourselves, and doth not himself repent, believe, love Christ, [and] obey the gospel for us, as he did satisfy the law for us.

Prop. XIX [22]

In this fore-explained sense it is that men in Scripture are said to be personally righteous. And in this sense it is that the faith and duties of believers are said to please God—viz. *as they are related to the covenant of grace, and not as they are measured by the covenant of works.*

Those that will not acknowledge that the godly are called righteous in Scripture by reason of a personal righteousness consisting in the rectitude of their own dispositions and actions, as well as in regard of their imputed righteousness, may be convinced from these scriptures, if they will believe them: Gen. 7:2, 18:23-24; Job 17:9; Pss. 1:5-6, 37:17-21, etc.; Eccl. 9:1-2; Ezek. 18:20-24, 33:12-18;

[19] John Saltmarsh, *Free Grace; or, The Flowings of Christ's Blood Free to Sinners* (London: Giles Calvert, 1646).

Matt. 9:13, 13:43, 25:37-46; Luke 1:6; Heb. 11:4; 1 Pet. 4:18; 2 Pet. 2:8; 1 John 3:7-12; Rev. 32:11; Matt. 10:41; Rom. 5:7 ('so their ways are called righteousness'); Pss. 15:2, 23:3, 45:7, etc.; Matt. 5:20, 21:32; Luke 1:75; Acts 10:35; Rom. 6:13-20; 1 Cor. 15:34; 1 John 2:29, 3:10; Eph. 4:24; etc.

Righteousness is the denomination of our actions or persons as they relate to some rule. This rule, when it is the law of man, and our actions suit thereto, we are then righteous before men. When this rule is God's law, it is either that of works or that of grace. In relation to the former there is none righteous, no not one, 'for all have sinned, and come short of the glory of God' [Rom. 3:23]. But in relation to the rule of the new covenant all the regenerate are personally righteous, because they all perform the conditions of this covenant and are properly pronounced righteous thereby. Neither can it be conceived how the works of believers should either please God, or be called righteousness, as they relate to that old rule, which doth pronounce them unrighteous, hateful, and accursed.

But the antinomians (and some other simple ones whom they have misled), if they do but hear a man talk of a righteousness *in himself*, or in any thing he can do thereto, they startle at such doctrine, and even gnash the teeth, as if we preached flat popery, yea, as if we cried down Christ and set up ourselves, not understanding the difference between the two sorts of righteousness—that of the old covenant, which is all out of us *in Christ*; and that of the new covenant, which is all out of Christ *in ourselves*, though wrought by the power of the Spirit of Christ.

Prop. XX [23]

In this sense also it is so far from being an error to affirm that faith itself is our righteousness, that it is a truth necessary for every Christian to know. That is, faith is our evangelical righteousness (in the sense before explained) as Christ is our legal righteousness.

This assertion, so odious to those that understand not its grounds, is yet so clear from what is said before that I need to add no more to prove it. For I have cleared before (1) that there must be a personal righteousness, besides that imputed, in all that are justified; and (2) that the fulfilling of the conditions of each covenant is our righteousness, in reference to that covenant. But faith is the fulfilling of the conditions of the new covenant; therefore it is our righteousness in relation to that covenant.

Question: In what sense then is faith said to be 'imputed to us for righteousness', if it be our righteousness itself?

Answer: Plainly thus: Man is become unrighteous by breaking the law of righteousness that was given him. Christ fully satisfieth for this transgression and buys the prisoners into his hands, and maketh with them a new covenant that whosoever will believe in him, who hath thus satisfied, it shall be as effectual for their justification as if they had fulfilled the law of works themselves. A tenant forfeiteth his lease to his landlord by not paying his rent. He runs deep in debt to him and is disabled to pay him any more rent for the future, whereupon he is put out of his house and cast into prison till he pay the debt. His landlord's son payeth it for him, taketh him out of prison, and putteth him in his house again as his tenant, having purchased house and all to himself. He maketh him a new lease in this tenor, that paying but a pepper corn yearly to him, he shall be acquit both from his debt and from all other rent for the future, which by his old lease was to be paid. Yet doth he not cancel the old lease, but keepeth it in his hands to put it in suit against the tenant if he should be so foolish as to deny the payment of the pepper corn. In this case the payment of the grain of pepper is imputed to the tenant, as if he had paid the rent of the old lease. Yet this imputation doth not extol the pepper corn, nor vilify the benefit of his benefactor who redeemed him. Nor can it be said that the purchase did only serve to advance the value and efficacy of that grain of pepper. But thus a personal rent must be paid for the testification of his homage. He was never redeemed to be independent as his own landlord and master. The old rent he cannot pay. His new landlord's clemency is such that he hath resolved this grain shall serve the turn.

Do I need to apply this in the present case, or cannot every man apply it? Even so is our evangelical righteousness, or faith, imputed to us for as real righteousness, as perfect obedience. Two things are considerable in this debt of righteousness: the value and the personal performance. The value of Christ's satisfaction is imputed to us, instead of the value of a perfect obedience of our own performing, and the value of our faith is not so imputed. But because there must be some personal performance of homage, therefore the personal performance of faith shall be imputed to us for a sufficient personal payment, as if we had paid the full rent, because Christ, whom we believe in, hath paid it, and he will take this for satisfactory homage. So it is in point of personal performance, and not of value, that faith is imputed.

Prop. XXI [25][20]

It is an improper speech of some divines that Christ first justifieth our persons, and then our duties and actions.

It is improper, in the best sense, because (1) it is contrary to the scripture use of the word 'justifying', which is the acquitting of us from the charge of breaking the law, and not from the charge of violating the new covenant; (2) it is against the nature of the thing, seeing justification (as you shall see anon) implieth accusation, but the esteeming a righteous action to be as it is doth not imply any accusation; (3) this speech, joining the justification of persons and actions together, doth seem to intimate the same kind of justification of both, and so doth tend to seduce the hearers to a dangerous error. For, if it be understood in the worst sense, it will overthrow the righteousness of Christ imputed and the whole scope of the gospel, and will set up the doctrine of justification by works. For if God do justify our works from any legal accusation, as he doth our persons, then it will follow that our works are just, and consequently we are to be justified by them.

Prop. XXII [26]

Neither can our performance of the conditions of the gospel be said to merit the reward, seeing there is nothing in the value of it, or any benefit that God receiveth by it, which may so entitle it meritorious; neither is there any proportion betwixt it and the reward.

Prop. XXIII [31]

The gospel doth establish, and not repeal, the moral law; and so is perfect obedience commanded, and every sin forbidden now as exactly as under the covenant of works.

Prop. XXIV [36]

The pardoning of sin is a gracious act of God, discharging the offender by the gospel-promise or grant from the obligation to punishment, upon consideration of the satisfaction made by Christ, accepted by the sinner and pleaded with God.

[20] JW omits Baxter's Thesis 24: 'This personal gospel righteousness is in its kind a perfect righteousness, and so far we may admit the doctrine of personal perfection.' In the explication Baxter denies perfect 'holiness' in this life, allowing only our perfect 'righteousness' in Christ. *Aphorismes*, 130-34.

I call pardon a 'gracious act', for if it were not in some sort gracious or free, it were no pardon. Let those think of this who say, 'We have perfectly obeyed the law *in Christ*, and are therefore righteous.' If the proper debt, either of obedience or suffering, be paid, either by ourselves or by another, then there is no place left for pardon. For when the debt is paid we owe nothing, except new obedience, and therefore can have nothing forgiven us. For the creditor cannot refuse the proper debt, nor deny an acquittance upon receipt thereof. But Christ having paid the value, and not the strict debt, this satisfaction the Father might have chosen to accept, which yet because he freely doth, therefore is his gracious act properly called pardon.

The ignorant antinomians think it cannot be a free act of grace if there be any condition on our part for enjoying it. As if, in the forementioned comparison, the tenant's redemption were the less free because his new lease requireth the rent of a pepper corn in token of homage. As if, when a pardon is procured for a condemned malefactor, upon condition that he shall not reject it when it is offered him, this was therefore no free pardon.

Prop. XXV [38-39][21]

Justification is a gracious act of God, by the promise or grant of the new covenant, acquitting the offender from the accusation and condemnation of the old covenant, upon consideration of the satisfaction made by Christ and accepted by the sinner. But final justification is a gracious act of God by Christ, according to the gospel, by sentence at his public bar, acquitting the sinner from the accusation and condemnation of the law pleaded against him by Satan, upon consideration of the satisfaction made by Christ, accepted by the sinner and pleaded for him.

Prop. XXVI [43]

The justification which we have in Christ's own justification is but conditional as to the particular offenders, and none can lay claim to it till he have performed the conditions, nor shall any be personally

[21] JW skipped Thesis 37, which distinguished between present and final justification, and here combines Baxter's next two theses, which define these in more detail.

justified till then. Even the elect[a] *remain personally unjust and unjustified, for all their conditional justification in Christ, till they do believe.*

Prop. XXVII [44]

Men that are but thus conditionally pardoned and justified, may be unpardoned and unjustified again for their non-performance of the conditions, and all the debt so forgiven be required at their hands, and all this without any change in God or in his laws.

Prop. XXVIII [45]

Yea, in case the justified by faith should cease believing, the Scripture would pronounce them unjust again, and yet without any change in God or Scripture, but only in themselves. Because their justification doth continue conditional as long as they live here. The Scripture doth justify no man by name, but all believers as such. Therefore, if they should cease to be believers, they would cease to be justified.

Prop. XXIX [47]

The new covenant accuseth no man as deserving its penalty but only those that perform not its conditions—that is, the finally unbelieving and impenitent rebels against Christ, their rightful Lord.

That the gospel doth not condemn men or threaten them with damnation for any sins but unbelief, I dare not speak or think. But that the gospel threateneth no man with damnation but unbelievers is out of all question. And consequently the proper sin threatened in the new covenant, as such, is unbelief—the rest are but left and settled on the sinner by this.

Prop. XXX [51]

If Satan should falsely accuse us of not performing the conditions of the new covenant, and so having no part in Christ's satisfaction, here

[a] N.B. Mr. Baxter held absolute Predestination. [In *Works* (1773) Wesley inserts the qualifier 'then held'.]

we must be justified only by our faith, or personal gospel-righteousness, and not by any thing that Christ hath done or suffered. For in all false accusations we must defend our innocency and plead not guilty.

To tell Satan that Christ hath fulfilled *the law for us*, when he is accusing us of not *fulfilling the gospel*, silly women are made believe, by antinomian teachers, that this is a solid way of comforting. But Satan is a better logician than to be baffled with such arguing. And as silly a shift it would be to tell him that Christ hath fulfilled the gospel-conditions *for us.*[22] The best is, these teachers do but spoil the comforts of believers, and not their safety, for in the case in hand we suppose the accusation to be false. But yet, by such grounds they may very easily overthrow the safety also of unbelievers, while they teach them how to comfort themselves *without faith*, or to look for all out of themselves *in Christ*.

Prop. XXXI [52]

We must not plead for our justification that Christ hath made us free from the very fact, nor from the sinfulness of the fact, nor from its desert of punishment. If Christ had done any of this for us, he must verify contradictories. But we must plead that the penalty is not due to our persons, notwithstanding the fact and its sinfulness and demerit, because Christ hath satisfied for all this.

For, (1) that the fact should be done and not done is a contradiction. (2) So is it that the fact should be sinful and not sinful. (3) Or that it should deserve death and not deserve it. Or that it should be a sin against that threatening law and yet not deserve the penalty threatened. Besides, if any of these three could have been taken off, what need Christ have died? But that which remission and justification freeth us from is the dueness of punishment to our persons, notwithstanding the dueness of it to the sin, because what is due to the sin is inflicted on the person of another already, even Christ.

Prop. XXXII [55]

Before it be committed it is no sin; and where there is no sin, the penalty is not due; and where it is not due, it cannot properly be forgiven; therefore sin is not forgiven before it be committed.

[22] *Works* (1773) omits the remainder of this paragraph.

Prop. XXXIII [57][23]

It is faith which justifieth men (1) in the nearest sense, directly and properly, as it is the fulfilling of the condition of the new covenant; [and] (2) in the remote and more improper sense, as it is the receiving of Christ and his satisfactory righteousness.

That it is faith in a proper sense that is said to justify, and not Christ's righteousness only, which it receives, may appear from the plain and constant phrase of Scripture, which saith he that believeth shall be justified, and that we are justified by faith, and that faith is imputed for righteousness. It had been as easy for the Holy Ghost to have said that Christ only is imputed, or his righteousness only, or Christ only justifieth, etc., if he had so meant.

That faith doth most directly and properly justify (as it is the fulfilling of the condition of the new covenant) appeareth thus. The new covenant only doth put the stamp of God's authority upon it, in making it the condition. A two-fold stamp is necessary to make it a current medium of our justification: (1) command, (2) promise. Now God hath neither commanded any other means, nor promised justification to any other; therefore it is that this is the only condition, and so only thus justifieth. When I read this to be the tenor of the new covenant ('whosoever believeth shall be justified'), doth it not tell me plainly why faith justifieth? Even because it pleaseth the Law-giver and Covenant-maker to make faith the condition of it.

That faith's receiving Christ and his righteousness is only the remote reason why it doth justify appears thus. I would ask any dissenter this question: Suppose that Christ had done all that he did for sinners, and they had believed in him thereupon, without any covenant promising justification to this faith. Would this faith have justified them? By what law? Or whence would they plead their justification at the bar of God? Well, but suppose that Christ, having done what he did for us, that he should, in framing the new

[23] JW skips Baxter's Thesis 56 (pp. 212-24), which takes up the debate in Reformed scholasticism over the various 'causes' of justification. Baxter argues against the more standard model of making Christ's 'satisfaction' the *formal cause* of justification, treating it instead as the *meritorious cause*. While JW likely considered this section too technical, he adopted the same classification in subsequent writings; see *Farther Appeal*, Pt. I, II.5-8, 11:112-15 in this edn.; Sermon 20, *The Lord Our Righteousness*, II.15, 1:460 in this edn.; and Sermon 43, *The Scripture Way of Salvation*, I.3, 2:157 in this edn.

covenant, have put in any other condition, and said, 'whosoever loveth God shall, by virtue of my satisfaction, be justified.' Would not this love have justified? No doubt of it. I conclude then thus: The receiving of Christ is as the silver of this coin. The gospel promise is as the King's stamp which maketh it current for justifying. If God had seen meet to have stamped anything else, it would have passed currently. Yet take this—faith is, even to our own apprehension, the most apt and suitable condition that God could have chosen. For, as far as we can reach to know, there cannot be a more rational and apt condition of delivering a redeemed malefactor from torment than that he thankfully accept the pardon and favour of redemption, and hereafter take his redeemer for his lord.

So that if you ask me, 'What is the formal reason why faith justifieth?' I answer: Because Christ hath made it the condition of the new covenant, and promised justification upon that condition. But if you ask me further, 'Why did Christ choose this, rather than anything else for the condition?' I answer: (1) To ask a reason of Christ's choice and commands is not always wise or safe. (2) But here the reason is so apparent that we may safely adventure to say that nothing could be more proportionable to our poverty, who have nothing to buy with, than thus freely to receive. Nothing could be more reasonable than to acknowledge him who hath redeemed us, and to take him for our Redeemer and Lord.

Prop. XXXIV [59]

Justification is not a single act, begun and ended immediately upon our believing, but a continued act which, though it be in its kind complete from the first, yet is it still in doing till the final justification at the Judgment Day.

This is evident from the nature of the act—it being, as I showed before, an act of God by his gospel. Now (1) God still continueth that gospel covenant in force. (2) That covenant still continueth justifying believers. (3) God himself doth continue to esteem them accordingly, and to will their absolution. This showeth you therefore [(1)] with what limitation to receive the assertion of our divines that remission and justification are *simul et semel* [24] performed; (2) that the justified and pardoned may pray for the continuance of

[24] Latin: 'simultaneously and in an instant'.

their pardon and[25] justification; and (3) that Christ's satisfaction and our faith are of continual use, and not to be laid by, when we are once justified, as if the work was done.

Prop. XXXV [60]

The bare act of believing is not the only condition of salvation by the new covenant, but several other duties also are parts of that condition.

I desire no more of those that deny this but that Scripture may be judge, and that they will put by no one text to that end produced till they give some other commodious, and not forced, interpretation.

1. Then that pardon of sin and salvation are promised upon condition of repenting, as well as believing, is undeniably asserted from these scriptures: Mark 1:15, 6:12; Luke 13:3-5; Acts 2:38, 3:19, 8:22, 17:30, 26:20-31, 11:18; Luke 24:47; Heb. 6:1; 2 Pet. 3:9.

2. That praying for pardon and forgiving others are conditions of pardon is plain [in] Matt. 6:12-15, 18:35; Mark 11:25-26; Luke 6:37, 11:4; 1 John 1:9; James 5:15; John 14:13-14; 1 John 5:15; Acts 8:22.

3. That love, and sincere obedience and works of love, are also parts of the condition appeareth in these scriptures: Luke 7:47; Matt. 5:44; Luke 6:27-35; John 11:12-17; 1 Cor. 16:22; James 1:12, 2:5; John 14:21; Prov. 8:17-21; John 16:27; Matt. 10:37; Luke 13:24; Phil. 2:12; Rom. 2:7-10; 1 Cor. 9:24; 2 Tim. 2:5-12; 1 Tim. 6:18-19; Rev. 22:14; Luke 11:28; Matt. 25:41-42; James 2:21-26.

Prop. XXXVI [61]

Therefore, though the non-performance of any one of these be threatened with certain death, yet there must be a concurrence of them all to make up the conditions which have the promise of life.

Therefore we oftener read death threatened to those that repent not than life promised to them that repent. And when you do read

[25] *Works* (1773) omits 'and pardoned' and 'pardon and'. This would avoid any suggestion that justification went beyond pardon to imputing the active righteousness of Christ. In debates on this topic JW had come to insist that 'justification is another word for pardon'; see Sermon 43, *The Scripture Way of Salvation*, I.3, 2:157 in this edn.

of life promised of any one of these, you must understand it in *sensu composito*,[26] as it stands conjunct with the rest, and not as it is divided. Though I think that in regard of their existence they never are divided (for where God giveth one, he giveth all), yet in case they were separated the gospel would not so own them as its entire conditions.

Prop. XXXVII [62]

Yet faith may be called the only condition of the new covenant, because all the rest are reducible to it—either being presupposed as necessary antecedents or means, or contained in it; or else implied as its immediate fruits, or necessary subservient means or consequents.

Subservient actions are in common speech implied in the principal. If the besieged be bound by articles to surrender a town to the besiegers at such a time, it need not be expressed in the articles that they shall withdraw their guards, and cease resistance, and open the gates, and yield up this house or that street, etc. All this is implied clearly in the articles of surrender.

So here, the great condition of believing doth include or imply all the rest:

1. Hearing the Word, consideration, conviction, godly sorrow, repentance from dead works, are implied as necessary means antecedent.

2. Knowledge of Christ, and assent to the truth of the gospel, as essential parts of faith.

3. Preferring of Christ above all in judgment, will, and affection is (in my judgment) the very essential property of true faith, differencing it from all false faith, and so an essential part of it.

4. Love, sincere obedience, and works of love are the immediate products of faith, as heat and light are of fire.

5. The praying for forgiveness, the forgiving of others, [and] the pleading of Christ's satisfaction, are both parts of this obedience, and necessary consequents of faith, and acts subservient to it for the attaining of its ends.

6. The denying and humbling of the flesh, the serious, painful,[27] constant use of God's ordinances—hearing, praying, meditating,

[26] Latin: 'a composite sense'.

[27] *Works* (1773) omits 'painful'. Compare the insistence that JW felt it necessary to add in 1760 to his sermon on self-denial that this had nothing to do with literally harming our bodies. Sermon 48, 'Self-Denial', I.14, 2:245 in this edn.

etc.—are both parts of the foresaid obedience and also the necessary means of continuing and exercising our faith.[28]

Prop. XXXVIII [63]

As it is God's method in giving the moral law, first to bring men to take him only for their God (which is therefore called the first and great commandment) and then to prescribe the particular duties, so is it the method of Christ in the gospel, first to establish with men his office and authority, and require an acknowledgment of them and subjection to them, and then to prescribe to them their particular duties in subordination.

Prop. XXXIX [64]

Faith therefore is the summary condition of the gospel, as love is the fulfilling of the law. As taking the Lord for our only God is the sum of the decalogue, implying or inferring all the rest, and so is the great commandment, so taking Christ[b] *for our only redeemer and Lord is the sum of the conditions of the new covenant, including, implying, or inferring all other parts of its conditions, and so the great command of the gospel.*

The full subjection to the authority commanding doth imply and infer subjection to the particular commands. Therefore God doth

[b] Although this is not the same definition (in terms) with that of our church, yet it is reducible to the same.

---

[28] JW omits Baxter's next paragraph:

> 'Strength of grace, assurance of pardon and salvation, persuasion of God's favour, settled peace of conscience, joy in this assurance and peace, the understanding of truths not fundamental or necessary in practice; all these are no properties of the condition of the covenant, but separable adjunct of faith tending to the well being of it'. (*Aphorismes*, 242-43)

At the time of preparing this extract, JW was just beginning to question whether a sense of assurance was necessarily connected with justifying faith. See Minutes, Aug. 2, 1745, *QQ*. 1-4, 10:149-50 in this edn. He would soon accept a position much like that of Baxter. See letter to CW, July 31, 1747, 26:254-55 in this edn.

still make this the sum of the conditions of the law, that they take him only for their God, or that they have no other gods but him. And when he contracteth his covenant into an epitome, it runs thus: 'I will be thy God, and thou shalt be my people' (Exod. 20:3, 23:13; Deut. 6:4, 8:19, 13:23, etc.; Josh. 24:2-16, etc.; Judg. 2:12-19, 10:13; 1 Sam. 8:8; 2 Kings 5:17, 17:7; Jer. 22:9, 7:23, 11:4, 30:22; Ezek. 36:28; Deut. 26:16-17, etc.). And as God's promise of taking us for his people doth imply his bestowing upon us all the privileges and blessings of his people, and so is the sum of all the conditions of the covenant on his part, even so our taking the Lord for our God, and Christ for our Redeemer and Lord, doth imply our sincere obedience to him, and is the sum of the conditions on our part.

Prop. XL [70]

Faith, in the largest sense, as it comprehendeth all the conditions of the new covenant, may be thus defined: It is when a sinner, by the Word and Spirit of Christ being thoroughly convinced of the righteousness of the law, the truth of its threatening, the evil of his own sin, and the greatness of his misery hereupon, and withal of the nature and offices, sufficiency and excellency of Jesus Christ, the satisfaction he hath made, his willingness to save, and his free offer to all that will accept him for their Lord and Saviour, doth hereupon believe the truth of this gospel and accept of Christ as his only Lord and Saviour, to bring him to God, his chiefest good, and to present him pardoned and just before him, and to bestow upon him a more glorious inheritance; and doth accordingly rest on him as his Saviour, and obey[29] *him as his Lord, forgiving others, loving his people, bearing what sufferings are imposed, diligently using his means and ordinances, and confessing and bewailing his sins against him, and praying for pardon; and all this sincerely and to the end.*

This is the condition of the new covenant at large. That all this is sometimes called faith is plain hence:

1. In that faith is oft called 'the obeying of the gospel', but the gospel commands all this (Rom. 10:16; 1 Pet. 1:22, 4:17; 2 Thess. 1:8; Gal. 3:1, 5:7; Heb. 5:9).

2. The fulfilling of the conditions of the new covenant is often called by the name of faith, as so opposed to the fulfilling of the

[29] Baxter: 'sincerely (though imperfectly) obey'. *Aphorismes*, 280.

condition of the old covenant, called works. But these forementioned are parts of the condition of the new covenant, and therefore implied in faith (Gal. 3:12, 23, 25).

Prop. XLI [73]

From what hath been said it appeareth in what sense faith only justifieth, and in what sense works also justify—viz. *(1) Faith only justifieth as it implieth all other parts of the condition of the new covenant.*[30] *(2) Faith only justifieth as the great master duty of the gospel, to which all the rest are reducible. (3) Faith only doth not justify in opposition to the works of the gospel, but those works do also justify, as the secondary remote parts of the condition of the covenant.*

I know this is the doctrine that will have the loudest outcries raised against it, and will make some cry out, 'Heresy!' 'Popery!' 'Socinianism!' and what not. For my own part, the Searcher of hearts knoweth that not singularity, affectation of novelty, nor any goodwill to popery provoketh me to entertain it. But that I have earnestly sought the Lord's direction upon my knees before I durst adventure on it, and that I resisted the light of this conclusion as long as I was able. But a man cannot force his own understanding if the evidence of truth force it not, though he may force his pen, or tongue, to silence or dissembling.

Prop. XLII [77]

That we are justified by sincere obedience to Christ, as the secondary part of the condition of our justification, is evident also from these following scriptures: Matt. 12:37; Mark 11:25-26; Luke 6:37; Matt. 6:12-15; 1 John 1:9; Acts 8:22; Acts 3:19; Acts 22:16; 1 Pet. 4:18; Rom. 6:16; 1 Pet. 1:2, 22.[31]

[30] JW omits 'and is so put in opposition to the works of the law, or the personal righteousness of the old covenant'. *Aphorismes*, 289. See n. 10 above (p. 63).

[31] Baxter devoted Thesis 75 to stressing how the teaching of James agrees on this point. JW could skip this thesis because the point was made earlier (Prop. XXXV, §3).

Prop. XLIII [78]

Our full justification, and our everlasting salvation, have the same conditions on our part. But sincere obedience is, without all doubt, a condition of our salvation, therefore also of our justification.

[1.] I say, 'our full justification' because, as I have showed, our first possession of it is upon our mere faith. But I think our glorification will be acknowledged to have the same conditions with our final justification at the bar of Christ.[32] And why not our entire continued justification on earth? You may object, 'Perseverance is a condition of our glorification, but not of our justification.' I answer: (1) Perseverance is nothing but the same conditions persevering. (2) As the sincerity of faith is requisite to our first possession of justification, so the perseverance of faith is the condition of persevering justification (see Heb. 3:14).

2. That obedience is a condition of our salvation is undoubted (Heb. 5:9). Christ is the author of eternal salvation to all them that obey him (so fully, Rom. 2:7-10; Rev. 22:14: 'Blessed are they that do his commandments, that they may have right to the tree of life, and may enter by the gates into the city.'). And hath that no hand in their justification which giveth them right to the tree of life?

Prop. XLIV [79]

This doctrine is no whit derogatory to Christ and his righteousness. For he that ascribeth to faith or obedience no part of that work which belongeth to Christ's satisfactory righteousness, doth not derogate from it. But he that maketh faith and obedience to Christ to be only the fulfilling of the conditions of the new covenant, and so to be only conditions of full justification by him, doth give them no part of the work of his righteousness, seeing he came not to fulfil the gospel but the law.

[32] JW let this affirmation of the connection of good works to final justification (as compared to first justification) stand in his abridgment. He had earlier criticized George Bull for a similar claim. *Journal*, June 24, 1741, 19:202-3 in this edn. Thirty years later JW would suggest that this was a mere verbal dispute and praise Bull as 'that great light of the Christian church'. Letter to Several Preachers and Friends, July 10, 1771, II.5 (vol. 28, this edn.). Baxter's affirmation of this point here, and in *The Saints' Everlasting Rest* (London: Underhill & Tyton, 1650), 158 (which JW reprinted in *Christian Library*, 37:92-93), may have played a role in JW's revised view of final justification.

Prop. XLV [80]

To conclude, it is most clear in Scripture that our justification at the great judgment will be according to our works and to what we have done in flesh, whether good or evil, which can be no otherwise than as it was the condition of that justification. And Christ will then give the reason of his publick sentence from men's keeping or breaking the conditions of his covenant. That so the mouths of all may be stopped, and the equity of his judgment may be manifest to all; and that he may there show forth his hatred to the sins, and not only to the persons of the condemned, and his love to the obedience, and not only to the persons of the justified.

Here I have these things to prove: (1) that the justifying sentence shall pass according to works, as well as faith; (2) that the reason is because they are parts of the condition.

[1.] For the first, see Matt. 25:21-23, 'Well done, good and faithful servant, thou hast been faithful over a few things, I will make thee ruler over many things. Enter thou into the joy of thy Lord.' And most plain is that from the mouth of the judge himself, describing the order of the process of that day (Matt. 25:34-35): 'Come ye blessed, inherit the Kingdom, etc. For I was hungry, etc.' So 1 Pet. 1:17, 'Who, without respect of persons, judgeth according to every man's work.' So 2 Cor. 5:10, 'We must all appear before the judgment seat of Christ, that every one may receive the things done in his body, according to that he hath done, whether good or bad.' So Rev. 20:12-13, 'They were judged every man according to his works.' Heb. 13:17; Phil. 4:17; Matt. 12:36; etc. But this is evident already.

2. As it is beyond doubt that Christ will then justify men according to their works, so it is evident that this is not only to discover the sincerity of their faith but that it is also as they are parts of that evangelical righteousness which is the condition of their justification.

1) The very phrases of the text import as much: Matt. 25:21-23, 'Well done, good and faithful servant, etc.' Matt. 25:34-35, 'For I was hungry, etc.' And in the rest, 'according to their works'. Can any more be said of faith than that we are justified or judged to life, both for it and according to it?

2) But the common opinion is that it is to satisfy the condemned world of the sincerity of the faith of the godly. But this cannot stand with the truth. For (1) it is clearly expressed a ground or reason of

the sentence, (2) and to the consolation and justification of the justified, and not to the satisfaction or conviction of others.

3) If God's justice engage him not to forget their work and labour of love (Heb. 6:10-12); if the dead in Christ be blessed because their works follow them (Rev. 15:13); if in every nation he that fears God and works righteousness be accepted of him (Acts 10:35); if men shall reap the fruit of well doing in good time (Gal. 6:7-9); if ministers save themselves in taking heed to themselves and to their doctrine (1 Tim. 4:16); if he that doth righteousness is righteous (1 John 3:7); if whatsoever good thing any man doth, the same he shall receive of the Lord (Eph. 6:8); if hearing and doing be building on a rock (Matt. 6:24); if the doers of God's will be the mothers, sisters, and brothers of Christ (Matt. 12:50); etc., then the mention of these works at judgment is more than to signify their sincerity to the condemned world.

Let me conclude with two or three cautionary queries concerning the inconvenience of the contrary doctrine.

Query 1. Doth it not needlessly constrain men to wrest most plain and frequent expressions of Scripture?

Q[uery] 2. Doth it not uphold that dangerous pillar of the antinomian doctrine that we must not work or perform our duties *for* life and salvation, but only *from* life and salvation; that we must not make the attaining of justification, or salvation, an end of our endeavours, but obey in thankfulness only, because we are saved and justified? A doctrine which, if it were reduced to practice by all that hold it (as I hope it is not), would undoubtedly damn them. For he that seeks not, and that striveth not to enter, shall never enter. Now if good works, or sincere obedience to Christ our Lord, be no part of the condition of our full justification and salvation, who will use them to that end? For how it can procure justification as a means, and not by way of condition, I cannot conceive.

Q[uery] 3. Whether this doctrine doth not tend to drive obedience out of the world? For if men do once believe that it is not so much as a part of the condition of their justification, will it not much tend to relax their diligence? I know mere love and thankfulness *should* be enough, and so they *will*, when all our ends are attained in our ultimate end. Then we shall have nothing to do but to love, and joy, and praise, and be thankful—but that is not yet. Sure as God hath given us the affections of fear and desire and hope, so he would have us use them for the attainment of our great ends. Therefore he that taketh down but one of all our motives to obedience helps to destroy obedience itself, seeing we have need of every motive that God hath left us.

Q[uery] 4. Doth it not much confirm the world in their imaginary faith? Sure that faith, which is by many thought to justify, is it that people most easily embrace—that is, the receiving of Christ for their Saviour, but not for their King, nor delivering themselves to be ruled by him.

Men are easily persuaded to believe that Christ will pardon and save them, and to expect justification from him alone. But it is the hardest thing in the world to persuade them really to take him for their Lord, and his Word for their law, and to endeavour faithful obedience accordingly. Surely the easiness of the former, and the difficulty of the latter, tells us that this hath more need to be preached than the other (though some think that nothing is preaching Christ but preaching him as a pardoning, justifying Saviour). Indeed among the Turks or Indians, that entertain not the gospel, it is as necessary to preach his pardoning office, yea and the verity of his natures and commission. Therefore the apostles, when they preached to Jews or pagans, did first and chiefly teach them the person and offices of Christ, and the great benefits which they might receive by him. But when they preach (as James) to professors of the Christian faith, they chiefly urge them to strive to enter, to fight that they might conquer, so to run that they may obtain, to lay violent hands upon the Kingdom and take it by force, and to be unwearied in laborious obedience to Christ their Lord—to be steadfast, unmoveable, always abounding in the work of the Lord, forasmuch as they know their labour is not in vain in the Lord.[33]

[*Query*] 5. Lastly, is not this excluding of sincere obedience from final justification the great stumbling block of papists, and that which hath had a great hand in turning many learned men from the Protestant religion to popery? When they see the language of Scripture in the fore-cited places so plain to the contrary. When Illyricus, Gallus, Amsdorsius, etc. shall account it a heresy in George Major to say that good works are necessary to salvation.[34] When even

[33] At the Conference immediately following publication of this extract, JW echoed this point in charging his preachers to 'preach Christ in all his offices'. Minutes (May 23, 1753), *Q.* 4, 10:263 in this edn.

[34] Baxter is referring to the 'Majoristic Controversy' aroused among German Lutherans in 1551 when George Major took up and emphasized Philip Melanchthon's moderating suggestion about good works playing a role in justification. While Major tried to clarify that he meant only that they were necessary for retaining salvation—not earning it—his position was vigorously attacked as opposed to the doctrine of justification by faith alone by Nicholas Amsdorsius Matthias Flacius (also known as Illyricus because of his birthplace), and Nicholas Gallus.

Melanchthon's credit is blasted for being too great a friend to good works, though he ascribe not to them the least part of the work or office of Christ. And when to this day many antinomian teachers, who are magnified as the only preachers of free grace, do assert that there is no more required to the perfect irrevocable justification of the vilest murderer or whoremaster but to believe that he is justified, or to be persuaded that God loveth him.

Do these men think that we are perfectly justified and saved already, before the absolving sentence at the Great Tribunal, or the possession of the Kingdom, for which we wait in hope? Indeed, when we have that perfect salvation we shall not need to seek it or labour to attain it, but must everlastingly be thankful to him that hath purchased it, and to him that hath bestowed it. But in the mean time, he that seeketh not shall not find, and he that runs not shall not obtain; no, not all that seek and run neither (Luke 13:24; Luke 12:31; 2 Tim. 2:5).

The common assertion then, *that good works do follow justification, but not go before it*, must be thus understood—*viz.* actual obedience goeth not before the first moment of justification. But yet it is as true: (1) That the taking of Christ for our Lord, and so delivering ourselves to his government, doth in order of nature go before our justification. (2) That actual obedience, as part of the condition, doth in order of nature go before our justification, as continued and confirmed. For though our marriage contract with Christ do give us the first possession, yet it is the marriage duties which must continue that possession. (3) That perseverance in faithful obedience doth, both in nature and time, go before our complete and final justification, and that as part of the condition of obtaining it. 'If we walk in the light, as he is in the light, we have fellowship one with another, and the blood of Jesus Christ his Son cleanseth us from all sin' (1 John 1:7).

'For being made perfect, he became the author of eternal salvation to all them that obey him' (Heb. 5:9). Of whom it shall be said, when they are glorified with him, 'These are they that came out of great tribulation, and have washed their robes in the blood of the Lamb, and made them white. Therefore they are before the throne of God, and serve him day and night in his temple, and he that sitteth on the throne shall dwell among them' (Rev. 7:14–15). To whom be glory for ever. Amen.

AN EXTRACT FROM THE *SHORTER CATECHISM* OF THE WESTMINSTER ASSEMBLY (1753)

An Introductory Comment

When Charles I was displaced, the Long Parliament appointed the Westminster Assembly (1643) to reform the Church of England. The Assembly included Episcopalian and Presbyterian members, as well as a small but influential group of Independents (due to the favor of Oliver Cromwell and the army). Their deliberations resulted in a proposed Confession of Faith, and both a larger and a shorter catechism—all with a decidedly Reformed theological tone. These were completed in the autumn of 1647 and approved by Parliament (with slight changes) on September 15, 1648.[1] The *Shorter Catechism* was largely the work of Anthony Tuckney (1599–1670), a Puritan divine and fellow of Cambridge. Although its time as a standard for the Church of England was brief, after 1662 it filled an important place (much more so than the *Larger Catechism*) in the lives of Baptists, Congregationalists, and Presbyterians in Britain.

The *Shorter Catechism* was often used by Dissenters as the basis for collected volumes of catechetical sermons. They also championed it as an exemplary survey of Christian teaching in its own right. A particularly relevant example is Samuel Palmer's insistence that 'our catechism is a most complete *System* of morality', in response to the charge of John Wesley's father, Samuel, that

[1] *The Humble Advice of the Assembly of Divines, now by authority of Parliament sitting at Westminster, concerning: I. A Confession of Faith; II. A Larger Catechism; and III. A Shorter Catechism* (London, 1648).

Dissenting academies had produced no important works of divinity.[2] This helps explain why John included this catechism in his *Christian Library* (1749–55). His aim in this fifty-volume collection was to digest the best of the 'practical divinity' published in English from the early seventeenth century to the present. Reformed works were central to much of this period, and Wesley included several representatives. He could hardly omit the *Shorter Catechism*, as their most widely used first-order form of practical divinity.

Wesley made clear in the preface to the *Christian Library* that selection of an item for inclusion did not indicate his full agreement with everything in it. Instead, one of his goals in abridging each item was to 'extract the gold out of baser mixtures'.[3] In the case of the *Shorter Catechism*, this involved the omission of six of the original 107 questions and revision of several others. The majority of the changes were related to the Assembly's affirmation of unconditional election and irresistible grace; but Wesley's commitment to Christian perfection also shines through, as does his concern about equating 'adoption' with baptism.[4] While these deletions are significant, it is also important to notice how much of the catechism remains—reflecting the broad extent of shared Christian conviction across the Reformed/Arminian divide. Wesley's editing of the *Shorter Catechism* embodies what he once said about the Assembly's *Larger Catechism*: 'To this I never subscribed; but I think it is in the main a very excellent composition. Which I shall therefore cheerfully endeavour to defend, so far as I conceive it is grounded on clear Scripture.'[5]

It is not certain which edition of the *Shorter Catechism* Wesley used for this abridgment. This poses little problem, as the basic text never varied from the original in editions through his life. We have

[2] Samuel Palmer, *A Vindication of the Learning, Loyalty, Morals, and most Christian Behaviour of the Dissenters toward the Church of England, in answer to Mr. Wesley's 'Defence'* (London: J. Lawrence, 1705), 93; cf. Samuel Wesley, *A Defence of a Letter Concerning the Education of Dissenters in Their Private Academies* (London: R. Clavel & J. Knaplock, 1704), 2-3.

[3] *Christian Library*, Preface, §9, 1:iv. JW soon had to admit that the press of time kept him from editing the items included as closely as he seemed to promise; cf. *Some Remarks on Mr. Hill's 'Review'*, I.1, vol. 13 in this edn.

[4] On Christian perfection, see notes 11, 14, and 18 below; on equating 'adoption' with baptism, see note 10. JW also shortened a few answers, deleting their opening that repeated the topic of the question. These occasions were not deemed necessary to note.

[5] *Doctrine of Original Sin*, Pt. II, III.1 (p. 240 below).

used the edition published in 1658 for comparison because this is the first one to include the full text of all the scripture references that Wesley includes (plus some not found in Wesley).[6] There is no clear evidence of Wesley adding any scripture references, and his main omissions are the subsidiary scriptures for the Ten Commandments and Lord's Prayer.

The text presented here is from the sole appearance of this work during Wesley's life, in 1753, in the *Christian Library*, 31:109-48. The extract was never published separately because Wesley did not consider this catechism accessible enough for the typical layperson or for children.[7] For more details see Bibliography, No. 165.

[6] *The Humble Advice of the Assembly of Divines . . . concerning a Shorter Catechism, with the proofs thereof at large out of the Scriptures* (London: John Rothwell, 1658). Many later edns. reduce the number of scripture references, so JW was likely using this edn. or a fairly direct descendant of it.

[7] See Sermon 120, 'Unity of the Divine Being', §10, 4:64 in this edn. Cf. the similar comment about the catechism in the BCP, JW letter to Mary Bishop, Mar. 15, 1777 (vol. 29 in this edn.).

AN

EXTRACT

FROM THE

ASSEMBLY's

Shorter Catechism;

WITH THE

PROOFS THEREOF

OUT OF THE

SCRIPTURES.

AN EXTRACT FROM THE SHORTER CATECHISM *OF THE WESTMINSTER ASSEMBLY*

Q. 1: What is the chief end of man?

A. Man's chief end is to glorify God,[a] and to enjoy him[b] for ever.

Q. 2: What rule hath God given to direct us how we may glorify and enjoy him?

A. The Word of God, which is contained in the Scriptures of the Old and New Testament,[c] is the only rule to direct us how we may glorify God, and enjoy him.

Q. 3: What doth the Scriptures principally teach?

A. The Scriptures principally teach what man is to believe concerning God, and what duty God requires of man.

Q. 4: What is God?

A. God is a Spirit,[d] infinite,[e] eternal,[f] and unchangeable,[g] in his being, wisdom,[h] power, holiness,[i] justice, goodness, and truth.[j]

Q. 5: Are there more gods than one?

A. There is but one only,[k] the living and true God.[l]

[a] 1 Cor. 10:31: 'Whether therefore ye eat or drink, or whatsoever ye do, do all to the glory of God.'

Rom. 11:36: 'For of him, and through him, and to him are all things; to whom be glory for ever. Amen.'

[b] Ps. 73:25: 'Whom have I in heaven but thee? And there is none upon earth that I desire besides thee.' [Ver.] 26: 'My flesh and heart faileth, but God is the strength of my heart, and my portion for ever.'

[c] 2 Tim. 3:16: 'All Scripture is given by inspiration of God, and is profitable for doctrine, for reproof, for correction, for instruction in righteousness.'

[d] John 4:24: 'God is a Spirit.'

[e] Job 11:7: 'Canst thou by searching find out God? Canst thou find out the Almighty unto perfection?'

[f] Ps. 90:2: 'From everlasting to everlasting, thou art God.'

[g] Jas. 1:17: 'The Father of lights, with whom is no variableness, neither the shadow of turning.'

[h] Ps. 147:5: 'Great is our Lord, and of great power; his understanding is infinite.'

[i] Rev. 4:8: 'Holy, holy, holy Lord God almighty, which was, and is, and is to come.

Rev. 15:4: 'Who shall not fear thee, O Lord, and glorify thy name? For thou only art holy.'

[j] Exod. 34:6: 'The Lord, the Lord God, merciful and gracious, long-suffering, and abundant in goodness and truth.' Ver. 7: 'Keeping mercy for thousands, forgiving iniquity, and transgression, and sin, and that will by no means clear the guilty.'

[k] Deut. 6:4: 'Hear, O Israel, the Lord our God is one Lord.'

[l] Jer. 10:10: 'But the Lord, he is the true God, he is the living God, and everlasting King.'

Q. 6: How many Persons are there in the Godhead?

A. There are three Persons in the Godhead, the Father, the Son, and the Holy Ghost;[m] and these three are one God, the same in substance, equal in power and glory.[n]

Q. 7:[1] What is the work of creation?

A. The work of creation is God's making all things[o] of nothing, by the word of his power,[p] in the space of six days, and all very good.[q]

Q. 8: How did God create man?

A. God created man male and female, after his own image,[r] in knowledge, righteousness, and holiness,[s] with dominion over the creatures.[t]

[m] Matt. 28:19: 'Go ye therefore, and teach all nations, baptizing them in the name of the Father, and of the Son, and of the Holy Ghost.'

[n] 1 John 5:7: 'For there are three that bear record in heaven, the Father, the Word, and the Holy Ghost; and these three are one.' [Wesley was aware of disputes over the authenticity of this verse; see Sermon 55, 'On the Trinity', §5, 2:378-79 in this edn.]

[o] Gen. 1, throughout: [Ver.] 1: 'In the beginning, God created the heaven and the earth.'

[p] Heb. 11:3: 'Through faith, we understand that the worlds were framed by the word of God.'

[q] Gen. 1:31: 'And God saw everything that he had made, and behold it was very good; and the evening and the morning were the sixth day.'

[r] Gen. 1:27: 'So God created man in his own image; in the image of God created he him; male and female created he them.'

[s] Col. 3:10: 'And have put on the new man, which is renewed in knowledge, after the image of him that created him.'

Eph. 4:24: 'And that ye put on the new man, which after God is created in righteousness and true holiness.'

[t] Gen. 1:28: 'And God blessed them; and God said unto them, Be fruitful and multiply, and replenish the earth, and subdue it, and have dominion over the fish of the sea, over the fowl of the air, and over every living thing that moveth upon the earth.'

---

[1] Here JW renumbers after omitting *QQ.* 7-8 of the orig:

'*Q.* 7. What are the decrees of God?

A. The decrees of God are his eternal purpose, according to the counsel of his will, whereby, for his own glory, he hath foreordained whatsoever comes to pass.'

'*Q.* 8. How doth God execute his decrees?

A. God executeth his decrees in the works of creation and providence.'

Wesley equated this conception of God's decrees with a rigid determinism of all that happens in the world; see *Thoughts upon Necessity*, I.7, II.4, vol. 13 in this edn.

Q. 9: What are God's works of providence?

A. God's works of providence are his most holy,[u] wise,[v] and powerful[w] preserving and governing all his creatures, and all their actions.[x]

Q. 10: What special act of providence did God exercise towards man in the estate wherein he was created?

A. When God had created man, he entered into a covenant of life with him, upon condition of perfect obedience,[y] forbidding him to eat of the tree of knowledge of good and evil, upon pain of death.[z]

Q. 11: Did our first parents continue in the estate wherein they were created?

A. Our first parents being left to the freedom of their own will, fell from the estate wherein they were created, by sinning against God.[a]

Q. 12: What is sin?

A. Sin is a transgression[2] of the law of God.[b]

Q. 13: What was the sin whereby our first parents fell from the estate wherein they were created?

[u] Ps. 145:17: 'The Lord is righteous in all his ways, and holy in all his works.'

Ps. 104:24: 'O Lord, how manifold are thy works! In wisdom hast thou made them all; the earth is full of thy riches.'

[v] Isa. 28:29: 'This also cometh forth from the Lord of hosts, which is wonderful in counsel, and excellent in working.'

[w] Heb.1:3: 'Upholding all things by the word of his power.'

[x] Ps. 103:19: 'His kingdom ruleth over all.'

Matt. 10:29: 'Are not two sparrows sold for a farthing? And one of them shall not fall to the ground without your Father.' Ver. 30: 'But the very hairs of your head are all numbered.'

[y] Gal. 3:12: 'The man that doth them shall live in them.'

[z] Gen. 2:17: 'But of the tree of knowledge of good and evil, thou shalt not eat of it; for in the day thou eatest thereof, thou shalt surely die.'

[a] Gen. 3:6: 'And when the woman saw that the tree was good for food, and that it was pleasant to the eyes, and a tree to be desired to make one wise; she took of the fruit thereof, and did eat, and gave also unto her husband with her, and he did eat.'

Eccles. 7:29: 'God hath made man upright.'

[b] 1 John 3:4: 'Sin is the transgression of the law.'

[2] 1658 orig.: 'Sin is any want of conformity unto, or transgression. . . .'

A. Their eating the forbidden fruit.[c]

Q. 14: Did all mankind fall in Adam's first transgression?

A. The covenant being made with Adam, not only for himself but for his posterity,[d] all mankind, descending from him by ordinary generation, sinned in him, and fell with him in his first transgression.[e]

Q. 15: Into what estate did the Fall bring mankind?

A. The Fall brought mankind into an estate of sin and misery.[f]

Q. 16: Wherein consists the sinfulness of that estate whereinto man fell?

A. The sinfulness of that estate whereinto man fell consists in the guilt of Adam's first sin,[g] the want of original righteousness,[h] and the corruption of his whole nature, which is commonly called original sin,[i] together with all actual transgressions which proceed from it.

[c] Gen. 3:6: 'And when the woman saw that the tree was good for food, and that it was pleasant to the eye, and a tree to be desired to make one wise, she took of the fruit thereof, and did eat, and gave also to her husband, and he did eat.'

[d] Gen. 1:28: 'And God blessed them, and God said unto them, be fruitful, and multiply, and replenish the earth.'

Gen. 2:16: 'And the Lord commanded the man, saying, Of every tree in the garden thou mayst freely eat.' Ver. 17: 'But of the tree of knowledge of good and evil, thou shalt not eat of it; for in the day that thou eatest thereof, thou shalt surely die.'

[e] Rom. 5:12: 'Wherefore, as by one man sin entered into the world, and death by sin; so death passed upon all men, for that all have sinned.' Ver. 18: 'By the offence of one, judgment came upon all men to condemnation.'

1 Cor. 15:21: 'For since by man came death, by man came also the resurrection of the dead.' Ver. 22: 'For as in Adam all die, even so in Christ shall all be made alive.'

[f] Rom. 5:12: 'By one man sin entered into the world, and death by sin, and so death passed upon all men, for that all have sinned.'

[g] Rom. 5:19: 'By one man's disobedience many were made sinners.'

[h] Rom. 3:10: 'There is none righteous, no, not one.'

[i] Eph. 2:1: 'You hath he quickened, who were dead in trespasses and sins.' Ver. 2: 'Wherein in time past ye walked according to the course of this world, according to the prince of the power of the air, the spirit that now worketh in the children of disobedience.'

Ps. 51:5: 'Behold, I was shapen in iniquity, and in sin did my mother conceive me.'

Q. 17: What is the misery of that estate whereinto man fell?

A. All mankind by their fall lost communion with God,[j] are under his wrath and curse,[k] and so made liable to all the miseries in this life,[l] to death itself, and to the pains of hell for ever.

Q. 18:[3] Who is the Redeemer of mankind?[4]

A. The Lord[5] Jesus Christ,[m] who being the eternal Son of God,[n] became man,[o] and so was, and continued to be God and man, in two distinct natures, and one person for ever.[p]

Q. 19: How did Christ, being the Son of God, become man?

[j] Gen. 3:8: 'Adam and his wife hid themselves from the presence of the Lord God, among the trees of the garden.' Ver. 24: 'So he drove out the man.'

[k] Eph. 2:3: 'And were by nature children of wrath, even as others.'

Gal. 3:10: 'Cursed is everyone that continueth not in all things which are written in the book of the law to do them.'

[l] Rom. 6:23: 'The wages of sin is death.'

[m] 1 Tim. 2:5: 'For there is one God, and one mediator between God and man, the man Christ Jesus.'

[n] John 1:14: 'And the Word was made flesh, and dwelt among us.'

Gal. 4:4: 'But when the fullness of the time was come, God sent forth his Son, made of a woman, made under the law.'

[o] Rom. 9:5: 'Whose are the fathers, and of whom, as concerning the flesh, Christ came; who is over all, God blessed for ever.'

Luke 1:35: 'And the angel answered and said unto her, The Holy Ghost shall come upon thee, and the power of the Highest shall overshadow thee; therefore also that holy thing which shall be born of thee shall be called the Son of God.'

Col. 2:9: 'For in him dwelleth all the fullness of the Godhead bodily.'

[p] Heb. 7:24: 'But this man, because he continueth ever, hath an unchangeable priesthood.' Ver. 25: 'Wherefore he is able also to save them to the uttermost that come unto God by him, seeing he ever liveth to make intercession for them.'

---

[3] JW again renumbers after omitting *Q.* 20:

'*Q.* 20. Did God leave all mankind to perish in the state of sin and misery?

A. God having out of his mere good pleasure, from all eternity, elected some to everlasting life, did enter into a covenant of grace to deliver them out of the state of sin and misery, and to bring them into [a] state of salvation by a Redeemer.'

[4] JW replaces orig. 'of God's elect' with 'mankind'.

[5] 658 orig. begins: 'The only Redeemer of God's elect is the Lord . . .'.

A. Christ, the Son of God, became man by taking to himself a true body[q] and a reasonable soul,[r] being conceived by the power of the Holy Ghost in the womb of the Virgin Mary and born of her,[s] and yet without sin.[t]

Q. 20: What offices doth Christ execute as our Redeemer?

A. Christ as our Redeemer executeth the offices of a prophet,[u] of a priest,[v] and of a king,[w] both in his estate of humiliation and exaltation.

Q. 21: How doth Christ execute the office of a prophet?

A. Christ executeth the office of a prophet in revealing to us,[x] by his Word,[y] and Spirit,[z] the will of God for our salvation.

[q] Heb. 2:14: 'Forasmuch then as the children are partakers of flesh and blood, he also himself likewise took part of the same.' Ver. 16: 'For verily he took not on him the nature of angels, but he took on him the seed of Abraham.'

Heb. 10:5: 'Wherefore when he cometh into the world he saith, Sacrifice and offering thou wouldst not, but a body hast thou prepared me.'

[r] Matt. 26:38: 'Then saith he unto them, My soul is exceeding sorrowful, even unto death.'

[s] Luke 1:31: 'Behold, thou shalt conceive in thy womb, and bring forth a son, and shalt call his name Jesus.'

[t] Heb. 4:15: 'For we have not an high priest which cannot be touched with the feeling of our infirmities; but was in all points tempted like as we are, yet without sin.'

[u] Acts 3:22: 'Moses truly said unto the fathers, a prophet shall the Lord your God raise up unto you of your brethren, like unto me. Him shall ye hear in all things whatsoever he shall say unto you.'

Heb. 12:25: 'See that ye refuse not him that speaketh. For if they escaped not who refused him that spake on earth, much more shall not we escape if we turn away from him that speaketh from heaven.' Compare with 2 Cor. 13:3.

[v] Heb. 5:5: 'So also Christ glorified not himself to be made an high priest; but he that said unto him, Thou art my Son, today have I begotten thee.' Ver. 6: 'Thou art a priest for ever, after the order of Melchizedek.'

[w] Ps. 2:6: 'Yet have I set my king upon my holy hill of Zion.' Ver. 8: 'Ask of me, and I will give thee the heathen for thine inheritance, and the uttermost parts of the earth for thy possession.'

Isa. 9 6: 'For unto us a child is born, unto us a son is given; and the government shall be upon his shoulder. And his name shall be called, wonderful, counsellor, the mighty God, the everlasting Father, the Prince of peace.' Ver. 7: 'Of the increase of his government and peace there shall be no end.'

[x] John 1:18: 'No man hath seen God at any time; the only begotten Son, which is in the bosom of the Father, he hath declared him.'

John 15:15: 'Henceforth I call you not servants; for the servant knoweth not what his Lord doeth. But I have called you friends; for all things that I have heard of my Father I have made known unto you.'

[y] John 20:31: 'These things are written that ye might believe that Jesus is the Christ, the Son of God, and that believing ye might have life through his name.'

[z] John 14:26: 'The Comforter, which is the Holy Ghost, whom the Father will send in my name, he shall teach you all things.'

Q. 22: How doth Christ execute the office of a priest?
A. Christ executeth the office of a priest in his once offering up himself a sacrifice to satisfy divine justice[a] and reconcile us to God,[b] and in making continual intercession for us.[c]

Q. 23: How doth Christ execute the office of a king?
A. Christ executeth the office of a king in subduing us to himself,[d] in ruling and defending us,[e] and in restraining and conquering all his and our enemies.[f]

Q. 24: Wherein did Christ's humiliation consist?
A. Christ's humiliation consisted in his being born, and that in a low condition,[g] made under the law,[h] undergoing the miseries of this life,[i] the wrath of God,[j] and the cursed death of the cross,[k] in being buried, and continuing under the power of death for a time.[l]

[a] Heb. 9:14: 'How much more shall the blood of Christ, who through the eternal Spirit offered himself without spot to God, purge your conscience from dead works to serve the living God.'

[b] Heb. 2:17: 'In all things it behoved him to be made like unto his brethren, that he might be a merciful and faithful high priest, in things pertaining to God, to make reconciliation for the sins of the people.'

[c] Heb. 7:24: 'But this man, because he continueth ever, hath an unchangeable priesthood.' Ver. 25: 'He is able to save them to the utmost that come unto God by him, seeing he ever liveth to make intercession for them.'

[d] Ps. 110, throughout. Ver. 3: 'Thy people shall be willing in the day of thy power, etc.'

[e] Isa. 33:22: 'The Lord is our judge, the Lord is our lawgiver, the Lord is our king; he will save us.'

[f] 1 Cor. 15:25: 'For he must reign till he hath put all his enemies under his feet.'

[g] Luke 2:7: 'And she brought forth her first-born son, and wrapped him in swaddling clothes, and laid him in a manger.'

[h] Gal. 4:4: 'God sent forth his Son, made of a woman, made under the law.'

[i] Isa. 53:2: 'For he shall grow up before him as a tender plant, and as a root out of a dry ground. He hath no form nor comeliness; and when we shall see him, there is no beauty that we should desire him.' [Ver.] 3: 'He is despised and rejected of men, a man of sorrows, and acquainted with grief.'

Luke 22:44: 'And being in an agony, he prayed more earnestly. And his sweat was as it were great drops of blood falling down to the ground.'

[j] Matt. 27:46: 'And about the ninth hour Jesus cried with a loud voice, My God, my God, why hast thou forsaken me?'

[k] Phil. 2:8: 'He humbled himself, and became obedient unto death, even the death of the cross.'

[l] Matt. 12:40: 'As Jonas was three days and three nights in the whale's belly, so shall the Son of man be three days and three nights in the heart of the earth.'

Q. 25: Wherein consisteth Christ's exaltation?

A. Christ's exaltation consisteth in his rising again from the dead on the third day,[m] in ascending up to heaven, and sitting at the right hand of God the Father,[n] and in coming to judge the world at the last day.[o]

Q. 26: How are we made partakers of the redemption purchased by Christ?

A. We are made partakers of the redemption purchased by Christ by the effectual application of it to us[p] by his Holy Spirit.[q]

Q. 27: How doth the Spirit apply to us the redemption purchased by Christ?

A. The Spirit applieth to us the redemption purchased by Christ by working faith in us,[r] and thereby uniting us to Christ.[6][s]

Q. 28:[7] What benefits do they that truly believe[8] partake of in this life?

[m] 1 Cor. 15:4: 'And that he was buried, and that he rose again the third day, according to the Scriptures.'

[n] Mark 16:19: 'So then, after the Lord had spoken unto them, he was received up into heaven, and sat on the right hand of God.'

[o] Acts 17:31: 'He hath appointed a day in the which he will judge the world in righteousness, by that man whom he hath ordained, whereof he hath given assurance unto all men, in that he hath raised him from the dead.'

[p] John 1:11: 'He came unto his own, and his own received him not.' [Ver.] 12: 'As many as received him, to them gave he power to become the sons of God.'

[q] Tit. 3:5: 'Not by works of righteousness which we have done, but according to his mercy he saved us, by the washing of regeneration, and renewing of the Holy Ghost.' [Ver.] 6: 'Which he shed on us abundantly, through Jesus Christ our Saviour.'

Eph. 1:13: 'In whom ye also trusted, after that ye heard the word of truth, the gospel of your salvation; in whom also, after that ye believed, ye were sealed with that Holy Spirit of promise.' [Ver.] 14: 'Which is the earnest of our inheritance, until the redemption of the purchased possession, unto the praise of his glory.'

[r] Eph. 2:8: 'By grace you are saved through faith; and that not of yourselves; it is the gift of God.'

[s] Eph. 3:17: 'That Christ may dwell in your hearts by faith.'

---

[6] 1658 orig.: '. . . to Christ in our effectual calling'.

[7] JW again renumbers, after omitting *Q.* 31:

'*Q.* 31: What is effectual calling?

A. Effectual calling is the work of God's Spirit whereby, convincing us of our sin and misery, enlightening our minds in the knowledge of Christ, and renewing our wills, he doth persuade and enable us to embrace Jesus Christ freely offered to us in the gospel.'

[8] JW replaces 'are effectually called' with 'truly believe'.

A.[9] Justification, sanctification,[t] and the several benefits which in this life do either accompany or flow from them.

Q. 29: What is justification?

A. Justification is an act of God's free grace wherein he pardoneth all our sins[u] and accepteth us as righteous in his sight,[v] only for the righteousness of Christ imputed to us,[w] and received by faith alone.[x]

Q. 30:[10] What is sanctification?

[t] 1 Cor. 1:30: 'Of him ye are in Christ Jesus, who of God is made unto us wisdom, and righteousness, and sanctification, and redemption.'

Rom. 3:24: 'Being justified freely by his grace, through the redemption that is in Jesus Christ.' [Ver.] 25: 'Whom God hath set forth to be a propitiation, through faith in his blood, to declare his righteousness for the remission of sins that are past, through the forbearance of God.'

Rom. 4:6: 'Even as David also describeth the blessedness of the man unto whom God imputeth righteousness without works.' [Ver.] 7: 'Saying, Blessed are they whose iniquities are forgiven, and whose sins are covered.' [Ver.] 8: 'Blessed is the man to whom the Lord will not impute sin.'

[u] Eph. 1:7: 'In whom we have redemption through his blood, the forgiveness of sins, according to the riches of his grace.'

[v] 2 Cor. 5:19: 'God was in Christ, reconciling the world unto himself, not imputing their trespasses unto them; and hath committed unto us the word of reconciliation.' [Ver.] 21: 'For he hath made him to be sin for us that knew no sin, that we might be made the righteousness of God in him.'

[w] Rom. 5:17: 'For if by one man's offence death reigned by one, much more they which receive abundance of grace, and of the gift of righteousness, shall reign in life by one, Jesus Christ. Therefore as by the offence of one judgment came upon all men to condemnation, even so by the righteousness of one the free gift came upon all men unto justification of life.' [Ver.] 19: 'As by one man's disobedience many were made sinners, so by the obedience of one shall many be made righteous.'

[x] Gal. 2:16: 'Knowing that a man is not justified by the works of the law, but by the faith of Jesus Christ, even we have believed in Jesus Christ, that we might be justified by the faith of Christ.'

---

[9] 1658 orig.: 'They that are effectually called do in this life partake of justification, adoption, sanctification, and . . . '.

[10] JW again renumbers after omitting *Q.* 34:

'*Q.* 34: What is adoption?

A. Adoption is an act of God's free grace, whereby we are received into the number, and have a right to all the privileges of the sons of God.'

JW's deletion of this question (and parallel revision of *QQ.* 32, 36) has puzzled many. James MacDonald insists that it was simply to reduce the length and to focus attention on justification and sanctification. *Wesley's Revision of the Shorter Catechism* (Edinburgh: G. Morton, 1906), 9, 57-60. That more was involved is

A. Sanctification is the work of God's free grace whereby we are renewed in the whole man after the image of God,[y] and are enabled[11] to die unto sin and live unto righteousness.[z]

Q. 31: What are the benefits which in this life do either accompany or flow from justification[12] and sanctification?

[y] Eph. 4:23: 'And be renewed in the spirit of your mind.' [Ver.] 24: 'And that ye put on the new man, which after God is created in righteousness and true holiness.'

Rom. 6:4: 'Therefore we are buried with him by baptism unto death; that like as Christ was raised up from the dead by the glory of the Father, even so we also should walk in newness of life.' [Ver.] 6: 'Knowing this, that our old man is crucified with him, that the body of sin might be destroyed, that henceforth we should not serve sin.'

[z] Rom. 8:1: 'There is therefore now no condemnation to them which are in Christ Jesus, who walk not after the flesh, but after the Spirit.'

---

suggested by the fact that JW also deleted the section of the Anglican Article 'Of Baptism' (Article 27) that described baptism as the instrument of our adoption when he prepared the Articles of Religion for the American Methodists in 1784 (see vol. 8 in this edn.). In both cases he seems to carefully avoid equation of 'adoption' with initiation into formal Christian status.

The reason for this avoidance is not hard to find. The events surrounding Aldersgate led JW to stress the distinction between those who were baptized, held church membership, and the like, but manifested only the 'faith of a servant' and those who enjoyed instead the 'faith of a son'. The distinctive quality of the latter faith was that it was not motivated by fear but sprang from strong assurance of God's love. The passage to which JW consistently appealed in defending this distinction was Rom. 8:15, 'Ye have not received the spirit of bondage again to fear; but . . . the Spirit of adoption, whereby we cry, Abba, Father.' This scriptural warrant led Wesley—after 1738—to define the Spirit's work of 'adoption' almost exclusively in terms of granting conscious assurance to those who are often already nominally Christian. Note, e.g., his reference to a 1739 sermon on this 'glorious scripture describing the state of every true believer in Christ, everyone who by faith is born of God'. *Journal*, Apr. 25, 1739, 19:51 in this edn. See also his 1746 programmatic sermon on Rom. 8:15, Sermon 9, 'The Spirit of Bondage and Adoption', 1:249-66 in this edn.

[11] JW revises the orig. 'enabled more and more' to 'enabled', making room for his characteristic affirmation of the possibility of Christian perfection in this life.

[12] JW again omits 'adoption' in the series.

A. Assurance of God's love, peace of conscience, joy in the Holy Ghost,[a] increase of grace,[b] and perseverance therein unto the end.[c]

Q. 32: What benefits do believers receive from Christ at their death?[13]

A. The souls of believers at their death pass into glory,[d] and their bodies rest[14] in their graves[e] till the resurrection.[f]

Q. 33: What benefits do believers receive from Christ at the resurrection?

A. At the resurrection believers, being raised up in glory,[g] shall be openly acknowledged and acquitted in the day of judgment,[h] and made perfectly blessed, in full enjoying of God[i] to all eternity.[j]

[a] Rom. 5:1: 'Being justified by faith, we have peace with God through our Lord Jesus Christ.' [Ver.] 2: 'By whom also we have access by faith into this grace wherein we stand, and rejoice in hope of the glory of God.' [Ver.] 5: 'And hope maketh not ashamed, because the love of God is shed abroad in our hearts, by the Holy Ghost which is given unto us.'

Rom. 14:17: 'For the kingdom of God is not meat and drink, but righteousness, and peace, and joy in the Holy Ghost.'

[b] Prov. 4:18: 'The path of the just is as the shining light, that shineth more and more unto the perfect day.'

[c] 1 John 5:13: 'These things have I written unto you that believe on the name of the Son of God, that ye may know that ye have eternal life.'

1 Pet. 1:5: 'Who are kept by the power of God through faith unto salvation.'

[d] Phil. 1:23: 'Having a desire to depart, and to be with Christ.'

Luke 23:43: 'And Jesus said unto him, Verily I say unto thee, today shalt thou be with me in paradise.'

[e] Isa. 57:2: 'He shall enter into peace; they shall rest in their beds, each one walking in his uprightness.'

[f] Job 19:26: 'And though after my skin worms destroy this body, yet in my flesh shall I see God.'

[g] 1 Cor. 15:43: 'It is sown in dishonour, it is raised in glory.'

[h] Matt. 10:32: 'Whosoever shall confess me before men, him also will I confess before my Father which is in heaven.'

[i] 1 John 3:2: 'When he shall appear, we shall be like him; for we shall see him as he is.'

[j] 1 Thess. 4:17: 'And so shall we ever be with the Lord.'

---

[13] 1658 orig.: '. . . at death'.

[14] 1658 orig.: 'The souls of believers are at their death made perfect in holiness, and do immediately pass into glory; and their bodies, being still united to Christ, do rest.' JW removed the restriction of the possibility of perfection to the moment of death.

Q. 34: What is the duty which God requireth of man?

A. The duty which God requireth of man is obedience to his revealed will.[k]

Q. 35: What did God at first reveal unto man for the rule of his obedience?

A. The rule which God at first revealed to man for his obedience was the moral law.[l]

Q. 36: Where is the moral law summarily comprehended?

A. In the Ten Commandments.[m]

Q. 37: What is the sum of the Ten Commandments?

A. The sum of the Ten Commandments is to love the Lord our God with all our heart, with all our soul, with all our strength, and with all our mind, and our neighbour as ourselves.[n]

Q. 38: What is the preface to the Ten Commandments?

A. I am the Lord thy God, which have brought thee out of the land of Egypt, out of the house of bondage—Exod. 20:2.

Q. 39: What doth the preface to the Ten Commandments teach us?

A. That because God is the Lord, and our God and Redeemer, therefore we are bound to keep all his commandments.[o]

Q. 40: What is the first commandment?

A. Thou shalt have no other Gods before me—Exod. 20:3.

Q. 41: What is required in the first commandment?

A. To know[p] and acknowledge God to be the only true

[k] Micah 6:8: 'He hath showed thee, O man, what is good; and what doth the Lord require of thee but to do justly, and to love mercy, and to walk humbly with thy God?'

[l] Rom. 2:14: 'When the Gentiles, which have not the law, do by nature the things contained in the law; these having not the law, are a law unto themselves.' [Ver.] 15: 'Which show the work of the law written in their hearts.'

[m] Deut. 10:4: 'And he wrote on the tables, according to the first writing the Ten Commandments.'

Matt. 19:17: 'If thou wilt enter into life, keep the commandments.'

[n] Matt. 22:37: 'Thou shalt love the Lord thy God with all thy heart, and with all thy soul, and with all thy mind.'

[o] Deut. 11:1: 'Thou shalt love the Lord thy God, and keep his charge, and his statutes, and his judgments, and his commandments alway.'

[p] 1 Chron. 28:9: 'And thou, Solomon my son, know thou the God of thy father.'

God, and our God,[q] and to worship and glorify him accordingly.[r]

Q. 42: What is forbidden in the first commandment?

A. The first commandment forbiddeth the denying or not worshipping and glorifying the true God as God, and our God, and the giving that worship and glory to any other which is due to him alone.

Q. 43: What are we specially taught by these words ('before me') in the first commandment?

A. These words ('before me') in the first commandment teach that God, who seeth all things, taketh notice and is much displeased with the sin of having any other God.

Q. 44: Which is the second commandment?

A. Thou shalt not make unto thee any graven image, or any likeness of anything that is in heaven above, or that is in the earth beneath, or that is in the water under the earth. Thou shalt not bow down thyself to them, nor serve them. For I the Lord thy God am a jealous God, visiting the iniquities of the fathers upon the children unto the third and fourth generation of them that hate me, and showing mercy unto thousands of them that love me and keep my commandments—Exod. 20:4-6.

Q. 45: What is required in the second commandment?

A. The receiving, observing, and keeping pure and entire all such religious worship and ordinances as God hath appointed in his Word.

Q. 46: What is forbidden in the second commandment?

A. The worshipping of God by images, or any other way not appointed by his Word.

Q. 47: What are the reasons annexed to the second commandment?

A. The reasons annexed to the second commandment are God's sovereignty over us, his propriety in us, and the zeal he hath to his own worship.

[q] Deut. 26:17: 'Thou hast avouched the Lord this day to be thy God, and to walk in his ways, and to keep his statutes, and his commandments, and his judgments, and to hearken to his voice.'

[r] Matt. 4:10: 'Thou shalt worship the Lord thy God, and him only shalt thou serve.'

Q. 48: Which is the third commandment?
A. Thou shalt not take the name of the Lord thy God in vain; for the Lord will not hold him guiltless that taketh his name in vain—Exod. 20:7.
[*Q.*] 49: What is required in the third commandment?
[*A.*] The holy and reverent use of God's names, titles, attributes, ordinances, Word, and works.
Q. 50: What is forbidden in the third commandment?
A. All profaning or abusing anything whereby God maketh himself known.
Q. 51: What is the reason annexed to the third commandment?
A. The reason annexed to the third commandment is: that however the breakers of this commandment may escape punishment from men, yet the Lord our God will not suffer them to escape his righteous judgments.
Q. 52: Which is the fourth commandment?
A. Remember the sabbath day, to keep it holy. Six days shalt thou labour and do all thy work; but the seventh day is the sabbath of the Lord thy God; in it thou shalt not do any work, thou, nor thy son, nor thy daughter, thy man-servant, nor thy maid-servant, nor thy cattle, nor thy stranger that is within thy gates. For in six days the Lord made heaven and earth, the sea, and all that in them is, and rested the seventh day; wherefore the Lord blessed the sabbath day, and hallowed it—Exod. 20:8-11.
Q. 53: What is required in the fourth commandment?
A. The keeping holy to God such set time as he hath appointed in his Word, expressly one whole day in seven, to be a holy sabbath to himself.
Q. 54: Which day of the seven hath God appointed to be the weekly sabbath?
A. Till the resurrection[15] of Christ, God appointed the seventh day of the week to be the weekly sabbath,[s] and the first day of the week ever since, to continue to the end of the world.[16]

[s] Acts 20:7: 'And upon the first day of the week, when the disciples came together to break bread, Paul preached unto them.'

---

[15] 1658 orig.: 'From the beginning of the world to the resurrection . . .'.
[16] 1658 orig.: '. . . world, which is the Christian Sabbath'.

Q. 55: How is the sabbath to be sanctified?

A. The sabbath is to be sanctified by an holy resting all that day, even from such worldly employments and recreations as are lawful on other days, and spending the whole time in the public and private exercises of God's worship, except so much as is to be taken up in works of necessity and mercy.

Q. 56: What are the sins forbidden in the fourth commandment?

A. The omission or careless performance of the duties required, and the profaning the day by idleness, or doing that which is in itself sinful, or by unnecessary thoughts, words, or works about worldly employments or recreations.

Q. 57: What are the reasons annexed to the fourth command[ment]?

A. The reasons annexed to the fourth commandment are God's allowing us six days of the week for our own employment, his challenging a special propriety in the seventh, his own example, and his blessing the sabbath day.

Q. 58: Which is the fifth commandment?

A. Honour thy father and thy mother, that thy days may be long in the land which the Lord thy God giveth thee—Exod. 20:12.

Q. 59: What is required in the fifth commandment?

A. The preserving the honour, and performing the duties, belonging to everyone in their several places and relations, as superiors, inferiors, or equals.

Q. 60: What is forbidden in the fifth commandment?

A. The neglecting of, or doing anything against, the honour and duty which belongs to everyone in their several places and relations.

Q. 61: What is the reason annexed to the fifth commandment?

A. A promise of long life and prosperity (as far as it shall serve for God's glory and their own good) to all such as keep this commandment.

Q. 62: Which is the sixth commandment?

A. Thou shalt not kill [—Exod. 20:13].

Q. 63: What is required in the sixth commandment?
A. All lawful endeavours to preserve our own life and the life of others.

Q. 64: What is forbidden in the sixth commandment?
A. The taking away of our own life or the life of our neighbour unjustly, or whatsoever tendeth thereunto.

Q. 65: What is the seventh commandment?
A. Thou shalt not commit adultery—Exod. 20:14.

Q. 66: What is required in the seventh commandment?
A. The preservation of our own and our neighbour's chastity, [in thought,][17] speech, and behaviour.

Q. 67: What is forbidden in the seventh commandment?
A. All unchaste thoughts, words, and actions.

Q. 68: What is the eighth commandment?
A. Thou shalt not steal—Exod. 20:15.

Q. 69: What is required in the eighth commandment?
A. The lawful procuring and furthering the wealth and outward estate of ourselves and others.

Q. 70: What is forbidden in the eighth commandment?
A. Whatsoever doth or may unjustly hinder our own or our neighbour's wealth and outward estate.

Q. 71: Which is the ninth commandment?
A. Thou shalt not bear false witness against thy neighbour—Exod. 20:16.

Q. 72: What is required in the ninth commandment?
A. The maintaining and promoting of truth between man and man, and of our own and our neighbour's good name, especially in witness bearing.

Q. 73: What is forbidden in the ninth commandment?
A. Whatsoever is prejudicial to truth or injurious to our own or our neighbour's good name.

Q. 74: Which is the tenth commandment?
A. Thou shalt not covet thy neighbour's house, thou shalt not covet thy neighbour's wife, nor his man-servant, nor his maid-servant, nor his ox, nor his ass, nor anything that is thy neighbour's—Exod. 20:17.

[17] 1658 reads: 'chastity, in heart, speech . . .'. JW's 1753 revision reads: 'chastity, speech . . .'. In his personal copy of the *Christian Library* (preserved at his house in London) JW restored the sense of 1658—apparently without consulting the Westminster vol.—by correcting the text to read, 'chastity, in thought, speech . . .' (see 31:135).

Q. 75: What is required in the tenth commandment?
A. Full contentment with our own condition, with a right and charitable frame of spirit towards our neighbour and all that is his.
Q. 76: What is forbidden in the tenth commandment?
A. All discontentment with our estate, envying or grieving at the good of our neighbour, and all inordinate motions and affections to anything that is his.
Q. 77:[18] Are all transgressions of the law equally heinous?
A. Some sins in themselves, and by reason of several aggravations, are more heinous in the sight of God than others.[t]
Q. 78: What doth every sin deserve?
A. Every sin deserveth God's wrath and curse, both in this life and that which is to come.[u]
Q. 79: What doth God require of us that we may escape the wrath and curse due to us for sin?
A. To escape the wrath and curse of God due to us for sin, God requireth of us faith in Jesus Christ, repentance unto life,[v] with the diligent use of all outward means whereby Christ communicateth to us the benefits of redemption.

[t] Ezek. 8:6: 'He said furthermore unto me, Son of man, seest thou what they do? Even the great abominations that the house of Israel committeth here, that I should go far off from my sanctuary? But turn thee yet again, and thou shall see greater abominations.' See ver. 13, 15.

Ps. 78:17: 'And they sinned yet more against him, by provoking the Most High in the wilderness.' See ver. 32, 56.

John 19:11: 'He that delivereth me unto thee hath the greater sin.'

[u] Eph. 5:6: 'Let no man deceive you with vain words; for because of these things cometh the wrath of God upon the children of disobedience.'

Gal. 3:10: 'Cursed is everyone that continueth not in all things that are written in the Book of the Law, to do them.'

Matt. 25:41: 'Then shall he say unto them on the left hand, Depart from me, ye cursed, into everlasting fire, prepared for the devil and his angels.'

[v] Acts 20:21: 'Testifying both to the Jews and also to the Greeks, repentance towards God, and faith towards our Lord Jesus Christ.'

Prov. 8:33: 'Hear instruction, and be wise, and refuse it not.' See ver. 34-35.

Isa. 55:3: 'Incline your ear, and come unto me. Hear, and your souls shall live, and I will make an everlasting covenant with you, even the sure mercies of David.'

---

[18] JW renumbers one final time, after omitting *Q.* 82:

'*Q.* 82: Is any man able perfectly to keep the commandments of God?

A. No mere man since the Fall is able in this life perfectly to keep the commandments of God, but doth daily break them in thought, word, and deed.'

Q. 80: What is 'faith in Jesus Christ'?

A. Faith in Jesus Christ is a saving grace[w] whereby we receive[x] and rest upon him alone for salvation,[y] as he is offered to us in the gospel.

Q. 81: What is repentance unto life?

A. Repentance unto life is a saving grace whereby a sinner, out of a true sense of his sin[z] and apprehension of the mercy of God in Christ,[a] doth, with grief and hatred of his sin, turn from it unto God,[b] with full purpose of and endeavours after new obedience.[c]

Q. 82: What are the outward means whereby Christ communicateth to us the benefits of redemption?

A. The outward and ordinary means whereby Christ communicateth to us the benefits of redemption are his ordinances, especially the Word, sacraments, and prayer.[19]

[w] Heb. 10:39: 'We are not of them that draw back unto perdition, but of them that believe to the saving of the soul.'

[x] John 1:12: 'As many as received him, to them gave he power to become the sons of God, even to them that believe on his name.'

Isa. 26:3: 'Thou wilt keep him in perfect peace whose mind is stayed on thee, because he trusteth in thee.' See ver. 4.

[y] Phil. 3:9: 'And be found in him, not having mine own righteousness, which is of the law, but that which is through the faith of Christ, the righteousness which is of God by faith.'

[z] Acts 11:18: 'Then hath God also to the Gentiles granted repentance unto life.'

Acts 2:37: 'When they heard this, they were pricked in their hearts, and said unto Peter, and to the rest of the apostles, Men and brethren, what shall we do?' See ver. 38.

[a] Joel 2:12: 'Therefore also now, saith the Lord, turn ye unto me with all your heart, and with fasting, and with weeping, and with mourning.' Also ver. 13.

Jer. 3:22: 'Return ye, backsliding children, and I will heal your backslidings. Behold, we come unto thee, for thou art the Lord our God.'

[b] Jer. 31:18: 'Turn thou me, and I shall be turned, for thou art the Lord my God.' See ver. 19.

Ezek. 36:31: 'Then shall ye remember your own evil ways, and your doings that were not good, and shall loathe yourselves in your own sight, for your iniquities, and for your abominations.'

[c] Ps. 119:59: 'I thought on my ways, and turned my feet unto thy testimonies.'

2 Cor. 7:11: 'For behold, this selfsame thing that ye sorrowed after a godly sort, what carefulness it wrought in you, yea, what clearing of yourselves, yea, what indignation, yea, what fear, yea, what vehement desire, yea, what zeal, yea, what revenge! In all things ye have approved yourselves to be clear in this matter.'

Isa. 1:16: 'Wash ye, make ye clean, put away the evil of your doings from before mine eyes; cease to do evil.' See ver. 17.

---

[19] 1658 orig.: '. . . especially his Word, sacraments, and prayer; all which are made effectual to the elect for salvation'.

Q. 83: How is the Word made effectual to salvation?

A. The Spirit of God maketh the reading,[d] but especially the preaching of the Word an effectual means of convincing and converting sinners,[e] and of building them up in holiness and comfort,[f] through faith unto salvation.[g]

Q. 84: How is the Word to be read and heard, that it may become effectual to salvation?

A. That the Word may become effectual to salvation we must attend thereunto with diligence,[h] preparation,[i] and prayer,[j] receive it with faith,[k] and love,[l] lay it up in our hearts,[m] and practise it in our lives.[n]

[d] Neh. 8:8: 'So they read in the Book, in the Law of God, distinctly, and gave the sense, and caused them to understand the reading.'

Acts 26:18: 'To open their eyes, and to turn them from darkness to light, and from the power of Satan unto God, that they may receive forgiveness of sins, and an inheritance among them which are sanctified by faith that is in me.'

Acts 20:32: 'And now, brethren, I commend you to God, and to the word of his grace, which is able to build you up, and to give you an inheritance among all them which are sanctified.'

Rom. 15:4: 'For whatsoever things were written aforetime, were written for our learning; that we through patience and comfort of the Scriptures might have hope.'

2 Tim. 3:15: 'And that from a child thou hast known the holy Scriptures, which are able to make thee wise unto salvation, through faith which is in Christ Jesus.' See ver. 16-17.

[e] Ps. 19:7: 'The law of the Lord is perfect, converting the soul; the testimony of the Lord is sure, making wise the simple.' See ver. 8.

[f] 1 Thess. 1:6: 'And ye became followers of us, and of the Lord, having received the Word in much affliction, with joy of the Holy Ghost.'

[g] Rom. 1:[1]6: 'I am not ashamed of the gospel of Christ, for it is the power of God unto salvation to everyone that believeth.'

[h] Prov. 8:34: 'Blessed is the man that heareth me, watching daily at my gates, waiting daily at the posts of my doors.'

[i] 1 Pet. 2:1: 'Wherefore laying aside all malice, and all guile, and hypocrisies and envies, and evil speakings.' See ver. 2.

[j] Ps. 119:18: 'Open thou mine eyes, that I may behold wonderful things out of thy law.'

[k] Heb. 4:2: 'The Word preached did not profit them, not being mixed with faith in them that heard it.'

[l] 2 Thess. 2:10: 'They received not the love of the truth, that they might be saved.'

[m] Ps. 119:11: 'Thy Word have I hid in mine heart, that I might not sin against thee.'

Luke 8:15: 'But that on the good ground are they which in an honest and good heart, having heard the Word, keep it, and bring forth fruit with patience.'

[n] Jas. 1:25: 'But whoso looketh into the perfect law of liberty, and continueth therein, he being not a forgetful hearer, but a doer of the Word, this man shall be blessed in his deed.'

Q. 85: How do the sacraments become effectual means of salvation?

A. The sacraments become effectual means of salvation, not from any virtue in them, or in him that doth administer them,[o] but only by the blessing of Christ and the working of his Spirit in them that by faith receive them.[p]

Q. 86: What is a sacrament?

A. A sacrament is an holy ordinance instituted by Christ, wherein by sensible signs Christ, and the benefits of the new covenant, are represented,[q] sealed, and applied to believers.[r]

Q. 87: What are the sacraments of the New Testament?

A. Baptism and the Lord's Supper.

Q. 88: What is baptism?

A. Baptism is a sacrament wherein the washing with water in the name of the Father, and of the Son, and of the Holy Ghost,[s] doth signify and seal our engrafting into Christ, and partaking of the benefits of the covenant of grace,[t] and our engagements to be the Lord's.[u]

[o] 1 Cor. 3:6: 'I have planted, Apollos watered; but God gave the increase.' See ver. 7.

[p] 1 Pet. 3:21: 'The like figure whereunto even baptism doth also now save us (not the putting away the filth of the flesh, but the answer of a good conscience towards God) by the resurrection of Jesus Christ.'

1 Cor. 12:13: 'For by one Spirit are we all baptized into one body, whether we be Jews or Gentiles, whether we be bond or free; and have been all made to drink into one Spirit.'

[q] Gen. 17:7: 'And I will establish my covenant between me and thee, and thy seed after thee, in their generations, for an everlasting covenant; to be a God unto thee, and to thy seed after thee.' See ver. 10.

[r] Rom. 4:11: 'And he received the sign of circumcision, a seal of the righteousness of the faith, which he had yet being uncircumcised.'

1 Cor. 11:23: 'For I have received of the Lord that which also I delivered unto you, that the Lord Jesus, the same night in which he was betrayed, took bread.' See ver. 26.

[s] Matt. 28:19: 'Go ye, therefore, and teach all nations, baptizing them in the name of the Father, and of the Son, and of the Holy Ghost.'

[t] Rom. 6:3: 'Know ye not that so many of us as were baptized into Jesus Christ, were baptized into his death?'

[u] Rom. 6:4: 'Therefore we are buried with him by baptism into death, that like as Christ was raised up from the dead by the glory of the Father, even so we also should walk in newness of life.'

Gal. 3:27: 'For as many of you as have been baptized into Christ have put on Christ.'

Q. 89: To whom is baptism to be administered?

A. Baptism is not to be administered to any that are out of the visible Church till they profess their faith in Christ and obedience to him,[v] but the infants of such as are members of the visible Church are to be baptized.[w]

Q. 90: What is the Lord's Supper?

A. The Lord's Supper is a sacrament wherein by giving and receiving bread and wine, according to God's appointment, his death is showed forth[x] and the worthy receivers are, not after a corporal and carnal manner but by faith, made partakers of his body and blood, and with all his benefits, to their spiritual nourishment and growth in grace.[y]

Q. 91: What is required in the worthy receiving of the Lord's Supper?

A. It is required of them that would worthily partake of the Lord's Supper that they examine themselves of their knowledge to discern the Lord's body,[z] of their faith to feed upon him,[a] of their repentance,[b] love, and new

[v] Acts 8:36: 'And as they went on their way they came unto a certain water. And the eunuch said, See, here is water; what doth hinder me to be baptized?'

Acts 2:41: 'Then they that gladly received his word were baptized.'

[w] Gen. 17:7: 'And I will establish my covenant between me and thee, and thy seed after thee, in their generations, for an everlasting covenant, to be a God unto thee, and to thy seed after thee.' See ver. 10.

Acts 2:38: 'And Peter said unto them, Repent and be baptized every one of you, in the name of Jesus Christ, for the remission of sins, and ye shall receive the gift of the Holy Ghost.' See ver. 39.

Col. 2:11: 'In whom also ye are circumcised with the circumcision made without hands, in putting off the body of the sins of the flesh, by the circumcision of Christ.' See ver. 12.

1 Cor. 7:14: 'For the unbelieving husband is sanctified by the wife, and the unbelieving wife is sanctified by the husband, else were your children unclean; but now are they holy.'

[x] Luke 22:19: 'And he took bread, and gave thanks, and brake it, and gave unto them, saying, This is my body which is given for you; this do in remembrance of me.' See ver. 20.

[y] 1 Cor. 10:16: 'The cup of blessing which we bless, is it not the communion of the blood of Christ? The bread which we break, is it not the communion of the body of Christ?'

[z] 1 Cor. 11:28: 'But let a man examine himself, and so let him eat of that bread, and drink of that cup.' See ver. 29.

[a] 2 Cor. 13:5: 'Examine ourselves, whether you be in the faith.'

[b] 1 Cor. 11:31: 'If we would judge ourselves, we should not be judged.'

obedience,[c] lest coming unworthily they eat and drink judgment to themselves.

Q. 92: What is prayer?

A. Prayer is an offering up of our desires to God,[d] for things agreeable to his will,[e] in the name of Christ,[f] with confession of our sins,[g] and thankful acknowledgment of his mercies.[h]

Q. 93: What rule hath God given for our direction in prayer?

A. The whole Word of God is of use to direct us in prayer, but the special rule of direction is that form of prayer which Christ taught his disciples,[i] commonly called the Lord's Prayer.

Q. 94: What doth the preface of the Lord's Prayer teach[20] us?

A. The preface of the Lord's Prayer, which is 'Our Father, which art in heaven', teacheth us to draw near to God with all holy reverence,[j] and confidence,[k] as children to a

[c] 1 Cor. 5:7: 'Purge out therefore the old leaven, that ye may be a new lump, as ye are unleavened. For even Christ our passover is sacrificed for us.' See ver. 8.

[d] Ps. 62:8: 'Trust in him at all times, ye people, pour out your hearts before him. God is a refuge for us.'

[e] Rom. 8:27: 'And he that searcheth the hearts knoweth the mind of the Spirit, because he maketh intercession for the saints, according to the will of God.'

1 John 5:14: 'And this is the confidence that we have in him, that if we ask anything according to his will, he heareth us.'

[f] John 16:23: 'Whatsoever ye shall ask the Father in my name, he will give it you.'

[g] Dan. 9:4: 'And I prayed unto the Lord my God, and made my confession.'

[h] Phil. 4:6: 'Be careful for nothing, but in everything by prayer and supplication, with thanksgiving, let your request be made known to God.'

[i] Matt. 6:9: 'After this manner therefore pray ye, Our Father which art in heaven, hallowed be thy name, etc.' See Luke 11:2-4.

[j] Isa. 64:9: 'Be not wroth very sore, O Lord, neither remember iniquity for ever. Behold, see, we beseech thee, we are all thy people.'

[k] Rom. 8:15: 'For ye have not received the spirit of bondage again to fear; but ye have received the spirit of adoption, whereby we cry, Abba, Father.'

[20] The word 'teach' was inadvertently printed twice in the *Christian Library*. JW marked the second occurrence for deletion in his personal copy.

father, able and ready to help us,[l] and that we should pray with and for others.[m]

Q. 95: What do we pray for in the first petition?

A. In the first petition, which is 'Hallowed be thy name', we pray that God would enable us, and others, to glorify him in all that whereby he maketh himself known; and that he would dispose of all things to his own glory.

Q. 96: What do we pray for in the second petition?

A. In the second petition, which is 'Thy kingdom come', we pray that Satan's kingdom may be destroyed, that the kingdom of grace may be advanced, ourselves and others brought into it, and kept in it, and that the kingdom of glory may be hastened.

Q. 97: What do we pray for in the third petition?

A. In the third petition, which is 'Thy will be done on earth as it is in heaven', we pray that God by his grace would make us able and willing to know, obey, and submit to his will in all things, as the angels do in heaven.

Q. 98: What do we pray for in the fourth petition?

A. In the fourth petition, which is 'Give us this day our daily bread', we pray that of God's free gift we may receive a competent portion of the good things of this life, and enjoy his blessing with them.

Q. 99: What do we pray for in the fifth petition?

A. In the fifth petition, which is 'And forgive us our debts, as we forgive our debtors', we pray that God, for Christ's sake, would freely pardon all our sins, which we are the rather encouraged to ask because by his grace we are enabled from our heart to forgive others.

Q. 100: What do we pray for in the sixth petition?

A. In the sixth petition, which is, 'And lead us not into temptation, but deliver us from evil', we pray that God

[l] Luke 11:13: 'If ye, then, being evil, know how to give good gifts unto your children, how much more shall your heavenly Father give the Holy Spirit to them that ask him!'

[m] Eph. 6:18: 'Praying always with all prayer and supplication in the Spirit, and watching thereunto with all perseverance, and supplication for all saints.'

Acts 12:5: 'Peter therefore was kept in prison, but prayer was made without ceasing of the church unto God for him.'

1 Tim. 2:1: 'I exhort, therefore, that first of all supplications, prayers, intercessions, and giving of thanks be made for all men.' See ver. 2.

would either keep us from being tempted to sin, or support and deliver us when we are tempted.

Q. 101: What doth the conclusion of the Lord's Prayer teach us?

A. The conclusion of the Lord's Prayer, which is, 'For thine is the kingdom, and the power, and the glory, for ever, Amen', teacheth us to take our encouragement in prayer from God only, and in our prayers to praise him, ascribing kingdom, power, and glory to him; and in testimony of our desire and assurance to be heard, we say, *Amen*.

THE DOCTRINE OF ORIGINAL SIN: ACCORDING TO SCRIPTURE, REASON, AND *EXPERIENCE* (1757)

An Introduction

JOHN Wesley's Arminian commitments are evident in his extract of the Westminster *Shorter Catechism* only indirectly, through what he chose to omit. These commitments shine through a bit more in his extended response to a book by John Taylor on the doctrine of original sin. But even here Wesley chose to keep them largely in the background. This is striking because Taylor was among the eighteenth-century Dissenters who sharply rejected Calvinism, shifting allegiance to the broad Arminian camp. The problem, in Wesley's view, was that Taylor's reactionary swing went to the opposite extreme, adopting a naively optimistic view of human nature.[1] Thus, Wesley targeted his response on criticizing Taylor's rationalist version of Arminianism, leaving it for readers to discern Wesley's alternative evangelical Arminianism.

To assist readers in such discernment, this introduction will place John Taylor's attack on the doctrine of original sin in historical context, give an overview of Taylor's argument and contemporary responses to it, and then sketch John Wesley's engagement with Taylor.

[1] See JW's letter to Sir Harry Trelawney, Aug. 1780 (vol. 29 in this edn.).

Enlightened and Rational Dissent in Eighteenth-Century Britain

While there were earlier marginal strands, the Dissenting churches in Britain mark their formal beginnings from the ejection of the Puritans in 1662, following the return of Charles II. Ejection proceedings focused on ministers, university dons, and schoolteachers who refused to accept the Book of Common Prayer and episcopacy. Accordingly, education of ministers (in their own academies) became a central institutional setting of eighteenth-century Dissent.

The Dissenting academies were fertile grounds for a wider engagement of Enlightenment emphases than in the Established Church. Anglican engagement was generally conservative in tone, highlighting the concern to preserve civilized society against any resurgence of religious enthusiasm (like the earlier Puritan revolution). It specifically championed continued support of constitutional monarchy and the Established Church. By contrast, Dissenting academies nurtured voices like Richard Price, Joseph Priestley, and Thomas Paine—some of the strongest critics of aristocracy and clericalism in the late eighteenth century, sounding Enlightenment themes more common on the European continent.

To be sure, there was diversity among Dissenters on these issues. Some resisted most Enlightenment emphases. The majority in the eighteenth century assumed a mediating stance like that evident in Anglican circles, where faith and inspiration could exceed (but not contradict) reason. But alongside such 'enlightened Dissent' was a more radical strand of 'rational Dissent', which placed increasing emphasis on reason in interpreting Scripture and judging claims for Christian belief.[2] This minority wing found its major locus in Presbyterian circles, who most valued an educated clergy. The Presbyterian John Taylor was an early formative voice.

[2] See the distinction between these varieties in the introduction to Knud Haakonssen, ed., *Enlightenment and Religion: Rational Dissent in Eighteenth-Century Britain* (New York: Cambridge University Press, 1996). The collection as a whole develops these points.

Central Disputed Themes of Rational Dissent

Before turning directly to Taylor, it will be helpful to identify two of the most debated tendencies in rational Dissent and the labels frequently used to brand or condemn it.

One tendency was rejection of major Calvinist emphases in soteriology.[3] Most representatives of this strand of Dissent were raised in the irenic moderate Calvinism of Richard Baxter. But they adopted a stronger emphasis than Baxter on the right and responsibility of individual rational judgment. They quickly became sharp critics of the notions of total depravity, unconditional reprobation, and the necessity of spiritual regeneration as a prerequisite to faith, as well as emphasis on the imputed righteousness of Christ in justification. In response, more traditional Calvinists labeled them Pelagian, Socinian, Arminian, and papist.[4]

These labels were frequently grouped together, with little attention to differences between Pelagius (*c.* 350–418), Faustus Socinus (1539–1604), Jacob Arminius (1560–1609), and standard Roman Catholic teachings. While these four shared a concern to place morality at the heart of religion, they differed significantly on how to do so. For example, Socinus assumed that this required rejecting both the notion of human inability for faith and good works (apart from restoring grace) and any required role for Christ's atoning death (stressing only his role as a human teacher and moral example). Pelagius may have held similar views, though this is hard to demonstrate because few of his writings have survived other than in quotations by his opponents.[5] By contrast, Arminius and

[3] See ibid., 4.

[4] See Isabel Rivers, *Reason, Grace and Sentiment: A Study of the Language of Religion and Ethics in England, 1660–1780* (New York: Cambridge University Press, 1991), 1:9. An early example would be Jean Gailhard, *God's Truth Vindicated against Man's Lies; or, An Answer to a Virulent Socinian, Popish, and Arminian Pamphlet* (London: for the author, 1703). Arminians, in turn, tended to equate Calvinist and antinomian.

[5] John Wesley, for one, thought that Pelagius had been caricatured in the attacks on him by those uncomfortable with his emphasis on holy living. See Sermon 68, 'The Wisdom of God's Counsels', §9, 2:555-56 in this edn.; letter to Alexander Coates, July 7, 1761 (vol. 27 in this edn.); and letter to John Fletcher, Aug. 16, 1775 (vol. 29 in this edn.). This explains his deletion of negative references to Pelagius in the extracts appended to *Doctrine of Original Sin*.

standard Roman Catholic teaching took the opposite stance on both issues.[6]

The other major tendency of the rationalist strand of Dissent that drew broad criticism was its growing rejection of the doctrine of the Trinity. Since Faustus Socinus also rejected this doctrine, opponents typically had this aspect in mind as well in labeling writers like John Taylor as Socinian. Their criticisms almost always added the additional label of Arian, arguing that Socinus had actually compounded the error of Pelagius in early soteriology with that of Arius (256–336) in early models of the doctrine of God.[7] Some opponents invoked the further negative label of deist, suggesting that the differences between Arians, Socinians, and deists were 'rather verbal than real'.[8]

More careful observers noticed the differences. While Arius stressed the supremacy of the Father over the Son in authority and being (rendering the Son literally the 'first-born' of the Father), he assumed that the Son had divine powers and preexisted the incarnation in Jesus of Nazareth. Arius also affirmed the Holy Spirit as a third member in the divine chain of beings. By contrast, Socinus focused on Jesus as a man (denying preexistence) and viewed the language of 'Holy Spirit' as another way of referring to the one God, not a distinct person in the Godhead.[9] Deists shared the focus of Socinus on the unity of God and the humanity of Jesus, but differed strongly from his suggestion that God's revelatory work was confined almost exclusively to the teaching and ministry of Jesus.[10] As such, the appropriate question about particular representatives of rational Dissent in relation to their understanding of God is whether they were more Arian, more Socinian, or more deist in tone.[11]

[6] See the helpful summary of Socinus, and comparison to Arminius, in Sarah Mortimer, *Reason and Religion in the English Revolution: The Challenge of Socinianism* (New York: Cambridge University Press, 2010), 13-26.

[7] See Nicholas Tyacke, *Aspects of English Protestantism, c. 1530–1700* (New York: Manchester University Press, 2001), 320-39.

[8] Anonymous, *A Dissertation on Deistical and Arian Corruption* (London, 1742), 1.

[9] This difference is highlighted, e.g., in Josiah Tucker, *A Brief and Dispassionate View of the Difficulties Attending to the Trinitarian, Arian, and Socinian Systems* (Gloucester: R. Raikes, 1774), 8-11. Some differentiation is also evident in CW's intercessory hymn 'For the Arians, Socinians, Deists, Pelagians, etc.', in *Hymns of Intercession for all Mankind* (Bristol: Farley, 1758), 28-29.

[10] See Mortimer, *Reason and Religion*, 17-21.

[11] See Maurice Wiles's discussion of Taylor in *Archetypal Heresy: Arianism through the Centuries* (New York: Oxford University Press, 1996), 143-46.

John Taylor as a Formative Influence on Rational Dissent[12]

John Taylor was born in 1694 in Scotforth, Lancashire (a village near Lancaster). His father was a timber merchant and member of the Church of England. His mother was a Dissenter. Her influence was the stronger on Taylor's early beliefs, leading him to enroll in 1709 as a pupil in the Dissenting academy in Whitehaven, Cumbria, run by Rev. Thomas Dixon (a disciple of the mediating theology of Richard Baxter and Edmund Calamy). Taylor moved on to study with Thomas Hill in Derby, finishing in 1716. In both settings he excelled in classical languages.

Taylor was ordained by the Presbyterian classis of Derby on April 11, 1716. In contrast with their Scottish kin, English Presbyterians were generally uneasy with requiring subscription to human creeds. While the Derby classis was small, it stood at the forefront of its English fellows in championing freedom of judgment in theological matters. Thus, Taylor's evaluation for ordination included no request to subscribe to the Westminster Confession. His response to the questions that he was asked stressed his personal commitment to unconstrained rational interpretation of Scripture.[13]

Taylor's first ministerial charge was at Kirkstead Abbey Chapel, in Lincolnshire. This was a small chapel that Daniel Disney, a staunch nonconformist, acquired in 1680 and supported for Presbyterian worship. Taylor served in this rather remote setting for eighteen years. Although this entailed financial hardship, it allowed him to devote extended time to studies. In 1733 Taylor accepted an invitation to become co-pastor with Peter Finch of a Presbyterian church in Norwich. Finch was in declining health, and Taylor soon took charge of the congregation. One of his accomplishments was to

[12] The following details draw from accounts of Taylor by his son and grandson: Edward Taylor, 'A Sketch of the Life of the late Dr. John Taylor of Norwich', *Universal Theological Magazine* 2, no. 7 (July 1804): 1-7; and John Taylor (1750–1826), *History of the Octagon Chapel, Norwich* (London: Charles Green, 1848), 19-39. See also the biography by G. T. Eddy, *Dr. Taylor of Norwich: Wesley's Arch-Heretic* (Peterborough: Epworth Press, 2003).

[13] See Taylor's account of the questions raised and answers given at his ordination, in Richard Taylor and John E. Taylor (great-grandsons), *The Principles and Pursuits of an English Presbyterian Minister of the Eighteenth Century; exemplified in a Selection from the Writings of Dr. John Taylor of Norwich* (London: T. Cadell, 1843), 20-22.

lead them in building an octagon-shaped chapel that was dedicated May 12, 1756. On first viewing this chapel, John Wesley opined that it was 'perhaps the most elegant one in all Europe'.[14] In October 1757 Taylor left Norwich to return to Lancashire and take on the role of divinity tutor in the newly opening Warrington Academy. His time in this role was short, with his death on March 5, 1761. The role was apparently also not an entirely happy fit between Taylor, his colleagues, and his students.[15]

With his move to the prominent pulpit in Norwich, Taylor became a key figure in the emerging rationalist strand of Dissent. There is some evidence that one of his early actions was to work through Samuel Clarke's *Scripture Doctrine of the Trinity* with the congregation. What is clear is that Taylor shared Clarke's emphasis on the sufficiency of Scripture for doctrine. This conviction undergirded Taylor's first publication in 1737, a defense of Joseph Rawson, a lay member of the Independent Dissenting congregation at Castle Gate in Nottingham, who was excluded from Communion by his pastor, James Sloss, for refusing to affirm the classical doctrine of the Trinity (using the language of three 'persons' in one 'substance').[16] Taylor's primary concern in this first tract was not to reject the Trinity per se, but to defend the right of Christians to speak of God solely in terms found within Scripture. This focus came through even more clearly in his response, a year later, to Rev. Sloss's defense of the excommunication. Taylor's response championed 'the sufficiency and perfection of Scripture, without the aids of human schemes, creeds, confessions, etc.'[17]

In 1740 Taylor published a major work, applying his conviction of the sufficiency of Scripture for doctrine to the classic Western Christian understanding of original sin.[18] This work gained much broader

[14] *Journal*, Nov. 23, 1757, 21:131 in this edn. Although JW commented derisively on the amount of money spent on ornamentation, he soon adopted the octagon as a favored shape for Methodist preaching-houses.

[15] See Herbert McLachlan, *Warrington Academy: Its History and Influence* ([Manchester:] Chetham Society, 1943), 42-46.

[16] John Taylor, *Narrative of Mr. Joseph Rawson's Case . . . With a Prefatory Discourse in Defence of the Common Right of Christians* (London: T. Cooper, 1737).

[17] John Taylor, *A Further Defence of the Common Rights of Christians, and the Sufficiency and Perfection of Scripture, without the Aids of Human Schemes, Creeds, Confessions, etc.* (London: R. Hett, 1738).

[18] John Taylor, *Scripture-Doctrine of Original Sin Proposed to Free and Candid Examination* (London: J. Wilson, 1740). Note the hyphen between the first two words of the title, which emphasizes Taylor's central methodological assumption.

attention—bringing Taylor both acclaim and criticism. Over the next two years he penned responses to some of the critics. The original volume, supplemented by these responses, went through four editions in English during the eighteenth century and was honored by a German translation.[19] We will consider this work more closely below.

Rather than carrying on an extended debate around *Scripture-Doctrine of Original Sin*, Taylor turned to related topics. In 1745 he issued *A Paraphrase with Notes on the Epistle to the Romans*. In the opening dedication to his congregation, Taylor reminded them, 'We may not indulge our conceits in matters of revelation. Every point advanced as Christian doctrine ought to be found in Scripture and explained by Scripture.'[20] One target of this reminder was a set of traditional Calvinist emphases on soteriology, as is evident in Taylor's comments on Romans 11 summarizing 'a just idea [of] what it is to preach Christ, or the gospel':

> 'Tis not telling people they are all *naturally corrupt*, under God's wrath and curse from the womb, and in a state of damnation till they come under the influences of a supposed efficacious, irresistible grace, which yet works in a sovereign way, arbitrarily and unaccountably. 'Tis not teaching that only a small, uncertain number among Christians are arbitrarily redeemed, elected, called, adopted, born again or regenerated, and that all the rest are by a sovereign, absolute, and eternal decree passed by, or reprobated. These are no principles of Christianity, but stand in direct contradiction of them, and have drawn a dark veil over the grace of the gospel.[21]

Taylor applied his Scripture-focused approach next to the doctrine of the atonement.[22] He presented biblical teachings on atonement within the paradigm of God's role as magistrate or governor of the universe. God does not pardon sin indiscriminately, Taylor suggested, because God is concerned for the public good. So God established a means of pardon designed to avoid propagating the spirit of rebellion, encouraging instead a 'loyal, well-affected temper throughout the whole community'.[23] Christ's death was integral to

[19] *Johann Taylors gewesenen Presbyterianischen Predigers zu Norwich schriftmätzige Lehre von der Erbsünde* (Frankfurt: s.n., 1769).

[20] John Taylor, *A Paraphrase with Notes on the Epistle to the Romans* (London: J. Waugh, 1745), ii.

[21] Ibid., 101.

[22] John Taylor, *The Scripture-Doctrine of the Atonement* (London: J. Waugh, 1751).

[23] See ibid., 104–5.

this design, not only as an example of God's pardoning love, but as the means that God in wisdom and goodness has 'judged fit and expedient to be done in order to the forgiveness of sin'.[24] Taylor's account echoed themes of the traditional penalty satisfaction model of atonement. But he carefully avoided (and indirectly rejected) emphases central to the substitutionary justification model prominent in Calvinist circles.[25]

The most detailed fruit of Taylor's focus on Scripture was a two-volume concordance of the Hebrew Bible published in the mid-1750s.[26] It was primarily in recognition of this work that Glasgow University bestowed on Taylor in early 1757 an unsolicited Doctor of Divinity degree. Among other publications he issued were a collection of tunes for Isaac Watts's poetic version of the Psalms, the sermon preached at the dedication of the Octagon Chapel, a critique of Francis Hutcheson's notion of the 'moral sense', Taylor's own scheme of moral philosophy used at Warrington, and a tract on debates over liturgical prayer in Dissenting congregations.[27]

Taylor's last publication was posthumous. An editor pulled together his lecture notes in doctrine at Warrington and issued them as *A Scheme of Scripture Divinity*. The methodological assumption of this collection is captured in its preface, which quotes the solemn charge that Taylor gave to students in his course at the beginning of each year:

> I. I do solemnly charge you, in the name of the God of truth and of our Lord Jesus Christ, who is the Way, the Truth, and the Life, and before whose judgment-seat you must in no long time appear, that in all your studies and inquiries of a religious nature, present or future, you do constantly, carefully, impartially, and conscientiously attend to evidence, as it lies in the Holy Scriptures, or in the nature of things and the dictates of reason. . . .

[24] Ibid., 91-92.

[25] See ibid., 22; and the discussion of these models in the introduction to JW's extract of Baxter's *Aphorisms* above (pp. 45-47).

[26] John Taylor, *The Hebrew Concordance*, 2 vols. (London: Waugh & Fenner, 1754–57).

[27] John Taylor, *A Collection of Tunes in Various Airs adapted to the Psalms taken out of Dr. Watts* (London: J. Waugh, 1750); *The Glory of Any House Erected for Worship . . . A Sermon preached at the Opening of the New Chapel in Norwich, May the 12th, 1756* (London: Waugh & Fenner, 1756); *An Examination of the Scheme of Morality advanced by Dr. Hutcheson* (London: Waugh & Fenner, 1759); *A Sketch of Moral Philosophy* (London: J. Waugh & W. Fenner, 1760); and *The Scripture Account of Prayer* (London: Waugh & Fenner, 1761).

II. That you admit, embrace, or assent to no principle, or sentiment, by me taught or advanced, but only so far as it shall appear to you to be supported and justified by proper evidence from revelation, or the reason of things. . . .

IV. That you study to live in peace and love with all your fellow-Christians; and that you steadily assert yourself, and freely allow to others, the unalienable rights of judgment and conscience.[28]

This charge exemplifies the central commitment of early rational Dissent—appeal to Scripture alone, *as interpreted by reason*. Taylor's writings played a major role in shaping the historical trajectory of the group, which moved from a mediating Calvinism into Arminianism and eventually on to Unitarianism. Some present Taylor as one of the founding Unitarians.[29] But this is anachronistic. He was an early transitional figure within the longer trajectory.

Consider his understanding of the Godhead. Taylor's opposition to requiring any account of the nature of God beyond the language of Scripture is often taken as a rejection of the doctrine of the Trinity. However, his comments typically focus on the monarchy or supremacy of the Father, echoing Samuel Clarke. These comments can be read in an Arian fashion. But Taylor never specifically affirmed that the Son had a beginning in time. His positive claims could equally be compared to Eastern Christian accounts of the Trinity.[30]

While Taylor might plausibly be read as an Arian, there is little warrant for equating his view of the Godhead with Faustus Socinus (as Wesley tended to do).[31] Taylor showed no hesitance with biblical language of the discrete work of the Holy Spirit in our lives. He accepted the preexistence of the Son; indeed, he insisted that a central feature of Christ's sacrificial love on the cross was that he emptied himself of that 'state of glory that he had with the Father before the world was'.[32] Taylor also affirmed an integral role for Christ's death in God's provision of forgiveness of sin. He differed from Socinus on all of these points.

[28] John Taylor, *A Scheme of Scripture Divinity* (London: Waugh & Fenner, 1762), vi-vii.

[29] See, e.g., William Turner, *Lives of Eminent Unitarians* (London: Unitarian Association, 1840), 1:299-346.

[30] This case is made in relation to Clarke in Thomas Pfizenmaier, *The Trinitarian Theology of Dr. Samuel Clarke* (New York: Brill, 1997).

[31] This is clearest in sermons from JW's waning years: Sermon 123, 'On Knowing Christ after the Flesh', §4, 4:99-100 in this edn; and Sermon 105, 'On Conscience', I.10, 3:484 in this edn. But see his more indirect charge in *Doctrine of Original Sin*, Pt. II, II.4 (pp. 237-38); and Pt. III, VIII.3 (p. 339).

[32] Taylor, *Scripture-Doctrine of Original Sin*, 34.

Allowing these differences concerning the nature of God, one might still charge Taylor with being Socinian in soteriology—that is, with assuming that humans have an ability for faith and good works *apart from restoring grace*. While Wesley chooses to use the related label of deist, this is his central charge against Taylor.[33] To consider the appropriateness of the charge, one needs a sense of Taylor's argument in *Scripture-Doctrine of Original Sin*.

Key Assumptions Guiding Taylor's 'Scripture-Doctrine of Original Sin'[34]

In the preface to his study Taylor explains his hyphenated title by insisting: 'I have made the revelation of God alone the rule of my judgment, not any schemes or opinions of men' (p. vii). Almost immediately he clarifies that this does not mean he is setting aside reason, for 'Scriptures can be no rule to us, if the understanding God hath given us is not a rule in judging of their sense and meaning' (p. 3). Rather, the 'opinions of men' that he is rejecting are traditional doctrinal claims that he judges to contradict both Scripture and reason. Taylor allows that many of these doctrinal claims appear early in the history of the Church, but characterizes them as corruptions 'by *priests* and *monks*' (p. 264) who mixed 'the forgery of man's imagination with the Truth of God' (p. 128).

This raises the obvious question of how to distinguish between human claims that are mere forgeries of our imagination and those that are clarifications of the truth of God. Taylor is clear about his guideline: 'Nothing ought to pass for divine revelation which is inconsistent with any of the known perfections of the divine nature' (p. 3). In typical early Enlightenment fashion, Taylor proceeds as if the relevant divine perfections are obvious. He seems unaware of (or ignores) debate running through Christian history over 1) which perfections most define the divine nature and 2) what implications attend these perfections. Taylor's stance on the initial aspect of this debate is not hard to discern—throughout the volume he emphasizes justice/goodness as God's primary divine perfection.

[33] See below, Pt. I, Preface, §§3-4 (pp. 157-58).

[34] The page numbers cited in this and the following section refer to the 3rd edn. of Taylor's *The Scripture-Doctrine of Original Sin* (London: J. Waugh, 1750), since this is the edn. that JW cites throughout his response.

The first implication that Taylor draws from the primacy of God's justice/goodness is that the 'image of God' in humanity is our reason, which enables us to develop all the habits of virtue (p. 7). As he enlarges a bit later,

> It is agreeable to [God's] wisdom and goodness to devise all methods of promoting virtue. For of all God's works intelligent beings are the most excellent, and the highest excellency of intelligent beings, and even of God himself, is virtue, or right action. . . . True virtue, or the right exercise of reason, is true worth. (p. 73)

The second implication of God's justice/goodness that Taylor takes as obvious is that authentic guilt must be personal, belonging only to the individual who performs a sinful act or deed (p. 13). On this basis, Taylor immediately dismissed the notion of later humans inheriting the *guilt* of the sin of Adam and Eve. But his deeper concern, and the focus of much of his study, was to demonstrate that this implication also undermined the notion of subsequent humanity inheriting moral *depravity* as a result of the sin of Adam and Eve (see p. 128).

The third implication of God's justice/goodness that Taylor draws is that Christ must bring salvation to sinful humanity *by way of moral means* (p. 16). He highlights Christ's doctrine, example, obedience, and death among these means. In each case his focus is on Christ's consummate virtue, for 'virtue is the only price which purchaseth every thing with God' (p. 72).

Synopsis of Taylor's 'Scripture-Doctrine of Original Sin'

With his central assumptions in mind, we can sketch briefly the flow of Taylor's book. This is helpful, in part, because this flow can be lost in the midst of Wesley's point-by-point rejoinders to Taylor.[35]

Taylor devotes the first part of his study (pp. 1-64) to analysis of five biblical texts that explicitly address the consequences of the sin of Adam and Eve: Genesis 2:17; Genesis 3:7-24; Romans 5:12-20;

[35] Leading Leslie Stephens, e.g., to characterize Pt. II–III of JW's response as 'a wearisome wrangle over texts'. *History of English Thought in the Eighteenth Century* (London: John Murray, 1902), 2:419.

1 Corinthians 15:21-22; and 1 Timothy 2:14. He casts his reflections as recovering a 'Hebrew' understanding of these texts—in contrast to the distortions of later Christian tradition (pp. 30-35).

The main argument running through this section is that only *physical* or *temporal* death was threatened for the sin of Adam and Eve, and only such death resulted from that sin.[36] This argument is developed in direct contrast to a traditional suggestion in most Christian theology that the result of their sin included *spiritual* death (or depravity of moral nature), for Adam and Eve and for their posterity. Taylor insists, for example, that Genesis 3 contains 'not one word of darkening or weakening their rational powers'; Adam and Eve are subjected only to sorrow, labor, and physical death (p. 19). He allows that these afflictions and mortality descend to all subsequent humanity *in consequence* of the transgression of Adam and Eve. But he denies that Scripture presents these realities as inflicted upon us as *punishments* for our parents' sin because punishment connotes guilt and we are not guilty of their sin (pp. 20-21). In fact, Taylor suggests that the afflictions resulting from the sin of Adam and Eve may actually be of *benefit* to their posterity, 'as they are a great advantage to our virtue, by mortifying our lusts and leading us to the fear and obedience of God, and the desires of a better world' (p. 21).

Closely correlated with his analysis of the human problem is Taylor's account of the solution. He contends that these biblical passages identify Christ's main benefit, as the 'Second Adam', to be restoring all humans to life *at the resurrection* (p. 24). Once again, he is rejecting a traditional claim that Christ also 'makes us alive' *now*, renewing our depraved moral nature to some degree (p. 47). Significantly, this is not because Taylor wants to downplay the importance of Christian obedience in the present world. He identifies obedience as second in importance only to Christ's gift of renewed life at the resurrection in the true biblical account of salvation (p. 61). But he relates the two as follows: 'The resurrection is revealed and assured as a motive to piety and virtue; and it is our own great fault if it turn not to our eternal happiness' (p. 62n).

This might appear to reduce Christ's role in salvation simply to his virtuous death, which gains our future resurrection. But Taylor

[36] See Taylor, *Scripture-Doctrine of Original Sin*, 7, 25, 27, 50, 63, 95, and 162. Taylor admits that Rom. 5 is the most difficult passage to limit in this way and argues his point at some length when considering it (pp. 30-31, 51-55).

insists that the grace and benefits of the redeemer 'overflow and abound far beyond the consequences or ill effect of the first offense' (p. 39). In creation God provided sufficient light to all ages and nations of the world for them to understand and practice their duty. God's gracious gift in Christ went further, erecting 'a new dispensation furnished with a glorious fund of light and truth, and all proper means and motives to deliver us from all iniquity and to purify us unto himself a peculiar people, zealous of good works' (p. 78; cf. p. 44). In short, we have the additional benefits of Christ's virtuous doctrine and example. If we open our hearts to these benefits and embrace the methods of salvation established in Christ, we will enjoy not just future life but present spiritual improvements (pp. 63-64).

In an appendix to Part I, Taylor considers two theological questions that could be posed even to his narrower reading of the consequences of the sin of Adam and Eve. The first concerns whether it is consistent with justice for the whole race to be subjected to (temporal) death by the disobedience of our first parents. Taylor insists that God never intended to leave us continually in death, and understood that experiencing death would help us form a just idea of the odious and destructive nature of sin (pp. 65-70). The second question is how the obedience of one man, Jesus Christ, could restore all humankind to life at the resurrection (pp. 70-83). Taylor's answer stresses Christ's consummate virtue (p. 72).

Having thus established the clear teachings of Scripture (as interpreted by reason) on the issue at hand, Taylor turns in Part II of his study (pp. 86-163) to the section in the *Larger Catechism* of the Westminster Assembly devoted to the 'scheme or opinion' of original sin.[37] He works through questions 22-29, noting the scriptural passages quoted as supporting each answer, and arguing that these passages are being misinterpreted. Once again Taylor rejects the notions of later humanity 'sinning in Adam', inheriting the guilt of a sin they did not commit, or being subjected to a sinful nature and misery because of their first parents' sin. Adding to his case, Taylor charges that the notion of inherited moral depravity renders sinning *natural* and *necessary* for fallen humanity, rather than an expression of

[37] Taylor insists that he casts no aspersions on the memory of the Assembly of Divines in challenging some of their propositions because he attributes the origin of these false teachings to the Church of Rome many years ago! *Scripture-Doctrine of Original Sin*, 125n26.

culpable choice (p. 125). And he specifically challenges the justice of God reprobating any person on account of Adam's sin (p. 157). If we are excluded from eternal glory, he insists, it is not due to Adam's guilt or inherited depravity but our own lack of 'love, compassion, and benevolence toward our fellow-creatures' (pp. 159-60).

Part III of Taylor's investigation (pp. 166-266) takes up issues related to the position he has staked out. He highlights seven possible objections and three questions for consideration. Wesley quotes all ten items in his response, so it is not necessary to enumerate them here.[38] But it is important to recognize Taylor's deepest concern emerging in this section. While Taylor argues against the notion of inherited depravity per se, his real target is the further assumption evident in the *Larger Catechism* that this depravity is TOTAL—that is, our 'natural' condition after the fall is such that all humans inevitably sin and are incapable even of recognizing their sinfulness, let alone repenting for it (cf. pp. 186, 224). On these terms, the only possibility of salvation is if our fallen 'nature' is renewed by a direct act of the Spirit of God. Taylor is well aware that the *Larger Catechism* (in *Q.* 30) limits this divine renewal to the 'elect', leaving the rest of humanity in their depraved incapacity, with its resulting reprobation. He protests that such a limited offer of salvation and such unconditional reprobation serve 'to embarrass religion with inextricable difficulties, and to fill the minds of Christians with endless perplexity and confusion' (p. 245).

How might one defend instead that God provides *all* humans with the possibility of eternal salvation, and correlated culpability for rejecting God's ways? Taylor's solution is to contend that the moral capacities of later humanity are not *totally* different from those of pre-fallen Adam. To make this case, he challenges a long-standing assumption that when God pronounced Adam 'good' (Gen. 1:31), it meant that Adam was perfect in every way—ideal physical condition, perfect knowledge, fully formed moral character, and so on. Taylor argues that this does not fit the general portrayal of Adam's initial condition in Scripture (pp. 170-76) and contests the passages offered in the *Larger Catechism* as proof for Adam's original perfect nature (pp. 176-86). On the specific question, 'How far is our present state the same with that of Adam in paradise?' Taylor concludes that human mental capacities are generally the same (allowing for individual variance). But Adam was created with maturity in bodily

[38] See Pt. II, sections IV-V, below (beginning p. 273).

stature and mental capacity (though not all knowledge), while we enter life in the ignorance and weakness of infancy. His body was healthy, while ours is subject to disease. And Adam's temptations were few, while ours are various (and propagated widely by culture). On the other hand, Adam had less divine assistance and grace than offered in the new dispensation by Christ (pp. 235-36). In short, all humans enter life with the basic integrity bestowed in God's gracious act of creation—moral ability and accountability.

Having traced his alternative account of the present human situation, Taylor turns to how his understandings of redemption and regeneration differ from those in a system built on inherited total depravity. Relating redemption largely to pardon, he insists that the ground of Christ's redeeming mission was not Adam's sin, but our sins (p. 241); and the condition for receiving that redeeming work is recognition of what we ourselves have done wrongly, not what we lost in Adam (p. 243). Similarly, he rejects the understanding of regeneration as a renewal (in the elect) of our totally depraved nature after the fall, defining it instead as 'gaining those habits of virtue and religion, which give us the real character of the children of God' (p. 246). He is quick to add that part of Christ's new dispensation is the promise of the Spirit's presence to 'assist our sincere endeavours after wisdom, and the habits of virtue' (pp. 254-55). But he stresses that 'it is fitting we should make a due use of the powers we already have, before we receive, and in order to our receiving, further help' (p. 256).

For Taylor, the powers we already have are gifts of God's grace bestowed through our creation in God's image. Thus, he did not champion nature over grace per se. But he insisted that humans have an ability for faith and good works apart from *restoring* grace. On this point, the soteriology he develops in *Scripture-Doctrine of Original Sin* is very similar to that of Socinus, whatever their other differences.

Contemporary Dissenting Responses to Taylor's 'Scripture-Doctrine of Original Sin'

Taylor concluded *Scripture-Doctrine* with the contention that the notion of total depravity blasphemes the holy God (p. 256). He surely anticipated that this position would spark debate, particularly in the broader Dissenting community.

One of the earliest responses was that of David Jennings (1691–1762), who issued anonymously *A Vindication of the Scripture-Doctrine of Original Sin* within months of Taylor's work being released.[39] Jennings was the son of John Jennings, who ran a moderate Dissenting academy after his ejection from the Church of England in 1662. Philip Doddridge, who studied in this academy, praised the way that the senior Jennings encouraged freedom of inquiry, affirming Scripture as the only standard of truth, and refusing to follow the doctrines of any single party, being instead 'sometimes a Calvinist, sometimes an Arminian and sometimes a Baxterian, as truth and evidence determine him'.[40] Raised in this moderate wing of the Dissenting tradition, David Jennings moved towards a more confessional stance as he rose to become, by 1744, professor of divinity in the academy in Moorfields, London, supported by William Coward's trust—a school that required students 'be instructed in the true Gospel doctrines, according as the same are explained in the Assembly's Catechism'.[41] Thus, while he pledged in *Vindication* to pursue the same course as Taylor in seeking truth as it is revealed in Scripture (p. 3), Jennings was quick to add, 'yet I look upon the Assembly's catechism to be, in the general, as excellent a summary of the Christian faith as any that is extant' (p. 48). He also mocked Taylor's insistence that he was not trying to disparage the Assembly (p. 46).

Jennings's rebuttal of Taylor could take a disparaging tone. He chose for an emblem on the title page the Greek text of Romans 1:22, 'Claiming to be wise, they became fools.' In this vein, he protested Taylor's self-confident tone (p. 110), charging him with perverting various texts of Scripture to present 'his own darling scheme' (pp. 113-14). Reversing and intensifying Taylor's depiction of the teaching of the *Larger Catechism*, Jennings branded Taylor's

[39] [David Jennings], *A Vindication of the Scripture-Doctrine of Original Sin, from Mr. Taylor's Free and Candid Examination of It* (London: R. Hett & J. Oswald, 1740).

[40] Philip Doddridge, letter to Rev. Samuel Clark, Sept. 1722, in J. E. Humphreys, ed., *The Correspondence and Diary of Philip Doddridge* (London: Colburn & Bentley, 1829), 1:155-56.

[41] For more details on Jennings and the academy in Moorfields, see John Hanby Thompson, *A History of the Coward Trust* (London: United Reformed Church History Society, 1988), 16-22; and J. W. Ashley Smith, *The Birth of Modern Education: The Contribution of the Dissenting Academies, 1660–1800* (London: Independent Press, 1954), 180-84.

scheme as 'a thick cloud of bigotry, prejudice and error . . . whereby the whole gospel is most wretchedly impoverished and deformed, and almost all the glory of it quite darkened'.[42]

Looking beyond such rhetorical flourishes, Jennings generally defended the traditional Calvinist interpretation of the biblical texts in question, taking for granted the roles of Adam and Christ as 'federal heads' that had developed in English Puritan theology.[43] He particularly defended limited atonement, insisting that Scripture does not teach that all humans share in the benefits of Christ as 'federal head' (pp. 30-32). Though he does not stress the point, those who do not share in these benefits are surely reprobated.

Perhaps the most significant point in Jennings's response to Taylor was his commendation of a book titled *The Ruin and Recovery of Mankind* as 'the most easy, rational, and scriptural account of the doctrine of original sin that has yet been published' (p. 11). This book, which had just been released anonymously, was by Jennings's friend and former mentor, Isaac Watts (1674–1748).[44] Watts was raised and trained as an orthodox Calvinist. But over the years he distanced himself from high Calvinism, to the dismay of early supporters like William Coward.[45] For example, he sided with those at Salters' Hall (in 1719) who refused to impose the formal doctrine of the Trinity on Independent ministers. He also balked at the idea of unconditional reprobation, developing a model of soteriology where the elect are assured salvation, while the possibility of salvation is extended to all other humans (the non-elect) on the condition of their response to the gospel.[46] By 1740, Watts was a leading figure of moderate Dissent, particularly in Congregational circles.

[42] Jennings, *Vindication*, 87; cf. Taylor, *Scripture-Doctrine of Original Sin*, 161.

[43] See David A. Weir, *The Origins of the Federal Theology in Sixteenth-Century Reformation Thought* (Oxford: Clarendon Press, 1990); and Michael McGiffert, 'The Perkinsian Moment of Federal Theology', *Calvin Theological Journal* 29 (1994): 117-48.

[44] [Isaac Watts,] *The Ruin and Recovery of Mankind* (London: R. Hett & J. Brackstone, 1740).

[45] See Arthur Paul Davis, *Isaac Watts: His Life and Works* (New York: Dryden Press, 1943); and Rivers, *Reason, Grace and Sentiment*, 164-204.

[46] This argument is developed in *Ruin and Recovery*, 224-53. JW found it so irenic that he extracted and published it the same year as *Serious Considerations concerning the Doctrines of Election and Reprobation* (London, 1740); see *Bibliography*, No. 42.

Watts had been at work on *Ruin and Recovery* for some time. The initial edition shows no awareness of Taylor. But Watts's project covered much of the same territory as Taylor's book, as evidenced by Watts's subtitle: 'An attempt to vindicate the scriptural account of these great events upon the plain principles of reason, with an answer to various difficulties relating to original sin, the universal deprivation of nature . . . '. Watts's general approach was more irenic than Taylor's, trying to reconcile traditional doctrines with Scripture whenever possible. This tone, combined with the systematic character of Watts's book, made it an ideal dialogue partner for Taylor.

Jennings's reference to Watts drew him to Taylor's attention, leading Taylor to issue *A Supplement to the Scripture-Doctrine of Original Sin* in 1741 addressing both writers.[47] Actually, Taylor largely dismissed Jennings because 'he seldom faces my argument' (p. v). So the *Supplement* interacts mainly with Watts, clarifying how Taylor differs from him on the various biblical texts and issues involved. Watts returned the favor the following year, incorporating responses to several of Taylor's points in the second edition of *Ruin and Recovery*.[48] Taylor in turn issued a set of *Remarks* on these additions.[49] The various forays illuminated the differences between the two authors, but introduced little new to the discussion.

In addition to largely dismissing Jennings, Taylor's *Supplement* totally ignored another Dissenting pastor who was vigorously challenging *Scripture-Doctrine of Original Sin*. This critic was Samuel Hebden (1692?–1747), who served the Independent chapel in Canterbury between 1714 and 1724, then assumed pastoral leadership of the Congregational church in Wrentham, Suffolk, until his death.[50] Since Wrentham is about twenty miles southeast of Norwich, it is likely that Hebden and Taylor were acquainted. What is certain is

[47] John Taylor, *A Supplement to the Scripture-Doctrine of Original Sin, etc.; Containing some Remarks upon two Books . . .* (London: Mary Fenner, 1741). Taylor notes in the preface that Jennings's reference brought Watts to his attention.

[48] [Isaac Watts,] *The Ruin and Recovery of Mankind*, 2nd edn. (London: James Brackstone, 1742).

[49] Taylor, *Remarks on such Additions to the Second Edition of 'The Ruin and Recovery of Mankind' as Relate to the Arguments advanced in the Supplement to the Scripture-Doctrine of Original Sin* (London: Mary Fenner, 1742).

[50] Cf. John Browne, *History of Congregationalism . . . in Norfolk and Suffolk* (London: Jarrold & Sons, 1877), 432; and Arthur F. Taylor, *The Free Churches of Canterbury* (London: Carey Kingsgate Press, 1930?), 42.

that Hebden considered Taylor's position a threat to Calvinist orthodoxy and was ready to challenge it on every front.

Hebden's first foray was to add a few footnotes and a focused appendix to two sermons he published in 1740 expounding the original perfection of Adam and the covenant of works that God established with Adam as our federal head (that is, the Puritan federal theology that Taylor rejected).[51] Early the next year Hebden issued a full-length book defending the teaching of the *Larger Catechism* against the criticisms of Taylor.[52] Not to miss an opportunity, he also added rebuttals of Taylor to a sermon he printed that year disproving baptismal regeneration.[53] Then, in 1743, he published a defense of *The Scripture-Doctrine of Imputed Sin and Righteousness*, taking Taylor again as his primary opponent.[54]

Hebden was a strong confessional Calvinist. He appealed often to the *Larger Catechism* and Puritan writers, as well as earlier historical precedent, in defending his position. He charged Taylor with maliciously misrepresenting the position of the Catechism on issues under debate and perverting Scripture to fit his system.[55] And he branded Taylor's system as sharing the errors of Pelagius, Socinus, and popery.[56] Although one might understand why Taylor would see little chance of productive engagement with Hebden, Taylor's choice to ignore him left unanswered the most staunchly Calvinist contemporary response to his position on original sin.

[51] Samuel Hebden, *Man's Original Righteousness; and God's Covenant with Adam, as a publick Person; asserted and plainly proved from the Scripture, as the basis of the true Doctrine of Original Sin. In two Sermons, with an appendix, relating to a Book lately published by the Reverend Mr. J. Taylor, of Norwich, against the Doctrine of Original Sin* (London: R. Hett & J. Oswald, 1740).

[52] Samuel Hebden, *The Doctrine of Original Sin, as laid down in the Assembly's Catechism, Explained; proved to be agreeable to Scripture and Reason* (London: R. Hett & J. Oswald, 1741).

[53] Samuel Hebden, *Baptismal Regeneration disproved; the Scripture Account of the Nature of Regeneration explained; and the Absolute Necessity of such a Change argued from the native corruption of Man since the Fall. With some remarks on some late passages in a late book against Original Sin* (London: R. Hett & J. Oswald, 1741).

[54] Samuel Hebden, *The Scripture-Doctrine of Imputed Sin and Righteousness Stated and Defended; Chiefly for Confuting what Socinian Writers (and the Reverend Mr. J. Taylor, in his late books against Original Sin) have Suggested, as to 'God's Imputing no Sin or Righteousness but what is Personal'* (London: J. Oswald, 1743).

[55] See Hebden, *Man's Original Righteousness*, 8; and *Doctrine of Original Sin*, 24n36.

[56] See Hebden, *Man's Original Righteousness*, 46; and *Doctrine of Original Sin*, iv.

There were continuing scattered engagements with Taylor across the Dissenting spectrum in England through the end of his life, though none that rose to the scope of the works of Hebden, Jennings, and Watts.[57] Concern about the impact of Taylor's arguments continued as well, particularly in the staunch Calvinist wing of Dissent. This concern was expressed graphically on the occasion of Taylor's death in 1761. A writer using the pseudonym 'Antisocinus' issued *The Arian's and Socinian's Monitor*.[58] This satirical treatise recounts a purported vision experienced by a former student of John Taylor. The student sees Taylor now in the sufferings of hell, being tormented by those around him whom his preaching and writings hardened against the truth, so that they went heedlessly into everlasting despair. An Arian Christology and rejection of the doctrine of inherited depravity are highlighted among the false teachings leading to this demise (pp. 29, 34). The vision closes with Taylor lamenting, 'Alas, I never saw the need of the operations of unfrustrable [that is, irresistible] grace till I arrived in eternity' (p. 44).

John Wesley's Engagement with Taylor's 'Scripture-Doctrine of Original Sin'

Given Taylor's framing of his challenge to the doctrine of original sin in explicit contrast with the Westminster *Catechism*, initial debate over his model centered in Dissenting traditions. But it did not take long for Anglicans who shared his Enlightenment convictions to begin affirming and rehearsing his arguments in broader venues.[59]

[57] Two significant responses were published in North America, but there is little evidence that Taylor knew of them: Samuel Niles, *The True Scripture-Doctrine of Original Sin Stated and Defended; In the way of Remarks on a Late Piece . . . by John Taylor* (Boston: Samuel Kneeland, 1757); and Jonathan Edwards, *The Great Christian Doctrine of Original Sin Defended; . . . a Reply to the Objections and Arguings of Dr. John Taylor* (Boston: Samuel Kneeland, 1758).

[58] Antisocinus, *The Arian's and Socinian's Monitor* (London: for the author, 1761). The author was John MacGowan (1726–80), who served in the mid-1750s as a local preacher in association with JW, until he became a convinced Calvinist. This change led to a stint as an Independent minister and eventually to ordination as a Particular Baptist. See *Blackwell Dictionary of Evangelical Biography* (1995), 2:71.

[59] See, e.g., the positive distillation of Taylor's argument by S___n in *Gentleman's Magazine* 17 (1747): 474-76; and the praise of Taylor's study of original sin in the opening to a review of his *Scripture-Doctrine of the Atonement* by William Rose in *Monthly Review* 4 (1751): 266-77.

It was inevitable that John Wesley would become aware of Taylor's work, since his role in the evangelical revival meant that Wesley often crossed the divide between the Anglican and the Dissenting communities. The first clear mention he makes is in August 1748:

> We came to Shackerley [Shropshire]. . . . Abundance of people were gathered before six; many of whom were disciples of Dr. Taylor; laughing at Original Sin, and, consequently, at the whole frame of Scriptural Christianity. O what a providence is it, which has brought us here also, among these silver-tongued Antichrists! Surely a few, at least, will recover out of the snare, and know Jesus Christ as their wisdom and righteousness![60]

When Wesley returned to Shackerley in April 1751, he records that he 'enlarged much more than I am accustomed to do, on the doctrine of original sin; and determined, if God should give me a few years' life, publicly to answer his [i.e., Taylor's] *new gospel*'.[61] Wesley reiterated this intention the following day to Rev. John Milner, vicar of Chipping, when he preached in his parish.[62] But Wesley's resolve soon wavered, in part because of his recognition of Taylor's expertise in the biblical languages.[63]

Whatever his doubts, continuing concern about the impact of Taylor's dismissal of original sin finally persuaded Wesley to prepare an extended rebuttal.[64] He started writing during a preaching tour in Ireland over the summer of 1756.[65] The bulk of Parts II–VI of the volume was composed during retreats to the home of

[60] *Journal*, Aug. 28, 1748, 20:245-46 in this edn.

[61] Ibid., Apr. 10, 1751, 20:383 in this edn.

[62] See John Milner's letter to JW, June 30, 1751, 26:467 in this edn.

[63] Note JW's passing comment in Pt. I, Preface, §2 (p. 156 below); and the disparaging comments about his hesitance in the MS diary of a book steward in Bristol (Nicholas Norton?) on Dec. 10, 1752 (pp. 104-9), http://www.divinity.duke.edu/sites/default/files/documents/cswt/Bristol_Steward_Diary.pdf.

[64] JW's resolve may have been deepened by William Mason, *Methodism Displayed, and Enthusiasm Detected; Intended as an Antidote against and a Preservative from the delusive principles and unscriptural Doctrines of a Modern Set of Seducing Preachers* (London: Henry Cooke 1756). Mason was defending William Romaine and other Calvinist evangelical preachers, who were being mocked as 'Methodists' by Anglican clergy. Mason highlighted the rejection of the doctrine of original sin by this 'modern set of seducing preachers' as the root of their attack on the evangelicals. See pp. 9-10, 23-24.

[65] See JW's letter from Limerick to his wife, June 18, 1756 (vol. 27 in this edn.).

Ebenezer Blackwell in Lewisham during the winter of 1756–57.[66] On March 25, 1757, the day after writing his conclusion, Wesley read it to a 'serious clergyman', and they were moved to pray for Dr. Taylor, hoping that God would show him 'the truth as it is in Jesus'.[67] Since Wesley was leaving London in mid-April for his regular preaching tour in the north of England, he entrusted the manuscript to his brother Charles, who took it to Bristol to oversee production and correction of the proofs. Before leaving, John drafted a proposal for subscriptions to the volume, which appeared in *Felix Farley's Bristol Journal* on April 16, 1757.[68] The completed volume (including an additional abstract from Thomas Boston that Wesley decided to add during the summer) was announced on November 19, 1757, in *Felix Farley's Bristol Journal*.

John Taylor's initial response to hearing that Wesley was preparing a volume critical of *Scripture-Doctrine of Original Sin* was reportedly to express surprise that 'that servant of God' was going to write against him.[69] After Wesley's *Doctrine of Original Sin* was published, Taylor was asked whether he intended to prepare an answer. He replied that he was not inclined to do so because it would merely be a 'personal controversy' between him and Wesley. Hearing this response, Wesley wrote Taylor a cordial letter in which he expressed his confidence that they could engage the topic without personal attacks, while insisting that the difference between them was not just of personal opinion but of the 'fundamental nature of Christianity'.[70] This letter seems to have encouraged Taylor to collect a few observations on Wesley's volume. Taylor died before publishing these observations, but they were issued by an editor of his papers in 1767.[71]

[66] The Preface is dated Nov. 30, 1756, Lewisham; the closing exhortation on Mar. 24, 1757, again in Lewisham.

[67] *Journal*, Mar. 25, 1757, 21:89 in this edn. (quoting Eph. 4:21). See also his lament the following week about Dr. Taylor's poison spreading even to Switzerland. *Journal*, Apr. 1, 1757, 21:90 in this edn.

[68] The Proposal will be included as an open letter in vol. 27 of this edn.

[69] Henry Moore, *Life of the Rev. John Wesley* (London: Kershaw, 1825), 2:409.

[70] Letter to John Taylor, July 3, 1759 (vol. 27 in this edn.).

[71] John Taylor, *A Reply to the Reverend John Wesley's Remarks on 'The Scripture-Doctrine of Original Sin'* (London: Waugh, 1767). This was also appended to the *Supplement* section of the 4th edn. of *Scripture-Doctrine of Original Sin* (London: M. Waugh, 1767), 229-48. Taylor's responses will be recorded in footnotes at the relevant locations in Pt. II and III below.

There is no evidence that Wesley became aware of Taylor's published reply; he certainly never answered it in print. Neither is there any evidence for Wesley's suggestion in 1780 that Taylor became convinced of the error of his Socinianism before his death, but could not bring himself to acknowledge this publicly![72]

Wesley's Focal Concern about Taylor's Dismissal of Original Sin

Turning to consider Wesley's rebuttal of Taylor's *Scripture-Doctrine of Original Sin*, it is helpful to identify first the focal concern that propelled him to write. In Wesley's proposal for subscribers to *Doctrine of Original Sin*, he lamented that many were confidently affirming that Taylor was *unanswerable* because he had not yet been answered. He then noted that this was not entirely true because there had been responses by Hebden, Jennings, and Watts. Why were these not sufficient? Wesley suggested that they had not rebutted Taylor systematically, working 'step by step, from the beginning of his book to the end'.[73]

But surely potential subscribers recognized that there was another significant difference in Wesley's proposed response to Taylor. It would be the first detailed critique of Taylor by an Anglican/Arminian writer! Wesley was clearly sensitive to this point, since he sought to preserve broad sponsorship by promising in the proposal to stay focused on the narrow topic of inherited depravity and our need for restoration in Christ—not touching on any other controversy between 'Remonstrants and Counter-Remonstrants' (that is, Arminians and Calvinists).

The Dissenting rebuttals of Taylor shared the goal (in varying degrees) of defending Calvinist soteriology, including limited and unconditional election to salvation. Hebden and Jennings also defended implicitly the inevitable reprobation of those who are not elect. Wesley, by contrast, shared Taylor's disdain for any soteriology

[72] Letter to Sir Harry Trelawney, Aug. 1780 (vol. 29 in this edn.). Among other problems with JW's claim, he has Taylor living past 80, while Taylor died at 67!

[73] *Felix Farley's Bristol Journal*, Apr. 16, 1757 (vol. 27 of this edn.).

implying unconditional reprobation.[74] On the broad scale Wesley and Taylor were fellow Arminians. So what did Wesley object to in Taylor's argument that touched on the 'fundamental nature of Christianity'?

While Wesley was clearly dissatisfied with Taylor's Christology, this was not the focus of his concern. In the proposal for publishing a rebuttal, Wesley identified the point in Taylor's work that threatened to undercut the cause of all revealed religion specifically as his dismissal of the doctrine of original sin. But this is still not focused enough.

One dimension of the doctrine of original sin in Western Christian theology is affirmation that the posterity of Adam and Eve inherit the *guilt* of their sin. While Wesley accepted this traditional claim, he had long contended that this inherited guilt was then canceled for *all* persons as one of the benefits of Christ's death.[75] As such, he could insist as vigorously as Taylor that no person will be sent to hell for the guilt of Adam's sin.[76]

A second dimension of the traditional doctrine of original sin in Western Christianity is the claim that Adam and Eve were originally immortal and became subject to physical death only after they sinned. The doctrine stresses that all subsequent persons inherit this mortality as their initial state. Since Taylor accepted this dimension of the traditional doctrine, it was not at issue for Wesley.

Rather, Wesley's concern focused on the third major dimension of the traditional doctrine of original sin, the claim that Adam and Eve not only lost their state of innocence when they sinned but also experienced a spiritual death, a weakening and corruption of their human faculties, and this corrupted state was passed on to their descendants.[77] As we have seen, Taylor argued at length against this notion of inherited depravity. He particularly rejected the claim that this depravity was so thorough-going that humans stand in need of a healing work of God's grace before they are capable of living in God's ways or even of recognizing their moral infirmity. Taylor's

[74] See Sermon 110, 'Free Grace', §§4-9, 3:545-47 in this edn., as well as the section devoted to debates with Calvinists in vol. 13 of this edn.

[75] See Minutes (June 25, 1744), *Q.* 16, 10:129 in this edn.

[76] See particularly *Predestination Calmly Considered* (1752), §34, vol. 13 in this edn.; and letter to John Mason, Nov. 21, 1776 (vol. 29 in this edn.).

[77] See his letter to Samuel Sparrow, Oct. 9, 1773 (vol. 28 in this edn.): 'With regard to original sin (I mean the proneness to evil which is found in every child of man). . . .'

alternative was to praise the ability for moral living that God has instilled in every human being and exhort his readers to use those abilities.

For Wesley, Taylor's denial of inherited depravity reflected a naively optimistic view of present human nature and behavior. More important, Wesley worried that it obscured the nature of the Christian gospel, which is the good news not just of forgiveness for sin but of *healing* for the infirmity and distortion of character that incline us to sinning. As Wesley put it in the preface to his response to Taylor, Christianity is essentially about 'healing the soul'; if persons are convinced (by Taylor's arguments) that they have no need of healing, they will not be open to the gospel offer of 'medicine to heal their sickness'.[78] As he reiterated later, 'none will come to the "physician" but "they that are sick", and are throughly sensible of it.'[79]

The Heart of Wesley's Evangelical Alternative to Taylor's Rationalist Arminianism

Taylor's response to Wesley on this point would surely be to remind him that inherited depravity was the base upon which traditional Calvinist soteriology established its affirmation of unconditional election, limited atonement, and the implied necessary reprobation of the non-elect. This base might allow for 'healing', but only of the elect! Wesley was no happier with such a restricted possibility of salvation than was Taylor. But what was his alternative? How did Wesley's evangelical Arminianism differ from Taylor's rationalist Arminianism?

The first way in which they differed concerns how they grounded their shared conviction of the universal possibility of salvation. Taylor preserved this possibility by emphasizing the gifts of God's grace bestowed in our creation in God's image, insisting that these gifts had not been significantly altered or weakened by the fall. By contrast, Wesley retained the notion that the abilities given in our initial creation were fatally impaired by the fall. But he then insisted that God had *restored* these abilities *in all persons*, as one of the

[78] Pt. I, Preface, §4 (p. 158 below).
[79] Pt. II, section VI.1 (p. 295 below).

benefits of Christ's redemption, to a sufficient degree that we are capable of sensing our need for further healing and turning to God as the physician of souls. This universal (partial) renewal of our fallen nature was one of the central benefits that Wesley came to assign to prevenient grace (or 'preventing' grace), as the foundational dimension of God's restoring work.[80]

What is the significance of Wesley's alternative approach to accounting for the universal possibility of human response to God? When Taylor dismissed a similar suggestion as positing a needless 'redundancy of grace', Wesley responded that this betrayed a woefully inadequate understanding of 'communion with God'![81] For Taylor, God's gracious initiative was complete, and now the ball was in our court. He insisted that we must make due use of the powers that God bestowed in creation and Christ's virtuous example before expecting to receive further divine help. Wesley concurred with Taylor on the importance of recognizing that God's grace undergirds (or 'accompanies') and responds to (or 'follows') every human good desire, but he insisted that God's grace also goes before (or 'prevents') every such desire.[82] God is not standing back, waiting to see how we will use the gracious gifts of creation. God is constantly engaging us, in the midst of the mess that we have made by misusing these gifts, inviting and enabling restored communion. This divine initiative to fallen humanity is not a 'redundancy of grace'; it is a heaping of 'grace upon grace',[83] which underscores the depth, continuity, and responsiveness of redemptive communion with God!

This points towards another difference between Wesley's evangelical Arminianism and the position of Taylor—the prominence and nature of the work of the Holy Spirit in salvation. Wesley charged that Taylor's 'scheme' of salvation rendered assistance from the Spirit needless, for humans are sufficient in themselves.[84]

[80] See esp. Sermon 85, 'On Working Out Our Own Salvation', II.1, 3:203 in this edn.; *Predestination Calmly Considered*, §47, vol. 13 in this edn.; and Sermon 43, 'The Scripture Way of Salvation', §I.2, 2:156-57 in this edn. Both 'preventing' and 'prevenient' carry over their meaning from the Latin: 'to come before'.

[81] See Pt. II, section II.17 (p. 267 below), responding to Taylor, *Scripture-Doctrine of Original Sin*, 149.

[82] See Pt. II, section VI.2 (p. 301 below), responding to Taylor, *Scripture-Doctrine of Original Sin*, 256.

[83] See Sermon 1, 'Salvation by Faith', §§1-3, 1:117-18 in this edn.

[84] Pt. II, section V.2 (p. 290 below).

Taylor protested that this was a gross misrepresentation of his view.[85] He had a point because Taylor does invoke the work of the Spirit on occasion. His most frequent mention is identifying the Spirit as the author of Scripture, the source of saving truth.[86] He also highlights the 'extraordinary effusion and miraculous gifts peculiar to the Apostolic Age'.[87] Most relevantly, Taylor affirms 'the communication and influence of the Spirit of God in all ages, to assist our sincere endeavours after wisdom, and the habits of virtue'.[88] This echoes Taylor's definition of being 'born of the Spirit' as being born 'into the right use and application of the natural powers, in a life of righteousness, godliness and sobriety'.[89] To which one must add his recognition that

> we are very apt, in a world full of temptation, to be deceived and drawn into sin by bodily appetites; when once we are under the government of those appetites, it is at least exceeding difficult, if not impracticable, to recover ourselves by the mere force of reason; and consequently that we stand in need of that life-giving Spirit which the Apostle mentions (Rom. 8:2).[90]

Thus, Taylor did affirm the assistance of the Spirit in salvation, but in a carefully delimited fashion. He is clear about the reasons for his caution: 'It is common to find [Calvinist] divines asserting that we are born again by some uncertain, arbitrary, and irresistible workings of the Spirit of God, which operate upon some few, and not upon others.'[91]

In other words, Taylor shied away from emphasizing the Spirit's agency in salvation in order to preserve the integrity of our human response. Wesley believed that Taylor leaned too far in the other direction. His evangelical alternative portrayed the agency of the Spirit permeating the entire process of salvation, inviting and enabling our response step-by-step, while refusing to effect it irresistibly:

[85] Taylor, *Reply* (1767), 239.

[86] See Taylor, *Scripture-Doctrine of Original Sin*, 19, 103, 104, 111, 225, 233.

[87] Ibid., 255.

[88] Ibid., 255-56.

[89] Ibid., 144.

[90] Ibid., 228.

[91] Ibid., 245-46.

> The life of God in the soul of a believer . . . immediately and necessarily implies the continual inspiration of God's Holy Spirit: God's breathing into the soul, and the soul's breathing back what it first receives from God; a continual action of God upon the soul, the re-action of the soul upon God; an unceasing presence of God, the loving, pardoning God, manifested to the heart. . . . [But] God does not continue to act upon the soul unless the soul re-acts upon God.[92]

Here was a truly dynamic, responsive model of 'communion with God' in the Christian life.

It will be helpful to the reader of *Doctrine of Original Sin* to bear in mind one further difference between the Arminianism of Taylor and that of Wesley. It rests in their differing assumptions about what enables authentic human moral action and accountability (that is, their moral psychology). Taylor assumes a strongly rationalist moral psychology. For him, God's greatest gift in our creation was the power of reason, to control and rightly order our appetites, affections, and passions. While the latter are innocent in themselves, they readily become excessive and disordered in our fallen world, leading to sinful actions. The way to overcome sinful actions is for reason to reassert its role in habituating affections and passions into their proper balanced state.[93] How is this possible? As Taylor summarizes it, 'Under the glorious light of the gospel we have very clear ideas of the divine perfections. . . . We see our duty to the utmost extent, and have the most cogent reasons to perform it . . . and [we have] the Spirit of God promised for our direction and assistance.'[94]

Wesley's response to this summary is telling: 'This sounds well. But will *knowledge* balance *passion*? Or are "rational powers" a counterpoise to sensual appetites? Will "clear ideas" deliver [us] from lust or vanity? Or *seeing* the duty to love our enemies enable us to practise it?'[95] In his youth, Wesley had actually embraced a rationalist moral psychology much like that of Taylor. But in the events surrounding Aldersgate he became increasingly convinced that 'all that can be said of the beauty and advantage of virtue and the deformity and ill effect of vice alone cannot resist, much less overcome

[92] Sermon 19, 'The Great Privilege of Those that Are Born of God', III.2-3, 1:442 in this edn.

[93] These themes permeate Taylor, but see particularly *Scripture-Doctrine of Original Sin*, 7, 215-17, 232-33, 248.

[94] Ibid., 233.

[95] Pt. II, section V.2 (p. 290 below).

and heal, one irregular appetite or passion'.[96] Then he experienced the 'heavenly, healing light' of the Spirit's assurance of God's pardoning love and found that this enabled him to love God and neighbor truly.[97] Sparked by this insight and drawing on a range of resources, Wesley's mature writings present an 'affectional' moral psychology that values the positive contribution of the emotions and passions as much as reason (indeed, refusing to separate as strongly between these as Taylor had done).[98] They present human action as *responsive*—evoked and sustained by what we experience holistically, not just by rational conviction or mere emotional sensation. And they insist that specific actions (holy or sinful) flow from holistic dispositions (which Wesley calls 'tempers'). Thus, when Taylor equated righteousness with 'right action', Wesley replied, 'Righteousness is properly and directly *a right temper* or *disposition of mind*, or a complex of all right tempers.'[99]

In short, while Taylor based his hope for authentic human holiness on the 'moral means' of rational persuasion, Wesley based his hope on the *promise* of God's *healing* love poured into human hearts by the Holy Spirit. This was the core of his evangelical Arminianism.

The Constraints of Wesley's Rhetorical Strategy in Doctrine of Original Sin

I have detailed these central differences between Taylor and Wesley because they are obscured a bit by Wesley's rhetorical strategy. As promised in the proposal for subscribers to the volume, Wesley stays focused on the topic of inherited depravity, avoiding other debates. In particular, he avoided traditional areas of dispute

[96] As he put it in the later Sermon 62, 'The End of Christ's Coming', §§1-3, 2:472-73 in this edn. Similar in Sermon 70, 'Case of Reason Impartially Considered', II.8-9, 2:598 in this edn.

[97] Cf. Sermon 9, 'Spirit of Bondage and Adoption', III.1-3, 1:260-61 in this edn.; and Sermon 77, 'Spiritual Worship', II.5, 3:96-97 in this edn.

[98] For more on this, see Randy L. Maddox, 'A Change of Affections: The Development, Dynamics, and Dethronement of John Wesley's "Heart Religion"', in Richard Steele, ed., '*Heart Religion' in the Methodist Tradition and Related Movements* (Metuchen, N.J.: Scarecrow Press, 2001), 3-31; and Kenneth J. Collins, 'John Wesley's Topography of the Heart: Dispositions, Tempers, and Affections', *Methodist History* 36 (1998): 162-75.

[99] Pt. III, section VIII.3 (p. 338 below).

between Calvinists and Arminians.[100] But this meant that some of his key convictions—like prevenient grace—remain largely in the background. They appear only in passing and are never explained in detail. This edition compensates for that reality by drawing attention to the most significant occasions in footnotes.

A related impact of Wesley's rhetorical strategy is that he generally concedes in passing or ignores those areas where he agrees with Taylor against Calvinist soteriology. For example, Taylor spends five pages showing that *Q.* 29 in the Westminster *Larger Catechism* asserts that all subsequent humanity are liable to punishment in this life and beyond because of Adam's sin *alone*.[101] Wesley omits the bulk of Taylor's argument and ignores his target, saying only: 'That all men are liable to these for Adam's sin *alone*, I do not assert. But they are so for their own outward and inward sins.'[102] When Wesley reiterates later, 'I believe none ever did or ever will die eternally, merely for the sin of our first father', Taylor rightly protested that Wesley was ignoring a principal effect that the *Catechism* assigns to original sin.[103] Nowhere in *Doctrine of Original Sin* does Wesley specifically articulate his conviction (in contrast to the *Larger Catechism*) that the inherited guilt of Adam's sin is cancelled for all persons by virtue of the death of Christ. Similarly, in his summary of Taylor's discussion of regeneration Wesley elides Taylor's deepest worry—those who attribute the new birth to 'some uncertain, arbitrary and irresistible workings of the Spirit of God, which operate upon some few, and not upon others'.[104] Again, this edition draws attention in footnotes to the most significant areas where Wesley would have shared Taylor's concern about traditional Calvinist soteriology.

Perhaps most significant, Wesley's rhetorical strategy often led him to omit parts of the argument of the Calvinist rebuttals of Taylor when Wesley drew extracts of these writers into his volume. Since Wesley does this without comment, it again obscures that his sensitivities on the point at issue may have stood closer to Taylor. Thus, this edition also draws attention in footnotes to the more important such deletions. Notice, for example, how many times

[100] Note how he emphasizes this point to James Hervey in *Answer to Hervey*, §17.5, vol. 13 in this edn.

[101] Taylor, *Scripture-Doctrine of Original Sin*, 156-61.

[102] Pt. II, section III.19 (p. 271 below).

[103] See Pt. III, section I.2; and Taylor's *Reply* (1767), 19.

[104] Cf. Taylor, *Scripture-Doctrine of Original Sin*, 245, to Pt. II, section VI.2 (p. 297, n. 266 below). See also Pt. II, section III.5, Obs. 3; and Pt. II, section III.10.

Wesley omits 'federal head' language and the identification of God's people as the 'elect' in his extract from Jennings in Part II, section I.16. Or Wesley's repeated omission of Hebden's pejorative comments on Pelagius in Parts V–VI. Surely the most interesting case is when Wesley totally rewrites a section of his extract of Watts (without acknowledging the fact!) to argue for the opposite of the position that Watts had taken on animal suffering.[105]

Some Recurrent Topics of Debate

Readers of Wesley's *Doctrine of Original Sin* may also benefit from brief observations on a few topics that appear repeatedly in debate between Taylor, his Dissenting critics, and Wesley.

The Nature of Adam as Created. One of these topics is Taylor's proposed model of Adam, as created with physical maturity but not absolutely perfect virtues, or knowledge of all truths and so on. Wesley responds satirically that 'the whole body of Christians in all ages' supposed that Adam was created perfect in every way 'till after seventeen hundred years a sweet-tongued orator arose, not only more enlightened than silly Adam, but than any of his wise posterity, and declared that the whole supposition was folly, nonsense, inconsistency, and blasphemy!'[106] This response is a bit surprising because the model had been defended the previous century by Jeremy Taylor, one of Wesley's favored authors.[107]

More important it is now recognized that there was a significant strand in the early Eastern Christian church (particularly those writing in Syriac) that read Genesis as teaching that Adam was created 'innocent' rather than 'perfect'; that is, more like a pristine child than a fully matured adult.[108] The most influential representative of this reading of Genesis is Irenaeus. We know that Wesley was familiar with Irenaeus's work *Against Heresies* because he discussed it at some length in his 1749 *Letter to Conyers Middleton.* But Irenaeus only hints at his model of Adam in this treatise. He develops it most

[105] See Pt. IV, section IV.3 (p. 392, n. 45 below).

[106] Pt. II, section IV, Obj. 1 (p. 276 below).

[107] Jeremy Taylor, *Unum Necessarium; or, The Doctrine and Practice of Repentance* (London: James Flesher, 1655), 363-74 (1705 edn., 329-37). There is no evidence, however, that JW read this specific work of Taylor.

[108] See Henri Rondet, *Original Sin: The Patristic and Theological Background* (Shannon, Ireland: Ecclesia Press, 1972), 37-50.

fully in *Demonstration of the Apostolic Preaching*, a work that remained unaccessible in the West until the early twentieth century.[109] Thus, Taylor's suggestion could appear to be a novel interpretation.

Romans 5:12 on Sin and Human Mortality. A second topic touched on by Wesley and many of his sources concerns the correct understanding of Romans 5:12. When St. Jerome prepared the Vulgate (which became the standard Bible for the Latin-speaking Western church), he rendered the Greek clause ἐφ' ᾧ πάντες ἥμαρτον as teaching that death spread to all humanity because all sinned *in Adam*. This translation was quickly enlisted in the West to explain why all humanity shared in the *guilt* of that original sin. By contrast, earlier Greek exegetes and many in the continuing Eastern Christian tradition argued that the original Greek clause should actually be rendered that 'death spread to all, such that all have sinned'. On this reading there is no consideration of participating in the guilt of Adam's sin, only inheriting the *consequence* of that sin—mortality and depravity, which lead us to sin as well.[110]

When Wesley published his *NT Notes* in 1755, he translated Romans 5:12: 'As by one man sin entered into the world, and death by sin, even so death passed upon all men, *in that all had sinned*' (emphasis added). This translation, drawn from Johann Bengel, follows the Western reading and could be taken to imply that all are subject to eternal death solely because of participating directly in Adam's sin. Within weeks of *NT Notes* appearing, Wesley received a letter questioning some of these implications. He replied that, on closer inspection, his original translation 'seemed to assert such an imputation of Adam's sin to his posterity as might make way for the "horrible decree" [unconditional reprobation]'.[111] Wesley promised to change the reading immediately. His alternative translation did not appear in print, however, until the third edition of *NT Notes* (1760–62). Here Wesley changed 'in that all *had* sinned' to 'in that all sinned'. He also added a note explaining the phrase 'sin entered into the world'—'Actual sin, and its consequence, a sinful nature'. Combined, these changes shift the focus from humanity's *guilt* for

[109] See Iain M. MacKenzie, *Irenaeus's Demonstration of the Apostolic Preaching* (Burlington, Vt.: Ashgate, 2002).

[110] See David Weaver, 'From Paul to Augustine: Romans 5:12 in Early Christian Exegesis', *Saint Vladimir's Theological Quarterly* 27 (1983): 187-206.

[111] Letter to Richard Tompson, June 28, 1755, 26:566-67 in this edn.

Adam's sin to the *depravity* inherited by all after Adam's sin; that is, they shift towards the more typical Eastern reading of the text.

Alternative Explanations for Present Human Depravity. A third topic that appears repeatedly in the sources Wesley engages is how to account for humans being born with a depraved moral nature. Most early Christian accounts emphasized a biological connection. Some took the language of Genesis 5:3 about Adam siring a son 'in his own likeness' as the key, arguing that in reproduction the entire nature of the parent (body *and* soul) is transmitted to the child (a view called 'traducianism'). The major objection to this model was that Genesis 2:7 presents the origination of Adam's soul as a distinct act from that of his body. On analogy, other early theologians argued that only the body is produced by human procreation, with each soul being created and instilled directly by God. But this leaves the problem of universal corruption. God would not have created our souls already corrupt, so how do they become so? The most common answer picked up on the negative use of 'flesh' in Scripture—the soul is instantly corrupted by its incorporation into fallen human flesh. The corruption of the flesh itself was again traced biologically to Adam.

Variants of these two models dominated Christian theology through the Reformation. The most significant alternative was championed in English Puritan circles, with their emphasis on covenant theology and strongly juridical models of sin and atonement. They insisted that humanity was not present in Adam biologically, but *representatively*. Adam was cast as the federal head or legal representative of all humanity when he accepted and broke God's original covenant. As such, Adam's guilt was *legally* imputable to all who were represented by him. His penalty would be as well. The corruption of every subsequent human's soul and body results from the imposition of that penalty.

In 1753 Wesley responded to an elaborate discussion of the various options for explaining the transmission of depravity: 'The fact I know, both by Scripture and by experience. I know it is transmitted: but *how* it is transmitted I neither know nor desire to know.'[112] Actually, he had shown some earlier interest. In an unpublished 1730 sermon, for example, Wesley sketched a strongly biological account of human corruption.[113] With his broader engagement of evangelical

[112] Letter to Dr. John Robertson, Sept. 24, 1753, 26:519 in this edn.

[113] Sermon 141, 'The Image of God', II.1-5, 4:296-99 in this edn.

voices in 1738, Wesley's comments of human corruption tended to reduce this biological emphasis and add mention of Adam as representative of humanity.[114]

Ambiguity about the options on this topic is evident in Wesley's engagement with Taylor and his abridgment of Taylor's Dissenting opponents. He leaves hints of various models in the texts while eliding extended discussions.[115] He specifically denies again the need to choose between the models.[116] At the same time, Wesley's repeated insistence that the curse on Adam was not simply physical death but spiritual death kept open room for a biological account. Shortly after publishing *Doctrine of Original Sin*, Wesley came across a traducian account of the transmission of depravity that he found convincing.[117] By the early 1780s he was championing this alternative in print.[118]

The Connection of Federal Theology to Imputation of Active Righteousness. Part of the reason that Wesley came to champion the traducian explanation of depravity was that he became uncomfortable with the alternative that stressed Adam and Christ as federal heads for all of humanity. In particular, he noted that Christ's headship was typically assumed in such federal theology to include the imputation of Christ's *active* righteousness to believers.[119] Wesley's hesitance about federal head language is evident in *Doctrine of Original Sin*, partly through the instances where he elides this language in his Dissenting sources. He is particularly careful to omit passages that specifically connect federal headship to imputation, like this example in Hebden:

[114] The best example is Sermon 5, 'Justification by Faith', I.5-9, 1:185-87 in this edn.

[115] See particularly Pt. IV, section III (pp. 378-84 below); and Pt. V, section III.3 (pp. 415-16 below).

[116] Pt. III, sections VII.1 and VII.2 (pp. 329, 331 below).

[117] The book was Henry Woolnor, *The True Original of the Soule* (London: Paine and Symmons, 1641). See JW's reference to reading it in *Journal*, Jan. 27, 1762, 21:350 in this edn.

[118] He published 'On the Origin of the Soul' in *Arminian Magazine* 5 (1782):146-49, 195-97; and followed this with a series extracting Woolnor in *Arminian Magazine* 6 (1783).

[119] See the discussion of JW's concern about imputing Christ's active righteousness to believers in the introduction to his extract of Baxter's *Aphorisms* (pp. 47-51 above).

If Adam was not the appointed federal Head of mankind, and if mankind did not fall in him, and if his sin is not imputed to all his descendants, it will follow that Christ is not the federal Head of all his, and that his righteousness is not imputed to them, so far as to acquit them from condemnation, and entitle them to eternal life. Every argument for justification by Christ implicitly confirms our fall in Adam.[120]

Wesley's hesitance can also be seen in the care with which he defends Adam as federal head 'in some sense' when engaging Taylor.[121] His primary concern is to insist that Adam's sin did not terminate with him, but affected his posterity (which would fit a 'traducian' model!).

Wesley distanced himself further from federal theology in the coming years, in the midst of his debates with James Hervey and others (gathered in volume 13 in this edition).

The Structure and Sources of Wesley's 'Doctrine of Original Sin'

It remains to comment briefly on the structure and sources of Wesley's volume. While this is the longest single monograph that Wesley ever published, it is a very hybrid piece.

Wesley's starting point is hinted at in the full form of his title: *The Doctrine of Original Sin According to Scripture, Reason, and Experience*. I have underlined *and* to show that Wesley put it in emphatic form on the title page. Taylor's appeal throughout was to Scripture, as interpreted by reason. One of Wesley's charges is that Taylor ignores the obvious experiential evidence for human depravity. Wesley makes this point at times by appeal to personal experience of the propensity to sin.[122] But its primary expression comes in Part I, which sketches an account of typical human behavior as much worse than Taylor admits. Wesley draws on a range of classical writers and current travel accounts of global cultures in making his case, as well as some contemporary poets and several selections from *Gulliver's Travels* by Jonathan Swift.

[120] Hebden, *Doctrine of Original Sin, as laid down in the Assembly's Catechism*, 85; cf. JW's alternative brief digest in Pt. VI, section V.3.4.iii (p. 441 below).

[121] See Pt. III, section VI.1 (p. 326 below).

[122] See, e.g., Pt. II, section IV, Obj. 3 (p. 280 below).

He concludes that these various sources demonstrate 'the overflowing of ungodliness, in every nation under heaven'.[123]

Part II is devoted to defending the scriptural method of accounting for this state. More specifically, Wesley works through Taylor's *Scripture-Doctrine of Original Sin* (in its third edition), seeking to rebut Taylor's argument that Scripture does not teach inherited depravity. Wesley sprinkles through his text several extracts from Daniel Jennings. He also inserts some passages from *Theron and Aspasio*, by his former student James Hervey, adding to a couple previous inserts in Part I. But the larger argument is Wesley's own.

In Part III Wesley moves to Taylor's *Supplement*, considering it in the same step-by-step manner, this time bringing in few other resources.

Having answered Taylor's arguments, Wesley could have wrapped up his project. But he decided to append to it further extracts from the earlier Dissenting rebuttals. Part IV provides an extract of Isaac Watts's *Ruin and Recovery of Mankind*. Wesley framed this extract so that it was not just additional support for his case but could provide readers a chance to see if they thought that Taylor did justice to Watts's book.

Then Wesley stitched together extracts from the various works of Samuel Hebden. He was drawn to do this in part because Taylor had ignored these pieces. In the original edition of *Doctrine of Original Sin* these extracts comprise Part V; when Wesley incorporated *Doctrine of Original Sin* in his collected *Works* (1773), he separated out the longest extract to stand on its own as Part VI (where it appears in this edition). In both settings, Wesley's conclusion to the volume came at the end of his extracts of Hebden. This marked the end of the manuscript that Wesley entrusted to his brother Charles in April 1757 to take to Bristol for typesetting, while John headed north on his preaching tour.

As part of his northern travels, John visited Edinburgh in early June 1757. There he was gifted by Mr. Walker with a copy of the tenth edition of Thomas Boston's *Human Nature in its Fourfold State*.[124] This work surveyed human existence in the four states of

[123] In one of the few reviews of *Doctrine of Original Sin* at the time of its appearance, Abraham Dawson focused on Pt. I, commenting that it presented the reader with 'a most unlovely picture of the human species'. Dawson showed his distaste for the argument by adding: 'Nor is it less false than foul'. *Monthly Review* 17 (1757): 445-46.

[124] Thomas Boston, *Human Nature in its Fourfold State*, 10th edn. (Edinburgh: Lumisden, 1753). This vol. survives, dated 1757 with JW's initials, in the archives of Kingswood School, Bath. Boston (1677–1732) was a strong Scottish Presbyterian representative of federal theology. Cf. A. T. B. McGowan, *The Federal Theology of Thomas Boston* (Carlisle: Paternoster, 1997); and Philip Graham Ryken, *Thomas Boston as Preacher of the Fourfold State* (Carlisle: Paternoster, 1999).

'innocence', 'nature', 'grace', and 'eternity'. Wesley decided to add an extract of the relevant portion (mainly Boston's treatment of the state of nature) to his already lengthy response to Taylor. The extract was delivered to Farley in mid-August. It was incorporated into the larger project by tagging it on as a distinct section at the end, without moving Wesley's original conclusion.

Wesley's Practice as Editor and Opponent

Given that *Doctrine of Original Sin* is a piece of apologetics or controversial theology, it is fitting to ask how fairly Wesley treats those whom he engages and appropriates. Some later writers have chided Wesley's volume for its 'excess of theological vituperation'.[125] But when Wesley's text is compared to the typical controversial writing of his day (like the Dissenting rebuttals of Taylor summarized above), I share Gerald Cragg's broader judgment that Wesley's controversial writing is relatively reasonable and self-possessed in tone.[126]

This said, there are times when Wesley's summaries of Taylor's argument or his selective quotation of that argument are less than ideal—either obscuring or caricaturing Taylor's point. I have tried to draw attention to the most significant examples in footnotes.

What readers will be less able to appreciate is how often Wesley's editorial rewriting of the sources he is using renders them more readable. Let me illustrate with a couple of examples:

Boston:	'Many call Christ their sweet saviour, whose consciences can bear witness they never sucked so much sweetness from him as from their sweet lusts, which are ten times sweeter to them than their saviour.'
Wesley:	'Many call him "dear" to whom their sins are ten times dearer than their Saviour.'[127]
Hebden:	'Mr. T[aylor]'s remark, then, though just, is disserviceable to his purpose, rather than otherwise.'
Wesley:	'But this rather hurts Mr. Taylor's cause than helps it.'[128]

[125] E.g., Turner, *Unitarians*, 1:314.

[126] See Cragg's reflections concerning Wesley's *Appeals* in 11:460-62 in this edn.

[127] Boston, *Human Nature in its Fourfold State*, 68; revised by JW in Pt. VII, section II.B.2.d.2.

[128] Hebden, *Scripture-Doctrine of Imputed Sin and Righteousness*, 22; revised by JW in Pt. V, section IV.2.

As the second example suggests, Hebden's prose is particularly turgid, and Wesley rewrites it more extensively than the other extracts. I have noted such editorial rewriting by Wesley only when there is possible theological significance.

Editions and Extracts of Doctrine of Original Sin

The edition of *Doctrine of Original Sin* published by Farley in 1757 was the only separate printing of the complete work during Wesley's life. Twenty-four copies of this printing remained in stock at Wesley's house when he died. It was clearly not a best seller. This is not surprising, given its length/cost and the nature of the step-by-step argument in Parts II–III.

Perhaps to bypass these factors, Wesley released Part I as a separate pamphlet titled *Dignity of Human Nature* in 1762, and his extract of Boston (Part VII) as a separate pamphlet titled *Doctrine of Original Sin* in 1784. But he did not abandon the longer treatment, including it in volume 21 of his collected *Works* in 1773.

In addition to these published forms, printer proofs for Parts I–III of the 1757 edition have survived (in Bridwell Library, Perkins School of Theology, Southern Methodist University). These proofs were used to prepare the errata page for that edition, with corrections appearing in Charles Wesley's hand.

The text presented here is based on the edition of 1757. For a stemma illustrating the transmission of the text through its various complete and partial appearances during Wesley's lifetime, together with the substantive variant readings, see the appendix (pp. 488-90). For further details see *Bibliography*, No. 222 (including 222.i and 222.ii).

THE

DOCTRINE

OF

ORIGINAL SIN:

ACCORDING TO

SCRIPTURE, REASON, *and* EXPERIENCE.

By *JOHN WESLEY.*

BRISTOL:
Printed by E. FARLEY, in *Small-Street,*
M.DCC.LVII.

THE DOCTRINE OF ORIGINAL SIN: ACCORDING TO SCRIPTURE, REASON, *AND* EXPERIENCE

The Preface

1. A few years ago a friend put into my hands Mr.[1] Taylor's *Doctrine of Original Sin*; which I read carefully over and partly transcribed—and have many times since diligently considered. The author is doubtless a person of sense, nay, of unusually strong understanding, joined with no small liveliness of imagination and a good degree of various learning. He has likewise an admirable command of temper, so that he almost everywhere speaks as one in good humour. Add to this that he has a smooth and pleasing, yet a manly and nervous[2] style. And all these talents he exerts to the uttermost on a favourite subject in the treatise before us, which he has had leisure for many years to revise, file, correct, and strengthen against all objections.

2. So finished a piece surely deserves the consideration of all those masters of reason which the age has produced. And I have long hoped that some of those would attempt to show how far the doctrine there laid down is true. And what weight there is in the arguments which are produced in confirmation of it. I know not how to believe that all the clergy in England are of the same opinion with this author. And certainly there are some whom all his skill in Greek, and even in Hebrew, does not make afraid. I should rejoice had any of these undertaken the task who are in many respects better qualified for it—particularly in this, that they have time upon their hands, they have full leisure for such an employment. But since none else will,[a]

[a] Since the writing of this I have seen several tracts, which I shall have occasion to take notice of hereafter. There are likewise many excellent remarks on this subject, in Mr. Hervey's *Dialogues.* [i.e., James Hervey *Theron and Aspasio; or a Series of Dialogues and Letters upon the most Important and Interesting Subjects*, 2 vols. (Dublin: Robert Main, 1755). Hervey (1714–58) was a former student of Wesley and a popular devotional writer. He had not written this work in direct response to Taylor, but JW judged the Eleventh Dialogue to be a strong defense of the doctrine of original sin; see letter to James Hervey, Oct. 15, 1756 (vol. 27 in this edn.). JW and Hervey (who had moved into the Calvinist Methodist fold) would soon lock in an extended debate over the nature of imputed sin and imputed righteousness. See vol. 13 in this edn.]

---

[1] *Works* (1773) changes throughout to 'Dr. Taylor'. Taylor was awarded the D.D. by Glasgow in April 1757.

[2] I.e., 'strong' or 'vigorous'; cf. *OED* (2nd edn.), def. 3.

I cannot but speak, though lying under many peculiar disadvantages. I dare not be silent any longer. Necessity is laid upon me to provide those who desire to know the truth with some antidote against that deadly poison which has been diffusing itself for several years through our nation, our Church, and even our universities. Nay, one (I hope only one) Father of the Church has declared that he knows 'no book more proper than this, to *settle the principles* of a young clergyman'.[3] Is it not time then for 'the very stones' to 'cry out'?[4]

3. For this is not a point of small importance, a question that may safely be determined either way. On the contrary, it may be doubted whether the scheme before us be not far more dangerous than open deism itself. It does not shock us like barefaced infidelity. We feel no pain, and suspect no evil, while it steals like 'water into our bowels', like 'oil into our bones'.[5] One who would be upon his guard in reading the works of Dr. Middleton[6] or Lord Bolingbroke[7] is quite open and unguarded in reading the smooth, decent writings of Mr. Taylor—one who does not *oppose* (far be it from him!) but only *explain* the Scripture; who does not *raise* any difficulties or objections against the Christian revelation, but only *removes* those with which it had been unhappily encumbered for so many centuries!

4. I said, 'than *open* deism'. For I can't look on this scheme as any other than *old* deism in a *new* dress, seeing it saps the very foundation of all revealed religion, whether Jewish or Christian. 'Indeed, my L[ady?], said an eminent man to a person of quality, I can't see that we have much need of Jesus Christ.'[8] And who might not say,

[3] Wesley apparently refers to an oral comment. The most probable candidate is Thomas Hayter, Bishop of Norwich (1749–61), who maintained friendly communication with Taylor through these years.

[4] Cf. Luke 19:40.

[5] Cf. Ps. 109:18.

[6] Conyers Middleton (1683–1750), whose *Free Inquiry into the Miraculous Powers which are supposed to have subsisted in the Christian Church . . .* (London: Manby & Cox, 1749) JW rebutted shortly after it appeared in *Letter to the Reverend Dr. Conyers Middleton*, vol. 14 in this edn.

[7] Henry St. John, first Viscount Bolingbroke (1678–1751), whose collected *Philosophical Works*, 5 vols. (London: Mallet, 1754) had recently been published. Some of his most deistic writings appeared here for the first time, sparking such responses as William Warburton, *A View of Lord Bolingbroke's Philosophy . . . in which his whole system of infidelity and naturalism is exposed and confuted* (London: J. and R. Tonson, S. Draper, & A. Millar, 1756).

[8] JW likely refers to Francis Hastings (1729–89), son of Selina, Countess of Huntingdon, who became Earl of Huntingdon in 1749. Hastings had recently returned to England after spending several years in Europe—particularly in France, where he was influenced by deistic thinkers. Cf. JW's similar comments on Lord Huntingdon in his letter to Mary Bishop, Feb. 7, 1778 (vol. 29 in this edn.).

upon this supposition, 'I can't see that we have much need of Christianity.' Nay, not any at all, for 'They that are whole have no need of a physician."[9] And the Christian revelation speaks of nothing else but the great Physician of our souls. Nor can Christian philosophy, whatever be thought of the pagan, be more properly defined than in Plato's words: it is θεραπεία ψυχῆς[10]—the *only true* 'method of healing a distempered soul'. But what need of this if we are in perfect health? If we are not diseased, we do not want a cure. If we are not sick, why should we seek for a 'medicine to heal our sickness'?[11] What room is there to talk of our being 'renewed in knowledge or holiness, after the image wherein we were created',[12] if we never have lost that image? If we are as knowing and holy now (nay, far more so) than Adam was immediately after his creation? If therefore we take away this foundation, that man is by nature foolish and sinful, 'fallen short of the glorious' image of 'God',[13] the Christian system falls at once—nor will it deserve so honourable an appellation as that of a 'cunningly devised fable'.[14]

5. In considering this *confutation of the Christian system* I am under some difficulty from Mr. Taylor's manner of writing. It is his custom to say the same thing (sometimes in different, sometimes in nearly the same words) six or eight, perhaps twelve or fifteen times, in different parts of his book. Now I have accustomed myself for many years to say one and the same thing once only. However, to comply with his manner as far as possible, I shall add at proper intervals extracts from others, expressing nearly the same sentiments which I have before expressed in my own words.

6. I am sensible, in speaking on so tender a point as this must needs be to those who believe the Christian system, there is danger of a warmth which does no honour to our cause, nor is at all countenanced by the revelation which we defend. I desire neither to show nor to feel this, but to 'speak the truth in love'[15] (the only warmth which the gospel allows), and to write with calmness, though not indifference. There is likewise a danger of despising our opponents,

[9] Mark 2:17.

[10] E.g., Plato, *Republic*, 585d. See also the n. on Sermon 44, 'Original Sin', III.3, 2:184 in this edn.

[11] Cf. Ps. 147:3 (BCP).

[12] Cf. Col. 3:10.

[13] Cf. Rom. 3:23.

[14] 2 Pet. 1:16.

[15] Cf. Eph. 4:15.

and of speaking with an air of contempt or disdain. I would gladly keep clear of this also, well knowing that a diffidence of ourselves is far from implying a diffidence of our cause—I distrust myself, not my argument. O that the God of the Christians may be with me! That his Spirit may give me understanding, and enable me to think and to[16] 'speak as the oracles of God',[17] without going from them to the right hand or to the left!

Lewisham,
Nov. 30, 1756

[16] Proof (1757) inserted this 'to', overlooked by the printer.
[17] 1 Pet. 4:11.

PART I
THE PAST AND PRESENT STATE OF MANKIND

Before we attempt to account for any fact we should be well assured of the fact itself. First therefore let us inquire what is the real state of mankind. And in the second place endeavour to account for it.

I. First, I say, let us inquire, What is the real state, with regard to knowledge and virtue, wherein mankind have been from the earliest times? And what state are they in at this day?

1. What is the state (to begin with the former branch of the inquiry) with regard to knowledge and virtue, wherein according to the most authentic accounts mankind have been from the earliest times? We have no authentic account of the state of mankind in the times antecedent to the deluge but in the writings of Moses. What then, according to these, was the state of mankind in those times? Moses gives us an exact and full account: God then 'saw that the wickedness of man was great, and that every imagination of the thoughts of his heart was only evil continually'.[b] And this was not the case of only part of mankind, but 'all flesh had corrupted his way upon the earth'. And accordingly God said, 'The end of all flesh is come, for the earth is filled with violence through them.' Only Noah was 'righteous before' God.[c] Therefore only he and his household were spared when God 'brought the flood upon the world of the ungodly'[18] and destroyed them all from the face of the earth.

Let us examine the most distinguishing features in this draft. Not barely the works of their hands, or the words of their tongue, but 'every imagination of the thoughts of' their 'heart was evil'. The contagion had spread itself through the inner man; had tainted the seat of their principles, and the source of their actions. But was there not some *mixture* of good? No. They were *only* evil. Not so much as a little leaven of piety, unless in one single family. But were there no *lucid intervals*? No happy moments wherein virtue gained the ascendency? None. Every imagination, every thought was only evil continually.[d]

[b] Gen. 6:5, 12-13.

[c] Chap. 7:1.

[d] Mr. Hervey's *Theron and Aspasio*, Dial[ogue] XI [1:352-53; abridged and slightly rephrased, with one unacknowledged interpolation—'unless in one single family'].

[18] 2 Pet. 2:5.

2. Such was the state of mankind for at least sixteen hundred years. Men were corrupting themselves and each other, and proceeding from one degree of wickedness to another, till they were all (save eight persons) ripe for destruction. So deplorable was the state of the moral world, while the natural was in its highest perfection. And yet it is highly probable that the inhabitants of the earth were then abundantly more numerous than ever they have been since, considering the length of their lives, falling little short of a thousand years, and the strength and vigour of their bodies, which we may easily gather from the time they were to continue—to say nothing of the fertility of the earth, probably far greater than it is at present. Consequently it was then capable of sustaining such a number of inhabitants as could not now subsist on the produce of it.

3. Let us next take a view of the 'families of the sons of Noah',[19] the inhabitants of the earth after the flood. The first remarkable incident we read concerning them is that while 'they were all of one language [. . .] they said one to another, Let us build a city and a tower, whose top may reach unto heaven, lest we be scattered abroad upon the face of the earth.'[20] It is not easy to determine what were the peculiar aggravations which attended this attempt. But it is certain there was daring wickedness therein, which brought upon them the very thing they feared. For 'the Lord' by 'confounding their language' (not their *religious worship*; can we suppose God would *confound* this?)[21] 'scattered them abroad upon the face of all the earth'.[e] Now whatever particulars in this account may be variously interpreted, thus much is clear and undeniable, that all these, that is, all the inhabitants of the earth, had again 'corrupted their way',[22] the universal wickedness being legible in the universal punishment.

[e] Gen. 11:4, 9.

---

[19] Gen. 10:32.

[20] Cf. Gen. 11:1, 4.

[21] This aside is aimed at Emanuel Swedenborg (1688–1772), who had recently published in Latin an 8-vol. set of the 'secrets' he found in Scripture, titled *Arcana Coelestia* (1749–56). The first vol., which includes his suggestion that Gen. 11:1-9 describes God confounding the unity of doctrine and inner worship that originally existed among humans, was released in English under the same title in 1750. Cf. JW's later 'Thoughts on the Writings of Baron Swedenborg', vol. 14 in this edn.

[22] Cf. Gen. 6:12.

4. We have no account of their reforming their ways, of any universal or general repentance, before God separated Abraham to himself, to be the father of his chosen people.[f] Nor is there any reason to believe that the rest of mankind were improved either in wisdom or virtue when Lot and Abraham 'separated themselves, and Lot pitched his tent toward Sodom'.[g] Of those among whom he dwelt it is particularly remarked, 'The men of Sodom' (and of all 'the cities of the plain')[23] 'were wicked, and sinners before the Lord exceedingly',[h] so that not even 'ten righteous persons' could be found among them; the consequence of which was that 'the Lord rained upon them brimstone and fire from the Lord out of heaven.'[i]

5. We have no ground to suppose that the other inhabitants of the earth (Abraham with his family and descendants excepted) had either the knowledge or the fear of God from that time till Jacob 'went into Egypt'.[24] This was then, as well as for several ages after, the great seat of learning, insomuch that 'the wisdom of the Egyptians'[25] was celebrated even to a proverb. And indeed for this end (as well as 'to save much people alive'[j]) did God 'send' Joseph 'into Egypt', even 'to inform their princes after his will, and to teach their senators wisdom'.[26] And yet not long after his death, as their 'king knew not Joseph',[27] so his people knew not God. Yea, they set him at defiance. They and their king provoked him more and more, and 'hardened their hearts' against him, even after they had 'seen his wonders in Egypt',[28] after they had groaned under his repeated vengeance. They still added sin to sin, till they constrained the Lord to destroy them with an utter destruction, till the divided 'waters returned and covered the chariots and horsemen and all the host of Pharaoh'.[29]

[f] Ibid., 12:1-2.
[g] Ibid., 13:11-12.
[h] Gen. 13:13.
[i] Ibid., 19:24.
[j] Ibid., 50:20.

---

[23] Gen. 13:12.
[24] Jer. 26:1; cf. Gen. 46:4-7.
[25] Acts 7:22.
[26] Cf. Ps. 105:22 (BCP).
[27] Exod. 1:8.
[28] Cf. Exod. 7:3, etc.
[29] Exod. 14:28.

6. Nor were the other nations who then inhabited the earth any better than the Egyptians, the true knowledge and spiritual worship of God being confined to the descendants of Abraham. 'He had not dealt so with other nations, neither had the heathens knowledge of his laws.'[k] And in what state were the Israelites themselves? How did they worship the God of their fathers? Why, even these were 'a stubborn and rebellious generation, a generation that set not their heart aright'.[l] 'They kept not the covenant of God, and refused to walk in his law.'[m] 'They provoked him at the sea, even at the Red Sea'[n]—the very place where he had so signally delivered them. 'They made a calf in Horeb, and worshipped the molten image',[30] where they had heard the Lord, but a little before, saying out of the midst of the fire, 'Thou shalt not make unto thyself any graven image. Thou shalt not bow down to them nor worship them.'[31] And how amazing was their behaviour during those whole forty years that they sojourned in the wilderness! Even while 'he led them in the daytime with a cloud, and all the night with a light of fire!'[o] Such were the knowledge and virtue of God's peculiar people (certainly the most knowing and virtuous nation which was then to be found upon the face of the earth) till God brought them into the land of Canaan—considerably more than two thousand years from the creation of the world.

None, I presume, will say there was any other nation at that time more knowing and more virtuous than the Israelites. None can say this while he professes to believe, according to the scriptural account, that Israel was then under a theocracy, under the immediate government of God; that he conversed with their subordinate governor 'face to face, as a man talketh with his friend';[32] and that God was daily through him conveying such instructions to them as they were capable of receiving.

[k] Ps. 147:20 [(BCP)].
[l] Ps. 78:8.
[m] Ps. 78:10.
[n] Ps. 106:7; Exod. 14:11-12.
[o] Ps. 78:14.

---

[30] Ps. 106:19.
[31] Cf. Exod. 20:4-5.
[32] Cf. Exod. 33:11.

7. Shall we turn our eyes for a moment from the scriptural to the profane account of mankind in the earliest ages? What was the general sentiment of the most polite and knowing nation, the Romans, when their learning was in its utmost perfection? Let one who certainly was no bigot or enthusiast speak for the rest. And he speaks home to the point:

> Fuit ante Helenam mulier teterrima belli
> Causa: sed ignotis perierunt mortibus omnes
> Quos venerem incertam rapientes, more ferarun
> Viribus editior caedebat, ut in grege taurus.[33]

> Full many a war has been for women waged
> Ere half the world in Helen's cause engaged;
> But unrecorded in historic verse
> Obscurely died those savage ravishers;
> Who like brute beasts the female bore away,
> Till some superior brute re-seized the prey.
> As a wild bull, his rival bull o'erthrown,
> Claims the whole subject herd, and reigns alone.[34]

I doubt he who gives this, not as his peculiar opinion, but as what was then a generally received notion, would scarce have allowed even so much as Juvenal:

> Pudicitiam Saturno rege moratam
> In terris . . .[35]

> Chastity did once, I grant, remain
> On earth, and flourished in old Saturn's reign.[36]

Unless one should suppose the reign of Saturn to have expired when Adam was driven out of paradise.

I cannot forbear adding another picture of the ancient dignity of human nature, drawn by the same masterly hand. Before men dwelt in cities, he says, this

[33] Cf. Horace, *Satires*, I.iii.107-10; changing '*cunnus*' to '*mulier*' and '*illi*' to '*omnes*'.

[34] The English form is not from any of the current translations. Henry Moore, who worked closely with both brothers, identifies CW as the translator. See Moore, *The Life of the Rev. John Wesley* (London: Kershaw, 1824–25), 2:366.

[35] Juvenal, *Satires*, vi.1-2.

[36] Probably CW's translation again (not from Dryden's standard translation).

Turpe pecus, glandem atque cubilia propter
Certabant pugnis, dein fustibus, atque ita porro
Pugnabant armis, quae post fabricaverat usus.[37]

The human herd, unbroken and untaught,
For acorns first, and grassy couches fought;
With fists, and then with clubs, maintain'd the fray,
Till urg'd by hate they found a quicker way
And forg'd pernicious arms, and learnt the art to slay.[38]

What a difference is there between this and the gay, florid accounts, which many moderns give of their own species!

8. But to return to more authentic accounts. At the time when God brought the Israelites into Canaan, in what state were the rest of mankind? Doubtless in nearly the same with the Canaanites; with the Amorites, Hittites, Perizzites, and the rest of the seven nations. But 'the wickedness' of these, we know, 'was full'.[39] They were corrupt in the highest degree. All manner of vice, all ungodliness and unrighteousness[40] reigned among them without control. And therefore the wise and just Governor of the world gave them up to a swift and total destruction.

9. Of Israel indeed we read that they 'served the Lord all the days of Joshua, and all the days of the elders that overlived Joshua'.[p] And yet even at that time they did not serve him alone; they were not free from gross idolatry. Otherwise there had been no need of his giving them that exhortation a little before his death: 'Now therefore put away the strange gods which are among you',[q] 'the gods which your fathers served on the other side of the river'[41] (Jordan). What gods these were we learn by the words of Amos, cited by St. Stephen:

[p] Josh. 24:31.
[q] Josh. 24:23.

---

[37] Cf. Horace, *Satires*, I.iii.100–102, changing '*Unguibus et*' to '*Certabant*'.

[38] The translation is again by CW, as in n. 34 above. The closing couplet was omitted from Proof (1757), but restored in a note by JW using 'urged' and 'forged'—an indication of JW's preferred styling of the silent 'e' at this time, even in verse. The 1757 final printed version was styled by the printer as 'urg'd' and 'forg'd'.

[39] Cf. Gen. 15:16.

[40] Cf. Rom. 1:18.

[41] Josh. 24:14.

'O ye house of Israel, have ye offered sacrifices to me by the space of forty years? Yea, ye took up the tabernacle of Moloch, and the star of your god Remphan, figures which ye made to worship them.'[r]

10. The sacred history of what occurred within a short space after the death of Joshua for some hundred years, even till the time that Samuel judged Israel, gives us a large account of their astonishing wickedness during almost that whole period. It is true, just 'when God smote them, then they sought him. They returned and inquired after God. Yet their heart was not right with him, neither were they steadfast in his covenant.'[s] And we find little alteration among them for the better in the succeeding ages. Insomuch that in the reign of Ahab, about nine hundred years before Christ, there were only 'seven thousand left in Israel who had not bowed the knee to Baal'.[t] What manner of men they were for the next three hundred years we may learn from the Books of Kings and from the prophets. Whence it fully appears that except [for] a few short intervals, they were given up to all manner of abominations, by reason of which the name of the Most High was the more abundantly blasphemed among the heathens. And this continued till their open rebellion against God brought upon the whole nation of the Jews (an hundred and thirty-four years after the captivity of the ten tribes, and about six hundred before Christ) those terrible and long deserved calamities which made them a spectacle to all that were round about them. The writings of Ezekiel, Daniel, and Jeremiah leave us no room to think that they were reformed by those calamities. Nor was there any lasting reformation in the time of Ezra, or of Nehemiah and Malachi; but they were still, as their forefathers had been, 'a faithless and stubborn generation'.[42] Such were they likewise, as we may gather from the Books of Maccabees and Josephus, to the very time when Christ came into the world.

11. Our blessed Lord has given us a large description of those who were then the most eminent for religion. 'Ye devour', says he, 'widows' houses, and for a pretence make long prayers. 'Ye make' your proselytes 'twofold more the children of hell than yourselves. Ye neglect the weightier matters of the law, judgment, mercy, and faith. Ye make clean the outside of the cup, but within are full of

[r] Acts 7:42-43.
[s] Ps. 78:34, 37.
[t] [Cf.] 1 Kgs. 19:18.

---

[42] Ps. 78:9 (BCP).

extortion and excess. Ye are like whited sepulchres, outwardly beautiful, but within full of dead men's bones, and of all uncleanness. Ye serpents, ye generation of vipers, how can ye escape the damnation of hell?'[u] And to these very men, after they had murdered that Just One, his faithful follower declared: 'Ye stiff-necked and uncircumcised in heart and ears, ye do always resist the Holy Ghost. As your fathers did, so do ye.'[v] And so they continued to do till the 'wrath' of God did indeed 'come upon them to the uttermost',[43] till eleven hundred thousand of them were destroyed, their city and temple levelled with the dust, and above ninety thousand sold for slaves and scattered into all lands.

12. Such in all generations were the lineal children of Abraham, who had so unspeakable advantages over the rest of mankind—'to whom pertained the adoption, and the glory, and the covenants, and the giving of the law, and the service of God, and the promises';[44] among whom therefore we may reasonably expect to find the greatest eminence of knowledge and virtue. If these then were so stupidly, brutishly ignorant, so desperately wicked, what can we expect from the heathen world, from them who had not the knowledge either of his law or promises? Certainly we cannot expect to find more goodness among them. But let us make a fair and impartial inquiry, and that not among wild and barbarous nations but the most civilized and refined. What then were the ancient Romans? The people whose virtue is so highly extolled, and so warmly commended to our imitation?[45] We have their character given by one who cannot deceive or be deceived, the unerring Spirit of God. And what account does he give of these 'best of men',[46] these heroes of antiquity? 'When they knew God', says he, at least as to his *eternity* and *power* (both implied in that appellation which occurs more than once

[u] [Cf.] Matt. 23:14, etc. [i.e., 14–15, 23, 25, 27, 33].
[v] Acts 7:51.

---

[43] 1 Thess. 2:16.
[44] Rom. 9:4.
[45] This may be a jab at James Burgh, *The Dignity of Human Nature* (London: Knapton, 1754). In his preface (p. vii) Burgh laments the current lack of virtue in British culture and contrasts the exemplary nature of several early Romans, including Cato the elder (see JW's counter in I.16 below). For reflections on a broad tendency following the settlement of 1688–89 for English aristocracy and gentry to extol Roman culture, see Philip Ayres, *Classical Culture and the Idea of Rome in Eighteenth-Century England* (Cambridge: Cambridge University Press, 1997).
[46] Most probably a reference to the familiar Latin phrase *vir optimus*.

in their own poet, '*Pater omnipotens*'—'Almighty Father'[47]) they 'glorified him not as God, neither were thankful'.[w] So far from it that one of their oracles of wisdom (though once he stumbled on that great truth, '*Nemo unquam vir magnus sine afflatu divino fuit*'[48]—'There never was any great man without the afflatus or inspiration of God', yet almost in the same breath) does not scruple to ask '*Quis pro virtute aut sapientia gratias Diis dedit unquam?*'[49] —'Whoever thanked God for virtue or wisdom?' No, why should he; since these are his own acquisition, the pure result of his own industry! Accordingly another virtuous Roman has left it on record as an unquestioned maxim:

Haec satis est orare Jovem, quae donat et aufert,
Det vitam, det opes, aequum mi animum ipse parabo.[50]

Enough for common benefits to pray,
Which Jove can either give, or take away.
Long life or wealth his bounty may bestow,
Wisdom and virtue to myself I owe.[51]

So 'vain were they become in their imaginations', so 'were their foolish hearts darkened'![x]

13. But this was only the first step. They did not stop here. 'Professing themselves wise', they yet sunk into such gross, astonishing folly as to 'change the glory of the incorruptible God' (whom they might have known even from their own writers to be

[. . .] *vastam* [. . .]
Mens agitans molem, et magno se corpore miscens[52]

[w] Rom. 1:21.
[x] Rom. 1:21, etc. [cf. the quotations below from Rom. 1:23-27].

[47] I.e., Virgil, as in *Aeneid*, iv.24, vii.141, xii.178.

[48] Cf. Cicero, *De Natura Deorum* (*On the Nature of the Gods*), ii.66: '*Nemo igitur vir magnus sine aliquo afflatu divino unquam fuit. . . .*'

[49] Cf. ibid., iii.36, where Cicero insists that virtue is a human achievement rather than a result of fortune or a divine gift.

[50] Horace, *Epistles*, I.xviii.111-12.

[51] This again was likely CW's translation. In Sermon 62, 'The End of Christ's Coming', §3, 2:473 in this edn., JW re-used this same material from Cicero and Horace, giving a different translation of Horace (likely his own).

[52] Cf. Virgil, *Aeneid*, vi.726-27, which reads
'*. . . totamque infus per artus*
Mens agitat molem, et magno se corpore miscet'.

. . . the all-informing soul
That fills the mighty mass, and moves the whole.[53])

'into an image made like to corruptible man, yea to birds', to 'beasts', to 'creeping things'! What wonder was it then that after they had thus 'changed his glory into an image' God 'gave them up to uncleanness, through the lusts of their own hearts, to dishonour their own bodies between themselves'? How justly, when they had 'changed the truth of God into a lie, and worshipped and served the creature rather than the Creator', did he 'for this cause', punishing sin by sin, 'give them up unto vile affections. For even the women did change the natural use into that which is against nature.' Yea, the modest honourable Roman matrons (so little were they ashamed!) wore their *Priapi*[54] openly on their breasts. And likewise the men 'burned in their lust one toward another, men with men working that which is unseemly'. What an amazing testimony of this is left us on record, even by the most modest of all the Roman poets!

Formosum pastor Corydon ardebat Alexim![55]

How does this pattern of heathen chastity avow, without either fear or shame, as if it were an innocent at least, if not laudable passion, their 'burning in lust one toward another'![56] And did men of the finest taste in the nation censure the song, or the subject of it? We read nothing of this. On the contrary, the universal honour and esteem paid to the writer, and that by persons of the highest rank, plainly shows that the case of Corydon, as it was not uncommon in any part of the Roman dominions, so it was not conceived to be any blemish, either to him or his master, but an innocent *infirmity*.

Meantime how delicate an idea of love had this favourite of Rome and of the Muses? Hear him explaining himself a little more fully on this tender point:

[53] JW frequently uses both the quotation from Virgil and varying translations; cf. *Earnest Appeal*, §19, 11:51 in this edn.; Sermon 74, 'Of the Church', §13, 3:50 in this edn.; and Sermon 77, 'Spiritual Worship', I.5, 3:92 in this edn.

[54] Phallic images of Priapus, the god of procreation.

[55] Virgil, *Eclogues*, ii.1; 'Corydon, the shepherd, was aflame for the fair Alexim' (Loeb).

[56] Cf. Rom. 1:27.

Eheu! quam pinqui macer est mihi taurus in agro!
Idem amor exitium est pecori, pecorisque magistro.[57]

Idem amor! The same love in the bull and in the man! What elegance of sentiment! Is it possible anything can exceed this? One would imagine nothing could, had not the same chaste poet furnished us with yet another scene more abundantly shocking than this:

Pasiphaen nivei solatur amore juvenci![58]

'He comforts Pasiphaë with the love of her milk-white bull!' *Nihil supra!*[59] The condoling a woman on her unsuccessful amour with a bull shows a brutality which nothing can exceed! How justly then does the Apostle add, as 'they did not like' or desire 'to retain God in their knowledge, God gave them over to an undiscerning mind, to do those things which are not convenient'.[60] In consequence of this they were 'filled with all unrighteousness',[61] vice of every kind, and in every degree. In particular 'with fornication' (taking the word in its largest sense, as including every sin of the kind) 'with wickedness, covetousness, maliciousness; with envy, murder, debate, deceit, malignity;[62] being 'haters of God',[63] the true God, the God of Israel, to whom they allowed no place among all their herd of deities; 'despiteful, proud, boasters',[64] in as eminent a degree as ever was any nation under heaven; 'inventors of evil things' in great abundance, of *mille nocendi artes*,[65] both in peace and war; 'disobedient to parents',[66] although duty to these is supposed to be inscribed on the hearts of the most barbarous nations; 'covenant-breakers',[67] even of those of the most solemn kind, those wherein the public faith was engaged by their supreme magistrate—which notwithstanding they

[57] Virgil, *Eclogues*, iii.100-101; 'Alas, alas! how lean is my bull amid the fattening tares! The same love is the bane of the herd and the herd's master' (Loeb).

[58] Ibid., vi.46; 'Now he solaces Pasiphaë with her passion for the snowy bull' (Loeb).

[59] 'Nothing can exceed this!'

[60] Rom. 1:28.

[61] Rom. 1:29.

[62] Ibid.

[63] Rom. 1:30.

[64] Ibid.

[65] Virgil, *Aeneid*, vii.338; 'a thousand forms of ill' (Loeb).

[66] Rom. 1:30.

[67] Rom. 1:31.

made no manner of scruple of breaking, whenever they saw good, only colouring over their perfidiousness by giving those magistrates into their hands with whom the *covenant* was made. And what was this to the purpose? Is the King of France or the Republic of Holland at liberty to violate their most solemn treaties at pleasure, provided they give up to the King of England the ambassador or general by whom that treaty was made? What would all Europe have said of the late Czar if instead of punctually performing the engagements made with the Porte when in his distress, he had only given up the persons by whom he transacted, and immediately broke through them all?[68] There is therefore no room to say

> *Modo Punica scripta supersint,*
> *Non minus infamis forte Latina fides.*[69]
>
> Perhaps, if the Carthaginian writings were extant,
> Roman faith would be as infamous as Punic.[70]

We need them not. In vain have they destroyed the Carthaginian writings, for their own sufficiently testify of them, and fully prove that in perfidy the natives of Carthage could not excel the senate and people of Rome.

14. They were as a nation ἄστοργοι, 'void of natural affection',[71] even to their own bowels. Witness the universal custom, which obtained for several ages in Rome and all its dependencies (as it had done before through all the cities of Greece), when in their highest repute for wisdom and virtue, of *exposing* their own new-born children, more or fewer of them, as every man pleased, when he had as many as he thought good to keep, throwing them out to perish by cold and hunger, unless some more merciful wild beast shortened their pain and provided them a sepulchre.[72] Nor do I remember a

[68] JW refers to a treaty that Peter the Great negotiated in 1711 when besieged by the army of the Ottoman Empire (whose government was called the 'Sublime Porte'), as described in Alexander Gordon, *The History of Peter the Great, Emperor of Russia* (London: Hitch & Hawes, 1755), 2:22-30. JW had recently read this work; see *Journal*, Jan. 30, 1756, 21:40-41 in this edn.

[69] The source of this epigram has not been located. The translation is likely JW's own.

[70] 'Punic faith' (*Punica fide*) was a synonym for 'treachery' among Roman writers; see. Sallust, *Jugurtha*, cviii.3. They alleged that this was their continual experience at the hands of the *Poeni* or Carthaginians.

[71] Cf. Rom. 1:31.

[72] See the description of this practice in Pliny the Younger, *Letters*, x.65-66.

single Greek or Roman, of all those that occasionally mention it, ever complaining of this diabolical custom or fixing the least touch of blame upon it. Even the tender mother in Terence, who had some compassion for her helpless infant, does not dare to acknowledge it to her husband without that remarkable preface: '*Ut misere superstitiosae sumus omnes*'[73]—'as we women are all miserably superstitious'.

15. I would desire those gentlemen who are so very severe upon the Israelites for killing the children of the Canaanites at their entrance into the land of Canaan to spend a few thoughts on this. Not to insist that the Creator is the absolute lord and proprietor of the lives of all his creatures; that as such he may at any time, without the least injustice, take away the life which he has given; that he may do this in whatsoever manner, and by whatever instruments, he pleases; and consequently may inflict death on any creature by whom he pleases, without any blame either to him or them—not to insist, I say, on this or many other things which might be offered, let us at present fix on this single consideration: the Israelites destroyed the children for some weeks or months, the Greeks and Romans for above a thousand years. The one put them out of their pain at once, doubtless by the shortest and easiest way. The others were not so compassionate as to cut their throats, but left them to pine away by a lingering death. Above all, the Hebrews destroyed only the children of their enemies. The Romans destroyed their own. O fair pattern indeed! Where shall we find a parallel to this virtue? I read of a modern who took up a child that fell from its mother's womb and threw it back into the flames. (Pure, genuine human nature!) And reason good, for it was the child of an heretic.[74] But what evil, ye worthies of ancient Rome, did ye find in *your own* children? I must still say this is without a parallel, even in the *papal* history.

16. They were 'implacable, unmerciful'.[75] Witness (one or two instances of ten thousand) poor, grey-headed Hannibal (whom very probably, had we any other accounts of him than those which were given by his bitterest enemies, we should have reverenced as one of the most amiable of men, as well as the most valiant of all the ancient

[73] Cf. Terence, *Self-Tormentor*, 649-50: '*Ut stultae et misere omnes sumus / Religiosae*'; 'With a woman's usual folly and miserable superstition' (Loeb).

[74] JW read this account in Daniel Neal, *History of the Puritans* (London: Richard Hett, 1732–38), 1:102.

[75] Rom. 1:31.

heathens), hunted from nation to nation, and never quitted[76] till he fell by his own hand.[77] Witness the famous suffrage, '*Delenda est Carthago*'[78]—'Let Carthage be destroyed.' Why? Because it was *imperii aemula*[79]—the rival of the Roman glory. These were open, undeniable evidences of the public, national *placability* and *mercy* of the *Romans*. Need instances of a more private nature be added? Behold then one for all—in that glory of Rome, that prodigy of virtue, the great, the celebrated Cato. Cato the elder, when any of his domestics had worn themselves out in his service and grew decrepit[80] with age, constantly turned them out to starve, and was much applauded for his *frugality* in so doing.[81] But what *mercy* was this? Just such as that which dwelt in Cato of Utica, who repayed the tenderness of his servant endeavouring to save his life, to prevent his tearing open his wound, by striking him on the face with such violence as to fill his mouth with blood.[82] These are thy gods, O deism! These the patterns so zealously recommended to our imitation!

17. And what was the real character of that hero whom Cato himself so admired? Whose cause he espoused with such eagerness, with such unwearied diligence? Of Pompey the Great? Surely never did any man purchase that title at so cheap a rate! What made him 'great'? The villainy of Perpenna,[83] and the treachery of Pharnaces.[84] Had not the one murdered his friend, the other rebelled against his father, where had been Pompey's greatness? So this

[76] An obsolete transitive use of 'quit'; if JW had intended the reflexive sense, the preceding conjunction would have been 'who' rather than 'and'.

[77] The story of Hannibal is told in Cornelius Nepos, *Excellentium Imperatorum Vitae*, bk. XXIII (his death found at XXIII.xii.5). Wesley published an abridged copy of this vol. for the students at Kingswood in 1749 (see *Bibliography*, No. 173).

[78] The phrase added by Cato the Elder to all his public utterances.

[79] Cf. Sallust, *Cataline War*, §10: '*Carthago aemula imperii Romani*'—'Carthage, jealous of Roman power'. In Proof (1757) Wesley's introductory phrase read, 'It was', to which he added in the margin 'Because'. The printer ignored this, and it was not recaptured in the printed errata.

[80] Orig., 'decrepid'.

[81] Plutarch, *Life of Cato Major*, iv.4.

[82] Cf. Plutarch, *Life of Cato the Younger*, lxx.6, for this basic story, though it lacks the detail of the mouth full of blood.

[83] JW would know this story from Velleius Paterculus, *Historiae Romanae* (II.xxx.1), a text that he assigned while a tutor at Oxford.

[84] Pharnaces' rebellion is mentioned in ibid., II.xi.1; and detailed in Cassius Dio Cocceianus, *Historia Romana*, xxxvii.12 (a work that JW cites in Sermon 38, 'A Caution Against Bigotry', I.8, 2:66-67 in this edn.).

stalking-horse of a party procured his reputation in the commonwealth. And when it was procured, how did he use it? Let his own poet, Lucan, speak:

> *Nec [. . .] Caesar ferre priorem,*
> *Pompeiusve parem potuit*[85]—
>
> Nor Caesar could to a superior look:
> Nor patriot Pompey could an equal brook![86]

'He would bear no equal!' And this a senator of Rome! Nay, the grand patron of the republic! But what a republican himself, when this principle was the spring of all his designs and actions! Indeed a less amiable character it is not easy to find among all the great men of antiquity—ambitious, vain, haughty, surly, and overbearing, beyond the common rate of men. And what virtue had he to balance these faults? I can scarce find one, even in Lucan's account.[87] It does not appear that in the latter part of his life he had even military virtues. What proof did he give of personal courage in all his war with Caesar? What instances of eminent conduct? None at all, if we may credit his friend Cicero, who complains heavily to Atticus that he acted like a madman and would ruin the cause he had undertaken to defend.[88]

18. Let none therefore look for *placability* or *mercy* in Pompey. But was there any unmercifulness in Caesar?

> Who than Julius hopes to rise,
> More brave, more generous, or more wise?[89]

[85] Cf. Lucan, *Civil War*, i.125-26:
Nec quemquam iam ferre potest Caesarve priorem
Pompeiusve parem.

[86] The translation again is likely by CW. It differs greatly from those of Sir Arthur Gorges (1614), Christopher Marlowe (1600), and Nicholas Rowe (1718), but suggests some echoes of that of Thomas May (1627):
Nor now can Caesar a superior brooke,
Nor Pompey brooke a peere . . .
Note in this regard JW's complaint about Francis Asbury's suggestion that 'Mr. Wesley and I are like Caesar and Pompey. He will bear no equal, and I will bear no superior'. JW's letter to Beverley Allen, Oct. 31, 1789 (vol. 31 in this edn.).

[87] Lucan attempts in *Civil War* to make Pompey a truly heroic figure, the peer of Caesar.

[88] Cf. Cicero, *Letters to Atticus*, 171.2.

[89] Samuel Wesley Jr. (1691–1739), 'On Happiness', stanza 4, in *Poems on Several Occasions* (London: S. Birt, 1736), 9.

Of his courage and sense there can be no doubt. And much may be said with regard to his contest with Pompey, even for the justice of his cause. For with him he certainly fought for life, rather than glory—of which he had the strongest conviction (though he was ashamed to own it) when he passed the Rubicon.[90] Nor can it be doubted but he was often *merciful.*[91] It is no proof of the contrary that he rode up and down his ranks during the Battle of Pharsalia and cried to those who were engaged with the pretty gentlemen of Pompey's army, '*Miles, faciem feri*'—'Soldier, strike at the face'.[92] For this greatly shortened the dispute with those who were more afraid of losing their beauty than their lives, and so prevented the effusion of much blood. But I cannot get over (to say nothing of the myriads of common Gauls whom he destroyed) a short sentence in his own *Commentaries: 'Vercingetorix per tormenta necatus*'.[93] Who was this Vercingetorix? As brave a man and (considering his years) as great a general as even Caesar. What was his crime? The love of his parents, wife, children, country, and sacrificing all things in the defence of them. And how did Caesar treat him on this account? He tortured him to death. O Roman mercy! Did not Brutus and Cassius avenge Vercingetorix rather than Pompey?[94] How well was Rome represented in the prophetical vision by that beast, 'dreadful and terrible', which had 'great iron teeth', and 'devoured and brake in pieces, and stamped under his feet'[95] all other kingdoms!

II. 1. Such is the state, with regard to knowledge and virtue, wherein, according to the most authentic accounts, mankind was from the earliest times, for above four thousand years. Such nearly did it continue during the decline and since the destruction of the Roman Empire. But we will waive all that is past, if it only appears that mankind is virtuous and wise at this day. This then is the point we are at present to consider. Are men in general now wise and virtuous?

[90] Cf. Lucan, *Civil War*, i.183-205; and Plutarch, *Life of Caesar*, xxxii.4-6.

[91] Years later JW inserted an account of an instance of 'Remarkable Clemency of Julius Caesar' in *Arminian Magazine* 9 (1786): 514.

[92] Florus, *Epitome of Roman History*, II.xiii.50.

[93] See Caesar, *Gallic War*, vii.4, which says of Vercingetorix, '*igne atque omnibus tormentis necat*'—'he kills with fire and every kind of torture'. Vercingetorix was the Arverian leader of a rebellion against Caesar in 52 B.C.

[94] I.e., when they assassinated Caesar on March 15, 44 B.C.

[95] Dan. 7:7.

Our ingenious countryman, Mr. Brerewood, after his most careful and laborious inquiries, computes that, supposing that part of the earth which we know to be inhabited were divided into thirty equal parts, nineteen of these are *heathen* still and of the remaining eleven six are *Mahometan* and only five *Christian*.[96] Let us take as fair and impartial a survey as we can of the heathens first, and then of the Mahometans and Christians.

2. And first, of the heathens. What manner of men are these, as to virtue and knowledge, at this day? Many of late who still bear the Christian name have entertained very honourable thoughts of the old heathens. They cannot believe them to have been so stupid and senseless as they have been represented to be—particularly with regard to idolatry, in worshipping birds, beasts, and creeping things.[97] Much less can they credit the stories told of many nations, the Egyptians in particular,

> Who are said to
> Have set the leek they after prayed to.[98]

But if they do not consider who they are that transmit to us these accounts, namely both those writers who, they profess to believe, spake 'as they were moved by the Holy Ghost',[99] and those whom perhaps they value more, the most credible of their contemporary heathens; if, I say, they forget this, do they not consider the *present* state of the heathen world? Now allowing the bulk of the ancient heathens (which itself is not easily proved) to have had as much understanding as the modern, we have no pretence to suppose they had more. What therefore they were we may safely gather from what

[96] Edward Brerewood, *Enquiries touching the Diversities of Languages and Religions through the chief parts of the world* (London: John Bill, 1614), 118. JW repeats this reference in *Letter to . . . Bishop of Gloucester*, II.9, 11:508 in this edn.; Sermon 63, 'The General Spread of the Gospel', §1, 2:485 in this edn.; and Sermon 112, 'Causes of the Inefficacy of Christianity', §3, 4:87 in this edn.

[97] JW is surely thinking of Andrew Michael Ramsay, *The Travels of Cyrus; to which is annexed a Discourse upon the Theology and Mythology of the Pagans* (London: Woodward & Peele, 1727), a book JW assigned to students at Lincoln College in 1730–31. In the annexed discourse Ramsay rejects the suggestion that their portrayals of deities in animal and insect forms demonstrate that Egyptians were idolaters.

[98] Cf. Matthew Prior, 'An Epistle to Fleetwood Shepherd, Esq.', lines 63-64:

> Egyptian gardeners thus are said to
> Have set the leeks they after prayed to.

[99] 2 Pet. 1:21.

they are—we may judge of the past by the present. Would we know then (to begin with a part of the world known to very early antiquity) what manner of men the heathens in Africa were two or three thousand years ago? Inquire what they are now, who are genuine pagans still, not tainted either with Mahometanism or Christianity. They are to be found in abundance either in Negroland,[100] or round the Cape of Good Hope. Now what measure of knowledge have the natives of these countries?[101] I do not say in metaphysics, mathematics, or astronomy. Of these it is plain they know just as much as do their four-footed brethren. The lion and the man are equally accomplished with regard to this knowledge. I will not ask what they know of the nature of government, of the respective rights of kings and various orders of subjects. In this regard an herd of men are manifestly inferior to an herd of elephants. But let us view them with respect to common life. What do they know of the things they continually stand in need of? How do they build habitations for themselves and their families? How select and prepare their food? Clothe and adorn their persons? As to their habitations, it is certain (I will not say our horses, particularly those belonging to the nobility and gentry, but) an English peasant's dogs, nay his very swine, are more commodiously lodged. And as to their food, apparel, and ornaments, they are just suitable to their edifices:

> Your nicer Hottentots think meet
> With guts and tripe to deck their feet;
> With downcast eyes on Totta's legs
> The lovesick youth most humbly begs,
> She would not from his sight remove
> At once his breakfast and his love.[102]

[100] A term for central and much of southern Africa. Wesley's is the first cited use in *OED* (2nd edn.); but he would have known it from Thomas Salmon, *A New Geographical and Historical Grammar* (London: William Johnston, 1749), 454.

[101] In the following description JW focuses on the 'Hottentots', one of the Khoisanid subgroups, closely related to the African 'bushmen'. He repeats here much of the description of this group in 'An Account of the Cape of Good Hope, by Mr. John Maxwell', *Philosophical Transactions* 25 (1706–7): 2423-34. JW regularly read this publication of the Royal Society. He would also have known the similar disparaging description of Hottentots in William Dampier, *Voyages Round the World* (London: Knapton, 1697–1709), 1:536-42, since he assigned this vol. to several students at Lincoln College in 1730–31.

[102] Cf. Matthew Prior, *Alma*, 937-42; where the orig. has 'downcast looks', 'The ogling youth', and 'his hopes remove'.

Such is the knowledge of these accomplished animals in things which cannot but daily employ their thoughts, and wherein consequently they cannot avoid exerting to the uttermost both their natural and acquired understanding.

And what are their present attainments in virtue? Are they not, one and all, 'without God in the world'?[103] Having either no knowledge of him at all, no conception of anything he has to do with them, or they with him. Or such conceptions as are far worse than none, as make him such a one as themselves. And what are their social virtues? What are their dispositions and behaviour between man and man? Are they eminent for justice? For mercy, or truth? As to mercy, they know not what it means, being continually cutting each other's throats, from generation to generation, and selling for slaves as many of those who fall into their hands as on that consideration only they do not murder. Justice, they have none. No courts of justice at all. No public method of redressing wrong. But every man does what is right in his own eyes,[104] till a stronger than he beats out his brains for so doing. And they have just as much regard to truth, cozening, cheating, and over-reaching every man that believes a word they say. Such are the moral, such the intellectual perfections, according to the latest and most accurate accounts, of the present heathens who are diffused in great numbers over a fourth part of the known world!

3. It is true that in the new world, in America, they seem to breathe a purer air and to be in general men of a stronger understanding and a less savage temper. Among these then we may surely find higher degrees of knowledge as well as virtue. But in order to form a just conception of them we must not take our account from their enemies, from any that would justify themselves by blackening those whom they seek to destroy. No, but let us inquire of more impartial judges concerning those whom they have personally known, the Indians bordering upon our own settlements, from New England down to Georgia.

We cannot learn that there is any great difference in point of knowledge between any of these, from east to west, or from north to south. They are all equally unacquainted with European learning, being total strangers to every branch of literature, having not the least conception of any part of philosophy, speculative or practical. Neither have they (whatever accounts some have given) any such thing as a regular civil

[103] Eph. 2:12.

[104] See Deut. 12:8, etc.

government among them. They have no laws of any kind, unless a few temporary rules made in and for the time of war. They are likewise utter strangers to the arts of peace, having scarce any such thing as an artificer in a nation. They know nothing of building, having only poor, miserable, ill-contrived huts, far inferior to many English dog-kennels. Their clothing, till of late, was only skins of beasts, commonly of deer, hanging down before and behind them. Now among those who have commerce with our nation it is frequently a blanket wrapped about them. Their food is equally delicate—pounded Indian corn, sometimes mixed with water, and so eaten at once, sometimes kneaded into cakes, meal and bran together, and half-baked upon the coals. Fish or flesh, dried in the sun, is frequently added to this, and now and then a piece of rough, fresh-killed deer.[105]

Such is the knowledge of the Americans, whether in things of an abstruser nature or in the affairs of common life. And this, so far as we can learn, is the condition of all, without any considerable difference. But in point of religion there is a very material difference between the northern and the southern Indians. Those in the north are idolaters of the lowest kind.[106] If they do not worship the devil appearing in person (which many firmly believe they do, many think incredible), certainly they worship the most vile and contemptible idols. It were more excusable if they only 'turned the glory of the incorruptible God into the image of corruptible man', yea or 'of birds, or four-footed beasts, or reptiles',[107] or any creature which God has made. But their idols are more horrid and deformed than anything in the visible creation, and their whole worship is at once the highest affront to the divine and disgrace to the human nature.

[105] This description carries strong echoes of an official SPG account: David Humphreys, *An Historical Account of the incorporated Society for the Propagation of the Gospel in Foreign Parts* (London: Joseph Downing, 1730), 278. JW records reading this account in his diary on July 12, 1737, 18:527 in this edn.

[106] JW's knowledge of northern Native Americans was secondhand, mainly through the eyes of Christian missionaries. Among his sources were Cotton Mather, *The Life and Death of the Renowned Mr. John Eliot, who was the first preacher of the Gospel to the Indians in America* (London: John Dunton, 1691), see esp. 83-89; and Jonathan Edwards, *An Account of the Life of the Late Reverend Mr. David Brainerd* (Boston: D. Henchman, 1749). JW included an extract of the life of Eliot in the *Christian Library* (50:267-335) and published *An Extract of the Life of . . . David Brainerd* in 1768 (see *Bibliography*, No. 310).

[107] Cf. Rom. 1:25 (*NT Notes*).

On the contrary, the Indians of our southern provinces do not appear to have any worship at all. By the most diligent inquiry from those who had spent many years among them, I could never learn that any of the Indian nations who border on Georgia and Carolina have any public worship of any kind—nor any private. For they have no idea of prayer. It is not without much difficulty that one can make any of them understand what is meant by *prayer*. And when they do, they cannot be made to apprehend that God will answer or even hear it. They say: 'He that sitteth in heaven is too high, he is too far off to hear *us*'. In consequence of which they leave him to himself, and manage their affairs without him.[108] Only the Chickasaws,[109] of all the Indian nations, are an exception to this.[110]

I believe it will be found on the strictest inquiry that the whole body of southern Indians, as they have no letters and no laws, so properly speaking have no religion at all.[111] So that everyone does what he sees good. And if it appears wrong to his neighbour, he usually comes upon him unawares and shoots or scalps him alive. They are likewise all (I could never find any exception) gluttons, drunkards, thieves, dissemblers, liars. They are 'implacable',[112] never forgiving an injury or affront, or being satisfied with less than blood. They are 'unmerciful',[113] killing all whom they take prisoners in war, with the most exquisite tortures. They are murderers of fathers, murderers of mothers, murderers of their own children. It being a common thing for a son to shoot his father or mother because they are old and past labour, and for a woman either to procure abortion

[108] JW is likely recalling one of his conversations with Tomochici, a *meeko* (or chief) of the Creek nation, with whom he had several religious conversations while in Georgia—cf. *Journal*, Feb. 14, 1736, 18:148-49 in this edn.; diary, Apr. 29, 1736 (18:381); diary, June 29, 1736 (18:398); diary, Apr. 11, 1737 (18:498); and JW's comment in *Journal*, Oct. 20, 1739 (19:108). See also below in Pt. II, III.6 (p. 247).

[109] Orig., 'Chicasaw', JW's normal spelling.

[110] Cf. JW's record of a conversation with five Chickasaw warriors that he included in a letter (July 20, 1736) that was published in *Gentleman's Magazine*, 25:464-66 in this edn.

[111] Much of this is distilled from JW's extended negative portrayal of the indigenous nations on his return from Georgia in his *Journal*, Dec. 2, 1737, §§21-28, 18:201-4 in this edn. These comments should be read in light of JW's initial 'romantic' assumptions about Native Americans prior to the Georgia venture, evidenced in his letter to John Burton, Oct. 10, 1735, 25:439 in this edn. Cf. J. Ralph Randolph, 'John Wesley and the American Indian: A Study in Disillusionment', *Methodist History* 10, no. 3 (1972): 3-11.

[112] Rom. 1:31.

[113] Ibid.

or to throw her child into the next river because she will go to the war with her husband. Indeed husbands, properly speaking, they have none. For any man leaves his wife, so called, at pleasure, who frequently in return cuts the throats of all the children she has had by him.

The Chickasaws alone seem to have some notion of an intercourse between man and a superior being. They speak much of their 'Beloved Ones', with whom, they say, they converse both day and night.[114] But their 'Beloved Ones' teach them to eat and drink from morning to night, and in a manner from night to morning. For they rise at any hour of the night when they wake, and eat and drink as much as they can, and sleep again.[115] Their Beloved Ones likewise expressly command them to torture and burn all their prisoners. Their manner of doing it is this. They hold lighted canes to their arms and legs and several parts of their body for some time, and then for a while take them away. They also stick burning pieces of wood into their flesh, in which condition they keep them from morning to evening. Such are at present the knowledge and virtue of the native heathens over another fourth of the known world.

4. In Asia, however, we are informed that the case is widely different. For although the heathens bordering on Europe, the thousands and myriads of Tartars, have not much to boast either as to knowledge or virtue.[116] And although the numerous little nations under the Mogul,[117] who retain their original heathenism, are nearly on a level with them, as are the inhabitants of the many large and populous islands in the eastern seas. Yet we hear high encomiums of the Chinese, who are as numerous as all these together—some late travellers assuring us that China alone has fifty-eight millions of inhabitants.[118] Now these have been described as men of the deepest

[114] Cf. letter to *Gentleman's Magazine*, July 20, 1736, 25:465 in this edn.

[115] The negative comments in these last two sentences were not in JW's letter in 1736, but come from an account of a conversation with a Frenchman that he reported in *Journal*, July 9, 1737, 18:185 in this edn., as his disillusionment was growing.

[116] 'Tartary' was the current title for a band of Central Asia separating China and Russia, running from Korea to Eastern Europe. See the description in Thomas Salmon, *Modern History; or, The Present State of all Nations*, 3rd ed., 3 vols. (London: T. Longman et al., 1744–46), 1:400-408. Wesley's description of China that follows almost certainly depends on Salmon (in this or an earlier edn.).

[117] The leader of the 'Mongolians', ruling land at this time that included northern India and Tibet. Cf. Salmon, *Modern History*, 1:193-278.

[118] See ibid., 1:4 (citing a travel account by Johannes Nieuhof).

penetration, the highest learning, and the strictest integrity. And such doubtless they are, at least with regard to their understanding, if we will believe their own proverb: 'The Chinese have two eyes, the Europeans one, and other men none at all.'[119]

And one circumstance, it must be owned, is much in their favour. They live some thousand miles off. So that if it were affirmed that every Chinese had literally three eyes, it would be difficult for us to disprove it. Nevertheless there is room to doubt even of their understanding. Nay, one of the arguments often brought to prove the greatness, to me clearly demonstrates the littleness of it—namely, the thirty thousand letters of their alphabet.[120] To keep an alphabet of thirty hundred letters could never be reconciled to common sense, since every alphabet ought to be as short, simple, and easy as possible. No more can we reconcile to any degree of common sense their crippling all the women in the empire by a silly, senseless affectation of squeezing their feet till they bear no proportion to their bodies, so that the feet of a woman at thirty must still be as small as they would be naturally when four years old.[121] But in order to see the true measure of their understanding in the clearest light, let us look not at women or the vulgar, but at the nobility, the wisest, the politest part of the nation. Look at the mandarins, the glory of the empire, and see any, every one of them at his meals, not deigning to use his own hands, but having his meat put into his mouth by two servants, planted for that purpose, one on his right hand, the other on his left![122] O the deep understanding of the noble lubber that sits in the midst, and

> *Hiat, ceu pullus hirundinis!*[123]
> Gapes, as the young swallow for his food.

Surely an English ploughman, or a Dutch sailor, would have too much sense to endure it. If you say, Nay, the mandarin would not

[119] This proverb is noted in ibid., 1:8.

[120] Salmon observed that ordinary Chinese know about 3,000 characters, while scholars may know more than 24,000. Ibid., 1:19. Other contemporary accounts suggest totals as high as 40,000 characters.

[121] This well-known practice is described in ibid., 1:9.

[122] Accounts of this custom trace back to a book first published in England in the 1490s: *The Voyages and Travels of Sir John Mandevile*. See p. 133 in 1705 edn. (London: Chiswell).

[123] Juvenal, *Satires*, x.231.

endure it but that *it is a custom*; I answer, Undoubtedly it is, but how came it to be a custom? Such a custom could not have begun, much less have become general, but through a general and marvellous want of common sense.

What their learning is now I know not. But notwithstanding their boast of its antiquity, it was certainly very low and contemptible in the last century, when they were so astonished at the skill of the French Jesuits and honoured them as almost more than human for calculating eclipses.[124] And whatever progress they may have made since in the knowledge of astronomy and other curious rather than useful sciences, it is certain they are still utterly ignorant of what it most of all concerns them to know. They know not God, any more than the Hottentots. They are all idolaters to a man. And so tenacious are they of their national idolatry that even those whom the French missionaries called converts yet continued, one and all, to worship Confucius and the souls of their ancestors. It is true that when this was strongly represented at Rome, by an honest Dominican who came from thence, a bull was issued out and sent over into China forbidding them to do it any longer.[125] But the good fathers kept it private among themselves, saying the Chinese were not able to bear it.

Such is their religion with respect to God. But are they not eminent for all social virtues, all that have place between man and man? Yes, according to the accounts which some have given. According to these they are the glory of mankind and may be a pattern to all Europe.[126] But have not we some reason to doubt if these

[124] JW embellishes a well-known account of the success of the astronomical calculations of Ferdinand Verbiest, S.J., which led the Chinese emperor to give the Jesuits charge of preparing the official Chinese calendar in 1644 (noted in passing in Salmon, *Modern History*, 1:19).

[125] JW refers to the papal bull '*Ex illa die*' issued by Clement XI in 1715. This account almost certainly relies on Johann Lorenz Mosheim, *Authentic Memoirs of the Christian Church in China* (London: Tonson & Draper, 1750); note Mosheim's affirmation of 'honest Castorani' (the Dominican) on p. 38, and his attack on the Jesuits for trying to keep the bull private on p. 35. The account of the fortunes of the Jesuits in Salmon, *Modern History* (1:28-30) ends at 1707. Likewise, Mosheim does not include these details in his *Ecclesiastical History* (London: Millar, 1755), which JW later abridged (see *Bibliography*, No. 420).

[126] JW surely has in mind, among others, Matthew Tindal, *Christianity as Old as the Creation; or, The Gospel, a Republication of the Religion of Nature* (London: [Thomas Astley], 1731). In this vol. Tindal suggests that Confucius taught the same moral truths as Jesus, but in a simpler and clearer manner (p. 314); affirms

accounts are true? Are pride and laziness good ingredients of social virtue? And can all Europe equal either the laziness or pride of the Chinese nobility and gentry? Who are either too stately or too indolent even to put the meat into their own mouths! Yet they are not too proud or too indolent to oppress, to rob, to defraud all that fall into their hands. How flagrant instances of this may anyone find even in the account of Lord Anson's *Voyage*![127] Exactly agreeing with the accounts given by all our countrymen who have traded in any part of China, as well as with the observation made by a late writer, in his *Geographical Grammar*:

> Trade and commerce, or rather cheating and overreaching, is the natural bent and genius of the Chinese. Gain is their god. They prefer this to everything besides. A stranger is in great danger of being cheated if he trusts to his own judgment. And if he employs a Chinese broker, it is well if he does not join with the merchant to cheat the stranger. [. . .]
>
> Their laws oblige them to certain rules of civility in their words and actions. And they are naturally a fawning, cringing generation—but the greatest hypocrites on the face of the earth.[128]

5. Such is the toasted virtue of those who are beyond all degrees of comparison the best and wisest of all the heathens in Asia. And how little preferable to them are those in Europe! Rather, how many degrees beneath them! Vast numbers of these are within the borders of Muscovy. But how amazingly ignorant! How totally void both of civil and sacred wisdom! How shockingly savage both in their tempers and manners! Their idolatry is of the basest and vilest kind. They not only worship the work of their own hands, but idols of the most horrid and detestable forms that men or devils could devise. Equally savage (or more so, if more can be), as is well known, are the natives of Lapland, and indeed of all the countries which have been

Leibniz's claim that the Chinese are better examples than the typical European Christian of all moral values (p. 371); and notes a milder suggestion of Ferdinand Navarette, a Jesuit missionary to China, about what the Chinese could teach the West about moral behavior (p. 372). JW's Oxford diary records that he read Tindal in Mar. 1731; cf. letter to Mary Pendarves, June 19, 1731, 25:288 in this edn.

[127] Cf. George Anson, *A Voyage Round the World* (London: Knapton, 1748), 510-46. This section describes at length the obstacles and extortion that Anson confronted when he put in at a Chinese port for needed repairs on his ship and concludes with a derogatory assessment of Chinese morality based on this experience. JW records reading Anson in *Journal*, Oct. 29, 1755, 21:33 in this edn.

[128] Salmon, *Geographical Grammar*, 410.

discovered to the north of Muscovy or Sweden.[129] In truth, the bulk of these nations seem to be considerably more barbarous, not only than the men near the Cape of Good Hope, but than many tribes in the brute creation.

Thus have we seen what is the present state of the heathens in every part of the known world. And these still make up, according to the preceding calculation, very near two-thirds of mankind. Let us now calmly and impartially consider what manner of men the Mahometans in general are.

6. An ingenious writer, who a few years ago published a pompous translation of the Koran, takes great pains to give us a very favourable opinion both of Mahomet and his followers.[130] But he cannot wash the Ethiop white.[131] After all, men who have but a moderate share of reason cannot but observe in his Koran, even as polished by Mr. Sale, the most gross and impious absurdities.[132] To cite particulars is not now my business. It may suffice to observe in general that human understanding must be debased to an inconceivable degree in those who can swallow such absurdities as divinely revealed. And yet we know the Mahometans not only condemn all who cannot swallow them to everlasting fire, not only appropriate to themselves the title of Mussulmen or 'true believers', but even anathematize with the utmost bitterness and adjudge to eternal

[129] JW would have recently seen the condescending description of peoples in these regions in an appendix of Gordon, *History of Peter the Great* (2:322-52), providing an account of 'Mr. Isbrant's Journey through Russia and Tartary to China'.

[130] See *Lives and Memorable Actions of many Illustrious Persons of the Eastern Nations* (London: J. Wilcox, 1739). The 1st edn. was attributed to George Sale (1697?–1736), but later edns. make clear his contribution was minimal. Sale had gained his reputation for *The Koran; commonly called the Alcoran of Mohammed, translated into English immediately from the original Arabic* (London: C. Ackers, 1733).

[131] An echo of Lucian, *Adversus Indoctum*, §28: 'Αἰθίοπα σμήχειν ἐπιχειρῶ', which in turn became a Latin proverb: '*Aethiopem dealbare*', of which there are several traces in JW's writings. See Sermon 63, 'The General Spread of the Gospel', §4, 2:487 in this edn., which also deals with Mahometans; and the related passage in Jer. 13:23, 'Can the Ethiopian change his skin?', as in *Journal*, Feb. 6, 1759, 21:177 in this edn.

[132] For an assessment of Islam that JW would have assumed was more 'reasonable' see Humphrey Prideaux, *True Nature of Imposture Fully Displayed in the Life of Mahomet* (London: William Rogers, 1697). JW's Oxford diary records that he read Prideaux in Sept. 1726, and his diary for Jan. 22-24, 1737, 18:465 in this edn., shows him returning to it. Cf. his appeal to Prideaux to counter another positive treatment of Mohammad in *Journal*, Nov. 23, 1767, 22:114 in this edn.

destruction all their brethren of the sect of Hali, all who contend for a figurative interpretation of them.[133]

That these men then have no knowledge or love of God is undeniably manifest, not only from their gross, horrible notions of him, but from their not loving their brethren. But they have not always so weighty a cause to hate and murder one another as *difference of opinion*. Mahometans will butcher each other by thousands without so plausible a plea as this. Why is it that such numbers of Turks and Persians have stabbed one another in cool blood? Truly, because they differ in the manner of *dressing their head*.[134] The Ottoman vehemently maintains (for he has unquestionable *tradition* on his side) that a Mussulman should wear a *round* turbant.[135] Whereas the Persian insists upon his liberty of conscience, and will wear it *picked before*. So, for this wonderful reason, when a more plausible one is wanting, they beat out each other's brains from generation to generation.

It is not therefore strange that ever since the religion of Mahomet appeared in the world the espousers of it, particularly those under the Turkish emperor, have been as wolves and tigers to all other nations, rending and tearing all that fell into their merciless paws, and grinding them with their iron teeth.[136] That numberless cities are razed from the foundation, and only their name remaining. That many countries which were once as the garden of God are now a desolate wilderness. And that so many once numerous and powerful nations are vanished away from the earth! Such was, and is at this day the rage, the fury, the revenge, of these destroyers of humankind!

7. Proceed we now to the Christian world. But we must not judge of Christians in general from those who are scattered through the

[133] Note Salmon's description of Persians as following the tradition of Islam traced back to Hali (i.e., Ali, the son-in-law of Mohammad) and called 'Chia', while the Turks follow the (Sunni) tradition traced back to Abubeker, and his stress of their hate for each other. *Modern History*, 1:361-62, 597. Salmon mentions that the Hali give more latitude to their religious leaders to bring new revelations, which may be the source of JW's assumption that they champion figurative interpretation.

[134] JW's source for this preposterous claim is unclear. Salmon mentions difference in the colors of Turkish and Persian turbans. Ibid., 1:314, 414. But he gives neither the following details nor any suggestion that differences over turbans contributed to their mutual antagonism.

[135] JW's *Dictionary* defines 'turbant' as 'A sort of cap worn by the Turks'.

[136] Dan. 7:7.

Turkish dominions—the Armenian, Georgian, Mingrelian[137] Christians—nor indeed from any others of the Greek communion. The gross, barbarous ignorance, the deep, stupid superstition, the blind and bitter zeal, and the endless thirst after vain jangling[138] and strife of words,[139] which have reigned for many ages in the Greek Church and well nigh banished true religion from among them, make these scarce worthy of the Christian name, and lay an insuperable stumbling-block before the Mahometans.[140]

8. Perhaps those of the *Romish* communion may say: 'What wonder that this is the case with heretics! With those who have erred from the Catholic faith, nay, and left the pale of the Church!' But what is the case with them who have not left that Church and who retain the Roman faith still? Yea, with the most zealous of all its patrons, the inhabitants of Italy, of Spain, and Portugal? Wherein do they excel the Greek Church, except in Italianism? Received by tradition from their heathen fathers, and diffused through every city and village. They may indeed praise chastity and rail at women as loudly as their forefather Juvenal. But what is the moral of all this?

Nonne putas melius, quod tecum pusio dormit?[141]

This, it must be acknowledged, is the glory of the Romish Church. Herein it does excel the Greek.

They excel it likewise in deism. Perhaps there is no country in the world, at least in that part of it which bears the Christian name, wherein so large a proportion of the men of education are absolute deists, if not atheists, as Italy. And from hence the plague has spread far and wide, through France in particular. So that did not temporal motives restrain, no small part of the French nobility and gentry

[137] Orig., 'Mengrelian', as in Salmon's *Geographical Grammar*, 395. With its own unwritten language, Mingrelia, along the eastern Black Sea, was subject at varying times to the Ottoman Empire, Iran, and Russia. Nestorianism was the dominant form of Christianity in the three neighboring groups named by JW, now known as the Assyrian Christians.

[138] 1 Tim. 1:6.

[139] See Ps. 31:20.

[140] JW elsewhere speaks more generically about the lives of *all* Christians being a stumbling block to the Mahometans. Cf. Sermon 63, 'The General Spread of the Gospel', §21, 2:495 in this edn.

[141] Juvenal, *Satires*, vi.34: 'How much better to take some boy bed-fellow' (Loeb). Cf. JW's criticism of teaching children the 'shameless Satires of Juvenal (even the sixth)' in *A Plain Account of Kingswood School*, §7, vol. 16 of this edn.

would pay no more regard to the Christian revelation than do the mandarins in China.

They excel still more in murder, both private and public. Instances of the former abound all over Italy, Spain, and Portugal. And the frequency of shedding blood has taken away all that horror which otherwise might attend it. Take one instance of a thousand. An English gentleman was some years ago at an entertainment in Brescia, when one who was near him whispered a few words in his ear which he did not well understand. He asked his host, 'What did that gentleman mean by these words?' And was answered: 'That he will murder you. And an Italian is never worse than his word in this. You have no way but to be beforehand with him.' This he rejected with abhorrence. But his host, it seems, being not of so tender a conscience, sent a stranger to him in the morning who said: 'Sir, look out of your window. I have done his business. There he lies. You will please to give me my pay.' He pulled out an handful of money, in great disorder, and cried, 'There, take what you will.' The other replied, 'Sir, I am a man of honour—I take only my pay,' took a small piece of silver, and retired.[142]

This was 'a man of honour' among the Christians of the Romish Church! And many such are to be found all over Italy, whose trade it is to cut throats, to stab, for hire, in cool blood. They have *men of conscience* too. Such were two of the Catholic soldiers under the famous Duke of Alva, who broke into the house of a poor countryman in Flanders, butchered him and his wife, with five or six children, and after they had finished their work sat down to enjoy the fruit of their labour. But in the midst of their meal conscience awaked. One of them started up in great emotion and cried out, 'O Lord! What have I done? As I hope for salvation, I have eaten flesh in Lent!'[143]

The same sort of *conscience* undoubtedly it was which constrained the late *most Christian* King, in defiance of the most solemn treaties—

[142] This vignette is not found in any of the well-known 'Grand Tour' accounts of British citizens on the Continent published by 1757. JW may be reporting an oral account.

[143] JW's source for this story is undetermined. It does not appear in the account of this general persecution in either John Foxe's *Acts and Monuments* or Samuel Clarke's *General Martyrologie* (two standards that JW abridged in the *Christian Library*). Nor has it been located in other anti-Catholic works of the time. While the specific story is likely apocryphal, the mission of the Spanish, Catholic Duke of Alva (Fernando Alvarez de Toledo) to subdue the Protestant Netherlands in 1568–73 was indeed brutal.

yea, of all ties divine and human—most graciously to murder so many thousands of his quiet, unresisting subjects; to order his dragoons, wherever they found the Protestants worshipping God, to fall in upon them, sword in hand, without any regard to sex or age.[144] It was *conscience*, no question, which induced so many of the Dukes of Savoy, notwithstanding the public faith engaged over and over, to shed the blood of their loyal subjects the Vaudois like water, to ravage their fields and destroy their cities.[145] What but *conscience* could move the good Catholics of a neighbouring kingdom in the last century to murder (according to their own account) two hundred and fifteen thousand Protestants in six months! A costly sacrifice this! What is an hecatomb, an hundred oxen, to two hundred thousand men? And yet what is even this to the whole number of victims who have been offered up in Europe since the beginning of the Reformation? Partly by war, partly by the Inquisition, and a thousand other methods of Romish cruelty? No less within forty years, if the computation of an eminent writer be just, than five and forty millions![146]

[144]JW refers to the persecution of Protestants in France after Louis XIV revoked the Edict of Nantes in 1685. Wesley had read an extended account of this persecution by the pastor of a Huguenot chapel in London: Stephen Abel Laval, *A Compendious History of the Reformation in France and of the Reformed Churches in that Kingdom . . . With an account of the late persecution*, 3 vols. (London: Woodfall, 1737–39). Cf. his comments in his *Journal*, Nov. 20, 1741, 19:239 in this edn.

[145]The 'Vaudois' (now called 'Waldenses') originated in the late 12th century under the leadership of Peter Valdes as a lay movement strongly critical of the worldliness of the clergy. They were soon excommunicated by Rome. In the 16th century they sought to align with the Reformers and by the early 17th century had found relative freedom in the Piedmont region of northern Italy (then under French control). Then, in 1655 the Duke of Savoy brutally attacked them. The massacre was halted finally by the intervention of Oliver Cromwell, and in 1664 France officially granted them limited liberty. This pact was set aside in 1685, with the revocation of the Edict of Nantes, and the Duke of Savoy attacked again, forcing most of the Vaudois to flee into Switzerland. JW may well have read *An Account of the late Persecution of the Protestants in the Valleys of Piedmont, by the Duke of Savoy and the French King, in the year 1686* (Oxford: John Crosley, 1688) as reprinted in Thomas Bray, *Papal Usurpation and Persecution*, vol. 2, Pt. I (London: Joseph Downing, 1712).

[146]Wesley's source is Johann Bengel, *Gnomon Novi Testamenti* (Tubingen: Philip Schram, 1742), on Rev. 18:24; also cited in Sermon 92, 'On Zeal', §1, 3:310 in this edn.; and Sermon 102, 'Of Former Times', §14, 3:449 in this edn. Bengel notes that some say more than 15 million Protestants were put to death between 1518 and 1548 through the instrumentality of the Inquisition, then adds that Hoë 'doubles this vast number from 1550–1580'. This is an apparent misreading of Matthias Hoë, *Commentariorum in beati apostoli et euangelistae Johannis Apocalypsin*, on Apoc. 17. See 1671 edn. (Leipzig), p. 99.

Such is the conscience, such the religion of Romish Christians! Of their Inquisition ('the house of mercy', as it is most unfortunately called) I should give some account, but that it has been largely described by others. Yet it may not be improper to give a specimen of that mercy which they show to those under their care. At the 'Act of Faith',[147] so called, which was celebrated some years ago when Dr. Geddes was in Portugal, a prisoner who had been confined nine years was brought out to execution. Looking up and seeing what he had not seen for so long a time, the sun in the midst of heaven, he cried out, 'How can any who sees that glorious creature worship any but the God that made it?' The father who attended immediately ordered a gag to be run through his lip[s], that he might speak no more.[148]

See the Christians, who have received all the advantages of education, all the helps of ancient and modern learning! 'Nay, but *we* have still greater helps than them. We who are *reformed* from the errors of popery. We who *protest* against all those novel corruptions with which the Church of Rome has polluted *ancient* Christianity. The enormities therefore of popish countries are not to be charged upon *us*. We are *Protestants*, and have nothing to do with the vices and villainies of Romish nations.'

9. Have we not? Are Protestant nations nothing concerned in those melancholy reflections of Mr. Cowley:

> If twenty thousand naked Americans were not able to resist the assaults of but twenty well-armed Spaniards, how is it possible for one honest man to defend himself against twenty thousand knaves who are all furnished *cap-a-pie*[149] with the defensive arms of worldly prudence, and the offensive too of craft and malice? He will find no less odds than this against him, if he have much to do in human affairs. [. . .] Do you wonder then that a virtuous man should love to be alone? It is hard for him to be otherwise. He is so when he is among ten thousand. Nor is it so uncomfortable to be alone without any other creature as it is to be alone in the midst of wild beasts. Man is to man all kind of beasts, a fawning dog, a roaring lion, a thieving fox, a robbing wolf, a dissembling crocodile, a treacherous decoy, and a rapacious vulture. The civilest, methinks, of all nations, are those whom we account

[147] The 'Act of Faith' (auto da fé in Portuguese) was the final stage of the Inquisition, a public reading of sentences and administration of punishment for those judged heretics.

[148] Cf. Michael Geddes, 'A View of the Inquisition in Portugal', in *Miscellaneous Tracts*, 3 vols. (London: Churchill, 1702–6), 1:423-50; this incident, p. 444. JW repeats this account in Sermon 91, 'On Charity', III.10, 3:305 in this edn.

[149] I.e., 'head-to-toe' (orig. '*cap-a-pe*').

the most barbarous. There is some moderation and good nature in the Toupinambaltians, who eat no men but their enemies, while we learned and polite and Christian Europeans, like so many pikes and sharks, prey upon everything that we can swallow.[150]

Are Protestant nations nothing concerned in that humorous but terrible picture drawn by a late eminent hand?[151]

> He was perfectly astonished (and who would not, if it were the first time he had heard it?) at the historical account I gave him of our affairs during the last century; protesting it was only an heap of conspiracies, rebellions, murders, massacres [. . .]; the very worst effects that avarice, faction, hypocrisy, perfidiousness, cruelty, rage, madness, hatred, envy, lust, malice, and ambition could produce.[152] . . . Even in times of peace, how many innocent and excellent persons have been condemned to death or banishment by great ministers practising upon the corruption of judges and the malice of factions! How many villains have been exalted to the highest places of trust, power, dignity, and profit! [. . .] By what methods have great numbers in all countries procured titles of honour and vast estates? [. . .] Perjury, oppression, subornation, fraud, pandarism were some of the most excusable. [. . .] For many owed their greatness to sodomy or incest, others to the prostituting of their own wives or daughters, others to the betraying of their country or their prince, more to the perverting of justice to destroy the innocent.[153]

Well might that keen author add: 'If a creature pretending to reason can be guilty of such enormities, certainly the corruption of that faculty is far worse than brutality itself.'[154]

Now are popish nations only concerned in this? Are the Protestant quite clear? Is there no such thing among them (to take one instance only) as 'perverting of justice', even in public courts of judicature? Can it not be said in any Protestant country:

[150] Abraham Cowley, 'The Dangers of an Honest Man in much Company', in *Works* (London: Henry Herringman, 1668), 132.

[151] Here begins a set of selections from Jonathan Swift, *Lemuel Gulliver's Travels into Several Remote Nations of the World*, 2 vols. (London: Benjamin Motte, 1726); cf. Frank Baker, 'Jonathan Swift and the Wesleys', *London Quarterly Review* 179 (1954): 290-300. JW's Oxford diary records reading this vol. shortly after its release (Nov. 14, 1726), reading it aloud to the Kirkham sisters a month later (Dec. 22-24, 1726), and reading it to his family at Epworth a couple of years later (July 10-16, 1730).

[152] Swift, *Gulliver's Travels*, bk. II, chap. vi (1:118-19); parenthetical material is JW's interpolation.

[153] Ibid., bk. III, chap. viii (2:109-13).

[154] Ibid., bk. IV, chap. v (2:68).

> There is a society of men among us, bred up from their youth in the art of proving, according as they are paid, by words multiplied for the purpose, that white is black, and black is white. [. . .] For example, if my neighbour has a mind to my cow, he hires a lawyer to prove that he ought to have my cow from me. I must hire another to defend my right, it being against all rules of law that a man should speak for himself. [. . .] In pleading they do not dwell on the merits of the cause, but upon circumstances foreign thereto. For instance, they do not take the shortest method to know what title my adversary has to my cow, but whether the cow be red or black, her horns long or short, whether the field she graze in be round or square, and the like. After which they adjourn the cause from time to time, and in ten or twenty years' time come to an issue. This society likewise has a peculiar cant and jargon of their own, in which all their laws are written. And these they take special care to multiply; whereby they have so confounded truth and falsehood, right and wrong, that it will take twelve years to decide whether the field left me by my ancestors for six generations belong to me or to one three hundred miles off.[155]

Is it in popish countries only that it can be said:

> It does not appear that any one perfection is required toward the procurement of any one station among you; much less that men are *ennobled* on account of their virtue, that priests are advanced for their piety or learning, judges for their integrity, senators for the love of their country, or counsellors for their wisdom.[156]

10. But there is a still greater and more undeniable proof that the very foundations of all things, civil and religious, are utterly out of course in the Christian as well as the heathen world. There is a still more horrid reproach to the Christian name, yea to the name of man, to all reason and humanity. There is *war* in the world! War between men! War between Christians! I mean between those that bear the name of Christ and profess to 'walk as he also walked'.[157] Now who can reconcile war (I will not say to religion, but) to any degree of reason or common sense?[158]

But is there not a cause? O yes, 'the causes of war' (as the same writer observes) 'are innumerable. Some of the chief are these:'

[155] Ibid. (2:71-77).

[156] Ibid., bk. II, chap. vi (1:120).

[157] Cf. 1 John 2:6.

[158] Although one would not sense it from this comment, Wesley did (reluctantly) support war as justified in some instances. See Theodore Weber, *Politics in the Order of Salvation* (Nashville: Kingswood Books, 2001), 353-88.

The ambition of princes, or the corruption of their ministers. Difference of opinion, as whether *flesh* be *bread*, or *bread* be *flesh*; whether the juice of the grape be *blood* or *wine*. What is the best *colour* for a coat, whether black, white, or grey? And whether it should be long or short? Whether narrow or wide? Nor are there any wars so furious as those occasioned by such difference of opinions.

Sometimes two princes make war to decide which of them shall dispossess a third of his dominions. Sometimes a war is commenced because another prince is too strong, sometimes because he is too weak. Sometimes our neighbours *want* the things which we have, or have the things which we want. So we both fight, until they take ours or we take theirs. It is a reason for invading a country if the people have been wasted by famine, destroyed by pestilence, or embroiled by faction; or to attack our nearest ally if part of his land would make our dominions more round and compact.[159]

Another cause of making war is this:

A crew are driven by a storm they know not where. At length they make land and go ashore. They are entertained with kindness. They give the country a new name; set up a stone or rotten plank for a memorial; murder a dozen of the natives, and bring away a couple by force. Here commences a new *right of dominion*. Ships are sent, and the natives driven out or destroyed. And this is done to civilize and convert a barbarous and idolatrous people.[160]

But whatever be the cause, let us calmly and impartially consider the thing itself. Here are forty thousand men gathered together on this plain. What are they going to do? See, there are thirty or forty thousand more at a little distance. And these are going to shoot them through the head or body, to stab them, or split their skulls, and send most of their souls into everlasting fire as fast as possibly they can. Why so? What harm have they done to them? Oh, none at all. They do not as much as know them. But a man who is King of France has a quarrel with another man who is King of England.[161] So these Frenchmen are to kill as many of those Englishmen as they can to prove the King of France is in the right. Now what an argument is this! What a method of proof! What an amazing way of deciding controversies! What must mankind be before such a thing as war could ever be known, or thought of upon earth? How shocking, how

[159] Swift, *Gulliver's Travels*, bk. IV, chap. v (2:62-64).

[160] Ibid., bk. IV, chap. xii (2:192-93).

[161] JW is commenting on what would become known as the Seven Years War, which had just erupted out of disagreement between France and England in May 1756.

inconceivable a want must there have been of common understanding, as well as common humanity, before any two governors or any two nations in the universe could once think of such a method of decision! If then all nations—pagan, Mahometan, and Christian—do in fact make this their last resort, what farther proof do we need of the utter degeneracy of all nations from the plainest principles of reason and virtue? Of the absolute want both of common sense and common humanity, which runs through the whole race of mankind?

In how just and strong a light is this placed by the writer cited before!

> I gave him a description of cannons, muskets, pistols, swords, bayonets; of sieges, attacks, mines, countermines, bombardments; of engagements by sea and land; ships sunk with a thousand men, twenty thousand killed on each side, dying groans, limbs flying in the air; smoke, noise, trampling to death under horses' feet, flight, pursuit, victory; fields strewed with carcasses left for food to dogs and beasts of prey; and farther, of plundering, stripping, ravishing, burning, and destroying. I assured him, I had seen an hundred enemies blown up at once in a siege, and as many in a ship, and beheld the dead bodies drop down in pieces from the clouds, to the great diversion of the spectators.[162]

Is it not astonishing, beyond all expression, that this is the naked truth? That within a short term of years this has been the real case in almost every part of even the Christian world? And meanwhile we gravely talk of the 'Dignity of our Nature' in its present state![163] This is really surprising, and might easily drive even a well-tempered man to say:

> One might bear with men if they would be content with those vices and follies to which nature has entitled them. I am not provoked at the sight of a pickpocket, a gamester, a politician, a suborner, a traitor, or the like. This is all according to the natural course of things. But when I behold a lump of deformity and diseases both in body and mind smitten with pride, it breaks all the measures of my patience. Neither shall I ever be able to comprehend how such an animal and such a vice can tally together.[164]

And surely all our declamations on the strength of human reason, and the eminence of our virtues, are no more than the cant

[162] Swift, *Gulliver's Travels*, bk. IV, chap. v (2:67).

[163] In ironic contrast, JW used this phrase as the title for a separate reprint of Pt. I of *The Doctrine of Original Sin* in 1762 (*Bibliography*, No. 222.i).

[164] Swift, *Gulliver's Travels*, bk. IV, chap. xii (2:197–98).

and jargon of pride and ignorance so long as there is such a thing as war in the world. Men in general can never be allowed to be reasonable creatures till they know not war any more.[165] So long as this monster stalks uncontrolled, where is reason, virtue, humanity? They are utterly excluded. They have no place. They are a name and nothing more. If even an heathen were to give an account of an age wherein reason and virtue reigned, he would allow no war to have place therein. So Ovid of the golden age:

> *Nondum praecipites cingebant oppida fossae; [. . .]*
> *Non galeae, non ensis erat. Sine militis usu*
> *Mollia securae peragebant otia gentes.*[166]

> Steep ditches did not then the towns surround,
> Nor glittering helm, nor slaughtering sword was found.
> Nor arms had they to wield, nor wars to wage,
> But peace and safety crowned the blissful age.

11. How far is the world at present from this state! Yet when we speak of the folly and wickedness of mankind, may we not except our own country, Great Britain and Ireland? In these we have such advantages for improvement both in knowledge and virtue as scarce any other nation enjoys. We are under an excellent constitution, which secures both our religious and civil liberty. We have religion taught in its primitive purity, its genuine, native simplicity. And how it prospers among us we may know with great ease and certainty. For we depend not on hearsay, on the report of others, or on subtle and uncertain reasonings, but may see everything with our own eyes, and hear it with our own ears. Well then, to make all the allowance possible, we will suppose mankind in general to be on a level with regard to knowledge and virtue, even with the inhabitants of our fortunate islands, and take our measure of them from the present undeniable state of our own countrymen.

In order to take a thorough survey of these let us begin with the lowest, and proceed upward. The bulk of the natives of Ireland are to be found in or near their little cabins throughout the kingdom, most of which are their own workmanship, consisting of four earthen walls, covered with straw or sods, with one opening in the side-wall

[165] See Isa. 2:4.

[166] Ovid, *Metamorphoses*, i.97, 99-100. The translation is likely by CW, not coming from any of the current English versions.

which serves at once for door, window, and chimney. Here in one room are the cow and pig, the woman with her children, and the master of the family. Now what knowledge have these rational animals? They know to plant and boil their potatoes, to milk their cow, and to put their clothes on and off, if they have any besides a blanket. But other knowledge they have none, unless in religion. And how much do they know of this? A little more than the Hottentots, and not much. They know the names of God and Christ and the Virgin Mary. They know a little of St. Patrick, the Pope and the priest, how to tell their beads, to say *Ave Maria* and *Pater-noster*; to do what penance they are bid, to hear Mass, confess, and pay so much 'for the pardon of their sins'. But as to the nature of religion, the life of God in the soul, they know no more (I will not say than the priest, but) than the beasts of the field.

And how very little above these are the numerous inhabitants of the northern parts of Scotland, or of the islands which lie either on the west or the north side of that kingdom? What knowledge have these? And what religion? Their religion usually lies in a single point, in implicitly believing the head of their clan, and implicitly doing what he bids.[y] Meantime they are, one and all, as ignorant of rational, scriptural religion as of algebra, and altogether as far from the practice as from the theory of it.

'But it is not so in England. The very lowest of the people are here better instructed.' I should be right glad to find it so. But I doubt a fair trial will show the contrary. I am afraid we may still say of thousands, myriads of peasants, men, women, and children throughout our nation:

> Wild as the untaught Indian's brood
> The Christian savages remain,
> Strangers, yea, enemies to God,
> They make thee spend thy blood in vain.[167]

[y] By a late Act of Parliament there is an happy alteration made in this particular [added in *Works* (1773); apparently referring to the 'Bill to Encourage the Improvement of Lands, Tenements, and Hereditaments . . . in Scotland', which was passed by Parliament in 1770].

[167] JW and CW, *Hymns for Those that Seek, and Those that Have Redemption in the Blood of Jesus Christ*, Hymn 31, stanza 3 (London: Strahan, 1747), 42. The orig. has 'Strangers and enemies . . .'.

The generality of English peasants are not only grossly, stupidly (I had almost said, brutishly) ignorant as to all the arts of this life, but eminently so with regard to religion and the life to come. Ask a countryman, What is faith? What is repentance? What is holiness? What is true religion? And he is no more able to give you an intelligible answer than if you were to ask him about the north-east passage.[168] Is there then any possibility that they should practice what they know nothing of? If religion is not even in their heads, can it be in their hearts or lives? It cannot. Nor is there the least savour thereof either in their tempers or conversation. Neither in the one nor the other do they rise one jot above the pitch of a Turk or an heathen.

Perhaps it will be said, 'Whatever the clowns in the midland counties are, the people near the sea-coasts are more civilized.' Yes, great numbers of them are, in and near all our ports—many thousands there are civilized by *smuggling*. The numbers concerned herein upon all our coasts are far greater than can be imagined. But what reason and what religion have these that trample on all laws, divine and human, by a course of thieving, or receiving stolen goods, of plundering their king and country? I say, king and country, seeing whatever is taken from the king is in effect taken from the country, who are obliged to make up all deficiencies in the royal revenue. These are therefore general robbers. They rob you and me, and every one of their countrymen, seeing had the king his due customs a great part of our taxes might be spared. A *smuggler*, then (and in proportion every *seller* or *buyer* of unaccustomed goods), is a thief of the first order, a highwayman or pickpocket of the worst sort. Let not any of those prate about reason or religion. It is an amazing instance of human folly that every government in Europe does not drive these vermin away into lands not inhabited.[169]

We are all indebted to those detachments of the army which have cleared some of our coasts of these public nuisances. And indeed many of that body have in several respects deserved well of their country. Yet can we say of *the soldiery* in general that they are men of reason and religion? I fear not. Are not the bulk of them void of almost all knowledge, divine and human? And is their virtue more eminent than their knowledge? But I spare them. May God be

[168] A sailing course north of Europe and Asia, still thought to be a practicable route to the East.

[169] JW the evangelist/pastor also called upon smugglers to recognize their wrong and change in *A Word to a Smuggler* (1767), vol. 15 in this edn.

merciful to them! May he be glorified by their reformation, rather than their destruction!

Is there any more knowledge or virtue in that vast body of men (some hundred thousands), the *English sailors?* Surely no. It is not without cause that a ship has been called 'a floating hell'. What power, what form of religion is to be found, in nine out of ten, shall I say? Or ninety-nine out of an hundred, either of our merchant-men or men of war? What do the men in them think or know about religion? What do they practise? Either sailors or marines? I doubt whether any heathen sailors, in any country or age, Greek, Roman, or barbarian, ever came up to ours for profound ignorance and barefaced, shameless, shocking impiety. Add to these, out of our renowned metropolis, the whole brood of porters, draymen, carmen, hackney coachmen, and—I am sorry to say—noblemen and gentlemen's footmen (together making up some thousands), and you will have such a collection of *knowing* and *pious* Christians as all Europe cannot exceed.

'But all men are not like these.' No, 'tis pity they should. And yet how little better are the retailers of brandy or gin, the inhabitants of blind alehouses, the oyster-women, fishwives, and other good creatures about Billingsgate,[170] and the various clans of peddlars and hawkers that patrol through the streets, or ply in Rag Fair[171] and other places of public resort. These likewise amount to several thousands, even within the bills of mortality. And what knowledge have they? What religion are they of? What morality do they practise?

'But these have had no advantage of education, many of them scarce being able to write or read.' Proceed we then to those who have had these advantages, the officers of the excise and customs. Are these in general men of reason? Who think with clearness and connection, and speak pertinently on a given subject? Are they men of religion? Sober, temperate? Fearing God and working righteousness?[172] Having a conscience void of offence toward God working righteousness? Having a conscience void of offence toward God and toward man?[173] How many do you find of this kind among them, men that fear an oath, that fear perjury more than death? That would

[170] Billingsgate, the fish market for London, was so associated with vulgar language and behavior that the name became a synonym for the same; see *OED* (2nd ed.).

[171] The used clothing market in London.

[172] See Acts 10:35.

[173] Cf. Acts 24:16.

die rather than neglect any part of that duty which they have sworn to perform? That would sooner be torn in pieces than suffer any man, under any pretence, to defraud his majesty of his just right? How many of them will not be deterred from doing their duty, either by fear or favour? Regard no threatenings in the execution of their office, and accept no bribes called 'presents'? These only are wise and honest men. Set down all the rest as having neither religion nor sound reason.

'But surely *tradesmen* have.' Some of them have both, and in an eminent degree. Some of our traders are an honour to the nation. But are the bulk of them so? Are a vast majority of our tradesmen, whether in town or country (I will not say religious, but) honest men? Who shall judge whether they are or no? Perhaps you think St. Paul is too strict. Let us appeal then to Cicero, an honest heathen. Now when he is laying down rules of honesty between man and man he proposes two cases:

1) Antisthenes brings a shipload of corn to Rhodes at a time of great scarcity. The Rhodians flock about him to buy. He knows that five other ships laden with corn will be there tomorrow. Ought he to tell the Rhodians this before he sells his own corn? Undoubtedly he ought, says the heathen. Otherwise he makes a gain of their ignorance, and so is no better than a thief or a robber.[174]

2) A Roman nobleman comes to a gentleman to buy his house, who tells him, 'There is another going to be built near it, which will darken the windows,' and on that account makes a deduction in the price. Some years after the gentleman buys it of him again. Afterward he sues the nobleman for selling it without telling him first that houses were built near which darkened the windows. The nobleman pleads, 'I thought he knew it.' The judge asks, 'Did you tell him or not?' And on his owning he did not, determines, 'This is contrary to the law, *Ne quid dolo malo fiat*' (let nothing be done fraudulently), and sentences him immediately to pay back part of the price.[175]

[174] JW takes the example from Cicero, *De Officiis* (*On Moral Obligations*), III.xii.50, with added dramatic details such as the name of the merchant, 'five other ships', and 'tomorrow'. In the ensuing imaginary debate between Diogenes and his disciple Antipater, Diogenes maintains that as long as the seller does not use trickery, he should get the best price he can. JW supports Antipater's position that you cannot 'honestly conceal from men what is to their advantage and well-being', but overstates it by describing the astute seller (in an allusion to John 10:1) as 'a thief or a robber'.

[175] See Cicero, *De Officiis*, III.xvi.66-67, which apparently is the situation from which JW manufactures a similar illustration. '*Dolus malus*' and the quotation of the law are probably a general reference to the same work, III.xv.61, *dolus malus* being a formal expression implying fraud or deceit.

Now, how many of our tradesmen come up to the heathen standard of honesty? Who is clear of *dolus malus*? Such fraud as the Roman judge would immediately have condemned? Which of our countrymen would not have sold his corn or other wares at the highest price he could? Who would have sunk his own market by telling his customers there would be plenty the next day? Perhaps scarce one in twenty. That one the heathen would have allowed to be an honest man. And every one of the rest, according to his sentence, is 'no better than a thief or a robber'.

I must acknowledge, I once believed the body of English *merchants* to be men of the strictest honesty and honour. But I have lately had more experience. Whoever wrongs the widow and fatherless knows not what honour or honesty means. And how very few are there that will scruple this? I could relate many flagrant instances.

But let one suffice. A merchant dies in the full course of a very extensive business. Another agrees with his widow that, provided she will recommend him to her late husband's correspondents, he will allow her yearly such a proportion of the profits of the trade. She does so and articles are drawn, which she lodges with an eminent man. This eminent man positively refuses to give them back to her, but gives them to the other merchant, and so leaves her entirely at his mercy. The consequence is, the other says, There is no profit at all. So he does not give her a groat. Now where is the honesty or honour, either of him who made the agreement or him who gave back the articles to him?

That there is honour, nay, and honesty, to be found in another body of men, among the gentlemen of the *law*, I firmly believe, whether *attorneys, solicitors*, or *counsellors*. But are they not thinly spread? Do the generality of attorneys and solicitors in Chancery love their neighbour as themselves?[176] And do to others what (if the circumstance were changed) they would have others do to them?[177] Do the generality of counsellors walk by this rule? And by the rules of justice, mercy, and truth?[178] Do they use their utmost endeavours, do they take all the care which the nature of the thing will allow, to be assured that a cause is just and good before they undertake to defend it? Do they never knowingly defend a bad cause, and so make

[176] Lev. 19:18, etc.
[177] See Matt. 7:12, etc.
[178] See Ps. 89:14.

themselves accomplices in wrong and oppression? Do they never deliver the poor *into* the hand of his oppressor,[179] and see that such as are in necessity have *not* right?[180] Are they not often the means of withholding bread from the hungry and raiment from the naked?[181] Even when it is their own, when they have a clear right thereto, by the law both of God and man? Is not this effectually done in many cases by protracting the suit from year to year? I have known a friendly bill preferred in Chancery by the consent of all parties, the manager assuring them a decree would be procured in two or three months. But although several years are now elapsed they can see no land yet. Nor do I know that we are a jot nearer the conclusion than we were the first day.[182] Now where is the honesty of this? Is it not picking of pockets and no better? A lawyer who does not finish his client's suit as soon as it can be done, I cannot allow to have more honesty (though he has more prudence) than if he robbed him on the highway.

'But whether lawyers are or no, sure the *nobility* and *gentry* are all men of reason and religion.' If you think they are all men of religion, you think very differently from your Master, who made no exception of time or nation when he uttered that weighty sentence, 'How difficultly shall they that have riches enter into the kingdom of heaven!'[183] And when some who seem to have been of your judgment were greatly astonished at his saying, instead of retracting or softening, he adds: 'Verily I say unto you, it is easier for a camel to go through the eye of a needle than for a rich man to enter into the kingdom of God.'[184] You think differently from St. Paul, who declares in those remarkable words, verified in all ages, 'Not many rich men, not many noble are called'[185] . . . and obey the heavenly

[179] See Jer. 21:12.

[180] See Ps. 82:3 (BCP).

[181] See Job 22:6-7.

[182] There is no other record of this specific instance, but for similar negative comments on the formal procedures and typical dynamics of Chancery suits, see his *Journal* for Dec. 27, 1744 (20:47 in this edn.); Dec. 19, 1759 (21:236-37); Feb. 21, 1761 (21:308), and July 3, 1761 (21:332-33). See also his diatribe against lawyers in *Farther Appeal*, II.20 (11:232-35).

[183] Cf. Mark 10:23. In his *NT Notes* JW follows the AV in the translation 'hardly'. There was no current translation using 'difficultly', though it is accurate to the Greek.

[184] Mark 10:25.

[185] Cf. 1 Cor. 1:26.

calling.[186] So many snares surround them that it is the greatest of all miracles if any of them have any religion at all. And if you think they are all men of sound reason, you do not judge by fact and experience. Much money does not imply much sense. Neither does a good estate infer a good understanding. As a gay coat may cover a bad heart, so a fair peruke[187] may adorn a weak head. Nay, a critical judge of human nature avers that this is generally the case. He lays it down as a rule:

Sensus communis in illa
Fortuna rarus[188]

'Common sense is rarely found in men of fortune.' 'A rich man', says he, 'has liberty to be a fool. His fortune will bear him out'—'*Stultitiam patiuntur opes*'. But '*tibi parvula res est*'[189]—'You have little money, and therefore should have common sense.'

I would not willingly say anything concerning those whom the providence of God has allotted for *guides* to others. There are many thousands of these in the Established Church, many among Dissenters of all denominations. We may add some thousands of Romish priests scattered through England and swarming in Ireland. Of these therefore I would only ask, 'Are they all moved by the Holy Ghost to take upon them that office and ministry'?[190] If not, they do not 'enter by the door into the sheepfold';[191] they are not *sent of God*. Is their 'eye single'?[192] Is it their sole intention in all their ministrations to glorify God and to save souls?[193] Otherwise, 'the light which

[186] Heb. 3:1.

[187] A wig or artificial head of hair.

[188] Cf. Juvenal, *Satires*, viii.73-74: '*Rarus enim ferme sensus communis in illa / Fortuna*'. JW quotes this accurately in his *Journal*, June 29, 1758, 21:156 in this edn.

[189] Cf. Horace, *Epistles*, I.xviii.28-29:

. . . meae (contendere noli)
Stultitiam patiuntur opes; tibi parvola res est . . .

'My wealth—don't try to rival me—allows of folly: your means are but trifling' (Loeb). There is no such quotation in Juvenal, although JW seems to imply that this is from him.

[190] BCP, Ordination of Deacons, bishop's first question.

[191] Cf. John 10:1.

[192] Cf. Matt. 6:22.

[193] JW addressed this question directly to his Anglican peers a year earlier in 'Address to the Clergy', I.3.1, II.2.1, vol. 16 in this edn. Cf. his similar charge to his lay assistants in Minutes (Aug. 3, 1745), §71, 10:159 in this edn.

is in them is darkness'.[194] And if it be, 'how great is that darkness'![195] Is their 'heart right with God'?[196] Are their 'affections set on things above, not on things of the earth'?[197] Else how will they themselves go one step in the way wherein they are to guide others? Once more, Are they 'holy in all manner of conversation, as he who hath called them is holy'?[198] If not, with what face can they say to the flock, 'Be ye followers of me, as I am of Christ'?[199]

12. We have now taken a cursory view of the present state of mankind in all parts of the habitable world, and seen in a general way what is their real condition, both with regard to knowledge and virtue. But because this is not so pleasing a picture as human pride is accustomed to draw, and because those who are prepossessed with high notions of their own beauty will not easily believe that it is taken from the life I shall endeavour to place it in another view, that it may be certainly known whether it resembles the original. I shall desire everyone who is willing to know mankind to begin his inquiry at home. First, let him survey himself, and then go on, step by step, among his neighbours.

I ask then first, Are you throughly pleased with *yourself*? Say you, Who is not? Nay, I say, Who is? Do you observe nothing in yourself which you dislike? Which you cannot cordially approve of? Do you never think too well of yourself? Think yourself wiser, better, and stronger, than you appear to be upon the proof? Is not this pride? And do you approve of pride? . . . Was you never *angry* without a cause? Or farther than that cause required? Are you not apt to be so? Do you approve of this? Do not you frequently resolve against it? And do not you break those resolutions again and again? Can you help breaking then? If so, Why do you not? . . . Are not you prone to *unreasonable desires*, either of pleasure, praise, or money? Do not you catch yourself desiring things not worth a desire—and other things more than they deserve? Are all your desires proportioned to the real, intrinsic value of things? Do not you know and feel the contrary? Are not you continually liable to 'foolish and hurtful desires'?[200] And do not you frequently relapse into them, knowing

[194] Cf. Matt. 6:23.
[195] Ibid.
[196] Cf. 2 Kgs. 10:15.
[197] Cf. Col. 3:2.
[198] Cf. 1 Pet. 1:15.
[199] Cf. 1 Cor. 11:1.
[200] 1 Tim. 6:9 (*NT Notes*).

them to be such; knowing that they have before 'pierced you through with many sorrows'?[201] Have you not often resolved against these desires? And as often broke your resolutions? Can you help breaking them? Do so. Help it if you can. And if not, own your helplessness.

Are you throughly pleased with your own life? *Nihilne vides quod nolis*? Do you observe nothing there which you dislike? I presume you are not too severe a judge here. Nevertheless I ask, Are you quite satisfied, from day to day, with all you say or do? Do you *say* nothing which you afterwards wish you had not said? *Do* nothing which you wish you had not done? Do you never speak anything contrary to truth or love? Is that right? Let your own conscience determine. Do you never do anything contrary to justice or mercy? Is that well done? You know it is not. Why then do you not amend? '*Moves, sed nil promoves*.'[202] You resolve and resolve, and do just as you did before.

Your *wife*, however, is wiser and better than you. Nay, perhaps you do not think so. Possibly you said once:

> Thou hast no faults, or I no faults can spy;
> Thou art all beauty, or all blindness I.[203]

But you do not say so now. She is not without faults. And you can see them plain enough. You see more faults than you desire, both in her temper and behaviour. And yet you can't mend them, and she either can't or won't. And she says the very same of *you*. . . . Do your *parents* or hers live with you? And do not they too exercise your patience? Is there nothing in *their* temper or behaviour that gives you pain? Nothing which you wish to have altered? Are you a parent yourself? Parents in general are not apt to think too meanly of their own offspring. And probably at some times you admire yours more than enough, you think there are none such. But do you think so upon cool reflection? Is the behaviour of all your *children*, of most, of any of them, just such as you would desire? Toward yourself, toward each other, and toward all men? Are their tempers just such

[201] 1 Tim. 6:10.

[202] Cf. Terence, Eunuch, 913:
Sophrona, the nurse: 'Moveo'. ('I'm moving.')
Chremes: '*Video, sed nil promoves*.' ('So I see, but not forward.')

[203] Christopher Codrington, 'To my Friend the Author', lines 5-6; prefixed in Samuel Garth, *The Dispensary*, 3rd ed. (London: John Nutt, 1699).

as you would wish: loving, modest, mild, and teachable? Do you observe no self-will, no passion, no stubbornness, no ill nature or surliness among them? Did you not observe more or less of these in every one of them before they were two years old? And have not those seeds ever since grown up with them, till they have brought forth a plentiful harvest?

Your *servants* or *prentices* are probably older than your children. And are they wiser and better? Of all those who have succeeded each other for twenty years, how many were good servants? How many of them did their work 'unto the Lord',[204] 'not as pleasing man but God'?[205] How many did the same work, and in as exact a manner, behind your back as before your face? They that did not were knaves. They had no religion. They had no morality. Which of them studied *your* interest in all things, just as if it had been his own?[206] I am afraid, as long as you have lived in the world, you have seen few of these black swans yet.[207]

Have you had better success with the *journeymen* and *labourers* whom you occasionally employ? Will they do the same work if you are at a distance which they do while you are standing by? Can you depend upon their using you as they would you should use them? And will they do this not so much for gain as for conscience' sake? Can you trust them as to the price of their labour? Will they never charge more than it is fairly worth? If you have found a set of such workmen, pray do not conceal so valuable a treasure, but immediately advertise the men and their places of abode for the common benefit of your countrymen.

Happy you who have such as these about your house! And are your *neighbours* as honest and loving as they? They who live either in the same or in the next house, do these love you as themselves? And do to *you* in every point as they would have you do to *them*? Are they guilty of no untrue or unkind sayings, no unfriendly actions toward you? And are they (as far as you see or know) in all other respects reasonable and religious men? How many of your neighbours answer this character? Would it require a large house to contain them?

[204] Rom. 14:8, etc.

[205] 1 Thess. 2:4.

[206] Cf. JW's hortatory 'Directions to Servants', vol. 15 in this edn.

[207] Black swans are proverbially rare.

But you have intercourse not with the next neighbours only, but with several *tradesmen*. And all very honest, are they not? You may easily make a trial. Send a child or a countryman to one of their shops. If the shopkeeper is an honest man he will take no advantage of the buyer's ignorance. If he does, he is no honester than a thief. And how many tradesmen do you know who would scruple it?

Go a little farther. Send to the market for what you want. 'What is the lowest price of this?' 'Five shillings, sir.' 'Can you take no less?' 'No, upon my word. It is worth it every penny.' An hour after he sells it for a shilling less. And it is really worth no more. Yet is not this the course (a few persons excepted) in every market throughout the kingdom? Is it not generally, though not always, cheat that cheat can? Sell as dear as you can, and buy as cheap? And what are they who steer by this rule better than a company of *Newgate birds*?[208] Shake them all together, for there is not a grain of honesty among them.

But are not your own *tenants*, at least, or your *landlord*, honest men? You are persuaded they are. Very good. Remember, then, an honest man's word is as good as his bond. You are preparing a receipt or writing for a sum of money which you are going to pay or lend to this honest man. Writing! What need of that? You do not fear he should die soon. You did not once think of it. But you do not care to trust him without it; that is, you are not sure but he is a mere knave. What, your landlord? Who is a justice of peace! It may be a judge! Nay, a member of Parliament! Possibly a peer of the realm! And cannot you trust this honourable (if not Right Honourable) man without a paltry receipt? I do not ask whether he is an whoremonger, an adulterer, a blasphemer, a proud, a passionate, a revengeful man. This it may be his nearest friends will allow. But do you suspect his honesty too?

13. Such is the state of the *Protestant Christians* in England. Such their virtue from the least to the greatest, if you take an impartial survey of your parents, children, servants, labourers, neighbours, of tradesmen, gentry, nobility. What then can we expect from *Papists*? What from *Jews, Mahometans, heathens?*

And it may be remarked that this is the plain, glaring, apparent condition of humankind. It strikes the eye of the most careless, inaccurate observer, who does not trouble himself with any more than their outside. Now it is certain, the generality of men do not wear

[208] *OED* (2nd edn.) cites this as the last of three examples implying 'gaol-birds' (i.e., prisoners).

their worst side outward. Rather, they study to *appear* better than they are and to conceal what they can of their faults. What a figure then would they make were we able to touch them with Ithuriel's spear![209] What a prospect would there be, could we anticipate the transactions of the great day! Could we 'bring to light the hidden things of darkness, and make manifest the thoughts and intents of the heart'![210]

This is the plain, naked fact, without any extenuation on the one hand or exaggeration on the other. The present state of the moral world is as conspicuous as that of the natural. Ovid said no more concerning both near two thousand years since than is evidently true at this day. Of the natural world he says (whether this took place at the fall of man, or about the time of the deluge):

> *Jupiter antiqui contraxit tempora veris,*
> *Perque hiemes, aestusque et inaequalis autumnos,*
> *Et breve ver spatiis exegit quattuor annum.* [211]

> The God of nature, and her sovereign King,
> Shorten'd the primitive perennial spring.
> The spring gave place, no sooner come than past,
> To summer's heat, and winter's chilling blast,
> And autumn sick, irregular and uneven:
> While the sad year through different seasons driven
> Obey'd the stern decree of angry heaven.

And a man may as modestly deny that spring and summer, autumn and winter, succeed each other, as deny one article of the ensuing account of the moral world.

> *Irrupit venae pejoris in aevum*
> *Omne nefas; fugere pudor, verumque, fidesque;*
> *In quorum subiere locum fraudesque dolique*
> *Insidiaeque, et vis, et amor sceleratus habendi.* [212]

[209] Ithuriel was one of the angels sent by Gabriel in Milton's *Paradise Lost* to search out Satan, who in disguise is threatening Adam and Eve. A touch of Ithuriel's spear reveals his true identity. See *Paradise Lost*, iv.810-13, 819.

[210] Cf. 1 Cor. 4:5.

[211] Ovid, *Metamorphoses*, i.116-18. The loose translation is almost certainly from the pen of CW, as indicated in Moore, *Wesley*, 2:366.

[212] Ibid., i.128-31; changing the orig.: '*inrupit*' to '*irrupit*', '*fugitque*' to '*fugere*', and '*dolusque*' to '*dolique*'. Again the translation is by CW, as noted in Moore, *Wesley*, 2:366-67.

A flood of general wickedness broke in
At once, and made the iron age begin.
Virtue and truth forsook the faithless race,
And fraud and wrong succeeded in their place.
Deceit and violence, the dire thirst of gold,
Lust to possess, and rage to have and hold.

What country is there now upon earth, in Europe, Asia, Africa, or America, be the inhabitants *pagans, Turks*, or *Christians*, concerning which we may not say:

Vivitur ex rapto: non hospes ab hospite tutus [. . .]
Filius ante diem patrios inquirit in annos;
Victa jacet pietas, et virgo caede madentes
Ultima caelestum terras astraea reliquit [213]

They live by rapine. The unwary guest
Is poison'd at the inhospitable feast.
The son, impatient for his father's death,
Numbers his years, and longs to stop his breath.
Extinguish'd all regard for God and man;
And justice, last of the celestial train,
Spurns the earth drench'd in blood and flies to heaven again.

14. Universal misery is at once a consequence and a proof of this universal corruption. Men are unhappy (How very few are the exceptions!) because they are unholy.[214] '*Culpam poena premit comes*'[215]—pain accompanies and follows sin. Why is the earth so full of complicated distress? Because it is full of complicated wickedness. Why are not you happy? Other circumstances may concur, but the main reason is because you are not holy. It is impossible in the nature of things that wickedness can consist with happiness. Roman heathen, tell the English heathens, '*nemo malus felix*'[216]—'no vicious man is happy'. And if you are not guilty of any gross outward vice, yet you have vicious tempers. And as long as these have power in your heart, true peace has no place. You are proud; you think too

[213] Ibid., i.144, 148-50. Translated by CW; see Moore, *Wesley*, 2:367.

[214] JW consistently conjoins happiness with holiness; see Outler's list of examples in 1:35n28, in this edn.

[215] Horace, *Odes*, IV.v.24; 'Vengeance follows close on guilt' (Loeb).

[216] Juvenal, *Satires*, iv.8; cf. Sermon 45, 'The New Birth', III.3, 2:195 in this edn.

highly of yourself. You are passionate, often angry without reason. You are self-willed, you would have your own will, your own way in everything. That is plainly, you would rule over God and man. You would be the governor of the world. You are daily liable to unreasonable desires. Some things you desire that are no way desirable, others which ought to be avoided, yea abhorred, at least as they are now circumstanced. And can a proud or a passionate man be happy? Oh no! Experience shows it is impossible. Can a man be happy who is full of self-will? Not unless he can dethrone the Most High. Can a man of unreasonable desires be happy? Nay, they 'pierce him through with many sorrows'.[217]

I have not touched upon envy, malice, revenge, covetousness, and other gross vices. Concerning these it is universally agreed by all thinking men, Christian or heathen, that a man can no more be happy while they lodge in his bosom than if a vulture was gnawing his liver.[218] It is supposed, indeed, that a very small part of mankind, only the vilest of men, are liable to these. I know not that, but certainly this is not the case with regard to pride, anger, self-will, foolish desires. Those who are accounted not bad men are by no means free from these. And this alone (were they liable to no other pain) would prevent the generality of men, rich and poor, learned and unlearned, from ever knowing what happiness means.

15. You think however you could bear yourself pretty well, but you have such an husband or wife, such parents and children, as are intolerable! One has such a tongue, the other so perverse a temper! The language of these, the carriage of those, is so provoking! Otherwise you should be happy enough. True, if both you and they were wise and virtuous. Meanwhile, neither the vices of your family nor your own will suffer you to rest.

Look out of your own doors. 'Is there any evil in the city, and *sin* hath not done it?'[219] Is there any misfortune or misery to be named whereof it is not either the direct or remote occasion? Why is it that the *friend* or *relation* for whom you are so tenderly concerned is involved in so many troubles? Have not you done *your* part toward making them happy? Yes, but they will not do their own. One has no management, no frugality, or no industry. Another is too fond of

[217] Cf. 1 Tim. 6:10.

[218] An allusion to the Greek legend of Tityus, father of Europa, who was spread out on the ground while vultures gnawed his liver (similar to Prometheus).

[219] Cf. Amos 3:6.

pleasures. If he is not what is called scandalously vicious, he loves wine, women, or gaming. And to what does all this amount? He might be happy, but *sin* will not suffer it.

Perhaps you will say, Nay, he is not in fault; he is both frugal and diligent. But he has fallen into the hands of those who have imposed upon his good nature. Very well, but still sin is the cause of his misfortunes. Only it is another's, not his own.

If you inquire into the troubles under which your neighbour, your acquaintance, or one you casually talk with, labours, still you will find the far greater part of them arise from some fault either of the sufferer or of others. So that still sin is at the root of trouble, and it is unholiness which causes unhappiness.

And this holds as well with regard to families as with regard to individuals. Many families are miserable through want. They have not the conveniences, if the necessaries of life. Why have they not? Because they will not work. Were they diligent they would want nothing. Or if not idle, they are wasteful. They squander away in a short time what might have served for many years. Others indeed are diligent, and frugal too—but a treacherous friend, or a malicious enemy has ruined them. Or they groan under the hand of the oppressor.[220] Or the extortioner has entered into their labours.[221] You see then, in all these cases want (though in various ways) is the effect of sin. But is there no rich man near? None that could relieve these innocent sufferers without impairing his own fortune? Yes, but he thinks of nothing less. They may rot and perish for him. See, more sin is implied in their suffering.

But is not the family of that rich man himself happy? No, far from it—perhaps farther than his poor neighbour's. For they are not content. Their 'eye is not satisfied with seeing, nor their ear with hearing'.[222] Endeavouring to fill their souls with the pleasures of sense and imagination, they are only pouring water into a sieve. Is not this the case with the wealthiest families you know? But it is not the whole case with some of them. There is a debauched, a jealous, or an ill-natured husband; a gaming, passionate, or imperious wife; an undutiful son, or an imprudent daughter; who banishes happiness from the house. And what is all this but sin in various shapes, with its sure attendant, misery?

[220] Jer. 21:12.
[221] John 4:38.
[222] Cf. Eccl. 1:8.

In a town, a corporation, a city, a kingdom, is it not the same thing still? From whence comes that complication of all the miseries incident to human nature, war? 'Is it not from the *tempers* which war in the soul?'[223] When nation rises up against nation, and kingdom against kingdom, does it not necessarily imply pride, ambition, coveting what is another's? Or envy, or malice, or revenge, on one side, if not on both? Still then sin is the baleful source of affliction. And consequently the flood of miseries, which covers the face of the earth, which overwhelms not only single persons, but whole families, towns, cities, kingdoms, is a demonstrative proof of the overflowing of ungodliness, in every nation under heaven.[224]

[223] Cf. 1 Pet. 2:11.

[224] In reprinting Pt. I in 1762 under the title *The Dignity of Human Nature*, JW added the following closing sentence: 'Such (if we can believe our eyes, ears, or experience) is the *present dignity of human nature!*'

PART II
THE SCRIPTURAL METHOD OF ACCOUNTING FOR THIS DEFENDED

I. 1. The fact then being undeniable, I would ask, How is it to be accounted for? Will you resolve it into the prevalence of *custom* and say, Men are guided more by *example* than reason? It is true. They run after one another like a flock of sheep (as Seneca remarked long ago), '*non qua eundum est, sed qua itur*'[1]—'not where they ought to go, but where others go'. But I gain no ground by this. I am equally at a loss to account for this custom.

How is it (seeing men are reasonable creatures, and nothing is so agreeable to reason as virtue) that the custom of all ages and nations is not on the side of virtue rather than vice? If you say, This is owing to bad *education*, which propagates ill customs, I own education has an amazing force, far beyond what is commonly imagined. I own too that as bad education is found among Christians as ever obtained among the heathens. But I am no nearer still. I am not advanced an hair's breadth toward the conclusion. For how am I to account for the almost universal prevalence of this *bad education*? I want to know when this prevailed first. And how came it to prevail. How came wise and good men (for such they must have been before *bad education* commenced) not to train up their children in wisdom and goodness? In the way wherein they had been brought up themselves? They had then no ill precedent before them. How came they to make such a precedent? And how came all the wisdom of after ages never to correct that precedent? You must suppose it to have been of ancient date. Profane history gives us a large account of universal wickedness—that is, universal 'bad education'—for above two thousand years last past. Sacred history adds the account of above two thousand more, in the very beginning of which (more than four thousand years ago) 'all flesh had corrupted their ways before the Lord'![2] Or, to speak agreeably to this hypothesis, were *very corruptly educated*. Now how is this to be accounted for, that in so long a tract of time no one nation under the sun has been able, by wholesome laws or by any other method, to remove this grievous evil? So that their

[1] Seneca, *De Vita Beata*, i.3.
[2] Cf. Gen. 6:12.

children, being *well educated*, the scale might at length turn on the side of reason and virtue?

These are questions which I conceive will not easily be answered to the satisfaction of any impartial inquirer. But to bring the matter to a short issue. The first parents who educated their children in vice and folly either were wise and virtuous themselves or were not. If they were not, their vice did not proceed from education. So the supposition falls to the ground. Wickedness was antecedent to bad education. If they were wise and virtuous, it cannot be supposed but they would teach their children to tread in the same steps. In no wise therefore can we account for the present state of mankind from *example* or *education*.

2. Let us then have recourse to the oracles of God. How do they teach us to account for this fact, that 'all flesh corrupted their way before God', even in the antediluvian world? That mankind was little, if at all, less corrupt from the Flood to the giving of the Law by Moses. That from that time till Christ came even God's chosen people were a 'faithless and stubborn generation',[3] little better, though certainly not worse, than the heathens who knew not God. That when Christ came 'both Jews and Gentiles were all under sin',[4] 'all the world was guilty before God'.[5] That even after the gospel had been preached in all nations, still the wise and virtuous were a 'little flock',[6] bearing so small a proportion to the bulk of mankind that it might yet be said, 'The whole world lieth in wickedness.'[7] That from that time 'the mystery of iniquity'[8] wrought even in the church, till the Christians were little better than the heathens. And lastly, that at this day 'the whole world'—whether pagan, Mahometan, or nominally Christian (little indeed is the flock which is to be excepted!)—again 'lieth in wickedness', doth not 'know the only true God',[9] doth not love, doth not worship him as God, hath not 'the mind which was in Christ',[10] neither 'walketh as he walked',[11] doth

[3] Ps. 78:9 (BCP).
[4] Cf. Rom. 3:9.
[5] Cf. Rom. 3:19.
[6] Luke 12:32.
[7] 1 John 5:19.
[8] 2 Thess. 2:7.
[9] Cf. John 17:3.
[10] Cf. Phil. 2:5.
[11] Cf. 1 John 2:6.

not practice justice, mercy, and truth,[12] nor do to others as they would others should do to them.[13] How, I say, do the oracles of God teach us to account for this plain fact?

3. They teach us that 'in Adam all die'.[a] That 'by' the first 'man came' both natural and spiritual 'death'.[14] That 'by' this 'one man sin entered into the world, and death' in consequence of sin; 'and' that from him 'death passed upon all men, in that all have sinned.'[b]

But you aver that 'no evil but *temporal death* came upon men in consequence of Adam's sin.'[c] And this you endeavour to prove by considering the chief Scriptures which are supposed to relate thereto.

The first you mention is Gen. 2:17, 'But of the tree of the knowledge of good and evil, thou shalt not eat of it. For in the day that thou eatest thereof thou shalt surely die.'

On this you observe: '*Death* was to be the consequence of his disobedience. And the *death* here threatened can be opposed only to that *life* God gave Adam when he created him.'[d] True. But how are you assured that God, when he created him, did not give him *spiritual*, as well as *animal* life?[15] Now *spiritual death* is opposed to *spiritual life*. And this is more than the *death* of the body.

'But this is pure conjecture, without a solid foundation. For no other *life* is spoken of before.'[[e]] Yes, there is. 'The image of God'[16]

[a] 1 Cor. 15:22, compared with Gen. 2 and 3.

[b] Rom. 5:12.

[c] Mr. [John] Taylor's [*The Scripture-*]*Doctrine of Original Sin* [(3rd edn.; London: J. Waugh, 1750)] Part I, to whom I address myself in what follows. What is quoted from him, generally in his own words, is enclosed in commas, ' '. [In this instance Wesley does not appear to be quoting a specific sentence, but giving a summary of the main thrust of Taylor's argument (cf. pp. 5-8, 63-64).]

[d] [Ibid.], p. 7. [Wesley tended to provide citations only when moving to a new page in Taylor's work, not to identify each quotation. This edn. adds citations when necessary, enclosed in square brackets, to identify every quotation.]

[[e]] [Ibid.]

---

[12] See Ps. 89:14.

[13] See Luke 6:31.

[14] 1 Cor. 15:21.

[15] John Taylor, *A Reply to the Reverend John Wesley's Remarks on 'The Scripture-Doctrine of Original Sin'* (London: Waugh, 1767), 7, here notes: 'I am assured of this by the reasons given *Supplem[ent]*, Section VIII'—i.e., pp. 122-25, which JW does not treat.

[16] Gen. 1:27.

is spoken of before.[17] This is not therefore pure conjecture, but is grounded upon a solid foundation, upon the plain Word of God.

Allowing then that 'Adam could understand it of no other *life* than that which he had newly received',[f] yet would he naturally understand it of *the life of God* in his soul, as well as of *the life of his body*.

'In this light, therefore, the sense of the threatening will stand thus: "Thou shall surely die;" as if he had said, "I have formed thee of the dust of the ground, and breathed into thy nostrils the breath of lives" '—both of *animal life* and of *spiritual life*[18]—' "and" ' in both respects ' "thou art become a living soul. But if thou eatest of the forbidden tree, thou shalt cease to be a living soul." '[19] For I will take from thee the lives I have given, and thou shalt die spiritually, temporally, eternally.[g]

But 'here is not one word relating to Adam's posterity. Though it be true, if he had died immediately upon his transgression all his posterity must have been extinct with him.'[h] It is true, yet 'not one word' of it is *expressed*. Therefore other consequences of his sin may be equally *implied*, though they are no more *expressed* than this.[20]

4. The second Scripture you cite is Gen. 3, from the seventh to the twenty-fourth verse.[i] On this you observe: here 'we have some consequences of our first parents' sin *before* God judged them, some appointed by his *judicial* sentence, and some which happened *after* that sentence was pronounced'.[j] 'Immediately upon their transgression they were seized with shame and fear. [. . .] Guilt will

[f] [Ibid.]
[g] Third edition, pp. [7-]8.
[h] [p. 8.]
[i] pp. 9-10.
[j] p. 11.

[17] Taylor, *Reply* (1767), 7: 'And the "image of God" is spoken of afterwards as belonging to the human nature now, as well as to Adam when first created, Gen. 9:6, Jas. 3:9.'

[18] Taylor had said 'the breath of life'. JW renders it plural and distinguishes animal and spiritual life. Taylor, *Reply* (1767), 8: 'חיים, life is of the plural number, but the sense is singular, as מים water, *tenebrae*, darkness, etc. And is so far from including spiritual life that it is applied to wicked men, who are destitute of spiritual life, to brutes who are incapable of it, Gen. 6:17–7:14, 15, 22.'

[19] While Wesley placed his quotation mark to suggest that the next sentence also comes from Taylor, it is actually a major revision of Taylor—adding spiritual death to the threat.

[20] Taylor, *Reply* (1767), 8: 'They may indeed be implied, except they are absurd, contradictory, and impossible.'

always be attended with shame, and a state of guilt is often in Scripture expressed by being *naked*. Exod. 32:25, "Moses saw that the people were naked. For Aaron had made them naked to their shame among their enemies." '[k] Certainly 'naked' does not mean *guilty* here, but either stripped of their ornaments[l] or of their swords, or their upper garment. 'Isa. 47:3, "Thy nakedness shall be uncovered, yea, thy shame shall be seen." '[m] Here also 'nakedness' does not mean *guilt*, but is to be taken literally, as manifestly appears from the words immediately preceding (ver. 2): 'Make bare the leg, uncover the thigh, pass over the rivers.' 'And Rev. 16:15, "Blessed is he that watcheth and keepeth his garments, lest he walk naked and they see his shame." '[n] The plain meaning is, lest he lose the graces he has received, and so be ashamed before men and angels.

'Their fear is described (ver. 8): "Adam and his wife hid themselves from the presence of the Lord God among the trees of the garden." They had no such fear while they were innocent, but now they were afraid to stand before their Judge.'[o]

This is all you can discern in the Mosaic account as the consequence of our first parents' sin *before* God judged them. Mr. Hervey discerns something more.[21] I make no apology for transcribing some of his words:

> Adam violated the precept, and as the nervous[22] original expresses it, 'died the death'. He before possessed a life incomparably more excellent than that which the beasts enjoy. He possessed a divine life, consisting, according to the Apostle, 'in knowledge, in righteousness, and true holiness'. This, which was the distinguishing glory of his nature, 'in the day that he eat' the forbidden fruit, was extinct.
>
> His understanding, originally enlightened with wisdom, was clouded with ignorance. His heart, once warmed with heavenly love, became 'alienated from God' his Maker. His passions and appetites, rational and regular before, shook off the government of order and reason. In a word, the whole moral frame was unhinged, disjointed, broken.
>
> The *ignorance* of fallen Adam was palpable. Witness that absurd attempt to 'hide himself' from the eye of *Omniscience*, among the trees of the garden. His *aversion*

[k] [pp. 11-12.]
[l] [Exod.] 33:5–6.
[m] [Taylor, *Scripture-Doctrine*, p. 12.]
[n] p. 12.
[o] pp. [12-]13.

[21] Ibid.: 'Rather, Mr. Hervey imagines something more.'
[22] I.e., 'strong' or 'vigorous'; cf. *OED* (2nd edn.), def. 3.

to the all-gracious God was equally plain. Otherwise he would never have fled from his Maker, but rather have hasted on the wings of desire into the place of the divine manifestation.

A strange variety of *disorderly* passions were evidently predominant in his breast. *Pride*, for he refuses to acknowledge his guilt, though he cannot but own the fact. *Ingratitude*, for he obliquely upbraids the Creator with his gift, as though it had been a snare rather than a blessing—'the woman thou gavest me'. The female criminal acts the same unhumbled part. She neither takes shame to herself, nor gives glory to God, nor puts up a single petition for pardon.

As all these disasters ensued upon the breach of the commandment, they furnish us with the best key to open the meaning of the penalty annexed. They prove beyond any argument that *spiritual death* and all its consequences were comprised in the extent of the threatening.[p]

5. However, 'no other could in justice be punishable for that transgression, which was their own act and deed only.'[q] If no other was justly 'punishable', then no other was *punished* for that transgression. But all men were *punished* for that transgression, namely, with death. Therefore all men were *justly punishable* for it.

By *punishment* I mean *suffering* consequent upon *sin*, or *pain* inflicted because of *sin* preceding. Now it is plain all mankind *suffer* death, and that this *suffering* is consequent upon Adam's *sin*. Yea, and that this *pain* is inflicted on *all men* because of *his* sin. When therefore you say, 'Death does descend to us in consequence of his transgression,'[r] you allow the point we contend for; and are very welcome to add, 'Yet it is not a *punishment* for his *sin*.' You allow the thing. Call it by what name you please.

But '*Punishment* always connotes *guilt*.'[s] It always connotes *sin* and *suffering*. And here are both. Adam sinned, his posterity *suffer*, and that in consequence of his sin.

But '*Sufferings* are *benefits* to us.'[t] Doubtless, but this does not hinder their being *punishments*. The pain I *suffer* as a *punishment* for *my own* sins may be a *benefit* to me, but it is a *punishment* nevertheless.

p [Hervey,] *Theron and Aspasio*, Dial. II [in fact, Dial. XI (1:342-43)].

q [Taylor, *Scripture-Doctrine*,] p. 13.

r p. 20.

s p. 21.

[t] [Ibid.]

But 'as they two only were guilty of the first sin, so no other but they two only could be conscious of it *as their sin*.'[u] No other could be conscious of it 'as their sin' in the same sense as Adam and Eve were. And yet others may 'charge it upon themselves' in a different sense, so as to judge themselves 'children of wrath'[23] on that account.

To sum up this point in Dr. Jennings'[24] words:

> If there be anything in this argument, that Adam's posterity could not be justly punishable for his transgression because it was his personal act and not theirs, it must prove universally that it is unjust to punish the posterity of any man for his personal crimes. And yet most certain it is that God has in other cases actually punished men's sins on their posterity. Thus the posterity of Canaan, the son of Ham, is punished with slavery for *his* sin.[v] Noah pronounced the curse under a divine *afflatus*, and God confirmed it by his providence. [. . .] So we do in fact suffer for Adam's sin, and that too by the sentence inflicted on our first parents. We suffer death in consequence of their transgression. Therefore we are, in some sense, guilty of their sin. I would ask, What is *guilt* but an obligation to suffer punishment for sin? Now since we suffer the same penal evil which God threatened to and inflicted on Adam for his sin, and since it is allowed we suffer this for Adam's sin, and that by the sentence of God appointing all men to die because Adam sinned, is not the consequence evident? Therefore we are all some way guilty of Adam's sin.[w]

6. 'The consequences appointed by the *judicial sentence* of God are found in that pronounced on the serpent, or the woman, or the man.'[x]

'The serpent is cursed (ver. 14-15). And those words in the fifteenth verse, "I will put enmity between thee and the woman, and between thy seed and her seed. He" (so the Hebrew)[25] "shall bruise thy head and thou shalt bruise his heel", [. . .] imply that God would appoint his only-begotten Son to maintain a kingdom in the world opposite to the kingdom of Satan, till he should be born of a woman,

[u] p. 14.

[v] Gen. 9:25, 27.

[w] [David Jennings, A] *Vindication of the [Scripture-]Doctrine of Original Sin* [(London, for R. Hett, 1740), pp. 7-8, 12-13, abridged and slightly paraphrased].

[x] [Taylor, *Scripture-Doctrine*,] p. 15.

---

[23] Eph. 2:3.

[24] Orig., 'Dr. J——'s'.

[25] JW is correcting Taylor's use of 'It'; see John Taylor, *The Scripture-Doctrine of Original Sin*, 3rd edn. (London: J. Waugh, 1750), 15.

and by his doctrine, example, obedience, and death, give the last stroke, by way of moral means, to the power and works of the devil.'[y]

I do not understand that expression, 'by way of *moral means*'. What I understand from the whole tenor of Scripture is that the eternal, almighty Son of God, 'who is over all, God, blessed for ever',[26] having reconciled us to God by his blood, creates us anew by his Spirit, and reigns till he hath destroyed all the works of the devil.

'Sentence is passed upon the woman (ver. 16) that she should bring forth children with more pain and hazard than otherwise she would have done.'[z] How? With 'more pain and hazard' than otherwise she would have done! Would she otherwise had *any pain* at all? Or have brought forth children with *any hazard*? Hazard of what? Certainly not of death. I cannot comprehend this.

'Lastly, the sentence upon the man (ver. 17-19) first affects the earth, and then denounces death upon himself. [. . .] After sentence pronounced, God having clothed Adam and Eve, drove them out of paradise'.[a]

Here 'observe (1) a curse is pronounced on the serpent and on the ground, but no curse upon the woman and the man'.[b] But a curse fell upon them in that very moment wherein they transgressed the law of God. For 'cursed is everyone that continueth not in all things which are' contained[27] 'in the law, to do them'.[28] Vainly therefore do you subjoin, 'Though they are subjected to sorrow, labour, and death, these are not inflicted under the notion of a curse'.[[c]] Surely they are, as the several branches of that curse which he had already incurred. And which had already not only 'darkened and weakened his rational powers', but disordered his whole soul.

'Observe (2) here is not one word of any other *death* but the dissolution of the body.'[[d]] Nor was it needful. He felt in himself that

[y] pp. [15-]16.
[z] p. 17.
[a] pp. [17-]18.
[b] p. 19.
[[c]] [Ibid.]
[[d]] [Ibid.]

---

[26] Rom. 9:5.

[27] It appears that JW, in order to forestall legalistic quibbling, deliberately suppressed the word 'written' in the AV translation because the relevant law was not at that time written down.

[28] Gal. 3:10.

spiritual death which is the prelude of *death everlasting*. 'But the words, "Dust thou art, and unto dust thou shalt return,"[29] restrain this death to this dissolution alone.'[e] 'This dissolution alone' is *expressed* in those words. But how does it appear that nothing more is *implied*? The direct contrary appears from your own assertions. For if these words refer clearly to those, 'And the Lord God formed man out of the dust of the ground, and breathed into his nostrils the breath of lives;'[30] and if 'the judicial act of condemnation clearly implieth the depriving him of that life which God then breathed into him;'[[f]] it undeniably follows that this judicial act implieth a deprivation of *spiritual* life as well as *temporal*, seeing God breathed into him both one and the other in order to his 'becoming a living soul'.[31]

It remains that the death *expressed* in the original threatening and *implied* in the sentence pronounced upon man includes all evils which could befall his soul and body—death temporal, spiritual, and eternal.

7. You next cite 1 Cor. 15:21-22, 'Since by man came death, by man came also the resurrection of the dead. For as in Adam all die, even so in Christ shall all be made alive.'[g]

On this you observe, (1) 'The Apostle is in this chapter proving and explaining *the resurrection*. It is this fact or event, and no other, which he here affirms and demonstrates.'[h]

If you mean, 'The *resurrection of the body to that life* which it enjoyed in this world is *the only thing* which the Apostle speaks of in this chapter', your assertion is palpably false. For he speaks therein of *that glorious life* both of soul and body which is not, cannot be enjoyed in this world.

You observe, (2) 'It is undeniable that *all* mankind "die in Adam", *all* are mortal in consequence of his sin.' (3) 'It is equally clear that "by Christ came the resurrection of the dead;" that "in Christ all" who die in Adam, that is, all mankind, "are made alive".'[i] It is neither clear nor true that St. Paul affirms this in either of the texts

[e] p. 20.
[[f]] [Ibid.]
[g] p. 22.
[h] p. 23.
[i] pp. [23-]24.

[29] Gen. 3:19.
[30] Gen. 2:7; for 'lives' see n. 18 above.
[31] Cf. Gen. 2:7.

before us. For in this whole chapter he speaks only of the resurrection of the just, of 'them that are Christ's' (ver. 23). So that from hence it cannot be inferred at all that 'all mankind' will be 'made alive'. Admitting then 'that "the resurrection of the dead" and being "made alive" are expressions of the same signification',[j] this proves nothing, since the Apostle affirms neither one nor the other of any but those 'who are fallen asleep in Christ' (ver. 18). It is of these only that he here asserts their 'death came by' the first, their 'resurrection by' the second Adam; or that 'in Adam they all died', 'in Christ they all are made alive'. Whatever life *they* all lost by means of Adam, *they* all recover by means of Christ.

'From this place we cannot conclude that any death came upon mankind in consequence of Adam's sin beside that death from which mankind shall be delivered at the resurrection.'[k]

Nay, from this place we cannot conclude that mankind in general shall be delivered from any death at all, seeing it does not relate to mankind in general, but wholly and solely to 'them that are Christ's'.

But from this place we may firmly conclude that more than the mere 'death' of the body 'came' even upon these 'by man', by Adam's sin, seeing 'the resurrection' which 'comes' to them 'by man', by Christ, is far more than the mere removal of *that death*. Therefore their 'dying in Adam' implies far more than the bare loss of the bodily life we now enjoy, seeing their 'being made alive in Christ' implies far more than a bare recovery of *that life*.

Yet it is true that whatever 'death came' on them 'by' one 'man' came upon all mankind, and that in the same sense wherein they 'died in Adam' all mankind died likewise. And that all mankind are not 'made alive in Christ', as they are, is not God's fault but their own.

I know not therefore what you mean by saying that after Doctor J[ennings] has proved this whole chapter, and consequently the two verses in question, to relate wholly and solely to the resurrection of the just, 'he leaves you in full possession of your argument'.[32] Surely if he proves this, he wrests your whole argument out of your hands. He leaves you not one shred of it.

[j] [p. 24.]
[k] p. 25.

---

[32] John Taylor, *A Supplement to the Scripture-Doctrine of Original Sin, etc.; Containing some Remarks upon two Books* . . . (London: Mary Fenner, 1741), Preface, p. vi.

8. 'We come now', you say, 'to the most difficult Scripture which speaks of this point, Rom. 5:12-19':[33]

> As by one man sin entered into the world, and death by sin, even so death passed upon all men, for that all have sinned.
>
> For until the law, sin was in the world. But sin is not imputed when there is no law.
>
> Nevertheless death reigned from Adam to Moses, even over them that had not sinned after the similitude of Adam's transgression, who is the figure of him that was to come.
>
> But not as the offence, so also is the free gift. For if through the offence of one many be dead, much more the grace of God, and the gift by grace, which is by one man, Jesus Christ, hath abounded unto many.
>
> And not as it was by one that sinned, so is the gift, for the judgment was by one offence unto condemnation, but the free gift is of many offences unto justification.
>
> For if by one man's offence death reigned by one, much more they who receive the abundance of grace and of the gift of righteousness shall reign in life by one Jesus Christ.
>
> Therefore as by the offence of one *judgment came* upon all men to condemnation, even so by the righteousness of one *the free gift came* upon all men unto justification of life.
>
> For as by one man's disobedience many were made sinners, so by the obedience of one shall many be made righteous.'[l]

On this you observe (1) that this passage 'speaks of temporal death and no other'.[m] That it speaks of temporal death is allowed, but not that it speaks of no other. How prove you this? Why, thus: 'He evidently speaks of that death which "entered into the world" by Adam's sin; that death which is common to "all mankind", which "passed upon all men", that death which "reigned from Adam to Moses", that whereby "the many", that is all mankind, "are dead".'[[n]] He does so. But how does it appear that the death which 'entered into the world' by Adam's sin, which is common to 'all mankind', which 'passed upon all men', which 'reigned from Adam to Moses',

[l] pp. [25-]26.
[m] p. 28 [i.e., 27].
[[n]] [pp. 27, 30.]

---

[33] Wesley alters the AV translation reproduced by Taylor in ver. 12 ('even' for 'and'), ver. 16 ('offence' added), and ver. 17 ('who' for 'which', 'the' added), all moves reflecting JW's translation in his recently published *NT Notes*. See the discussion of debates over translating Rom. 5:12 in the introduction (pp. 148-49 above).

and whereby the 'many', that is, all mankind, 'are dead'—how, I say, does it appear from any or all of these expressions that this is *temporal death ONLY*? Just here lies the fallacy. 'No man', say you, 'can deny that the Apostle is here speaking of that death.'[o] True. But when you infer, 'therefore he speaks of that *only*', we deny the consequence.

9. You affirm, (2) 'By "judgment to condemnation" (ver. 16, 18) he means the being adjudged to the fore-mentioned *death*. For the *condemnation* inflicted by the *judgment* of God (ver. 16) is the same thing with *being dead* (ver. 15).'[p] Perhaps so, but that this is merely the *death of the body* still remains to be proved. As, on the other hand, that 'the *gift*, or *free gift*' opposed thereto, is merely *deliverance from that death*.

You add, 'In all the Scriptures there is recorded but one "judgment to condemnation", one sentence, one judicial act of condemnation, which "came upon all men".'[q] Nay, in *this sense* of the word there is not one—not one *formal sentence* which was *explicitly* and *judicially* pronounced upon *all mankind*. That which you cite, Gen. 3:17, 19, was not. Neither does all that sentence in fact 'come upon all men'. 'Unto dust shalt thou return' does come upon all, but that other part does not, 'In sorrow shall thou eat of it all the days of thy life.' This was *formally pronounced*, and actually fulfilled upon Adam. But it is not fulfilled upon all his posterity.

10. You affirm, (3) 'These words in the nineteenth verse, "As by one man's disobedience many were made sinners," mean the same as those in the eighteenth, "As by the offence of one judgment came upon all men to condemnation." '[r] Not exactly the same. The being 'made sinners' is different from the being *judged*, *condemned*, or *punished* as such. You subjoin, 'But these words, "By the offence of one judgment came upon all men to condemnation" answer in sense to those (ver. 17) "By one man's offence death reigned by one." '[s] Neither is this exactly true. 'Condemnation' came first, and in consequence of this 'death reigned'. You add, 'And by *death* most certainly is intended no other than *temporal death*.'[t] Most certainly this cannot be proved. Therefore it does not follow, 'That these words, "By

[o] [p. 27.]
[p] pp. 27[-28].
[q] p. 29 [i.e., pp. 28-29n.].
[r] p. 30 [i.e., 29].
[s] p. 30.
[t] [Ibid.]

one man's disobedience many were made sinners," mean no more than "By one man's disobedience" mankind were made subject to temporal death.' 'Review', you say, 'this reasoning, and see if you can find any flaw in it.'[u] There are several, but the grand flaw lies in the very first link of the chain. You have not yet proved that 'Death throughout this passage means *only* the death of the body.'[34]

[u] [Ibid.]

---

[34] Taylor, *Reply* (1767), 8-11:

'The proof that the death from which all mankind are released at the resurrection is the only death which came upon all mankind in consequence of Adam's sin is very evident from the antithesis or opposition between the members of the following sentences: Rom. 5:18, "Therefore, as by the offence of one (judgment came) upon *all men* to condemnation, even so by the righteousness of one (the free gift came) upon *all men* unto justification of life." 1 Cor. 15:21-22, "For since by man came *death*, by man came also the *resurrection of the dead*" (that is, of all the dead, for it follows,) "For as in Adam *all* die, even so in Christ shall *all* be made alive" (or restored to life). He speaks evidently of the general resurrection of all men, and not of the *just* only. For the erroneous principle which some of the new Christian converts at Corinth advanced was this (ver. 12), "that there is no resurrection (at all) of the dead".'

'It is plainly against this general proposition that the Apostle immediately argues (ver. 13), "But if there is no resurrection (at all) of the dead, then is not Christ risen; (ver. 14) and if Christ be not risen, etc." (Ver. 18) "Then they also who are fallen asleep in Christ are perished" (or totally lost, because upon this supposition they will not be raised from the dead). (Ver. 29) "Else what shall they do who are baptized for the dead, if the dead rise not at all (εἰ ὅλως νεκροὶ οὐκ ἐγείρονται)?" If none of the dead are to be raised. It is plain that his argument relates, not only to the resurrection of the *just*, or the glory which they would enjoy above other men, but to the resurrection of all men in general, even that resurrection without which even believers in Christ would not only have a less degree of life than they expected, but would *perish* (ἀπώλοντο) or be totally lost; and without which the Apostle himself expected no manner of advantage from all his labours and sufferings; (ver. 32) on the contrary, "if the dead rise not, let us eat and drink, for tomorrow we die", and there is an end of us.

Thus he *argues*; but when he *explains* the resurrection, and what would follow upon it, he dwells, as he naturally would, upon the case of those "who are Christ's at his coming" (ver. 23, and ver. 35, etc.), in order to show the Christians to whom he wrote what a glorious prospect was set before them, and to animate them "in the work of the Lord" (ver. 58). Now the two verses, namely 21-22, belong to the argumentative part of his discourse, and are therefore, as the expressions plainly declare, to be understood of the resurrection of all mankind. Consequently the death from which all mankind shall be released at the resurrection is the only death which came upon all mankind in consequence of Adam's sin. But supposing he speaks in those two verses only of the resurrection of the *just*, he speaks only of their bodies, or the restoration of that life which was extinguished by death in this world, as appears plainly from the whole chapter, and therefore can mean no other death but that when he said, "for since by man came death", "for as in Adam all die".'

This flaw is not amended by your observing that St. Paul was a Jew, and wrote to Jews as well as Gentiles; that he often uses Hebrew idioms, and that the Hebrew word which signifies 'to be a sinner', in [the conjugation] Hiphil, signifies *to condemn*, or *make* (i.e. *declare*), *a man a sinner* by a judicial sentence; [or] that you can (by the help of your concordance) produce fifteen Hebrew texts in which the word is so taken![v] For if it would follow from hence that 'by the offence of one, judgment came upon all men to condemnation', is just equivalent with 'by one man's disobedience many were made sinners',[[w]] still this does not prove that the death in question is no other than temporal death.

But indeed it does not follow that two expressions are just equivalent because one Hebrew word may contain them both. Nor can it therefore be inferred from hence that 'many were made sinners' is just equivalent with 'judgment came upon all men to condemnation'. Rather the former expression answers to 'all have sinned', the latter to 'death passed upon all men'. *Sin* is the cause of their *condemnation*, and not the same thing with it.

You go on. 'Besides all this, it is here expressly affirmed that the many are "made sinners" by the disobedience of *another* man." '[x] It is expressly affirmed, and by an inspired apostle. Therefore I firmly believe it. 'But they can be made sinners by the disobedience of *another* in no other sense than as they are *sufferers*.'[y] How is this proved? We grant, the Hebrew words for 'sin' and 'iniquity' are often used to signify 'suffering'.[[z]] But this does not prove that the phrase 'were made sinners' signifies only, they 'were made sufferers'.

'So Christ was made sin for us.'[a]—No, not *so*; but as he was 'made an offering for sin'. 'He suffered on account of the sins of men, and so he "was made sin".'[[b]] Yes, a sin-offering. But it is never said, he 'was made a sinner'.[35] Therefore the expressions are not parallel. But he need not have been 'made sin' at all, if we had not been 'made

[v] [Cf.] pp. 31-32.
[[w]] [p. 33.]
[x] p. 33.
[y] p. 34.
[[z]] [Cf. p. 34n.]
[a] p. 35 [citing 2 Cor. 5:21].
[[b]] [Ibid.]

[35] JW is again seeking to avoid a 'substitutionary justification' model of atonement; cf. his extract of Baxter's *Aphorisms* (above in this vol.).

sinners' by Adam. 'And men suffer on account of Adam's sin, and so *they* are "made sinners".'[c] Are they made sinners *so only*? That remains to be proved.

'It seems then confirmed beyond all doubt that "by one man's disobedience many were made sinners" meaneth only, by Adam's sin the many, that is, all mankind, "were made subject to death".'[d] He that will believe it (taking death in the common sense) may. But you have not confirmed it by one sound argument.

11. You affirm, (4) 'The Apostle draws a comparison between Adam and Christ, between what Adam did, with the consequences of it, and what Christ did, with the consequences of that. And this comparison is the main thing he has in view.'[e]

This is true. 'The comparison begins at the twelfth verse, "Wherefore as by one man sin entered into the world, and death by sin".—There he stops awhile, and brings an argument to prove that death came on mankind through Adam's transgression.'[f] He does so, but not before he had finished his sentence, which literally runs thus: 'As by one man sin entered into the world, and death by sin, even so death passed upon all men, in that all had sinned.'[36] The comparison therefore between Adam and Christ begins not at the twelfth but the fourteenth verse. Of this you seem sensible yourself when you say, 'Adam is the *pattern of him that was to come*. Here a *new* thought starts in the Apostle's mind.'[g] For it was not a *new* thought starting into his mind *here*, if it was the same which he began to express at the twelfth verse.

You proceed, 'The extent of the *free gift* in Christ answers to the extent of the consequences of Adam's sin; nay, abounds far beyond them. This he incidentally handles (ver. 15-17), and then resumes his main design (ver. 18-19), half of which he had executed in the

[c] [Ibid.]
[d] [Ibid.]
[e] p. 36.
[f] pp. 37-38.
[g] pp. [38-]39.

[36] JW now alters the AV translation even further than in I.8 above, giving his own translation as published in *NT Notes* in 1755. See the summary of debate over this translation, and how JW revised his translation, in the introduction (pp. 148-49 above).

twelfth verse.'[h] Not one jot of it. That verse is a complete sentence, not half of one only. And the particle 'therefore' prefixed to the eighteenth verse shows that the discourse goes straight forward, and that this as well as the nineteenth verse are closely connected with the seventeenth.

Allowing then 'that the Apostle draws a comparison between the "disobedience of Adam", by which all men are "brought under condemnation", and the "obedience of Christ", by which all men are (in some sense) "justified unto life";'[i] still it does not appear either that this *condemnation* means no more than the *death of the body*, or that this *justification* means no more than the *resurrection of the body*.

12. You affirm, (5) 'The whole of the Apostle's argument stands upon these two principles, that by the *offence of one* death passed upon all men, and by the *obedience of one* all are justified.'[j]

This is allowed. But I cannot allow your interpretation of 'sin is not imputed when there is no law,' or (as you would oddly, and contrary to all precedent, translate it, 'where law is not in being'.) 'The sins of mankind', say you, 'were not *imputed*, were not taxed with the forfeiture of life, because the law which subjects the transgressor to death was not then in being. For it was abrogated upon Adam's transgression, and was not again in force till revived by Moses.'[k] On this I would ask, (1) Where is it written that 'the law which subjected the transgressor to death was "abrogated by Adam's transgression"?' I want a clear text for this.[37] (2) Suppose it was, how does

[h] [p. 39.]
[i] p. 40.
[j] [Ibid.]
[k] p. 41.

[37] Taylor, *Reply* (1767), 11:

'A misrepresentation. I do not say that the law was abrogated *by* Adam's transgression (transgression doth not abrogate the law), but that it was abrogated *upon* (that is, soon after) Adam's transgression, namely, when grace was introduced. And the very texts under consideration (Rom. 5:13, 14) prove that it was then abrogated, till it was revived by Moses.'

The misunderstanding arises because Taylor is operating with a model of discrete 'dispensations', where the later Mosaic law had no application to those who lived prior to Moses. See *Scripture-Doctrine*, 41. Wesley's contrary assumption that there is a basic accountability to the core of the Mosaic law through the breadth of God's dealings with humanity is evident in Sermon 34, 'The Original, Nature, Properties, and Use of the Law', 2:4-19 in this edn.

it appear that it was not again in force till 'revived by Moses'? (3) Did not that law, 'whoso sheddeth man's blood, by man shall his blood be shed',[38] 'subject the transgressor to death'? And was it 'not in force' after Adam's transgression and before Moses? (4) What do you mean by that ambiguous expression, 'were not taxed with the forfeiture of life'? Your argument requires that it should *mean*, 'were not punished, or punishable with death'.

But is this true? Were not the sins of the men of Sodom and indeed the whole antediluvian world punished with death during that period?[l] Was not every wilful, impenitent transgressor, during this whole time, subject to death everlasting?

Neither can I allow that unnatural interpretation of 'them who had not sinned after the similitude of Adam's transgression', 'had not sinned against law, making death the penalty of their sin, as Adam did'.[m] Do not the words obviously mean, 'Had not sinned, by any *actual* sin, as Adam did'?

Nay, 'the Sodomites and antediluvians are no objection to this.' That is strange indeed! But how so? 'Because extraordinary interpositions come under no rule but the will of God.' What is that to the purpose? Their sins were actually punished with death 'during that space wherein you say mankind were not subject to death for their transgressions'. They *were* subject to death for their transgressions—as God demonstrated by those 'extraordinary interpositions'.[n]

You add: 'That law, "Whoso sheddeth man's blood, by man shall his blood be shed," makes death the penalty of murder.'[o] It does, and thereby overthrows your whole assertion. 'No, For (1) it was not enacted till the year of the world 1657.'[p] Well, and if it had been enacted only the year before Moses was born, it would still have destroyed your argument. But (2) 'It is given as a rule for magistrates in executing justice, and not as a declaration of the penalty of sin to be inflicted by God himself.'[q] What then? What does it

[l] ver. 5 [i.e., Gen. 9:5].
[m] [Taylor, *Scripture-Doctrine*,] p. 42.
[n] [pp. 42-43n.]
[o] [p. 43n., citing Gen. 9:6]
[p] [Ibid.]
[q] [Ibid.]

[38] See Gen. 9:6.

matter whether the penalty annexed by God were inflicted by God or man? However, I suppose, this punishment on the antediluvians and on Sodom and Gomorrah was 'inflicted by God himself.' But (3) 'None of these were *made mortal* by those sins.'[r] Certainly, infallibly true! And yet the case of any of these abundantly proves that the law was in force from Adam to Moses even according to your own definition of it, 'A rule of duty, with the penalty of death annexed, as due to the transgressor from God.'[s]

13. You affirm, (6) 'The consequences of Adam's sin answer those of Christ's obedience. But not exactly, "Not as the offence, so is the free gift. For if through the offence of one many be dead, *MUCH MORE* the grace" (or favour) "of God and the gift" (the benefits that are) "by grace, which is by one man Jesus Christ, hath *ABOUNDED* unto many" (ver. 15). That is, he hath in Christ bestowed benefits upon mankind far exceeding the consequences of Adam's sin, in erecting a new dispensation, furnished with a glorious fund of light and truth, means and motives.'[t] This is true—but how small a part of the truth! What a poor, low account of the Christian dispensation!

You go on, (ver. 16) ' "Not as it was by one that sinned, so is the gift. For the judgment was by one (offence) to condemnation; but the free gift is of many offences unto justification." That is, the grace of God in Christ discharges mankind from the consequences of Adam's one offence.'[u] Does it entirely discharge them from these consequences?[39] From sorrow, and labour, and death? Which you affirmed a while ago to be the *only* consequences of it that affect his posterity. It 'also sets them quite to rights with God, both as to a conformity to the law and eternal life.'[v]

Is not this allowing too much? Is it well consistent with what you said before? 'In the nineteenth verse the Apostle concludes the whole argument: "As by one man's disobedience many were made sinners,

[r] [Ibid.]
[s] p. 43 [n.]
[t] pp. 43-44 [citing Rom. 5:15].
[u] [p. 44.]
[v] [Ibid.]

[39] Taylor, *Reply* (1767), 11: 'Yes, doubtless it is intended to discharge them from all those in the future world. But the Apostle is speaking of death only, and my comment is to be understood of that only.'

so by the obedience of one shall many be made righteous." '[w] Were 'made sinners', you aver, means only were 'made mortal'. If so, the counterpart, 'made righteous', can only mean, *made immortal.* And that you thought so then appears from your citing as a parallel text 'In Christ shall all be made alive', which you had before asserted to mean only, shall be 'raised from the dead'.[x]

14. 'Hence it followeth, (1) that the *ABOUNDING* of God's *grace*, and the blessings by that grace, doth not respect the consequences of Adam's sin, hath no reference to his transgression, but to the grace of God and the obedience of Christ.'[y] 'The *ABOUNDING* of God's grace', you inform us, 'has reference to the grace of God.' Most sure. But this does not prove that it has 'no reference' to the consequences of Adam's sin. If we gain more blessing by Christ than we lost by Adam it is doubtless *abounding grace*.[40] But still it has a reference to Adam's transgression and the consequences of it. It is over these that it abounds. Therefore it has a manifest *respect* to them.

'It followeth, secondly, that in the eighteenth and nineteenth verses the Apostle considers the effects of Christ's obedience only so far as they answer to and reverse the consequences of Adam's disobedience, *the additional* benefits flowing therefrom having been mentioned apart in the fifteenth, sixteenth and seventeenth verses.'[z] In those verses the Apostle does undoubtedly show how the blessing by Christ *abounded* over the curse by Adam. But what then? How does this prove that the eighteenth and nineteenth verses do not respect all the benefits mentioned before? Without question they do. They are a general conclusion, not from one, but all the preceding verses.

'Again observe, that the *justification to life* is such a justification as comes upon *all men*.'[a] It *may*, in some sense. But *does* it in fact?

[w] [p. 29.]
[x] [Cf.] p. 29 and seq. [and I.10 above].
[y] p. 45.
[z] p. 46.
[a] p. 47.

[40] JW firmly believed that God's abounding grace would restore the fallen creation to a state with greater capacities and blessings than it had in the beginning; cf. Sermon 59, 'God's Love to Fallen Man', 2:423-35 in this edn.; and Sermon 63, 'The General Spread of the Gospel', §27, 2:499 in this edn.

According to your sense of it, it comes upon none. For if it means the discharging men from the consequences of Adam's sin, and if the only consequences of that sin are sorrow, labour, and death, it is manifest no man upon earth is *justified* to this day.[41]

But you go on. 'As *justification to life* comes upon all men.'[b]— No, not in the proper, scriptural sense of 'justification'. That term is never once in the Bible used for the *resurrection*, no more than for heaven or hell.

It may be proper here once for all to observe that what St. Paul says of 'abounding grace' is simply this: (1) The condemnation came by *one offence* only, the acquittal is from *many offences*. (2) They who receive this shall enjoy a far higher blessing by Christ than they lost by Adam. In both these respects the consequences of Christ's death *abound* over the consequences of Adam's sin. And this whole blessing by Christ is termed in the eighteenth verse 'justification', in the nineteenth 'being made righteous'.

'Further, the phrase "being made righteous", as well as "being made sinners", is an Hebrew way of speaking.'[c] I do not allow that. Both the phrases καθὶστασθαι δίκαιοι or ἁμαρτωλοὶ are pure and good Greek. That therefore there is any Hebraism at all in these expressions cannot be admitted without proof. If then the same Hebrew word does signify to 'make righteous' and to 'acquit in judgment', it does not follow that the Greek word here translated 'made righteous' means only 'being acquitted'. You yourself say the contrary.[42] You but now defined this very *gift*, 'the benefits that are by grace'. And in explaining those very words, 'The free gift is of many offences unto justification', affirmed, 'That is, the grace of God in Christ not only discharges mankind from the consequences of

[b] [Ibid.]
[c] p. 49 [i.e., 48].

[41] JW appears to misunderstand Taylor at this point. Recall that Taylor focused the consequence of Adam's sin for his posterity primarily on the introduction of final mortality (that this life was all they got). His point here is to distinguish between the gift that Christ gives to all humans—resurrecting all to life after death—and the further gifts of Christ's teaching and example that make it more likely one's afterlife will be one of blessing rather than suffering.

[42] Taylor rejects the way that JW uses the following quotation to incorporate the benefits of sanctification into the discussion, insisting: 'This is a misrepresentation of my sense.' *Reply* (1767), 12.

Adam's sin, but also sets them quite to rights with God, both as to a conformity to the law, and as to eternal life.'[d] And is this no more than 'acquitting them in judgment'? Or 'reversing the sentence of condemnation'?

Through this whole passage it may be observed that 'the gift', 'the free gift', 'the gift by grace', mean one and the same thing, even the whole benefit given by the *abounding* grace of God, through the obedience of Christ: *abounding* both with regard to the fountain itself, and the streams—*abundant* grace producing *abundant* blessings.

If then these verses are 'evidently parallel to those, 1 Cor. 15:21-22',[e] it follows even hence that 'dying' and 'being made alive' in the latter passage do not refer to the body only; but that 'dying' implies all the evils temporal and spiritual which are derived from Adam's sin; and 'being made alive' all the blessings which are derived from Christ, in time and in eternity.

Whereas therefore you add, 'It is now evident surely beyond all doubt' (strong expressions!) 'that the consequences of Adam's sin here spoken of are no other than the "death" which comes upon all men,'[f] I must beg leave to reply. It is not evident at all. Nay, it is tolerably evident, on the contrary, that this 'death' implies all manner of evils to which either the body or soul is liable.

15. You next reconsider the twelfth verse, which you understand thus: ' "Death passed upon all men, for that all have sinned", namely in Adam. All "have sinned", that is, are subjected to death through that one offence of his.'[g]

You said before, ' "Death passed upon all men" means, All were by a judicial sentence made subject to death.'[h] And here you say, ' "All have sinned" means, All have been subjected to death.'[i] So the Apostle asserts, 'All were subjected to death, because all were subjected to death!' Not so. *Sin* is one thing, *death* another; and the former is here assigned as the cause of the latter.

Although the criticism on ἐφ' ᾧ is liable to much exception,[j] yet I leave that and the Hebrew citations as they stand because, though

[d] p. 44.
[e] [p. 49.]
[f] p. 50.
[g] p. 51.
[h] [Cf. p. 27; and I.8 above.]
[i] [p. 51.]
[j] p. 52 [i.e., Taylor's excursus on this phrase in a long note, running pp. 51-55].

they may cause many readers to admire your learning, yet they are not to the point.[43]

'Seeing then the phrase "All are made sinners" hath been *demonstrated* to signify, "All are subjected to death by a judicial sentence"; and seeing the Apostle's whole argument turns on this point, that all men die through the one offence of Adam; who can doubt but "all have sinned" means the same with "all are made *sinners*"?'[k] I do not doubt it. But I still deny that either phrase means no more than 'all are in a state of suffering'.

16. In order fully to clear this important text, I shall here subjoin some of Dr. Jennings's remarks:

The Apostle having treated in the preceding chapter[s] of the cause and manner of a sinner's justification before God, namely through the merits[44] of Christ, and by faith in his blood; and having spoken of the fruits of justification in the former part of this chapter; he proceeds in the verses before us to illustrate our salvation by Christ by comparing it with our ruin by Adam. He compares Adam with Christ,[45] and shows how what we lost by the one is restored by the other, with abundant advantage. He makes Adam to be a figure or type of Christ; considering them both as public persons,[46] representing, the one all his natural descendants, the other all his spiritual seed; the one, Adam, all mankind, who are 'all guilty before God'; the other, Christ, all those 'who obtain the righteousness of God, which is by faith, to all them that believe'.[l]

Concerning the consequences of Adam's sin upon his posterity we have here the following particulars:

i. That 'by one man sin entered into the world'. That the whole world is some way concerned in Adam's sin. And this indeed is evident, because,

ii. Death, which is 'the wages of sin', and the very punishment threatened to Adam's first transgression, 'entered by sin and passed upon all men', is actually inflicted on all mankind. Upon which it is asserted in the next words,

[k] pp. 53-54.

[l] [Jennings,] *Vindication of the Scripture-Doctrine of Original Sin*, pages 18-35 [here, 18-19].

---

[43] For the debate over translating this clause, see the introduction (pp. 148-49 above).

[44] David Jennings had said 'righteousness' of Christ. *A Vindication of the Scripture-Doctrine of Original Sin, from Mr. Taylor's Free and Candid Examination of It* (London: R. Hett & J. Oswald, 1740), 18. Wesley changes to 'merits', reflecting the argument in his extract of Baxter's *Aphorisms* (above in this vol.).

[45] JW omits 'as two federal heads'. *Vindication*, 18.

[46] JW omits 'political heads, and federal representations'. Ibid., 19.

iii. That all have sinned: 'Even so death passed upon all men, for that all have sinned.' All men then are deemed sinners in the eye of God, on account of that one sin of which alone the Apostle is here speaking. And,

iv. Not only after, but before and 'until the law' (given by *Moses*), 'sin was in the world', and men were deemed sinners and accordingly punished with death,through many generations. Now 'sin is not imputed where there is no law: nevertheless death reigned from Adam to Moses.' Plainly showing that all mankind during that whole period had sinned in Adam, and so died, in virtue of the death threatened to him. And death could not then be inflicted on mankind for any actual sin, because it was inflicted on so many infants who had neither eaten of the forbidden fruit, nor committed any actual sin whatever, and therefore 'had not sinned' in any sense, 'after the similitude of Adam's transgression'. Therefore,

v. It was 'through the offence of one that many are dead' (ver. 15). 'By one offence death reigned by one' (ver. 17). And seeing the sin of Adam is thus punished in all men it follows,

vi. That they were all involved in that sentence of condemnation which God passed upon him. 'The judgment was by one to condemnation' (ver. 16). 'By one offence judgment came upon all men to condemnation' (ver. 18). And since it is so plain that all men are actually punished for Adam's sin, it must needs follow,

vii. That they 'all sinned in Adam'. 'By one man's disobedience[47] many were made sinners.' They were so *constituted sinners* by Adam's sinning as to become liable to the punishment threatened to his transgression.[48]

Between Adam and Christ, the type and the antitype, St. Paul draws the parallel in the following particulars:

i. Both have done something by which many others are affected, who either lose or gain by what they did: 'Through the offence of one many are dead. By one the gift of grace hath abounded to many' (ver. 15).

ii. That which the first Adam did, by which many (i.e. all) men receive hurt, was *sin, offence*, and *disobedience*. They all suffer 'by one that sinned' (ver. 16), 'by the offence of one, by one man's disobedience' (ver. 18-19). That which the second Adam did by which many, that is all[49] who believe, receive benefit is righteousness and obedience: 'by the righteousness of one, by the obedience of one' (ver. 18-19).

iii. The detriment which all men[50] receive through Adam is that they 'are made sinners', that 'judgment is come upon them to condemnation', in consequence of which death, the wages of sin, is inflicted on every one of them. The benefit which all believers[51] receive through Christ is *grace*, or the favour of God. Justification, righteousness or sanctification, and eternal life. 'The grace of God, and the gift by

[47] JW omits 'as their Federal Head'. Ibid., 22.
[48] JW omits a section on the notion of being a federal head. Ibid., 23.
[49] JW omits 'to whom he is Federal Head'. Ibid., 23.
[50] Jennings reads: 'all those whose Federal Head Adam was'. Ibid., 24.
[51] Jennings reads: 'all those whose Federal Head Christ is'. Ibid.

grace, hath by one man, Jesus Christ, abounded to many. By the righteousness of one the free gift came upon all men (who receive it) to justification of life. By the obedience of one many are made righteous' (ver. 15, 18, 19).

Thus the Apostle shows the parity between the effects of Adam's sin and of Christ's righteousness. Only in two instances he shows that the effect of the latter vastly exceeds the effect of the former.

i. It removes many sins besides that one sin of Adam which so affected all his posterity. 'If through one offence many be dead, *MUCH MORE* the grace of God by Jesus Christ hath abounded to many. The judgment was by one to condemnation. But the free gift is of many offences unto justification' (ver. 15-16).

ii. Christ raises believers[52] to a far happier state than that which Adam enjoyed in paradise. '*MUCH MORE* they who receive abundance of grace and of the gift of righteousness shall *REIGN* in life by one, Jesus Christ' (ver. 17).[m]

17. Your paraphrase on the text,[n] being only a repetition of what you had said over and over before, does not require any separate consideration. Only I must observe a few mistakes which have not occurred before. [(1)] 'The resurrection is the first and fundamental step in the gospel salvation.'[o] No. 'He shall save his people from their sins.'[53] This is the first and fundamental step.[54] (2) You have very grievously mistaken the meaning of four texts in the sixth of St. John.[p] 'This is the Father's will, that of all which he hath given me I should lose nothing, but should raise it up again at the last day.'[q] 'This is the will of him that sent me, that everyone that seeth the Son and believeth on him should have everlasting life, and I will raise him up at the last day.'[r] 'No man can come to me except the Father draw him, and I will raise him up at the last day.'[s] 'Whoso eateth my flesh and drinketh my blood hath eternal life, and I will raise him up at the last day.'[t] Now you cite all these texts as relating

[m] [Ibid., pp. 20-25].

[n] [Taylor, *Scripture Doctrine*,] pp. 55-64.

[o] p. 61.

[p] [pp. 61-62n.]

[q] ver. 39.

[r] ver. 40.

[s] ver. 44.

[t] ver. 54.

---

[52] Jennings reads: 'his people' (ibid., 25); i.e., the elect.

[53] Matt. 1:21.

[54] Taylor, *Reply* (1767), 12: 'A misrepresentation. See *Script. Doct.*, p. 61.' For Taylor, the restoring to *all* humans of life after death is prior logically to providing the gracious means for this afterlife to be blessed.

to the *general resurrection*.[55] Whereas not one of them relates to it at all. They are all promises made to true believers only, and relate wholly and solely to the 'resurrection of the just'.[56]

18. It remains then, all that has been advanced to the contrary notwithstanding, that the only true and rational way of accounting for the general wickedness of mankind in all ages and nations is pointed out in those words, 'In Adam all die.' In and through their first parent *all* his posterity *died* in a spiritual sense. And they remain wholly 'dead in trespasses and sins'[57] till the second Adam makes them alive. 'By' this 'one man sin entered into the world, and passed upon all men'.[58] And through the infection which they derive from him all men are and ever were 'by nature'[59] entirely 'alienated from the life of God, without hope, without God in the world'.[60]

[II.] 1. Your *Appendix* to the first part of your book is wholly employed in answering two questions. 'One is, "How is it consistent with justice that all men should die by the disobedience of one man?" The other, "How shall we account for all men's rising again by the obedience of another man, Jesus Christ?" '[u]

You may determine the former question as you please, since it does not touch the main point in debate. I shall therefore take no farther pains about it than to make a short extract of what Dr. J[ennings] speaks on the head:

2. As to the first question, Mr. T[aylor] gets rid of all difficulty that may arise from the consideration of God's justice by ascribing it wholly to his goodness, that 'death passed upon all men'. 'Death', he tells us, is 'upon the whole a benefit.' It is certain that believers in Christ receive benefit by it. But this gentleman will have death to be an original benefit, and that to all mankind, merely intended 'to increase the vanity of all earthly things, and to abate their force to delude us'. He afterward displays the benefit of shortening human life to its present standard: 'That death

[u] [Taylor, *Scripture-Doctrine*,] p. 65.

[55] Ibid.: 'A misrepresentation. It is false. I cite them as relating to the gospel salvation in eternal life, or as they relate to the "resurrection of the just".' Note *Scripture-Doctrine*, 62n, where Taylor stresses that restoration to eternal life is not a 'blessing' for the unjust.

[56] Luke 14:14.

[57] Eph. 2:1.

[58] Rom. 5:12.

[59] Eph. 2:3.

[60] Eph. 4:18.

being nearer to our view might be a powerful motive to regard less the things of a transitory world.' But does the 'nearer view of death' in fact produce this effect? Does not the common observation of all ages prove the contrary? Has not covetousness been the peculiar vice of old age? As death is nearer to the view we plainly see that men have more and more regard for the things of a transitory world. We are sure therefore that death is no such benefit to the generality of men. On the contrary, it is the king of terrors to them, the burden of their lives, and bane of their pleasures. To talk therefore of death's being a benefit, an original benefit, and that to all mankind, is to talk against the common sense and experience of the whole world.

'Tis strange death should be originally given by God as a benefit to man, and that the shortening of man's life afterward should be designed as a farther benefit—and yet that God should so often promise his peculiar people long life as the reward of obedience, and threaten them with death as a punishment of disobedience!

But 'the Scripture', he says, 'affirms that sufferings are the chastisement of our heavenly Father, and death in particular'. But does not every chastisement suppose a fault? Must he not be a cruel Father who will chasten his children for no fault at all? If then God does but chasten us for Adam's sin, the fault of it must some way lie upon us. Else we suppose God's dealings with his children to be unreasonable and unrighteous.[v]

3. I would only add two or three obvious questions. (1) Did God propose death as a benefit in the original threatening? (2) Did he represent it as a benefit in the sentence pronounced on Adam, 'Dust thou art, and unto dust thou shalt return'?[61] (3) Do the inspired writers speak of God's 'bringing a flood on the world of the ungodly'[62] as a *benefit* or a *punishment*? (4) Do they mention the destruction of Sodom and Gomorrah as designed for a benefit to them? (5) Is it by way of benefit that God declares, 'The soul that sinneth, it shall die'?[63] Certainly this point is not defensible. Death is properly not a benefit but a punishment.

4. The other question is: 'How shall we account for all men's rising again by the obedience of another man, Jesus Christ?'[w]

'To set this in a clear light I ask another question, [. . .] What was it that gave the glorious personage emblemized by "the Lamb" (Rev. 5:1, etc.) his superior *WORTHINESS*, his prevailing *INTEREST*

[v] [Jennings] *Vindication*, p. 36, etc. [i.e., pp. 36-41].
[w] [Taylor, *Scripture-Doctrine*,] p. 70.

[61] Gen. 3:19.
[62] 2 Pet. 2:5.
[63] Ezek. 18:4, 20.

IN GOD,[64] beyond all others in heaven and earth? It was his *being slain*, that is, his *obedience* to God, and *goodwill* to men; it was his consummate *VIRTUE*. "Thou art worthy."—Why? Because thou hast exhibited to God such an instance of *virtue, obedience*, and *goodness*. Thou hast sacrificed thy life in the cause of truth, and hast redeemed us by that act of the highest obedience.'[x]

With what extreme wariness is this whole paragraph worded! You do not care to say directly, 'Jesus Christ is either a little God or he is no God at all.'[65] So you say it indirectly, in an heap of smooth, laboured, decent circumlocutions. Yet permit me to ask, was 'that *act* of obedience the *original* and *sole* ground' of his prevailing *INTEREST IN GOD* and of his *WORTHINESS*, not only 'to open the book', but 'to receive' from all the armies of heaven 'the power, and the riches, and the wisdom, and the strength; and the honour and the glory, and the blessing'?[y] And is this *act* the *original* and the *sole* ground why 'all men' must 'honour him even as they honour the Father'?[66] Yea, and why 'every creature which is in the heaven, and on the earth, and under the earth, and on the sea, and all that are in them, say, To him that sitteth on the throne and to the Lamb is the blessing, and the honour and the glory and the power, for ever and ever!'[z]

To 'him that sitteth on the throne and to the Lamb.'—Does that mean, to the great God and the little God? If so, when all 'creatures in heaven and earth', all throughout the universe, thus 'honour him even as they honour the Father',[67] are they not doing him too much honour? 'My glory', saith the Lord, 'I will not give to another.'[68] How comes it then to be given to 'the Lamb'?

5. You proceed: 'The *WORTHINESS* of Christ is his consummate *VIRTUE*, *obedience* to God and *benevolence* to his creatures.'[a] Is this the *only* ground of his *WORTHINESS* to be 'honoured even

[x] pp. 71-72 [i.e., 70-72].
[y] Rev. 5:12.
[z] [Rev.] 5:13.
[a] [Taylor, *Scripture-Doctrine*, p. 72.]

[64] Wesley adds this emphasis; cf. Taylor, *Scripture-Doctrine*, 72.
[65] JW is implying that Taylor is at least an Arian and perhaps Socinian in his view of Christ. See discussion in the general introduction above, pp.120, 125.
[66] Cf. John 5:23.
[67] Ibid.
[68] Isa. 42:8.

as the Father'? Is it on this ground *alone* that 'all the angels of God' are to 'worship him'?[69] Or rather, because 'in the beginning', from everlasting, he 'was with God and was God'?[70]

'Virtue is the only *price* which *purchaseth* everything with God. True *VIRTUE*, or the right exercise of reason, is true *worth*, and the only *valuable consideration* which prevails with God.'[b]

Do you then conceive this to be the exact meaning of St. Paul when he says, 'Ye are bought with a price'?[71] And that where he speaks of 'the Church of God which he hath purchased with his own blood',[72] he means, with his 'own *VIRTUE*'? Agreeably to which, 'Thou hast redeemed us by thy blood'[73] must mean by the 'right exercise of thy reason'! Well then might Father Socinus say, '*Tota redemptionis nostrae per Christum metaphora*'—'the whole metaphor of our redemption by Christ'.[74] For on this scheme there is nothing *real* in it.

'It was not the mere *natural power* or strength of the Lamb, but his most *excellent character*.'[c]—Sir, do you 'honour the Son, even as you honour the Father'?[75] If you did, could you possibly talk of him in this strain?

However, all this does not affect the question. But it still remains an unshaken truth that all men's *dying* in Adam is the grand cause why 'the whole world lieth in wickedness'.[76]

Newington, Jan. 18, 1757

[III.] 1. In your *Second Part* you profess to 'examine the principal passages of Scripture which divines have applied in support of the

[b] pp. [72-]73.
[c] [pp. 73-74.]

[69] Heb. 1:6.
[70] John 1:1.
[71] 1 Cor. 6:20.
[72] Acts 20:28.
[73] Rev. 5:9.
[74] This is an exact quotation of the opening summary of Faustus Socinus, *De Jesu Christo Servatore, hoc est, cur & qua ratione Jesus Christus noster servator sit* (Raków: Alexius Rocecki, 1594), Pt. II, chap. 2 (p. 76). Wesley was likely citing from Socinus, *Opera omnia*, 2 vols. (Irenopoli, 1656), 2:143. JW also quotes this phrase in his letter to George Whitefield, Apr. 27, 1741, 26:60 in this edn.; and letter to John Robertson, Sept. 24, 1753, 26:522 in this edn.
[75] Cf. John 5:23.
[76] 1 John 5:19.

doctrine of original sin, particularly those cited by "the Assembly of Divines" in their *Larger Catechism'*.[d] To this I never subscribed; but I think it is in the main a very excellent composition. Which I shall therefore cheerfully endeavour to defend, so far as I conceive it is grounded on clear Scripture.[77]

But I would first observe in general, with Dr. J[ennings], that there are two kind of texts in the ensuing collection: 'some that *directly prove*, others that *properly illustrate* the doctrine of original sin. And there are so many in which it is either directly spoken of, or evidently implied, that the author might well have spared his observation, "The Scripture speaks very sparingly of the consequences of Adam's sin upon us, because as these are freely reversed to mankind by Christ, we are not so much concerned to know them."[e] The fact here affirmed is equally true with the reason assigned for it'.[78]

2. The first proposition in the *Catechism* which relates to original sin is this:[79]

'The covenant being made with Adam as a public person, not for himself only but for his posterity, all mankind descending from him by ordinary generation sinned with[80] him, and fell with him in that first transgression.'

Acts 17:26. 'God hath made of one blood all nations of men'. . . .[f]
I believe Dr. J[ennings]'s remark here will suffice:

> This is quoted to prove that all mankind descend from Adam. But Mr. T[aylor] adds, 'that is, hath made all the nations of the world of one species, endowed with the same faculties'. And so they might have been, if all men had been created singly and separately, just as Adam was. But they could not then, with any propriety of language, have been said to be 'of one blood'. This Scripture therefore is very pertinently quoted to prove what it is brought for. That 'Adam was a public person, including all his posterity, and consequently that all mankind descending from him by ordinary generation sinned in him, and fell with him in his first transgression',

[d] pp. 87-88 [i.e., 86-87].
[e] p. 50.
[f] pp. 91-92.

---

[77] For indication of some places where JW thought it was *not* in line with the clear teachings of Scripture, see his abridgment of *Shorter Catechism* (above in this vol.).

[78] Jennings, *Vindication*, 48-49.

[79] Taylor is working in serial order through *QQ*. 22-29 of the *Larger Catechism*.

[80] Taylor, *Scripture-Doctrine*, accurately quoting the *Larger Catechism, Q*. 22, said 'sinned in him' (p. 91).

the Assembly have proved very methodically and substantially. First from Gen. 2:16-17, where death is threatened to Adam in case of his sinning; then from Rom. 5:12-20 and 1 Cor. 15:21-2[2], where we are expressly told that 'all men die in Adam', and that 'by his offence, judgment is come upon all men to condemnation.'[g]

Prop[osition]. 'All mankind sinned in him, and fell with him in that first transgression.'[h] Which they prove by Gen. 2:16-17, compared with Rom. 5:12-20.

On this you remark, 'The threatening, "Thou shalt surely die," is addressed to Adam personally. And therefore nothing can be concluded thence with regard to Adam's posterity.'[i] Is this consequence good? Was not the sentence also grounded on this threatening, 'Unto dust thou shalt return', personally directed to him? And is this nothing to his posterity?[81] Nay, does it not from this very consideration appear that all his posterity were concerned in that threatening, because they are all partakers of the death which was so threatened to Adam?

'But we cannot gather from Rom. 5 or 1 Cor. 15 "that all mankind sinned in Adam", if we understand *sinned* as distinguished from *suffering*.'[[j]] It has been largely proved that we can, and that *sinning* must necessarily be understood there as distinguished from *suffering*.

'But the Apostle says, "The offence of one" brought death into the world, whereas had all mankind sinned in Adam when he sinned, then that offence would not have been "the offence of one", but of *MILLIONS*.'[k] It might be in one sense the offence of *millions*, and in another 'the offence of one'.

'It is true, Adam's posterity so "fell with him in that first transgression" that if the threatening had been immediately executed he would have had no posterity at all.'[[l]] The threatening! What was the threatening to them?[82] Did not you assure us, in the very last page,

[g] [Jennings,] *Vindication*, p. 49, etc. [i.e., 49-50].
[h] [Taylor, *Scripture-Doctrine*,] pp. 93-94.
[i] p. 94.
[[j]] [Ibid.]
[k] p. 95 [i.e., 94-95].
[[l]] [p. 95.]

[81] Taylor, *Reply* (1767), 12: 'We could not have certainly known that this sentence affected Adam's posterity had not the Apostle told us that it did, Rom. 5:12-20. We might have supposed that we died for our own offences, or by the mere will and pleasure of God.'

[82] Ibid., 13: 'The *execution* of the threatening, of which I am speaking, was of great importance to them.'

'The threatening is addressed to Adam personally; and therefore nothing can be concluded from thence with regard to his posterity'?[m]

And here you say their very 'existence did certainly fall under *the threatening* of the law and into the hands of the judge to be disposed of as he should think fit'.[n] 'As he should think fit'! Then he might without any injustice have deprived them of all blessings—of being itself, the only possible ground of all! And this, for 'the sin of another'!

You close the article thus: 'We cannot from those passages conclude that mankind by Adam's offence incurred any evil but *temporal death*!'[o] Just the contrary has been shown at large.

3. Their second proposition is, 'The fall brought mankind into a state[83] of sin and misery.'[p]

To prove this they cite Rom. 5:12, a proof which all the art of man cannot evade; and Rom. 3:23, 'All have sinned, and come short of the glory of God.' 'But this', you say, 'means only, Jews as well as Gentiles, men of all nations, "have sinned".'[q] Nay, it is most certain, as Dr. J[ennings] observes, that he

> means all men of all nations, or he means nothing to the purpose of his conclusion and his inferences (ver. 19-22). The Apostle concludes from the view he had given before of the universal corruption of mankind that 'every mouth must be stopped, and all the world become guilty before God' (ver. 19). From whence he draws two inferences: (1) 'Therefore by the works of the law there shall no flesh be justified.' (2) The only way of justification for all sinners is 'by faith in Jesus Christ'. 'For there is no difference' as to the way of justification; 'for all have sinned and come short of the glory of God.' And therefore whoever they are whom Mr. T[aylor] excludes from this 'all' ('all have sinned')[84] he must likewise excuse from having any need of justification by Christ.[r]

[m] [p. 94.]
[n] [p. 95.]
[o] [Ibid.]
[p] p. 96.
[q] p. 97 [i.e., 96-97].
[r] [Jennings,] *Vindication*, p. 50, etc. [i.e., pp. 51-52].

[83] Taylor, *Scripture-Doctrine*, accurately quoting the *Larger Catechism, Q.* 23, said 'estate' (p. 96).

[84] Taylor, *Reply* (1767), 13: 'I exclude none from that "all".'

Be this as it may, it is certain, (1) that mankind are now *in a state of sin and suffering*. (2) That they have been so in all ages, nearly from the time that Adam fell. Now if his fall did not *bring them into* that state, I would be glad to know, What did?

4. Their third proposition is: 'Sin is any want of conformity to[85] or transgression of the law of God, given as a rule to the reasonable creature.' 'This', you say, 'has no immediate relation to our present design.'[s] But it had to theirs, which was to illustrate the preceding assertion, 'that the fall of Adam brought mankind into a state of sin', in both these senses of the word.

5. Their fourth proposition is: 'The sinfulness of that state[86] into which man fell consists in the guilt of Adam's first sin, the want of that righteousness wherein he was created, and the corruption of his nature, whereby he is utterly indisposed, disabled, and made opposite to all that is spiritually good, and wholly inclined to evil,[87] and that continually, which is commonly called original sin, and from which do proceed all actual transgressions.'

On the first article of this you say: 'Adam's first sin was attended with consequences which affect all his posterity. But we could not on account of his sin become obnoxious to *punishment*.'[t] By *punishment* I mean *evil* suffered on account of *sin*. And are we not obnoxious to any evil on account of Adam's sin?

To prove the rest of the proposition they cite first, Rom. 3:10-20. On which you remark, 'The Apostle is here speaking of Jews and Gentiles, not in a *personal*, but in a *national* capacity. "The mouth", says he, of all sorts of people "is stopped", and both Jews and Gentiles are "brought in guilty". For I have proved that there are transgressors among the Jews as well as among the Gentiles.'[u] Not at all. If he proved no more than this not one person would 'become guilty before God'. Not one 'mouth', of Jew or Gentile, would 'be stopped' by showing 'there were Jewish as well as heathen transgressors'.

[s] [Taylor, *Scripture-Doctrine*,] p. 98.
[t] p. 99.
[u] p. 102.

---

[85] Taylor, *Scripture-Doctrine*, accurately quoting the *Larger Catechism*, *Q.* 24, said 'unto' (p. 98).

[86] Taylor, ibid., accurately quoting the *Larger Catechism*, *Q.* 25, said 'estate' (pp. 89, 98).

[87] Taylor, ibid., accurately quoting the *Larger Catechism*, *Q.* 25, said 'all evil' (pp. 89, 100).

I proceed to your observations.

'*Obs*. 1. In this whole section there is not one word of Adam.'[v] There is enough in the next chapter but one. The Apostle first describes the effect, and afterward points out the cause.

'*Obs*. 2. He is here speaking not of all men, but of the Jews, of those *alone* who were "under the law" (ver. 19), and proving from their own writings that there were great corruptions among them as well as other people.'[w]

He is speaking of them *chiefly*, but not of them *only*, as appears from the ninth verse: 'We have before proved both Jews and Gentiles, that they are all under sin. As it is written, There is none righteous' (neither among the Jews nor Gentiles) 'no, not one.' Does this respect them in their *national* only, not *personal* capacity? Does it prove no more than 'that there were great corruptions among the Jews as well as other people'?

'*Obs*. 3. The section consists of several quotations out of the Old Testament. But, (1) none of them, taken separately, speaks of any depravity of nature, but of habits of wickedness, which men had themselves contracted.'[x] They do speak of habits which men had contracted themselves. But do they speak of these *only*? The way to know this is, not to 'take them *separately*', not to consider the precise meaning wherein they were occasionally spoken by David, Solomon, or Isaiah, but to take them *conjointly*, as they are here put together by the Holy Ghost to form the character of all mankind.

On one of them, '*separately* taken', you say: 'How could God "look down from heaven to see if there were any that did seek God", if he knew all mankind were *naturally* disabled from seeking him?'[y] Why not, if whatever they were by *nature*, the *grace of God* was more or less given to all? Though they were 'wholly inclined to all evil by nature', yet by *grace* they might recover all goodness.[88]

[v] [Ibid.]
[w] pp. [102-]103.
[x] p. 103.
[y] [Ibid., citing Ps. 14:2.]

[88] Taylor had quoted the *Catechism* more fully here, '. . . all mankind were naturally corrupted, and "utterly indisposed, disabled and made opposite unto all that is spiritually good, and wholly *and continually* inclined to all evil"'. *Scripture-Doctrine,* 103, emphasis added. JW is invoking his personal conviction about universal prevenient grace without admitting that it is not affirmed in the document that Taylor is specifically criticizing.

You affirm, (2) 'In none of these places does God speak strictly of every individual Jew under David or Solomon. Very many were bad, but some were good.'[z] They were; though by grace, not nature. But among all those of whom God speaks by St. Paul, 'there was none' good or 'righteous, no, not one'—every individual, whether Jew or heathen, was 'guilty before God'.

'I conclude therefore, (1) that none of these texts refer to any corruption common to all mankind.'[a] Perhaps they do not, as spoken by David. But they do as spoken by St. Paul. 'I conclude, (2) such a general corruption as admits of no exception was not necessary to the Apostle's argument.'[b] Absolutely necessary. Had it not included 'every individual person, no person's mouth' would have been 'stopped'.

These texts therefore do 'directly and certainly prove' that at the time when the Apostle wrote every individual Jew and Gentile (except only those who were 'saved by grace')[89] *were all under sin.*[90] That 'there was none of them righteous, no, not one. None that understood' or 'that sought after God'.[91] This was the fact. And who can find out a more rational way of accounting for this universal wickedness than by an universal corruption of our nature, derived from our first parent?

6. The next proof is Eph. 2:1-3, 'And you hath he quickened, who were dead in trespasses and sins. Wherein in time past ye walked, according to the course of this world, according to the prince of the power of the air, the spirit that now worketh in the children of disobedience. Among whom also we all had our conversation in times past, in the desires of our flesh, fulfilling the desires of the flesh and of the mind; and were by nature the children of wrath, even as others.'

1) 'Nothing is here intimated of any ill effects of Adam's sin upon us.'[c] No? Not if we are 'children of wrath by nature'?

[z] p. 104 [i.e., 104-5].
[a] pp. 106-7.
[b] [p. 107.]
[c] p. 108.

---

[89] Cf. Eph. 2:5, 8.

[90] Contrast Taylor's insistence that these texts 'directly and certainly prove no more than that there were in those times, even among the Jews some, and sometimes great numbers, that were wicked'. *Scripture-Doctrine*, 107-8.

[91] Cf. Rom. 3:10-11.

2) 'The Ephesians were Gentiles converted to the faith.'[d] Yea, and Jews also. In this very passage the Apostle speaks of both, first the Gentile, then the Jewish converts.

3) 'In these verses he is describing their wretched state while they were in Gentile darkness'[e]—and while they were in Jewish darkness, the Jews having been just as wicked before their conversion as the heathens. Both the one and the other had 'walked' till then 'in the vanity of their mind, having their understanding darkened', being equally 'dead in trespasses and sins', equally 'alienated from the life of God through the blindness of their heart'[92]—a very lively description, not so much of a wicked life, as of an evil nature.

4) 'When he saith they were "dead in trespasses and sins", he speaks of their personal iniquities.'[f] (True, both of *heart* and *life*.[93] I must make some variation in the rest of your paraphrase.)[94] ' "Wherein", saith he, "in times past ye", heathens particularly, "walked", inwardly and outwardly, "according to the prince of the power of the air, the spirit that now"—still—"worketh in the children of disobedience. Among whom we Jews also had our conversation", being as "dead in trespasses and sins" as you.'

'Therefore, (5) when he adds, "and were by nature the children of wrath, even as others", he cannot mean, they were liable to wrath "by" that "nature" which they brought into the world.'[g] Why not? This does not follow from anything you have said yet. Let us see how you prove it now. 'This nature is no other than God's own work. The nature of every man comes out of the hands of God.'[h] The same may be said of those who are still 'dead in trespasses and sins'. Their *original nature* came from God, and was no other than God's own work. Yet the *present corruption* of their nature came not from God, and is not his work. 'Consequently the *nature* of every person

[d] [Ibid.]
[e] [Ibid.]
[f] p. 109.
[g] p. 110.
[h] [Ibid.]

[92] Eph. 4:17-18.

[93] Remember JW's mature moral psychology, that sinful acts flow from a sinful heart (or tempers). See the introduction (pp. 144-45 above).

[94] In the following quotation Wesley inserts as his own emphases the phrases 'heathens particularly', 'inwardly and outwardly', and 'still'. Cf. Taylor, *Scripture-Doctrine*, 109.

when brought into being is just what God sees fit it should be.'[i] This is true of the *original nature* of mankind, when it was first 'brought into being'. But it is not true of our 'present corrupt nature'. This is not what God sees fit it should be. 'It is his power alone that forms it.'[j] Yes, that forms us *men*. But not that forms us *sinful men*. 'To say the nature he gives is the object of his wrath is little less than blasphemy.'[k] As he gave it, it is not the object of his wrath. But it is as it is defiled with sin. 'Far was it from the Apostle to depreciate our *nature*.'[l] True, our *original nature*. But never did man more deeply depreciate our *present, corrupt nature*.[95] 'His intent is to show the Ephesians, they were "children of wrath", through the "sins in which they walked".'[m] Yea, and through 'the desires of the flesh and the mind' mentioned immediately before—'through the vanity of their mind', through 'the blindness of their hearts, past feeling, alienated from the life of God.' Is he 'not here speaking of their *nature*, but of the vicious course of life they had led'?[n] 'He well understood the worth of the human nature'[o]—he did, both in its *original*, and in its *present* state—'And elsewhere shows, it was endowed, even in the heathens, with light and power sufficient to know God, and obey his will.'[p] In what heathens, in Europe, Asia, Africa, or America, is nature now endowed with this light and power?[96] I have never found it in any heathen yet—and I have conversed with many, of various nations. On the contrary, I have found one and all deeply ignorant of the very end of their existence. All of them have confirmed what an heathen *meeko* (or chief) told me many years ago, 'He that sitteth in heaven knoweth *why he made man*. But we know nothing.'[97]

[i] [Ibid.]
[j] [Ibid.]
[k] [Ibid.]
[l] [Ibid.]
[m] [Ibid.]
[n] p. 111.
[o] [Ibid.]
[p] [Ibid.]

[95] In other writings, JW insists that no one actually exists solely in this state of corrupt nature, apart from the initial restoring presence of God's prevenient grace; e.g, Sermon 85, "On Working Out Our Own Salvation," III.3-4, 3:207 in this edn.

[96] Compare JW's suggestion in his later years that God may have taught some heathens all the essentials of true religion by an inward voice. Sermon 106, 'On Faith', I.4, 3:494 in this edn.

[97] Wesley is likely recalling one of his conversations with Tomochici, a *meeko* of the Creek nation; cf. above, Pt. I, II.3 (p. 180, n. 108).

'But St. Paul says, "When the Gentiles which have not the law do by nature the things contained in the law, they are a law to themselves." This supposes they might have done them "by nature", or their *natural powers*.'[q] But how does it appear that 'by nature' here means 'by their *mere* natural powers'? It is certain, they 'had not the' written 'law'. But had they no *supernatural assistance*? Is it not one God, 'who works in' us and in them, 'both to will and to do'?[98] They who by *this help* do the things contained in the law we grant 'are not the objects of God's wrath'.[r]

'Again, he affirms, the Gentiles had light sufficient to have seen God's eternal power and godhead.'[s] They had. But how does it appear that this was the *merely natural* light of their own *unassisted* reason?[99] If they had assistance from God, and did not use it, they were equally 'without excuse'. 'Nay, if their nature was corrupt, and therefore they "did not glorify God", they had a fair excuse.'[t] True, if God had not offered them grace to balance the corruption of nature. But if he did, they are still 'without excuse'—because they might have conquered that corruption and would not. Therefore we are not 'obliged to seek any other sense of the phrase, "by nature", than "by the nature" we bring into the world'.[100]

However, you think you have found another. ' "By nature" may signify "really and truly". [. . .] Thus St. Paul calls Timothy γνήσιον τέκνον, his "own, genuine son in the faith"—not to signify he was the *child* of the Apostle, but that he was a *real* imitator of his faith. In like manner he calls the Ephesians φύσει τέκνα, "genuine children of wrath", not to signify they were related to *wrath* by their *natural birth*, but by their *sin* and *disobedience*.'[u]

This is simply begging the question, without so much as a shadow of proof. For the Greek word in one text is not the same, nor any way related to that in the other. Nor is there the least resemblance

[q] [Ibid.]
[r] [Ibid.]
[s] Rom. 1:19-21 [cited by Taylor, *Scripture-Doctrine*, pp. 111-12].
[t] [Taylor, *Scripture-Doctrine*,] p. 112.
[u] p. 113 [i.e., a distillation of 112-14].

[98] Phil. 2:13.

[99] As JW insists in his comment on Rom. 3:14 in *NT Notes* (1755), 'this also, strictly speaking, is by preventing grace'.

[100] Taylor had claimed we *are* obliged to seek some other sense than this. Cf. *Scripture-Doctrine*, 112.

between the Apostle's calling Timothy his 'own son in the faith', and his affirming that even those who are now 'saved by grace' were 'by nature children of wrath'.

To add therefore, 'not as they came under "condemnation by the offence of Adam" '[v] is only begging the question once more. Though it is true, they had afterwards inflamed their account by 'their own "trespasses and sins" '.

You conclude, ' "By nature", therefore, may be a metaphorical expression, and consequently is not intended' ('May be' in the premise, 'is not' in the conclusion! A way of arguing you frequently use) 'to signify "nature" in the proper sense of the word, but to mean they were *really* and *truly* children of wrath.'[w] But where is the proof? Till this is produced I must still believe, with the Christian Church in all ages, that all men are 'children of wrath by nature' in the plain, proper sense of the word.

7. The next proof is Rom. 5:6, 'While we were yet without strength, in due time Christ died for the ungodly.' You answer, (1) 'The Apostle is here speaking not of mankind in general, but *of the Gentiles only*, as appears by the whole thread of his discourse from the beginning of the Epistle.'[x] From the beginning of the Epistle to the sixth verse of the fifth chapter is the Apostle speaking *of the Gentiles only*? Otherwise it cannot appear 'by the whole thread of his discourse from the beginning of the Epistle'. 'But it appears especially from Chap. 3, ver. 9: "What then? Are we Jews better than they Gentiles?" '[y] Nay, from that very verse he speaks chiefly of the Jews. And you yourself, a few pages ago,[z] roundly affirmed 'that he there spoke of *the Jews only*'.[101]

[v] [p. 114.]
[w] p. 114.
[x] p. 115 [i.e., 114-15].
[y] [Ibid.]
[z] p. 102, etc.

[101] Taylor, *Reply* (1767), 13:

'This paragraph, with the two following, is a gross misrepresentation. The whole thread of his discourse, from the beginning of the Epistle, may clearly prove that the Apostle is speaking of the Gentiles only in Rom. 5:6, though he may, in the preceding thread of his discourse, mention the Jews, by way of comparing them with the Gentiles.'

And will you affirm that in the fourth chapter likewise 'he is speaking of the Gentiles only'? Is it not manifest that he does not speak of them at all in a considerable part of that chapter? How then does it appear, by 'the whole thread of his discourse from the beginning of the Epistle', that 'he is here speaking not of mankind in general, but of the Gentiles only'?

However, you boldly go on: 'Having established the point that the Gentiles have as good a title to God's favour as the Jews'[a]—How? Is this the only, or the chief point which St. Paul establishes in the fourth chapter? Is not his main point throughout that chapter to prove that both Jews and Gentiles were *justified by faith*? Or is he 'speaking this not of mankind in general, but of the Gentiles *only*'? 'He proceeds, Chapter 5:1, "Therefore being justified by faith, we Gentiles have peace with God." '[b] In the same manner you thrust in the word Gentiles into each of the following verses. Had then the Gentiles only 'peace with God'? You might with more colour have inserted Jews in every verse. For of them *chiefly* the Apostle had been speaking. To say that 'he principally speaks *of* and *to* the Gentiles, to the end of the sixth chapter',[c] is another assertion which cannot be proved. It is therefore by no means true that 'he is in this verse speaking of the Gentiles, in contradistinction to the Jews.'[d]

You affirm, (2) 'By the same argument, he here considers the Gentiles only in a *body*, as distinguished from the *body* of the Jews. For so he does all along in the four first chapters.'[e] No, not in one of them. If he had, the 'mouth' of no one individual person had been 'stopped'. On the contrary he speaks both here and all along of every individual, that everyone might believe in him 'who died for' *every one* of 'the ungodly'.

You affirm, (3) 'In this verse he describes the condition of the converted Gentiles when in their heathen state, in which they 'were without strength' [(Rom. 5:6)], unable to recover themselves. They were *ungodly*, yea *sinners*, and *enemies* to God.'[f] And were not the unconverted Jews also *sinners*, and *enemies to* God, *ungodly*, and *without strength* to recover themselves? These four characters therefore are no proof at all 'that the Gentiles only are here spoken of'.

[a] p. 116.
[b] [Ibid.]
[c] p. 117.
[d] [Ibid.]
[e] [Ibid.]
[f] p. 118.

'Their *sin* and *enmity* and *ungodliness* consisted in their *wicked works*.'[g] Primarily in their *wicked tempers*.[102] But how came all men, Jews and Gentiles, to have those wicked *tempers*, and to walk in those wicked *works*? How came they all, till converted, to be 'dead in sin' and 'without strength' to recover from it? Unless 'in Adam all died',[103] in a deeper sense than you are willing to allow.

You sum up your argument thus: 'The Apostle is not speaking here of all mankind's being corrupted in Adam, but of the Gentiles being corrupted by the idolatry and wickedness into which they had plunged themselves, and out of which they were unable to recover themselves without the extraordinary interposal of divine grace.'[h]

If this was the case of the heathens only, then the Jews were not 'without strength', but were able to recover themselves from their wickedness without any such interposal! But with regard to the heathens I ask, (1) Was this the state of all heathen nations, or of some only? (2) If of some only, which were they that were not corrupted? (3) If it was the state of all heathen nations, how came it to be so? How was it that there was not one uncorrupted nation on earth? (4) How could any heathen nation be in this state? 'Without strength'? 'Unable to recover themselves' from sin without the extraordinary interposal of the divine grace? Since you are clear in this, that 'all the Gentiles are endowed with light and power sufficient to know God, and perform obedience to his will, by their *natural powers* of reason and understanding'.[i] If you say, 'They were once endowed with these powers, but now they had cast them away;' I am not satisfied still. What, did all nations cast away their 'natural powers' of reason and understanding? Surely not! But if not, how came they all to plunge themselves into this dreadful corruption?

8. Another proof is Rom. 8:7-8, 'The carnal mind is enmity against God. For it is not subject to the law of God, neither indeed can be. So then they that are in the flesh cannot please God.'

On this you observe, 'Here is not one word of Adam, or any consequence of his sin upon us.'[j] The whole passage speaks of that corruption of our nature which is the consequence of Adam's sin.

[g] [Ibid.]
[h] p. 120.
[i] p. 111.
[j] [p. 120.]

[102] JW again invokes his mature moral psychology. See introduction (pp. 144-45 above).
[103] 1 Cor. 15:22.

The plain and obvious sense of it is this.[104] Ver. 3, 'What the law could not do' ('in that it was weak through the flesh'—too weak to contend with our corrupt nature), God hath done; 'sending his own Son', he hath 'condemned that sin' which was 'in our flesh'—hath given sentence that it should be destroyed. Ver. 4, 'That the righteousness of the law might be fulfilled in us, who walk not after the flesh, but after the Spirit'—who are guided in all our thoughts, words, and actions not by corrupt nature, but by the Spirit of God. Ver. 5, 'They that are after the flesh'—who are still guided by corrupt nature—'mind the things of the flesh'—have their thoughts and affections fixed on such things as gratify corrupt nature; 'but they that are after the Spirit', who are under his guidance, 'mind the things of the Spirit'—think of, relish, love the things which the Spirit hath revealed, which he moves us to, and promises to give us. Ver. 6, 'For to be carnally minded', to 'mind the things of the flesh', of our corrupt nature, 'is death'— the sure mark of spiritual death, and the way to death everlasting. 'But to be spiritually minded', to *mind* the things of the Spirit, 'is life'—the sure mark of spiritual life, and the way to life everlasting; and attended with the *peace of God*, and *peace with God*, which otherwise can have no place. Ver. 7, 'Because the carnal mind', the mind, taste, inclination, the whole bias of our evil nature, 'is enmity against God. For it is not subject to the law of God, neither indeed can be'—being as opposite thereto as hell to heaven. Ver. 8, 'So then they that are in the flesh'—still unrenewed by the Spirit, still following the bent of corrupt nature[105]—'cannot please God.' Every man now may see whether this passage does not strongly *illustrate* the depravity of our nature.

9. The last proof of this part of the proposition is Gen. 6:5, 'God saw that the wickedness of man was great in the earth, and that every imagination of the thoughts of his heart was only evil continually.' And below, ver. 11, 'The earth was corrupt before God, and the earth was filled with violence.'[k]

[k] p. 122.

[104] Taylor argues that 'the plain and obvious sense' of this text is that those who do the 'things of the flesh' cannot please God, but that it says nothing about human nature being corrupt ever since Adam. *Scripture-Doctrine*, 121.

[105] Taylor, *Reply* (1767), 13: 'In this paragraph "corrupt nature" is arbitrarily inserted.'

'Mankind', you say, 'was universally debauched into lust and sensuality, rapine, and violence.'[l] And how came this *universal wickedness*, if all mankind were quite upright by nature? You answer, 'They had corrupted themselves; so the text, ver. 12: "All flesh had corrupted his way upon the earth." This expression does not necessarily imply any more than that "all flesh", all men, "were corrupted".'[m] But taking it literally I ask, How came all flesh to *corrupt themselves*? 'Oh, by Seth's posterity intermarrying with the Cainites.'[n] But how came 'all the Cainites' to 'corrupt themselves'? And 'all the Sethites' to follow, not reform them? If the balance was even, if nature leaned neither way, there ought to have been as many *good* as *bad* still. And the Sethites ought to have reformed as many of the children of Cain as the Cainites corrupted of the children of Seth. How came it then that *only* 'Noah was a just man'? And does one good man amidst a world of the ungodly prove that the 'nature of mankind in general is not corrupted'?[106] Or rather strongly prove that it is? It does not prove that Noah himself was not naturally inclined to evil; but it does, that the world was.

'But if the corruption of nature was the reason why the old world was destroyed, it is a reason for the destruction of the world at any time.'[o] This *alone* was never supposed to be the reason, but their actual wickedness added thereto.

You add, 'It may be urged that God said (Gen. 8:21), "I will not again curse the ground for man's sake. For the imagination of man's heart is evil from his youth." But the *Hebrew* particle כי sometimes signifies *although*.'[p] That does not prove that it signifies so here. But what if it does? What if the texts be rendered, 'Though the imagination of man's heart is evil from his youth'? Even thus rendered it implies as strongly as it did before that *man's heart* is naturally inclined to evil.

[l] [Ibid.]
[m] [Ibid.]
[n] [Ibid.]
[o] p. 123.
[p] [Ibid.]

[106] Taylor had cited the exception of Noah to disprove the assumption of universal corruption. Cf. *Scripture-Doctrine*, 122-23.

The Hebrew word translated 'youth'[q] is always applied to *childhood* or *tender age*.[107] [In] Isa. 7:16, נער signifies 'a little child'. And none of the texts you have cited prove the contrary. Heman, the author of the 88th Psalm, was doubtless 'afflicted from his youth' or *childhood*. The Babylonians mentioned [in] Isa. 47:12 may well be supposed to have been trained up in the way of their fathers from their 'earliest childhood'. And the plain meaning of Jeremiah, Chap. 3:24-25, 'Shame hath devoured the labour of our fathers from our youth. . . . We lie down in our shame, for we have sinned against the Lord our God, we and our fathers from our youth,' is, ever since we began to think or act, we have gone astray from God.

10. The preceding texts were brought to prove (and they do abundantly prove it)[108] that our nature is deeply corrupted, inclined to evil, and disinclined to all that is spiritually good, so that without supernatural grace we can neither will nor do what is pleasing to God. And this easily accounts for the wickedness and misery of mankind in all ages and nations, whereby experience and reason do so strongly confirm this scriptural doctrine of *Original Sin*.

Yet it will not 'follow that men are no *moral agents*'.[r] If you ask, 'Why, how are they capable of performing duty?' I answer, by grace, though not by nature. And a measure of this is given to all men.[109]

Nor does it follow 'that we can by no means help or hinder that sin which is *natural* to us'.[s] Yes, we can. Anger, for instance, is *natural* to me—yea, irregular, unreasonable anger. I am *naturally* inclined to this, as I experience every day. Yet *I can help it*, by the grace of God, and do so as long as I watch and pray.

Dr. J[ennings] answers this assertion more at large:

[q] p. 124.
[r] p. 125.
[s] [Ibid.]

---

[107] JW is responding to Taylor's argument that the phrase about man's heart being evil 'from his youth' (Gen. 8:21) simply signifies 'the greatness and long duration of a thing', not its actual beginnings. *Scripture-Doctrine*, 124n.

[108] Taylor had insisted it was 'clear and certain that they prove no such thing'. Ibid., 124-25.

[109] Here is another clear allusion to JW's developed doctrine of prevenient grace, but he again carefully avoids mentioning the target of Taylor's attack, the limitation of renewing grace to the 'elect' in the *Larger Catechism*, *Q*. 30. This is the very reason that Wesley deleted the parallel question (*Q*. 20) from his abridgment of the *Shorter Catechism* (see above in this vol.).

'If sin be natural, then it is necessary.'[t] If by sin is meant the corrupt bias of our wills, that indeed is natural to us, as our nature is corrupted by the fall. But not as it came originally out of the hand of God. Therefore it is improperly compared to the appetites of hunger and thirst, which might be in our *original nature*. Now this bias of the will is certainly evil and sinful, and hateful to God. Whether we have contracted it ourselves, or whether we derive it from Adam, makes no difference. A proud or passionate temper is evil, whether a man has contracted it himself, or derived it from his parents. Therefore the inference, 'if natural, and' (in some sense) 'necessary, then no sin', does by no means hold.

But if by *sin* be meant sinful actions, to which this corrupt bias of the will inclines us, it remains to be proved that a corrupt bias of the will makes the actions necessary, and consequently not sinful. And indeed, if a corrupt bias makes sin to be necessary, and consequently to be no sin, then the more any man is inclined to sin, the less sin he can commit. And as that corrupt bias grows stronger, his actual sinning becomes more necessary. And so the man instead of growing more wicked grows more innocent.[u]

11. That this doctrine has been long 'held in the Church of Rome'[v] is true. But so it has in the Greek Church also.[110] And so far as we can learn in every Church under heaven, at least from the time that God spake by Moses.

From this infection of our nature (call it 'original sin' or what you please)[111] spring many, if not all, actual sins. And this St. James plainly intimates, even according to *your* paraphrase on his words: ' "every man is tempted", is overcome by temptation, "when he is drawn away by his own lust," his own *irregular desire*—where the Apostle charges the wickedness of men on its proper cause, their "own lust".'[w] Very true. And *irregular desire* is (not so much a fruit

[t] [Ibid.]
[u] [Jennings,] *Vindication*, p. 68, etc. [i.e., pp. 68-69].
[v] [Taylor, *Scripture-Doctrine*,] p. 126 n.
[w] [pp. 126-27; citing Jas. 1:14.]

[110] JW is correct that the Eastern Christian church also accepted the reality of inherited depravity as the *consequence* of the sin of Adam and Eve. What he does not make clear is that Eastern Christian theologians generally rejected the notion that we inherit the *guilt* of their sin.

[111] Note JW's apparent ambivalence about the term 'original sin', probably because it does not focus solely on inherited depravity. When describing the reality of sinfulness in his sermons, Wesley more commonly turns to terms like 'inbred sin' or 'inbred corruption'. See, e.g., the index of passages on 'Original Sin' in the *Sermons*, 4:728 in this edn.; the term itself occurs in none of the passages! Likewise, when JW referred to Sermon 44, 'Original Sin', among his pastors, he called it a sermon on 'Inbeing Sin' or 'Indwelling Sin'. See respectively the *Minutes* of the 1766 Conference, *Q*.27, 10:324 in this edn., and the 'Large' *Minutes* (1780–89), §57, 10:927 in this edn.

as a) part of original sin. For to say, 'Eve had *irregular desires* before she sinned'[x] is a contradiction,[112] since all irregular desire is sin.

12. Another proof that *actual* sins spring from *original* is Matt. 15:19, 'Out of the heart proceed evil thoughts, murders, adulteries, fornications, thefts, false witness, blasphemies.'

'But what has this text to do with Adam's sin?'[y] It has much to do with the point it is brought to prove, namely, that *actual* sin proceeds from *original, evil works* from an *evil heart*. Do not therefore triumph over these venerable men (as you have done again and again) because a text cited in proof of one clause of a proposition does not prove the whole.[113]

But 'neither of these texts proves that all our wickedness proceeds from our being corrupted by Adam's sin.'[z] But they both prove what they were brought to prove, that all outward wickedness proceeds from inward wickedness. Those pious men therefore did not 'mix the forgery of their own imagination with the truth of God'.[114]

But 'if all actual transgressions proceed from Adam's sin, then he is the only guilty person that ever lived. For if his sin is the cause of all ours, he alone is chargeable with them.'[a]

TRUE—if all our transgressions so proceed from his sin that we cannot possibly avoid them. But this is not the case. By the grace of God we may 'cast away all our transgressions'.[115] Therefore if we do not, they are chargeable on ourselves.[116] We *may* live, but we *will* die.

[x] p. 127.
[y] [p. 128.]
[z] p. 128.
[a] [Ibid.]

[112] Taylor, *Reply* (1767), 14: 'Whether it be or be not a contradiction, I have not spoke in that manner.'

[113] JW is responding to Taylor's demurral: 'I desire it may be observed that I have no design to asperse the memory of the Assembly of Divines, either here or in any other part of the book. 'Tis my opinion they were a body of men not inferior either in understanding or integrity to any in those days.' *Scripture-Doctrine*, 125n.

[114] Taylor had said that *any one* who takes these texts to prove that Adam's sin is the cause of our wickedness, by serving as the source of our corrupt nature, 'manifestly mixeth the forgery of his own imagination with the truth of God'. Ibid., 128.

[115] Cf. Ezek. 18:31.

[116] JW is again assuming the *universal* restoration of the ability to recognize and resist sin in prevenient grace, which restores universal culpability.

Well, but 'on these principles, all actual sins proceed from Adam's sin, either by necessary consequence, or through our own choice; or partly by one, and partly by the other.'[b] Yes, partly by one and partly by the other. We are inclined to evil, antecedently to our own choice. By grace we may conquer this inclination. Or we may *choose* to follow it, and so commit actual sin.

13. Their fifth proposition is: 'Original sin is conveyed from our first parents to[117] their posterity by natural generation, so as all that proceed from them in that way are conceived and born in sin.'[c]

In proof of this they urge, Ps. 51:5, 'Behold, I was shapen in iniquity, and in sin did my mother conceive me.'[d]

On this you observe, 'The word which we translate "shapen" signifies to "bring forth" or "bear". So here it means, "Behold I was brought forth or born in iniquity." '[e]

Suppose it does (which is not plain, for you cannot infer from its meaning so *sometimes* that it means so here), what have you gained? If David was 'born' in iniquity it is little different from being 'shapen' therein.

That the Hebrew word does not always mean 'to be born', but rather to be 'shapen', 'formed', or 'made', evidently appears from Ps. 90:2, where it is applied to the 'formation' of the earth. And in this very text the Seventy render it by ἐπλάσθη,[118] a word of the very same import. It is therefore here very properly rendered 'shapen'. Nor can it be more exactly translated.

But 'the word יחמתני *properly* signifies *warmed me*.'[f] You should say, *literally* signifies. But it signifies *conceived me* nevertheless. And so it is taken [in] Gen. 30:38, 39, 41, etc., 31:10. 'Nay, it signifies there the *act of copulation*. So several translators render it.'[g] And several render it otherwise. So this does not determine the point either way.

[b] p. 129.
[c] p. 130.
[d] p. 131.
[e] [Ibid.]
[f] [Ibid.]
[g] pp. 132-33.

[117] Taylor misquotes the *Larger Catechism, Q.* 26, saying 'to' rather than 'unto' (p. 130); but see p. 89, where he had it correctly.

[118] The Septuagint actually gives the verb (πλάσσω) in the infinitive form: πλασθῆναι. JW has rendered it (on purpose or by faulty memory) in the aorist passive form.

It must therefore be determined by the sense. Now for what end did Jacob put the 'pilled rods before the cattle'?[119] That the lambs might be marked as the rods were. And when is it that females of any kind mark their young? Not in that act, but sometime after, when the foetus is either forming or actually formed. Throw a plum or a pear at a woman before *conception*, and it will not mark the foetus at all. But it will if thrown while she is *conceiving*, or after she has conceived, as we see in a thousand instances.[120] This observation justifies our translators in rendering the word by 'conceiving' in all those places.

And indeed you own, 'David could not apply that word to his mother in the sense wherein you would apply it to the cattle.'[h] You therefore affirm, it means here 'to nurse'.[i] You may as well say, it means 'to roast'. You have as much authority from the Bible for one interpretation as for the other. Produce, if you can, one single text in which יחם signifies to 'nurse', or anything like it.

You stride on, (1) 'The verse means, "In sin did my mother nurse me." (2) That is, I am "a sinner from the womb". (3) That is, "I am a great sinner." (4) That is, "I have contracted strong habits of sin." '[j] By this art you may make the most expressive texts mean just anything or nothing.

'So Ps. 58:3, "The wicked are estranged from the womb. They go astray as soon as they are born, telling lies." That is, my unjust persecutors in Saul's court are exceedingly wicked.'[k] If this was all

[h] [p. 133.]
[i] p. 134.
[j] [Ibid.]
[k] [Ibid.]

[119] Cf. Gen. 30: 8.

[120] Wesley is reflecting the broadly shared view of medicine up to his time (going back to Galen), that the form of the fetus can be 'marked' by incidents that capture the 'imagination' of the mother. A good survey of this traditional assumption, and of some emerging challenges to it in JW's time, can be found in Lester S. King, *The Philosophy of Medicine: The Early Eighteenth Century* (Cambridge, Mass.: Harvard University Press, 1978), 152-81. JW would have encountered this general assumption in Nicholas Malebranche's *Treatise Concerning the Search for Truth* (Oxford: Lichfield, 1694), 58-60. But his most direct source in this instance is likely John Maubray, *The Female Physician* (London: James Holland, 1724), who describes this phenomenon (pp. 57-63) with direct reference to Gen. 30:8 (p. 60) and specifically highlights the potential impact of pears and plums (p. 368). Note as well JW's claim that his elder brother Samuel bore a 'mulberry' birthmark due to his mother's longing for mulberries; in 'Remarks on the Count de Buffon's *Natural History*', *Arminian Magazine* 5 (1782): 547.

David meant, what need of זרו—'are alienated'? And that from the *bowels* of their mother? Nay, but he means as he speaks. They are 'alienated from the life of God', from the time of their coming into the world. From the time of their birth they 'knew not the way of truth'.[121] Neither can, unless they are 'born of God'.

You cite as a parallel text, ' "Thou wast called a transgressor from the womb," that is, set to iniquity by prevailing habits and customs'.[l] Nay, the plain meaning is, the Israelites in general had never kept God's laws since they came into the world.

Perhaps the phrase 'from the womb' is once used figuratively, namely, Job 31:18. But it is manifest that it is to be literally taken [in] Isa. 49:1, 'The Lord hath called me from the womb, from the bowels of my mother hath he made mention of my name'.[122] For, (1) this whole passage relates to Christ, these expressions in particular. (2) This was literally fulfilled when the angel was sent while he was yet in the womb, to order that his 'name' should be 'called Jesus'.[123] This is not therefore barely 'an hyperbolical form of aggravating sin',[m] but an humble confession of a deep and weighty truth, whereof we cannot be too sensible.

'But you have no manner of ground to conclude that it relateth to Adam's sin.'[n] Whether it relates to Adam's personal sin or no, it relates to a *corrupt nature*. This is the present question, and your pulling in Adam's sin only tends to puzzle the reader.

But how do you prove (since you *will* drag this in) that it does not relate to Adam's sin?

Thus: '1) In the whole Psalm there is not one word about Adam or the effects of his sin upon us.'[o] Here, as usual, you blend the two questions together—the ready way to confound an unwary reader. But first, to the first. 'In the whole Psalm there is not one word about Adam. Therefore it relateth not to him.' Just as well you may argue:

[l] [Ibid., citing Isa. 48:8.]
[m] [p. 135.]
[n] p. 136.
[o] [Ibid.]

---

[121] Cf. 2 Pet. 2:2.

[122] Taylor suggested that this use was probably also figurative, meaning early in one's life. *Scripture-Doctrine*, 135.

[123] Cf. Matt. 1:21.

'In the whole Psalm there is not one word about Uriah.[124] Therefore it relateth not to him.' The second assertion, 'There is not one word of the effects of his sin,' is a fair begging the question.

'2) The psalmist is here charging himself with his own sin.'[p] He is—and tracing it up to the fountain.

'3) But according to our version he does not charge *himself* with his sin, but *some other* person. He throws the whole load of his sin from off himself on God who shaped him, and his mother who conceived him.'[q]

What you say might have had weight if he had offered this in *excuse* of his sin, or even in extenuation of it. But does he do this? Does he in fact 'throw the whole blame or any part of it from off himself'? Just the reverse. He acknowledges and bewails *his own* total *iniquity*; not to *excuse*, but to abase himself the more before God for his *inward* as well as *outward* wickedness.

And yet he might, in perfect consistency with this when God had caused 'the bones which had been broken to rejoice',[125] cry out, 'I will praise thee, O God. For I am fearfully and wonderfully made'.[126] Yea, and repeat all that follows in the same Psalm—which proves so much and no more, that every foetus in the womb is formed by the power and wisdom of God. Yet it does not follow that the sin transmitted from the parent 'must be attributed to God'.[127]

'But how could he with pleasure reflect upon his formation, or praise God for it?'[r] As I can at this day—though I know I was 'conceived in sin, and shapen in iniquity'.[128] But 'where sin abounds, grace does much more abound'.[129] I lose less by Adam than I gain by Christ.

[p] [Ibid.]
[q] [pp. 136-37.]
[r] [p. 137.]

---

[124] Taylor, *Reply* (1767), 14: 'But there is a sufficient intimation in the title of the Psalm.' That is, the AV includes a traditional description of Ps. 51 as being a psalm that David wrote after being confronted about committing adultery with Bathsheba, the wife of Uriah.

[125] Cf. Ps. 51:8.

[126] Ps. 139:14. Taylor had quoted this verse as evidence the psalmist did not look upon himself as corrupt when born. *Scripture-Doctrine*, 137. By inserting the prior psalm, JW is portraying it as the praise of one who has been given *new* life.

[127] Taylor, *Scripture-Doctrine*, 137: 'Now if God *shaped* him in the womb, and if he was *then* and *there shapen in iniquity*, pray, tell me, By whom was he *shapen in iniquity*?'

[128] Cf. Ps. 51:5.

[129] Rom. 5:20.

This also perfectly consists with the following verse, ' "Behold, thou desirest truth", or, it is thy will that we should have truth, "in the inward parts".'[130] Thou art willing to remove all that 'iniquity' wherein 'I was shapen', to 'give me a clean heart, and renew a right spirit within me.' 'And in the hidden part thou hast made me to know wisdom.'[131] Thou hast 'shown me what was good'.[132] So that I am every way without excuse. I knew thy will and did it not.

'But if after all you will adhere to the literal sense of this text, why do you not adhere to the literal sense of that text, "This is my body," and believe *transubstantiation*?'[s] For those very reasons which you suggest: (1) Because it is grossly 'absurd to suppose that Christ speaks of' what he then held in his hands as his *real, natural body*.[t] But it is no way absurd to suppose the Psalmist was *conceived in sin*. (2) 'The sense of "This is my body" may be clearly explained by other Scriptures, where the like forms of speech are used.'[u] But there are no other Scriptures where the like forms with this of David are used in any other sense. (3) '*Transubstantiation* is attended with consequences hurtful to piety.'[v] But the doctrine of original sin, and faith grounded thereon, is the only foundation of true piety.[133]

14. The next proof is Job 14:4, 'Who can bring a clean thing out of an unclean? Not one.'

On this you observe, 'Job is here speaking of the weakness of our nature, not with regard to sin, but to the shortness and afflictions of life.'[w] Certainly with regard both to the one and the other. For though in the 1st and 2nd verses he mentions the shortness and troubles of life, yet even these are mentioned with a manifest regard

[s] p. 138.
[t] [pp. 138-39.]
[u] [p. 139.]
[v] [Ibid.]
[w] p. 139.

---

[130] Taylor, *Scripture-Doctrine*, 138, citing Ps. 51:6. Taylor was arguing that this verse is *not* consistent with the assumption that this psalm teaches that all since Adam are 'conceived in sin'.

[131] Ps. 51:6, 10.

[132] Cf. Mic. 6:8.

[133] JW is disagreeing with Taylor on each of these three points. Taylor had argued (1) that it is absurd to assume the psalmist means he was conceived in sin, (2) that he has shown other texts where this expression is used in a figurative sense, and (3) that the doctrine of original sin has consequences hurtful to true piety. *Scripture-Doctrine*, 139.

to sin. This appears from the very next verse: ' "And dost thou open thy eyes upon such a one," to punish one already so wretched, "and bringest me into judgment with thee" '[x] by chastising me still more? It then immediately follows, ' "Who can bring a clean thing out of an unclean? Not one." '[y] It does therefore by no means appear that 'Job is here speaking *only* with regard to the shortness and troubles of life'.[z]

Part of the following verses run thus (ver. 16-17): 'Now thou numberest my steps. Dost thou not watch over my sin? My transgression is sealed up in a bag, and thou sewest up mine iniquity.' Let anyone judge, then, whether Job in this chapter does not speak of the sinfulness as well as the mortality of human nature.

Not that he 'urges his *natural pravity* as a reason why he should not be "brought into judgment".'[a] No more than David urges his being 'shapen in wickedness' as an excuse for that wickedness.[134] Rather Job (as well as David) humbly acknowledges his total sinfulness, confessing that he *deserved* the *judgment*, which yet he prays God not to inflict.

15. Another proof is Job 15:14, 'What is man that he should be clean, and he that is born of a woman, that he should be righteous?'

On this you observe, ' "Born of a woman" signifies no more than *a man*.'[b] Often it does not; but here it is emphatical. 'The phrase indeed includes *frailty* and *imperfection*.'[c] How can that be? Was Adam made *frail* and *imperfect*? And have you forgot that every man is now *born* in as good a state as Adam was *made* at first?[135] 'But it is not to be understood as the reason why man is unclean and unrighteous.'[d] From the placing of the words one would really judge it was. And how do you prove it is not? Why, 'Job and his friends use this

[x] p. 140 [quoting Job 14:3].
[y] [Ibid., quoting Job 14:4.]
[z] [p. 140.]
[a] p. 141.
[b] [Ibid.]
[c] p. 142.
[d] [Ibid.]

---

[134] Taylor had not claimed that either Job or David personally urged that inborn pravity released him from accountability, but that this was the *logical* implication of 'the common scheme of Original Sin'. Ibid., 141.

[135] JW is speaking sarcastically here. Taylor will soon argue against the common model of Adam being created with perfect knowledge and perfect character. Cf. ibid., 170-75, 235-36.

manner of speech in other places of this book. "Shall mortal man be more just than God? Shall a man be more pure than his Maker?" '[e] Nay, this is not the 'manner of speech' which is in question. So you are here quite wide of the mark.

However that is, 'How can man be justified with God? Or how can he be clean that is born of a woman?'[f] And does not this point at original sin? You say, No. For 'if Job and his friends had known that the reason of our uncleanness and imperfection was our receiving a corrupted nature from Adam, they ought to have given this reason of it.'[[g]] And do they not, in the very words before us? You say, 'No. They turn our thoughts to a quite different reason, namely, the uncleanness of the best of creatures in his sight.'[[h]] This is not a different reason, but falls in with the other. And the natural meaning of these texts is, 'How can he be clean that is born of a woman', and so conceived and born in sin? 'Behold, even to the moon, and it shineth not,' compared with God; 'yea, the stars are not pure in his sight! How much less man that is a worm!'[i] In how much higher and stricter a sense is man impure that carries about with him his mortality, the testimony of that *unclean* nature which he brought with him into the world![136]

Shall mortal man be more just than God? ' "Shall a man be more pure than his Maker?" '[j] Shall man dare to arraign the justice of God? To say, God punishes him more than he deserves? 'Behold, he puts no trust in his servants, and his angels he chargeth with folly.' Many of these left their first estate. Even their wisdom was not to be depended on. 'How much less in them that dwell in houses of clay,'[k] whose bodies, liable to pain, sickness, death, are standing monuments of the folly and wickedness which are deep rooted in their souls.

[e] Job 4:17 [quoted p. 142].
[f] Job 25:4 [quoted p. 142].
[[g]] [Taylor, *Scripture-Doctrine*, p. 142.]
[[h]] [Ibid.]
[i] Job 25:4[-6].
[j] [Taylor, *Scripture-Doctrine*,] p. 143 [quoting Job 4:17].
[k] Job 4:17, etc. [i.e., 4:18-19, both quoted by Taylor, *Scripture-Doctrine*, p. 143].

[136] Here and in quoting the following verses, Taylor affirms that our nature at birth is mortal and infirm, but he denies that it is 'unclean' or already guilty and incapable of any good action. Cf. ibid., 143.

'What is man, that he shall be clean, and he which is born of a woman, that he should be righteous? Behold, he putteth no trust in his holy ones.' Yea, the heavens 'are not pure in his sight'. His holy angels have fallen, and the highest creatures are not pure in comparison of him. 'How much more abominable and filthy', in the strictest sense, 'is man', every man born into the world? 'Who drinketh iniquity like water',[l] iniquity of every kind, so readily, so naturally, as being so throughly agreeable to 'the desires of' his 'flesh, and of' his 'mind'?[137]

You conclude the head thus: 'Man in his present weak and fleshly state cannot be clean before God.'[m] Certainly as clean as the moon and stars at least, if he be as he was first created. He was 'made but a little lower than the angels'.[138] Consequently he was then far higher and more pure than these, or the sun itself, or any other part of the material creation. You go on: 'Why cannot a man be clean before God? Because he is conceived and born in sin? No such thing. But because if the purest creatures are not pure in comparison of God, much less a being subject to so many infirmities as a mortal man.'[n] Infirmities! What then? Do *innocent* infirmities make a man 'unclean before God'? Do labour, pain, bodily weakness, or mortality, make us 'filthy and abominable'? Surely not. Neither could they make a man pure from sin, less pure than the moon and stars. Nor can we conceive Adam as he came out of the hands of God to have been in any sense 'less clean' than these. All these texts therefore must refer to that sinful impurity which every man brings into the world.

You add: 'Which is a demonstration to me that Job and his friends were wholly strangers to this doctrine.'[o] A demonstration of a peculiar kind! I think neither mathematical nor logical.

16. The last proof is John 3:6, 'That which is born of the flesh is flesh, and that which is born of the spirit is spirit.'

Here by 'flesh' Mr. Taylor understands nothing else but the mere 'parts and powers of a man'. And by 'being born of the flesh' the being 'born of a woman', with

[l]Job 15:14, etc. [i.e., 15-16, quoted by Taylor, *Scripture-Doctrine*, p. 143].
[m][Taylor, *Scripture-Doctrine*, p. 143.]
[n][Ibid.]
[o]p. 144.

---

[137]Eph. 2:3.
[138]Ps. 8:5.

'the constitution and natural powers of a man'.[p] Now let us suppose that human nature is not at all corrupted, and let us try what sense we can make of other Scriptures where the word 'flesh' is used in opposition to 'spirit', as it is here. Rom. 8:1, 'There is no condemnation to them who walk not after the flesh, but after the spirit'—that is, not after the pure, uncorrupted constitution and powers of man. Again, ver. 8, 'They that are in the flesh cannot please God'—that is, they that have the parts and powers of a man. Again, 'If ye live after the flesh ye shall die'[139]—that is, if ye live suitably to the constitution and powers of your nature. Once more, how shall we understand 'the flesh lusteth against the spirit, and the spirit against the flesh' (Gal. 5:17), if 'flesh' means nothing but the pure and uncorrupted powers of human nature?

But this text, John 3:6,[140] is according to Mr. Taylor so far from implying any corruption of our nature that 'on the contrary it supposes we have a nature susceptible of the best habits, and capable of being born of the Spirit.'[q] And whoever denied it? Whoever supposed that such a corruption of nature as for the present disables us for spiritual good renders us incapable of being 'born of the Spirit'?[r]

'But if natural generation is the mean[s] of conveying a sinful nature from our first parents to their posterity, then must itself be a sinful and unlawful thing.'[s] I deny the consequence. You may transmit to your children a nature tainted with sin, and yet commit no sin in so doing.

Again. 'We produce one another only as the oak produces the acorn. The proper production of a child is from God. But if God produces a foetus which has sinful dispositions, he produces those dispositions.'[t] Your argument proves too much. It would prove God to be the author of all *actual* (as well as *original*) sin. For 'it is the power of God under certain laws and established rules'[u] which produces not only the *foetus*, but all the *motion* in the universe. It is his power which so violently expands the air on the discharge of a pistol or cannon. It is the same which produces muscular motion, and the circulation of all the juices in man. But does he therefore produce adultery or murder? Is he the cause of those *sinful motions*? He

[p] [Ibid.]
q p. 145.
r [Jennings, *Vindication*], p. 78, etc. [i.e., pp. 78-79].
[s] [Taylor, *Scripture-Doctrine*, p. 145.]
t p. 146.
[u] [Ibid.]

139 Rom. 8:13.
140 Orig., 'John 3:3'—an uncorrected error; Jennings's original is correct.

is the cause of the *motion* (as he is of the foetus); of the *sin*, he is not. Do not say, This is too fine a distinction. Fine as it is, you must necessarily allow it. Otherwise you make God the direct author of all the sin under heaven. To apply this more directly to the point. God does produce the foetus of man, as he does of trees, empowering the one and the other to propagate each after its kind. And a *sinful man* propagates after his kind, another *sinful man*. Yet God *produces*, in the sense above mentioned, *the man*, but not *the sin*.[141]

17. Their sixth proposition is: 'The fall brought upon mankind the loss of communion with God,[v] his displeasure and curse, so as we are by nature children of wrath,[w] bondslaves to Satan,[x] and justly liable to all punishments in this world and that which is to come.'[y]

In proof of the first clause of this proposition they cite Gen. 3:8, 10, 24. On this you observe, 'Adam and Eve by their sin did forfeit communion with God. But God did not take the forfeiture.'[z] Surely he did, when 'they were afraid, and hid themselves from his presence.' 'But afterward they had frequent communion with him.'[[a]] This does not prove they did not lose it before.

'But their posterity did not. Abel had communion with him, and so had the patriarchs and prophets. And so have we at this day. So that as we could not justly have lost this communion by Adam's sin, it is true, in fact, that we have not lost it. We still have "fellowship with the Father and the Son".'[b]

[v] Gen. 3:8, 10, 24.
[w] Eph. 2:2-3.
[x] 2 Tim. 2:26.
[y] Gen. 2:17, . . . Rom. 6:23.
[z] [Taylor, *Scripture-Doctrine*,] p. 147.
[[a]] [pp. 147-48.]
[b] p. 148 [quoting 1 John 1:3].

[141] Taylor, *Reply* (1767), 14:

'*W[esley]*. God produces the *man*, but not the *sin*, as in murder he causeth the muscular *motion*, but not the *sin*.

'*T[aylor]*. The nature of a man cannot be produced without those qualities which belong to it when it is produced. But muscular motion or power may be caused without applying that motion or power to the act of murder. Suppose God causes the motion or power, it is the wicked agent that applies it to murder, who might, if he had pleased, have applied it to a better purpose.'

Could we not justly by Adam's sin have lost our very existence? And if we[142] had not existed, could we have had communion with God? 'But we have not lost it in fact. We still have "fellowship with the Father and with the Son".' Who have? All men born into the world? All Jews, and Turks, and heathens? Have all that are called Christians? Have the generality of Protestants 'fellowship with the Father and the Son'? What fellowship? Just as much as light has with darkness, as much as Christ has with Belial. The bulk of mankind, Christians as well as heathens, Protestants as well as Papists, are at this day, and have been ever since they were born, 'without God', ἄθεοι, 'atheists in the world'.[143]

We need not therefore say, 'Their fellowship with God is owing to his mercy through a Redeemer.'[144] They have none at all—no fellowship with 'the only true God, and with Jesus Christ whom he hath sent'.[145] Indeed they have no great need of Jesus Christ, according to your account, seeing '*All* that God's grace doth for us in Christ, to repair what we lost in Adam, is raising us up at the last day!'[c] You add, 'And therefore communion with God is either the same grace which was vouchsafed to Adam, continued to us' (to every man born into the world, as naturally as seeing or hearing!) 'or, if there be anything extraordinary in it' (Which you judge can hardly be allowed!), 'it belongs to the redundancy of grace, which has no relation to anything we lost by Adam.'[d] That that whole passage has relation to what we lost in Adam has been shown already. But what conception you have of 'communion with God' is easily seen by this wonderful account of it.

'However, this text gives no intimation that Adam's posterity lost communion with God for his sin.'[e] It shows that Adam did so. And all his posterity has done the same. Whence is this, unless from his sin?

Ver. 24, 'So he drove out the man. And he placed at the east of the garden of Eden cherubim and a flaming sword, which turned every way, to keep the way of the tree of life.' Although God is equally

[c] [pp. 148-49.]
[d] [p. 149.]
[e] [Ibid.]

---

[142] Orig.: 'he', corrected in the errata to *Works* (1773).
[143] Eph. 2:12.
[144] Taylor suggested this possibility, only to reject it. *Scripture-Doctrine*, 148.
[145] Cf. John 17:3.

present in every place, yet this was a clear token that man had not now that near communion with him which he had enjoyed before his sin.

18. *Prop.* 'The fall brought upon mankind God's displeasure and curse, so as we are by nature the children of wrath.'

'The text on which this is grounded, Eph. 2:2-3, we have considered before.'[f] And those considerations have been answered at large.

You add: 'How mankind could be *justly* brought under God's displeasure for Adam's sin we cannot understand. On the contrary, we do understand *it is unjust*. And therefore, unless our understanding or perception of truth be false, *it must be unjust*. But understanding must be the same in all beings, as far as they do understand. Therefore if we understand that *it is unjust*, God understands it to be so too.'[g]

Plausible enough. But let us take the argument in pieces. 'How mankind could be justly brought under God's displeasure for Adam's sin we cannot understand.' I allow it. I cannot understand, that is, clearly or fully comprehend, the deep of the divine judgment therein. No more than I can how 'the whole' brute '*creation*' through his sin should have been 'made subject to vanity', and should 'groan together', in weakness, in various pain, in death, 'until this day'.[146] 'On the contrary, we do understand, *it is unjust*.' I do not understand it is. It is quite beyond my understanding. It is a depth which I cannot fathom. 'Therefore unless our understanding or *perception of truth* be false, it *must be unjust*.' Here lies the deceit. You shift the terms, and place as equivalent those which are not equivalent. Our *perception of truth* cannot be false, our *understanding* or *apprehension of things may*. 'But understanding must be the same in all beings.' Yes, in the former sense of the word, but not the latter. 'Therefore if we understand (apprehend) *it is unjust*, God understands it so too.' Nay verily: 'As the heavens are higher than the earth, so are' his 'thoughts higher than' our 'thoughts.'[147]

[f] p. 150.
[g] p. 151 [i.e., 150-51.]

[146] Cf. Rom. 8:20, 22.
[147] Isa. 55:9.

'What a God must he be, who can curse his innocent creatures before they have a being! Is this thy God, O Christian?'[148] Bold enough! So Lord B[olingbroke], 'Is Moses's God your God?'[149] He is mine. Although he said, 'Cursed be Canaan,'[150] including his posterity, before they had a being. And although he now permits millions to come into a world which everywhere bears the marks of *his displeasure*. And he permits human souls to exist in bodies which are (*how* we know not, but the fact we know)[151] 'conceived and born in sin',[152] by reason whereof all men coming into the world are 'children of wrath'.[153] But he has provided a Saviour for them all.[154] And this fully acquits both his justice and mercy.

19. *Prop*. 'So as we are by nature bondslaves to Satan'[h]—2 Tim. 2:26, 'And that they may recover themselves out of the snare of the devil who are taken captive by him at his will.'

But you say, 'The Apostle speaks this of the unconverted Gentiles, who were slaves to Satan, not through Adam, but through their own fault.'[i] Both one and the other. But how does it appear that he speaks this of the Gentiles only?

Without offering at any proof of this, you go on: 'The clause, "taken captive by him", is spoken not of the devil, but of "the servant of the Lord". For thus the place should be rendered: "That they may awake out of the snare of the devil, being revived by him", that is, the servant of the Lord, "to his", that is, God's, "will".'[j]

[h] p. 152.
[i] [Ibid.]
[j] p. 153.

---

[148] Taylor, *Scripture-Doctrine*, 151. Taylor goes on to say, 'But so far is God from cursing his innocent creatures, that he hath not only turned the sentence of mortality into a general good, but hath also supplied a *superabundance* of grace in his Son.'

[149] Cf. above, Preface, §3. For Bolingbroke's criticism of Moses' 'unworthy notions of a Supreme Being', see his *Letter Occasioned by One of Archbishop Tillotson's Sermons, in Philosophical Works* (London, 1754), 5:365-75.

[150] Gen. 9:25.

[151] See the discussion of this topic in the introduction (pp. 149-50 above).

[152] Cf. Ps. 51:5.

[153] Eph. 2:3.

[154] Once again JW quietly ignores that the *Larger Catechism*, which Taylor is criticizing, limits Christ's saving work to the 'elect'.

Well, the proof. 'The word ζωγρέω signifies to *revive*, and so here, to restore men to life and salvation.'[k] As a proof of this sense of the word you cite Luke 5:10. But this rather proves the contrary. For there it has nothing to do with *reviving*. We read in the verse before of the 'fishes which they had taken', alluding to which Jesus 'said unto Simon, From henceforth thou shalt catch men'[155]—'take them captive' in the gospel net. Although therefore it were allowed (which cannot be done) that 'his' related not to the word immediately preceding, but to another which stands three verses off,[156] yet even this would avail nothing, since the sense which you impose upon ζωγρέω is what it will by no means bear.

You say indeed, 'It always means to *take alive* or *save alive*.'[l] It does mean, 'to take alive'. But you bring not one authority to prove that it ever means, 'to save alive'. It therefore 'suits the devil and his snare'[157] admirably well. For he does not take therein those who are 'free among the dead',[158] but those who are *alive* in a natural, though *dead* in a spiritual sense.

'But however this be, they were not led captive through Adam's sin, but their own wickedness.'[m] They were 'bondslaves to Satan' (which was the point to be proved) through Adam's sin, and their own wickedness.

'Yea, but what an inconsistency must that be in the divine dispensations and in the Scriptures, if it can be made appear from them that God hath for *no fault* of *ours*, but *only* for Adam's *one* sin, put us all into the hands of the devil, when he hath been in all ages providing means to preserve or rescue mankind from him!'[n] What can be made appear from the Scriptures is this. That from Adam 'sin passed upon all men'.[159] That hereby all men, being by nature 'dead in sin', cannot of themselves resist the devil. And that consequently all who will not accept of help from God are 'taken captive by Satan at his will'.[160] And there is no inconsistency between this and any of the divine dispensations.

[k] [Ibid.]
[l] p. 154 [n].
[m] p. 155.
[n] p. 156.

[155] Luke 5:9-10.
[156] As Taylor argued, *Scripture-Doctrine*, 154n.
[157] Cf. 2 Tim. 2:26.
[158] Ps. 88:5.
[159] Cf. Rom. 5:12.
[160] 2 Tim. 2:26.

Prop. 'And justly liable to all punishments in this world and that which is to come.'

That all men are liable to these for Adam's sin *alone*, I do not assert.[161] But they are so for their own outward and inward sins, which through their own fault spring from the infection of their nature. And this I think may fairly be inferred from Rom. 6:23, 'The wages of sin is death'[o]—its due reward, death—temporal, spiritual, and eternal. God grant we may never feel it so!

20. You conclude this part: 'I cannot see that we have advanced one step further than where we were at the conclusion of the first part, namely, that the consequences of Adam's first sin upon us are labour, sorrow, and mortality, and no other.'[p]

The contrary to this having been so largely proved, instead of repeating those proofs over again, I shall close this part with that beautiful description of the present state of man which Mr. Hervey gives us from Mr. Howe's *Living Temple*: 'Only', says he, 'let me hint that it considers the human soul as originally "an habitation of God through the Spirit".'[162]

That he hath withdrawn himself, and left this his temple desolate, we have many sad and plain proofs before us. The *stately ruins* are visible to every eye, and bear in their front (yet extant) this doleful inscription, '*HERE GOD ONCE DWELT*.' Enough appears of the admirable structure of the soul of man to show the divine presence did sometime reside in it; more than enough of vicious deformity to proclaim he is now retired and gone. The *lamps* are extinct, the *altar* overturned; the light and love are now vanished which did, the one shine with so heavenly brightness, the other burn with so pious fervour. The *golden candlestick* is displaced to make room for the throne of the prince of darkness. The sacred *incense*, which sent up its rich perfumes, is exchanged for a poisonous hellish vapour. The comely *order* of this house is all turned into confusion; the beauties of holiness into noisome impurities; the house of prayer into a den of thieves. Thieves of the worst kind; for

[o] pp. 157-58.
[p] p. 162.

---

[161] In five pages (156-61) that are the nerve center of *Scripture-Doctrine*, Taylor makes clear that it is the intent of the framers of this proposition to assert precisely that Adam's sin *alone* renders all subsequent humanity liable to eternal punishment from birth. He suggests that this proposition derives more from the influence of their 'scheme' than from Scripture and rejects its implication of unconditional reprobation.

[162] James Hervey, *Theron and Aspasio; or a Series of Dialogues and Letters upon the most Important and Interesting Subjects*, 2 vols. (Dublin: Robert Main, 1755), 1:332.

every lust is a thief, and every theft is sacrilege. The noble powers which were designed and dedicated to *divine contemplation* and *delight* in God, are alienated to the service of the most despicable idols, and employed in the vilest embraces—to behold and admire lying vanities, to indulge and cherish lust and wickedness.

There is not now a *system*, an entire table of coherent truths to be found, or a frame of holiness, but some shivered parcels. And if any with great toil and labour apply themselves to draw out here one piece, and there another, and set them together, they serve rather to show how exquisite the divine workmanship was in the *original composition*, than to the excellent purposes for which the whole was at first designed. Some pieces agree, and own one another; but how soon are our inquiries nonplussed and superseded! How many attempts have been made, since that fearful fall and ruin of this fabric, to compose again the truths of so many several kinds into their distinct orders, and make up frames of science or useful knowledge! And after so many ages, nothing is finished in any kind. Sometimes truths are misplaced; and what belongs to one kind is transferred to another, where it will not fitly match. Sometimes falsehood inserted, which shatters or disturbs the whole frame. And what with much fruitless pains is done by one hand is dashed in pieces by another; and it is the work of a following age to sweep away the fine-spun cobwebs of a former. And those truths which are of greatest use, though not most out of sight, are least regarded. Their tendency and design are overlooked, or they are so loosened and torn off that they cannot be wrought in so as to take hold of the soul, but hover as faint, ineffectual notions, that signify nothing.

Its very *fundamental powers* are shaken and disjointed, and their order toward one another confounded and broken. So that what is judged *considerable* is not *considered*, what is recommended as *lovely* and *eligible* is not loved and chosen. Yea, 'the truth which is after godliness' is not so much disbelieved as *hated*, or 'held in unrighteousness', and shines with too feeble a light in that malignant darkness which 'comprehends it not'. You come amidst all this confusion into the ruined palace of some great prince, in which you see, here the fragments of a noble pillar, there the shattered pieces of some curious imagery, and all lying neglected and useless among heaps of dirt. He that invites you to take a view of the soul of man gives you but such another prospect, and doth but say to you, 'Behold the desolation!' All things rude and waste. So that should there be any pretence to the divine presence, it might be said, 'If God be here, why is it thus?' The faded glory, the darkness, the disorder, the impurity, the decayed state in all respects of this temple, too plainly show, *The GREAT INHABITANT is gone!*[163]

Newington, Jan. 21

[163] Ibid., Dial. X (1:332-34); quoting John Howe, *The Living Temple* (London: R. Clavell, 1702), 2:139-43. Wesley's appreciation for Howe led him to include an abridgment in *Christian Library*, vol. 48 (1755). JW may have introduced Howe's work to Hervey, his former student at Oxford.

[IV.] In your *Third Part* you propose, first to answer some objections and queries, and then to consider the connection of the doctrine of original sin with other parts of religion.

'*Obj.* 1. Are we not in worse moral circumstances than Adam was before he fell?'

'I answer, (1) If by "moral circumstances" you mean the state of religion and virtue, it is certain the greatest part of mankind ever were and still are very corrupt. But this is not the fault of their nature, but occasioned by the abuse of it, in prostituting reason to appetite, whereby in process of time they have sunk themselves into the most lamentable degrees of ignorance, superstition, idolatry, injustice, debauchery.'[q]

But how came this? How came all nations thus to 'abuse their nature', thus to 'prostitute reason to appetite'? How came they all to sink into this 'lamentable ignorance, superstition, idolatry, injustice, debauchery'? How came it that half of them, at least, if their nature was uncorrupt, did not use it well? Submit appetite to reason, and rise, while the other sunk? 'Process of time' does not help us out at all. For if it made the one half of mankind more and more vicious, it ought by the same degrees to have made the other half more and more virtuous. If men were no more inclined to one side than the other, this must absolutely have been the event. Turn and wind as you please, you will never be able to get over this. You will never account for this fact, that the bulk of mankind have in all ages 'prostituted their reason to appetite', even till they sunk into 'lamentable ignorance, superstition, idolatry, injustice, and debauchery', but by allowing their very nature to be in fault, to be more inclined to vice than virtue.[164]

'But if we have all a corrupt nature, which, as we cannot, so God will not, wholly remove in this life, then why do we try to reform the world?'[r] Why? Because, whether the corrupt nature be wholly removed or no, men may be so far reformed as to 'cease from evil',[165] to be 'renewed in the spirit of their mind',[166] and 'by patient

[q] p. 168.
[r] [pp. 168-69, summarized.]

[164] Taylor, *Scripture-Doctrine*, had been contesting the language in the *Larger Catechism* about being 'wholly inclined to all evil continually' (p. 169).
[165] Cf. Isa. 1:16.
[166] Cf. Eph. 4:23.

continuance in well-doing', to 'seek' and find 'glory and honour and immortality'.[167]

'I answer, (2) If by "moral circumstances" you mean *provision and means for spiritual improvement,* those given us through Christ are far greater than Adam had before he sinned.'[s] To those who believe in Christ they are. But above four-fifths of the world are Mahometans or pagans still. And have these (immensely the greater part of mankind—to say nothing of popish nations) greater 'provision and means for spiritual improvement' than Adam before he sinned?

'But if, (3) by "moral circumstances" you mean *moral*' (rather *natural*)[168] '*abilities* or *mental powers*' (a consideration quite foreign to the question) 'I answer, The Scriptures nowhere compare our faculties with Adam's. Nor know I how we can judge, but by comparing the actions of Adam in innocence with what men have performed since.'[t] Yes, we can judge thus. There could be no defect in Adam's understanding when he came first out of the hands of his Creator. But there are essential defects in mine and yours, and every man's whom we know—our *apprehension* is indistinct, our *judgment* false, our *reasoning* wrong, in a thousand instances. So it always was; and so it is still, after all the care we can possibly take. Therefore 'our faculties are' *not* 'as sound and fit for right action as Adam's were before he sinned'.[169]

'But any man of common understanding might have "dressed and kept the garden" as well as he.'[[u]] I can neither affirm nor deny this. For we know not *how* he 'dressed and kept' it.

'Nor doth it appear that in "giving names" to all the creatures he showed any extraordinary penetration into their natures. For that the names he gave truly expressed the several qualities of them is a mere fiction, without any foundation in Scripture history or the

[s] pp. 169[-70].
[t] p. 170.
[[u]] [pp. 170-71, citing Gen. 2:15.]

---

[167] Rom. 2:7.

[168] Cf. JW's distinction between the moral image and the natural image in Sermon 45, 'The New Birth', I.1, 2:188 in this edn.

[169] Cf. Taylor, *Scripture-Doctrine*, 170, where he sets up the argument that runs over the next several pages, disputing the common Western Christian model of Adam being created with perfect knowledge, wisdom, etc.

names of animals in the original Hebrew.'[v] This is really strange! That any man of learning should be so hardy as to affirm this, after the numberless instances which have been produced of Hebrew names expressing the most essential property of each animal.

And is this supposition likewise 'without any foundation in Scripture history'? What is that, Gen. 2:19? 'And the Lord God brought every beast of the field, and every fowl of the air, unto Adam, to see what he would call them', to make proof of his understanding. 'And whatsoever Adam called every living creature, that was the name thereof.' Now whether those names were Hebrew or no (which you *affect* to doubt) can it be supposed that God would have permitted them to stand if they had not suited the nature of each creature? 'Tis bold therefore to affirm that 'many of his posterity would have given names to them as well as he, and that therefore this is not a proof that he had any capacity superior to us'.[w]

You proceed, 'Surely his eating the forbidden fruit is no evidence of superior [moral] abilities.'[x] And it is no evidence of the contrary, seeing (as you yourself observe) 'What his *special* temptation was we do not know.'[[y]] Therefore neither do we know whether any of his posterity could have overcome it, much less that 'many of his posterity have overcome temptations more violent than his'.[[z]] All this is talking in the dark, 'not knowing what we say, neither whereof we affirm'.[170]

'And now let any man see whether there be any ground in revelation for exalting Adam's nature as divines have done, who have affirmed that all his faculties were eminently perfect, and entirely set to the love and obedience of his Creator. . . . And yet these same suppose him to have been guilty of the vilest act that ever was committed.'[a]

They suppose Adam to have been created holy and wise, like his Creator, and yet capable of falling from it. They suppose farther that through temptations of which we cannot possibly judge he did fall from that state; and that hereby he brought pain, labour, and sorrow

[v] p. 171.
[w] p. 172 [i.e., 171-72].
[x] p. 173.
[[y]] [Ibid.]
[[z]] [p. 174.]
[a] pp. 175-76.

[170] Cf. 1 Tim. 1:7.

on himself and all his posterity—together with death, not only temporal, but spiritual, and (without the grace of God) eternal. And it must be confessed that not only a few divines, but the whole body of Christians in all ages, did suppose this, till after seventeen hundred years a sweet-tongued orator arose, not only more enlightened than silly Adam, but than any of his wise posterity, and declared that the whole supposition was folly, nonsense, inconsistency, and blasphemy![171]

'*Obj*. 2. But do not the Scriptures say, Adam was created after God's own image? And do his posterity bear that image now?'[b]

'The Scriptures do say, Gen. 1:27, "God created man in his own image." But whatever that phrase means here, it doubtless means the same in Gen 9:6: "Whoso sheddeth man's blood, by man shall his blood be shed. For in the image of God made he man." Certainly it has the same meaning in both places, for the latter plainly refers to the former. And thus much we may fairly infer from hence, that "the image of God" wherein "man was" at first "created", whereinsoever it consisted, was not utterly effaced in the time of Noah. Yea, so much of it will always remain in all men as will justify the punishing murderers with death.'[c] But we can in no wise infer from hence that that entire image of God in which Adam was at first created now remains in all his posterity.

The words of Gen 5:3, rendered literally, are, 'He begat in his likeness, according to his image.' 'Adam', says Mr. Hervey, 'was "created in the image of God". After his fall the sacred historian varies his style, and with a remarkable peculiarity, as well as propriety, says, "Adam begat a son in his own likeness." ' (So it must be translated according to all the rules of grammar, Adam being the nearest antecedent.) 'That every reader may advert to this melancholy but important truth it is enforced by a very emphatical repetition, "after his own image", as contradistinguished from that "image of God" mentioned in the preceding verse; which expressions are evidently intended to denote the difference between the state in which Adam was created and Seth begotten.'[172]

[b] [p. 176.]
[c] p. 177 [i.e., 176-77].

[171] See the discussion of this response in the introduction (pp. 147-48 above).
[172] Hervey, *Theron and Aspasio*, Dial. XI (1:340-41).

'The two following texts are brought by the Assembly to show what the image of God was in which Adam was made. Col. 3:10, "And have put on the new man, which is renewed in knowledge after the image of him that created him." Eph. 4:24, "Put on the new man, which after the image of God is created in righteousness and true holiness." I answer, These texts are parallel. "The old man" means a wicked life, "the new man", a good life; to which they were formed and *created* by the gospel dispensation. And this "new man", this new life, is "after the image", that is, agreeable to the nature, "of God".'[d] As you advance no proof of this perfectly new interpretation, I leave it to shift for itself.

To disprove the common interpretation you add: 'Adam could not be originally created in "righteousness and true holiness", because habits of holiness *cannot* be created without our knowledge, concurrence, or consent. For holiness in its nature implies the choice and consent of a moral agent, without which it *cannot* be holiness.'[e]

What is holiness? Is it not, essentially, love? The love of God and of all mankind? Love producing 'bowels of mercies, humbleness of mind, meekness, gentleness, long-suffering'?[173] And *cannot* God shed abroad this love in any soul, without his concurrence? Antecedent to his knowledge or consent? And supposing this to be done, will love change its nature? Will it be no longer holiness? This argument can never be sustained—unless you would play upon the word 'habits'. Love is holiness wherever it exists. And God *could* create either men or angels, endued from the very first moment of their existence with whatsoever degree of love he pleased.[174]

You 'think, on the contrary, it is demonstration, that we cannot be righteous or holy, we cannot *observe* what is right, without our own free and explicit choice'.[f] I suppose you mean, *practise* what is right.

[d] pp. 178-79.
[e] pp. [179-]80.
[f] [p. 180.]

---

[173] Cf. Col. 3:12.
[174] Taylor, *Reply* (1767), 14-15:
'That is to say, he could create them in the highest degree of love to objects they were not acquainted with. Which is absurd. No man can love what he doth not first know is lovely. And therefore the faculty of knowledge must be exercised before he can love. And therefore, though men or angels may be endued with a capacity of love, they cannot be endued with love itself from the first moment of their existence.'

But a man may *be* righteous before he *does* what is right, holy in heart before he is holy in life. The confounding these two all along seems to be the ground of your strange imagination that Adam 'must choose to be righteous, must exercise thought and reflection before he *could be* righteous'. Why so? 'Because righteousness is the right *use and application* of our powers.'[g] Here is your capital mistake. No, it is not. It is the right *state* of our powers. It is the right *disposition* of our *soul*, the right *temper* of our *mind*.[175] Take this with you, and you will no more dream that 'God *could not* create man in righteousness and true holiness;' or that 'to talk of wanting that "righteousness in which Adam was created" is to talk of nothing we want'.[h]

On Rom. 2:14 you observe: 'This text clearly proves that natural reason and understanding is a rule of action to all mankind, and that all men ought to follow it. This therefore overthrows the whole doctrine of original sin.'[i]

How do you prove the consequence? May not men have *some* reason left, which in *some measure* discerns good from evil, and yet be deeply fallen, even as to their understanding, as well as their will and affections?

On Eccles. 7:29, 'God hath made man upright, but they have found out many inventions', you say: '"Man" here means all mankind; "upright", endued with powers to know and perform their duty.'[j] You offer no proof for either of these assertions. And without it I cannot receive them.

[g] [pp. 180-81.]
[h] p. 181 [cf. Eph. 4:24].
[i] p. 183.
[j] [p. 184.]

---

[175] Ibid., 15-16:

'Therefore this right *state, disposition, temper*, must be considered antecedently to and separately from all exercise of thought, or any other use or application of our powers. And so must be considered antecedently to and separately from all desire, and all choice of right action. And therefore, can with no propriety be called righteousness or true holiness, which must at least imply a desire and choice of righteous or holy action, but must be no more than a capacity of righteousness or holiness. It be said, "This *disposition, state*, or *temper* is an inclination to righteousness", I answer—an inclination to righteousness before a man knows and hath considered what righteousness is, is an absurdity, an inclination to he knows not what, or to nothing. Adam therefore must not only be created, but also must know and consider what righteousness was before he could be so much as inclined or disposed to it.'

Again, '"They"' (you say) 'means mankind in general.'[k] I rather believe it means our first parents, who are by Moses likewise comprehended under the common name of 'man', or rather אדם (Adam). So Gen. 5:2, 'God called their name Adam in the day when they were created.' And in the day that they fell, whoever reads Gen. 3 will see, 'they found out' not one, but 'many inventions'.[176] This text therefore in its obvious meaning teaches both the original uprightness and subsequent fall of man.

From all these texts it manifestly appears, (1) that man was created in the image of God; (2) that this image consisted not only in his rational and immortal nature, and his dominion over the creatures, but also *in knowledge*, actual knowledge, both of God and of his works, in the right *state* of his intellectual powers, and in *love*, which is *true holiness*.

'*Obj*. 3. But do we not derive from Adam a moral *taint* and *infection*, whereby we have a *natural propensity* to sin?'

'I answer, We have many natural appetites and passions, which, if they grow irregular, become sinful. But this does not amount to a *natural propensity* to sin.'[l] But is not pride sin? Is not idolatry sin? And is it not idolatry to 'love the creature more than the Creator'?[177] Is not revenge sin? Is it not sin to 'look upon a woman' so as 'to lust after her'?[178] And have not all men a natural propensity to these things? They have all then a *natural propensity* to sin. Nevertheless this propensity is not *necessary*, if by necessary you mean *irresistible*.[179] We can resist and conquer it too, by the grace which is ever at hand.[180]

This *propensity* to pride, to revenge, to idolatry (call it *taint*, or anything) cannot be pleasing to God,[181] who yet in fact does permit

[k] [p. 185.]
[l] p. 186.

[176] Cf. Taylor, *Scripture-Doctrine*, 185: 'Which demonstrateth the text refers to other inventions besides that *one* which our first parents found out, even to all the inventions in all ages.'

[177] Cf. Rom. 1:25.

[178] Cf. Matt. 5:28.

[179] Taylor goes on: 'For I presume by a natural propensity is meant a necessary inclination to sin, or that we are necessarily sinful from the original bent and bias of our natural powers.' *Scripture-Doctrine*, 186.

[180] I.e., universally restored prevenient grace.

[181] Taylor had said, 'That we are weak and liable to temptation is the will of God, holy and good, and for glorious purposes to ourselves'. *Scripture-Doctrine*, 186.

that it should descend from Adam to his latest posterity. And 'we can neither help nor hinder'[m] its descending to us. Indeed we can heap up plausible arguments to prove the impossibility of it. But I *feel* it, and the argument drops. Bring ever so many proofs that there can be no such thing as motion. I *move*, and they vanish away.

'But nature cannot be *morally corrupted* but by the choice of a moral agent.'[n] You may play upon words as long as you please, but still I hold this fast. I (and you too, whether you will own it or no) am inclined, and was ever since I can remember, antecedently to any choice of my own, to pride, revenge, idolatry. If you will not call these moral *corruptions*, call them just what you will. But the fact I am as well assured of as that I have any memory or understanding.

'But some have attempted to explain this intricate affair.'[o] I do not commend their wisdom.[182] I do not attempt to explain even how I, at this moment, stretch out my hand, or move my finger.

One more of your assertions I must not pass over. 'It is absurd to say infection is derived from Adam, independent of the will of God. And to say it is by his will, is to make him the author of the pollution.'[p] We answer, It is not derived from Adam independent of the will of God—that is, his permissive will. But our allowing this does not make him the author of the pollution.

'*Obj.* 4. But do not the vices of parents often infect their children?'[q] I know not well either how to affirm or deny it.[183]

'*Obj.* 5. How can we account for children's beginning so soon to sin but by supposing they have a natural propensity to it?'

'I answer, Who can tell how soon they begin?'[r] Then they begin, when they first show wrong tempers, such as plain, undeniable frowardness, revenge, self-will, which is as soon as they have any exercise of reason. So that the use of reason and the abuse generally

[m] [Cf. p. 187.]
[n] p. 187 [i.e., 188].
[o] p. 188.
[p] pp. 189[-90].
[q] pp. 190-91.
[r] p. 192.

[182] Taylor is referring to the traditional model where union with the material body is what corrupts the soul that God has created in spotless purity, a model Taylor soundly critiques. See *Scripture-Doctrine*, 188-89. JW is refusing to endorse or defend this model.

[183] In *Works* (1773), 21:178, JW inserts the alternative: 'I think we cannot deny it.'

commence and grow up together. As soon as their faculties appear at all, they appear to be disordered, the wrong *state* of their powers being easily inferred from their continual wrong *application* of them.

'But if parents were wise and virtuous themselves, and then endeavoured to bring up their children virtuously, there would be less wickedness in the world.'[s] There would. But this does not reach the point. Nor that 'undisciplined children contract bad habits'.[t] I have known wise and virtuous parents who did earnestly labour to bring up their children virtuously; and disciplined them with all possible care, from the very first dawn of reason.[184] Yet these very children showed *bad tempers*, before it was possible they should 'contract *bad habits*'. They daily evidenced the *wrong state* of all their faculties, both of their understanding, will, and affections, just contrary both to the examples and instructions of all that were round about them. Here then these *wrong* tempers were not owing to 'the fault of careless or ungodly parents';[u] nor could be rationally accounted for but by supposing those children to have a *natural propensity* to evil.

It is indeed a general rule, 'Train up a child in the way he should go, and when he is old he will not depart from it.'[v] And there is much truth in that observation: 'Foolishness is bound in the heart of a child, but the rod of correction shall drive it far from him.'[w] That is, prudent correction is the most probable means which you can use to remove that foolishness. Yet this no way contradicts what is [a] matter of daily experience, that they have a *natural propensity* to evil. Nay, the latter of these texts strongly confirms it. For if there be no such propensity, how comes 'foolishness' (that is, wickedness, in the language of Solomon) to be 'bound in the heart of a child'? Of every child, of children in general, as the phrase manifestly imports. It is not from education here. It is supposed to be antecedent to education, whether good or bad. 'Oh, foolishness means only *strong appetite*.'[x]

[s] [Ibid.]
[t] [p. 193.]
[u] [Ibid.]
[v] Prov. 22:6.
[w] [Prov. 22,] ver. 15.
[x] [Taylor, *Scripture-Doctrine*,] p. 193.

[184] Indeed, JW exhorted all parents to do so. See Sermon 94, 'Of Family Religion', 3:334-46 in this edn.; and Sermon 95, 'On the Education of Children', 3:347-60 in this edn.

Yes, strong *appetite to evil*. Otherwise it would not call for 'the rod of correction', or need to be 'driven far from him'.

'*Obj*. 6. Might not Adam's posterity be said to *sin in him*, as *Levi* is said to "pay tithes in Abraham"?'[y]

If the querist means, not to prove a doctrine already proved, but only to illustrate one expression by another, your answer, 'that it is a bold figure',[z] does not at all affect him. It is so. But still it may be pertinently cited to illustrate a similar expression.

'*Obj*. 7. "But there is a law in our members which wars against the law of our minds, and brings us into captivity to the law of sin and death." And does not this prove that we come into the world with *sinful propensities*?'[a]

You answer, (1) 'If we come into the world with them, they are *natural*; but if *natural*, *necessary*; and if *necessary*, then no sin.'[b]

If the consequence were good with regard to what is so *natural* and *necessary* as to be *irresistible*, yet certainly it is not good with regard to those propensities which we may both resist and conquer.[185]

You answer, (2) 'The Apostle does not in this chapter speak of any man as he comes into the world, but as he is afterward depraved and corrupted by his own wicked choice.'[c]

Where is the proof? How does it appear that he does not speak of men corrupted both by choice and by nature?

You answer, (3) 'He does not speak of himself, or any regenerate man, but of a Jew under the power of sin.'[d] Nay, your argument proves he does not speak of any Jew. For in order to prove 'the Apostle does not speak of himself,' you say, 'The persons of whom he speaks were "before the commandment came", i.e. before they came under the law, "once without the law". But the Apostle never was

[y] Heb. 7:9 [see Taylor, *Scripture-Doctrine*, p. 194].
[z] [Taylor, *Scripture-Doctrine*,] p. 195.
[a] p. 199.
[b] p. 200.
[c] [Ibid.]
[d] p. 200.

[185] Taylor makes this same general point in a footnote, distinguishing between being born with dispositions that *are* sinful and being born with dispositions that can *become* sinful. He assumes that the first option would imply irresistible propensities and that this is what is being affirmed in the Westminster *Catechism*. See *Scripture-Doctrine*, 200n.

"without the law".' No, nor any Jew. 'For he was born, and continued "under the law" till he was a Christian.' So did all the Jews, as well as he. 'And therefore it cannot be true that he' or any Jew whatever 'was "without the law" before he came under it.'[e] So you have clearly proved that the Apostle does not in this passage speak of any Jew at all.

But why do you think he does speak of Jews? Nay, of them only? It 'appears', you say, 'from ver. 1: "I speak to them that know the law." For the Gentiles never were "under the law".'[f] Yes, they were. All the Gentiles who were 'convinced of sin'[186] were 'under the law' in the sense here spoken of—under the *condemning power* of the law 'written in their hearts',[187] for transgressing which they were under the wrath of God. And this whole chapter, from the 7th to the 24th verse, describes the state of all those, Jews or Gentiles, who *saw* and *felt* the wickedness both of their hearts and lives, and groaned to be delivered from it.

Many passages in your paraphrase on the former part of this chapter are liable to much exception; but as they do not immediately touch the point in question, I pass on to the latter part.

Ver. 14. ' "I am carnal, sold under sin." He means a willing slavery.'[g] Quite the contrary, as appears from the very next words: 'For that which I do, I allow not. For what I would, I do not; but what I hate, that I do.' 'What I hate.' Not barely, 'what my reason disapproves',[188] but what I really detest and abhor, yet cannot help.

Ver. 17. ' "Now then, it is no more I that do it, but sin that dwelleth in me." It is my sinful propensities, my indulged appetites and passions.'[h] True. But those propensities were antecedent to that indulgence.

[e] [p. 201.]
[f] [pp. 200-201.]
[g] p. 216 [citing Rom. 7:14, with Taylor's comment in a footnote].
[h] p. 217.

---

[186] Cf. John 8:46.
[187] Rom. 2:15.
[188] Cf. Taylor, *Scripture-Doctrine*, 216:
'The sin which the sinner commits is what he doth not allow with his understanding and reason. For what his reason approves and dictates, that he doth not; but what he hateth, what is abhorrent from his reason, that he doth . . . not the choice of his own reason, but the dictates of his irregular passions.'

'But the Apostle cannot mean that there is something in man which makes him sin whether he will or no. For then it would not be sin at all.'[[i]] Experience explains his meaning. I have felt in me a thousand times something which made me transgress God's law, whether I would or no.[189] Yet I dare not say that 'transgression of the law'[190] was 'no sin at all'.

Ver. 18. 'For I know that in me, that is, in my flesh' (not my 'fleshly appetites' only, but my whole nature while unrenewed) 'dwelleth no good thing.' 'For to will' indeed 'is present with me'—not barely 'that natural faculty, the will', but an actual will to do good, as evidently appears from the following words, 'but how to perform that which is good I find not'—I have the desire, but not the power.[191]

Ver. 19. 'For the good that I would', that I desire and choose, 'I do not; but the evil which I would not', which I hate, 'that I do.'[192]

Ver. 20. 'Now if I do that I would not, it is no more I, but sin that dwelleth in me'—but 'the prevalency of sensual affections', yea, sinful tempers of every kind, 'settled and ruling in my heart', both by nature and habit.[j]

Ver. 21. 'I find, then, that when I would do good', when I choose and earnestly desire it,[193] I cannot; 'evil is present with me'—as it were gets in between.

Ver. 22. 'For I delight in the law of God, after the inward man'—my mind, my conscience approves it.

Ver. 23. 'But I see another law in my members which warreth against the law in my mind'—'another principle of action, which fights against my reason' and conscience, 'and bringeth me into captivity to the law of sin which is in my members'—which 'captivates and enslaves me to the principle of wickedness'. (Strange language

[[i]] [p. 217n.]
[j] p. 218.

---

[189] Taylor, *Reply* (1767), 16: 'That cannot be true. Such notions must embolden foolish men in wickedness, when they have been taught to imagine, they cannot help doing wickedly.'

[190] 1 John 3:4.

[191] Taylor's paraphrase of this verse equated 'flesh' with 'fleshly appetites' and took 'to will' as referring to the natural faculty of the will. Cf. *Scripture-Doctrine*, 217.

[192] Cf. ibid., 218: 'For what good actions his reason chooses, those he, the man in the flesh, doth not. On the contrary, he doth that wickedness which his reason disapproveth.'

[193] Taylor spoke of this as when one's 'reason approveth obedience'. Ibid.

for *you* to use!) 'Seated in the lusts of the flesh'[k]—seated indeed in all my tempers, passions, and appetites, which are the several members of 'the old man'.

Ver. 24. 'O wretched man that I am. Who shall deliver me from the body of this death?' 'He is under the power of such passions as his own reason disapproves, but is too weak to conquer. And N.B., being a Jew, he stands condemned to eternal death by the law. How shall such a wretched Jew be delivered from sinful lusts, and the curse of the law?'[l] Did then none but a Jew ever cry out under the burden of sin, 'Wretched man that I am'? Are none but Jews 'under the powers of such passions as their own reason disapproves, but is too weak to conquer'? And does the law of God 'condemn to eternal death' no sinners beside Jews? Do not Christians also (in the wide sense of the word) groan to be 'delivered from the body of this death'? With what truth, with what sense, can you restrain this passage to a Jew any more than to a Turk?

I cannot but observe upon the whole, the question is, Does not Rom. 7:23 show that we come into the world with sinful propensities? (This is all that is pertinent in the objection awkwardly proposed, p. 199.)[194] But instead of keeping to this, you spend above twenty pages in proving that this chapter does not describe a regenerate person! It may, or it may not.[195] But this does not touch the question, Do not men come into the world with sinful propensities?

We have undoubtedly an additional proof that they do in the words of Jeremiah 17:9, 'The heart is deceitful above all things, and desperately wicked. Who can know it?' On this you descant (one instance of a thousand of your artful manner of declaiming in order to forestall the reader's judgment, and 'deceive the hearts of the

[k] p. 219.

[l] [Ibid.]

---

[194] I.e., *Obj.* 7, above.

[195] A long stream of Western Christian exegesis, including Calvin and the Puritans, read Rom. 7 as expressing the struggle of regenerated saints with the sinful inclinations that remained within them. Arminius challenged this standard Reformed view, citing several early Christian writers (particularly Eastern voices) who believed Paul was describing here the state of the unregenerate sinner; see his *Dissertation on the True and Genuine Sense of the Seventh Chapter of the Epistle to the Romans* (Latin original, 1613). JW's comments on Rom. 7 in *NT Notes* (1755) clearly sided with Arminius. He later published an extract of John Kettlewell in the *Arminian Magazine* (3:625-36) rejecting the Reformed reading. But in keeping with his stated desire to avoid other debates, JW avoids stating his own views here.

simple'):[196] 'Christians too generally neglecting the study of the Scripture, content themselves with a few scraps, which though wrong understood, they make the test of truth, in contradiction to the whole tenor of revelation. Thus this text has been misapplied to prove that every man's heart is so desperately wicked that no man can know how wicked his heart is.'[m] O what πιθανολογία[197]—persuasiveness of speech! After reading this I was much inclined to believe, without going a step further, that this text had been 'generally misunderstood'. I thought probably it has been misapplied, and does not assert that every man's 'heart is desperately wicked'. But no sooner did I read over the very verses you cite than the clear light appeared again. Ver. 5, 'Cursed be the man that trusteth in man, and whose heart departeth from the Lord.'[n] That 'man' whom we are not to trust in means man in general cannot be denied. After repeating the intermediate verses, you yourself add, 'He subjoins a reason (ver. 9), which demonstrates the error of trusting in man: "The heart is deceitful above all things, and desperately wicked. Who can know it?" This text therefore does not mean, who can know his own heart, but another's.'[[o]] Whether it means one or both, it positively asserts that 'the heart of man', of men in general, of every man, 'is desperately wicked'. Therefore as to the main point contained therein, Christians do not 'understand it wrong,'[p] neither misapply it at all.

When I say, 'I feel I have a "wicked heart" ', another thing which you do not understand,[198] I mean this, I feel much pride remaining in my heart, much self-will, much unbelief. Now I really believe

[m] p. 224.
[n] p. 225 [quoting Jer. 17:5].
[[o]] [Ibid.]
[p] p. 224.

---

[196] Rom. 16:18.
[197] Col. 2:4.
[198] Cf. Taylor, *Scripture-Doctrine*, 226-28:
'To hear some Christians talk, one would imagine they thought it their duty, and a mark of sincerity and goodness, to be always complaining of corrupt and desperately wicked hearts. . . . It is manifestly true that while we are in the body we shall be exercised with the infirmities and passions thereof. But this is not our corruption or wickedness, but the trial of our virtue and holiness in resisting and subduing every irregular appetite. And it is the real character of every true Christian, not that he feels he hath a corrupt and wicked heart, but that he "crucifieth the flesh with the affections and lusts" (Gal. 5:24) "and perfecteth holiness in the fear of the Lord".'

pride and self-will and unbelief to be essentially wicked tempers. Therefore in whatever heart they remain (and they remain in yours as well as mine), that is a 'wicked heart'.

After a long pause, you return to the seventh[199] of the Romans, and affirm, 'We cannot from anything in that chapter infer that we came into the world with sinful dispositions derived from Adam, for the Apostle says nothing about Adam.'[q] He had said enough in the fifth chapter of the cause. Here he only describes the effect, the state of those who are now 'brought to the birth', but 'there is not yet strength to bring forth'.[200]

'Nor can we infer from hence that any man sins through a principle which it was never in his power to command. For then it would be no sin.'[[r]] Upon this I would only ask, Are you assured that no man transgresses God's law (whether you will call it sin or not) through a principle which it was never in his power to command? At least not for any time together? Every passionate man can confute you in this.[201] He has sad experience of the contrary.

[V.] To those objections which you have, in some sort, answered, you subjoin the following questions.

Quest. 1. 'Is not the doctrine of original sin necessary to account for the being of so much wickedness in the world?'[s]

You answer: 'Adam's nature, it is allowed, was not sinful, and yet he sinned. Therefore this doctrine is no more necessary to account for the wickedness of the world than to account for Adam's sin.'[[t]] Yes, it is. I can account for one man's sinning, or an hundred, or even half mankind, suppose they were evenly poised between vice and virtue, from their own choice, which might turn one way or the

[q] p. 229.
[[r]] [Ibid.]
[s] p. 231.
[[t]] [pp. 231-32.]

[199] Orig., 'eighth'; an uncorrected error in all edns.
[200] Isa. 37:3.
[201] Taylor, *Reply* (1767), 16: 'Every passionate man hath a power to command and govern his passion, if he chooses. But you, who vindicate and justify your passion as what you cannot help, upon a pretended principle of religion, are never likely to command your passion.'

other. But I cannot possibly on this supposition account for the general wickedness of mankind in all ages and nations.[202]

Again:

If men were never drawn into sin any other way than as Adam was, namely by temptations offered from without, there might be something in this answer. But there are numberless instances of men sinning though no temptation is offered from without. It is necessary, therefore, some other account should be given of their sinning than of Adam's. And how to account for the universal spread of sin over the whole world without one exception, if there were no corruption in their common head, would be an unsurmountable difficulty.[u]

Quest. 2. 'How then are we born into the world?'

You answer, 'As void of actual knowledge as the brutes.'[v]

And can you really imagine that text (Job 11:12), 'Vain man would be wise' (evidently spoken of man in general) 'though a man be born like a wild ass's colt', implies no more than 'Men are born void of actual knowledge'? Do we need inspiration to make this discovery, that a new-born child has no actual knowledge? Is man compared to 'a wild ass', of all animals the most stupid, to teach us no more than this? Yea, 'a wild ass's colt'? Does not this intimate anything of intractableness, sullenness, stubbornness, perverseness?

How keenly is the comparison pointed! Like the *ass*, an animal stupid even to a proverb. Like the *ass's colt*, which must be still more egregiously stupid than its dam. Like the *wild ass's colt*, which is not only blockish, but stubborn and refractory; neither has valuable qualities by nature, nor will easily receive them by discipline. The image in the original is yet more strongly touched. The particle 'like' is not in the Hebrew, 'born a wild ass's colt'; or, as we should say in English, 'a mere wild ass's colt'.[w]

Yes, 'We are born with many sensual appetites and passions; but every one of these are *in themselves good*.'[x] I grant all the appetites

[u] [Jennings,] *Vindication*, p. 110.
[v] [Taylor, *Scripture-Doctrine*,] p. 232.
[w] [Hervey,] *Theron and Aspasio*, Dial. XIII [2:9n].
[x] [Taylor, *Scripture-Doctrine*, p. 232.]

[202] Ibid., 17: 'This is an idle way of talking. The "general wickedness of mankind" hath always and everywhere been the wickedness of single persons. And therefore we may account for the wickedness of any number of single persons in the same way that we account for the wickedness of any one man.'

and passions originally implanted in our nature *were* good in themselves. But are all that now exist in us good? 'If not, they become evil only by excess or abuse.'[y] First, this may be doubted. I do not know that love of praise, of power, of money, 'become evil only by abuse'. I am afraid these and other passions which we have had from our infancy are evil *in themselves*. But be that as it may, in how few do we find even the more innocent passions and appetites clear of excess or abuse? 'But all that is wrong in them is from habit.'[z] This cannot be allowed as universally true. The little children of wise and pious parents have not yet contracted ill habits. Yet before they can go alone they show such passions as are palpably excessive, if not evil in themselves.

But whatever they are in themselves, here is the 'grand difficulty, of which you give us no manner of solution. Whence comes it to pass that those appetites and passions, which no doubt were at first kindly implanted in our nature by an holy God, are now become so excessive or irregular that no one man from the beginning of the world has so resisted them as to keep himself pure and innocent?'[203]

'But without these appetites and passions our nature would be defective, sluggish, or unarmed. Nor is there any one of them which we can at present spare.'[a] We could very well spare the excess and irregularity of them all, and possibly some of the passions themselves, as love of praise, and love of revenge. The love of God would more than supply the place of both—neither does it suffer us to be *sluggish* or *inactive*. Nor does calm, Christian fortitude leave us *unarmed* against any danger which can occur. 'But our reason would have nothing to struggle with.'[b] O yes. Not only all our reason, but all the grace we have received, has enough to struggle with, even when 'we' do 'not wrestle with flesh and blood'. We are still abundantly 'exercised' by 'principalities and powers and spiritual wickedness in high places'.[204]

[y] [pp. 232-33.]
[z] [p. 233.]
[a] [p. 232.]
[b] p. 233.

---

[203] An uncited paraphrase from Jennings, *Vindication*, 110-11.
[204] Cf. Eph. 6:12.

'On the other hand, we are born with rational powers, which grow gradually capable of the most useful knowledge. And we under the gospel have clear ideas of the divine perfections: we see our duty, and the most cogent reasons to perform it.'[c] This sounds well. But will *knowledge* balance *passion*? Or are 'rational powers' a counterpoise to sensual appetites? Will 'clear ideas' deliver men from lust or vanity? Or *seeing* the duty to love our enemies enable us to practise it?[205] What are 'cogent reasons' opposed to covetousness or ambition? A thread of tow that has touched the fire.[206] 'But the Spirit of God is promised for our assistance.'[d] Nay, but what need of him, upon your scheme? Man is sufficient for himself.[207] 'He that glorieth', on this hypothesis, must glory in himself, not 'in the Lord'.[208]

Quest. 3. 'How far is our present state the same with that of Adam in paradise?'

'I suppose our mental capacities are the same as Adam's, only that some are above, some below his standard. Probably there are many in the world much below Adam in rational endowments. But possibly the force and acuteness of understanding was much greater in our Sir Isaac Newton than in Adam.'[e]

I do not apprehend this requires any answer. He that can believe it, let him believe it.

[VI.] 'We are next to inquire upon what true grounds those parts of religion stand which the Schoolmen have founded upon the doctrine of original sin, particularly the two grand articles of Redemption and Regeneration.'[f]

In what century did the Schoolmen write? How long before St.

[c] [Ibid.]
[d] [Ibid.]
[e] p. 235.
[f] [pp. 237-38.]

---

[205] See the discussion of JW's mature moral psychology in the introduction (pp. 144-45 above).

[206] 'Tow' is a general term for flax or wool fibres, all of which would burn readily.

[207] Taylor, *Reply* (1767), 17: 'This is a gross misrepresentation. I never thought or asserted anything like it.'

[208] Cf. 1 Cor. 1:31.

Augustine (to go no higher)?[209] A sad specimen this of 'the honesty and impartiality with which you deliver your sentiments'![210]

1. *Redemption*

'Our fall, corruption, and apostasy in Adam has been made the reason why the Son of God came into the world and "gave Himself a ransom" for us.'[g]

And undoubtedly it is the reason. Accordingly the very first promise of the Redeemer was given presently after the fall. And given with a manifest reference to those evils which came on all men through Adam's transgression. Nor does it appear from any Scripture that he would have come into the world at all had not 'all men died in Adam'.[211]

You yourself allow, 'The Apostle affirms (Rom. 5:18-19) that by "the righteousness and obedience of Christ" all men are delivered from the condemnation and sentence they came under through Adam's disobedience; and that thus far the redemption by Christ stands in connection with Adam's transgression.'[h]

'But the redemption by Christ extends far beyond the consequences of Adam's transgression.'[i] It does. Men receive far greater blessings by Christ than those they lost by Adam. But this does not prove that our fall in Adam is not the ground of our redemption by Christ.

Let us once more consider the text itself. Ver. 15, 'But not as the offence, so is the free gift. For if through the offence of one many be dead, much more the grace of God and the gift by grace'—the blessing which flows from the mere mercy of God—'which is by one man, Jesus Christ, hath abounded unto many.' Ver. 16, 'For not as it

[g] [p. 238.]
[h] p. 238.
[i] [Ibid.]

---

[209] JW seems to be chastising Taylor for diverting attention from the fact that the doctrine of original sin goes back to the early Church, not just medieval theologians.

[210] Cf. Taylor's Preface to *Scripture-Doctrine*, vii-viii:

'I have made the revelation of God alone the rule of my judgment, not any schemes or opinions of men. . . . I have honestly endeavoured to set things in a just light. . . . I add a hearty wish that we may all so seriously, closely, impartially, peaceably, and in the spirit of love, study the Scriptures, that . . . an entrance may be ministered unto us abundantly into his everlasting kingdom.'

[211] Cf. 1 Cor. 15:22.

was by one that sinned, so is the gift. For the judgment was by one' offence 'to condemnation, but the free gift is of many offences unto justification.' In this respect first, the free gift by 'Christ hath abounded much more' than the loss by Adam. And in this secondly, ver. 17, 'If by one man's offence *DEATH*', spiritual and temporal, leading to death eternal, '*REIGNED* by one' over his whole posterity, 'much more they who receive the abundance of grace and of the gift of righteousness', the free gift of justification and sanctification, 'shall *REIGN* in life' everlasting 'by one, Jesus Christ.'[212] Let anyone who calmly and impartially reads this passage judge, if this be not the plain, natural meaning of it.

But let us now observe your comment upon it. 'Here the Apostle asserts a grace of God which *already* hath *abounded*, beyond the effects of Adam's sin upon us.'[j] It has, upon them that are justified and sanctified, but not upon all mankind.[213]—'And which has respect, not to his *one offence*'—not to that only—'but' also 'to the *many offences* which men have personally committed. Not to the *DEATH* which *REIGNED* by him.'—Yes, verily. But over and above the removal of this, it hath also respect 'to the *LIFE* in which *they who receive* the *abounding grace* shall *REIGN* with him for ever'.[[k]]

Thus far you have proved just nothing. But you go on: 'The death consequent on Adam's sin is reversed by the redemption in Christ. But this is not the whole end of it by far. The grand reason and end of redemption is "The grace of God, and the gift by grace".'[l] Infallibly it is. But this is not a different thing, but precisely the same with the 'free gift'. Consequently your whole structure raised on the supposition of that difference is a mere castle in the air.[214] But if 'the

[j] p. 239.
[[k]] [Ibid.]
[l] p. 239 [quoting Rom. 5:15].

[212] Taylor quoted these three verses from Rom. 5 without additions. *Scripture-Doctrine*, 239. Note JW's insertions, particularly in ver. 17.

[213] JW's point is that the full benefits of God's abounding grace are experienced only in justification and sanctification. He is clear that a 'degree' of that benefit is experienced by all persons—in prevenient grace. Letter to John Mason, Nov. 21, 1776 (vol. 29 in this edn.); and Sermon 85, 'On Working Out Our Own Salvation', II.1, 3:203-4 in this edn.

[214] Taylor, *Reply* (1767), 17: 'A misrepresentation. I never supposed or affirmed that "the grace of God" and "the gift by grace" was different from the "free gift".'

gift by grace' and 'the free gift' are the very same thing, and if 'the gift by grace' is 'the grand reason and end of redemption', then our fall in Adam, to which you allow 'the free gift' directly refers, is 'the reason of Christ's coming into the world'.

'But the Scriptures of the New Testament (excepting Rom. 5:12-19 and 1 Cor. 15:21-22) always assign the actual wickedness of mankind as the reason of Christ's coming into the world.'[m] They generally do assign this, their outward and inward wickedness. But this does not exclude the wickedness of their nature, springing from their fall in Adam. Rather this, which is expressed in those two places at least, is presupposed in all places. Particularly in the beginning of the Epistle to the Romans, where he describes the enormous wickedness both of the Jews and Gentiles.

'Tis true, he begins his discourse with an account of the actual transgressions of the idolatrous Gentiles. Afterwards (chapter 3) he treats of the depravity and corruption of all mankind, and then proceeds (chapter 5) to show that we are all 'made sinners' by Adam, and that 'by his offence judgment is come upon all men to condemnation'. The Apostle's method is clear and natural. He begins with that which is most obvious, even actual sin, and then proceeds to speak of original sin, as the joint cause of the necessity of redemption for all men. But which way can we infer that because he begins with the mention of actual sins, in order to demonstrate the necessity of redemption, therefore he excludes original out of the account?[n]

Neither can we infer that because it is not expressly mentioned in other texts, therefore it is not implied.[215]

'But the Redeemer himself saith not one word of redeeming us from the corruption of nature derived from Adam. And seeing he spake exactly according to the commission which the Father gave him, we may safely conclude, it was no part of his commission to preach the doctrine of original sin.'[o]

Just as safely may we conclude that it was no part of his commission to teach and make known to men the 'many things' which he 'had to say to' his apostles before his death, which they 'could not' then 'bear' (John 16:12), but which according to

[m] p. 240.
[n] [Jennings,] *Vindication*, pp. 116-17.
[o] [Taylor, *Scripture-Doctrine*,] p[p]. 242[-43].

[215] JW referenced here Taylor, *Scripture-Doctrine*, 241-42, where Taylor cites a number of verses that talk about the gift of grace without mentioning original sin.

his promise he afterwards taught them by his Spirit, and by them to the world. It makes no difference as to the ground of our faith whether a doctrine was delivered by Christ himself or by his apostles, and whether it be written in any of the four Gospels or of the divine epistles. There is only this difference. The epistles were wrote after the resurrection and ascension of Christ, therefore after the full commencement of the Gospel dispensation. Whereas the discourses of Christ recorded in the Gospels were delivered before the Gospel dispensation was properly begun. Therefore we are to look for the peculiar doctrines of Christ rather in the epistles than in the Gospels. However, Christ did speak of this, and referred to it more than once, during his personal ministry; particularly in his discourse with Nicodemus, and Matthew 23. But it is not surprising that he did not speak so largely of redeeming us from sin, original or actual, by the price of his blood, before that price was actually paid, as the apostles did afterward. He considered the littleness of their knowledge with the violence of their prejudices.[216] Therefore we have no cause to be surprised that no more is said on this head in those discourses which Christ delivered before his death. But *to us he has told it* plainly, and *we do find* the doctrines of original sin and redemption from it by Jesus Christ, *distinguished emphatically* in almost every page of the inspired epistles.[217]

To sum up this: (1) Christ speaks very sparingly of many things whereof his apostles have spoken largely. (2) Yet he does speak of the corruption of our nature (which St. Paul expressly tells us is derived from Adam), particularly in the 23rd of St. Matthew and the 3rd of St. John. (3) Wherever he speaks of 'saving that which was lost', he in effect speaks of this, especially Matthew 18:11, where he mentions 'little children' as lost, which could not be by actual sin. (4) There was the less need of our Lord's speaking much on this head, because it was so fully declared in the Old Testament, and was not questioned by any of those false teachers against whom he was chiefly concerned to warn his disciples.

You add: 'It has been delivered as a fundamental truth that no man will come to Christ, the second Adam, who is not first throughly convinced of the several things he lost in the first Adam.'[p]

[p] p. 243.

[216] Taylor, *Reply* (1767), 17-18:

'But it is always supposed that the doctrine of original sin is clearly taught in the Old Testament, with which the apostles were well acquainted. How then could they be ignorant of it or prejudiced against it? How could they be unacquainted with it if they felt a corrupt nature in their own breasts as plainly and certainly as Mr. W[esley] feels it in his? Were they not as religious, sensible, and conscientious men as Mr. W[esley]?'

[217] Jennings, *Vindication*, 117-20 (an unmarked citation).

This is a fundamental truth. None will come to Christ as a redeemer till he is throughly convinced, he wants a redeemer. No man ever will come to him as a saviour till he knows and feels himself a *lost* sinner. None will come to the 'physician' but 'they that are sick',[218] and are throughly sensible of it—that are deeply convinced of their sinful tempers, as well as sinful words and actions. And these tempers they well know were antecedent to their choice, and came into the world with them. So far, 'every man who comes to Christ is first convinced of the several things he lost by Adam,' though he may not clearly know the source of that corruption which he sees and feels in his own heart and life.

'But why does our Lord never mention Adam, or the corruption of our nature through him!'[q] He does mention this corruption, and he presupposes it in all his public discourses. He does not mention it largely and explicitly for the reasons above recited. 'But the apostles are wholly silent on this head in their sermons recorded in the Acts, and in their epistles too.'[r] Are they 'wholly silent' in their epistles? This is a violent mistake. And as to their sermons, it may be observed: (1) That we have not one whole sermon of any one apostle recorded in the Acts; nor, it may be, the twentieth part of one. (2) That it was not needful for them to prove what none of their hearers denied—no, not even the heathens. Even these allowed the corruption of human nature. Even these received it as an undeniable fact,

Vitiis nemo sine nascitur[219]

No man is born without vices.

These acknowledged (as Seneca expresses it) '*Omnia in omnibus vitia sunt*'[220]—'All vices are in all men.' These saw, there were hardly any good men to be found upon the face of the earth, and openly testified it:

[q] [Ibid.]
[r] pp. 243-44.

---

[218] Cf. Matt. 9:12, etc.
[219] Horace, *Satires*, I.iii.68.
[220] Seneca, *De Beneficiis* (*On Benefits*), IV.xxvii.3.

Rari quippe boni: numero vix sunt totidem quot
Thebarum portae, vel divitis ostia Nili [221]

The good lie scattered in this barren soil,
Few as the gates of Thebes, or mouths of Nile.

They had also among them some faint account of the cause of that overflowing corruption. So Horace, immediately after he had asserted the fact,

Audax omnia perpeti
Gens humana ruit per vetitum nefas . . .

Lawless and unrestrained the human race
Rushes through all the paths of daring wickedness—
glances at the cause of it, in their fabulous manner:

Audax Japeti genus
Ignem fraude mala gentibus intulit.
Post ignem aetheria domo
Subductum, macies, et nova febrium
Terris incubuit cohors,
Semotique prius tarda Necessitas
Lethi corripuit gradum.[222]

Prometheus first provoked the heavenly Sire,
Purloining Jupiter's authentic fire.
Evil, from hence derived, and brooding pain,
And strange disease with all the ghastly train,
Poured in upon the wretched sons of men;
While hasty fate quickened the ling'ring pace
Of distant death, unveiled the monster's face,
And gave into his hands our whole devoted race.[223]

[221] Juvenal, *Satires*, xiii.26-27. The translation is possibly from CW. The Loeb edn. has: 'For honest men are scarce; hardly so numerous as the gates of Thebes or the mouths of the enriching Nile.' (This number was seven in each instance.)

[222] Horace, *Odes*, I.iii.25-26, 27-33.

[223] The translation is likely by CW (see Pt. I, n. 34, pp. 164 above). The closing line was corrected to this form in Proof (1757), where the original read: 'And gave into his hands the whole of our devoted race.'

I observe, (3) it was neither needful nor proper for an apostle in his first sermon to a congregation wholly unawakened to descant upon original sin. No man of common sense would do it now. Were I to preach to a certain congregation at Norwich[224] I should not say one word of Adam, but endeavour to show them that their lives, and therefore their hearts, were corrupt and abominable before God.

You conclude this head: '*Guilt imputed* is *imaginary guilt*, and so no object of *redemption*.'[s] I dare not say so as to my own particular. I pray God of his tender mercy to free me from this and all other guilt, 'through the *redemption which is in* Jesus Christ'![225]

2. *Regeneration*

'Why must we be *born again*?' (You subjoin the common, but as you suppose, absurd answer:) 'Because we are *born in sin*. Nature is averse to all good and inclined to all evil. Therefore we must be *born again*, before we can please God.'[t]

In order to confute this you assert: 'Then it cannot be *our duty* to be born again, nor consequently *our fault*, if we are not; because it is not in *our power*.'[u] It is, by grace, though not by nature. By this we may all be born again. Therefore it is *our duty*; and if we fall short herein it is *our own fault*.[226]

'But being born again does really signify the gaining those habits of virtue which make us children of God.'[v] Then St. Paul ought to have said, not 'ye are all the children of God, by faith in Christ Jesus',[227] but, 'ye are all the children of God, by gaining habits of virtue'!

[s] [p. 244.]
[t] p. 245.
[u] [Ibid.]
[v] p. 246.

---

[224] I.e., the Octagon Chapel, John Taylor's congregation.

[225] Cf. Rom. 3:24.

[226] JW does not address Taylor's point:

'It is common to find Divines asserting that we are born again by some uncertain, arbitrary and irresistible workings of the Spirit of God, which operate upon some few, and not upon others. Though the same divines tell us that if any are not born again they shall be condemned to everlasting torments. Which is to embarrass religion with inextricable difficulties, and to fill the minds of Christians with endless perplexity and confusion.' (*Scripture-Doctrine*, 245).

[227] Gal. 3:26.

Nay, but according to the whole tenor of Scripture the being 'born again' does really signify the being inwardly changed by the almighty operation of the Spirit of God—changed from sin to holiness, renewed in the image of him that created us.[228] And why must we be so changed? Because 'without holiness no man shall see the Lord'.[229] And because without this change all our endeavours after holiness are ineffectual. God hath indeed 'endowed us with *understanding*, and given us abundant means'.[w] But our understanding is as insufficient for that end as are the outward means if not attended with inward power.

You proceed to explain yourself at large. 'Christ informs us that "except a man be born again, he cannot see the kingdom of God",[x] and thereby teaches us':

1) 'That God hath erected a kingdom, united in and under him, for his glory, and men's mutual happiness.'[y]

2) 'He will finally admit none into it who are not disposed to relish and promote the happiness of it.'[z] (Both these propositions I willingly allow.)

3) 'All wickedness is quite contrary to the nature and end of this kingdom. Therefore no wicked men can be fit members of it. Unless there be a full persuasion that reverence, love, and obedience are due to God' (I add, and unless it be actually paid to him; otherwise that 'persuasion' but increases our condemnation); 'unless his favour is preferred before all other enjoyments whatsoever; unless there be a delight in the worship of God, and in converse with him; unless every appetite be brought into subjection to reason' (add, and reason to the Word of God), 'how can any man be fit to dwell with God, or to do him service in his kingdom?'[a]

4) 'It is one thing to be born into God's creation, another to be born into his peculiar kingdom. [. . .] In order to an admittance into his peculiar kingdom it is not enough for an intelligent being to exist.'[b] I do not know that. Perhaps it is not possible for God to

[w] [Cf. ibid.]
[x] p. 246 [citing John 3:3].
[y] pp. 246–47.
[z] p. 247.
[a] pp. 247–48.
[b] pp. 250–51.

[228] See Col. 3:10.
[229] Cf. Heb. 12:14.

create an intelligent being without creating it duly subject to himself, that is, a subject of his peculiar kingdom. It is highly probable the holy angels were subjects of his peculiar kingdom from the first moment of their existence. Therefore the following peremptory assertion, and all of the like kind, are wholly groundless: 'It is *absolutely necessary* before any creature can be a subject of this that it learn to employ and exercise its powers suitably to the nature of them.'[c] It is not necessary at all. In this sense surely, God 'may do what he will with his own'.[230] He may bestow his own blessings as he pleases. 'Is thine eye evil, because he is good?'[231]

The premises then being gone, what becomes of the conclusion? 'So that the being *born* into God's peculiar kingdom depends upon a *right use and application* of our life and being; and is the privilege only of those wise spirits who attain to an *habit* of true holiness.'[d]

This stands without any proof at all. At best, therefore, it is extremely doubtful. But it must appear extremely absurd to those who believe God can *create* spirits both wise and holy; that he can stamp any creature with what measure of holiness he sees good, at the first moment of its existence.

The occasion of your running into this absurdity seems to be that you stumbled at the very threshold. In the text under consideration our Lord mentions two things, the *new birth* and the *kingdom of God*. These two your imagination blended into one. In consequence of which you run on with 'born into his kingdom' (a phrase never used by our Lord nor any of his apostles), and an heap of other *crude expressions* of the same kind—all betraying that *confusedness of thought* which alone could prevent your usual clearness of language.

Just in the same manner you go on: 'Our first parents in paradise were to form their minds to an habitual subjection to the law of God, without which they could not be received into his spiritual kingdom.'[e] This runs upon the same mistaken supposition, that God *could not create them* holy. Certainly he could and did. And from the very moment that they were created their minds were in subjection to the law of God, and they were members of his spiritual kingdom.

[c] [p. 251.]
[d] [pp. 251-52.]
[e] p. 252.

[230] Cf. Matt. 20:15.
[231] Cf. ibid.

'But if Adam was originally perfect in holiness' (say *perfectly holy*, made in the moral image of God), 'what occasion was there for any farther trial?'[f] That there might be room for farther holiness and happiness. Entire holiness does not exclude growth. Nor did the *right state* of all his faculties entitle him to that full reward which would have followed the *right use* of them.

'Upon the whole, regeneration, or gaining habits of holiness, takes in no part of the doctrine of original sin.'[g] But regeneration is not 'gaining habits of holiness'. It is quite a different thing. It is not a natural but a supernatural change; and is just as different from the gradual 'gaining habits', as a child's being *born* into the world is from his *growing* up into a man. The *new birth* is not (as you suppose) the *progress*, or the *whole* of sanctification, but the *beginning* of it—as the natural *birth* is not the whole of life, but only the entrance upon it.[232] He that is 'born of a woman'[233] then begins to live a natural life, he that is 'born of God'[234] then begins to live a spiritual. And if every man 'born of a woman' had spiritual life already, he would not need to be 'born of God'.

'However, I allow the Spirit of God assists our endeavours. But this does not suppose any natural pravity of our minds.'[h] Does not his 'quickening'[235] then suppose we were *dead*? His 'opening our eyes'[236] suppose we were *blind*? And his 'creating us anew'[237] imply something more than the *assisting our endeavours*? How very slender a part in sanctification will you allow to the Spirit of God! You seem very fearful of doing him too much honour, of taking from man the glory due to his name![238]

Accordingly you say, 'His aids are so far from supposing the previous *ineptitude*[239] of our minds' (to the being 'born again') 'that our

[f] [Ibid.]
[g] p. 254.
[h] p. 255 [i.e., 254–55].

---

[232] Cf. Sermon 43, *The Scripture Way of Salvation*, I.4, 2:158 in this edn.; and Sermon 45, 'The New Birth', IV.3, 2:198 in this edn.
[233] Job 14:1, etc.
[234] 1 John 3:9, etc.
[235] Rom. 4:17.
[236] Cf. Matt. 20:33.
[237] Cf. Eph. 2:10.
[238] Contrast Ps. 29:2, etc.
[239] Original in JW 'inaptitude'; but in Taylor, 'ineptitude'. *Scripture-Doctrine*, 255.

previous desire of the Spirit's assistance is the condition of our receiving it.'[i] But who gave us that desire? Is it not God 'that worketh in us to will', to *desire*, as well as 'to do'?[240] His grace does *accompany* and *follow* our desires; but does it not also *prevent*, go before them?[241] After this we may *ask* and *seek* farther assistance. And if we do, not otherwise, *it is given*.

I cannot but add a few words from Dr. Jennings:

> Mr. Taylor believes 'the influence of the Spirit of God to assist our sincere endeavours is spoken of in the gospel, but never as supposing any natural pravity of our minds'. But certain it is that Christ opposeth our being 'born of the Spirit' to our being 'born of the flesh'.[242] 'That which is born of the flesh is flesh, and that which is born of the spirit is spirit' (John 3:[6]). Therefore the influence of the Spirit in regeneration supposeth something that we are *born* with, which makes such an influence necessary to our being *born again*. And if this be not some natural pravity, let our author tell us what it is. It is plain it is not any ill habit afterward acquired, for it is something that we are *born* with. And if to be 'born of the flesh' means only 'to have the parts and powers of a man', and if these parts and powers are all 'pure and uncorrupted', we have no need of any such influence of the Spirit to be superadded to our natural powers. Without this *our* own *sincere endeavours* will suffice for attaining all 'habits of virtue'.[j]

[VII.] I proceed to your conclusion: 'Is it not highly injurious to the God of our nature, whose hands have formed and fashioned us, to believe our nature is originally corrupted?'[k] It is. But the charge falls not on *us*, but *you*. We do not believe our nature is 'originally corrupted'. It is *you* who believe this, who believe our nature to be in the same state, moral and intellectual, as it *originally* was! Highly injurious indeed is this supposition to the God of our nature. Did he *originally* give us such a nature as this?[243] So like that of 'a wild ass's

[i] [p. 255.]
[j] [Jennings,] *Vindication*, p[p]. 125[-26]
[k] [Taylor, *Scripture-Doctrine*,] p. 256.

---

[240] Cf. Phil. 2:13.

[241] Taylor had said, 'It is highly fitting we should make a due use of the powers we already have, before we receive, and in order to our receiving further help.' *Scripture-Doctrine*, 256.

[242] Taylor, *Reply* (1767), 18: 'In this paragraph "being born of the flesh" is turned into "something that we are born with", whereas it rather denotes something we are born without.'

[243] Ibid.: 'Why then do you call the supposed corruption of your nature original sin, or the sin of your original, if your nature is not originally corrupted?' Note that Wesley and Taylor are using 'original' in two different senses!

colt'?[244] So stupid, so stubborn, so intractable! So prone to evil! Averse to good! Did 'his hands form and fashion us' *thus?*[245] No wiser or better than men at present are? If I believed this, that men were *originally* what they are now; if you could once convince me of this, I could not go so far as to be a deist—I must either be a Manichee[246] or an atheist. I must either believe there was an evil God, or that there was no God at all.

'But to disparage our nature is to disparage the work and gifts of God.'[l] True. But to describe the corruption of our nature as it is, is not disparaging the work of God. For that corruption is not his work. On the other hand, to say it is, to say God created us as corrupt as we are now, with as weak an understanding and as perverse a will—this is disparaging the work of God, and God himself, to some purpose!

'But doth not this doctrine teach you to transfer your wickedness and sin to a wrong cause? Whereas you ought to blame yourself alone, you lay the whole blame upon Adam.'[m] I do not. I know God is willing to save me from all sin, both original and actual. Therefore if I am not saved, I must lay the whole blame upon myself.

'But what good end does this doctrine promote?'[[n]] The doctrine that we are by nature 'dead in sin', and therefore 'children of wrath',[247] promotes *repentance*, a true knowledge of ourselves, and thereby leads to *faith* in Christ, to a true knowledge of Christ crucified. And faith worketh love; and by love, all holiness both of heart and life. Consequently, this doctrine promotes (nay, and is absolutely, indispensably necessary to promote) the whole of that religion which the Son of God lived and died to establish.

'We are told, indeed, that it promotes humility. But neither our Lord nor his apostles, when inculcating humility, say a word about natural corruption.'[[o]] Supposing (not granting) that they did not, yet it cannot be, in the very nature of the thing, that any whose

[l] p. 257.
[m] p[p]. [257-]258.
[[n]] [p. 258.]
[[o]] [p. 258n.]

---

[244] Job 11:12; cf. above, section V, Question 2.
[245] Cf. Job 10:8.
[246] A member of the sect founded by Manichaeus (3rd century A.D.), who represented Satan as co-eternal with God.
[247] Cf. Eph. 2:1, 3.

nature is corrupt should be humble, should know himself, without knowing that corruption.

'But what can be more destructive to virtue than to represent sin as altogether *unavoidable?*'[p] This does not follow from the doctrine. Corrupt as we are, through almighty grace we may avoid all sin.

But it is destructive of virtue. For 'if we believe we are by nature worse than the brutes, what wonder if we act worse than brutes?'[q] Yea, if we *are* so, what wonder if we *act* so! And this it is absolutely certain men do, whether they believe one way or the other. For they who do not believe this live no better than those that do. Therefore if 'the generality of Christians have been the most wicked, lewd, bloody, and treacherous of all mankind',[r] it is not owing to this belief. But in truth they have not been so. Neither are they at this day. The generality of Christians, so called, are perhaps but little better, yet surely they are no worse, either in tempers or actions, than the rest of mankind. The generality of Jews, yea, of Turks and pagans, are full as 'lewd, bloody, and treacherous' as they.

You go on. ''Tis surprising that Christians' (you mean those of them who believe original sin) 'have lost even a sense of the beneficence of God in giving them a rational nature.'[s] Nay, surely Christians have lost that rational nature itself, or they retain it to very little purpose, if 'the generality of them are the most wicked, lewd, bloody, and treacherous of all mankind'! They ought 'to be humbled' for yielding to those evil propensities which through the grace of God they may conquer. And they who do conquer ought to be continually 'thanking God' for this and all his benefits.

With great decency you proceed: 'Who can believe that to be a revelation from God which teacheth so absurd a doctrine? I make no doubt, this, with other like principles, have filled our land with infidels.'[t] However, the gentlemen who disclaim these absurd principles of original sin, redemption, and regeneration, may very easily convert those infidels—since there is scarce any room for contention left between them.

[p] p. 259.
[q] [Ibid.]
[r] [Cf. ibid.]
[s] p. 260.
[t] [pp. 260-61.]

'Is not this doctrine hurtful to the power of godliness, as it diverts men from the heavenly and substantial truths of religion?'[u] Just the reverse. There is no possibility of the power of godliness without it. The power of godliness consists in the love of God and man—this is heavenly and substantial religion. But no man can possibly 'love his neighbour as himself'[248] till he loves God. And no man can possibly love God till he truly believes in Christ. And no man truly believes in Christ till he is deeply convinced of his own sinfulness, guiltiness, and helplessness.[249] But this no man ever was, neither can be, who does not know he has a corrupt nature.

This doctrine, therefore, is the 'most proper' of all others 'to be instilled into a child'.[250] That it is by nature a 'child of wrath',[251] under the guilt and under the power of sin. That it can be saved from wrath only by the merits, and sufferings, and love of the Son of God. That it can be delivered from the power of sin only by the inspiration of his Holy Spirit. But that by his grace it may be renewed in the image of God, perfected in love, and made meet for glory.

But 'must it not lessen the due love of parents to children to believe they are the vilest creatures in the world?'[v] Far from it, if they know how God loves both them and theirs, vile and sinful as they are. And it is a certain fact that no parents love their children more tenderly than those who firmly believe this doctrine. And that none are more careful to 'bring them up in the nurture and admonition of the Lord'.[252]

But 'how can young people "remember" their "Creator" without horror if he has given them life under such deplorable circumstances?'[[w]] They can remember him with pleasure, with earnest thankfulness, when they reflect 'out of' what a 'pit' he hath 'brought

[u] p. 261.
[v] p. 262.
[[w]] [Ibid.]

---

[248] Mark 12:33, etc.

[249] What JW fails to add here, but stresses elsewhere, is the witness of the Holy Spirit *assuring* us of God's love in Christ. Perhaps this is another of those 'disputed doctrines' that he was carefully avoiding in this treatise.

[250] Taylor claimed it would be better to instill in children the conviction that they were 'born under the smiles of heaven, endowed with noble capacities, and formed in love, for the glory of God and [their] own happiness, if [their] goodness is not despised and neglected'. *Scripture-Doctrine*, 261-62.

[251] Cf. Eph. 2:3.

[252] Eph. 6:4.

them up';[253] and that if 'sin abounded', both by nature and habit, 'grace' did 'much more abound'.[254]

You conclude: 'Why should we subject our consciences to tales and fables, invented by priests and monks?'[x] This fable, as you term it, of original sin, could not be invented by Romish priests or monks, because it is by many ages older than either, yea, than Christianity itself.

I have now weighed, as my leisure would permit, all the arguments advanced in your three parts. And this I have done with continual prayer, that I might know 'the truth as it is in Jesus'.[255] But still I see no ground to alter my sentiments touching the general corruption of human nature. Nor can I find any better or any other way of accounting for that general wickedness which has prevailed in all nations, and through all ages, nearly from the beginning of the world to this day.

Lewisham, Jan. 25, 1757

[x] p. 264.

[253] Ps. 40:2.
[254] Rom. 5:20.
[255] Cf. Eph. 4:21.

PART III
AN ANSWER TO MR. TAYLOR'S SUPPLEMENT

You subjoin to your book a very large *Supplement*, in answer to Dr. Jennings and Dr. Watts. All that they have advanced I am not engaged to defend, but such parts only as affect the merits of the cause.

You divide this part of your work into eight sections. The first treats

[I.] *Of Imputed Guilt*

[1.] And here you roundly affirm: 'No *action* is said in Scripture to be *imputed* to any person for righteousness or condemnation but the *proper act and deed* of that person.'[a]

Were then the 'iniquities and sins'[1] which were put upon the scapegoat his own 'proper act and deed'? You answer, 'Here was no imputation of sin to the goat. It was only a figurative way of signifying the *removal of guilt* from the penitent Israelites, by the goat's going into the wilderness.'[b] But how could it be a 'figure' of any such thing if no *guilt* was *imputed* to him?

> Aaron is commanded to 'put the iniquities of Israel' upon the scapegoat (Lev. 16:21). And this goat is said to 'bear the iniquities of the people' (ver. 22). This was plainly an *imputation*. Yet it could not possibly be an imputation of anything done by the animal itself. The effects also which took place upon the execution of the ordinance indicate a translation of guilt. For the congregation was cleansed, but the goat was polluted. The congregation *so cleansed* that their iniquities were borne away, and to be found no more; the goat so *polluted* that it communicated defilement to the person who conducted it into a land not inhabited.[c]

In truth the scapegoat was a figure of him 'on whom the Lord laid the iniquities of us all' (Isa. 53:6). 'He bore our iniquity' (ver. 11).

[a] [John Taylor, A] *Supplement [to the Scripture-Doctrine of Original Sin, etc.; Containing some Remarks upon two Books* . . . (London: Mary Fenner, 1741)], p. 7.
[b] [pp. 7-8.]
[c] [Hervey] *Theron and Aspasio* [Dial. II (1:41-42)].

[1] Cf. Lev. 16:21-22.

'He bare the sin of many' (ver. 12). The prophet uses three different words in the original, of which the first does properly signify the *meeting together*; the last, the *lifting up* a weight or burden. This burden it was which made him 'sweat as it were great drops of blood, falling to the ground'.[2] 'But *iniquity* and *sin* sometimes signify *suffering*.'[d] Yes; *suffering for sin*, the effect being put for the cause. Accordingly what we mean by, 'Our sins *were imputed to him*', is he was punished for them—'He was wounded for our transgressions; he was bruised for our iniquities.'[3] He 'who knew no sin' but what was thus imputed, 'was made sin', a sin-offering, 'for us'.[4] 'It pleased the Lord' (your own words) 'to bruise him, in order to the expiation of our sins.'[e]

[2.] 'But with regard to parents and their posterity, God assures us children "shall not die for the iniquity of their fathers".'[f] No, not eternally. I believe none ever did or ever will die eternally, merely for the sin of our first father.[5]

[3.] 'But the Scripture never speaks of *imputing* any *sin* to any person, but what is the act of that person.'[g] It was but now you yourself observed that by 'our sins were *imputed to* Christ' we mean, 'he suffered for them'.[6] Our sins, then, were imputed to Christ. And yet these sins were not the act of the person that suffered. He did not commit the sin which was thus *imputed* to him.

[4.] But 'no just constitution can punish the *innocent*.'[h] This is undoubtedly true. Therefore God does not look upon infants as innocent, but as involved in the *guilt* of Adam's sin. Otherwise death, the *punishment* denounced against that sin, could not be inflicted upon them.

[d] [Taylor] *Supplement*, p. 8.
[e] p. 10.
[f] [pp. 10-11; quoting Deut. 24:16.]
[g] pp. 13-14.
[h] p. 16.

---

[2] Luke 22:44.
[3] Isa. 53:5.
[4] Cf. 2 Cor. 5:21.
[5] John Taylor, *A Reply to the Reverend John Wesley's Remarks on 'The Scripture-Doctrine of Original Sin'* (London: Waugh, 1767), 19: 'This is denying one principal article of original sin. See Assembly's Catechism.'
[6] Ibid.: 'This is a misrepresentation. I never observed any such thing.' Taylor is rejecting JW's loose paraphrase of the argument of *A Supplement to the Scripture-Doctrine of Original Sin, etc.; Containing some Remarks upon two Books . . .* (London: Mary Fenner, 1741), 8-10.

[5.] 'It is allowed the posterity of Ham and Gehazi, and the children of Dathan and Abiram, suffered for the sins of their parents.'[i] It is enough. You need allow no more. All the world will see, if they *suffered* for them, then they were *punished* for them. Yet we do not 'confound *punishment* with *suffering*, as if to *suffer* and to be *punished* were the same thing'. *Punishment* is not barely *suffering*, but *suffering for sin*—to *suffer* and to be *punished* are not the same thing. But to *suffer for sin* and to be *punished* are precisely the same.[7]

If therefore the children of Dathan and Abiram 'suffered for the sins'[8] of their parents, which no man can deny, then they were *punished* for them. Consequently it is not true that 'in the instances alleged the parents only were *punished* by the sufferings of the children'.[j] If the children 'suffered for those sins', then they were *punished* for them. Indeed sometimes the parents too were punished by the sufferings of their children—which is all that your heap of quotations proves—and sometimes they were not. But however this were, if the children 'suffered for their sins', they were *punished* for them.

It is not therefore 'evident that in all these cases, children are considered not as *criminals*, involved in guilt, but as the *enjoyments* of their parents, who alone are *punished* by their sufferings'.[k] On the contrary, it is very evident that the children of Canaan were *punished* for the sin of Ham. And that the children of Dathan and Abiram were punished with death, as 'involved in the guilt' of their parents.

[6.] 'On the other hand, the virtues of an ancestor may convey great advantages to his posterity. But no man's posterity can be *rewarded* for their ancestor's virtue.'[l] The point here in dispute between Dr. Watts and you is whether the thing concerning which you are agreed should be expressed by one *term* or another. You both agree (and no man in his senses can deny) that in all ages God has, on account of pious ancestors, given many blessings to their

[i] [pp. 16-17.]
[j] pp. 17-18.
[k] p. 18.
[l] p. 21.

---

[7] Taylor, *Reply* (1767), 19: 'To *suffer* in consequence of another man's sin, in which I had no hand, directly or indirectly, and to be *punished* for it, cannot be precisely the same.'

[8] Cf. Num. 16:23-35.

offspring. But he thinks these blessings should be termed *rewards* (and so do all the world). You say they should not. The fact is plain either way. God does continually, and did in all ages, give numberless blessings to the children on account of the piety of their fathers. And it is certain, *blessings given on account of virtue* have been hitherto termed 'rewards' both by God and man.

You conclude this section: 'Thus it appears, the distinction between *personal sin* and *imputed guilt* is without any ground in Scripture.'[m] Just the contrary appears, namely, that *guilt* was *imputed* to the scapegoat, to the children of wicked parents, and to our blessed Lord himself, without any *personal sin*. The distinction therefore is sound and scriptural.

Sect. II

Of the Nature and Design of our Afflictions and Mortality

[1.] That God *designs* to bring good out of these is certain. But does this prove they have not the *nature* of *punishments*? Did Adam himself suffer any *affliction*? Any toil or pain? Doubtless he did, long before he returned to dust. And can we doubt but he received spiritual good from that pain? Yet it was a *punishment* still, as really such as if it had consigned him over to everlasting punishment. This argument therefore is of no weight: 'God draws good out of punishments, therefore they are no punishments at all.'[9] However, then, the sufferings wherein Adam's sin has involved his whole posterity may 'try and purify us, in order to future and everlasting happiness',[n] this circumstance does not alter their *nature*. They are *punishments* still. See B[axter]'s *Aph*[*orisms*].[10]

Let 'afflictions, calamities, and death itself, be means of improving in virtue',[o] of healing or preventing sin, this is no manner of

[m] p. 22.
[n] p. 23.
[o] p. 24.

[9] This is not a quotation, but JW's articulation of an apparent assumption of Taylor in *Supplement*, 22-28.

[10] I.e., Richard Baxter's *Aphorismes of Justification* (London: Francis Tyton, 1649), of which JW published an extract in 1745 (above in this vol., pp. 45-88). JW surely has in mind Baxter's Thesis 9 (pp. 60-61), which appears in his extract as Prop. VI. This cryptic addition may have been a memorandum accidentally left in the printed text—it disappeared from *Works* (1773).

proof that they are not *punishments*. Was not God able to heal or prevent sin without either pain or death? Could not the Almighty have done this as easily, as speedily, and as effectually, without these as with them? Why then did he not? Why did Adam's sin bring these on his whole posterity? Why should one man suffer for another man's fault? If you say, to cure his own, I ask: (1) What necessity was there of any suffering at all for this? If God intended *only* to cure his sin, he could have done that without any suffering. I ask, (2) Why do infants suffer? What sin have they to be cured thereby? If you say, 'It is to heal the sin of their parents, who sympathize, suffer with them'[11]—in a thousand instances this has no place. The parents are not the better, nor any way likely to be the better, for all the sufferings of their children. Their sufferings, therefore, yea, and those of all mankind which are entailed upon them by the sin of Adam, are not the result of mere *mercy*, but of *justice* also. In other words, they have in them the nature of *punishments*, even on us and on our children. Therefore children themselves are not innocent before God. They suffer, therefore they deserve to suffer.

[2.] And here another question arises.[12] What benefit accrues to the brute creation from the sufferings wherein their whole race is involved through the sin of the first man? The fact cannot be denied. Daily experience attests what we read in the oracles of God, that 'the whole creation groaneth together, and travaileth in pain to this day.'[13] A considerable part of it groans to God under the wantonness or cruelty of man. Their sufferings are caused, or at least greatly increased, by our luxury or inhumanity—nay, and by our *diversions*! We draw *entertainment* from the pain, the death of other creatures! Not to mention several entire species, which at present have such natural qualities that we are obliged to inflict pain, nay, perhaps death upon them, purely in our own defence. And even those species which are out of the reach of men are not out of the reach of suffering. 'The lions do lack and suffer hunger,'[14] though they are as it were sovereigns of the plain. Do they not acknowledge this, when

[11] JW has actually cast in more positive terms Taylor's suggestion that God may allow the sin of the parent to be punished in the sufferings of the child as a motive to deter parents from impiety and wickedness. Cf. *Supplement*, 19-20.

[12] JW is raising this question; Taylor does not even hint at it in this context. Wesley will even more explicitly insert his view on this issue into his extract of Watts in Pt. IV, below (pp. 392-93, n. 45).

[13] Cf. Rom. 8:22.

[14] Cf. Ps. 34:10.

'roaring for their prey', they 'seek their meat from God'?[15] And what shall we say of their helpless prey? Is not their lot more miserable still? Now what benefits, I say, have these from their sufferings? Are they also 'tried and purified thereby'? Do sufferings 'correct their inordinate passions, and dispose their minds to sober reflections'? Do they 'give them opportunity of exercising kindness and compassion, in relieving each other's distresses'?[16] That I know not. But I know by this and a thousand proofs that when man, the lord of the visible creation, rebelled against God, every part of the creation began to 'suffer on account of his sin'.[17] And to 'suffering on account of sin' I can give no properer name than that of *punishment*.

[3.] 'It was to reclaim offenders that an extraordinary power was exercised, either immediately by our Lord himself or by his apostles, of inflicting bodily distempers and in some cases death itself.'[p] I do not remember any more than one single case wherein one of the apostles 'inflicted death'. I remember no instance recorded in Scripture of their 'inflicting bodily distempers'. (The blindness inflicted on Elymas[18] cannot be so termed without great impropriety.) And certain I am that our Lord himself inflicted neither one nor the other.

The citations in the next page prove no more than that we may reap benefit from the *punishments* of others.[q] But though either we or they reap benefit from them, yet they are *punishments* still.

[4.] 'We do not here consider death and suffering as they stand in the threatening of the law.'[r] You are sensible, if we did, all mankind must acknowledge them to be *punishments*.[19] And this is the very light wherein we do and must consider them in the present question. We consider death and suffering as they stand in that threatening, 'Thou shalt surely die.'[20] That this was denounced to all mankind we know,

[p] p. 25.
[q] p. 26.
[r] p. 27.

[15] Cf. Ps. 104:21 (BCP).

[16] Taylor offered these three explanations to account for *human* suffering in our state of probation. Cf. *Supplement*, 23.

[17] Cf. 1 Pet. 3:18.

[18] Acts 13:8-11.

[19] Wesley has taken this last quotation out of context. Taylor was stipulating that he was not considering death and suffering as related only to the law (i.e., the old covenant) but as 'altered and rectified by grace'. *Supplement*, 27.

[20] Gen. 2:17.

because it is executed on all. Therefore considering *suffering* and *death* as so *threatened* and *executed*, we cannot deny that they are *punishments*—punishments not on Adam only, but on all that in fact do either *die* or *suffer*.

To sum up this point. Although the wisdom and mercy of God do 'bring good out of evil'. Although God *designs* to extract blessings from punishments, and does it in numberless instances. Yet this does not alter the *nature* of things, but *punishments* are *punishments* still. Still this name properly belongs to all *sufferings* which are *inflicted on account of sin*; and consequently it is an evident truth that the whole animate creation is *punished* for Adam's sin.

Sect. III
The Argument taken from the Calamities and Sinfulness of Mankind considered

[1.] 'The subject of our present inquiry is threefold: (1) Whether mankind be under God's displeasure antecedently to their actual sins. (2) Whether our nature be corrupt from the beginning of life. And (3) whether these propositions can be proved from the *calamities* and *sinfulness* of mankind.'[s]

Whether they can or no, they have been fully proved from Scripture. Let us now inquire if they may not be proved from the state of the world.

[2.] But you think Dr. Watts[21] 'has here laid too great stress on supposition and imagination'.[[t]] In proof of which you cite from him the following words:

> Can we *suppose* that the blessed God would place his innocent creatures in such a dangerous habitation? Can we *suppose* that among the roots, and the herbs, and the trees which are good for food, the great God would have suffered deadly poison to spring up here and there? Would there have been any such creatures in our world as bears and tigers? Can we ever *imagine* the great and good God would have appointed men to be propagated in such a way as would necessarily give such exquisite pain and anguish to the mothers that produce them, if they had been all accounted in his eyes a race of holy and sinless beings?[u]

[s] pp. 30-31.
[[t]] [p. 31.]
[u] p. 31 [citing Watts, *Ruin*, pp. 14-24].

---

[21] In his *Supplement* Taylor did not name the authors of the two works, referring to them as 'the Vindicator' (Jennings) and 'R.R.' (Watts, as author of *Ruin and Recovery*).

I answer, It is not true 'that too great stress', or any stress at all, is 'here laid on *mere* supposition and imagination'. Your catching at those two words *suppose* and *imagine* will by no means prove it. For the meaning of them is plain. 'Can we *suppose* the blessed God would do this' is manifestly the same with, 'How can we reconcile it with his essential attributes?' In like manner, 'Can we ever *imagine*' is plainly equivalent with, 'Can we possibly conceive?' So that the occasional use of these words does not infer his laying any stress on supposition and imagination. When therefore you add, 'Our *suppositions* and *imaginations* are not a just standard by which to measure the divine dispensations',[v] what you say is absolutely true, but absolutely foreign to the point.

Some of the questions which you yourself ask, to expose his, it is not so easy to answer. 'Would innocent creatures have been thrust into the world in so contemptible circumstances? And have been doomed to grow up so slowly to maturity and the use of reason? Would they when grown up have been constrained to spend so much time in low and servile labour? Would millions have been obliged to spend all their days, from early morn till evening, in hewing stone, sawing wood, heaving, rubbing, or beating the limb of an oak or a bar of iron?'[w] I really think they would not. I believe all this toil, as well as the pain and anguish of women in child-birth, is an evidence of the fall of man, of the sin of our first parents, and part of the *punishment* denounced and executed first on them, and then on all their posterity.

[3.] You add: 'He doth not consider this world as a state of trial, but as if it ought to have been a seat of happiness.'[x] There is no contrariety between these. It might be a state of trial, and of happiness too. And such it certainly was to Adam in paradise. Whether he was holy or no, he was undoubtedly happy. A state of trial, therefore, does not necessary imply any kind or degree of natural evil. And accordingly the Creator himself assures us, there was none originally in his creation. For so I read at the conclusion of it: 'And God saw everything that he had made; and behold, it was very good.'[y]

'But natural evil *may be* mixed with a state of trial. Consequently this world *could not* be built for a seat of happiness.'[z] Admirable

[v] p. 32.
[w] pp. 32-33.
[x] pp. 34-35.
[y] Gen. 1:31.
[z] [Taylor, *Supplement*, p. 35.]

drawing of consequences! 'It *may be*, therefore it *could not* be otherwise.'[22] Whatever *may be*, God himself here tells us *what was*. And from his own declaration it is infallibly certain, there was no *natural evil* in the world till it entered as the punishment of *sin*.

[4.] 'Neither doth he take a future state into his representation.'[a] No, nor is there any need he should, when he is representing the present state of the world as a *punishment* of Adam's sin.

[5.] 'Nor doth he take into his argument the goodness of God.'[b] Not into *this* argument. That is of after consideration. So the texts you have heaped together on this head also are very good. But what do they prove?

[6.] 'He supposes our sufferings to be mere punishments.'[[c]] I suppose they are *punishments* mixed with mercy. But still they are *punishments*—they are 'evils inflicted on account of sin'.

'We find in fact that the *best of men* may be made *very unhappy* by calamities and oppressions.'[d] It cannot be. The *best of men* cannot be made unhappy by any calamities or oppressions whatsoever. For they 'have learned, in every' possible 'state, therewith to be content'.[23] In spite of all calamities they 'rejoice evermore',[24] and 'in everything give thanks'.[25]

[7.] 'From punishments inflicted on *particular persons* he infers that *all men* are under the wrath of God. But to infer the state of *the whole* from the case of *some* is not a fair way of arguing.'[e] No. The punishments inflicted on particular persons prove nothing but with regard to those on whom they are inflicted. If therefore *some men* only suffer and die, this proves nothing with regard to the rest. But if *the whole* of mankind suffer and die, then the conclusion reaches *all men*.

[8.] 'He is not quite just in pronouncing the present form of the earth "irregular, abrupt, and horrid", and asking "Doth it not bear

[a] p. 36.
[b] p. 37.
[[c]] [p. 38.]
[d] p. 39.
[e] p. 40.

[22] Taylor, *Reply* (1767), 20: 'A misrepresentation. The consequence is drawn from other premises besides "natural evil". See *Supplement*, p. 35.'

[23] Cf. Phil. 4:11.

[24] 1 Thess. 5:16.

[25] 1 Thess. 5:18.

strongly on our sight, the ideas of ruin and confusion, in vast broken mountains, dreadful cliffs and precipices, immense extents of waste and barren ground?" If this be the case, how can "the invisible things of God" be "clearly seen from" such a ruined "creation"?'[f] Perfectly well. 'His eternal power and godhead',[26] the existence of a *powerful* and *eternal* Being, may still be inferred from these his works, grand and magnificent, though in ruin.[27] Consequently, these leave the atheist 'without excuse'.[28] And whatever objections he might form (as Lucretius[29] actually does) from these palpable blemishes and irregularities of the terraqueous globe, the scriptural account of *natural* flowing from *moral* evil will easily and perfectly solve them. All which is well consistent with the words of the Psalmist, 'O Lord, how manifold are thy works! In wisdom hast thou made them all: the earth is full of thy riches!'[g] So undoubtedly it is, though it bears so visible signs of *ruin* and *devastation*.

'We have no authority from Scripture to say that the earth, in its *present constitution*, is at all different from what it was at its first creation'.[30] Certainly we have, if the Scripture affirms that God *said*, after Adam sinned, 'Cursed is the ground for thy sake. Thorns and thistles shall it bring forth to thee';[31] and that 'the earth was of old, standing out of the water, and in the water',[32] till God destroyed it for the sin of its inhabitants.

[9.] You go on. 'I cannot agree that "disease, anguish, and death have entered into the bowels and veins of multitudes by an innocent

[f] pp. [40-]41 [quoting Watts, *Ruin*, pp. 11-17].
[g] p. 42 [quoting Ps. 104:24].

---

[26] Rom. 1:20.
[27] See Milton, *Paradise Lost*, ii.305, 'majestic, though in ruin'.
[28] Rom. 1:20.
[29] See Lucretius, *De Rerum Natura* (*On the Nature of Things*), v.195-234, etc.
[30] Taylor, *Reply* (1767), 20: 'A misrepresentation of my sense. See *Supplement*, p. 42.' Here the orig. reads: '. . . we have no authority from Scripture to say that the earth looks like a "ruin", or that its "present constitution", so far as *R. R.* here considers it, is at all different from what it was when upon a review God pronounced it and all its furniture "very good".' JW's basic summary is therefore accurate, though he gives no hint of the continuation: 'Consequently we have no authority from Scripture to say that the present form and furniture of the earth carry in them evident tokens of God's displeasure against the inhabitants of it.'
[31] Cf. Gen. 3:17-18.
[32] Cf. 2 Pet. 3:5.

and fatal mistake, of pernicious plants and fruits for proper food." '[h] Why not? Doubtless *multitudes* have perished hereby, if we take in the account of all ages and nations. *Multitudes* also have been 'the living prey of bears and tigers, wolves, and lions'. And *multitudes* have had 'their *flesh* and bones crushed and churned between the jaws of panthers and leopards, sharks and crocodiles'.[33] And would these things have come upon mankind were it not on account of Adam's sin?

Yet you think we have 'now a more extensive dominion over all creatures than Adam had even in his innocence. Because we have the liberty of eating them, which Adam never had.'[i] This will not prove the point. That I have the liberty to eat a *lamb* does not prove that I have dominion over *a lion*. Certainly I have not dominion over any creature which I can neither *govern* nor *resist*. Yea, and if 'the dread of' me is 'on every beast and fowl',[34] this does not prove that I have any 'dominion over' them. I know, on the contrary, that not only a tiger or a bear, but even a dove will not stoop to my dominion.

[10.] 'However, we have no authority to say Man himself was cursed, though the ground was.'[j] Yes, we have, the authority of God himself: 'Cursed is every man that continueth not in all the things'[35] which God hath commanded. The moment therefore that he sinned Adam fell under this curse.[36] And whether the *toil* and *death* to which he and his posterity were sentenced, and the *pain* of *child-birth*, be termed *curses* or no,[k] sure it is they are *punishments*,[37] and heavy ones too, though mercy is often mixed with judgment.

[h] p. 43 [quoting Watts, *Ruin*, p. 17].
[i] pp. 44-[45].
[j] p. 45.
[k] pp. 46-50.

---

[33] JW is citing approvingly two quotations from Isaac Watts, *Ruin and Recovery of Mankind*, 2nd edn. (London: James Brackstone, 1742), 19, 22, which Taylor had rejected as exaggerations of the negative dimensions of our present situation (*Supplement*, 43).

[34] Cf. Gen. 9:2.

[35] Gal. 3:10.

[36] Taylor, *Reply* (1767), 20: 'True. But this curse did not come into any part of the sentence which God pronounced upon Adam after he had sinned.'

[37] Taylor argued that the 'labours of life' are better viewed as wholesome exercise. Cf. *Supplement*, 50.

[11.] The main argument follows, taken from the state of mankind in general with regard to religion. But you say, 'It is impossible we should make a just estimate of the wickedness of mankind.'[l] Yes, an *exactly* just estimate of the *precise* degree of wickedness in the whole world. But it is very possible, nay, very easy, to make an estimate in the gross, with such a degree of justness as suffices for the present question.

Indeed you 'think we carry our censures of the heathens too far'.[m] I dare not carry them so far as to say, No heathen shall be saved. But this I say: I never knew an heathen yet (and I have personally known many out of various nations) who was not a slave to some gross vice or other. Bad therefore as nominal Christians are, I cannot yet place them on a level with the heathens—not even with the mild, courteous, conversable heathens who border on Georgia and Carolina. Much less would I say, 'Possibly the heathens may be *less vicious* than the Christian world in general.'[n] If I believed this I should bid adieu to Christianity, and commence heathen without delay.

[12.] 'But if we allow mankind to be ever so wicked, suppose there is not one upon earth who is truly righteous, it will not follow that men are *naturally* corrupt. For a sinful action does not infer a sinful nature. If it does, then Adam brought a sinful nature with him into the world. But if we cannot infer from Adam's sin that his nature was originally corrupt, neither can we infer from the wickedness of all mankind, be it ever so great, that they have a sinful nature.'[o]

The consequence is not good.[38] 'If one man's committing a sin does not prove that he was naturally inclined to evil, then the wickedness of all mankind for six thousand years will not prove that they are naturally inclined to evil.'[p] For we may easily account for one man's committing sin, though he was not naturally inclined to evil, but not so easily for 'all flesh corrupting themselves',[39] for the wickedness of all mankind in all ages. It is not possible rationally to

[l] p. 51.
[m] [Ibid.]
[n] [Ibid.]
[o] pp. 52-53.
[p] [p. 53.]

---

[38] Taylor, *Reply* (1767), 20: 'See the remark on p. 205.' This refers to Taylor's comment on Pt. II, section V (see p. 288, n. 202 above).

[39] Cf. Gen. 6:12.

account for this, for the general wickedness of mankind, for such a majority of men through all generations being so corrupt, but on the supposition of their having a corrupt nature. Sin in one or a few cases does not prove a sinful nature. But sin overspreading the earth, does. Nor is your argument drawn from the sin of the angels[q] of any more force than that drawn from the sin of Adam—unless you can prove that as great a majority of angels as of men have rebelled against their Creator.

[13.] 'Again. If our first parents felt *fear* and *shame*, and yet their nature was not originally corrupt, then it will not follow that ours is so, notwithstanding our uneasy and unruly passions.'[40] Empty sound! Had anyone said to Adam, 'Your nature was originally corrupt, for you feel uneasy and unruly passions,' would he not readily have answered, 'But these began at such an hour. Till then my nature was without either pain or corruption'. Apply this to any child of Adam, and if he can answer in like manner, 'Till such an hour no uneasy or unruly passion had any place in my breast,' we will then grant these passions no more prove a corrupt nature in the sons than in their first father. But no man can answer thus. You and I and every man must acknowledge that uneasy and unruly passions are coeval with our understanding and memory, at least, if not with our very being.

[14.] 'Again. Adam by his sin brought sufferings on himself and his posterity. Yet it does not follow that his nature was corrupt. Therefore, though others by their sins bring sufferings on themselves and their posterity, it will not follow that their nature is corrupt, or under the displeasure of God.'[r] Two very different things are here blended together. The corruption of their nature is one thing, the displeasure of God another. None affirms that those sufferings which men by their sins bring on themselves or posterity

[q] [Cf.] p. 54.
[r] [p. 55.]

[40] This is a misleading abridgment of Taylor, *Supplement*, 54-55:

'If our first parents had animal passions which they indulged in eating the forbidden fruit . . . and thereby introduced into their breasts the uneasy perturbations of fear and shame, and yet their nature was not originally corrupt; . . . then it will follow, notwithstanding the inward anguish that springs from all our uneasy and unruly passions of every kind, that our nature . . . is not corrupt from birth, but made in the image and favour of God.'

prove that their nature is corrupt. But do not the various sufferings of all mankind prove that they are under the displeasure of God? It is certain no sufferings came upon Adam till he was under the displeasure of God.

[15.] 'Again. If our first parents by their sin brought suffering both on themselves and others, and yet their nature was not originally corrupt, nor under the displeasure of God, it clearly follows that the nature of those who suffer purely in consequence of their sin is not originally corrupt, nor are they under God's displeasure.'[s] This argument is bad every way. For, (1) at the time when Adam brought the sentence of suffering both on himself and others, his nature was corrupt, and he was under the actual displeasure of God. But (2) suppose it were otherwise, all you could possibly infer with regard to his posterity is that their suffering does not prove their corruption, or their being under the displeasure of God. How could you think their suffering would prove them *not corrupt*? Not under God's displeasure? Therefore neither this nor the preceding argument (seeing both are utterly inconclusive) take off anything that Dr. Watts has said touching the present state of the world, as a proof of God's displeasure, and the natural corruption of man. So far therefore is 'his argument from the sinfulness and misery of mankind from being altogether insufficient in every part',[t] that it is strong and conclusive, anything you have advanced to the contrary notwithstanding.

You add: '*Suffering* may happen where there is *no sin*, as in the case of brutes and infants; or where there is the most perfect innocence, as in the case of our blessed Lord.'[u] Absolutely true. That is, where there is no *personal* sin, but only *sin imputed*. There was no *personal sin* in our blessed Lord. There can be none either in brutes or infants. He suffered therefore for the sin of others, which were thus *imputed* to him. As is the sin of Adam to infants, who suffer death through him. And in some sense to the whole creation, which was 'made subject to vanity, not willingly',[41] but on account of his transgression. But where there is no sin, either personal or imputed, there can be no suffering.

[s] [p. 56.]
[t] [p. 57.]
[u] [Ibid.]

[41] Rom. 8:20.

[16.] 'I may add, From the present state of things a directly opposite argument may be taken, from the enjoyments and comforts, the good things and blessings, which abound in the world. I might ask, Are these creatures, so well provided for, under God's displeasure? Are they not the care of his goodness? Does he not love them, and delight to do them good?'[v] I answer, God does still give us many good things, many enjoyments, comforts, and blessings. But all these are given through 'the seed of the woman',[42] they are all the purchase of his blood. Through him we are still the care of the divine goodness, and God does delight to do us good. But this does not at all prove, either that we have not a sinful nature, or that we are not, while sinful, under his displeasure.

Sect. IV
Some Consequences of the Doctrine of Original Sin

1. 'By this doctrine some have been led to maintain that men have not a sufficient power to perform their duty. But if so, it ceases to be their duty.'[w] I maintain that men have not this power by nature. But they have or may have it by grace.[43] Therefore it does not cease to be their duty. And if they perform it not, they are without excuse.

2. 'Hence some maintain that we have no reason to thank our Creator for our being.'[x] He that will maintain it may. But it does by no means follow from this doctrine. Since whatever we are by nature, we may by grace be children of God and heirs of the kingdom of heaven.

'But unthankfulness is a natural consequence of this doctrine, which greatly diminishes, if not totally excludes the goodness and mercy of God'.[y] St. Paul thought otherwise. He imagined the total ungodliness and impotence of our nature to be the very thing which most of all illustrated the goodness and mercy of God. 'For a good man', says he, 'peradventure one would even dare to die. But God commendeth', unspeakably, inconceivably, beyond all human

[v] pp. 58-61 [i.e., pp. 57-61].
[w] pp. 63-69.
[x] pp. 70-73.
[y] p. 74.

---

[42] Cf. Gen. 3:15; Gal. 4:4.
[43] For JW, it is by *prevenient grace*, as the foundational dimension of God's restoring work, but he characteristically avoids specifying this Arminian commitment.

precedent, 'his love to us, in that while we were yet without strength Christ died for the ungodly'.[44] Here is the ground, the real and the *only* ground for true Christian thankfulness. Christ died for the ungodly that were without strength. Such as is every man by nature. And till a man has been deeply sensible of it, he can never truly thank God for his redemption—nor consequently for his creation, which is in the event a blessing to those only who are 'created anew in Christ Jesus'.[45]

3. 'Hence, some have poured great contempt upon human nature. Whereas God himself does not despise mankind, but thinks them worthy of his highest regards.'[z] To describe human nature as deeply fallen, as far removed both from virtue and wisdom, does not argue that we despise it. We know by Scripture, as well as by sad experience, that men are now unspeakably foolish and wicked. And such the Son of God knew them to be when he laid down his life for them. But this did not hinder him from loving them, no more than it does any of the children of God.

[4.] You next consider what Dr. Watts observes with regard to infants. 'Mankind', says he, 'in its younger years, before it is capable of proper moral action, discovers the principles of iniquity and the seeds of sin. What young ferments of spite and envy, what native malice and rage, are found in the little hearts of infants, and sufficiently discovered by their little hands and eyes, and their wrathful countenances, even before they can speak!'[a] You answer, 'Our Lord gave us different ideas of them, when he taught his apostles to become *as little children*.'[[b]] Not at all. They may be imitable in some respects, and yet have all the tempers above described. And it is certain they have, as any impartial observer will be convinced by his own eyes. Nor is this any way contradicted by St. Paul's words, 'In wickedness (κακία) be ye children',[c] untaught, unexperienced; or by those of David, 'My soul is even as a weaned child.'[d]

'But we discover in them also the noble principles of reason and understanding, with several tempers which are capable of

[z] p. 75 [i.e., pp. 74-75].
[a] pp. 77-78 [quoting Watts, *Ruin*, p. 35].
[[b]] [p. 78.]
[c] 1 Cor. 14:20 [cited p. 78].
[d] Ps. 131:2 [quoted p. 78].

[44] Rom. 5:6-8.
[45] Eph. 2:10.

improvement, whereby they may be trained up in a good way; and numbers in all ages of the world have risen to very considerable degrees of excellence.'[e] All this is true. But it is not at all inconsistent with the account of them given above, by which it clearly appears that they are strongly inclined to evil, long before any ill *habits* can be contracted.

Sect. V
A general Argument taken from what God has declared concerning Mankind at the Restoration of the World after the Deluge

[1.] 'There are three passages from which divines infer the excellency of Adam's state and nature above ours: (1) Gen. 1:28, "And God blessed them and said unto them, Be fruitful and multiply and replenish the earth." '[f] With this I have nothing to do, for I infer nothing from it with regard to the present question. '(2) "Have dominion over the fish of the sea, and over the fowl of the air, and over every living thing that moveth upon the earth." (3) Gen. 1:27, "God created man in his own image, in the image of God created he him." '[g] 'From these three particulars they deduce the superiority of Adam's nature above ours. But the very same marks of excellency are more expressly pronounced by God upon the human nature when the race of mankind was to be propagated anew from Noah and his sons.'[h]

[2.] 'i) Gen. 9:1, "And God blessed Noah and his sons." '[i] With regard to this whole passage I must observe that God did not pronounce any blessing at all either on him or them till Noah had 'built an altar unto the Lord, and had offered burnt-offerings on the altar'.[46] Then it was that 'the Lord smelled a sweet savour;'[47] accepted the sacrifice which implied faith in the promised seed, and for his sake restored in some measure the blessing which he had given to Adam at his creation. And said, 'Be fruitful and multiply, and replenish the earth.'[48] On this I need only observe, Had Adam

[e] [Taylor, *Supplement*, pp. 78-80.]
[f] [p. 84.]
[g] pp. 84[-85].
[h] p. 85.
[i] [Ibid.]

---

[46] Gen. 8:20.
[47] Gen. 8:21.
[48] Gen. 9:1.

stood, or had not his fall affected his posterity, there would have been no need of this, for they would have 'multiplied and replenished the earth' in virtue of the original blessing.

'ii) Ver. 2, "The fear of you and the dread of you shall be upon every beast of the earth, and upon every fowl of the air, and upon all that moveth upon the earth. Into your hands they are delivered. [Ver. 3] Every moving thing that liveth shall be meat for you. Even as the green herb have I given you all things." '[j] On this likewise I would observe, What need was there of any such power over the creatures to be given to man, if he had not forfeited his former power? Had man remained subject to God, the creatures would have remained subject to him, by virtue of God's original constitution. And why was it, but because man had lost this power, that God here in some degree restores it?

But hence you 'infer that all that power is restored, yea, more than all; that we have a *more* extensive dominion granted to us over the brutal world than was originally given to Adam'.[k] It has been commonly thought that Adam had full dominion over the creatures, subject to him by a kind of instinct. Whereas we have only so far power over them that by labour and vigilance we may use or subdue them. But how do you prove that we have a fuller dominion than he had? By those words, 'The fear and the dread of you shall be upon all. Into your hands they are delivered. Even as the green herb have I given you all things.' Nay, 'the fear and the dread of you shall be upon them' does not imply any *dominion* at all. A wolf may *fear* me, who yet does not *obey* me. I *dread* a viper, but I do not *obey* it. And those words, 'Into your hands they are delivered,' are plainly equivalent with, 'I have given you all things, even as the green herb'—namely *for food*; you may feed on any of them. So far therefore is this text from 'expressly pronouncing'[l] a 'more extensive dominion'[m] given to Noah over the brutal world than was originally given to Adam, that it does not express any *proper dominion* at all.

'iii) Ver. 6, "Whoso sheddeth man's blood, by man shall his blood be shed. For in the image of God made he man"[n]—namely at the creation. And some remains of the natural 'image of God', as we are

[j] [pp. 85-86.]
[k] p. 86.
[l] [p. 87.]
[m] [p. 86.]
[n] [Ibid.]

spiritual and immortal beings, are even now to be found in every man, sufficient to justify the putting a murderer to death. St. James alludes to the same Scripture when he says, 'Therewith bless we God, and curse men who were made' (τοὺς γεγονότας, not 'are made')[49] 'after the similitude of God.'[o] But what does all this prove? That the being 'created in the image of God' 'is *more expressly pronounced* upon Noah and his sons than it was originally on Adam'?[p] I think no man of sense will say this in cool blood.

Of 'the three particulars' then which you brought to prove the superiority of Noah over Adam in innocence, the first proves no more than that God gave to both the blessing of *fruitfulness*. The second, far from proving that Noah had a 'more extensive dominion' over the brute creation than Adam, hardly proves that he had any dominion over them at all. And the third proves only this, that the image of God wherein man was made at first is not *totally* lost now.

Yet you say, 'These three particulars contain all the privileges conferred on Adam at first. And every one of these is *expressly* repeated, and *more emphatically* and extensively pronounced upon man, after *the judgment* passed on Adam had come upon his posterity.'[q] *Expressly? More* emphatically? *More* extensively? Where? I am sure not in the Bible.

[3.] However, you pompously add (*sicut tuus est mos*):[50] 'This is to me a clear and undoubted *demonstration*,

'i) That "the judgment which came upon all men to condemnation" did noways alter the primary relation in which God stood to man and man to God.'[r] Certainly it was altered thus far: God was a *condemner*, and man was *condemned*. And though 'God is still the God and Father of mankind',[s] yet it cannot be said that he is so to unregenerate men, men who are as yet 'dead in sin'[51] and 'children of wrath',[52] 'as much' or in the same sense 'as he was to Adam in

[o] Jas. 3:9 [quoted p. 86].
[p] [Taylor, *Supplement*, p. 87.]
[q] p. 87.
[r] [Ibid.]
[s] [Ibid.]

[49] JW is correcting Taylor's translation in *Supplement*, 86.
[50] 'after your usual manner'. Cf. Horace, *Satires*, I.ix.1, '*sicut meus est mos*', 'after my usual manner'.
[51] Eph. 2:5.
[52] Eph. 2:3.

innocence'.[t] Adam then was surely 'the son of God', as no other man is till 'born of the Spirit'.[53] The power to become the sons of God is now given to none till they 'believe on his name'.[54]

'ii) That the love, regards, and providence of God toward mankind in general are still the *very same* as to man at his first formation.'[u] His *providence* is still over all his works.[55] But he cannot *regard* or *delight* in *sinful* man in the *very same* manner wherein he delighted in him when *innocent*.

'iii) That our nature as derived from Noah has just the same endowments, natural and moral, with which Adam was created.'[v] This does not follow from anything that has yet been said. If it stands of itself, it may.

'iv) That whatever came upon us from "the judgment to condemnation" came no farther than was consistent with that blessing, pronounced upon Noah as well as Adam, "Be fruitful and multiply." '[w] This is undoubtedly true. Otherwise the human species could not have been continued. 'So that "the condemnation" which "came upon all men" cannot infer the *wrath* of God upon mankind.'[x]—It *may*, notwithstanding that they 'increase and multiply';[56] it *must*, if they are 'by nature children of wrath'[57]—'but only as subjecting us to such evils as were perfectly consistent with his blessing, declared to Adam as soon as he came out of his Maker's hands'[y]—namely with the blessing, 'Increase and multiply'—'and consequently to such evils as God might justly have subjected mankind to before Adam sinned'[z]—Whether God could justly have done this or not, what a consequence is this! 'If God gave that blessing, "Increase and multiply," to men in general, as well as he did to

[t] [Ibid.]
[u] p. 88.
[v] [Ibid.]
[w] [Ibid., quoting Rom. 5:16; Gen. 1:28.]
[x] [p. 87, quoting Rom. 5:16.]
[y] pp. [88–]89.
[z] [p. 89.]

[53] John 3:6.
[54] John 1:12.
[55] See Ps. 145:9 (BCP).
[56] JW alters the biblical 'be fruitful and multiply' used by Taylor (Gen. 1:22, etc.) to the phrase in the BCP Collect for the 4th Sunday after Trinity and continues using this form to the end of the section.
[57] Eph. 2:3.

Adam, then men in general are not "children of wrath" now, any more than Adam was at his creation.'[58]

'v) It is no less evident that when St. Paul says, "By the disobedience of one many" (or all) "were made sinners," he cannot mean, they "were made sinners" in any sense inconsistent with the blessing pronounced on man in innocence.'[a] True, not in any sense inconsistent with that blessing, 'Increase and multiply.' But this blessing is no way inconsistent with their being 'by nature children of wrath'.

[4.] 'From all which I conclude that our state with regard to the blessing of God, and the dignity and faculties of our nature (unless debased by our own sins) is not inferior to that in which Adam was created.'[b] Be this so or not, it cannot be concluded from anything that has gone before. But we may still believe that men in general are 'fallen short of the glory of God',[59] are deprived of that glorious image of God wherein man was originally created.[60]

Sect. VI

The notion of Adam's being a Federal Head, or Representative of Mankind, considered[c]

[1.] My reason for believing he was so in some sense is this.[61] Christ was the *representative* of mankind when God 'laid on him the iniquities of us all', and 'he was wounded for our transgressions'.[62] But Adam was a type or *figure* of Christ. Therefore he was also in some sense our *representative*. In consequence of which 'all died in him', as 'in Christ all shall be made alive'.[63]

[a] [Ibid., quoting Rom. 5:19.]
[b] p. 90.
[c] pp. 94[-113].

---

[58] This is a misleading summary of Taylor's argument in *Supplement*, 88-89. Taylor does reject the notion that the situation of later humans is dramatically different from that of Adam, but by insisting that Adam, too, was subject from the beginning to such evils as are consistent with God's blessing and goodness.

[59] Rom. 3:23 (*NT Notes*).

[60] See Col. 3:10.

[61] Taylor devotes this section to a strong critique of the notion of Adam as 'federal head', noting its direct connection to imputed sin and righteousness. JW's concern is not to defend 'federal theology', but to clarify the 'sense' in which he wants to talk about Adam and Christ as representative of humanity. See the discussion of this broader issue in the introduction (pp. 150-51 above).

[62] Isa. 53:5-6.

[63] Cf. 1 Cor. 15:22.

But as neither 'representative' nor 'federal head' are Scripture words, it is not worth while to contend for them. The thing I mean is this: the state of all mankind did so far depend on Adam that by his fall they all fell into sorrow and pain and death, spiritual and temporal. And all this is noways inconsistent with either the justice or goodness of God, provided all may recover through the *Second Adam* whatever they lost through the *first*. Nay, and recover it with unspeakable gain, since every additional temptation they feel, by that corruption of their nature which is antecedent to their choice, will if conquered by grace be a means of adding to that 'exceeding and eternal weight of glory'.[64]

This single consideration totally removes all reflections on the divine justice or mercy, in making the state of all mankind so dependent on the behaviour of their common parent. For not one child of man finally loses thereby, unless by his own choice. And everyone who 'receives the grace of God in Christ'[65] will be an unspeakable gainer. Who then has any reason to complain, even of having a nature inclined to evil? Seeing the more opportunities he has of fighting, the more of conquering; and seeing the greater is the difficulty of obtaining the victory, the brighter is the crown of glory.

Now if Adam and Christ did not stand or fall, obey and suffer, for mankind, how can the death of others be the consequence of Adam's offence, the life of others the consequence of Christ's obedience? How could all men be in any sense *constituted sinners* by the one, or *constituted righteous* by the other?

[2.] To explain this a little farther in Mr. Hervey's words:

> By *federal head* or *representative* I mean what the Apostle teaches, when he calls Christ 'the second Man',[d] and 'the last Adam'.[66] The last? How? Not in a numerical sense; not in order of time. But in this respect, that as Adam was a public person, and acted in the stead of all mankind, so Christ likewise was a public person, and acted in behalf of all his people; that as Adam was the first general representative of mankind, Christ was the second and the last (there never was, and never will be any other); that what they severally did in this capacity was not intended to *terminate* in themselves, but to affect as many as they severally represented. [. . .]

[d] 1 Cor. 15:47.

---

[64] 2 Cor. 4:17.
[65] Cf. 2 Cor. 6:1.
[66] 1 Cor. 15:45.

This does not rest on a single text, but is established again and again in the same chapter. The divinely wise Apostle, foreseeing the prejudices which men would entertain against this doctrine, as lying quite out of the road of reason's researches, has inculcated and re-inculcated this momentous point. 'Through the offence of one, many are dead. . . . The judgment was by one to condemnation. . . . By one man's offence death reigned by one. . . . By the offence of one, judgment came upon all men to condemnation' [Rom. 5:15-18]. And that there may remain no possibility of mistaking his meaning, or eluding his argument, he adds, 'By one man's disobedience many were made sinners.'[67]

All these expressions demonstrate that Adam (as well as Christ) was a *representative* of all mankind. And that what he did in this capacity did not *terminate* in himself, but affected all whom he represented.

[3.] After vehemently cavilling at the terms, you yourself allow the thing. You say, 'If what was lost by "the disobedience of one" person might afterward be recovered by "the obedience" of another, then matters would have stood upon an equal footing.'[e] And this is indeed the truth. For 'all that was lost to us by Adam's *disobedience* is fully recovered by Christ's *obedience*, however we *denominate* the relation in which the one or the other stands to us'.[68]

[4.] In this we agree, but not in what follows. 'By "law" in the fifth of the Romans, as in several other places, the Apostle does not mean barely a rule of duty, but such a *rule with the penalty of death threatened to every transgression of it*. Such was the law given by Moses'.[f] That is, 'a rule to every transgression of which the penalty of death was threatened'. Not so. There were a thousand transgressions of it to which death was not threatened. Observe, by death we now mean temporal death, according to the whole tenor of your argument.[69]

[e] [Taylor, *Supplement*,] p. 113.
[f] p. 114.

[67] James Hervey, *Theron and Aspasio; or a Series of Dialogues and Letters upon the most Important and Interesting Subjects*, 2 vols. (Dublin: Robert Main, 1755), Dial. V (1:136-37). The following two sentences are also presented as if they were a continuation of this quotation, but seem instead to be JW's summary of Hervey's argument. Note how he shifts the primary attention to Adam. JW soon found it necessary to insist to Hervey that such a representative role for Christ did not entail the imputation of Christ's active righteousness to believers. See *Answer to Hervey* (1765), vol. 13 in this edn.

[68] JW discretely omits from this quotation Taylor's specification of what was lost by Adam's disobedience (and regained by Christ's obedience): '—*viz.* natural life'. Cf. *Supplement*, 113. So, they do not *fully* agree.

[69] Taylor, *Reply* (1767), 20: 'A misrepresentation. By "death" in law I always mean, as the Scripture means, *eternal* death.'

But is it not said, 'Cursed is everyone that continueth not in all things written in the law, to do them?'[g] It is. But whatever this *curse* implied, it did not imply temporal death. For a man might neglect to do many 'things written in the law', and yet not be punishable with death.

[5.] Neither can I agree with your interpretation of Rom. 7:9. ' "I was alive without the law once"—namely before the giving of the law at Mount Sinai. The Jew was then alive. That is, because he was not *then* under the law he was not slain by his sin. His sin was not so imputed to him as to subject him to death. "But when the commandment came" with the penalty of death annexed, "sin revived"—acquired full life and vigour'—(How so? One would have expected just the contrary!)— ' "and I died", that is, was a dead man in law, upon the first transgression he committed.'[h] Beside many other objections to this strange interpretation, an obvious one is this. It supposes every transgression punishable with death. But this is a palpable mistake. Therefore all that is built on this foundation falls to the ground at once.

[6.] Upon the whole, whatever objections may lie against Dr. Watts's method of explaining it, it appears from clear Scripture and from your own words that Adam was the *representative* of mankind.

Sect. VII

Of the Formation of our Nature in the Womb[i]

[1.] Before I say anything on this head, I must premise that there are a thousand circumstances relating to it concerning which I can form no conception at all, but am utterly in the dark. I know not how my body was fashioned there, or when or how my soul was united to it. And it is far easier in speaking on so abstruse a subject to pull down than to build up. I can easily object to any hypothesis which is advanced, but I cannot easily defend any.

And if you ask me how, in what determinate manner, sin is *propagated*, how it is transmitted from father to son, I answer plainly, I cannot tell. No more than I can tell how man is propagated, how a body is transmitted from father to son. I know both the one and the other fact. But I can account for neither.[70]

[g] [Gal. 3:10, quoted on p. 115.]
[h] [Taylor, *Supplement*,] p. 116.
[i] p. 129.

[70] See the discussion of this topic in the introduction (pp. 149-50 above).

[2.] Thus much however is plain, that 'God is the Maker of every man who comes into the world.'[j] For it is God alone who gives man power to propagate his species. Or rather, it is God himself who does the work, by man as an instrument—man (as you observed before) having no other part in producing man than the oak has in producing an acorn. God is really the producer of every man, every animal, every vegetable in the world; as he is the true *primum mobile*,[71] the spring of all motion throughout the universe. So far we agree. But when you subsume, 'If it is the power of God whereby a sinful species is propagated, whereby a *sinful father* begets a *sinful son*, then God is the author of *sin*; that sinfulness is chargeable upon him'[k]—here we divide; I cannot allow the consequence, because the same argument would make God chargeable with *all the sinful actions* of men. For it is the power of God whereby the murderer lifts up his arm, whereby the adulterer perpetrates his wickedness, full as much as it is his power whereby an acorn produces an oak or a father a son. But does it follow that God is chargeable with the sin? You know it does not follow. The power of God, vulgarly termed *nature*, acts from age to age under its fixed rules. Yet he who this moment supplies the power by which a *sinful action* is committed is not chargeable with the *sinfulness* of that action. In like manner, it is the power of God which from age to age continues the human species, yet he who this moment supplies the power whereby a *sinful nature* is propagated (according to the fixed rules established in the lower world) is not chargeable with the *sinfulness* of that nature. This distinction you must allow, as was observed before, or charge God with all the sin committed under heaven. And this general answer may suffice any sincere and modest inquirer, without entangling himself in those minute particulars which are beyond the reach of human understanding.

'But does not God *create* the nature of every man that comes into the world?'[l] He does not, in the proper sense of the word 'create'.

[j] p. 138.
[k] [p. 135.]
[l] [Cf. ibid.]

[71] The *primum mobile* (primary moving power) was a conception added to the Ptolemaic system of astronomy, a supposed outermost sphere of the universe, revolving round the earth from east to west every 24 hours. Cf. *A Farther Appeal,* Pt. II, II.14, 11:226 in this edn.; and 'A Thought on Necessity', V.6, in *Arminian Magazine* 3 (1780): 485-92 (and vol. 13 in this edn.).

The Scripture plainly affirms the contrary. 'On the seventh day he rested from all his work which God created and made.'[m] 'The works' which God *created* 'were finished from the foundation of the world.' And as soon as they were finished, God 'ceased from his work',[n] namely from his work of *creating*. He therefore now (not *creates*, but) produces the body of every man, in the same manner as he produces the oak, only by supplying the power whereby one creature begets another, according to what we term 'the laws of nature'. In an higher sense he is the *Creator* of all souls. But *how* or *when* he does or did create them I cannot tell. Neither can I give any account *how* or *when* he unites them to the body. Likewise *how* we are *conceived* in sin I know not. But I know *that* we are so conceived. God hath said it. And I know he will be 'justified in his saying, and clear when he is judged'.[72]

[3.] It is certain that God is the Maker of every man. But it is neither certain nor true that he 'makes every man in the womb, both soul and body, *as immediately as he made Adam*;' and that therefore 'every man comes out of the hands of God as properly as Adam did.'[o] To interpret any Scriptures as affirming this is to make them flatly contradict other Scriptures. God *made* Adam by *immediate creation*; he does not *so make* every man, or any man beside him. Adam came *directly* out of the hands of God, without the *intervention* of any creature. Does every man *thus come* out of the hands of God? Do no creatures now *intervene*?

[4.] 'But if God produces the *nature* of every man in the womb, he must produce it with all the qualities which belong to that nature, as it is *then* and *so* produced.'[p] So, if God produces the *action* of every man in the world, he must produce it with all the qualities which belong to that action, as it is *then* and *so* produced.[73] 'For it is

[m] Gen. 2:2-3.
[n] Heb. 4:3, 10.
[o] [Taylor, *Supplement*,] p. 140.
[p] [Ibid.]

---

[72] Cf. Ps. 51:4 (BCP).
[73] Taylor, *Reply* (1767), 21:

'Very true. You run a parallel in this and the following paragraphs between God's producing an *action* and his producing the *nature* of every man in the womb, in order to disprove what I have advanced concerning the latter. But your instance of God's producing an *action* hath a contrary force and effect. For it confirms my assertions in every particular respect. Your principle is false, that God produces every *sinful action* in the world. God gives the *power* by which every action is performed; but it is the agent who produces the action, by the power which he hath received from God; and therefore it is the agent alone who is chargeable with the sinfulness of the action.'

impossible, God should produce our *nature*, and not produce the *qualities* it has when produced.'[q] For it is impossible God should produce an *action*, and yet not produce the *qualities* it has when produced. 'No *substance* can be made without some qualities. And it must necessarily, as soon as it is made, have those qualities which the maker gives it, and no other.'[r] No *action* can be produced without some qualities. And it must necessarily, as soon as it is produced, have those qualities which the producer gives it, and no other. You see what this argument would prove, if it proved anything at all.

[5.] We will trace it a little farther. 'If God produces the *nature* of every man in the womb, with all its *qualities*, then whatever those qualities are, they are the *will* and the *work* of God.'[s] So, if God produces the *action* of every man in the world, with all its *qualities*, then whatever those qualities are, they are the *will* and the *work* of God. Surely no. God does (in the sense above explained) produce the *action* which is *sinful*. And yet (whether I can account for it, or no) the *sinfulness* of it is not his *will* or *work*. He does also produce the *nature* which is *sinful* (he supplies the power by which it is produced). And yet (whether I can account for this or no) the *sinfulness* of it is not his *will* or *work*. I am as sure of this as I am that there is a God, and yet impenetrable darkness rests on the subject. Yet I am conscious my understanding can no more fathom this deep than reconcile man's free will with the foreknowledge of God.

[6.] 'Consequently those *qualities* cannot be *sinful*.'[t] This consequence cannot hold in one case unless it holds in both. But if it does, there can be no sin in the universe.

[7.] However, you go on. ''Tis highly dishonourable to God to suppose he is displeased at us for what he himself has infused into our nature.'[u] It is not allowed that he has 'infused sin into our *nature*', no more than that he infuses sin into our *actions*; though it is *his power* which produces both our actions and nature.

I am aware of the distinction that man's *free will* is concerned in the one case, but not the other; and that on this account God cannot be charged with the sinfulness of human actions. But this does by no means remove the difficulty. For (1) does not God know what

[q] [Ibid.]
[r] [Ibid.]
[s] [p. 141.]
[t] [Ibid.]
[u] p. 142.

the murderer or adulterer is about to do, what use he will make of that *power to act* which he cannot have but from God? (2) Does he not at the instant supply him with that power whereby the *sinful action* is done? God therefore *produces* the *action* which is *sinful*. It is his *work*, and his *will* (for he *works* nothing but what he *wills*). And yet the *sinfulness* of the action is neither his *work* nor *will*.

'But can those passions or propensities be *sinful* which are neither caused nor consented to by me?'[v] I answer, spite, envy, and those other passions and tempers which are manifestly discernible even in little children, are certainly *not virtuous*, not morally good, whether you term them *sinful* or not. And it is as certain these exist before they are consented to, much less caused by those that feel them. 'But *sin*, if it is unavoidable, is no sin.'[w] Whether you term it 'sin' or not, it is contrary to the nature of God, and a transgression of his holy and good law.

[8.] 'But a *natural-moral evil* is a contradiction; for if it be *natural*, it cannot be *moral*.'[x] That tempers contrary to the nature and the law of God are *natural* is a point of daily experience. But if you do not choose to call these *morally evil*, call them what you please. All I aver is that such tempers do exist in us antecedent to our choice.

[9.] 'But if the *actual sins* of men proceed from a corrupt nature, they are unavoidable, and consequently no sins at all.'[y] *Actual sins* may proceed from a corrupt nature and yet not be *unavoidable*. But if actions contrary to the nature of God were unavoidable, it would not follow that they were innocent.[74]

[10.] To the question, 'How comes it to pass that our passions and appetites are now so irregular and strong that not one person has resisted them so as to keep himself pure and innocent?'[z] you answer by another question, 'How came Adam not to keep himself pure and innocent?'[a] There is no parity between the one case and the other. I can account for any one man's committing sin, supposing him to be naturally upright, as easily as for Adam's committing it. And one

[v] [Ibid.]
[w] p. 143.
[x] [Ibid.]
[y] p. 144.
[z] [p. 145, quoting Jennings, *Vindication*, p. 110.]
[a] p. 145.

[74] Taylor, *Reply* (1767), 22: 'But it follows, if they are unavoidable, that I who do them am innocent.'

person, as well as Adam, though naturally inclined to neither, might choose either good or evil. And on this supposition he would be as likely to choose one as the other. But the case is extremely different if you place Adam on one side, and all mankind on the other. It is true, 'The nature of sin is not altered by its being general.'[b] But the case is very widely altered. On this or that man it may 'come, just as it came upon Adam, by his own choice and compliance with temptation'.[c] But how comes it that all men under the sun should *choose* evil rather than good?[75] How came all the children of Adam from the beginning of the world till now to comply with temptation? How is it that in all ages the scale has turned the wrong way with regard to every man born into the world? Can you see no difficulty in this? And can you find any way to solve that difficulty but to say with the Psalmist, we were 'shapen in iniquity, and in sin did our mothers conceive us'?[76]

Sect. VIII
Of Original Righteousness

[1.] Original righteousness is said to be 'that moral rectitude in which Adam was created. His reason was clear, and sense, appetite, and passion were subject to it. His judgment was uncorrupted, and his will had a constant propensity to holiness. He had a supreme love to his Creator, a fear of offending him, and a readiness to do his will.'[d] 'When Adam sinned, he lost this moral rectitude, this image of God in which he was created, in consequence of which all his posterity come into the world destitute of that image.'[e]

In order to remove this mistake you reconsider some of the texts on which it is grounded. Col. 3:9-10, 'Lie not one to another, seeing ye have put off the old man with his deeds, and have put on the new man, which is renewed in knowledge after the image of him that created him.' Eph. 4:22-24, 'That ye put off, concerning the former conversation, the old man which is corrupt, according to the deceitful lusts, and be renewed in the spirit of your mind, and put on the new man, which after God is created in righteousness and true holiness.'

[b] [Ibid.]
[c] [pp. 145-46.]
[d] [pp. 147-48, quoting Watts, *Ruin*, pp. 4-6, 106.]
[e] p. 148 [Taylor's further summary of Watts].

[75] Ibid.: 'Because they choose it, just as Adam did, by yielding to temptation.'
[76] Cf. Ps. 51:5.

[2.] On this you affirm: 'The *old* and *new man* here do not signify a course of life. But the "old man" signifies the *heathen*, the "new man" the Christian *profession*.'[f]

This you prove (1) from 'Eph. 2:15, "Christ abolished the enmity, to make (or *create*) in himself of twain one new man." '[g] Does this only mean 'one new' *profession*? It evidently means *one church*, both of Jews and Gentiles.

You prove it (2) from Col. 3:8-12, where 'the Apostle tells the Colossian Christians that "now" they were obliged to "put off anger", and "to put on bowels of mercies"; to admit the Christian spirit into their hearts, and to practise Christian duties; for this reason, because they had "put off the old man", and had "put on the new". This shows "the new man" was something they might have "put on", and yet be *defective* in personal, internal holiness.'[h] True. Defective so far as still to want more—more 'bowels of mercies, meekness, long-suffering'. But this does not show that 'the new man' does not mean the principle both of internal and external holiness. The consciousness of having received this is a strong motive both to depart from evil and to labour after a continual increase of every holy and heavenly temper.[77] Therefore here likewise 'the putting off the old and the putting on the new man' does not mean an *outward profession*, but a real, inward change, a renewal of soul *in righteousness and true holiness*.

You prove it (3) from Eph. 4:22, 24. Here, you say, 'He considers "the putting off the old" and "putting on the new man" as a duty. They had done it by *profession*, and therefore were obliged to do it *effectually*.'[i] They had done it *effectually*. So the whole tenor of the Apostle's words implies: 'Ye have not so learned Christ. If so be' (rather, 'seeing that')[78] 'ye have been taught by him . . . that ye put off the old man . . . and be renewed in the spirit of your mind; and that ye put on the new man, which after God is created in

[f] pp. 150-51.
[g] [p. 150.]
[h] [p. 151.]
[i] [Ibid.]

[77] This reflects JW's mature distinction between the 'new birth' and 'sanctification' proper. Cf. Sermon 43, 'The Scripture Way of Salvation', I.4, 2:158 in this edn.; and Sermon 45, 'The New Birth', IV.3, 2:198 in this edn.

[78] JW again corrects the AV, quoted by Taylor, to his own translation in *NT Notes*.

righteousness and true holiness.'[j] The Apostle here manifestly speaks not of a lesson they 'had not learned', but of one which God had 'taught' them already, and thence exhorts them to walk worthy of the blessing they had received, to be 'holy in all manner of conversation'.[79]

But, (4) 'The *putting on the new man* is one thing, and the *creating* him is another. He must *first* be created, and *then* put on.'[k] No. He is *created* and *put on* at the same time, the former word more directly referring to God who creates, the latter to man who is created. 'But God', you say, '*created the new man* when he erected the gospel-dispensation, as appears from Eph. 2:15, 19-22.'[[l]] I answer, i) If those latter verses are explanatory of that expression 'one new man' in the fifteenth, then it does not mean *one outward profession*, but the *one church* of living believers in Christ. ii) The expression in the fifteenth verse is not the same with that we are now considering. Neither is the meaning of that and this expression the same. 'One new man' means *one church* and nothing else. 'The new man' means quite another thing—the work of God in every individual believer.

You say, (5) 'The *old man and the new*, and the *new man's being renewed and created*, and the *renewing* of the Ephesians all refer not to any corruption of nature but to their late wicked life.'[m] What? Does their being 'renewed in the spirit of their mind' refer only to their wicked *life*? If you had not affirmed this I should really wonder at your affirming quickly after, 'In all other places of Scripture except 2 Cor. 4:16, "renewing" relates only to a vicious course of life;'[n] seeing you immediately confute yourself by both the following citations: 'Be not conformed to this world, but be ye transformed by the renewal of your mind'[o]—unless 'the mind' be only another expression for 'a vicious course of life'. 'We ourselves also were sometimes foolish, disobedient, deceived, serving diverse lusts and pleasures; living in malice and envy, hateful and hating one

[j] Eph. 4:20-24.
[k] [Taylor, *Supplement*,] p. 152.
[[l]] [Ibid.]
[m] p. 153.
[n] p. 154.
[o] Rom. 12:2 [quoted p. 154].

[79] 1 Pet. 1:15.

another.'[p] Do these words imply nothing but 'a vicious course of life'? No inward *corruption* at all? 'But after that the loving-kindness and love of God our Saviour toward man appeared . . . he saved us by the renewing of the Holy Ghost.'[q] From what? From a vicious course of life only? Nay, but from *foolishness* of heart also, from error, from malice, hatred, *envy*, evil *desire*—all which are *inward corruptions*.

You add: 'From all this we may gather that God's "creating the new man after his own image in righteousness and true holiness" means his erecting the Christian Church with a view to promote righteousness and holiness among men. For "we are God's workmanship, created in Christ Jesus unto good works".'[r] Surely you do not cite this verse also to prove that the *renewing of our mind* implies no *inward change*? It must be something more than an *outward profession* or the reforming a vicious course of life by reason of which we are said to be God's 'workmanship, created anew in Christ Jesus'.

These texts therefore do manifestly refer to 'personal internal holiness',[80] and clearly prove that this is the chief part of that 'image of God' in which man was originally created.

[3.] The other text which you reconsider is Eccles. 7:29, 'God hath made man upright, but they have sought out many inventions.'[s] But this, you say, does not mean that God made man *righteous*, but that he 'made him *right*, as having those powers, means, and encouragements, by a due use of which he may become *righteous*'.[t] In order to prove that this is the true meaning of the words you affirm (1) 'that *man* here is not to be understood of Adam, but of all mankind'.[u] This cannot be granted without full proof. You affirm (2) 'This appears from the latter part of the sentence: they "sought out many inventions".'[v] Adam and Eve did so, in and after their fall. This therefore proves nothing. You affirm (3) the word *Jashar*

[p] [Titus 3:3; quoted p. 154.]
[q] Titus 3:4-5 [quoted p. 154.]
[r] [Taylor, *Supplement*,] p. 155 [quoting Eph. 2:10].
[s] pp. 156-60.
[t] [p. 158.]
[u] [Ibid.]
[v] [p. 160.]

[80] Cf. Taylor, *Supplement*, 155. He is not denying the importance of 'personal internal holiness', but the assumption that it is simply infused. He argues that developing such holiness is 'our duty', which Paul 'exhorts us to perform'.

(which we translate 'upright') 'does not always imply *uprightness* or *righteousness*'.[w] But this is its proper meaning, as will appear to any who seriously considers the following texts: (1) Deut. 12:25, 'When thou shalt do that which is *right* in the sight of the Lord.' It is taken in the very same sense [in] ver. 28, chaps. 13:18, and 21:9. In all these texts it undeniably implies *morally good* or *righteous*. (2) Deut. 32:4, 'A God of truth and without iniquity; just and *right* is he.' Psalm 25:8, 'Good and *upright* is the Lord.' (3) Psalm 33:4, 'The word of the Lord is *right*.' Hos. 14:9, 'The ways of the Lord are *right*.' (4) Psalm 32:11, 'Be glad and rejoice, ye *righteous*.' Psalm 33:1, 'Rejoice in the Lord, O ye *righteous*.' In the very same sense it occurs in numberless places. As the word is therefore properly applied to God himself, to his word, his providences, and his people, in all which cases it must necessarily mean *righteous*, we cannot lightly depart from this its proper signification.

But you think there is a necessity of departing from it here, because 'to say, God *created* Adam *righteous* is to affirm a contradiction, or what is inconsistent with the very nature of righteousness. For a righteousness wrought in him without his knowledge or consent would have been no righteousness at all.'[x] You may call it by any name you like better. But we must use the old name still, as being persuaded that the love of God, governing the senses, appetites, and passions, however or whenever it is wrought in the soul, is true, essential righteousness.

Nay, 'Righteousness is *right action*.'[y] Indeed it is not. Here (as we said before) is your fundamental mistake. It is a *right state of mind*, which differs from *right action* as the cause does from the effect. Righteousness is properly and directly *a right temper* or *disposition of mind*, or a complex of all right tempers.

For want of observing this you say, 'Adam could not *act* before he was created. Therefore he must exist, and use his intellectual powers, *before* he could be righteous.'[z] But 'according to this reasoning', as Dr. Jennings observes, 'Christ could not be righteous at his birth'.[a] You answer, 'He existed before he was made flesh.'[b] I reply, He did, as God. But the man Christ Jesus did not. Neither therefore

[w] [Ibid.]
x p. 161.
[y] [Ibid.]
[z] [Ibid.]
[a] [Jennings, *Vindication*, p. 95; quoted on pp. 161-62.]
[b] [p. 162.]

did he 'use his intellectual powers'. According to your reasoning, then, the man Christ Jesus 'could not be righteous at his birth'.

The doctor adds, 'Nay, according to this reasoning, God could not be righteous from eternity; because he must exist *before* he was righteous'.[c] You answer, 'My reasoning would hold even with respect to God, were it true that he ever did begin to exist. But neither the existence nor the holiness of God was prior to each other.'[d] Nay, but if his existence was not prior to his holiness, if he did not exist *before* he was holy, your assertion that every being must *exist before* it is *righteous* is not true.

Besides (to pursue your reasoning a little farther), if God did always *exist*, yet unless you can prove that he always *acted* it will not clear your argument. For let him exist millions of ages, he could not be *righteous* (according to your maxims) before he *acted right*.

One word more on this article. You say, 'My reasoning would hold good even with respect to God, were it true that he ever did begin to exist.' Then I ask concerning the Son of God, Did he ever begin to exist?[81] If he did not, he is the one, eternal God (for there cannot be two Eternals). If he did, and your reasoning hold good, when he began to exist he was not righteous.

[4.] 'But St. John saith, "He that doth righteousness is righteous." '[e] Yes, it *appears* he is, by his *doing* or practising *righteousness*. 'But where doth the Scripture speak one word of a righteousness *infused into us*?'[f] Where it speaks of 'the love of God' (the essence of righteousness) 'shed abroad in our hearts'.[82]

And cannot God by his almighty power infuse any good tempers into us? You answer: 'No. No being whatever can do for us that which *cannot be at all* if it be not *our own choice*, and the effect of *our own industry* and exercise. But all good tempers are the effect of *our own* industry and exercise. Otherwise they *cannot be at all.*'[g]

Nay then, it is certain they *cannot be at all*. For neither lowliness, meekness, long-suffering, nor any other good temper, can ever be

[c] p. 162 [quoting Jennings, *Vindication*, p. 95].
[d] [p. 162.]
[e] [Ibid., citing 1 John 3:7.]
[f] [Ibid.]
[g] [p. 163.]

[81] JW is pushing Taylor again on his supposed Arian or Socinian Christology.
[82] Rom. 5:5. This is one of JW's favorite passages. See, e.g., the number of appearances in the Scripture index to his sermons, 4:672 in this edn.

the effect of *my own industry* and *exercise*. But I verily believe they may be the effect of God's Spirit, working in me whatsoever pleaseth him (See Isa. 26:12).[83]

You add, 'The thing cannot exist unless *we* choose, because *our choosing* to do what is right is the very thing which is to exist.'[h] No. The thing which is to exist is *a right state of mind*. And it is certain, God can give this to any creature, at the very first moment of its existence. Nay, it may be questioned whether God can create an intelligent being in any other state.

[5.] 'But an *habit* is gained by repeated acts. Therefore *habits* of righteousness could not be created in man.'[i] Mere playing upon words! He *could be*, he *was* created full of love. Now, whether you call this an *habit* or no, it is the sum of all righteousness.

'But this love is either under the government of my will or it is not.'[j] It is. The love of God which Adam enjoyed was under the government of his will. 'But if so, it could be *righteous* only so far as applied to *right action* in heart and life.'[k] Stop here. The love of God is *righteousness* the moment it exists in any soul. And it must exist before it can be applied to action. Accordingly it was righteousness in Adam the moment he was created. And yet he had a power either to follow the dictates of that *love* (in which case his righteousness would have endured for ever) or to act contrary thereto. But *love* was *righteousness* still, though it was not irresistible.

[6.] 'I might add, Adam's inclination to sin (for he could not sin without a sinful inclination) must be so strong as to overcome his' (supposed) 'inbred propensity to holiness, and so malignant as to expel that principle at once and totally. Consequently, the supposed *original righteousness* was consistent with a sinful propensity *vastly stronger and more malignant than ever was or can be in any of his posterity*; who cannot sin against such resistance, or with such dreadful consequences. Thus *original righteousness* in Adam proves far worse than original sin in his posterity.'[l]

[h] [Ibid.]
[i] [pp. 163-64.]
[j] [p. 164.]
[k] p. 164.
[l] p. 166.

[83] Note JW's more characteristically Arminian resolution of this tension in Sermon 85, 'On Working Out Our Own Salvation', 3:199-209 in this edn.

[7.] I have set down your argument at large that it may appear in its full strength. Now let us view it more closely. [(1)] 'Adam could not sin without a *sinful inclination.*' The sentence is ambiguous. Either it may mean 'Adam could not *choose ill* without some *sinful temper* preceding,' and in this sense it is false; or, he could not commit *outward sin* without first *inclining*, that is, *choosing* so to do. (2) 'This his *sinful inclination* (or *temper*) was so strong as to overcome his inbred propensity to holiness.' It was not any *sinful inclination* (in this sense) which overcame his propensity to holiness, but strong temptation from without. How strong we know not; and the circumstances of it, we know not. (3) 'This his *sinful inclination* was so malignant as to expel that principle at once and totally.' Not by any *sinful inclination*, but by yielding to temptation, he did lose the love and image of God.[84] But that this was *totally* and *at once* we have no authority to affirm. (4) 'Consequently original righteousness in Adam was consistent with a *sinful propensity* "vastly stronger and more malignant than ever was or can be in any of his posterity".' It was consistent with no *sinful propensity* at all, but barely with a *power of yielding to temptation*. It declined in the same proportion, and by the same degrees, as he did actually yield to this. And when he had yielded entirely, and eaten the fruit, *original righteousness* was no more. Therefore the fifth proposition, 'Thus *original righteousness* proves to be *FAR WORSE* than *original sin*', is flourish. What a figure does this fair argument make, now it is turned inside out!

From all this it may appear that the doctrine of *original righteousness*, as well as that of *original sin*, hath a firm foundation in Scripture, as well as in the attributes of a wise, holy, and gracious God.[85]

As you do not offer any new argument in your conclusion,[86] I need not spend any time upon it.

[84] Taylor, *Reply* (1767), 22:

'In this paragraph it is affirmed that Adam sinned barely by yielding to temptation, without any previous sinful propensity or inclination. But he could not possibly yield to temptation without choosing to do so. He must previously *choose* to yield before he yielded. He could not choose to yield without being inclined to yield. Or he could not choose to yield to temptation against his inclinations. And if he was inclined to do a sinful action, such inclination must be sinful.'

[85] Contrast Taylor, *Supplement*, 167: 'From all this it appears to me that the common scheme of *original righteousness*, as well as that of *original sin*, is without any foundation in scripture, or the reason and nature of things.'

[86] Ibid., 167-76.

[Sect. IX.]

You subjoin *Remarks* on Dr. Watts's *Additions* to his book.[87] Some of these deserve a serious consideration.

1. 'Either the new-created man loved God supremely, or not. If he did not, he was not innocent, since the very law and light of nature require such a love to God. If he did, he stood disposed for every act of obedience. And this is true holiness of heart.'[m]

You answer (in many words): 'The new-created man did not love God supremely. For before he could love God the powers of his mind must have been quite finished, and actually exercised'.[[n]] And doubtless the very moment he was created they were quite 'finished', and 'actually exercised', too. For man was not *gradually formed* by God, as a statue is by an human artificer, but 'He spake the word, and they were made; he commanded, and they were created'.[88] And as light and heat were not subsequent to the creation of the sun, but began to exist with it, so that the moment it existed it shone; so spiritual light and heat, knowledge and love were not subsequent to the creation of man, but they began to exist together with him. The moment he existed, he knew and loved.[89]

2. 'If the new-made creature had not a propensity to love and obey God, but was in a state of mere indifference to good or evil, then his being put into such an union with flesh and blood, among a thousand temptations, would have been an overbalance on the side of vice. But our reason can never suppose that God, the wise, just, and good, would have placed a new-made creature in such a situation'.[[o]]

This argument cannot be answered unless it can be showed, either (1) that in such a situation there would not have been an overbalance on the side of vice, or (2) that to place a new-made creature in a situation where there was such an overbalance was consistent with the wisdom, justice, and goodness of God.

[m] p. 186 [quoting Watts, *Ruin*, p. 5].
[[n]] [pp. 186-87.]
[[o]] [p. 187, quoting Watts, *Ruin*, p. 6.]

[87] I.e., John Taylor, *Remarks on such Additions to the Second Edition of 'The Ruin and Recovery of Mankind' as Relate to the Arguments advanced in the Supplement to the Scripture-Doctrine of Original Sin* (London: Mary Fenner, 1742), which has been appended to Taylor's *Supplement* in this 3rd edn.
[88] Ps. 148:5 (BCP).
[89] Taylor, *Reply* (1767), 22: 'But he must *know* before he could *love*.'

But instead of showing, or even attempting to show this, you feebly say, 'I do not think the reason of man by any means sufficient to direct God in what state to make moral agents'. (O that you had always thought so! How much vain, yea, mischievous reasoning had then been spared!) 'But however Adam's propensities and temptations were balanced, he had freedom to choose evil as well as good'.[p] He had. But this is no answer to the argument, which like the former remains in its full force. How could a wise, just, and good God place his creature in such a state as that the scale of evil should preponderate?[90] Although it be allowed he is *in a measure* free still, the other scale does not 'fly up and kick the beam'.[91]

3. 'Notwithstanding all the cavils which have been raised, yet if these two texts (Eph. 4:24, Col. 3:10) are considered together, their obvious meaning will strike an honest and unbiased reader. "The new man", or the principle of true religion in the heart, is created by God after his moral image, in that righteousness and true holiness wherein man was at first created.'[q]

You answer, 'I have endeavoured to prove the contrary, and he does not offer to point out any one mistake in my interpretations.'[r] I have pointed out more than one.

4. 'If these are the qualifications with which such a new-made creature should be endued, and these the circumstances wherein from the wisdom, justice, and goodness of God we should expect him to be situated, then by a careful survey of what man is now, compared with what he should be, we may easily determine whether man

[p] pp. 187-88.
[q] p[p]. [188-]189 [quoting Watts, *Ruin*, p. 6].
[r] [p. 189.]

---

[90] Taylor, *Reply* (1767), 23:

'Whatever weight you lay in the scale of virtue and obedience, it is certain the other scale of evil and disobedience did preponderate, and the scale of virtue and obedience did actually "fly up and kick the beam". You get no advantage, therefore, by magnifying the moral state in which you suppose Adam was created, seeing it turns out just as bad upon your scheme as upon mine. And you are as much obliged as I am to answer your own question, "How could a wise, just, and good God, etc." '

[91] JW extends the metaphor of the balance in a figurative reference to a familiar phrase describing the sudden drop of one side of a pair of scales (familiar, but somewhat unusual, as is indicated by Taylor's use of quotation marks to enclose it in the previous note). Cf. Milton, *Paradise Lost*, iv.1004, where in the Eternal's scales are weighed Satan's chances in a war against God, so light that his scale 'quick flew up and kicked the beam'.

is at present such a creature as the great and blessed God made him at first.'[s]

You answer (in abundance of words, the sum of which is this): 'Our circumstances are, on the whole, far better than Adam's were. For he was under that severe law, "transgress, and die." '[t] He was so, but this does not prove the point. Still, balancing the single disadvantage (if such it was; for even that may be disputed) with the numerous advantages he was possessed of, with the holiness and happiness which he enjoyed, and might have enjoyed for ever, it does by no means appear that the present circumstances of mankind in general are better than Adam's were.

5. 'God did not give Noah dominion over the brute creatures in so ample a manner as he did to Adam. Fear indeed fell on the brutes, but this does not sufficiently preserve man from their outrage. In the innocent state, no man would have been poisoned or torn by serpents or lions as now.'[u]

You answer: 'The second grant runs, "The *fear* of you and the *dread* of you shall be upon *every* beast of the field, and upon *every* fowl of the air, and upon *all* that moves on the earth, and upon *all* the fishes of the sea. Into your hands they are delivered. *Every* moving thing that liveth shall be meat for you. Even as the green herb I have given you *all* things." Now this grant is more extensive than the first.'[v] It is as to *food*, but not as to *dominion*. The liberty of eating an animal does not necessarily imply any dominion over it at all. 'But the *fear* and *dread* of every beast are the effects of dominion in man, and the subjection in brutes.'[w] Nay, neither does *fear* necessarily imply *dominion*. I may *fear* what has not dominion over me, and what I am not *subject* to. And those animals may *fear* me over which nevertheless I have not dominion, neither are they *subject* to me. I *fear* every viper, yea, every poisonous spider. And they *fear* me. Yet neither has dominion over the other. *Fear* therefore and *dread* may be in an high degree, and yet no *dominion* at all. 'But they are "all delivered into our hands".'[x] Yes, *for meat*—as the very next words explain that expression. Whatever, therefore, it may import in other Scriptures, the meaning of it here is plain and certain.

[s] [p. 189, quoting Watts, *Ruin*, p. 11.]
[t] p. 190.
[u] [Ibid., quoting Watts, *Ruin*, pp. 27-28.]
[v] p. 191 [quoting Gen. 9:2-3].
[w] [Ibid.]
[x] [Ibid.]

6. 'Would God have exposed the pure and innocent works of his hands to such unavoidable perils and miseries as arise from bears, tigers, serpents, precipices, volcanoes, etc.?'[y]

You answer, 'He did expose innocent Adam to a *peril* and *misery* greater than all these put together, even to a tempting devil.'[z] I reply, (1) This did not imply any *unavoidable* 'misery' at all. (2) It implied no more 'peril' than God saw was needful as a test of his obedience. Therefore this is no parallel case. So this argument also stands unanswered.

7. 'It has been said indeed, If Adam fell into sin though he was innocent, then among a million of creatures everyone might sin, though he was as innocent as Adam. I answer, there is a possibility of the event, but the improbability of it is as a million to one. I prove it thus. If a million of creatures were made in an equal probability to stand or fall, and if all the numbers from one to one million inclusively were set in a rank, it is plainly a million to one that just any single proposed number of this multitude should fall. Now the total sum is one of these numbers, that is, the last of them. Consequently, it is a million to one against the supposition that the whole number of men should fall. And this argument will grow still ten thousand times stronger if we suppose ten thousand millions to have lived since the creation.'[a]

Your argument stood thus. 'If we can't infer from Adam's transgression that his nature was originally corrupt, neither can we infer from the transgressions of all mankind that their nature is originally corrupt.'[b] It is answered, 'If a million of creatures were made in an equal probability to stand or fall, it is a million to one they should not all fall.' You reply, 'This is no answer to my argument.'[c] Surely it is—and a direct answer. That *one man* sinned does not prove he had a corrupt nature.[92] Why? Because (supposing him free to choose

[y] [Ibid., quoting Watts, *Ruin*, p. 22.]
[z] pp. 191-92.
[a] pp. 194-95 [quoting Watts, *Ruin*, p. 47].
[b] [p. 196, quoting *Supplement*, p. 52.]
[c] p. 196.

---

[92] Taylor, *Reply* (1767), 23:

'Nor by the same argument that another sinned, nor that a third sinned, and so on, till we come to ten thousand millions. All the sinners in that vast number are each of them single sinners, and therefore if the sin of any single man doth not prove that he had a corrupt nature, no more will the sin of any other single man, till you come to any the greatest number of men, prove that he, or any one of them, hath a corrupt nature.'

good or evil) it was as probable he should sin as not, there being no odds on one side or the other. But that *all men* should sin does prove they have a corrupt nature, because it is not as probable that *all men* should sin as that *one man* should, the odds against it being as a million or rather ten thousand millions to one. Either therefore we must allow that mankind are more inclined to evil than to good, or we must maintain a supposition so highly improbable as comes very near a flat impossibility.

And thus much you yourself cannot but allow: 'The reasoning may hold good where all circumstances agree to make the *probability equal* with regard to every individual in this supposed million.'[d] And how can the *probability* be other than *equal*, if every individual be as wise and as good as Adam? But be it equal or no, you say: 'The case is not to be estimated by the laws of *equal probability*, but of *infection*. For when sin is once entered into a body of men it goes on not according to the laws of *chance*' (is this precisely the same with *equal probability*?), 'but the laws, as I may say, of *infection*.'[e] But how came sin to 'enter into a body of men'?[93] That is the very question. Supposing first a *body of sinners*, sin may assume the nature of a contagion. But the difficulty lies against supposing any 'body of sinners' at all. You say indeed, 'One sinner produces another, as the serpent drew in Eve, the first sin and sinner being like "a little leaven" which "leavens the whole lump".'[f] All this I can understand, supposing our nature is inclined to evil. But if not, why does not one good man produce another, as naturally as one sinner produces another?[94] And why does not righteousness spread as fast and as wide among mankind as wickedness? Why does not this 'leaven leaven the whole lump' as frequently, as readily, and as throughly as the other? These 'laws of infection' (so called) will therefore stand you in no stead. For (to bring the matter still more to a point) suppose Adam and Eve newly 'infected' by sin. They had then none to 'infect', having no child. Afterward they repented and found mercy. Then Cain was born. Now surely neither Adam nor Eve would 'infect' him! Having

[d] [Ibid.]
[e] [Ibid.]
[f] [Ibid.]

[93] Ibid., 24: 'Just as it enters into every individual which composes that body; with this addition, that they often corrupt one another.'

[94] Ibid.: 'Doubtless one good man doth at least sometimes produce another, and sometimes a considerable number.'

suffered so severely for their own sin, which therefore they must needs guard him against. How then came he to be a sinner? 'Oh, by his own choice, as Seth was righteous.' Well. Afterwards both wicked Cain and good Seth begat sons and daughters. Now was it not just as probable one should *infect* his children with goodness as the other with wickedness? How came then Cain to transmit vice any more than Seth to transmit virtue? If you say: 'Seth did transmit virtue. His posterity was virtuous till they mixed with the vicious offspring of Cain',[95] I answer, (1) How does that appear? How do you prove that all the posterity of Seth were virtuous? But (2) if they were, why did not this mixture amend the vicious rather than corrupt the virtuous?[96] If our nature is equally inclined to virtue and vice, vice is no more *contagious* than virtue. How then came it totally to prevail over virtue, so that 'all flesh had corrupted themselves before the Lord'?[97] *Contagion* and *infection* are nothing to the purpose, seeing they might propagate good as well as evil.

Let us go one step farther. Eight persons only were saved from the general deluge. We have reason to believe that four, at least, of these were persons truly virtuous. How then came vice to have a majority again among the new inhabitants of the earth?[98] Had the nature of man been inclined to neither, virtue must certainly have had as many votaries as vice. Nay, suppose man a reasonable creature, and supposing virtue to be agreeable to the highest reason, according to all the rules of probability the majority of mankind must in every age have been on the side of virtue.[99]

[95] Both this and the prior response are hypothetical, not quotations from Taylor.

[96] Taylor, *Reply* (1767), 24: 'Because the virtuous, being left to the freedom of their own will, as Adam was, yielded to temptation, as he did.'

[97] Cf. Gen. 6:12; Judg. 2:19.

[98] Taylor, *Reply* (1767), 24: 'I do not know that vice had a majority among them. But if it had, it was because they yielded to temptation, as Adam did.'

[99] Ibid., 25:

'A greater part of mankind in every age may have been on the side of virtue than is commonly imagined. But whereas Mr. W[esley] strenuously asserts that the majority of mankind in any age was very far from being on the side of virtue, it will follow from his argument in this place that we must suppose man to be "no reasonable creature", nor virtue to be the "highest reason". For he saith, upon these suppositions, according to all the rules of probability the majority of mankind in every age must have been on the side of virtue.'

8. 'Some have reckoned up a large catalogue of the instances of divine goodness, and would make this as evident a proof that mankind stands in the favour of God as all the other instances are of an universal degeneracy of man, and the anger of God against them. But 'tis easy to reply. The goodness of God may incline him to bestow a thousand bounties upon criminals. But his justice and goodness will not suffer him to inflict miseries in such an universal manner where there has been no sin to deserve them, either in parents or children.'[g]

You answer, 'There is more than enough sin among mankind to deserve all the sufferings God inflicts upon them. And the Scriptures represent those sufferings as disciplinary, for correction and reformation.'[h] What, *all* the sufferings of *all* mankind? This can in no wise be allowed. Where do the Scriptures say that *all* sufferings, those of infants in particular, are purely *disciplinary*,[100] and intended only 'for correction and reformation'? Neither can this be reconciled to matter of fact. How did the sufferings of Grecian or Roman infants[101] tend to their correction and reformation?[102] Neither do they tend to the correction or reformation of their parents, or of any other persons under heaven. And even as to adults: if universal suffering is a proof of universal sin; and universal sin could not take place unless men were naturally prone to evil; then the present sufferings of mankind are a clear and strong evidence that their nature is prone to evil.

9. 'Notwithstanding all God's provision for the good of man, still the Scripture represents men, while they are in their fallen state, as destitute of God's favour and without hope.'[i]

[g] [pp. 199-200, quoting Watts, *Ruin*, p. 73.]
[h] [p. 200.]
[i] [p. 207, quoting Watts, *Ruin*, p. 121.]

---

[100] Ibid.: 'Where the Scriptures speak of death, or any calamity inflicted upon children, such calamities are represented as disciplinary to parents. See *Supplement*, p. 80.'

[101] A note in Proof (1757) at this point, apparently by JW, calls for this addition: 'how do the sufferings of ten thousand African infants'. The printer overlooked it.

[102] Taylor, *Reply* (1767), 26:

'The barbarous way of exposing their newborn children had a tendency to produce in the minds of the considerate an abhorrence of all such unnatural and worse than brutish practices, and to show them how sadly their morals were corrupted. And as for the innocent babes, it was a mercy to them to be delivered out of the hands of such cruel and barbarous parents.'

You answer, 'How can men be "destitute of God's favour" when he has vouchsafed them a Redeemer?'[j] By 'destitute of God's favour' we mean, 'children of wrath',[103] objects of God's displeasure. And because they were so the Redeemer was given, to *reconcile* them *to* God by his own blood. But notwithstanding this, *while* we and 'they were in' our 'fallen state', we were all objects of God's displeasure.

'But how can they be "without hope" when he *hath given* them *the hope of eternal life*?'[k] All men who are not born again, born of God, are *without hope* at this day. God indeed 'hath given', but they have not *accepted* 'the hope of eternal life'.[104] Hence the bulk of mankind are still as void of *this hope* as are the beasts that perish. And so (the Scripture declares) are all men *by nature*, whatever difference grace may make. 'By nature' all are 'children of wrath', without 'hope, without God in the world'.[105]

10. 'Doth that man write the sincere sense of his own mind and conscience who charges the expression, "Adam was on trial for us all" with this inference, "that we are none of us in a state of trial now, but Adam alone was upon trial for us all"? We have owned and granted that men are now in a state of trial: but this is upon the foot of a new covenant.'[l]

You answer: 'What can be more evident than that according to this scheme Adam alone was to be upon trial for us all, and that none of Adam's posterity are upon personal trial?'[m] Do you not see the ambiguity in the word 'alone'? Or do you see and dissemble it? Dr. Watts supposes that *Adam alone*, that is, *this single person*, was on trial for all men. Does it follow from hence that Adam *alone*, that is, *no other person*, was ever in a state of trial? Again: If 'no person but Adam was upon trial for all men', will it follow, '*No person but* Adam was *upon trial at all*'? It is really hard to think that you here 'speak the sincere sense of your own mind and conscience'.

You go on: 'He supposes all mankind are still under the original covenant with Adam, according to which he *alone* was upon trial for

[j] p. 207.
[k] [pp. 207-8.]
[l] [p. 208, quoting Watts, *Ruin*, p. 133.]
[m] [p. 209.]

[103] Eph. 2:3.
[104] Titus 1:2; 3:7.
[105] Eph. 2:12.

us all, and none of his posterity are upon personal trial.'[n] He does not suppose any man to be so under that covenant as to supersede his being upon personal trial. Yourself add: 'I knew he owned, we are upon personal trial, and that all mankind are now under the covenant of grace. But how can either of these consist with the scheme?'[o] Both of them consist with it perfectly well. (1) Adam *alone* or *single* was, in some sense, on trial for all mankind, according to the tenor of the old covenant, 'Do this and live.' (2) Adam fell, and hereby the sentence of death came on him and all his posterity. (3) The new covenant was given, whereby all mankind were put into a state of personal trial. Yet still, (4) death, the penalty of the old covenant, came (more or less) on all mankind. Now all this is well consistent with itself, as well as with the tenor of Scripture.

11. 'Mankind is represented as one collective body in several verses of the fifth chapter to the Romans.'[p]

You answer: 'St. Paul always distinguishes between Adam and *all men*, his posterity, and does not consider *Adam with all men*, as one creature.'[q] What then? This does not prove that he does not *represent mankind* (Adam's posterity) *as one collective body*.

12. 'All that is contained in *the blessing* given to Noah is consistent with *the curse* which came on all men by the first sin. But that *curse* is not consistent with *the original blessing* which was given to Adam.'[r]

You answer: 'The blessing given to Noah was the *very same* which was given to Adam.'[s] This is palpably false. The blessing which was given to Adam included: (1) freedom from pain and death, (2) dominion over the whole brute creation. But that given to Noah did not include either. Yet you affirm, 'It is renewed to Noah, without any manner of alteration, after pain and death were introduced into the world!'[t] And do *pain* and *death*, then, make 'no manner of alteration'?[106]

[n] [Ibid.]
[o] [pp. 209-10.]
[p] p. 211 [quoting Watts, *Ruin*, p. 183].
[q] [Ibid.]
[r] [Ibid., quoting Watts, *Ruin*, p. 185.]
[s] p. 212.
[t] [Ibid.]

---

[106] Taylor, *Reply* (1767), 26: 'No. For the same blessing is given to Noah, and all that were to descend from him, as is given to Adam, and to all that were to descend from him. This plainly shows that you should make an alteration in your sentiments.'

13. 'The dominion over the brutes given to Adam was not given to Noah.'[u]

You answer, 'Our killing and feeding upon them is the highest instance of *dominion* over them.'[v] It is no instance of it at all. I may shoot a bear and then eat him, yet I have no dominion, unless it be over his carcass.

[u] [Ibid., quoting Watts, *Ruin*, p. 187.]
[v] p. 213.

PART IV
EXTRACTS FROM DR. WATTS AND MR. HEBDEN

I have now considered what is material in your *Doctrine of Original Sin*, with *the Supplement and Reply to Dr. Watts*. And this I purposely did before I read the doctor's book. But how was I surprised on reading it to observe the manner wherein you have treated it, of which I could not be a judge before![1] The frame which he had so beautifully and strongly connected, you have disjointed and broken in pieces, and given us nothing but mangled fragments of it, from which it is impossible to form any judgment of the whole. In order therefore to do justice to that great and good man, as well as to his argument, I subjoin an extract of so much of that work as directly affects the main question.[2]

I the rather subjoin this and the following extracts for these two reasons: (1) Because what has gone before, being purely argumentative, is dry and less profitable to the generality of readers. (2) Because they contain one, uniform, connected scheme of the great doctrine which I have been hitherto defending, and which after the objections have been removed out of the way may be more clearly understood and firmly embraced.

[I.] *Introduction*[a]

Man is a creature made up of an animal body and a rational mind, so united as to act in a mutual correspondence according to certain laws appointed by his Creator. Now suppose the blessed God, who is perfect in wisdom and power, in justice and goodness, were to

[a] [Isaac Watts,] *Ruin and Recovery of Mankind* [2nd edn. (London: James Brackstone, 1742)]. p. 1.

[1] It is possible that Wesley had forgotten reading the 1st edn. of *Ruin and Recovery* in 1740 when it appeared, and immediately publishing an extract of Watts's Question XIII as *Serious Considerations concerning the Doctrines of Election and Reprobation* (see *Bibliography*, No. 42). After all, Watts had published that edn. anonymously. Or JW may not have read the *whole* of Watts's book until now, focusing earlier on the chap. dealing with reprobation.

[2] For biographical details on Watts and an account of his interactions with Taylor, see the introduction (pp. 133-34 above).

form such a new creature, with what qualifications may we conceive such a creature would be endowed by a Being of such goodness, justice, and wisdom?

1.[b] We cannot but conceive he must have a *perfection of natural powers, both of body and spirit*, as united together, suited to his present circumstances.

Not that we need conceive *man* would be made so perfect a being as God could make him. For the wisdom of God plainly designed to display itself in the different ranks and orders of his creation. Nor is it reasonable to suppose man would be made at first with such sublime perfections as he himself might afterwards arrive at by a wise improvement of his powers. But still the creature which was designed to bear the nearest likeness of his Maker in this lower world must have powers perfectly sufficient for his present well-being, and acting in that station wherein God had placed him. All[c] his senses must be clear and strong, his limbs vigorous and active, his body healthy in all the inward and outward parts of it, and every natural power in its proper order. For God would surely form such a creature in a state of perfect ease, without any original malady of nature to give him pain or sorrow.[d] Nor could there be any tendency in his body to pain or disease while he remained without sin.

And as the *powers of his body* must be thus perfect, so *the faculties of his soul* must have their *perfection*, too.

His *understanding* must have that knowledge both of God and his creatures which was needful for his happiness. Not that he was formed with all knowledge in arts and sciences, but with such as was requisite to his peace and welfare. His reason must be clear, his judgment uncorrupted, and his conscience upright and sensible.

This[e] leads me to speak of his *moral perfection*. A rational creature, thus made, must not only be *innocent* as a tree, but must be formed *holy*. His *will* must have an inward bias to virtue. He must have an inclination to please that God who made him, a supreme love to his Creator, a zeal to serve him, and a tender[3] fear of offending him.

[b] p. 2 [Wesley marks transitions to a new page in the original at (or near) the point that the transition occurs. His placement is retained in this edn.].

[c] p. 3.

[d] p. 4.

[e] p. 5.

---

[3] JW substitutes 'tender' for Watts's 'holy'. Cf. Isaac Watts, *Ruin and Recovery of Mankind*, 2nd edn. (London: James Brackstone, 1742), 5.

For either the new created man loved God supremely or not. If he did not, he was not innocent, since the law of nature requires a supreme love to God. If he did, he stood ready for every act of obedience. And this is *true holiness of heart*. And indeed, without this how could a God of holiness love the work of his own hands?

There must be also in this creature a regular subjection of the inferior powers to the superior. Sense and appetite and passion must be subject to reason. The mind must have a power to govern these lower faculties, that he might not offend against the law of his creation.

He[f] must also have his heart inlaid with love to the creatures, especially those of his own species, if he should be placed among them, and with a principle of honesty and truth in dealing with them. And if many of these creatures were made at once, there would be no pride, malice, or envy, no falsehood, no brawls or contentions among them, but all harmony and love.

This universal righteousness, which is the *moral image* of God, is far the noblest part of that image in which Moses represents man to have been originally created. The same writer assures us that when God surveyed all his works he pronounced them 'very good'! Agreeably to what Solomon assures[g] us that God 'made man upright'.

'Tis true, the *natural image* of God in which man was created consisted in his spiritual, intelligent, and immortal nature, and his *political image* (if I may so speak), in his being Lord of this lower creation. But the chief, the *moral* part of his image, we learn from St. Paul to have been the rectitude of man's nature—who in his Epistle to the Ephesians says that the image of God in which man is to be *renewed*, and consequently in which he was *made*, consists 'in righteousness and true holiness'.[h]

2. From the justice and goodness of God we may infer that though man was made *free* with a power[i] to choose either evil or good, that he might be put into a state of probation, yet he had a *full sufficiency of power to preserve himself in love and obedience to his Creator*, and to guard himself against every temptation.

[f] p. 6.
[g] p. 7.
[h] Chap. 4:24.
[i] p. 8.

3. 'Tis highly[j] probable, from the goodness of God, that such a creature would be *made immortal.* 'Tis true, the great God, as Sovereign Lord of his creatures, might take away all that he had given. But 'tis hard to suppose that he ever would have destroyed an intelligent creature who had continued to serve and please him.

'Tis also probable that he was endued with power to arrive at higher degrees of excellency and happiness than those in which he was formed at first. And hereby he was greatly encouraged both to watch against every sin and to use all zeal and diligence in improving the powers he had received.

4. We[k] may add that *the habitation* in which a God of infinite goodness would place such an innocent and holy creature would be furnished with *all the necessaries and conveniences* of life, and prepared for his *delight* as well as *safety*. And so Moses tells us that the first created pair were placed in Eden, a garden of pleasure, and were made lords of all therein, of all the creatures, animal and vegetable, that were round about them.

Neither can we conceive that anything destructive or hurtful could be found in this delightful habitation but what man would have sufficient notice of, with sufficient power to oppose or avoid it.

5.[l] And if this creature had power to propagate its kind, the child must be innocent and holy, and equally capable of persevering in virtue and happiness.

Now if we may judge from the wisdom, justice, and goodness of God that these are the qualifications with which such a new-made creature would be endued, these the circumstances in which he would be situated, then by a careful survey of what mankind is now we may easily judge whether man is now such a creature as the great and blessed God made him at first. And this is the subject of the ensuing inquiry.

[II.] *Question* I

Is[m] *man in his present circumstances such a creature as he came out of the hands of God his Creator?* We may derive a full answer to this inquiry from the following considerations.

[j] p. 9.
[k] p. 10.
[l] p. 11.
[m] p. 12.

1. This earth, which was designed for the habitation of man, carries evident tokens of ruin and desolation, and does not seem to be ordained in its present form and circumstances for the habitation of innocent beings, but is apparently fit for the dwelling-place of creatures who are degenerate and fallen from God.

It is granted that the beauty and order of this lower world, even in its present constitution, and the wonderful texture, composition, and harmony of the several parts of it, both in air, earth, and sea, do still illustriously display[n] the power, wisdom, and goodness of their Creator. Yet it must be confessed also that there are glaring proofs of the terrors of his justice and the execution of his vengeance.

Is not the present shape of our earth, in its divisions of seas and shores, rude and irregular, abrupt and horrid?[4] Survey a map of the world and say, Does the form of it strike our eyes with any natural beauty and harmony? Rather does it not strongly bear on our sight the ideas of ruin and confusion? Travel over the countries of this globe, or visit several parts of this island. What various appearances of a ruined world! What vast broken mountains hang over the heads of travellers! What stupendous cliffs and promontories rise, high and hideous to behold! What dreadful precipices, which make us giddy to look down, and are ready to betray us into destruction! What immense extents are there in many countries of waste and barren ground! What vast and almost impassable[5] deserts![o] What broad and faithless morasses, which are made at once both deaths and graves to unwary travellers! What huge ruinous caverns, deep and wide, big enough to bury whole cities!

What resistless deluges of water, in a season of great rains, come rolling down the hills, bear all things before them, and spread spacious desolation! What roaring and tremendous waterfalls in several parts of the globe! What burning mountains, in[p] whose caverns are

[n] p. 13.
[o] p. 14.
[p] p. 15.

[4] The assumption behind this and the following paragraph is that there were no horrid precipices, or deserts, on earth in its original created state. This was a broadly shared view, which Wesley reflects in his own Sermon 56, 'God's Approbation of His Works', 2:387-99 in this edn.

[5] JW changes Watts's 'hideous and unpassable' to 'vast and almost impassable'. He also inserts the word 'unwary' in the next sentence. Cf. Watts, *Ruin*, 13-14. One senses a higher appreciation of the naturalist's task of exploring such topography in Wesley.

lakes of liquid fire, ready to burst upon the lower lands! Or they are a mere shell of earth, covering prodigious cavities of smoke and furnaces of flame, and seem to wait a divine command to break inward and bury towns and provinces in fiery ruin.

What active treasures of wind are pent up in the bowels of the earth, ready to break out into wide and surprising mischief! What huge torrents of water rush and roar through the hollows of the globe we tread! What dreadful sounds and threatening appearances from the region of meteors in the air! What clouds charged with flame, ready to burst on the earth and discompose and terrify all nature!

When I survey such scenes as these I cannot but say within myself, 'Surely this earth, in these rude and broken appearances, this unsettled and dangerous state, was designed as a dwelling for some unhappy inhabitants who did or would transgress the laws of their Maker and merit[q] desolation from his hand. And he hath here stored up his magazines of divine artillery against the day of punishment.'

How often have the terrible occurrences of nature in the air, earth, and sea, and the calamitous incidents in several countries, given a strong confirmation of this sentiment!

What destructive storms have we and our fathers seen even in this temperate island of Great Britain! What floods of water and violent explosions of fire do we read of in the histories of the world! What shocking convulsions of the globe, stretching far and wide under the affrighted nations! What huge disruptions of the caverns of the earth, with tremendous bellowings, which have filled its inhabitants with terror and astonishment, and made wide devastations! Would a good and gracious Being have originally so formed the inanimate[r] parts of this lower world as to produce such deadly concussions therein, and such desolating appearances, had he not designed it for the habitation of such creatures as he foresaw would deserve these strokes of his indignation?[6]

[q] p. 16
[r] p. 17.

[6] JW omits a section (*Ruin*, 17-18) where Watts appeals to John Woodward's *Essay toward a Natural History of the Earth* (London, 1695) for evidence of how the deluge has wreaked havoc on the upper crust of the earth. JW did not find this account amenable to Scripture. Cf. Sermon 56, 'God's Approbation of His Works', I.2, 2:389 in this edn.

And thus both Moses and St. Peter suppose God to[s] have laid up stores of ruin and destruction within the bowels of the earth, that he might break open his[t] dreadful treasures of flood and fire at proper seasons, to drown and to burn the world, together with the sinful inhabitants thereof.

Now the great God, who appointed such prodigious quantities both of water and fire to be reserved in the bowels of the earth, and among the clouds of heaven, for such a foreseen day of general destruction, did also doubtless prepare the materials of all the lesser[u] storms and hurricanes, earthquakes and floods, and convulsions of nature, and treasured up for these purposes his magazines of wind and flood and fire in the earth. And is this an habitation prepared for the residence of pure and holy beings? Is this such a peaceful place as a kind Creator would have formed for innocent creatures? 'Tis absurd to imagine this of a God so wise, so righteous, and so merciful!

2. Let us take a survey of the vegetables which grow out of the earth, with the brute animals which are found on the surface of it, and we shall find more reasons to conclude that man, the chief inhabitant, is not such as he came first out of his Maker's hand.

It must be granted here again that the wisdom and goodness of the Creator are amazingly[v] displayed in the animal and the vegetable world, beyond the utmost reach of our thoughts or praises. But still we may have leave to inquire whether, if man had continued innocent, among the numerous herbs and flowers fitted for his support and delight, any plants or fruits of a malignant, mortal nature would have grown out of the earth, without some plain mark or caution set upon them?

Can we suppose that among the roots, herbs, and trees good for food the great God would have suffered mischief, malady, and deadly poison to spring up here and there, without any sufficient distinction that man might know how to avoid them? This is the case in our present world—disease, anguish, and death have entered into the bowels and veins of multitudes by an innocent and fatal mistake of these pernicious things for proper food.

[s] p. 18.
[t] p. 19.
[u] p. 20.
[v] p. 21.

There was indeed 'the tree of knowledge' in paradise. But man was expressly cautioned against it. And certainly, had he continued holy, no poisonous plant[w] would have been suffered to grow on the earth without either some natural mark set upon it or some divine caution to avoid it.

Proceed to the animal world. There are many creatures indeed which serve the use or pleasure of man. But are there not many other sorts which he is neither able to govern[x] nor to resist? And by which all his race are exposed, whenever they meet them, to wounds and anguish and death?

If man had not sinned, would there have been in the world any such creatures as bears and tigers, wolves and lions, animated with such fierceness and rage, and armed with such destructive teeth and talons? Would the innocent children of men have ever been formed to be the living prey of these devourers? Were the life and limbs of holy creatures made to become heaps of agonizing carnage? Or would their flesh and bones have been given up to be crushed and churned between the jaws of panthers and leopards, sharks and crocodiles? Let brutes be content to prey on their fellow brutes, but let man be their lord and ruler.

If man[y] were not fallen, would there have been so many tribes of the serpent kind, armed with deadly venom? Would such subtile and active mischiefs have been made and sent to dwell in a world of innocents? And would the race of all these murderers and destructive animals have been propagated for six thousand years in any province of God's dominion, had not its rational inhabitants been in rebellion against God?

What are the immense flights of locusts which darken the sky, and lay the fields desolate? What are the armies of hornets or mosquitoes[7] that frequently make a pleasant land almost intolerable? If they are found in the heats of Africa,[8] and of the East and West Indies, one would think they should not infest the polar regions, if the Creator had not designed them for a scourge to the nations on all sides of the globe.

What[z] are the innumerable host of caterpillars but so many messengers of the anger of God against a sinful race? And since we can

[w] p. 22.
[x] p. 23.
[y] p. 24.
[z] p. 25.

[7] Orig., 'muscatoes', as in Watts.
[8] Orig., 'Africk', while Watts had 'Africa'.

neither resist nor subdue them, we may certainly infer that we are not now such favourites of heaven as God at first made us.

The troublesome and pernicious tribes of animals, both of larger and smaller size, which are fellow-commoners with us on this great globe, together with our impotence to prevent or escape their mischiefs, is a sufficient proof that we are not in the full favour and love of the God that made us, and that he has quartered his armies, his legions, among us, as princes do in a rebellious province.

It is true all these are trials for man during his state of probation. But a[a] state of probation for innocent man would not have included *death*—much less a violent and bloody, or a lingering and painful death. Accordingly our return to dust is mentioned by Moses as a curse[b] of God for the sin of man. And when once life is forfeited by all mankind, then a painful death may properly become a part of the further trial of such creatures as are to rise again, and any pious sufferers may be rewarded by a happy resurrection. But a painful death could never be made a part of the trial of innocent creatures, who had never forfeited life, nor were ever legally subjected to death.

Upon the whole, therefore, such noxious and destructive plants and animals could not be made to vex and disturb, to poison and destroy, a race of innocent intellectual beings.

3. The[c] manner of our entrance into life is another proof of universal sin. Would the great and good God have appointed intellectual animals, had they been sinless, to be propagated in such a way as should necessarily give such exquisite pain and anguish to the mothers who bring them forth? And if the contagion had not been universal, why should such acute pangs attend almost every female parent? Are not the multiplied sorrows with which the daughters of Eve bring forth an evident token that they are not in their original state of favour with that God who created them and pronounced a blessing upon them in their propagation?[d]

[a] p. 26.

[b] p. 27.

[c] p. 28.

[d] The author has been censured here for not dropping a tear over the fair sex under their sorrows and acute pains. But he imagines, he has been dropping tears in every page, and that over every part of mankind. [Watts added this note to his 2nd edn., responding to this censure in John Taylor, *A Supplement to the Scripture-Doctrine of Original Sin, etc.; Containing some Remarks upon two Books* . . . (London: Mary Fenner, 1741), 47-48. Wesley quotes it, then adds his comment:] Undoubtedly he has. And if so, how unjust, how cruel is that censure!

Moses[e] informs us that God 'blessed' the first pair, and bid them 'be fruitful and multiply, and replenish the earth and subdue it;' and soon after tells us that these 'multiplied sorrows' in child-birth are a curse from an offended God. Surely the curse is not as old as the blessing. But sin and sorrow came in together, and spread a wide curse over the birth of man, which before stood *only* under a divine benediction. Not that the blessing is now quite taken away, though the pains of child-bearing are added to it. And daily experience proves, this curse is not taken away by the blessing repeated to Noah.

4. Let us consider in the next place how the generality of mankind are preserved in life. Some few[9] have their food without care or toil. But the millions of human creatures, in all the nations of the earth, are constrained to support a wretched life by hard labour.[f] What dreadful risks of life or limbs do multitudes run to purchase their necessary food! What waste of the hours of sweet repose, what long and slavish and painful toils by day, do multitudes sustain in order to procure *their* daily nourishment! 'Tis 'by the sweat of their brows' they obtain 'their bread'; 'tis by a continual exhausting their spirits that many of them are forced to relieve their own hunger, and to feed their helpless offspring.

If we survey the lower ranks of mankind even in England, in a land of freedom and plenty, a climate temperate and fertile, which abounds with corn and fruits and rich variety of food, yet what a hard shift do ten thousand families make to support life! Their whole time is devoured by bodily labour, and their souls almost eaten up with gnawing cares to answer that question, What shall I eat, and what shall I drink? Even in the poorest and coarsest manner! But if we send our thoughts to the sultry regions[g] of Africa, the frost and snows of Norway, the rocks and deserts of Lapland and Northern Tartary, what a frightful thing is human life! How is the rational nature lost in slavery, and brutality, and incessant toils, and hardships! They are treated like brutes by their lords, and they live like dogs and asses, among labours and wants, hunger and weariness, blows and burdens without end. Did God appoint this for innocents?

[e] p. 29.
[f] p. 30.
[g] p. 31.

[9] JW omits '. . . there are indeed whom Divine Providence has raised to riches and plenty, and . . .' Cf. Watts, *Ruin*, 29.

Is the momentary pleasure of eating and drinking a recompense for incessant labour? Does it bear any proportion to the length of toil, pain, and hazard wherewith the provisions of life are procured? Moses thought not. When he[h] speaks of man's 'eating bread in the sweat of his brows' he acknowledges this to be another of the curses of God for the sin of man.

'Tis strange that any man should say, 'In this sentence of God no curse is pronounced upon either Adam's body, soul, or posterity;' that 'the sorrow of child-bearing is not inflicted as a curse;' that 'the labours of life were increased, but not as a curse;' that 'death was not a curse.' I would fain ask what is a *curse*, if some natural evil pronounced and executed upon a person or thing be not so? Especially when it is pronounced on account of sin, and by God himself, as supreme Governor and Judge? And even the curse on the ground falls properly on the person who tills it.

It is granted, God can turn curses into blessings. Yet these evils were originally pronounced and inflicted as a *curse* or *punishment of sin*, as it is written, 'cursed is everyone who continueth not in all things.' And that death was designed as a curse on man for sin is evident, for Christ 'suffered' that 'curse for us'.[10]

5. Consider the character of mankind in general with regard[i] to religion and virtue, and it will be hard to believe they bear the image of their common father in knowledge and holiness. Some, I grant, are renewed in his image.[11] But the bulk of the world are of another stamp, and sufficiently show there is some fatal contagion spread through this province of God's dominion. So St. John tells us that except the few who are 'born of God', 'the whole world lieth in wickedness'.

And can we think of that gross and stupid ignorance of God which reigns through vast tracts of Asia, Africa, and America, and

[h] p. 32.
[i] p. 33.

[10] This and the preceding paragraph come from a footnote that Watts added to his 2nd edn., responding to Taylor, which JW has now moved into the regular text. Cf. *Ruin*, 32.

[11] Watts had said that some 'are restored to some degrees of conformity to Him that made them. They become his children by repentance and return to God, by a divine change passed upon their natures, and they enjoy a share of his special love'. *Ruin*, 33. JW's alternative suggests greater possible renewal in the image of Christ.

the thick darkness which buries all the heathen countries[j] and reduces them almost to brutes. Can we think of the abominable idolatries, the lewd and cruel rites of worship which have been spread through whole nations, the impious and ridiculous superstitions which are now practised among the greatest part of the world. And yet believe the blessed God would put such wretched polluted workmanship out of his pure hands?

Can we survey the desperate impiety and profaneness, the swearing and cursing and wild blasphemy that is practised day and night among vast multitudes of those who profess to know the true God. Can we behold that almost universal neglect of God, of his fear, his worship, and the obedience due to him, which is found even among them who are called Christians. And yet imagine that these bear that image of God in which they were created?

Nor have men forgot God only, but they seem also to have abandoned their duties to their fellow-creatures also. Hence the perpetual practices of fraud and villainy in the commerce of mankind. The innumerable instances of oppression and cruelty which run through the world. The pride[k] and violence of the great, the wrath, ambition, and tyranny of princes, and the endless iniquities and mischiefs that arise from malice, envy, and revenge in lower people. If we add to these the impure scenes of lust and intemperance which defy the day and pollute the darkness, with the monstrous barbarities which are continually committed by the heathen savages in Africa and America (some of whom kill and roast their fellow-creatures, and eat up men as they eat bread), and by the Christian savages in the Inquisition established in Asia,[12] as well as in many parts of Europe—can we still imagine that mankind abide in that state wherein they came from the hands of their Maker?

That far the[l] *greatest number of men are evil* was the known sentiment of the wiser heathens. They saw and bewailed the undeniable fact, though they knew not how to account for it. 'Οἱ πλείονες κακία—'most men are wicked'—was a common observation among them. Even the poets could not but see this obvious truth. So Virgil

[j] p. 34.
[k] p. 35.
[l] p. 37.

[12] JW adds this reference to Asia. Cf. Watts, *Ruin*, 35.

brings in Anchises, telling his son, 'Few are happy in the other world'—'*Pauci*[m] *laeta arva tenemus*'.[13]

And in this life Horace remarks of men in general, '*Nitimur in vetitum semper, cupimusque negata*'[14]—'we are always desiring and pursuing forbidden things.' Nay, he says, '*Vitiis nemo sine nascitur*'[15]—'No man is born without vices;' and gives this character of young men in general, '*Cereus in vitium flecti; monitoribus asper*'.[16] Seneca says just the same: '*Pejora juvenes facile praecepta audiunt*'[17]—'young men readily hearken to evil counsels; they are soft as wax to be moulded into vice, but rough and rugged to their best monitors.'[18]

Juvenal abounds with the same accounts of human nature:

Quae tam festa dies, ut cesset prodere furem?
Ad mores Natura recurrit
Damnatos, fixa et mutari nescia.
Quisnam[n] *hominum est, quem tu contentum videris uno*
Flagitio?
Dociles imitandis
Turpibus ac pravis omnes sumus.[19]

6. And[o] not only they of riper age, but even those of tender years discover the principles of iniquity and seeds of sin. What young ferments of spite and envy, what native wrath and rage, are found in the little hearts of infants, and sufficiently discovered by their hands and

[m] p. 38.
[n] p. 39.
[o] p. 41.

[13] Virgil, *Aeneid*, vi.739. JW gives his own translation and adds the identification of Watts's 'ghost' as Anchises. Cf. Watts, *Ruin*, 38.

[14] This quotation is actually from Ovid, *Amores*, III.iv.17. Watts misidentified it. Cf. *Ruin*, 38.

[15] Horace, *Satires*, I.iii.68. Translation was given by Watts.

[16] Horace, *De Arte Poetica* (*The Art of Poetry*), 163.

[17] Seneca, *Thyestes*, 309.

[18] This translation gives the Seneca quotation first, then picks up the prior quotation from Horace.

[19] JW omitted Watts's English translation for these four quotations from Juvenal's *Satires*: 'What day is there that does not show us some new malefactors?' (xiii.23-24); 'Nature recurs to its own wicked manners, is fixt in it, and knows not how to change' (xiii.239-40); 'How few persons will you find contented with one sort of wickedness?' (xiii.243-44); 'We are all very forward to learn and imitate whatever is base and wicked' (xiv.40-41). Cf. Watts, *Ruin*, 40.

eyes and countenances, before they can speak or know good from evil! What additional crimes of lying and deceit, obstinacy and perverseness, proceed to blemish their younger years!

How[p] little knowledge or thought of God their Creator and Governor is found in children when they can distinguish good and evil! What an utter disregard of him that made them, and of the duties they owe to him! And when they begin[q] to act according to their childish age, how little sense have they of what is morally *right* and *good*! How do evil passions or irregular appetites continually prevail in them! Even from their first capacity of acting as moral creatures, how are they led away to practise falsehood and injury to their playfellows, perhaps with cruelty or revenge! How often are they engaged in bold disobedience to their parents or teachers! And whence does this arise? What is the root that brings forth such early bitter fruit?

It cannot be imputed to custom, education, or example, for many of these things appear in children before they can take any notice of ill example, or are capable of imitating them. And even where there are only[r] good examples about them, and where the best and earliest instructions are given them and inculcated with the utmost care, yet their hearts run astray from God. The far greatest part of them visibly follow the corrupt influences of sense, appetite, passion, and manifest very early the evil principles of stubbornness, pride, and disobedience.

7. To[s] give a still fuller confirmation of this truth, that mankind have a corrupt nature in them, let it be observed that where persons have not only had all possible helps of education from their parents, but have themselves taken a religious turn betimes, what perpetual hindrance do they find within themselves! What inward oppositions work in their heart, and perhaps interrupt their holy course of life! What vanity of mind, what irregular appetites, what forgetfulness of God, what evil thoughts and tendencies of heart rise up, in contradiction to *their* best purposes! Insomuch that 'there[t] is not a just man upon earth', who through his whole life 'doth good and sinneth not'.

[p] p. 42.
[q] p. 43.
[r] p. 44.
[s] p. 45.
[t] p. 46.

To sum up the three last considerations: If the bulk of mankind are grossly sinful, and if every individual without exception is actually a sinner against the law of his Creator; if sinful propensities appear even in our most tender years, and every child becomes an actual sinner almost as soon as it becomes a moral agent; then we have just reason to conclude that there is some original taint spread through the whole race of men from their birth.

It has been[u] said, indeed, that 'if the first man fell into sin, though he was innocent and perfect, then among a million of men every one might sin, though he was as innocent and perfect as Adam'.[20]

I answer, There is a bare possibility of the event, but the improbability of it is in the proportion of a million to one.

And I prove it thus. If a million of creatures were made in an equal probability to stand or fall, and if all the numbers from *one* to *one million* inclusively were set in a rank, 'tis a million to one that just any single proposed number of all these should fall by sin. Now the total sum is one of these numbers, that is, the last of them. Consequently it is a million to one against the supposition that the whole number of men should fall.

And yet farther, if they were all made (as the goodness of God seems to require) in a greater probability of standing than falling, then it is abundantly more than a million[v] to one that all should sin without exception. And the argument grows still ten thousand times stronger if we suppose ten thousand millions to have lived since the creation.

8. That man is a fallen creature appears farther from hence: no man is able by his present natural powers to perform[w] that law of his Creator which is still written upon his heart.

Does not this law require us to love God with all our heart, to do to others as we would they should do to us, and to govern our senses, appetites, and passions by the rules of reason? Does it not require that these things, whether they regard God, ourselves, or others, should be done perfectly, without defect? Doth it not demand[x] that we should fear, honour, and trust the great God, and obey all his

[u] p. 47.
[v] p. 48.
[w] p. 49.
[x] p. 50.

[20] JW infelicitously omits Watts's clarification of the point of this argument: '. . . and that this is a better account of so universal an apostacy'. Watts, *Ruin*, 47.

will in a perfect manner? Doth it not prescribe constant justice, truth, and goodness toward our neighbour, without one covetous wish, one act of the will, or tongue, or hand, contrary to truth or love? Does it not demand that every sense, appetite, and passion should be perfectly subject to reason? How is there a man on earth who can say, 'I am able by my *natural powers* to do this'?

Even the[y] outward temptations to which man is exposed are evidently too strong to be effectually and constantly resisted by his now enfeebled reason and conscience. While at the same time his will, his appetites and passions, have a powerful propensity to comply with them.

Now[z] would a just, a wise, and a merciful God have formed intellectual creatures in such a wretched state, with powers and capacities so much below their duties that they break his law daily and continually, and are not able to help it?

Should it be said, 'God cannot require more than we are able to perform,' you have an answer in your own bosom. For (1) you know and feel God does require this, even by the law he has written in your heart; yet (2), you feel you are not able to perform it, untie or cut the knot how you may.[21]

Should it be said[a] again, 'God pities and pardons feeble creatures,' I answer: (1) According to the covenant of grace he does, but not according to the law of creation. But (2) did God make some of his noblest creatures so feeble in their original state as continually to offend and want pardon? Did he give them such a law as should never, never be fulfilled by any one of them? Would a God who adjusts the proportions of all things with the exactest wisdom give a law to his creatures so disproportionate to their original powers that even in the state of their creation they are under a necessity of breaking it, and stand in need of daily forgiveness? Does not this single consideration prove that man is now a degenerate being, and not such as he was at first created by the wise, the righteous, the merciful God?

[y] p. 51.
[z] p. 52.
[a] p. 54.

[21] JW inserts this 'experiential' appeal in place of Watts's insistence that God is justified in continuing to hold fallen humanity accountable for what Adam could 'perform' in his unfallen state. Cf. ibid., 53.

If you[b] who are most unwilling to acknowledge the fall of man would but look into yourself daily and observe all the sinful and irregular turns of your own heart—how propense you are to folly in greater or less instances, how soon appetite and passion oppose reason and conscience, how frequently you fall short of the demand of the perfect law of God, how thoughtless and forgetful you are of your Creator, how cold and languishing your affection to him, how little delight you have in virtue or in communion with God—could you think you are such an innocent and holy creature as God at first created you? And that you have been such even from your childhood? Surely a more accurate observation of your own heart must convince you that you yourself are degenerate from the first rectitude of your nature.[22]

9. Another[c] proof of the degeneracy of mankind is this—they are evidently under the displeasure of God, which could not be in their primeval state. As we have taken a short view of *the sins of men*, let us also briefly survey *the miseries of mankind*, and see how these consist with their being in the favour of God.

Think on the thousands of rational creatures descending hourly to the grave—a few by some sudden stroke, but far the greater part by painful and slow approaches. The grave! A dark and shameful prison! Which would never have been made for creatures persisting in innocence and abiding in the favour of him that gave them life and being. Death is the wages of sin. And from this punishment of sin none of mankind can claim a discharge.

Had they stood, can we think any of them would have died? Much less, every one of them? And especially that half the human race should have been doomed to die before seven years old! Before[d] they reach the tenth part of the present age of man, or have done anything in life worth living for!

But let us proceed to other miseries that attend us, and hasten us down to the grave.

Think next of the multitudes that are racked day and night by the gout and stone, the cholic and rheumatism, and all manner of acute

[b] p. 55.
[c] p. 56.
[d] p. 57.

[22] Ever the preacher, JW transforms this entire paragraph from Watts's third-person description ('If those who . . .') to second-person exhortation ('If you who . . .'). Cf. ibid., 55.

and painful diseases. And then say, would a merciful God have contrived these torments for sinless creatures? Think of the dismal scenes of war and bloodshed that have by times overspread all nations. Cast your thoughts on a field of battle, where thousands of men are destroyed[e] like brute beasts, and perish by sharp and bloody strokes or by the fatal engines of death. See thousands more lie on the cold ground, with their flesh and limbs battered and torn, wounded and panting in extreme anguish, till the murmuring soul takes its flight.[23] Are these the signals of their Maker's love, and of his image in which they were created?

Think[f] of the numbers that are swallowed up in the mighty waters, by the rage of stormy winds and seas. Review the multitudes which have been swept away by the pestilence, or consumed by the tedious agonies of famine. Would famine and pestilence, with all the train of lingering horrors which attend them, have ever been made for innocent creatures, to have swept away whole nations of them of every age and sex, men, women, and children without distinction?

Think[g] yet again, what numbers of men have been crushed into miseries and death, and buried by earthquakes. Or have had their bones broken, their limbs disjointed, and their flesh painfully battered, by the fall of houses—perhaps buried alive in the ruins of entire towns or villages, while their neighbours have been drowned in multitudes by the dismal eruptions of water, or destroyed by deluges of liquid fire bursting out of the earth. Would a God of goodness and justice have treated innocent creatures in this manner?

Carry your thoughts to the countries of those savages where thousands of their conquered enemies or prisoners of war are offered in sacrifice to their idols, or tortured and roasted to death by slow fires! Add this to all the former miseries, and then let calm reflection say whether this world does not look like a province half forsaken of its gracious Governor!

Some[h] perhaps will say, it is but a small part of mankind who are involved in these dreadful calamities; and they may suffer peculiar afflictions for their own personal iniquities.

[e] p. 58.
[f] p. 59.
[g] p. 60.
[h] p. 61.

[23] While Watts is rightly honored for his poetic gifts, it is striking that JW substituted this last phrase for Watts's more prosaic '. . . and die by degrees'. Cf. ibid., 58.

I answer, take a just survey of those who have suffered thus, and there is not the least reason to think, they were sinners above others. Do not these calamities spread through whole countries, and involve the best and the worst of men together? Whole nations suffer by them at once. And indeed such is the corruption of human nature that wherever they come they find none innocent. And it is the general situation of mankind, under the just displeasure of God, which exposes them to such destruction.

But to proceed.[i] Think of the innumerable common misfortunes that attend human life! What multitudes perish by these in one week! And how much larger a number do these accidents injure, and fill their lives with pain, though they are not brought immediately to the grave! Think of the mischiefs which one part of mankind in every place are continually contriving or practising against the other. Take a view of these extensive and reigning evils, and then say whether this world be not a part of the creation of God which bears plain marks of its Creator's displeasure!

Much is added to the heap of human miseries by the sorrows that arise from the daily loss of our dearest comforts. What groans and wailings of the living surround the pillows of dying friends or relations! What[j] symptoms of piercing distress attend the remains when they are conveyed to the grave! By such losses the comforts of future life lose their relish, and the sorrows are doubly embittered.

In the civilized parts of the world there is scarce one person sick or in pain, miserable or dying, but several others sustain a considerable share of misery by the strong ties of nature or friendship. This diffuses a personal calamity through whole families. This multiplies human miseries into a new and endless number. Add to this not only the unkindness or falsehood of those from whom we expected the tenderest affection, but the[k] anguish which springs from all our own uneasy and unruly passions. Bring in here all the wrath and resentment in the hearts of men, all the envy and malice that burn within, all the imaginary fears, and the real terrors of future distress coming upon us, all the rage and despair of lost blessings that were once within our hopes, and all the ferments of animal nature which torment the spirit all day, and forbid our nightly repose. Would mankind be in such a condition as this if they were still in the favour of their Maker?

[i] p. 62.
[j] p. 63.
[k] p. 64.

'Yes, men may make miseries for themselves, and be punished by them. But compare the sorrows which any man[l] necessarily suffers with the comforts he enjoys, and the one will balance the other. Or if his sorrows outweigh his comforts, this may be necessary in a state of trial; and God will reward the overbalance of sufferings hereafter.'

I answer, There is no reason to think the far greater part of mankind will have any reward hereafter. And if not, how shall we account for this overbalance of sufferings with regard to them? Therefore we cannot[m] reasonably impute the superior sorrows merely to their being in a state of probation, but rather to the displeasure of the righteous Creator and Governor of the world.

10. To make this still clearer. Not only those who are grown up in the practice of iniquity, who may be punished for their own sins, but all mankind in their very infancy bear the tokens of God's displeasure.

Before children are capable of committing sin they are subject to a thousand miseries. What[n] anguish and pain are they frequently exposed to, even as they are coming into the world, and as soon as they are entered into it! What agonies await their birth! What numerous and acute maladies are ready to attack them! What gripes, what convulsions, what inward torments, which bring some of them down to death within a few hours or days after they have begun to live! And if they survive a few months, what torture do they find in breeding their teeth, and other maladies of infancy which can be told only by shrieks and tears, and that for whole days and nights together! What additional pains do they often sustain by the negligence of their mothers, or cruelty of their nurses! Whereby many of them are brought down to the grave, either on a sudden, or by slow and painful degrees.[24]

And[o] what shall we say of whole nations in elder times, and some even at this day, who when they cannot or will not maintain them, expose their children in the woods, to be torn and devoured by the next wild beast that passes by? Add to this the common calamities in which infants are involved by fire, earthquake, pestilence. And there

[l] p. 65.
[m] p. 66.
[n] p. 67.
[o] p. 68.

---

[24] JW omits a section (ibid., 69-71) where Watts speculates about what birth and early childhood might have been like if there had been no fall.

are a thousand other accidents which attend them, whereby their members, their natural powers, receive dismal injuries, so that perhaps they drag on life with blindness, deafness, lameness, or distortion of body or limbs. Sometimes they languish on to manhood, or even old age, under sore calamities which began almost as soon as their being and which are only ended by death.

Now[p] as these sufferings cannot be sent upon them to correct their personal sins, so neither are they sent as a trial of their virtue, for they have no knowledge of good or evil. Yet we see multitudes of these little, miserable beings. And are these treated as innocent creatures? Or rather as under some general curse, involved in some general punishment?

'But[q] may not these sufferings of children be for the punishment of the sins of their parents?'

Not with any justice or equity, unless the sins of the parents are imputed to their children. Besides, many of the parents of these suffering children are dead or absent, so as never to know it. And how in these cases can it be a punishment for their parents' sin any otherwise than as it is a general punishment for the sin of their first parent?

'But God recompenses them for these sufferings hereafter.' Where does the Scripture affirm this?[25] Besides, many of them grow up to manhood. And if they prove wicked and are sent to hell at last, what recompense have they for their infant sufferings? Or will you say, God punished them before they had sinned because he knew beforehand they would sin? Yet farther. What wise or good design can this their punishment answer, when no creature can know what they are punished for, if it be not for that which affects all mankind?

'But how are such miseries reigning among his creatures consistent with the goodness of God?' Perfectly well, if[r] we consider mankind as a sinful, degenerate part of God's creation. 'Tis most

[p] p. 69.
[q] p. 71.
[r] p. 73.

---

[25] Watts:

'Are all the children which die secured of heaven either by reason or Scripture? If the infant seed of Abraham and his pious followers are taken to dwell with God *as their God*, are the children of wicked parents as happy too? Are you sure they are not subject to any pains hereafter? Or that their souls are not annihilated at death?' (Ibid., 71-72).

abundant goodness that they have any comforts left, and that their miseries are not doubled. Now the inspired writers do consider mankind as fallen from God, and so his goodness is evident in a thousand instances, though it must be confessed, there are also a thousand instances of his just hatred of sin and his righteous punishments among all nations.

11. If we[s] put together all these scenes of vice and misery, it is evident that creatures lying in such deplorable circumstances are not such as they came out of the hands of their Creator, who is wise, holy, and good. His *wisdom*, which is all harmony and order, would not suffer him to frame a whole race of beings under such wild and innumerable disorders, moral as well as natural. His *holiness* would not permit him to create beings with innate principles of iniquity; nor his *goodness* to produce a whole order of creatures in such circumstances of pain, torment, and death.

Could[t] the holy and blessed God originally design and frame a whole world of intelligent creatures in such circumstances that every one of them coming into being, according to the laws of nature, in a long succession of ages, in different climates, of different constitutions and tempers, and in ten thousand thousand different stations and conditions of life; that every one of them should break the laws of reason, and more or less defile themselves with sin; that every one should offend his Maker, every one become guilty in his sight; every one expose himself to God's displeasure, to pain and misery and mortality, without one single exception? If men were such creatures as God at first made them, would not one man, among so many millions, have made a right use of his reason and conscience, and so have avoided sin and death? Would this have been the universal consequent of their original constitution, as framed by the[u] hand of a wise, holy, merciful God? What can be more absurd to imagine than this! Surely God made man upright and happy; nor could all these mischiefs have come directly from our Creator's hand.

Is it objected that 'still the greater part of men have more moral good than evil in them, and have more pleasure than pain; and therefore, on the whole, *mankind is not sinful and miserable*; and that even the best human constitutions lay some innocent persons under

[s] p. 74.
[t] p. 75.
[u] p. 76.

unavoidable hardships.' I answer:[v] (1) In order to pronounce a man *miserable* he must have more pain than pleasure. But in order to pronounce a man a *sinner* there is no need that his moral evil should exceed his good. If a man had an hundred virtues, one vice would make him a criminal in the sight of God. One transgression of the law of his Creator would lay him under his just displeasure. He that keeps the whole law, except in one point, affronts that authority which requires all obedience. All men therefore are under this condemnation. They are *sinners every one of them*.

As to misery, let it be supposed (though by no means granted) that there are many whose pleasures exceed their uneasinesses. Yet 'tis certain, there are more whose pains[w] and uneasinesses far exceed their pleasures. And it is hard to conceive how this should be if all men were innocent and happy by nature.

I answer, (2) Men are not able to frame such constitutions in every case as shall secure happiness to all the innocent. Their narrow views of things do not enable them to provide against all future inconveniences. But it is not thus with the Creator and Governor of all things. He views at once all possibles and all futures. Therefore he is well able to guard against any inconvenience that might befall innocent beings.

I answer,[x] (3) Though the bulk of mankind were happy in the present constitution of things, this gives no manner of satisfaction to any one individual who is unhappy, without any demerit. The advantage of the majority is no reason at all why anyone innocent should suffer. If anyone therefore, man or child, and much more if numbers of them, have more pain than pleasure, they must be involved in some guilt, which may give just occasion to their misery.

12. To enforce this,[y] after the survey of these pains and sorrows, let us consider what are the pleasures of the bulk of mankind. Cast a glance at the sports of *children* from five to fifteen years of age. What toys and fooleries are these! Would a race of wise and holy beings waste so many years of early life in such wretched trifles? And as for our *manly years*, what are the greatest part of the delights of men but silly and irrational, if not grossly sinful? What are the pleasures even of the *rich* and *great* to relieve them under the common

[v] p. 77.
[w] p. 78.
[x] p. 79.
[y] p. 80.

sorrows of life? If they be not luxury and intemperance, are they not furniture and equipage, finery of dress, and gay appearances? To shine[z] in silks of various dye, and blaze in the splendor of gold and jewels? Now would wise and holy creatures have made this the matter of their joy and pleasure, 'My coat is gayer than yours, and I have more glittering things about me than you have!'

Others call for *cards* or *dice* to divert their trouble and pass away their time. How inexpressibly trifling are these sports, if mere diversion be sought therein! But if the design be gain, how is the game mingled with uneasy fears, with the working of various passions! Which in case of disappointment and loss often break out into wrath and fury.

Again,[a] what multitudes drench themselves in gross sensualities as their chief delight! They make a god of their belly, till they overload nature, and make haste to disease and death. They drown their cares and their senses together. Or they bury them in sensual impurities.

Others release themselves from the troubles of life by gadding abroad and mixing with impertinent company. Some delight in wanton jests, in foolish merriment, in mean and trifling conversation—a little above the chattering of monkeys in a wood, or the chirping of crickets upon a hearth. Nay, perhaps it is their diversion to rail at their neighbours, to murder[b] the reputation of the absent. This is their mirth and recreation, these their reliefs against the common miseries of human life.

But would a race of innocent beings fly to such mean and foolish or criminal refuges from pain as these? Would they pursue such vain or vile delights? Would they become rivals to the beasts of the field? Or sport themselves, as devils do, in accusing their fellow-creatures? Surely if we survey the very *pleasures*, as well as the *sorrows*, of the bulk of mankind, we may learn from thence that we are by no means such creatures as we were originally created.

I need add but one more proof of the general ruin of human nature. We are all[c] posting to the grave. Every one of us are succeeding our neighbours into some unknown invisible world. And we all profess to believe this. Yet how exceeding few are solicitous about

[z] p. 81.
[a] p. 82.
[b] p. 83.
[c] p. 84.

this great and awful futurity! Though we are exposed to so many sins and miseries in this life, and are hastening visibly and hourly to the end of it, yet how few are there that make any careful preparation for a better state than this! What multitudes are daily running down into darkness, speeding to an endless duration in an unknown country, without any earnest inquiries about their manner of existence there! They walk over the busy stage of life, they toil and labour, or play and trifle awhile here, and then plunge into a strange unseen world, where they will meet with a just and holy God, whose wisdom will assign them a place and portion suited to their own character. Now[d] were men indeed wise and holy, could they remain so ignorant and thoughtless of that state into which they are all hasting? Or could a gracious God create a race of beings in such a stupid insensibility of their eternal interests, so unsuited to the felicities of an immortal spirit, and so negligent of all preparations for them?

Upon[e] this whole survey, reason must join in this mournful confession, that there must be some spreading poison which has tainted our nature, made us so sinful and miserable, so thoughtless of the future and unprepared for it. There must have been some general revolt of mankind from their Creator, whereby they have ruined their innocence and peace and provoked the anger of their Maker. Whereby they become exposed to such wretched circumstances, even in their infancy and childhood, as well as when they grow to years of ripe understanding.[26]

And[f] methinks when I take a just survey of this world, with all the inhabitants of it, I can look upon it no otherwise than as a grand and magnificent structure in ruins, wherein lie millions of rebels against their Creator, under condemnation to misery and death—who are at the same time sick of a mortal distemper, and disordered in their minds even to distraction. Hence proceed those numberless follies and vices which are practised here, and the righteous[g] anger of an offended God visible in ten thousand instances. Yet are there

[d] p. 85.
[e] p. 86.
[f] p. 89.
[g] p. 90.

[26] JW omits a section (ibid., 87-89) where Watts recapitulates the preceding survey.

proclamations of divine grace, health, and life sounding among them, though very few take any notice thereof. Only here and there one attends to the call, and complies with the proposals of peace. His sins are pardoned and healed.[27] And though his body goes down to the dust for a season, his soul is happy with God—while the bulk of those criminals, despising all the offers of mercy, perish in their own wilful madness.

What[h] is the chief temptation that leads some men to deny so glaring a truth? Is it that they cannot give a satisfactory account of some of the difficulties that attend it? Nay, many, even of the heathen philosophers, believed it, from their own experience and their daily survey of mankind—though they were utterly at a loss how to account for it. And what if we could not assign a sufficient and satisfactory reason for it? Or show how this spreading degeneracy began, or how it came to take place so universally? What if we were still at a loss to explain how all this guilt and misery came upon us? Must we therefore deny the things which we see, and hear, and feel daily?

Can we account for all the secret things in the creation of God? And must we deny whatever we cannot account for? Does any man[i] refuse to believe that the infinite variety of plants and flowers, in all their beauteous colours and forms, grow out of the same earth, because he does not know all the springs of their vegetation? Do men doubt of a loadstone's drawing iron to itself because they cannot find out the way of its operation? Are we not sure that food nourishes our bodies, and medicines relieve our pains? Yet we know not all the ferments and motions of those atoms by which we are relieved and nourished. Why then should we deny that degeneracy of our nature which admits of so full and various proof, though we are not able to account for every circumstance relating to it, or to solve every difficulty that may attend it?

[h] p. 91.
[i] p[p]. 92[-93].
[j] p. 94.

---

[27] JW omits Watts's qualification '. . . of his worst distempers'. Ibid., 90.

[III.] *Question[s]* II, VIII

How[j] *came Vice and Misery to overspread Mankind in all Nations and in all Ages?*

Heathen philosophers could never answer this. But Christians may, from the oracles of God.[28]

These inform us that the first man was a[k] *common head* and *representative of all mankind*; and that he by sinning against his Maker lost his own holiness and happiness, and exposed himself and his posterity (whom he naturally produced and whom he legally represented) to the displeasure of his Maker, and so spread sin and misery through his whole offspring.[29]

So St. Paul:[l] 'As by one man sin entered into the world, and death by sin, even so death passed upon all men, for that all have sinned.'[30] All are esteemed in some sort guilty before God, though they 'did not sin after the similitude of Adam's transgression'. They did not commit actual personal sin against a known law as Adam did.[31]

[k] p. 102.
[l] Rom. 5:12; p[p]. 104[-5].

---

[28] JW omits Watts's elaboration of three possible answers: (1) all souls preexisted and fell together (as per Origen), (2) the original Parent sinned and has passed down the resulting fallen nature by mere natural propagation (i.e., traducianism), or (3) Adam sinned as our 'Federal Head' on the condition that we would receive the results of his act. In this elaboration Watts strongly rejects the first model. He treats the second as a legitimate option, while suggesting his reservations about it. Cf. *Ruin*, 95-101, and the discussion of this topic in the introduction (pp. 149-50 above).

[29] In this paragraph JW omits Watts's crucial description of Adam as our *legal* representation. He also obscures the hesitancy with which Watts opts for the third model. Watts's very next paragraph begins, 'I must confess I am not fond of such a scheme or hypothesis of deriving some sort of guilt from a surety or representative, though I know it has been embraced by a considerable part of Christians ancient and modern. No, I would gladly renounce it, because of some great difficulties attending it, if I could find another way to relieve the much greater difficulties. . . .' Ibid., 102.

Watts goes on to suggest a few practical reasons the third option is the least problematic (ibid., 103-4) and ends by saying it explains best Rom. 5:12, where JW picks up his argument again. Watts's footnote on p. 105 stresses again that it is finally Scripture that leads him to opt for the imputation model.

[30] See the summary of debate over this passage in the introduction (pp.148-49 above).

[31] JW skips Watts's Questions III–VII (*Ruin*, 106-55). In Questions III–V Watts defends the justice of God choosing to establish Adam as our legal representative. In Question VI he defends the assumption that the distorted passions and appetites of the body (passed down from our parents) corrupt the soul that God creates and instills in each person. And in Question VII he attempts to respond to objections about the wisdom or justice of God allowing pure souls to be thus corrupted by union with the body; his response comes close to reclaiming traducianism. Question VIII (beginning, p. 156) turns to the biblical warrant for the model of Adam as representative, and JW once again picks up the discussion in this vein.

[1.] This may more fully appear from the following particulars.[m]

1) It is plainly taught us in Scripture that God at first created one man and woman called Adam and Eve. And from them is derived the whole race of mankind: 'God hath made of one blood', as the Apostle observes, 'all nations of men, to dwell on all the face of the earth'.

2) God created man[n] at first in a holy and happy state in his own likeness, and in his favour. 'And God said, let us make man in our own image, after our likeness.'[o] And that none of the brute creation might molest him, but all of them be for his service, he said, 'Let them have dominion over the fish and the fowl and the cattle. . . . So God created man in his own image.' And what this image consisted in, beside his spiritual and immortal nature, and his dominion over other creatures, we are told by St. Paul, where he speaks of the 'new man, which', says he, 'after God', that is after the likeness of God, 'is created in righteousness and true holiness'.[p] So Solomon[q] assures us, God 'made man upright'. And Moses says, when God had finished all his creation, God 'saw everything that he had made, and behold it was very good'. It was all according to his idea and his will, and well-pleasing in his sight. Man, the last of his creatures, as well as all the rest, 'was very good', was holy and happy.

3) God originally appointed that Adam when innocent should produce an offspring in his own holy image. And on the other hand, that if he sinned he should propagate his kind in his own sinful image. The former is allowed. The latter may be gathered from Gen. 5:1-3, 5: 'In the day that God created man, in the likeness of God made he him. . . . And Adam lived an hundred and thirty years' after his loss of the image of God, 'and begat a son in his own likeness, after his image,' that is his own sinful and mortal image.

It[r] is not to be supposed that Moses in this brief history of the first generations of men should so particularly repeat 'the image and likeness of God' in which Adam was created, unless he had designed to set the comparison in a fair light, between Adam's begetting a son 'in his own' sinful and mortal 'image', whereas he himself was created 'in' God's holy and immortal 'image'.

[m] p. 159.
[n] p. 160.
[o] Gen. 1:26.
[p] Eph. 4:24.
[q] p. 161.
[r] p. 162.

4)[s] God was pleased to put the man whom he had made upon a trial of his obedience for a season. He placed him in a garden of Eden (or pleasure) and gave him a free use of all the creatures, only forbidding him to eat of the fruit of one tree, 'the tree of the knowledge of good and evil. For in the day', said he, 'that thou eatest of it, thou shalt surely die.' In which threatening were doubtless included all evils: death spiritual, temporal, and eternal.

5) As Adam was under a law, whose sanction threatened death upon disobedience, so doubtless God favoured him with a[t] covenant of life, and a promise of life and immortality upon his obedience.

6)[u] Adam broke the law of his Maker, lost his image and his favour, forfeited the hope of immortality, and exposed himself to the wrath of God, and all the punishment which he had threatened. In consequence of which he was now painfully afraid of him in whom he before delighted, and foolishly endeavoured to 'hide himself from the presence of the Lord'.

7)[v] Adam after his sin propagated his kind, according to the law of nature—not in the moral image or likeness of God, not 'in righteousness and true holiness', but in his own sinful likeness, with irregular[w] passions, corrupt appetites and inclinations. To this degeneracy Job manifestly refers in those expressions: 'What is man that he should be clean, or the son of man that he should be righteous?' 'Who can bring a clean thing out of an unclean? Not one.' And David says the same thing: 'Behold, I was shapen in iniquity, and in sin did my mother conceive me.'

This is not an hyperbolical aggravation of David's early sins and propensity to evil from his childhood. But the text is strong and plain in asserting sin some way to belong to his very conception, and to be conveyed from his natural parents, which is a different idea from his actual sins, or propensity to sin in his infancy. It shows the cause both of this propensity and of his actual sins, which operated before he was born. So that if original pravity be not so conveyed and derived as is here asserted, the words are not an *exaggeration of what is*, but a *downright fiction of what is not*.[32]

[s] p. 163.
[t] p. 164.
[u] p. 168.
[v] p. 170.
[w] p. 171.

[32] JW skips a section (ibid., 171-74) giving more biblical warrant on this point.

8) As[x] Adam produced his offspring like himself, destitute of the image of God, so he produced them[y] destitute of the favour of God, under the same condemnation with himself. So Job: 'Man that is born of a woman is of few days, and full of trouble'[z]—i.e., his short life and his troubles proceed from his very birth, his propagation from sinful and mortal parents. Otherwise God would not have appointed his noblest creature in this world to have been 'born to trouble'. Yet this is the case. 'Man is born to trouble, as the sparks fly upward.'[a] Naturally; for it is owing to his birth and his natural derivation from a sinful stock. We are a miserable race, springing from a corrupted and dying root, prone to sin and liable to sorrows and sufferings.

[2.] In[b] proof of this sentence of condemnation and death coming upon all mankind for the sin of Adam, we need only read from the twelfth verse of the fifth chapter of St. Paul's Epistle to the Romans. On which I observe:

1) Here[c] Adam and Christ are set up as distinct heads or representatives of their several families. Adam was the head of all mankind, who became sinful and mortal through his sin. Christ was the head of all believers, who obtain pardon and life through his righteousness.[33] To prove this headship of Adam the Apostle says, 'until the law', that is, from the creation, till the law of Moses, 'sin was in the world; but sin is not imputed where there is no law.' That is, where[d] there is no law or constitution of duty or penalty at all. Yet, saith he, 'Death reigned from Adam to Moses.' Yet sin was imputed and punished by death, even upon all mankind, both small and great, before the law given by Moses. The inference is, therefore there was some law or constitution during all the time from Adam to Moses, in virtue of which sin was imputed to mankind, and death accordingly executed upon them. Now what law or constitution could this be beside that which was said to Adam, as a representative of his whole posterity, 'In the day thou sinnest thou shalt die'?

[x] p. 174.
[y] p. 175.
[z] Chap. 14:1.
[a] Job 5:7.
[b] p. 176.
[c] p. 177.
[d] p. 178.

---

[33] Cf. Watts: 'Christ was the head of the new creation, or of the saints who obtain righteousness and life by divine grace'. Ibid., 177.

2) The Apostle carries his argument yet farther: 'Sin was imputed', and 'death reigned', or was executed 'even upon those who had not sinned after the similitude of Adam's transgression', who had not broken an express command as Adam had done. This manifestly refers to infants. Death reigned over them. Death was executed upon them. And this must be by some constitution which in some sense imputed sin to them who had not committed actual sin. For without such a constitution sin would never have been imputed, nor death executed on children.

Yet,[e] 3) death did not come upon them as a mere *natural* effect of their father Adam's sin and death, but as a proper and *legal* punishment of sin. For 'tis said, his sin brought 'condemnation' upon all men.[f] Now this is a *legal* term, and shows that death is not only a natural but a *penal* evil, and comes upon infants as guilty and *condemned*. Not for their own actual sins, for they had none, but for the sin of Adam their *legal* head, their appointed representative.

In the eighteenth verse the expression is very strong: 'By the offence of one, judgment came upon all men to condemnation.' All[g] the children of Adam, young and old, are *condemned* for this *one offence*. But farther,

4) In the original it is not, 'by the offence of one', but 'by one offence'. By the single offence of Adam, when he stood as the head of all his offspring, and brought sin and death upon them by his disobedience—as, in the following verse, 'by one man's disobedience many were made', or *constituted*, 'sinners', that is, became liable to guilt and death. And so in the sixteenth verse *one* single *offence* is represented as condemning through Adam, and stands in opposition to the *many offences* which are pardoned through Christ.

5)[h] There is a yet farther proof in this chapter that Adam conveyed sin and death to his posterity, not merely as a natural parent but as a common head and representative of all his offspring. As Adam and Christ are here said to be the two springs of sin and righteousness, of death and life to mankind, so the one is represented as a *type* and *figure* of the other. In this very respect Adam was a 'figure' or *type* 'of Christ'.[i] And for this very reason Christ is called 'the

[e] p. 179.
[f] [Rom. 5] ver. 18.
[g] [p. 180.]
[h] p. 181.
[i] [Rom. 5] ver. 14.

second man', 'the last Adam'.[j] As one was the spring of life, so the other was the spring of death, to all his seed or offspring.

Now Christ is a spring of life, not only as he conveys sanctification or holiness to his seed, but as he procures for them justification and eternal life, by his personal obedience. And so Adam is a spring of death, not only as he conveys an unholy nature to his[[k]] seed, to all men, but as he brings 'condemnation' to eternal death upon them by his personal disobedience. And this is the chief thing which the Apostle seems to have in his eye throughout the latter part of this chapter: the conveyance of condemnation and death to the seed of Adam, of justification and[[l]] eternal life to the seed of Christ, by the means of what their respective heads or representatives had done.

[3.][m] But some object, 'All the blessings which God gave at first to Adam consisted in these three particulars: (1) the *blessing of propagation*, (2) *dominion over the brutes*, (3) *the image of God*. But all these three are more expressly and emphatically pronounced to Noah and his sons than to Adam in paradise.'

I answer,[n] if we review the history and context, we shall find the blessing of Adam and that of Noah very widely differ from each other, in all the three particulars mentioned.

1) The blessing of Adam relating to propagation was without those multiplied pains and sorrows which after the first sin fell upon women in bearing children. It was also a blessing of sustentation or nourishment, without hard toil and the sweat of his brow. It was a blessing without a curse on the ground, to lessen or destroy the fruitfulness thereof. It was a blessing without death, without returning to dust. Whereas the blessing of Noah did not exclude death, no, nor the pains of childbirth, nor the earning our bread by the sweat of our brow.

2) To Adam[o] was given 'dominion over the brutes'. To Noah it was only said, 'The fear of you and the dread of you shall be upon every beast.' But notwithstanding this fear and dread, yet they frequently sting men to death, or bite and tear them in pieces. Whereas no such calamity could ever have befallen innocent Adam or his innocent offspring.

[j] 1 Cor. 15:47-49.
[[k]] [p. 182.]
[[l]] [p. 183.]
[m] p. 183 [i.e., 184].
[n] p. 186.
[o] p. 187.

3) 'The[p] image of God' in which Adam was created consisted eminently in righteousness and true holiness. But that part of 'the image of God' which remained after the fall, and remains in all men to this day, is the *natural image* of God, namely the spiritual nature and immortality of the soul—not excluding the *political image* of God, or a degree of dominion over the creatures still remaining. But the moral image of God is lost and defaced, or else it could not be said to be 'renewed'.[q] It is then evident that the blessing given to Adam in innocency and that given to Noah after the flood differ so widely that the latter was consistent with the condemnation or curse for sin and the former was not. Consequently mankind does not now stand in the same favour of God as Adam did while he was innocent.

Thus it appears that the Holy Scripture both in the Old and New Testament give[s] us a plain and full account of the conveyance of sin, misery, and death, from the first man to all his offspring.

[IV.] *The First Essay*[34]
Do the present Miseries of Man alone prove his Apostasy from God?

Sect. 1
A General Survey of the Follies and Miseries of Mankind

Upon[r] a just view of human nature, from its entrance into life till it retires behind the curtain of death, one would be ready to say concerning man, 'Is this the creature that is so superior to the rest of the inhabitants[s] of the globe as to require the peculiar care of the Creator in forming him? Does he deserve such an illustrious description as even the heathen poet has given us of him?'

Sanctius his animal, mentisque capacius altae
Deerat adhuc, et quod dominari in cetera posset.
Natus homo est, sive hunc divino semine fecit[35]
Ille opifex rerum mundi melioris origo [. . .]
Finxit in effigiem moderantum cuncta deorum.

[p] p. 188.
[q] p. 189.
[r] p. 359.
[s] p. 360.

[34] JW has reached the end of Watts's description of the *ruin* of humanity, so he omits the remainder of the main text (*Ruin*, 190-355), jumping to the first of two relevant essays that Watts included as an appendix.

[35] Orig., '*cretum*' (as in Watts).

Pronaque cum spectent animalia cetera terram,
Os homini sublime dedit, caelumque videre[36]
Iussit, et erectos ad sidera tollere vultus.[37]

A creature of a more exalted kind
Was wanting yet, and then was man designed.
Conscious of thought, of more capacious breast,
For empire formed, and fit to rule the rest.
Whether with particles of heavenly fire
The God of nature did his soul inspire, [. . .]
And moulding up a mass in shape like ours,
Formed a bright image of th' all-ruling powers.
And while the mute creation downward bend
Their sight, and to their earthy mother tend,
Man looks aloft, and with erected eyes,
Beholds his own hereditary skies.

Now[t] if man was formed in the image of God, certainly he was a holy and a happy being. But what is there like holiness or happiness now found running through this rank of creatures? Are there any of the brutal kind that do not more regularly answer the design of their creation? Are there any brutes that we ever find acting so much below their original character, on the land, in the water, or the air, as mankind does all over the earth? Or are there any tribes among them through which pain, vexation, and misery are so plentifully distributed as they are among the children of men?

Were[u] this globe of earth to be surveyed from one end to the other by some spirit of a superior order, it would be found such a theatre of folly and madness, such a maze of mingled vice and misery, as would move the compassion of his refined nature to a painful degree, were it not tempered by a clear sight of that wise and just providence which strongly and sweetly works in the midst of all, and will

[t] p. 361.
[u] p. 362.

[36] Orig., '*tueri*' (as in Watts).
[37] Ovid, *Metamorphoses*, i.76-79, 83-86; apparently quoted by Watts from memory, with a couple of errors, as JW, too, was prone to do. Watts provides as well the translation by Dryden.

in the end bring good out of all evil, and justify the ways of God with man.[38]

Sect. 2[v]

A Particular View of the Miseries of Man

But to waive for the present the sins and follies of mankind, may we not infer from his miseries alone that we are degenerate beings, bearing the most evident marks of the displeasure of our Maker?

View the histories of mankind, and what is almost all history but a description of the wretchedness of men under the mischiefs they bring upon themselves and the judgments of the great God? The scenes of happiness and peace are very thin set among all the nations, and they are rather a transient[w] glimpse here and there than anything solid and durable. But if we look over the universe, what public desolations by plague and famine, by storms and earthquakes, by wars and pestilence! What secret mischiefs reign among men, which pierce and torture the soul! What smarting wounds and bruises, what pains and diseases attack and torment the animal frame!

Where[x] is the family of seven or eight persons wherein there is not one or more afflicted with some troublesome malady or tiresome inconvenience? These indeed are often concealed by the persons who suffer them, and by the families where they dwell. But were they all brought together, what *hospitals* or *infirmaries* would be able to contain them?

What toils and hardships, what inward anxieties and sorrows, disappointments and calamities are diffused through every age and country! Do not[y] the rich feel them as well as the poor? Are they not all teased[39] with their own appetites, which are never satisfied? And their impetuous passions give them no rest. What keen anguish of mind arises from pride, and envy, and resentment! What tortures

[v] p. 363.
[w] p. 364.
[x] p. 365.
[y] p. 366.

[38] The last portion of this sentence (beginning 'which strongly') is by Wesley. Cf. *Ruin*, 362. For other examples of JW's characteristic description of God's providence working 'strongly and sweetly', see Sermon 15, 'The Great Assize', II.10, 1:365 in this edn.; Sermon 66, 'The Signs of the Times', II.9, 2:530 in this edn.; and Sermon 118, 'On the Omnipresence of God', II.1, 4:43 in this edn.

[39] Orig., 'teized'.

does ambition, or disappointed love, or wild jealousy, infuse into their bosoms! Meanwhile the poor, together with inward vexations and corroding maladies of the mind, sustain likewise endless drudgeries in procuring their necessary subsistence. And how many of them cannot after all procure even food to eat and raiment to put on!

Survey man through every state. See first what a figure he makes at his entrance into life! 'This animal', says Pliny, 'who is to govern the rest of the creatures, how he lies bound hand and foot all in tears, and begins his life in misery and punishment'.[40] If we trace the education of the human race from the cradle to mature age, especially among the poor, who are the bulk of all nations, the wretchedness of mankind will farther appear. How are they everywhere dragged up[z] in their tender age, through a train of nonsense, madness, and miseries! What millions of uneasy sensations do they endure in infancy and childhood by reason of those pressing necessities which for some years they can tell only in cries and groans, and which their parents either are so poor they cannot relieve, or so savage and brutish that they will not! How wretchedly are these young generations hurried on through the folly and weakness of childhood, till new calamities arise from their own ungoverned appetites and impetuous passions! As youth advances, the ferments of the blood rise higher and the appetites and passions grow much stronger, and give more abundant vexation to the race of mankind than they do to any of the brutal creation. And whereas[a] the all-wise God, for kind reasons, has limited the gratification of these appetites by rules of virtue, perhaps these very rules, through the corruption of our nature, irritate mankind to greater excesses.

Would the affairs[b] of human life in infancy, childhood, and youth have ever been in such a sore and painful situation if man had been such a being as God at first made him, and had continued in the favour of his Maker? Could divine wisdom and goodness admit of these scenes were there not a degeneracy through the whole race,

[z] p. 367.
[a] p. 368.
[b] p. 370.

[40] Pliny, *Natural History*, VII.i.3 (Loeb: '[the human child] . . . when successfully born he lies with hands and feet in shackles, weeping—the animal that is to lord it over all the rest, and he initiates his life with punishment because of one fault only, the offence of being born').

which by the just permission of God exerts itself some way or other in every stage of life?

Follow mankind to the age of public appearance upon the stage of the world. And what shall we find there but infinite cares, labours, and toil, attended with fond hopes almost always frustrated with endless crosses and disappointments, through ten thousand accidents that are every moment flying across this mortal stage? As for the poor,[c] how does the sultry toil exhaust their lives in summer, and what starving wretchedness do they feel in winter! How is a miserable life sustained among all the pains and fatigues of nature, with the oppression, cruelty, and scorn of the rich?

Let us follow on the track to the close of life. What a scene is presented us in old age! How innumerable and how inexpressible are the disasters and sorrows, the pains and aches, the groans and wretchedness, that meet man on the borders of the grave, before they plunge him into it!

And indeed is there any person on earth, high or low, without such distresses and difficulties, such crossing accidents and perplexing cares, such painful infirmities in some or other part of life, as must pronounce mankind upon the whole a miserable being? Whatever scenes of happiness seem to attend him in any shining hour, a dark cloud soon casts a gloom over them, and the pleasing vision vanishes as a dream.

And what are the[d] boasted pleasures which some have supposed to balance the sorrows of life? Are not most of them owing in a good degree to some previous uneasiness? 'Tis the pain of hunger which makes food so relishing, the pain of weariness that renders sleep so refreshing. And as for the blessings of love and friendship among neighbours and kindred, do they not often produce as much vexation as satisfaction? Not indeed of themselves, but by reason of the endless humours and follies, errors and passions of mankind.

Again. Do[e] not the very pleasures of the body prove the ruin of ten thousand souls? They may be used with innocence and wisdom; but the unruly appetites and passions of men continually turn into a curse what God originally designed for a blessing.

Think again how short and transient are the pleasures of life in comparison of the pains of it! How vanishing the sweetest

[c] p. 371.
[d] p. 373.
[e] p. 374.

sensations[f] of delight! But in many persons and families, how many are the days, the months, the years, of fatigue, or pain, or bitter sorrow? What pleasure of the animal frame is either as lasting or as intense as the pain of the gout or stone? How small is the proportion of sensible pleasure to that of pain, or trouble, or uneasiness! And how far is it overbalanced by the maladies or miseries, the fears or sorrows of the greatest part of mankind!

As for intellectual pleasures, how few are there in the world who have any capacity for them! And among those few, how many differences and contentions! How many crossing objections, bewildered inquiries, and unhappy mistakes are mingled with the enjoyment! So that 'he who increaseth knowledge increaseth sorrow', saith the wisest of men. And upon the whole computation he writes on this also, 'vanity and vexation of spirit'.

To[g] talk then of real happiness to be enjoyed in this life (abstracted from the foretaste of another) is contrary to all the common sense and experience of every thinking man. Without this 'taste of the powers of the world to come', I know[h] not what wise man would willingly come into these scenes of mortality, or go through them with any patience.

What, to be trained up from infancy under so many unavoidable follies, prejudices, and wretched delusions through the power of flesh and sense? To be sunk into such gross ignorance both of our souls, our better selves, and of the glorious Being that made us? To lie under such heavy shades of darkness, such a world of mistakes and errors, as are mingled with our little faint glimpses and low notices of God our Creator? What, to be so far distant from God, and to endure such a long estrangement from the wisest and best of beings in this foolish and fleshly state, with so few and slender communications with or from him?

What, to feel so many powerful and disquieting appetites, so many restless and unruly passions, which want the perpetual guard of a jealous eye, and a strong restraint over them? Otherwise they will be ever breaking out into some new mischief.

What, to be ever surrounded with such delights of sense as are constant temptations to folly and sin? To[i] have scarce any joys but

[f] [p. 375.]
[g] p. 376.
[h] p. 377.
[i] p. 378.

what we are liable to pay dear for by an excessive or irregular indulgence? Can this be a desirable state? For any wise being who knows what happiness is, to be united to such a disorderly machine of flesh and blood, with all its uneasy and unruly ferments?

Add to this another train of inbred miseries which attend this animal frame. What wise spirit would willingly put on such flesh and blood as ours, with all the springs of sickness and pain, anguish and disease in it? What, to be liable to the racking disquietudes of gout and stone, and a thousand other distempers! To have nature worn out by slow and long aches and infirmities, and lie lingering many years on the borders of death before we can find a grave!

Solomon[j] seems to be much of this mind when after a survey of the whole scheme of human life in its variety of scenes (without the views of hereafter) he declares, 'I praised the dead who were already dead more than the living who are yet alive.'[k] And indeed it[l] appears that the miseries of life are so numerous as to overbalance all its real comforts, and sufficiently to show that mankind now lie under evident marks of their Maker's displeasure, as being degenerated from that state of innocence wherein they were at first created.

Sect. 3
Objections answered

But it is objected: 'If human life in general is miserable, how is it that all[m] men are so unwilling to die?'

I answer, (1) because they fear to meet with more misery in another life than they feel in this. So our poet:

> The[n] weariest and most loathed worldly life
> That pain, age, penury, and imprisonment
> Can lay on nature, 'tis a paradise
> To what we fear of death.[41]

And in another place:

[j] p. 380.
[k] Eccles. 4:2.
[l] p. 381.
[m] [p. 382.]
[n] p. 383.

[41] Shakespeare, *Measure for Measure*, III.i.129-32.

If by the sleep of death we could but end
The heart-ache and the thousand natural shocks
That flesh is heir to, 'twere a consummation
Devoutly to be wished. O who would bear
The oppressor's wrongs, the poor man's contumely,
The insolence of office, and the spurns
That[o] patient merit of th' unworthy takes,
With all the long calamities of life;
When he himself might his quietus make
With a bare bodkin? Who would bear such burdens,
And groan and sweat under a weary life,
But that the dread of something after death,
That undiscovered country, from whose border
No traveller returns, puzzles the will,
And makes us rather bear those ills we have,
Than fly to others which are all unknown.[42]

If[p] you say, 'But the heathens knew nothing of a future life; and yet they, too, in all their generations have been unwilling to die. Nor would they put an end to their own life, were it never so miserable.' I answer, Most of the ancient (as well as the modern) heathens had some notions of an after-state, and some fears of punishment in another life for sins committed in this. And in the politer nations they generally supposed self-murderers in particular would be punished after death:

Proxima deinde tenent maesti loca, qui sibi letum
Insontes peperere manu, lucemque perosi
Projecere animas. Quam vellent aethere in alto
Nunc et pauperiem et duros perferre labores!
Fata obstant: duraque palus innabilis unda
Alligat, et novies Styx interfusa coercet.[43]

[o] p. 384.
[p] p. 385.

[42] Shakespeare, *Hamlet*, III.i.61-64, 70-71, 73-82. Watts had added an extra line as the fifth: 'the whips and scorns of time'. JW removed the line, restoring Shakespeare's text.

[43] Cf. Virgil, *Aeneid*, vi.434-39. JW inserted the Latin text, Watts giving only the English (from Dryden). Cf. Wesley, Sermon 99, 'The Reward of Righteousness', II.(III).9, 3:411 in this edn.

The next in place and punishment are they
Who prodigally threw their lives away.
Fools, who repining at their wretched state,
And loathing anxious life have hurried on their fate.
With late repentance now they would retrieve
The bodies they forsook, and wish to live:
All pain and poverty desire to bear,
To view the light of heaven, and breathe the vital air.
But fate forbids: the Stygian floods oppose,
And with nine circling streams the captive souls enclose.[44]

I answer,[q] (2) suppose this love of life and aversion to death are found even where there is no regard to a future state, this will not prove that *mankind is happy*, but only that the God of nature hath wrought this principle into the souls of all men, in order to preserve the work of his own hands.[[r]] So that reluctance against dying is owing to the natural principle of self-preservation, without any formed and sedate judgment whether it is best to continue in this life or not, whether life has more happiness or misery.

It may be objected, secondly, if brutes[s] suffer nearly the same miseries with mankind, and yet have not sinned, how can these miseries prove that man is an apostate being?[45]

[q] p. 386.
[[r]] [p. 387.]
[s] p. 389.

---

[44] Watts gave the English translation of Dryden; JW substituted the translation by Christopher Pitt.

[45] Without any indication in the text, JW inserts an answer to this question in the following two paragraphs that is entirely in his own voice. It argues the *reverse* of the answer that Watts had given! Watts spends nearly six pages (*Ruin*, 389-94) elaborating the various means by which animals suffer, arguing that humans provide only a small portion of this suffering. He then admits that many theologians have attributed the ultimate source of all animal suffering to the curse coming from the fall, but specifically *rejects* this suggestion. While he allows that humans often abuse other creatures by our perverse wills, he insists that most animal suffering has no special reference to human sin. More specifically, he takes it to be clear in Scripture that humans alone were created immortal and that it was part of God's creation design that wild beasts kill one another and be used for human food and raiment. Ibid., 394-96. Turning to moral issues, Watts discounts the concern for animal pain, siding with those like Descartes who view animals as mere matter, with no sense of pain and pleasure. Ibid., 396-98. Even if we allow that they do sense pain and pleasure, he next insists that they experience a far lower ratio of pain to pleasure than

I answer, It is by reason of man's apostasy that even brute animals suffer. 'The whole creation groaneth together' on his account, 'and travaileth together in pain to this day.' For the brute 'creation was made subject to vanity', to abuse, pain, corruption, death, not 'willingly', not by any act of its own, 'but by reason of him that subjected it'[46]—of God, who in consequence of Adam's sin, whom he had appointed lord of the whole lower world, *for his sake* pronounced this curse (not only on the ground, but) on all which was before under his dominion.

The misery, therefore, of the brute creation is so far from being an objection to the apostasy of man that it is a visible standing demonstration thereof. If beasts suffer, then man is fallen.

Sect. 4

The Apostasy of Man proved by Scripture and Reason

But[t] whether or no the *miseries* of mankind alone will prove their apostasy from God, it is certain these together with the *sins* of man are an abundant proof that we are fallen creatures. And this I shall now endeavour to show both from the express[u] *testimony of Scripture*, from the *necessity of renewing grace*, and from a *survey of the heathen world*.

First, the Scripture testifies that an universal degeneracy and corruption is come upon all the sons and daughters of Adam. 'Every imagination of the thoughts of the heart of man is only evil continually.'[v] Yea, 'evil from his youth'.[w] 'The Lord looked down from heaven upon the children of men, to see if there were any that did understand and seek God. They are gone out of the way. There is none that doth good, no not one.'[x] 'There is not a just man upon earth who doth good and sinneth not.'[y] 'All we like sheep have gone

[t] p. 409.
[u] p. 410.
[v] Gen. 6:5.
[w] Chap. 8:21.
[x] Ps. 14:2-3.
[y] Eccles. 7:20.

do humans (ibid., 398-99), particularly if we recall that their sense of pain is transitory while we can remember our pains. Ibid., 399-402. For JW's alternative conviction that human sin is the primal source, and a continuing primary agent, for animal suffering, see Sermon 60, 'The General Deliverance', 2:437-50 in this edn.

[46] Rom. 8:20; the text for JW's sermon 'The General Deliverance'.

astray, we have turned every one to his own way'[z]—different wanderings, but all[[a]] wanderers. 'There is none righteous, no not one. There is none that doth good, no not one. Every mouth is stopped, and all the world become guilty before God. All are fallen short of the glory of God, because all have sinned.'[b] 'If one died for all, then were all dead;'[c] that is, spiritually dead, 'dead in trespasses and sins'.[47]

Now can we suppose that all God's creatures would universally break his law, run into sin and death, defile and destroy themselves, and that without any one exception, if it had not arisen from some root of bitterness, some original iniquity which was diffused through them all, from their very entrance into the world? 'Tis utterly incredible that every single person among the millions of mankind should be born pure and innocent, and yet should all, by free and voluntary choice, everyone for himself for near six thousand years together, rebel against him that made them, if there were not some original contagion spread through them all at their entrance into life!

Secondly, the same thing appears from the scriptural doctrine of our recovery by divine grace. Let us consider in what manner the Scripture represents that great change which must be wrought in our souls in order to our obtaining the favour and image of God, and future happiness.[d] 'Except a man be born again, he cannot see the kingdom of God.' In other Scriptures it is represented that they must be 'born of the Spirit'. They must be 'born of God'.[e] They must be 'created anew in Christ Jesus unto good works'.[f] They must 'be quickened',[g] or raised again from their 'death in trespasses and sins'. They must 'be renewed in their spirit, or created after the image of God in righteousness and true holiness'. They must 'be reconciled to God by Jesus Christ'. They must be 'washed from their sins in his blood'. Since 'all have sinned and come short of the glory

[z] Isa. 53:6.
[[a]] [pp. 411-12.]
[b] Rom. 3:10, 12, 19, 23.
[c] 2 Cor. 5:14.
[d] p. 413.
[e] John 3:3, 6, 8.
[f] Eph. 2:10.
[g] [Eph. 2] ver. 5.

[47] Eph. 2:1.

of God', therefore if ever they are saved they must be 'justified freely by his grace, through the redemption that is in Christ Jesus'. Now[h] can anyone suppose God to have made so many millions of creatures as have come into the world from Adam till now, which have all entered the world innocent and holy, and yet not one of them should retain his image in holiness, or be fit for his favour, without being 'born again', 'created anew', 'raised from the dead', 'redeemed', not with corruptible things, but 'with the blood of his own Son'? Do not all these representations prove that every man is born with some original contagion, and under some criminal imputation in the sight of God? Else would not one among all these millions be fit to be made a partaker of his favour without such amazing purifications as require the blood of the Son of God, and the almighty operation of his Spirit? Do not all these things show that mankind in their present generations are not such creatures as God at first made them?

The[i] same great truth we may learn, thirdly, from even a slight survey of the heathen nations. A few days ago I was viewing, in the map of the world, the vast Asiatic empires of Tartary and China, and a great part of the kingdom of the Mogul, with the multitude of islands in the East Indies. I went on to survey all the southern part of Africa, with the savage nations of America. I observed the thousands, or rather millions, who dwell on this globe, and walk and trifle and live and die there, under the heaviest cloud of ignorance and darkness, not knowing God nor the way to his favour; who are drenched in gross impieties and superstitions, who are continually guilty of national immoralities, and practise idolatry, malice and lewdness, fraud and falsehood, with scarce any regret or restraint.

Then sighing within myself I said, 'Tis not many years since these were all infants, and they were brought[j] up by their parents who knew not God, nor the path that leads to life and happiness. Are not these unhappy children born under difficulties almost unsurmountable? Are they not laid under almost an impossibility of breaking their way of themselves through so much thick darkness, to the knowledge, the fear, and the love of him that made them? Dreadful truth indeed! Yet, so far as I can see, certain and incontestable. Such, I fear, is the case of those of human race who cover at present the far greatest part of the globe.

[h] p. 414.
[i] p. 415.
[j] p. 416.

Then I ran back in my thoughts four or five thousand years, and said within myself, What multitudes in every age of the world have been born in these deplorable circumstances! They are inured from their birth to barbarous customs and impious practices. They have an image of the life of brutes and devils wrought in them by their early education. They have had the seeds of wretched wickedness sown, planted, and cultivated in them, by the savage instructions of those that went before them. And their own imitation of such horrible examples has confirmed the mischief, long[k] before they knew or heard of the true God—if they have heard of him to this day. Scarce any of them have admitted one thoughtful inquiry whether they follow the rules of reason, or whether they are in the way of happiness and peace, any more than their parents before them. As they are born in this gross darkness, so they grow up in the vile idolatries and all the shameful abominations of their country, and go on to death in the same course. Nor have they light enough, either from without or from within, to make them ask seriously, 'Is there not a lie in my right hand?' 'Am I not in the way of destruction?'

St. Peter[l] says indeed that 'in every nation he that feareth God and worketh righteousness is accepted of him'. But if there were very few (*among the Jews*) who feared God, very few in those learned nations of the Gentiles, how much fewer, may we suppose, are in those barbarous countries which have no knowledge, either divine or human!

But[m] would this have been the case of those unhappy nations, both of the parents and their children, in an hundred long successions, had they been such a race of creatures as they came out of the hand of the Creator? If those children had been guiltless in the eye of God could this have been their portion? In short, can we suppose the wise and righteous and merciful God would have established and continued such a constitution for the propagation of mankind which should naturally place so many millions of them so early in such dismal circumstances, if there had not been some dreadful and universal degeneracy spread over them and their fathers, by some original crime, which met and seized them at the very entrance into life?

[k] p. 417.
[l] p. 419.
[m] p. 420.

[V.] *The Second Essay*
A Plain Explication of the Doctrine of
Imputed Sin *and* Imputed Righteousness[n]

This doctrine has been attended with many noisy controversies in the Christian world. Let us try whether it may not be set in so fair and easy a light as to reconcile the sentiments of the contending parties.

When[o] a man has broken the law of his country, and is punished for so doing, 'tis plain that 'sin is imputed to him'. His 'wickedness is upon him'. He 'bears his iniquity'. That is, he is reputed or accounted guilty—he is condemned and dealt with as an offender.

On the other hand, if an innocent man who is falsely accused is acquitted by the court, sin *is not imputed to him*, but *righteousness is imputed to him*; or to use another phrase, 'his righteousness is upon him'.

Or, if a reward be given a man for any righteous action, this righteous act *is imputed to him.*

Farther, if a man has committed a crime, but the prince pardons[p] him, then he is 'justified from' it, and his fault is 'not imputed to him'.

But if a man, having committed treason, his estate is taken from him and his children, then they 'bear the iniquity of their father' and his sin is 'imputed to them' also.

If a man lose his life and estate for murder, and his children thereby become vagabonds, then the *blood* of the person murdered is said to *be upon the murderer*, and *upon his children* also. So the Jews: 'His blood be on us and on our children'—let us and our children be punished for it.

Or[q] if a criminal had incurred the penalty of imprisonment, and the state were to permit a friend of his to become his surety, and to be confined in his room, then his crime is said to be *imputed to his surety*, or to be *laid upon him*; he *bears the iniquity* of his friend by suffering for him. Meantime the crime for which the surety now suffers *is not imputed* to the real offender.

And should we suppose the prince to permit this surety to exert himself in some eminent service to which a reward is promised, and

[n] p. 427.
[o] p. 428.
[p] p. 429.
[q] p. 430.

all this in order to entitle the criminal to the promised reward, then this eminent service may be said *to be imputed* to the criminal—that is, he is rewarded on the account of it. So in this case both what his friend has done and suffered is imputed to him.

If[r] a man do some eminent service to his prince, and he with his posterity are dignified on account of it, then the service performed by the father is said to *be imputed to the children also.*

Now if among the histories of nations we find anything of this kind, do we not easily understand what the writers say? Why then do we judge these phrases when they are found in the inspired writers to be so hard to be understood?

[1.] But it may be asked, How can[s] the acts of the parent's treason be *imputed to his* little *child*? Since those acts were quite out of the reach of an infant, nor was it possible for him to commit them.

Or how can the eminent service performed by a father be *imputed to his child*, who is but an infant?

I answer, (1) Those[t] acts of treason or acts of service are by a common figure said to be 'imputed to the children' when they suffer or enjoy the consequences of their father's treason, or eminent service—though the *particular actions* of treason or service could not be practised by the children. This would easily be understood should it occur in an human history. And why not when it occurs in the Sacred Writings?

I answer, (2) *Sin* is taken either for an *act of disobedience* to a law, or for the *legal result* of such an act—that is, the *guilt* or *liableness* to *punishment*. Now when we say, The *sin* of a traitor is 'imputed to[u] his children' we do not mean that the *act* of the father is charged upon the child, but that the *guilt* or liableness to punishment is so transferred to him that he suffers banishment or poverty on account of it.

In like manner *righteousness* is either particular *acts* of obedience to a law, or the *legal result* of those actions, that is, a *right to the reward* annexed to them.

And so when we say, 'The righteousness' of him that has performed some eminent act of obedience 'is imputed to his children,' we do not mean that the particular *act* of the father is charged on the

[r] p. 431.
[s] p. 432.
[t] p. 433.
[u] p. 434.

child, as if he had done it; but that the *right to reward*, which is the result of that act, is transferred to his children.

[2.] Now[v] if we would but thus explain every text of Scripture wherein either *imputed sin* or *imputed righteousness* is mentioned (whether in express words, or in the plain meaning of them), we should find them all easy and intelligible.

Thus[w] we may easily understand how the *obedience* of Christ is imputed to all his seed, and how the *disobedience* of Adam is imputed to all his children.

To confirm this I would add these three remarks:

1) There are several histories in Scripture where expressions of the same import occur.

So Gen. 22:16[-18], 'Thy seed shall possess the gate of his enemies, because thou hast obeyed my voice.' Here Abraham's *obedience*, that is, the result of it, is *imputed* to his posterity.

So[x] Num. 25:11[-13], God 'gave to' Phinehas 'and his seed after him the covenant of an everlasting priesthood, because he was zealous for his God', and slew the criminals in Israel. This was so *imputed to his children* that they also received the reward of it.

Thus the sin of Achan was so *imputed to* his children that they were all stoned on account of it (Josh. 7:24). In like manner the covetousness of Gehazi was *imputed* to his posterity (2 Kings 5:27) when God by his prophet[y] pronounced that the 'leprosy should cleave unto him and to his seed for ever'.

2) The Scriptures both of the Old and New Testament use the words 'sin' and 'iniquity' (both in Hebrew and Greek) to signify not only the criminal *actions* themselves but also the *result* and[z] *consequences* of those actions, that is, *the guilt* or *liableness to punishment*—and sometimes the *punishment* itself, whether it fall upon the original criminal, or upon others on his account.

In the same manner the Scriptures use the word 'righteousness', not only for *acts* of obedience but also the *result* of them, that is, *justification* or *right to a reward*. A moderate study of some of those texts where these words are used, may convince us of this.

So Job 33:26, God 'will render to a man his righteousness'—that

[v] p. 435.
[w] p. 436.
[x] p. 437.
[y] p. 438.
[z] p. 439.

is, the reward of it. Hos. 10:12, 'Sow to yourselves in righteousness, till the Lord come and rain righteousness upon you'—that is, till he pour down the rewards or fruits of it upon you.

I[a] might add here that in several places of St. Paul's epistles 'righteousness' means 'justification' in the passive sense of the word.

So Rom. 10:4, 'Christ is the end of the law for righteousness to everyone that believeth'—that is, in order to the justification of believers. Rom. 10:10, 'With the heart man believeth unto righteousness'—that is, so as to obtain justification. Gal. 2:21, 'If righteousness', that is, justification, 'come by the law, then Christ is dead in vain.' This particularly holds where the word λογίζομαι or 'impute' is joined with 'righteousness'. As Rom. 4:3, 'Abraham believed God, and it was imputed to him for righteousness.' Rom. 4:5, 'His faith is counted to him for righteousness.' It is not ἀντι or ὑπέρ, 'for' or 'instead of' righteousness; but εἰς δικαιοσύνην—'in order to justification' or acceptance with God.

And in other places of Scripture 'a work', whether good or evil, is put for the *reward* of it. Job. 34:11, 'The work of a man will he render unto him'—that is, the recompense[b] of it. So St. Paul desires Philemon to impute any wrong he had received from Onesimus to himself—that is, not the evil *action*, but the *damage* he had sustained.

Indeed when *sin* or *righteousness* are said 'to be imputed' to any man, on account of what himself hath done, the words usually denote both the good or evil actions themselves and the legal result of them. But when the *sin* or *righteousness* of one person is said 'to be imputed' to another, then generally those words mean only the result thereof, that is a liableness to punishment on the one hand, and to reward on the other.

But[c] let us say what we will to confine the sense of the *imputation of sin and righteousness* to the *legal result*, the reward or punishment *of good or evil actions*. Let us ever so explicitly deny the imputation of *the actions* themselves to others. Still Mr. Taylor will level almost all his arguments against *the imputation of the actions themselves*, and then triumph in having demolished what we never built, and refuting what we never asserted.[48]

[a] p. 440.
[b] [p. 441.]
[c] p. 444 [i.e., 445n].

---

[48] JW has moved this footnote to Watts's 2nd edn. into the text and made the reference to Taylor explicit. Cf. *Ruin*, 445n.

3. The[d] Scripture does not, that I remember, anywhere say in express words that 'the sin of Adam is imputed to his children', or that 'the sins of believers are imputed to Christ', or that 'the righteousness of Christ is imputed to believers'. But the true meaning of all these expressions is sufficiently found in several places of Scripture.

Yet[e] since these express words and phrases of the *imputation of Adam's sin to us*, of *our sins to Christ*, and *of Christ's righteousness to us*, are not plainly written in Scripture, we should not impose it on every Christian to use these very expressions. Let everyone take his liberty, either of confining himself to strictly scriptural language, or of manifesting his sense of these plain scriptural doctrines in words and phrases of his own.

But if these words were expressly written in the Bible, they could not reasonably be interpreted in any other sense than this which I have explained by so many examples, both in Scripture, history, and in common life.

I[[f]] would only add, if it were allowed, that the very *act* of Adam's disobedience was imputed to all his posterity, that all the same sinful *actions* which men have committed were imputed to Christ, and the very *actions* which Christ did upon earth were imputed to *believers*. What greater punishments would the posterity of Adam suffer? Or what greater blessings could believers enjoy, beyond what Scripture has assigned, either to *mankind*, as the result of the sin of Adam; or to Christ, as the result of the sins of *men*; or to *believers*, as the result of the righteousness of Christ?[49]

[d] p. 446.
[e] p. 447.
[[f]] [p. 452.]

[49] JW omits the Third Essay that Watts appended to his text, which defends the transfer of Adam's 'guilt' to later humanity, and our 'guilt' to Christ. *Ruin*, 454-76.

PART V
THE DOCTRINE OF ORIGINAL SIN, ETC.

I believe every impartial reader is now able to judge whether Mr. Taylor has solidly answered Dr. Watts or no. But there is another not inconsiderable writer whom I cannot find he has answered at all, though he has published four several tracts professedly against Mr. Taylor—of which he could not be ignorant, because they are mentioned in the *Ruin and Recovery of Human Nature*. I mean, the Revd. Mr. Samuel Hebden, Minister at Wrentham in Suffolk.[1] I think it therefore highly expedient to subjoin a short abstract of these also—the rather because the tracts themselves are very scarce, having been for some time out of print.

[I.][2] Eccles. 7:29

Lo, this only have I found, that God made man upright; but they have sought out many inventions.

In[a] the preceding verse Solomon had declared how few wise and good persons he had found in the whole course of his life. But lest any should blame the providence of God for this, he here observes that these were not what God made man at first; and that their being what they were not was the effect of a wretched apostasy from God. The original words stand thus: 'Only, see thou, I have found. . . .'

[b] 'Only'. This word sets a mark on what it is prefixed to, as a truth of great certainty and importance. . . . 'See (observe) thou.' He invites every hearer and reader in particular to consider what he was about to offer. 'I have found.' I have discovered this certain truth, and assert it on the fullest evidence: 'that God made man upright; but they have sought out many inventions'.

[a] p. 3 [Again Wesley's citations denote the beginnings of the new pages to which he turns in his extract.]

[b] p. 4.

[1] For details on Samuel Hebden and his various rebuttals of Taylor, see the introduction (p. 134–35 above).

[2] The first two sections of Part V distill the two sermons in Samuel Hebden, *Man's Original Righteousness; and God's Covenant with Adam* (London: R. Hett & J. Oswald, 1740).

The Hebrew word ישר which we render 'upright' is properly[c] opposed to *crooked, irregular, perverse*. It is applied to things, to signify their being *straight* or agreeable to rule. But it is likewise applied both to God and man, with the *words* and *works* of both. As applied to God, the *ways* of God, the *word* of God, it is joined with 'good' (Psalm 25:8), with 'righteous' (Psalm 99:137), with 'true' and 'good' (Neh. 9:13), where mention is made of 'right judgments, true laws, good statutes'. The 'uprightness' with which God is said to 'minister judgment to the people' answers to 'righteousness'. In a word, *God's uprightness* is the moral rectitude of his nature, infinitely wise, good, just, and perfect. The *uprightness of man* is his conformity of heart and life to the rule he is under, which is the law or will of God. Accordingly we read of 'uprightness of heart' (Ps. 36:10, Job 33:3), and 'uprightness of way' or conversation (Ps. 37:14, and often elsewhere). 'The upright man' throughout the Scripture is a truly good man, a man of integrity, an holy person.[d] In Job 1:1, 8; 2:3, 'upright' is the same with 'perfect' (as in Ps. 37:37, and many other places), and is explained by 'one who feareth God and escheweth evil'. In Job 8:6 it is joined, and is the same with, 'pure'. In the same sense it is taken—to mention but a few out of many texts which might be produced: Prov. 10:29, 'The way of the Lord is strength to the upright, but destruction shall be to the workers of iniquity.' Chap. 11:3, 'The integrity of the upright shall guide them, but the perverseness of transgressors shall destroy them.' Ver. 6, 'The righteousness of the upright shall deliver them, but transgressors shall be taken in their own naughtiness.' Ver. 11, 'By the blessing of the upright the city is exalted.' Chap. 15:8,[3] 'The sacrifice of the wicked is an abomination to the Lord, but the prayer of the upright is his delight.' Chap. 21:29, 'A wicked man hardeneth his face, but as for the upright, he directeth his way.' From even these texts it manifestly appears that 'uprightness' as applied to man is the very same with 'righteousness', 'holiness', or 'integrity' of heart and conversation.[4]

[c] p. 5.
[d] p. 6.

---

[3] JW corrects Hebden's mistaken citation from '15:3' to '15:8'. Cf. Hebden, *Man's Original Righteousness*, 6.

[4] JW substituted 'holiness' for Hebden's 'goodness', and added the focus 'of heart and conversation'. Cf. ibid.

When therefore Solomon says, 'God made man upright,' the plain undeniable meaning is, God at first formed man[e] righteous or holy; although 'they have sought out many inventions'. 'They'—this refers to Adam, which is both a singular and a plural noun. 'They', our first parents, and with them their posterity, 'have sought out many inventions', many contrivances, to offend God and injure themselves. These 'many inventions' are opposed to the 'uprightness', the simplicity of heart and integrity with which our first parents, and mankind in them, were *originally* made by God.

The doctrine of the text, then, is that God at his creation 'made man upright' or *righteous*; not only *rational*, and a *free agent*, but *holy*.[5] Therefore[f] to maintain that 'man neither was nor could be formed holy, because none can be holy but in consequence of his own choice and endeavour', is bold indeed![6] To prove the contrary, and justify Solomon's assertion, I offer a few plain arguments.

1. Moses in his account of the creation writes, 'And God said, Let us make man in our own image.'[7] Now[g] that righteousness or holiness is the principal part of this image of God appears from Eph. 4:22, 24, and Col. 3:9-10—on which passages I observe: (1) By 'the old man' is not meant *an heathenish life* or an ungodly conversation, but a *corrupt nature*.[8] For the Apostle elsewhere speaks of 'our old man' as 'crucified with Christ'; and here distinguishes from it their 'former conversation', or sinful actions, which he calls 'the deeds of the old man'. (2) By 'the new man' is meant, not *a new course of life* (as the Socinians interpret it)[9] but a *principle of grace*, called by St. Peter 'the hidden man of the heart' and a 'divine nature'. (3) To[h]

[e] p. 7.
[f] p. 8.
[g] p. 9.
[h] p. 10.

---

[5] JW omits a section (ibid., 7-8) where Hebden says of Adam, 'Though holiness, or a supreme love to God, was in a sense supernatural to him, it being superadded to the essential powers and faculties of his nature as a man, it was however thus far natural to him that it was concreated with his rational powers.'

[6] Hebden's footnote (ibid., p. 7 n. h) here states: 'To this purpose Mr. J. Taylor speaks in his late treatise of *Original Sin*.'

[7] JW omits a section that includes a criticism of the way 'Pelagians' (among others) understand the nature of 'the Image of God'. Ibid., 8.

[8] JW omits 'or a habitual propensity to sin'. Cf. ibid., 9.

[9] Hebden's footnote (ibid., p. 9 n. l) stresses that Taylor adopts this Socinian interpretation.

'put off the old man' (the same as to 'crucify the flesh') is to subdue and mortify our corrupt nature.[10] To 'put on the new man' is to stir up and cultivate that gracious principle, that new nature. 'This', saith the Apostle, 'is created after God, in righteousness and true holiness.' 'It is created': which cannot properly be said of a *new course of life*, but may of a *new nature*. It is created 'after God', or 'in his image and likeness', mentioned by Moses. But what is it to be 'created after God', or 'in his image'? It is to be 'created in righteousness and true holiness' (termed 'knowledge', the practical knowledge of God, Col. 3:10). But[i] if to be 'created after God', or 'in his image and likeness', is to be 'created in righteousness and true holiness', and if that principle of righteousness and holiness by which we are 'created unto good works' is a 'new man', a 'divine nature', it is easy to infer that man was at first created *righteous* or *holy*.

2. All things as at first made by God 'were very good'. Nor indeed could he make them otherwise. Now a *rational* being is *not good*, unless his *rational* powers are all devoted to God. The goodness of man as a rational being must lie[j] in a devotedness and consecration to God. Consequently man was at first thus devoted to God, otherwise he was *not good*. But this devotedness to the love and service of God is true righteousness or holiness. This righteousness, then, this goodness or uprightness, this regular and due state or disposition of the human mind, was at first natural to man. It was wrought into his nature, and con-created with his rational powers. A *rational* creature, as such, is capable of knowing, loving, serving, living in communion with the Most Holy One. Adam at first either did or did not use this capacity; either he knew and loved God or he did not. If he did not, he was not *very good*, no, nor *good* at all; if he did, he was upright, righteous, holy.

3. When God vested man with dominion over the other creatures, how was he qualified for exercising that dominion unless he had in himself a principle of love and obedience to the supreme Governor? Did not God form[k] the creatures obedient to man to confirm man in his loving obedience to God? Or did he create them with a

[i] [p. 11.]
[j] p. 12.
[k] p. 13.

[10] JW substitutes 'our corrupt nature' for Hebden's 'the corrupt principle which every renewed soul feels, laments, and abhors in itself'. Cf. ibid., 10.

disposition to depend on and obey man as their lord, and not create man with a disposition to obey and live dependent on the Lord of all? But this disposition is uprightness. Therefore God 'made man upright'.

4. Either man was created with principles of love and obedience, or he was created an enemy to God. One of these must be. For as all the duty required of man as a rational being is summarily comprised in love—a supreme love to God, and a subordinate love to others for his sake—so there can be no medium between a rational creature's loving God, and not loving, which is a degree of *enmity* to him. Either, O man, thou lovest God, or thou dost not. If thou dost, thou art holy or righteous; if thou dost not, thou art indisposed to serve him in such a manner and with such a frame of spirit as he requires. Then thou art an[l] enemy to God, a rebel against his authority. But God could not create man in such a state, in a state of enmity against himself. It follows that man was created a lover of God, that is, righteous and holy.

In a word,[m] can you prove either that man was not 'created after God', or that this does not mean being 'created in righteousness and true holiness'? Was not man, as all creatures, good in his kind? And is a *rational* creature 'good' unless all its powers are devoted to God? Was not man duly qualified at first to exercise dominion over the other creatures? And could he be so qualified without a principle of love and obedience to their common Lord? Lastly, can any man prove either that man could be *innocent* if he did not love the Lord his God with all his heart, or that such a love to God is not *righteousness* and true *holiness*?[11]

[n]From the doctrine of man's *original righteousness* we may easily conclude that of *original sin*. [o]For this reason it is that some so earnestly protest against *original righteousness*, because they dread looking on themselves as *by nature* fallen creatures and 'children of wrath'. If man was not holy at first, he could not fall from a state of

[l] p. 14.
[m] p. 15.
[n] p. 20.
[o] p. 21.

[11] JW omits a long section (*Man's Original Righteousness*, 17-20) where Hebden refuses to assert that Adam was created 'as perfect as he could have been' or 'as perfect as the glorified saints', but also rejects the suggestion Adam was essentially like a child at creation.

holiness, and consequently the first transgression exposed him and his posterity to nothing but temporal death. But on the other hand, if *man was made upright* it follows: (1) That man when he fell lost his original righteousness, and therewith his title to God's favour and to communion with God. (2) That he thereby incurred not only temporal but *spiritual death*. He became 'dead in sin' and 'a child of wrath'. And (3) that all his posterity are born with such a nature, not as man had at first, but as he contracted by his fall.

[II.] Gen. 2:16-17[12]

And the Lord God commanded the man, saying,
Of every tree of the garden thou mayst freely eat.
But of the tree of knowledge of good and evil, thou shalt not eat of it.
For in the day that thou eatest thereof thou shall surely die.[13]

[p]God forbade man to eat of this tree in token of his sovereign authority, and for the exercise of man's love,[q] and the trial of his obedience. The words added, 'In the day thou eatest thereof thou shalt surely die,' or literally, 'In dying thou shall die,' mean, not only 'Thou shalt certainly die,' but 'Thou shalt suffer every kind of death.' Thy *soul* as well as thy *body* shall die. And indeed if God made man *upright* or *holy*; if man at first enjoyed 'the life of God', including holiness joined with blessedness; and if the miserable state of the *soul* (as well as the dissolution of the body) is in Scripture termed 'death'; it plainly follows that the original threatening includes nothing less than a loss of man's original uprightness, of his title to God's favour, and a life of happy communion with God.

The words mean farther, 'Thou[r] shalt instantly die' as soon as ever thou eatest. And so he did. For in that instant his original righteousness, title to God's favour,[s] and communion with God being lost, he was spiritually dead, 'dead in sin', his soul was dead to God, and his body liable to death, temporal and eternal.[14]

[p] p. 26.
[q] p. 27.
[r] p. 28.
[s] p. 29.

[12] 'Sermon II,' ibid., beginning on p. 23.

[13] After quoting the scripture, JW omits a long section of Hebden that described Adam as the 'federal head' of humanity. Ibid., 23-26.

[14] JW omits Hebden's comment that most divines believe Adam was later forgiven and saved, and Hebden's endorsement of this conclusion. Cf. ibid., 28, 29.

And as there is a *threatening* of *death* expressed in these words, so a *promise of life* is implied. The threatening death only in case of disobedience implied that otherwise he should not die.[15] And even[t] since the fall, the law of God promises life to obedience, as well as threatens death to disobedience, since the tenor of it is: 'Do this and live'; 'If thou wilt enter into life, keep the Commandments.'

[1.] [u]Now a law given by God with a promise of life and a threatening of death, consented to by man, is evidently a *covenant*. For what is a covenant but a mutual agreement of two or more parties on certain terms? Now in this sense God *covenanted* with man and man *covenanted* with God. God gave a law, promising life in case of obedience, threatening death in case of disobedience. And man accepted of the terms. Here therefore was a real *covenant*.

But to guard this against objections I add:

1) We do not affirm that God visibly appeared, and formally treated with Adam as one man with another. Without so formal[v] a procedure God could and doubtless did signify to him on what terms he was to expect life or death.

2) We do not assert that God promised to translate him to heaven. But without question he made Adam sensible that if he continued obedient he should continue happy, whether in paradise or some other region.

3) If[w] one greatly superior will freely condescend to treat with an inferior, this does not disannul the mutual agreement, or hinder its having the nature of a *covenant*. So God entered into a proper covenant with Abraham of old, and with his people in the gospel. And if so, much more might he do so with man, when perfectly *upright* toward God.

[2.] And this covenant was made with Adam not only for *himself*, but likewise for all his *posterity*.[16] This appears,

[t] p. 30.
[u] p. 31.
[v] p. 32.
[w] p. 33.

[15] This sentence is Wesley's terse positive reformulation of a convoluted section where Hebden criticizes the suggestion that God did not give Adam a promise of life at the same time as the initial threatening of death. Cf. ibid., 29-30.

[16] This is JW's rephrasing of Hebden's affirmation that Adam was the 'federal or legal representative of all who were, in an ordinary way, to descend from him'. Cf. ibid., 33.

1)[x] From the tenor of the original threatening, compared with the present state of mankind. For it is evident that every one of his posterity is born *liable to death*; that the *death* to which all are liable was not threatened but in case of man's *sinning*; that man was not liable to *death* till he *sinned*, and his being so was the result of the threatening; and that the Scripture constantly points at sin as the sole cause of *death*, and of all *suffering*. But if all mankind are born liable to *that* which was originally threatened only to *sin*, then all mankind are accounted sinners, and as such are concerned in the *original threatening*, and consequently in the *original promise*.

2)[y] From 1 Cor. 15:22, 'In Adam all die.' Here the Apostle speaks not of both our parents, but of Adam singly (as also Rom. 5), to denote our peculiar relation to him. The 'all' mentioned are all his natural descendants, who 'all die in' or *through* 'him'—that is, are liable to death on account of their relation to him. And it is not only a *bodily death* that is here spoken of; for it stands opposed not to a bare revival of the body, but to a happy and glorious resurrection, such as 'they that are Christ's' will partake of at his Second Coming. For of this resurrection, not that of the ungodly, the Apostle is speaking throughout this chapter. But[z] they could not 'die in Adam' if they did not in some sense *sin in him*, and fall *with him*; if the covenant had not been made with him, not for himself only, but for all his posterity.

3) From verse 45 and 47 of the same chapter. The 'first man' and 'the second man', 'the last Adam', are here opposed. Now why is Christ, notwithstanding the millions of men intervening between Adam and him, and following after his birth, called 'the second man', and the 'last Adam'? We have an answer Rom. 5:12, 14, etc., where Adam is said to be 'a figure of' Christ. And the resemblance between them is shown to lie in this, that as *sin* and *death* descend from one, so *righteousness* and *life* from the other. Consequently what Christ is with regard to all his spiritual seed, that Adam is with regard to all his natural descendants, namely, a *public person*, a *federal head*, a *legal representative*—one with whom

[x] p. 34.
[y] p. 35.
[z] p. 36.

the covenant was made, not only for himself, but also for his whole posterity.[17]

[III.] John 3:5-6[18]

Except a man be born of water and of the spirit, he cannot enter into the kingdom of God. That which is born of the flesh is flesh; and that which is born of the Spirit is Spirit.

In[a] this text we have 1) the new birth described, 2) the necessity of it insisted on, [and] 3) the original corruption of every child of Adam observed, as that from which the necessity of such a change arises.

1. The new birth is here described.[19] Whatever[b] this implies, the Spirit of God is the sole author of it. He does not help a man to regenerate himself, but takes the work into his own hands. A child of God, as such, is 'not born of blood'—does not become so by a descent from pious parents. He is not 'born of the will of the flesh'—is not renewed by the power of his own carnal will; 'nor of man', of any man whatsoever, 'but of God'—by the sole power of his Spirit.[20]

In[c] regeneration the Holy Spirit mortifies 'the old man', corrupt nature, and breathes a principle of life into the soul, a principle of faith, of sincere love, and willing obedience to God.[21] He[d] who was

[a] [p. 4.]
[b] [p. 5.]
[c] [p. 6.]
[d] [p. 7.]

[17] JW adds the last phrase to explain the meaning of 'federal head', but a very similar definition was given earlier by Hebden. Ibid., 33. JW then omits a long section (ibid., 37-45) explaining and defending how Adam can be our legal and federal head, as well as an appendix (ibid., 46-51) where Hebden gives his summary of Taylor's position on original sin.

[18] This section extracts Samuel Hebden, *Baptismal Regeneration Disproved* (London: R. Hett & J. Oswald, 1741).

[19] JW omits a section where Hebden downplays physical baptism, arguing that being 'born of the Spirit' or inwardly renewed is sufficient for salvation, whether one has been baptized in water or not. *Baptismal Regeneration*, 4-5.

[20] JW omits Hebden's further insistence that regeneration is owed solely to 'the sovereign will of God' and 'the divine effectual working of the Spirit of God'. Ibid., 6.

[21] JW omits Hebden's elaboration: 'to express the matter in words plainer perhaps to some, he forms the soul to a fixed habitual disposedness for all obedience, and to as fixed habitual a dislike and aversion to all sin'. Ibid.

'dead in sin' is now 'dead to sin',[22] and[e] 'alive to God through Jesus Christ'. God[f] has 'created in him a clean heart', and 'renewed a right spirit within him'. He has 'created' him 'unto good works', and 'written' his 'law in his heart'. But[g] if the Spirit of God is the sole agent in the work of regeneration; if the soul of man has no active interest or concern in his 'being born again'; if man was created holy, and regeneration re-instamps that holy image of God on the soul; if 'the new man' is 'created after God in righteousness and true holiness'; if the corruption of nature (termed 'the old man' or 'flesh') is not contracted by imitation or custom, but is an inbred, hereditary distemper, coeval with our nature; if[h] all truly good works are the fruits of a good heart, a good principle wrought in the soul;[23] it plainly follows that the faith, hope, love, fear which distinguish the children of God from others are not of the nature of *acquired* but of *infused habits* or principles.[24] To say, then, that 'holiness must be the effect of a man's own choice and endeavour, and that by a right use of his natural powers every man may and must attain an habit of holiness, that is, "be born again",'[25] however pleasing it may be to human vanity, is contrary to the whole tenor of Scripture.

[e] [p. 8.]
[f] [p. 8.]
[g] [p. 10.]
[h] [p. 11.]

---

[22] JW omits a long section where Hebden asserts that 'Indwelling sin is the chief burden of a renewed soul' and stresses the need for those who have been regenerated to carry on a continual opposition to 'the old man', to continually loathe the corruption they feel in themselves, and to long for that final release from this life into God's presence—where they can finally live 'without ever once sinning against him more'. Ibid., 7-8.

[23] JW omits Hebden's continuation: 'and "works done before the grace of Christ, and the inspiration of his Spirit, are not pleasant to God, but have the nature of sin," as every subscriber of the Articles of the Church of England solemnly asserts'. Ibid., 11. When Wesley abridged the Articles of Religion to send to the Methodists in North America in 1784, he deleted Article XIII, which Hebden was quoting.

[24] This is JW's distillation of Hebden's extended argument (*Baptismal Regeneration*, 9-12) against people (like Taylor) who restrict regeneration to just forgiveness and scoff at 'infused habits' as a scholastic invention. Hebden traces the language of infused habits to pre-Augustinian fathers and highlights it in Anglican standards.

[25] Hebden was quoting Taylor.

And[i] all the scriptural expressions on this head are grounded on the real nature of things. *Sin* is of the nature of *filth* and *corruption*. It pollutes the whole man, and renders him as an *unclean* thing in the sight of God. When[j] therefore the Spirit of God removes this[26] he is said to 'create a clean heart', to 'purify the heart', to 'sprinkle clean water upon' us, to 'wash' us 'from' our 'filthiness'. And this cleansing efficacy is in the text expressed by being 'born of water and of the spirit'.[27]

When[k] therefore our Lord speaks of being 'born of the spirit', his plain meaning is, There is a spiritual cleansing you must partake of, mentioned in those promises, 'I will sprinkle clean water upon you, and ye shall be clean. From all your filthiness and from all your idols will I cleanse you.' 'A new heart also will I give you, and a new spirit will I put within you. And I will take away the stony heart, and I will give you an heart of flesh.' These promises give us a plain description of the Spirit's regenerating work; without experiencing which our state is miserable now, and will be much more so hereafter.[28]

2. For[l] this spiritual renovation of the soul is indispensably necessary. Without it none can 'enter the kingdom of heaven', either the kingdom of grace or of glory.[29]

[i] [p. 12.]
[j] [p. 13.]
[k] [p. 14.]
[l] [p. 20.]

---

[26] JW substitutes 'removes this' for Hebden's 'forms the soul to an holy temper and disposition'. Cf. *Baptismal Regeneration*, 13.

[27] Hebden launches at this point into a long section (ibid., 13-19) disputing the necessity of water baptism or any notion of 'baptismal regeneration'. He argues at length that this text focuses on 'the water of the Spirit', or the Spirit's inward regenerating work, not on the water of baptism. It eventually becomes clear that, for Hebden, water baptism is best understood as 'an appointed sign of regeneration'. Ibid., 18; cf. 40.

[28] JW carefully extracts this single paragraph from Hebden's six-page digression on the relationship of regeneration to baptism. Thereby he prevents equating 'regeneration' or the 'new birth' with baptism. Cf. his insistence that they are not the same in Sermon 45, 'The New Birth', §IV.1-2, 2:196-98 in this edn.

[29] JW's revision of Hebden in this and the next two paragraphs is significant. Hebden had equated the 'kingdom of grace' and the 'kingdom of glory', taking both to signify God's gift of final salvation—as contrasted with the gift of present spiritual renovation. See *Baptismal Regeneration*, 20. In keeping with his broader practice, JW revises so that 'kingdom of grace' refers to the *present* experience of the Spirit's renewing power, while 'kingdom of glory' is restricted to final salvation. Cf. Sermon 26, 'Sermon on the Mount VI', §III.8-10, 1:581-84 in this edn.

1) 'Except[m] a man be born of the spirit he cannot enter into the kingdom of' *grace*: he cannot be a loyal subject of Jesus Christ. By nature we are subjects of Satan. And such we must remain unless renewing grace 'translate us into the kingdom of God's dear Son'.

2) Consequently,[n] 'except we are born' again 'we cannot enter into the kingdom' of *glory*. Indeed, supposing he could be admitted there, what could an unregenerate sinner do in heaven? He could not possibly have any relish either for the business, the company, or the enjoyments of that world.

3. Our[o] Lord having asserted the absolute necessity of the new birth, to show the ground of this necessity adds, 'That which is born of the flesh is flesh; and that which is born of the spirit is spirit.' Here observe,

1) Our Lord opposes *flesh* and *spirit* to each other, which opposition we often meet with. Whatever therefore is meant by these two, they denote things opposite.

2) He speaks here of two several *births*, which are distinctly mentioned.

3) The former of these two is spoken of as that which renders the other so necessary. Because 'that which is born of the flesh is flesh', therefore 'we must be born of the spirit'. Therefore this great change must be wrought in us, or we cannot 'enter into the kingdom of God'.

4) If the latter of these is made necessary by the former, then to be 'born flesh' is to be born corrupt and sinful. And[p] indeed the word 'flesh' is very frequently taken for the corrupt principle in man. It is always so taken when it stands opposed to 'the spirit', or to that inwrought principle of obedience which itself also (taking the name of its author) is sometimes termed 'spirit'.

Now in the text, whatever or whoever is born of a man since the fall is denominated 'flesh'. And that 'flesh' is here put, not for sinless *frailty*, but sinful corruption, we learn from its being opposed to the *spirit*. Christ[q] was born *frail*, as well as we, and in this sense

[m] [p. 21.]
[n] [p. 22.]
[o] [p. 23.]
[p] [p. 24.]
[q] [p. 25.]

was *flesh*. Yet being without sin, he had no need to be 'born of the spirit'. This is not made necessary by any sinless infirmities, but by a sinful nature only. This alone is opposite to 'the spirit'; thus therefore we must understand it here.

But Mr. Taylor says, 'To[r] be born of the flesh is only to be naturally born of a woman.'[30] I answer, Is not 'flesh' opposed to 'spirit' in this verse? Is it not the Spirit of God which is spoken of in the latter clause, together with the principle of grace, which is in every regenerate person? And is anything beside sinful corruption opposite to the Spirit of God? No certainly. But if so, and if wherever 'flesh' is opposed to 'the spirit' it implies sinful corruption, then it is evident to be 'born of the flesh' is to be the sinful[31] offspring of sinful parents, so as to have need of the renewing influences of the Holy Spirit on that account, even from our birth.

If[s] to 'walk after the flesh', as opposed to 'walking after the spirit', is to follow our sinful inclinations; if[t] to 'be in the flesh' opposed to 'being in the spirit', is to be in a state of sin; if 'the flesh' and 'the spirit' are two contrary principles which counteract each other[32] (Gal. 5:16–17); if 'the works of the flesh' and 'the lusts of the flesh' are opposed to 'the spirit' and 'the fruit of the Spirit'; then to be 'born of the flesh' must signify more than barely to be born of a woman. Had Adam transmitted a pure nature to his descendants, still each of them would have been born of a woman, but they would have had no necessity of being 'born of the Spirit', or renewed by the Holy Ghost.

But[u] what is that corruption of nature which the Scripture terms 'flesh'? There are two branches of it: (1) A want of original righteousness. (2) A natural propensity to sin.

[r] [p. 26.]
[s] [p. 27.]
[t] [p. 28.]
[u] [p. 29.]

---

[30] Cf. John Taylor, *The Scripture-Doctrine of Original Sin*, 3rd edn. (London: J. Waugh, 1750), 144.

[31] In both this and the next instance, JW's 'sinful' substitutes for Hebden's 'corrupt degenerate'. Cf. *Baptismal Regeneration*, 26.

[32] Note that JW deletes the remainder of Hebden's sentence: 'in every truly good person (he being while in this world renewed but imperfectly) and hinder even the *best* from doing what they would do'. Ibid., 28.

1) A want of original righteousness. God created man righteous. Holiness was con-natural to his soul, a principle of love and obedience to God. But when he sinned he lost this principle. And every man is now born totally void both of the knowledge and love of God.

2) A natural propensity to sin is in every man. And this is inseparable from the other. If man is born and grows up without the knowledge or love of God, he is born and grows up propense to sin, which includes two things: an aversion to what is good, and an inclination to what is evil.

We are naturally averse to what is good. 'The[v] carnal mind is enmity against God.' Nature does not, will not, cannot submit to his holy, just, and good law. Therefore 'they that are in the flesh cannot please God.' Being averse to the will, law, and ways of God, they are utterly indisposed for such an obedience as the relation between God and man indispensably requires.

And as we are all naturally averse to what is good, so we are naturally inclined to what is evil. Even young children of themselves run into evil, but[w] are with difficulty brought to practise what is good. No sooner do they discover reason than they discover evil, unreasonable dispositions. And these, discovering themselves in everyone, even from his early childhood, manifestly prove the inbred and universal corruption of human nature.

But[x] why is this corruption termed 'flesh'? Not because it is confined to the body. It is the corruption of our whole nature, and is therefore termed 'the old man'. Not because it consists merely in a repugnance of the sensual appetites to reason. This is but one branch of that corruption. The whole of it is far more extensive. Not because it is primarily seated in the body. It is primarily seated in the soul. If 'sin reigns in our mortal bodies', it is because the sinful soul uses the bodily members as 'instruments of unrighteousness'.[33]

'Nay,[y] all which those words, "That which is born of flesh is flesh," mean is this. All men, being descended of frail and mortal

[v] [p. 30.]
[w] [p. 31.]
[x] [p. 32.]
[y] [p. 37.]

[33] JW omits a long section (ibid., 32-37) surveying the debate on how depravity is inherited and arguing strongly for an 'imputation' model. Cf. the discussion of this topic in the introduction (pp. 149-50 above).

parents, are like them, *frail* and *mortal*. In consequence of Adam's sin, all[z] his descendants die.'[34]

I answer, 1) Though this is true, it is not the whole truth. Nor is it the proper truth of the text, which speaks of our being 'born of the flesh' as the reason why we must be 'born of the Spirit'.

2) It is not consistent with the moral perfections of God for sinless creatures to be born *mortal*. Death in every sense[a] of the word is 'the proper wages of sin'. *Sin* has the same causal influence on death as the obedience of Christ has on eternal life.

3) We were not only born *mortal*, but 'children of wrath'—we who are now regenerate, as well as others.

4) The Scripture ascribes both our *mortality* and *corruption* to our relation to Adam. 'In him all die.' 'Through the offence of one, many', all mankind, 'are dead,' liable to death. Again, 'By the disobedience of one', the same, 'many are constituted sinners.' Therefore when our Lord says, 'That which is born of the flesh is flesh,' he means not only that we and our parents are *mortal*, but that all mankind derive *spiritual* as well as temporal *death* from their first father.[35]

[IV.] *The Scripture Doctrine of Imputed Sin and Righteousness*[36]

'Sin'[b] is a 'transgression of the law', of that law of God to which a rational creature is subject. 'Righteousness' is a fulfilment of, or

[z] [p. 38.]
[a] [p. 39.]
[b] p. 1.

[34] Cf. Taylor, *Scripture-Doctrine*, 144-45.

[35] JW omits the final five pages (*Baptismal Regeneration*, 40-44), where Hebden offers practical reflections that include another strong denial of 'baptismal regeneration' (40) and an emphasis on 'how small is the number of truly regenerate Christians' (42). He also omits the appendix (ibid., 45-56), which offers further critiques of baptismal regeneration.

[36] Wesley now turns to Hebden, *The Scripture-Doctrine of Imputed Sin and Righteousness Stated and Defended; Chiefly for Confuting what Socinian Writers (and the Reverend Mr. J. Taylor, in his late books against Original Sin) have Suggested, as to 'God's Imputing no Sin or Righteousness but what is Personal'* (London: J. Oswald, 1743). JW reduces this work to about one-tenth its original size. Hebden had set forth three propositions: (1) Adam's first sin was imputed to his posterity, (2) these

conformity to that law. This is the proper scriptural sense of the words.[c] But as sin involves the creature in *guilt*, that is, a liableness to punishment, the same words are often used to denote either *sin* itself or *guilt* and *punishment*. On the other hand, *righteousness* denotes not only a fulfilling of the law but also a *freedom from guilt and punishment*. Yea, and sometimes all the 'rewards of righteousness'.

Accordingly,[d] to 'impute sin' is either to impute *sin itself*, or *guilt* on the account of it. To impute *sin itself* to a person is to account him a transgressor of the law, to pronounce him such, or to treat him as a transgressor. To *impute guilt* to a person is to account him obnoxious to a threatened punishment, to pronounce him so, or to inflict that punishment. So to *impute righteousness*, properly so called, is to *account* him a fulfiller of the law, to *pronounce* him so to be, and to *treat* him as righteous. And to *impute righteousness* as opposed to *guilt* is to *account*, to *pronounce*, and to *treat* him as guiltless.

Thus much is agreed. But the point in question is, 'Does God impute[e] no *sin* or *righteousness* but what is *personal*?' Mr. Taylor positively asserts he does not. I undertake to prove that he does—that he imputes Adam's first sin to all mankind, and our sins to Christ.[37]

1. God imputes Adam's *first sin* to all mankind. I do not mean that the[f] *actual commission* of it was imputed to any beside himself (it was impossible it should). Nor is the *guilt* of it imputed to any of his descendants, in the full latitude of it, or in regard to its attendant circumstances. It constitutes none of them *equally guilty* with him. Yet both that *sin* itself, and a degree of *guilt* on account of it, are

[c] p. 2.
[d] p. 5. [i.e., p. 3]
[e] p. 5.
[f] p. 6.

sins were imputed to Christ, and (3) the righteousness of Christ was imputed for justification to true believers. JW retained a part of the introduction, parts of the first and second propositions, and the closing portion of Hebden's summary and exhortation. The convoluted divisions and subdivisions of the work apparently proved confusing to Hebden himself. Wesley's numbering adds to the confusion by repeating numbers without making clear their relationship to each other. Here we drop the 'I.' which Wesley prefixed to the introduction, and alter his 'I.' and 'II.' for the propositions to '1.' and '2.' in order to regularize them in the structure of JW's work as a whole.

[37] Hebden announced a third point he would try to prove—that Christ's righteousness is imputed to many for their justification. *Imputed Sin*, 5. Wesley omits this announcement and the later section on this point. Ibid., 49-79.

imputed to all his posterity. The *sin* itself is imputed to them as included in their head. And on this account they are reputed *guilty*, are 'children of wrath', liable to the threatened punishment. And this cannot be denied, supposing i) man's original righteousness, ii) Adam's being the federal head of all mankind.

1) Man's[g] original righteousness has been largely proved.[38] Let me add only an[h] argument *ad hominem*.[39] Supposing (not granting) that the Son of God is no more than the first of creatures, either he was *originally righteous* or he was not. If he was not, then time was when he was not 'the Holy One of God'; and possibly he never might have been such; no, nor *righteous at all*; but instead of that as *ungodly, guilty*, and *wretched* as the devil himself is. For the best creature is (Mr. Taylor grants) alterable for the worse, and the best when corrupted becomes the worst. Again, if the Son of God was a mere creature, and as such made without[i] righteousness (which every creature must be, according to Mr. Taylor) then he was not—could not be—at first as righteous, as like God, as the holy angels are now, yea, or as any holy man on earth is. But if these suppositions are shockingly absurd, if the Son of God could not have become as bad as the devil, if he never was unrighteous, if he was not originally less holy than angels and men are now, then the assertion 'that righteousness must be the effect of a creature's antecedent choice and endeavour'[40] falls to the ground.

'But the Hebrew word *jashar*', Mr. Taylor says, 'does not generally signify a moral character.'[41] This is one of the numerous critical mistakes in this gentleman's books. Of the more than 150 texts in which *jashar*, or the substantive *josher*, occurs, there are very few which do not confirm our interpretation of Eccles. 7:29. 'But *jashar* is applied to various things not capable of moral action.' It is. And what then? Many of those applications are neither for us nor against

[g] p. 7.
[h] p. 9.
[i] p. 10.

[38] Here Hebden rehearses (and Wesley skips) his arguments on Eccl. 7:29 in his earlier sermon (i.e., section I above).

[39] Hebden is reminding readers of Taylor's supposedly Arian Christology.

[40] See Taylor, *Scripture-Doctrine*, 180; and John Taylor, *A Supplement to the Scripture-Doctrine of Original Sin, etc.; Containing some Remarks upon two Books . . .* (London: Mary Fenner, 1741), 162.

[41] Taylor, *Supplement*, 156.

us. Some make strongly for us, as when 'tis applied to the *words* or *ways* of God and man. But the question[j] now is, what it signifies when applied to God, or to *moral agents*, and that by way of opposition to a vicious character and conduct. Is it not in the text before us applied to man as a moral agent, and by way of opposition to a corrupt character and conduct? No man can deny it. Either therefore prove that *Jashar*, when opposed, as here, to a corrupt conduct and character, does not signify 'righteous', or acknowledge the truth, that God 'created man upright' or 'righteous'.

To evade the argument from Eph. 4:24 Mr. Taylor first says, ' "The old man" means an "heathenish life",' and then says, '*The old* and *new man* do not signify a course of life.'[42] What then do they signify? Why, '*The*[[k]] *old man*', says he, 'relates to the Gentile state; and *the new man* is either the Christian state or the Christian Church, body, society.' But for all this, he says again a page or two after, '*The old* and *new man*, and the *new man's* being renewed, and the *renewing* of the Ephesians, do all manifestly refer to their *Gentile state* and "wicked course of life", from which they were lately converted.'[43]

When then the Apostle says (Rom. 6:6), 'Our old man is crucified with Christ,' is it the *Gentile state* or *course of life* which was so crucified? No, but the *corrupt nature*, the 'body of sin', as it is termed in the same verse. And 'to put off the old man'[l] is (according to St. Paul) to 'crucify' this, 'with its affections and desires'. On the other hand 'to put on the new man' is to cultivate the divine principle which is formed in the soul of every believer by the Spirit of Christ. It is this of which it is said: i) It is *created*; and in regard to it we are said to be [m]'created unto good works'. ii) It is *renewed*; for it is indeed no other than original righteousness restored. iii) It is *after* God, after his image and likeness, now stamped afresh on the soul. iv) It consists in *righteousness* and *holiness*, or that *knowledge* which comprehends both.

Again. To that argument, 'Either man at first loved God, or he was an enemy to God,' Mr. Taylor gives only this slight, superficial

[j] p. 11.
[k] p. 12.
[l] p. 13.
[m] p. 14.

---

[42] Ibid., 150.
[43] Ibid., 152-53.

answer: 'Man could not love God before he knew him'[44]—without vouchsafing the least notice of the arguments which prove that man was not created without the knowledge of God. Let[n] him attend to those proofs, and either honestly yield to their force, or, if he is able, fairly confute them.

The Doctrine of *Original Sin* presupposes,

2) Adam's being the federal head of all mankind.[45] Several proofs of this having been given already, I need not produce more till those are answered.[46]

2. God imputes our *sins* or the *guilt* of them to Christ. He consented to be responsible for them, to suffer the punishment[o] due for them. This sufficiently appears from Isa. 53, which contains a summary of the Scripture doctrine upon this head. 'He hath borne our griefs and carried our sorrows.' The[p] word '*nasa*' ('borne') signifies: (1) to *take up* somewhat, as on one's shoulders; (2) to *bear* or *carry* something weighty, as a porter does a burden; (3) to *take away*. And in all these senses it is here applied to the Son of God. He 'carried'—as a strong man does an heavy burden (the clear, indisputable sense of the other word '*sabal*')[47]—'our sorrows', the sufferings of various kinds, which were due to our sins. 'He was[q] wounded for our transgressions, and bruised for our iniquities.' 'Wounds' and 'bruises' are put for the whole of his sufferings, as his 'death' and 'blood' frequently are. He was 'wounded' and 'bruised', not for sins of his own, not *merely* to show God's hatred of sin, not *chiefly* to give us a pattern of patience; but *for our sins*, as the proper, impulsive cause. *Our sins* were the procuring cause of all his sufferings. His sufferings were the penal effects of our sins. 'The chastisement[r] of our peace', the punishment necessary to procure it, 'was' laid 'on him', freely submitting thereto; 'and by his stripes' (a part of his sufferings again put for the whole) 'we are healed'. Pardon, sanctification, and final

[n] p. 15.
[o] p. 16.
[p] p. 17.
[q] p. 18.
[r] p. 19.

---

[44] Ibid., 186.

[45] Hebden, *Imputed Sin*, 15: 'Adam's being ordained by God the federal Head, or legal representative of all his natural discendants.'

[46] Hebden refers to his sermon on Gen. 2:15-17 (distilled in section II above).

[47] Parenthetical material is JW's addition. Cf. Hebden, *Imputed Sin*, 17.

salvation are all purchased and bestowed upon us.[48] Every *chastisement* is for some *fault*. That laid on Christ was not for his own but ours, and was needful to reconcile an offended[s] Lawgiver and offending guilty creatures to each other. So 'the Lord laid on him the iniquity of us all', that is, the punishment due to our iniquity.

'Tis[t] true, as Mr. Taylor says, '*Sin* and *iniquity* often signify *affliction* or *suffering*.'[49] But why? Because 'tis usual for a *cause* to give denomination to its *effect*. And so the consequences of *sin* are called by the[u] same name. But this rather hurts Mr. Taylor's cause than helps it. For *sufferings* could with no propriety be called *sin* if they were not the proper effects of it. Man in innocence was liable to no *suffering* or *sorrow*—he was indeed tried, but not by *suffering*. All sorrow was introduced by sin, and if man is 'born to trouble' it is because he is born 'in sin'. God indeed does 'afflict' his children for 'their good', and turns even *death* into a blessing. Yet as it is the effect of *sin*, so is it in itself an *enemy* to all mankind. Nor would any man have been either tried or corrected by *affliction* had it not been for *sin*.

The[v] *Lord's laying on Christ the iniquity of us* all was eminently typified by the high priest 'putting all the iniquities' of Israel on the scapegoat, who then *carried* them *away*. 'But[w] the goat', says Mr. Taylor, 'was to suffer nothing.'[50] This is a gross mistake. It was a *sin-offering* ([Lev. 16,] ver. 5), and as such was to 'bear upon him all the iniquities' of the people into the wilderness, and there (as the Jewish doctors unanimously hold) to suffer a violent death, by way of *punishment*, instead of the people, for their sins 'put upon him'. Yet Mr. Taylor says, 'Here was no *imputation of sin*.'[51] No! What is the difference between 'imputing sins' and 'putting them upon' him? This is just of a piece with a *sin-offering* that suffered nothing—

[s] p. 20.
[t] p. 21.
[u] p. 22.
[v] p. 23.
[w] p. 24.

[48] Hebden said only '. . . were purchased for us'. Ibid., 19. JW adds the emphasis on them being bestowed upon us.

[49] Taylor, *Supplement*, 8-9.

[50] Ibid., 7.

[51] Ibid.

a creature turned loose into a land the properest[x] for its subsistence, while bearing upon him all the iniquities of God's people![52]

Thus[y] Christ 'redeemed us from the curse of the law, being made a curse for us'.[z] Mr. Taylor, when he wrote his late books, was not apprised of the usual Scripture meaning of this awful word 'curse'. 'Tis often put to signify *the legal punishment of sin*. What the law of God threatens against transgressors, or the threatening itself, is frequently called by this name. What signifies then his trifling observation that 'God inflicted *no curse* on our first parents (Gen. 3:16-18)'?[53] That is, he did not say in so many words, '*Cursed art thou*, O man, or, O woman.' But God's 'cursing the ground for man's sake' was really *a curse* pronounced against *him*; and what the Lord said to the woman was really *a curse*, a penalty, legally inflicted on *her*. For God is then said to 'curse' when he either *threatens* to punish or actually *punishes* his creatures for sin (see Deut. 27:15, etc.; Chap. 28:16, etc.; Jer. 17:5; Zech. 5:3).[54]

To conclude. Either[a] we must allow *the imputation of* Adam's *sin*, whatever difficulties attend it, or renounce *justification by Christ* and *salvation through* the merit of his blood. Accordingly the Socinians do this. Whether Mr. Taylor does, let every thinking man judge, after having weighed what he writes, particularly at pp. 72-73 of his *Scripture-Doctrine*: 'The *worthiness* of Christ is his consummate *virtue*. It is *virtue* that carrieth every cause in heaven. *Virtue* is the only price which purchaseth everything with God. [. . .] True *virtue*, or the right exercise of reason,[b] is true *worth*, and the only *valuable*

[x] p. 25.
[y] p. 39.
[z] p. 40.
[a] p. 80.
[b] p. 81.

[52] JW omits Hebden's extended reflections (*Imputed Sin*, 25-34) on Isa. 53:7-12, which elaborate on Christ's suffering in graphic terms and argue it must be ascribed to 'the hands of the divine vindictive justice' (Ibid., 26).

[53] Taylor, *Scripture-Doctrine*, 19; cf. *Supplement*, 45-50.

[54] Wesley omits Hebden's reflections on some questions often raised about Christ's sufferings, including Hebden's rejection of the notion of Christ 'descending into hell'. *Imputed Sin*, 42-48. He also omits the entirety of Hebden's defense of his Proposition III: 'The righteousness of Christ, as a surety, is imputed for justification to all true believers'. Ibid., 49-79. This latter omission includes Hebden's lament about how Calvinism has been challenged in recent decades by Arminianism, Pelagianism, and Socinianism. Ibid., 77.

consideration, the only *power* which prevails with God.' These passages are indeed connected with others which carry with them a show of ascribing honour to Christ and *grace*. But the fallacy lies open to every careful, intelligent, unprejudiced reader. He ascribes to Christ a singular *worthiness*; but 'tis nothing more than a superior degree of the same kind of worthiness which belongs to every *virtuous* man. He talks of Christ's consummate *virtue*, or his obedience to God, and goodwill to man. And to this *virtue* of his, *as imitated by us*, he would teach us to ascribe our acceptance with God; which is indeed to ascribe it to ourselves, or to our own *virtue*, to *works of righteousness done by us*, in direct opposition to the whole tenor of the gospel. To what dangerous lengths are men carried by an *ignorance* of God as infinitely holy and just, by a fond conceit of their own abilities, and a resolved opposition to the doctrine of original sin! Rather than allow this they renounce Christ as the *meritorious procurer* of salvation for sinners. They may *seem* indeed to acknowledge him as such, and talk of 'eternal life as given by God through his Son'. But all this is mere show, and can only impose on the ignorant and unwary. They dare not profess in plain terms that Christ has *merited salvation for any*; neither can they consistently allow this, while they deny original sin.

Let not any then who regard[c] their everlasting interests entertain or even tamper with doctrines which, how plausibly soever recommended, are contrary to many express texts, nay, to the whole tenor of Scripture, and which cannot be embraced without renouncing an humble dependence on Christ, and rejecting the gospel method of salvation.

God[d] grant every reader of this plain treatise may not only be convinced of the truth and importance of the Scripture doctrines maintained therein, but invincibly confirmed in his attachments to them by an experimental knowledge of their happy influence on faith, holiness, and comfort! Then shall we gladly say, We who are made sinners by the disobedience of Adam, are made righteous by the obedience of Christ. His righteousness entitles us to a far better inheritance than that we lost in Adam. In consequence of being justified through him, we shall 'reign in life' with him. Unto whom, with God the Father, and the sanctifying, comforting Spirit, be ascribed all praise forever!

[c] p. 82.
[d] p. 83.

PART VI[1]

THE DOCTRINE OF ORIGINAL SIN EXPLAINED AND VINDICATED

The phrase 'original sin', so far as we can discover, was first used in the fourth century. The first who used it was either St. Chrysostom or Hilary, some of whose words are these: 'The Psalmist says, "Behold, I was conceived in iniquities, in sins did my mother conceive me."[a] He acknowledges that he was born under *original sin*, and the law of sin'. Soon after Hilary's time,[b] St. Augustine and other Christian writers brought it into common use.[2]

The scriptural doctrine of original sin may be comprised in the following propositions:[c]

[a] p. 2. [Wesley's page notation in this selection is more haphazard than normal. He fails to note several pages, and the placement of the note occurs as often in the middle of the page being abstracted as at the beginning. The missing notes have been added (in square brackets) in this edn., placed to mark the beginning of new pages in Hebden.]

[b] p. 3.

[c] p. 8.

---

[1] This separate designation is given to the final Hebden extract only in Wesley's *Works* (1773), 21:385. It is the longest of the extracts from Hebden, abridging *The Doctrine of Original Sin, as laid down in the Assembly's Catechism, explained* (London: R. Hett & J. Oswald, 1741).

[2] JW omits Hebden's description of Augustine:

'whom a very particular experience of the workings of corrupt nature, and the free effectual grace of God, thoroughly qualified to oppose those errors of Pelagius, and his adherents, which the Christian Church has generally voted to be wicked and dangerous, on account of their over-rating the powers of fallen nature, and derogating not a little from the freeness and efficacy of divine grace' (*Doctrine*, 3).

Indeed, JW omits *every* negative reference to Pelagius in this piece by Hebden (to be noted as they occur). He also omits all references critical of Daniel Whitby (the first on p. 4), whose Arminian *Treatise concerning Original Sin* (London: John Noon, 1739) had been commended to JW by his father and would be published by JW as a serialized extract in *Arminian Magazine* vols. 8–12 (1785–89).

I. Man was originally made righteous or holy.

II. That original righteousness was lost by the first sin.

III. Thereby man incurred death of every kind; for,

IV. Adam's first sin was the sin of a *public person*, one whom God had appointed to represent all his descendants.

V. Hence all these are from their birth 'children of wrath', void of all righteousness, and propense to sin of all sorts.

I add, VI,[d] this is not only a truth agreeable to Scripture and reason, but a truth of the utmost importance, and one to which the Churches of Christ from the beginning have bore a clear testimony.

I. Man was originally made righteous or holy, formed with such a principle of love and obedience to his Maker as disposed and enabled him to perform the whole of his duty with ease and pleasure. This has been proved already. And this wholly overturns Mr. Taylor's fundamental aphorism, 'Whatever is natural is necessary, and what is necessary is not sinful.'[3] For if man was originally righteous or holy, we may argue thus. It was at first *natural* to man to love and obey his Maker. Yet it was not *necessary*—neither as *necessary* is opposed to *voluntary* or *free* (for he both loved and obeyed *freely* and *willingly*), nor as *necessary* means *unavoidable* (this is manifest by the event), no, nor as *necessary* is opposed to *rewardable*. For had he continued to love and obey he would have been rewarded with everlasting happiness. Therefore that assertion, 'Whatever is *natural* is *necessary*,' is palpably, glaringly false. Consequently, what is natural,[e] as well as what is acquired, may be good or evil, rewardable or punishable.[4]

II. Man's original righteousness was lost by the first sin. Though he was made righteous, he was not made immutable. He was free to

[d][p. 9.]
[e]p. 10.

---

[3]John Taylor, *The Scripture-Doctrine of Original Sin*, 3rd edn. (London: J. Waugh, 1750), 125. Wesley omits 'This maxim, so much depended on by the Pelagians, Socinians, and all deniers of the doctrine of original sin, is really no better than a piece of thin sophistry, and what men of learning, studious in the Scripture, should be ashamed to insist on'. Hebden, *Doctrine*, 10.

[4] The last two sentences are Wesley's summation, not an extract. Note as well that JW skips at this point a selection of quotations by Hebden (*Doctrine*, 11-13) of early Christian writers in defense of the idea of original righteousness. JW will come back to retrieve some of these quotations for section VI of this extract.

stand or fall. And he soon fell and lost[f] at once both the favour and image of God.

This fully appears 1, from the account which Moses gives of our first parents, Gen. 3, where we read, (1) 'The eyes of them both were opened, and they knew that they were naked'. That is, they were conscious of guilt, and touched with a pungent sense of their folly and wickedness. They began to find their nakedness irksome to them, and to reflect on it with sinful emotions of soul. (2) Immediately they were indisposed for communion with God, and struck with such a dread of him as could not consist with true love (ver. 8). (3) When questioned by God, how do they prevaricate, instead of confessing their sin and humbly imploring forgiveness! Which proves not only their having sinned, but their being as yet wholly impenitent. (4) The judgment passed upon them was a proof of their being[g] guilty in the sight of God. Thus was man's original righteousness lost. Thus did he fall both from the favour and image of God.

This appears 2, from the guilt which inseparably attends every transgression of the divine law. I say every transgression, because every sin virtually contains all sin. For 'whosoever keepeth the whole law, and offendeth in one point, he is guilty of all.' Every single offence is a virtual breach of all the commands of God. There is in every particular sin the principle of *all* sin—namely, the contempt of that sovereign authority which is equally stamped upon every command. When, therefore, our first parents ate the forbidden fruit,[h] they not only violated a particular precept but the entire law of God. They could not sin in one instance without virtually transgressing the whole law of their creation; which being once done, their title to God's favour and their original righteousness were both lost.

This appears 3, from the comprehensive nature and aggravating circumstances of the first transgression. For it implied (1) *Unbelief.* Man did not dare to break the divine command till he was brought to question[i] the truth of the divine threatening. (2) *Irreverence of God.* Reverence is a mixture of love and fear. And had they continued in their first love and filial fear, they could not so soon have

[f] p. 14.
[g] p. 15.
[h] p. 16.
[i] p. 17.

broken through the sole command of God. (3) *Ingratitude*. For what a return did they hereby make to their Creator for all his benefits! (4) *Pride* and *ambition*. Affecting to be 'as gods, knowing good and evil'. (5) *Sensuality*. The woman looked upon the fruit with an irregular appetite. Here the conflict between *reason* and *sense* began. To talk of such a conflict in man before he fell[5] is to represent him as in a degree sinful and guilty even while innocent. For *conflict* implies *opposition*. And an opposition of *appetite* to *reason* is nothing else than a repugnance to the law of God. But of this our first parents were no way guilty till their innocence was impaired, till they were led by the temptation of the devil to desire the forbidden fruit. (6) *Robbery*—for the fruit[j] was none of theirs. They had no manner of right to it. Therefore their taking it was a flat robbery of God, which cannot be less criminal than robbing our fellow-creatures. So comprehensive was the nature, so aggravated the circumstances, of man's first transgression.[6]

III. Hereby he incurred death of every kind; not only temporal, but also *spiritual* and *eternal*. By losing his original righteousness he became not only mortal as to his body, but also spiritually dead, 'dead to God', 'dead in sin'—void of that principle which St. Paul

[j] p. 18.

---

[5] JW omits 'as do the Pelagians and Socinians'. Hebden, *Doctrine*, 17.

[6] Wesley omits a section (ibid., 18-20) where Hebden tries to answer the objection that Adam could not have sinned so easily if he was created with a habit or principle of original righteousness. Hebden responds that we must simply take Scripture at its word, but then adds an edifying reflection that may have led to JW's omission:

'If the gracious principle planted and preserved in every sincere convert is not extinguished by continued sinful defects, and incidental acts of aggravated sinning (as in the case of David, Peter, and other backsliding saints); and if this "seed of God", this "divine nature", this "new creature", this "new man", as it is called, may and does, during the present state, consist with sinful corruption felt, lamented, abhorred, strove and prayed against; this is owing to the special grace of the New Covenant, which promises renewing grace, persevering strength, and a being preserved safe into God's heavenly Kingdom, to all the heirs of salvation. With what love and thankfulness to the God of all grace does the sincere, humble, judicious Christian remember these precious, suitable, necessary promises of God's everlasting covenant when he seriously reflects on his own experienced proneness to backslide, with the inconstancy of the best creatures, left to themselves, and the speedy apostacy of his first father, though created (as Scripture assures him he was) with original righteousness, or true holiness?' (Ibid., 19).

terms 'the[k] life of God' (Eph. 4:18), St. John, 'eternal life abiding in us' (1 John 3:15). A creature formed with a capacity of knowing, loving, and serving God must be either 'dead in sin' or 'alive to God'. Adam in his primitive state was 'alive to God', but after he had sinned, 'dead in sin', as well as 'dead in law'.

But Mr. Taylor is sure only temporal death was to be the consequence of his disobedience.[7] 'For death is the loss of life, and must be understood according to the nature of the life[l] to which it is opposed.'[8] Most true. And the life to which it is here opposed, the life Adam enjoyed till lost by sin, was not only *bodily life*, but that principle of holiness which the Scripture terms 'the life of God'. It was also a title to eternal life. All this therefore he lost by sin. And that justly. For 'death is the' *due* 'wages of sin', death both temporal, spiritual, and eternal.[9]

IV.[[m]] Adam's first sin was the sin of a public person, one whom God had appointed to represent all his descendants.[10]

This also has been proved. In one sense, indeed, [n]Adam's sin *was not ours*. It was not our personal fault, our actual transgression. But in another sense it *was ours*. It was the sin of our common representative.[11] And as such St. Paul shows it is imputed to us and all his descendants. Hence,

V. All these are from their birth 'children of wrath', void of all righteousness, and propense to sin of all sorts.[12]

In order to clear and confirm this proposition I intend,

[k] p. 20.
[l] p. 21.
[[m]] [p. 23.]
[n] p. 25.

---

[7] JW omits comparison of Taylor to ancient Pelagians. Ibid., 21.

[8] Taylor, *Scripture-Doctrine*, 7.

[9] JW omits a section (Hebden, *Doctrine*, 21-23) containing another critique of Pelagians.

[10] Hebden described Adam as 'by God's appointment the federal Head of all his natural descendants'. Ibid., 23.

[11] Hebden reads: 'our federal head'. Ibid., 25.

[12] Hebden reads: 'We no sooner become Adam's children, then we are fallen degenerate creatures. From him, our sinning Father and Head, we derive a degree of guilt, and a corrupt nature, which renders us not only liable, but inclinable, to acts of sinning, and a continuance in sin, to our utter and final undoing.' Ibid.

1. To consider a text which proves original sin in the full extent of it.[o]

2. To explain some other texts which relate either to the *guilt* or the *corruption* we derive from our first parents.

3. To add some arguments which Mr. Taylor has taken no notice of, or touched but very slightly.

4. To answer objections.

And 1, to consider that text, Eph. 2:3, 'and were by nature children of wrath, even as others'. In the beginning of the chapter St. Paul puts the Ephesians in mind of what God had done for them. This led him to observe what they had been before their conversion to God. They had been 'dead in trespasses and sins', but were not 'quickened', made alive to God. They had 'walked according to the prince of the power of the air, the spirit that worketh with energy[13] in the children of disobedience'. 'Among' such, saith the Apostle, 'we all had our conversation in times past', the whole time before our conversion 'fulfilling[p] the desires of the flesh and of the mind, and were by nature children of wrath, even as others'. On this I observe

1) The persons spoken of are both the believing Ephesians and the Apostle himself. For he says not, 'ye were', speaking in the second person (as he had done verse[s] 1, 2), but 'we were', plainly with a design the more expressly to include himself. Indeed, had he still spoken in the second person, yet what is here affirmed would have been true of *him* as well as *them*. But for the sake of more explicitly including himself he chose to say 'we were': you, Ephesians, who were descended of heathen parents, and *I*, who was born in the visible church.

2) The 'wrath' here spoken of means, either God's displeasure at sinners or the punishment which he threatens and inflicts[q] for sin.

3) 'Children of wrath' is an Hebraism, and denotes persons worthy of or liable to wrath. And this implies the being sinners, seeing sin only exposes us to God's displeasure and the dreadful effects of it.

[o] p. 26.
[p] p. 27.
[q] p. 28.

---

[13] The AV translates νῦν ἐνεργοῦντος in Eph. 2:2 as 'that now worketh'. Hebden added with emphasis 'that now, *and always*, worketh'. Ibid., 27. JW, transliterating the Greek, changes this to 'that worketh with energy' (but he retained the wording of the AV in *NT Notes*).

4) This charge the Apostle fixes on himself and them, as they had been before their conversion. He does not say 'we are', but 'we were children of wrath'.[r]

5) He speaks of himself and the converted Ephesians as having been so 'equally with others'. There is an emphasis on the words 'even as others', even as the stubborn Jews and the idolatrous heathens,[14] even as all who are still 'strangers and enemies' to Christ. These are still 'children of wrath'. But whatever difference there is between us and them, *we were* once what *they are* now.

6) He expressly says, 'we were children of wrath even as others, by nature', or, from our birth. He does not say, we became so, by *education* or by *imitation*, or by *custom* in sinning. But to show us when it is that we commence sinners, by what means we become 'children of wrath', whence it is that we are *so prone to evil*[[s]] *from our infancy*, and to imitate bad, rather than good examples, he says, 'we were children of wrath *by nature*'—we were born fallen creatures. We came into the world sinners, and as such *liable to wrath*, in consequence of the fall of our first father.

But it is affirmed i) that '*by nature* means by *habit* or *custom*'.[15] I answer, Though the term 'nature', with some qualifying expression annexed, is sometimes taken for inveterate custom, yet 'tis never so taken when put singly, without any such qualifying expression. When therefore the Apostle says absolutely, 'we were[t] children of wrath by nature', this, according to the constant sense of the words, must mean we were so from our birth.

It is affirmed ii) that 'because the original words stand thus, τέκνα φύσει ὀργῆς, "children by nature of wrath", therefore "children by nature" means only *truly* and *really* children of wrath.' I answer, The consequence is good for nothing. For let the words stand how they will, it is evident that τέκνα φύσει are 'children by birth', or such as are born so, in distinction from those who become such afterward.

[r] p. 29.
[[s]] [p. 30.]
[t] p. 31.

[14] Hebden read: 'blind hard-hearted Jews and blind idolatrous heathens'. *Doctrine*, 29.

[15] JW omits Hebden's reference to Daniel Whitby, Jeremy Taylor, and Henry Hammond—all favorites of JW—as ones who make this claim. Cf. ibid., 30.

It is affirmed iii) 'that φύσει, 'by nature', signifies no more than *truly* or *really*.'[16] I answer: (1) 'Tis not allowed that any good Greek writers ever use the word in this sense.[u] (2) Whatever others do, the writers of the New Testament always use it in another sense. So Gal. 2:15, 'We who are Jews by nature', φύσει Ἰουδαῖοι—that is, 'we who are born Jews', in contradistinction to proselytes. Gal. 4:8, 'Ye did service to them which by nature are no gods', μὴ φύσει οὖσιν θεοῖς—persons or things which are partakers of no *divine nature*. Rom. 2:14, 'The Gentiles do by nature the things contained in the law'—that is, by their own natural powers, without a written law. Neither here nor anywhere else does the word φύσει signify no more than *really* or *truly*.

It remains then that the word which we render 'by nature' does really so signify. And[[v]] yet it is allowed, we are not so guilty *by nature* as a course of actual sin afterward makes us. But we are antecedent to that course 'children of wrath', liable to some degree of wrath and punishment. Here then from a plain text, taken[w] in its obvious sense, we have a clear evidence both of what divines term 'original sin imputed', and of 'original sin inherent'. The former is the sin of Adam so far reckoned *ours* as to constitute us in some degree guilty. The latter a want of original righteousness, and a corruption of nature. Whence it is that from our infancy we are averse to what is good and propense to what is evil.

I am 2, to explain some other texts which relate either to the *guilt* or the *corruption* which we derive from our first parents.

Gen. 5:3. Here 'the image of Adam', in which 'he begat a son' after his fall, stands opposed to 'the image of God', in which man was at first created. Moses had said (ver. 1): 'In the day that God created man, in the likeness of God made he him.' In this, speaking of Adam as he was after the fall, he does not say he begat a son 'in the likeness of God', but he 'begat a son in his own likeness, after his image'. Now this must refer to Adam either as *a man*; or as *a good man*, or as *a mortal, sinful man*. But[x] it could not refer to him merely

[u] p. 32.
[[v]] [p. 33.]
[w] p. 33 [i.e., p. 34].
[x] p. 35.

---

[16] JW omits Hebden's ascription of this gloss to Pelagius and Grotius. Cf. ibid., 31.

as a man. The inspired writer could not design to inform us that Adam begat a man, not a lion or an horse. It could not well refer to him *as a good man*. For it is not said, Adam begat a son who at length became pious like himself, but he 'begat a son in his own likeness'. It refers to him therefore as a *mortal, sinful* man, giving us to know that the mortality and corruption contracted by the fall descended from Adam to his son. Adam, a sinner, begat a sinner like himself. And if Seth was thus a sinner *by nature*, so is every other descendant of Adam.[y]

Mr. Taylor takes no notice of the antithesis between 'the likeness of God' (ver. 1), and 'the likeness of Adam' (ver. 3). On the other hand, he[17] speaks of these two as one, as if Seth had been *born* in the very same image of God wherein Adam was *made*. But this cannot be admitted, because Adam had now lost his original righteousness. It must therefore be 'the likeness' of *fallen, corrupted Adam* which is here intended.

Gen. 6:5. 'And God saw that the wickedness of man was great in the earth, and that every imagination of the thoughts of his heart was only evil continually.' Here Moses, having observed, as the cause of the flood that God 'saw that the wickedness of man was great', to account for this general wickedness adds 'every imagination of the thoughts of his heart was evil', yea, was *only evil*, and that *continually*. The heart of man is here put[z] for his soul. This God had formed with a marvellous thinking power. But so is his soul debased that 'every imagination', figment, formation 'of the thoughts' of it, 'is evil', only evil, 'continually' evil. Whatever it forms within itself, as a thinking power, is an *evil formation*. This Moses spoke of the antediluvians. But we cannot confine it to them. If all their actual wickedness sprung from the evil formations of their corrupt heart, and if consequently they were sinners from the birth, so are all others likewise.

Gen. 8:21.[a] 'I will not again curse the ground any more for man's sake, for the imagination of man's heart is evil from his youth. Neither will I again smite any more every living thing.' I will not be provoked to this by the wickedness of mankind, for they are inclined to

[y] p. 36.
[z] p. 37.
[a] [p. 38.]

[17] JW omits 'and other Pelagians'. Cf. ibid., 36.

sin from their childhood. Was I therefore to do this as often as they deserve, I must be continually destroying the earth. The word יצר, 'imagination' (as was observed before), includes the thoughts, affections, inclinations, with everything which the soul, as a thinking being, forges and frames within itself. And the word we render 'youth' includes childhood and infancy, the earliest age of man, the whole time from his birth—or (as others affirm) from his formation in the womb.

Indeed Mr. Taylor would translate the text, 'Although the imagination[b] of man's heart should be evil from his youth'. But, (1) though the particle כי sometimes signifies 'although', yet 'for' is its common meaning. And we are not to recede from the usual signification of a word without any necessity. (2) If we read 'although', it will not at all invalidate our proof. For still the plain meaning of the words would be, I will not send another general flood, although every figment or formation of the heart of every man is evil from his earliest infancy.

Job 5:6-7. 'Although affliction cometh not forth of the dust, yet man is born to trouble, as the sparks fly upwards.'[c] The word which is here rendered 'affliction' sometimes signifies 'iniquity'. For what reason[[d]] but to show that these two, 'sin' and 'affliction' are inseparable? Sin is the cause of affliction, and affliction, of whatever kind, is the genuine effect of sin. Indeed it is incompatible with the justice and mercy of God to appoint afflictions of any kind for the innocent. If Christ suffered, it was because the sins of others were imputed to him. If then everyone of the posterity of Adam 'is born to trouble', it must be because he is born a sinner. Man was not originally made to suffer. Nor while he preserved his innocence was he liable to suffering of any kind. Are the angels, or any pure, sinless creatures, liable to any sorrow or affliction? Surely no. But every child of Adam is. And it is in consequence of his sin that the present life of man is short and afflictive—of which[[e]] the very heathens were deeply sensible. They also saw that 'great travail is created for every man, and an heavy yoke is upon the sons of Adam, from the day that they go out of their mother's womb till the day that they return to the mother of all things' [Ecclus. 40:1].

[b] p. 39.
[c] p. 40.
[[d]] [p. 41.]
[[e]] [p. 42.]

Job 11:12. 'Vain man would be wise, though man be born like a wild ass's colt'—in the original, 'though man be born' (will be born in every age) 'the colt of a wild ass'. Mr. Taylor owns, 'We are born quite ignorant.'[f] But this is far from reaching the plain import of the text, in which man as born into the world is compared to an animal most remarkably stupid and intractable. And such all the sons of Adam naturally are, particularly with regard to the things of God—from their infancy slow to learn what is good, though impetuously propense to learn and practise what is evil.[g]

Job 14:4 and *15:14.* I join these because the latter confirms the former. 'Who can bring a clean thing', or person, 'out of an unclean? Not one.' This is express. Job had been reflecting on the sorrowful, uncertain, imperfect state of all Adam's children in the present world (ver. 1-3). Then he carries his thoughts to the spring of such a state, the original corruption of man. 'Who', what creature, can make an innocent, righteous person proceed from a parent defiled by sin? 'Not one.' Through the whole Scripture we may observe, *sin* is described[h] as *uncleanness*, and a sinner as an unclean thing. On the contrary, holiness is expressed by *cleanness* of heart and hands, and the righteous man is described as *clean*. Agreeably to which the text asserts the natural impossibility of any man's being born *clean*, guiltless and sinless, because he proceeds from them who are *unclean*, guilty and defiled with sin.

The Septuagint[i] translates the text: 'Who shall be clean from filth? Not one. Even though his life on earth be a single day.' And this rendering, though not according to the Hebrew, is followed by all the Fathers, and shows what was the general belief of the Jews before Christ came into the world.

'But since *the heavens* and *stars* are represented[j] as *not clean* compared to God, may not man also be here termed "unclean" only as compared with him?'[18] I answer: (1) The heavens are manifestly compared with God. But man is not, in either of these texts. He is here described, not as he is in comparison of God, but as he is absolutely in himself. (2) When 'the heavens' and 'man' are

[f] p. 43 [citing Taylor, *Scripture-Doctrine*, 232].
[g] p. 44.
[h] [p. 45.]
[i] [p. 46.]
[j] p. 45. [After jumping ahead briefly, Wesley returns to p. 45.]

[18] A summary of Taylor's argument in *Scripture-Doctrine*, 143.

mentioned in the same text, and man is set forth as *unclean*, his *uncleanness* is expressed by his being *unrighteous*: and that always means guilty or sinful. Nor indeed is the innocent frailty of mankind[k] ever in Scripture termed 'uncleanness'.

Psalm 51:5. 'Behold, I was shapen in iniquity,[l] and in sin did my mother conceive me.' The Psalmist here confesses, bewails, and condemns himself for his natural corruption, as that which principally gave birth to the horrid sins with which he had been overtaken. 'Behold!' He prefixes this to render his confession the more remarkable, and to show the importance of the truth here declared: 'I was shapen'. This passive verb denotes somewhat in which neither David nor his parents had any active concern. 'In' or 'with' 'iniquity', and 'in' or 'with' 'sin did my mother conceive me'. The word[m] which we render 'conceive' signifies properly to *warm* or to *cherish by warmth*. It does not therefore so directly refer to the act of *conceiving* as to the *cherishing* what is conceived, till the time of its birth. But either way the proof is equally strong for the corruption of mankind from their first existence.[19]

Psalm 58:3-4. 'The wicked are estranged from the womb.[n] They go astray as soon as they are born, speaking lies.' 'They are estranged from the womb.' Strangers and averse to true, practical religion from the birth. 'They go astray as soon as they are born, speaking lies.' Not that they actually speak lies as soon as they are born. But they naturally incline that way, and discover that inclination as early as is possible.[o]

Prov. 22:15.[p] 'Foolishness is bound in the heart of a child; but the rod of correction shall drive it far from him.' *Chap. 29:15*. 'The rod and reproof give wisdom; but a child left to himself bringeth his mother to shame.' These passages put together are a plain testimony of the inbred corruption of young children. 'Foolishness', in the former, is not barely 'appetite, or a want of the knowledge attainable by

[k] p. 46.
[l] p. 47.
[m] p. 48.
[n] p. 51.
[o] p. 52.
[p] [p. 53.]

[19] JW omits a section (Hebden, *Doctrine*, 48-50) criticizing Daniel Whitby's argument that the early Church writers prior to Augustine did not affirm original sin from this passage.

instruction'. Neither of these deserve that sharp correction. But it is an indisposedness to what is good, and a strong propensity to evil. This 'foolishness is bound in the heart of a child'; 'tis rooted in his inmost nature. It is, as it were, 'fastened to him by strong cords'—so the original word signifies. From this corruption of heart in every child it is that 'the rod[q] of correction' is necessary to 'give' him 'wisdom'. Hence it is that 'a child left to himself', without correction, 'brings his mother to shame'. If a child were born equally inclined to virtue and vice, why should the wise man speak of 'foolishness', or wickedness, as fastened so closely to his heart? And why should 'the rod and reproof' be so necessary for him? These texts therefore are another clear proof of the corruption of human nature.

Matt. 15:18-19; Mark 7:20–23. Those things[r] 'which proceed out of the mouth come from the heart, and they defile the man. For from within, out of the heart, proceed evil thoughts, adulteries, murders. . . . All these things come from within, and defile the man'. Our Lord[s] here teaches that all evil thoughts, words, and actions, of every kind, flow out of the heart, the soul of man, as being now averse to all good and inclined to all evil.[20]

Rom. 5:12-19. Let the reader please to read the[t] whole passage very carefully. The Apostle here discourses of Adam and Christ as two representatives or public persons, comparing the *sin* of the one with the *righteousness* of the other.

On this I observe: 1) The 'one man' spoken of throughout is Adam, the common head of mankind. And to him (not to the devil or Eve) the Apostle ascribes the introduction of *sin* and *death*. The

[q] [p. 54.]
[r] p. 55.
[s] p. 56.
[t] p. 66.

[20] JW omits a large section (ibid., 56-66) with the primary theme of the continuing presence of the 'old man' or 'sinful nature' in believers. He was surely uncomfortable with such claims by Hebden as these: 'even the best Christians complain to this purpose; they cannot love, fear, trust in, pray to, in any respect serve, their God as they would do. Let them desire ever so earnestly, pray ever so frequently and fervently, and labour ever so diligently, they cannot reach the sinless purity of heart and practice which their souls, as renewed, earnestly and constantly incline to' (61); 'the sinful corruption that sincere Christians feel, lament, and abhor in themselves, is so firmly radicated that they can never get rid of it, on this side [of] death' (62); and 'the most perfect Christians in this world are most feelingly sensible of, and deeply affected with, their great defects and imperfections' (64).

devil was the first sinner, and Eve, seduced by him, sinned before her husband.[21] Yet the Apostle saith, 'By *one man* sin entered into the world.' 'Through the offence of *one*, many are dead.' 'The judgment was by *one* to condemnation.' 'Death reigned by one.' 'By the offence of *one* judgment came upon all men.' 'By *one man's* disobedience many were made sinners.' Now why should the Apostle lay all this on Adam, whose sin was posterior both to the devil's and Eve's, if Adam was[u] not appointed by God the federal head of mankind? In regard to which the Apostle points at him singly as the 'type' or 'figure of him that was to come'.[22] According to Mr. Taylor's[23] doctrine he should rather have said, 'By *the devil* sin entered into the world', or, 'Through the disobedience *of Eve* many were made sinners.' But instead of this he fixes[v] on our first father alone as bringing sin and death on all his posterity.

2) The *sin, transgression, offence, disobedience* here spoken of was Adam's eating the forbidden fruit. 'Tis remarkable that as the Apostle throughout his discourse arraigns *one man* only, so he ascribes all the mischief done to *one single offence* of that one man. And as he then stood in that special relation of federal as well as natural head to his descendants, so upon his committing that one sin, this special relation ceased.

3) The 'all' (ver. 12, 18) and 'the many' (ver. 15, 19) are all the natural descendants of Adam, equivalent with 'the world' (ver. 12), which means the inhabitants of it.[w]

4) The effects of Adam's sin on his descendants the Apostle reduces to two heads, sin and death. 'By one man sin entered into the world, and death by sin;' and so 'death passed on all men, for that all have sinned'.[24] 'Sin' sometimes means *punishment*, but[x] not here.

[u] [p. 67.]
[v] p. 67 [i.e., p. 68].
[w] p. 69.
[x] [p. 70.]

---

[21] JW omits 'and proved a tempter to him. But though she was the first sinner of mankind, and the occasion of sin to our first father . . .'. Cf. ibid., 66.

[22] JW omits a section where Hebden notes that some interpreters treat both Adam and Eve as representatives of mankind and then argues to the contrary that the first man stood in a more special relation to all his natural descendants. Cf. ibid., 67.

[23] Hebden (ibid.) also referred to Daniel Whitby; JW omits.

[24] Wesley omits Hebden's recognition (ibid., 69) that this translation of the last clause of this verse (ἐφ' ᾧ πάντες ἥμαρτον) is contested, including a reference to a recent argument for the translation more typical among early Greek Christian theologians—namely, that 'death spread to all, *such that all have sinned*'. Cf. the introduction (pp. 148–49 above).

Sin and *death* are here plainly distinguished. The common translation is therefore right, and gives us the true meaning of the words. 'Death passed upon all men, for that all have sinned', namely, in or with their first father. And this agrees with the context, the purport of which is that all have sinned and are therefore liable to the death originally threatened, is evident from this, that 'until the law sin was in the world'. In the ages that preceded the law of Moses, all men were sinners in the sight of God. 'But sin is not imputed where there is no law.' None can be sinners in the sight of God if they are not transgressors of some[y] law, for the transgressing of which they are reputed guilty. 'Nevertheless death reigned' all the time 'from Adam to Moses', over all mankind. Now if none is liable to death but for sin, if 'sin is not imputed where there is no law', and if notwithstanding this all mankind in all ages have died—infants themselves, who cannot actually sin, not excepted—it is undeniable that guilt is imputed to all for the sin of Adam. Why else are they liable to that which is inflicted on none but for sin?

This is the purport of the Apostle's arguing (ver. 12-14), which having led him to mention Adam as a figure of Christ, he then draws a parallel between them. The substance of it is this: as through the 'offence of Adam many are dead', as 'by the disobedience' of him 'many are made sinners', so through the righteousness or 'obedience of Christ many[25] are made righteous'. But how are many dead, or made sinners, through the disobedience of Adam? His first sin[z] so far affects[26] all his descendants as to constitute them guilty, or liable to all that death which was contained in the original threatening.

But Mr. Taylor avers: 'To "be made sinners" means only to be subjected to temporal death'.[27]

I answer: 1) Whatever it means, the disobedience of Adam had a proper causal influence upon it, just as the obedience of Christ has upon our being made righteous.

2) What 'to be made sinners' means must be learnt from the opposite to it, in the latter part[a] of the verse. Now allowing the Apostle to be his own interpreter, 'being made righteous' is the same with

[y] [p. 71.]
[z] p. 72.
[a] p. 73.

[25] Hebden reads: 'all belonging to him'. Ibid., 71.
[26] Hebden reads: 'is imputed to'. Ibid., 72.
[27] Taylor, *Scripture-Doctrine*, 30.

justification (ver. 16). Of this he had treated largely before. And through the whole of his discourse 'to be justified' is to be acquitted from guilt and *accepted of God* as righteous.[28] Consequently 'to be made sinners' is to be *condemned of God*, or to be 'children of wrath', and that on account of Adam's sin.[29]

1 Cor. 15:21-22. 'By man came death. In Adam all die.'[b] Let the reader please to bear in mind the whole of the two verses and the context. By 'man' in the 21st verse is meant Adam. The 'all' spoken of are all his natural descendants. These 'all die'—that is, as his descendants, are liable to death, yea to death everlasting. That this is the meaning appears hence: that the 'being made alive', to which this dying stands opposed, is not a mere recovery of life but a blessed resurrection to a glorious immortality.[30] Hence I observe, (1) Man[c] was originally immortal as well as righteous. In his primitive state he was not liable to death. (2) Death is constantly ascribed to sin, as the sole and proper cause of it. As it was threatened only for sin,[d] so the sentence was not pronounced till after man had sinned. (3) All men are mortal from their birth. As soon as they begin to live they are liable to death, the punishment denounced against sin, and sin only. (4) This is the genuine effect of the first sin of our first father. The Apostle does not attribute it to the devil. Neither does he say 'in Adam and Eve all die'. But here also he mentions Adam singly. Him he speaks of as 'a figure of Christ' (ver. 45, 47-48). And here as the sole author of death, to all his natural descendants. 'In Adam', or on account of his fall, 'all' of mankind in every age 'die.' Consequently, *in him all sinned.* With him all fell, in his first transgression. That they are all born liable to the legal punishment of sin proves him the federal as[e] well as natural head of mankind, whose sin is so far imputed to all men that they are born 'children of wrath', and liable to death.

[b] p. 74.
[c] p. 75.
[d] p. 76.
[e] p. 77.

---

[28] JW omits Hebden's elaboration: 'or entitled to the eternal life promised, in consideration of Christ's obedience to the death, and through faith in his blood'. *Doctrine*, 73.

[29] JW omits Hebden's elaboration: 'accounted ours, or imputed to us, as the sin of our federal Head'. Ibid.

[30] JW omits another reference to Adam as the legal, federal head of mankind. Ibid., 74.

[3.] Thus have I considered a large number of texts which testify of *original sin, imputed and inherent*. Some are more express than others; of which kind are Job 14:4; Psalm 51:5, 56:3; Rom. 5:12, etc.; 1 Cor. 15:22; Eph. 2:3. That in Ephesians presents us with a direct proof of the entire doctrine. Those in Romans and Corinthians relate directly to *original sin imputed*, and are but consequential proofs of original corruption. The rest refer particularly to *this*, and are but consequential proofs of *original sin imputed*.

And as this doctrine stands impregnable on the basis of Scripture, so it is perfectly agreeable to[f] sound reason, as may appear from a few plain arguments which confirm this Scripture doctrine.

1) If the first man was by God's appointment, as has been shown, the federal head of all his descendants, it follows that when Adam sinned and fell, they all sinned in him and fell with him. And if they did, they must come into the world both guilty and unclean.

'But we had no hand in Adam's sin, and therefore cannot be guilty on account of it.'

This 'We had no hand in it' is ambiguous. It means either, 'We did not actually join therein'—which no one denies; or, 'We were wholly unconcerned in it'—the contrary to which has been fully proved.[31]

2) Since[[g]] Adam's posterity are born liable to death, which is the due 'wages of sin', it follows that they are *born sinners*. No art can set aside the consequence.[32]

3) Either[[h]] Christ is the Saviour of infants, or he is not. If he is not, how is he 'the Saviour of all men'? But if he is, then infants are sinners. For he suffered death for sinners only. He 'came to seek and save' only 'that which was lost'; to 'save his people from their sins'. It follows that infants are sinners; that they are lost, and without Christ are undone for ever.

4) The consequences of the contrary opinion are shockingly absurd:

[f] p. 79.
[[g]] [p. 81.]
[[h]] [p. 83.]

---

[31] JW omits the section (ibid., 80-81) where Hebden argues that the guilt of Adam's sin can be imputed to us because he was our federal head, but that Adam's repentance was not imputed to us because God has ordained our righteousness and life to come through another—Christ.

[32] JW omits Hebden's reference to the Pelagians. Ibid., 81.

i) If original sin is not, either death is not the wages of sin, or there is punishment without guilt. God[i] punishes innocent, guiltless creatures. To suppose which is to impute iniquity to the Most Holy.

ii) If we are not sinners by nature, there are sinful actions without a principle, fruit growing without a root. 'No. Men contract sinful habits *by degrees*, and *then* commence sinners.' But whence is it that they contract those habits so easily and speedily? Whence is it that as soon as ever we discover reason, we discover sinful dispositions? The early discoveries of reason prove a principle of reason planted in our nature. In like manner the early discoveries of sinful dispositions[j] prove those dispositions planted therein.

iii) If we were not ruined by the first Adam, neither are we recovered by the second.[33] If the sin of Adam was not imputed to us, neither is the righteousness of Christ.

iv) If we do not derive a *corrupt nature* from Adam, we do not derive a *new nature* from Christ.

v)[[k]] A denial of original sin not only renders baptism needless with regard to infants, but represents a great part of mankind as having no need of Christ or the grace of the new covenant. I now speak of infants in particular, who if not 'guilty before God', no more need the merits[34] and grace of the second Adam than the brutes themselves.

Lastly, [vi)] a denial of original sin contradicts the main design of the gospel, which is to humble vain man, and to ascribe to God's *free grace*, not man's *free will*, the whole of his salvation. Nor indeed can we let this doctrine go without giving up at the same time the

[i] p. 84.
[j] p. 85.
[[k]] [p. 86.]

---

[33] This summary sentence is from Hebden, but JW omits the preceding explication:

'If Adam was not the appointed federal Head of mankind, and if mankind did not fall in him, and if his sin is not imputed to all his descendants, it will follow that Christ is not the federal Head of all his, and that his righteousness is not imputed to them, so far as to acquit them from condemnation, and entitle them to eternal life. Every argument for justification by Christ implicitly confirms our fall in Adam'. (Cf. ibid., 85).

See the discussion of this omission in the introduction (pp. 150-51 above).

[34] Hebden read: 'righteousness'. *Doctrine*, 86.

greatest part, if not all, of the essential articles of the Christian faith. If we give up this, we cannot defend either justification by the merits of Christ, or the renewal of our natures by his Spirit. Mr. Taylor's book is not therefore subversive of a particular branch, but of the whole scheme of Christianity.

VI.[l] The doctrine therefore of original sin is not only a truth agreeable to Scripture and reason, but a truth of the utmost importance. And it is a truth to which the Churches of Christ from the beginning have borne a clear testimony.

Few truths, if any, are more necessary to be known, believed, and throughly considered. For if we are not acquainted with this, we do not know ourselves. And if we do not know ourselves, we can't rightly know Christ and the grace of God. And on this knowledge of Christ and the grace of God depends the whole of our salvation. St. Augustine therefore well remarks, 'Christianity lies properly in the knowledge of what concerns Adam and Christ.'[35] For certainly if we do not know Christ, we know nothing to any purpose. And we cannot know Christ without some knowledge of what relates to Adam, who was 'the figure of him that was to come'.

'But if this doctrine is so important, why is so little said of it in Scripture, and in the writings of the ancients?'[36]

This is a grand mistake. We totally deny that the Scripture says little of it. Mr. Taylor indeed affirms, 'There are but five passages of Scripture that plainly relate to the effects of Adam's fall.'[37] Not so. Many Scriptures, as has been shown, plainly and directly teach us this doctrine. And many others deliver that from which it may be rationally and easily deduced. Indeed the whole doctrine of salvation by Christ and divine grace implies this. And each of its main branches, justification and regeneration, directly leads to it. So does the doctrine of man's original righteousness,[m] than which nothing is more clearly revealed.

[l] [p. 87.]
[m] p. 88.

---

[35] Hebden gives no source for this quotation in Augustine. It is likely, at best, a paraphrase.

[36] This question is not from Taylor, who assigned no authority to post-Scripture tradition and traced this 'false' doctrine back to the 'Roman church'. Cf. *Scripture-Doctrine*, 126n. Hebden is now turning to the claim of Anglicans like Gilbert Burnet that the notion of total depravity and unconditional election is not found prior to Augustine. See Burnet, *An Exposition of the Thirty-Nine Articles of the Church of England* (London: R. Chiswell, 1699), vi.

[37] Taylor, *Scripture-Doctrine*, 5.

And if the writers before St. Augustine say little concerning it, is not the reason plain? The occasions of their writing did not lead them to enlarge on what none had ever opposed or denied. For none had ever opposed or denied this doctrine. 'Who', says Vincentius Lirinensis before Celestius,[38] 'denied all mankind to be involved in the guilt of Adam's transgression?'[39] Yet they are not silent concerning it. Justin Martyr speaks of 'mankind as fallen under death and the deceit of the serpent',[40] of 'all Adam's descendants as condemned for his sin, and all that are Christ's as justified by him'.[41] In Irenaeus there are numerous, strong, express testimonies, both to *original righteousness* and *original sin* in the full extent: 'What we lost in Adam, that is, a being "after the image and likeness of God", this we recover by Christ'.[42] Again, 'They who receive the engrafted word return to the ancient nature of man, that by which he was made "after the image and likeness of God" '.[43] He likewise speaks of our 'sinning in Adam'.[44] 'In the first Adam', says he, 'we offended God; in the second Adam we are reconciled'.[45] And frequently, of 'man's losing the image of God by the fall, and recovering it by Christ'.[46] Tertullian says, 'Man was in the beginning deceived, and therefore condemned to death; upon which his whole race became infected, and partakers of his condemnation'.[47] Cyprian is express in his Epistle to Fidus.[n] Origen says, 'The curse of Adam is common to all.'[48] Again, 'Man by sinning lost the image and likeness of God'.[49]

[n] p. 93. [Actually in this and the next paragraph Wesley gathers together text and footnotes from pp. 92-93 and from Hebden's earlier appeal to the Fathers on pp. 12-13.]

---

[38] JW omits Hebden's identification of Celestius as 'that monstrous disciple of Pelagius'. *Doctrine*, 88.

[39] Vincent of Lérins, *Commonitory*, XXIV.

[40] Justin Martyr, *Dialogue with Trypho*, chap. 88.

[41] This is not actually a quotation but a summary of the argument of ibid., chaps. 88–95.

[42] Irenaeus, *Against Heresies*, III.20.

[43] Ibid., V.10.

[44] Ibid., V.1.

[45] Ibid., V.16.

[46] E.g., ibid., III.18.

[47] Tertullian, *De Testimonio Animae* (*Testimony of the Soul*), chap. 3.

[48] Origen, *Against Celsus*, IV.40.

[49] Hebden gives no source for this quotation, and no exact match has been found.

And again, 'No one is clean from the filth of sin, even though he is not above a day old'.[50]

'The whole of me', says Nazianzen, 'has need of being saved, since the whole of me fell, and was condemned for the disobedience of my first father'.[51] Many more are the testimonies of Athanasius, Basil, Hilary—all prior to St. Augustine. And how generally since St. Augustine this important truth has been asserted is well known. Plain it is, therefore, that the Churches of Christ from the beginning have borne clear testimony to it.

To conclude.[52] 1. This is a scriptural doctrine. Many plain texts directly teach it.

2. It is a rational doctrine, throughly consistent with the dictates of sound reason. And this, notwithstanding there may be some circumstances relating thereto which human reason cannot fathom.[o]

3. It is a practical doctrine. It has the closest connection with the life, power, and practice of religion. It leads man to the foundation of all Christian practice, the knowledge of himself, and hereby to the knowledge of God, and the knowledge of Christ crucified. It prepares him for, and confirms him in, just conceptions of the dependence of his salvation on the merits of Christ for justification, and the power of his Spirit for inward and outward holiness.[53] It humbles the natural pride of man. It excludes self-applause and boasting, and points out the true and only way whereby we may fulfil all righteousness.

[o] p. 91. [N.B. Although Wesley by this note pays testimony to its prototype in Hebden, pp. 91-92, this whole conclusion is so completely rewritten as to be virtually original. Only two words in the first point come from Hebden, none in the second, less than a third of those in the third, and only six in the fourth.]

---

[50] Origen, *De Principiis* (*On First Principles*), IV.1.31.

[51] See Gregory of Nazianzus, 'Letter to Cledonius against Apollinaris', Epistle 101.

[52] JW omits a section just prior to this conclusion where Hebden argues that the reason so many apparently wise and learned writers have recently rejected the doctrine of original sin is that 'whatever they know, they are ignorant of Christ, the grace of God, and themselves. They are strangers to the life of God. With the Bible in their hands, some skill in the original languages, etc., they know nothing of vital, experimental religion. On which account, let them be ever so conceited of themselves and scornful of such as differ from them, they are none of the most competent judges of such scripture truth' (*Doctrine*, 89).

[53] Hebden had said: '. . . confirms him in just conceptions of the dependance of his salvation on the righteousness and grace of the Second Adam'. Ibid., 91.

4. It is an experimental doctrine. The sincere Christian day by day carries the proof of it in his own bosom, experiencing that in himself which is abundantly sufficient to convince him that 'in him' by nature 'dwelleth no good thing',[54] but that 'it is God' alone 'who worketh in him, both to will and to do of his good pleasure'.[55]

Lewisham, March 23, 1757

[Wesley's Conclusion]

I have now gone through, as my leisure would permit, this whole complicated question: and I have spoken on each branch of it with plainness and openness, according to the best light I have at present. I have only a few words more to add, and that with the same openness and simplicity.

What I have often acknowledged I now repeat. Were it not on a point of so deep importance, I would no more enter the lists with Dr. Taylor[56] than I would lift my hand against a giant. I acknowledge your abilities of every kind: your natural and acquired endowments, your strong understanding, your lively and fruitful imagination, your plain and easy, yet nervous style. I make no doubt of your having studied the original Scriptures for many years. And I believe you have moral endowments, which are infinitely more valuable and more amiable than all these. For (if I am not greatly deceived) you bear *goodwill to all men*. And may not I add, you *fear* God?

Oh, what might not you do with these abilities! What would be too great for you to attempt and effect? Of what service might you be, not only to your own countrymen but to all that bear the Christian name! How might you advance the cause of true, primitive, scriptural Christianity! Of solid, rational virtue! Of the deep, holy, happy, spiritual religion which is brought to light by the gospel! How capable are you of recommending not barely *morality* (the duty of man to man) but *piety*, the duty of man to God! Even, the 'worshipping him in spirit and in truth'![57] How well qualified are you to explain, enforce, defend, even 'the deep things of God'![58] The nature of the

[54] Rom. 7:18.

[55] Cf. Phil. 2:13.

[56] JW finally realized that he had not given Dr. Taylor his appropriate title. He does so here and alters 'Mr.' to 'Dr.' throughout the reprint in his collected *Works*.

[57] John 4:24.

[58] 1 Cor. 2:10.

kingdom of God *within us*! Yea, the *interiora regni Dei*![59] (I speak on supposition of your having 'the unction of the Holy One',[60] added to your other qualifications.) And are you, whom God has so highly favoured, among those who serve the opposite cause? If one might transfer the words of a man to him, might not one conceive him to say, Καὶ σὺ εἶ ἐκείνων; καὶ σὺ, τέκνον[61]— Are *you* disserving the cause of *inward* religion? Labouring to destroy the *inward* kingdom of God? Sapping the foundation of all true, *spiritual worship*? Advancing *morality* on the ruins of *piety*? Are *you* among those who are overthrowing the very foundations of *primitive, scriptural Christianity*? Which certainly can have no ground to stand upon if the scheme lately advanced be true. What room is there for it till men *repent*? Know themselves? Without this, can they know or love God? O why should *you* block up the way to repentance? And consequently, to the whole religion of the heart? 'Let a man be a fool', says the Apostle, 'that he may be wise.'[62] But *you* tell him he is *wise* already, that every man is by nature as wise as Adam was in paradise. He gladly drinks in the soothing sound, and sleeps on and takes his rest.[63] We beseech those who are *mad* after earthly things to take knowledge of the dreadful state they are in, to return to their Father and beg of him 'the spirit of love and of a sound mind'.[64] You tell them they are of 'a sound mind' already. They believe, and turn to their husks again. Jesus comes to 'seek and save that which is lost'.[65] You tell the *men of form* (though as dead to God as a stone) that they are *not lost*; that (inasmuch as they are free from gross sins) they are in a good way, and *will* undoubtedly *be saved*. So they live and die, without the knowledge, love, or image of God, and die eternally!

[59] 'The internal things of the Kingdom of God.' JW takes this phrase from the Latin title of a collection of spiritual tracts by Francis Rous, *Interiora regni Dei tribus tractatibus reprasentata: academia coelesti, grandi oraculo, mystico matrimonio Christi cum ecclesia* (London, 1655). Cf. JW's translation of the preface to this collection in his introduction to an abridgment of the first tract (*The Heavenly Academy*) in *Christian Library*, 16:215.

[60] 1 John 2:20.

[61] 'Are you also one of them? *You*, lad?' Suetonius, *Lives of the Twelve Caesars: The Deified Julius*, 82.3. The words of Julius Caesar as Brutus stabbed him. Cf. '*Et tu Brute*!' in Shakespeare, *Julius Caesar*, III.i.77. See JW's use of the phrase in his *Principles of a Methodist*, Preface, §1, 9:48 in this edn., and a use by Charles Wesley in his letter to John, Mar. 16-17, 1741, 26:54 in this edn.

[62] Cf. 1 Cor. 3:18.

[63] See Matt. 26:45.

[64] 2 Tim. 1:7.

[65] Luke 19:10.

'They *will* be saved.' But *are* they *saved* already? We know all real Christians are. If they are, if these are possessed of the present salvation[66] which the Scripture speaks of, what is that salvation? How poor, dry, dull, shallow, superficial a thing! Wherein does it excel what the wiser heathens taught, nay, and perhaps experienced? What poor pitiable creatures are those Christians, so called, who have advanced no higher than this! You see enough of these on every side—perhaps even in your own congregation. What knowledge have they of the things of God? What love to God, or to Christ? What heavenly-mindedness? How much of 'the mind which was in Christ Jesus'?[67] How little have they profited by all your instructions! How few are wiser and better than when you knew them first? O take knowledge of the reason why they are not. That doctrine will not 'make them wise unto salvation'.[68] All it can possibly do is to shake off the leaves. It does not affect the branches of sin. Unholy tempers are just as they were. Much less does it strike at the root: pride, self-will, unbelief, heart-idolatry remain undisturbed, and unsuspected.

I am grieved for the people who are thus seeking death in the error of their life.[69] I am grieved for *you*, who surely desire to teach them the way of God in truth. O sir, think it possible that you may have been mistaken! That you may have leaned too far to what you thought the better extreme. Be persuaded once more to review your whole cause, and that from the very foundation. And in doing so you will not disdain to desire more than natural light. O that 'the Father of glory may give unto you the spirit of wisdom and revelation'! May he 'enlighten the eyes of your understanding, that you may know what is the hope of his calling, and what the riches of the glory of his inheritance in the saints'.[70]

Lewisham, March 24, 1757

[66] Cf. Ps. 46:1.
[67] Cf. Phil. 2:5.
[68] Cf. 2 Tim. 3:15.
[69] Wis. 1:12.
[70] Cf. Eph. 1:17-18.

PART VII[a]
THE DOCTRINE OF ORIGINAL SIN, ETC.

Because of the unspeakable importance of thoroughly understanding this grand foundation of all revealed religion, I subjoin one more extract relating both to the original and the present state of man.[1]

[I.][2] 'God[[b]] *made man upright*.'[3] By 'man' we are to understand our *first parents*, the archetypal pair, the root of mankind. This 'man' was made *right* (agreeably to the nature of God, whose work is perfect), without any imperfection, corruption, or principle of corruption in his body or soul. He was made *upright*, that is *straight* with the will and law of God, without any irregularity in his soul. God *made* him thus. He did not first *make* him and then make him *righteous*; but in the very making of him he *made* him *righteous*—righteousness was *concreated* with him. With the same breath that God breathed into him a living soul, he breathed into him a *righteous* soul.[4]

[A.] This[[c]] righteousness was the conformity of all the faculties and powers of his soul to the moral law, which implied three things.

[a] Mr. [Thomas] Boston's *Four-fold State of Man* [i.e., *Human Nature in its Four-fold State,* 10th edn. (Edinburgh: Lumisden, 1753)].

[[b]] [p. 2. Wesley did not list the page numbers for this extract, perhaps as a result of his last-minute decision to include it.]

[[c]] [p. 4.]

---

[1] For details on Thomas Boston, as well as JW's late decision to add this extract to a MS that was already completed (thus, the conclusion in Pt. VI!), see the introduction (pp. 152-53 above).

[2] In his hasty abridgment, JW incorporated haphazardly various enumerations of points in Boston's original. We provide a consistent numbering to facilitate reference. There are six levels of numbering, following this pattern: I. – A. – 1. – a. – 1) – a).

[3] Eccl. 7:29, the text for the discourse that constituted Boston's Pt. I.

[4] JW omits Boston's introduction to the other three states (pp. 2-4), including a section where Boston asserts: 'God made man habitually righteous, man was to make himself actually righteous. The former was the stock God put in his hand. The latter, the improvement he should have made of it'. *Four-fold State of Man* [i.e., *Human Nature in its Fourfold State*, 10th edn. (Edinburgh: Lumisden, 1753)], 4.

First, his *understanding* was a lamp of *light*. He was made after God's image, and consequently could not want knowledge, which is a part thereof. And a perfect *knowledge of the law*[d] was necessary to fit him for universal obedience, seeing no obedience can be according to the law unless it proceed from a sense of the command of God requiring it. 'Tis true Adam had not the law writ on tables of stone, but it was written upon his mind. God impressed it upon his soul, and made him a *law to himself*, as the remains of it even among the heathens testify. And seeing man was made to be the mouth of the creation, to glorify God in his works, we have ground to believe he had an exquisite *knowledge of the works of God*. We have a proof of this in his giving names to the beasts of the field and the fowls of the air, and these such as express their nature. 'Whatsoever Adam called every living thing, that was the name thereof.' And the dominion which God gave him over the creatures, soberly to use them according to his will (still in subordination to the will of God), implies a knowledge of their *natures*.

Secondly, his will lay *straight* with the will of God. There was no corruption in his will, no bent or inclination to evil, for that is sin, properly so called, and therefore inconsistent with that *uprightness* with which it is expressly said he was endued at his creation. The will of man was then *naturally* inclined to God and goodness, though *mutably*. It was disposed by its original make to follow the Creator's will, as the shadow does the body. It was not left in an equal balance to good and evil. For then he had not been *upright*, or conformable[5] to the law, which no more can allow the creature not to be inclined to God as his end, any more than it can allow man to be a God to himself.

Thirdly,[e] his affections were regular, pure, and holy.[f] All his passions, yea all his *sensitive* motions and inclinations were subordinate to his reason and will, which lay straight with the will of God. They were all, therefore, pure from all defilement, free from all disorder or distemper, because in all their motions they were duly subjected to his clear reason and his holy will. He had also an *executive power* answerable to his will—a power to do the good which he *knew*

[d] [p. 5.]
[e] [p. 6.]
[f] [p. 7.]

[5] Boston: 'habitually conformable'. Ibid., 5.

should be done and which he *inclined* to do, even to fulfil the whole law of God. If it had not been so, God would not have required perfect obedience of him. For to say that the Lord 'gathereth where he hath not strawed' is but the blasphemy of a slothful servant.

[B.] From what has been said it may be gathered that man's original righteousness was *universal* and *natural*, yet *mutable*.

1. It was universal, both with respect to the subject of it, the whole man, and the object of it, the whole law. It was diffused through the *whole* man; it was a blessed leaven that leavened the whole lump.[g] Man was then holy in soul, body, and spirit. While the soul remained untainted, the members of the body were consecrated vessels and instruments of righteousness. A combat between reason and appetite—nay, the least inclination to sin—was utterly inconsistent with this *uprightness* in which man was created, and has been invented to veil the corruption of man's nature, and to obscure the grace of God in Christ Jesus. And as this righteousness spread through the whole man, so it respected the whole law. There was nothing in the law but what was agreeable to his reason and will. His soul was shapen out, in length and breadth, to the *commandment*, though exceeding broad. So that his original righteousness was not only perfect in parts but in degrees.

2. As it was universal, so it was *natural* to him.[6] He was created with it. And it was necessary to the perfection of man as he came out of the hand of God, necessary to constitute him in a state of integrity. Yet,

3. It was mutable. It was a righteousness which might be lost, as appears from the sad event. His will was not indifferent to good and evil. God set it towards good only, yet did not so fix it that it could not alter. It was movable to evil, but by man himself only.

Thus[h] was man made *originally righteous*, being 'created in God's own image' (Gen. 1:27), which consists in 'knowledge, righteousness, and holiness' (Col. 3:10; Eph. 4:24). All that God made 'was very good', according to their several natures (Gen. 1:31). And so man was morally good, being 'made after the image' of him who is 'good and upright' (Ps. 25:8). Without this he could not have

[g] [p. 8.]
[h] [p. 9.]

[6] Wesley omits '. . . and not supernatural in that state. Not that it was essential to man as man; for then he would not have lost it without the loss of his being, but it was connatural to him'. Ibid., 8.

answered the end of his creation, which was to know, love, and serve his God. Nay, he *could not* be created otherwise. For he must either have been *conformable* to the law in his powers, principles, and inclinations, or not. If he was, he was *righteous*; if not, he was a *sinner*, which is absurd and horrible to imagine.

[C.] [1.] And as man was *holy*, so he was *happy*. He was full of peace as well as of love. [2.] And[i] he was the favourite of heaven. He bore the image of God, who cannot but love his own image. While he was alone in the world, he was not alone; for he had free, full *communion with God*. As yet there was nothing to turn away the face of God from the work of his own hands, seeing sin had not as yet entered, which alone could make the breach.[7]

[3.] He[j] was also *lord of the world*, universal emperor of the whole earth. His Creator gave him 'dominion over the fish of the sea, the fowl of the air, and everything that moveth on the earth'.[8] He was God's deputy-governor in the lower world. And this his dominion was an image of God's sovereignty.[9] Thus was man 'crowned with glory and honour', having 'all things put under his feet'.

[4.] Again,[k] as he had perfect *tranquillity* in his own breast, so he had a *perfect calm without*. His heart had nothing to reproach him

[i] [p. 10.]
[j] [p. 13.]
[k] [p. 14.]

[7] JW omits a long section on the various covenants in Scripture. Ibid., 10-12.

[8] JW omits 'He gave him a power soberly to use and dispose of the creatures in the earth and sea and air'. Ibid., 13. For JW, our 'dominion' over the animals was that we might *care* for them, not use and dispose of them! See Sermon 60, 'The General Deliverance', I.6, 2:444 in this edn.

[9] JW omits 'This was common to the man and the woman. But man had one thing peculiar to him, to wit, that he had dominion over woman also (1 Cor. 11:7). Behold how the creatures came to him to own their subjection and to do him homage as their lord, and quietly stood before him, till he put names on them as his *own*.' Ibid. Boston is reflecting a traditional reading of Gen. that depicts women as created inferior and subordinate to males. JW initially accepted this traditional reading, reproducing without change the comments of Johann Bengal on 1 Tim. 2:11-14 about woman as 'originally the inferior' and 'more easily deceived' when he published *NT Notes* in 1755. But by 1765 JW was endorsing Matthew Henry's comment that Adam and Eve were 'both made in God's likeness; and therefore between the sexes there is not that great difference and inequality which some imagine' by including it in the note on Gen. 5:2 in *Explanatory Notes upon the Old Testament*. This omission in his excerpt of Boston suggests that JW was already questioning whether Scripture clearly taught that God instituted dominion of men over women.

with, and without there was nothing to annoy him. His beautiful body was not capable of injuries from the air. It[l] was liable to no *diseases* or *pains*. And though he was not to live idle, yet *toil, weariness*, and *sweat of the brows* was not known in this state.

[5.] Lastly,[m] he was immortal. He would never have died if he had not sinned. Death was threatened only in case of sin. The perfect constitution of his body, which came out of God's hand 'very good', and the righteousness of his soul, removed all *inward* causes of death. And God's special care of his innocent creature secured him against *outward* violence. Such were the holiness and the happiness of man in his original state.[10]

[II.] But[n] there is now a sad alteration in our nature.[11] It is now entirely corrupted. Where at first there was nothing evil, there is now nothing good. I shall

First, prove this.

Secondly, represent this corruption in its several parts.

Thirdly, show how man's nature comes to be thus corrupted.

[A.] First, I shall prove both by God's Word and by men's experience and observation, that man's nature is corrupted.

1. For proof from God's Word let us consider:

a. How it takes particular notice of fallen Adam's communicating his image to his posterity. Gen. 5:3: 'Adam[o] begat a son in his own likeness, after his image.' Compare this with ver. 1: 'In the day that God created man, in the image of God made he him.' Behold here how the 'image' after which man was 'made' and the 'image' after which he is 'begotten' are opposed. Man was *made* in the likeness of God—an holy and righteous God *made* an holy and righteous creature. But fallen Adam *begat* a son, not in the likeness of God, but in his 'own likeness': corrupt, sinful Adam begat a corrupt, sinful son. For as the image of God included *righteousness* and *immortality*, so this image of fallen Adam included *corruption* and *death*. Moses, giving us in this chapter the first bill of mortality that ever was in the

[l] [p. 15.]
[m] [p. 16.]
[n] [p. 25.]
[o] [p. 26.]

---

[10] JW omits Boston's conclusion of the first section and introduction to the second section. *Fourfold State*, 16-25.

[11] This begins the extract from Boston's Pt. II, 'The State of Nature', which comprises by far the larger portion of JW's resulting text.

world, ushers it in with this observation, that *dying Adam* begat *mortals*. Having sinned he became *mortal*, according to the threatening. And so he 'begat a son in his own likeness', sinful and therefore *mortal*, and so 'sin and death passed on all'.

Let us consider, b. that text Job 14:4: 'Who can bring a clean thing out of an unclean? Not one.' Our first parents were unclean; how then can we be clean? How could our immediate parents be clean? Or how shall our children be so? The *uncleanness* here mentioned is a *sinful* uncleanness, for it is such as makes man's days 'full of trouble'. And it is *natural*, being derived from unclean parents. 'How can he be clean that is born of a woman?' God can 'bring a clean thing out of an unclean'. And did so in the case of the man Christ, but no other can. Every person, then, that is born according[p] to the course of nature is born unclean. If the root be corrupt, so are the branches. Neither is the matter mended, though the parents be holy. For they are such by *grace*, not by *nature*, and they beget their children as men, not as holy men. Wherefore, as the circumcised parent begets an uncircumcised child, so the holiest parents beget unholy children, and cannot communicate their grace to them as they do their nature.[12]

c. Hear our Lord's determination of the point, John 3:6: 'That which is born of the flesh is flesh.' Behold, the corruption of all mankind—all are 'flesh'. It does not mean all are *frail* (though that is a sad truth too; yea, and our natural frailty is an evidence of our natural corruption), but all are *corrupt* and *sinful*, and that *naturally*. Hence our Lord argues that because they are 'flesh', therefore they 'must be born again', or they 'cannot enter into the kingdom of God' (ver. 3, 5). And as the *corruption* of our nature evidences the absolute necessity of *regeneration*, so the necessity of regeneration proves the corruption of our nature. For why should a man need a *second* birth if his nature were not ruined in the *first* birth? Even infants must be born again, for this rule admits of no exception. And therefore they

[p] [p. 27.]

---

[12] JW may have left in this specific point to answer a question that he had been debating shortly before with Richard Tompson about why two sanctified parents (who were 'freed' from sin) would pass on a depraved nature to their child. See Tompson's letter to John Wesley, July 10, 1755, §18, 26:571 in this edn.; JW's reply to Tompson, July 25, 1755, 26:575 in this edn.; Tompson's follow-up letter to JW, Aug. 15, 1755, §27, 26:580 in this edn.; and JW's second reply to Tompson, Feb. 2, 1756 (vol. 27 in this edn.).

were circumcised under the Old Testament, as having 'the body of the sins of the flesh' (which is conveyed to them by natural generation), the whole old man, 'to put off' (Col. 2:11). And now by the appointment of Christ they are to be baptized; which[q] shows they are unclean, and that there is no salvation for them but 'by the washing of regeneration, and renewing of the Holy Ghost'.

d. We 'are by nature children of wrath'. We are worthy of, and liable to, the wrath of God, and that 'by nature'; and therefore doubtless we are by nature sinful creatures. We are condemned before we have done good or evil, under the curse ere we know what it is. But 'will a lion roar in the forest while he hath no prey?' Will an holy and just God roar in his wrath against man, if he be not by his sin made a prey for wrath? No, he will not. He cannot. We conclude, then, that according to the Word of God, man's nature is a corrupt nature.

2. If[r] we consult *experience*, and observe the case of the world in the things that are obvious to any person, we shall by its fruits easily discover the root of bitterness. I shall instance but in a few.

a. Who sees not a flood of *miseries* overflowing the world? Everyone at home and abroad, in city and country, in palaces and cottages, is groaning under some unpleasing circumstance or other. Some are oppressed with poverty or want. Some chastened with pain or sickness. Some are lamenting their losses. None is without a cross of one sort or another. No man's condition is so soft but there is some thorn of uneasiness in it. And at length death, 'the wages of sin', comes and sweeps all away. Now what but sin has opened the sluice? There is not a complaint or sigh heard in the world, or a tear that falls from our eye, but it is an evidence that man is fallen as a star from heaven. For God 'distributeth sorrows in his anger' (Job 21:17). This is a plain proof of the corruption of nature, forasmuch as those that have not actually sinned have their share of these sorrows, yea, and draw their first breath weeping. There are also graves of the smallest as well as the largest size. And there are never wanting some in the world who, like Rachel, are 'weeping for their children, because they are not'.

b. How early does this corruption of nature appear! It is soon discerned which way the bias of the heart lies. Do not the children of fallen Adam, before they can go alone, follow their father's footsteps?

[q] [p. 28.]
[r] [p. 29.]

What pride, ambition, curiosity, vanity, wilfulness, and averseness to good appear in them! And when they creep out of infancy there is a necessity of using 'the rod of correction to drive away the foolishness that is bound in their heart'.

c. Take[s] a view of the outbreakings of sin in the world. 'The wickedness of man is yet great in the earth.' Behold the bitter fruits of corrupt nature! 'By swearing and lying and killing and stealing and committing adultery they break out' (like the breaking forth of waters) 'and blood toucheth blood.' The world is filled with all manner of filthiness, wickedness, and impiety. And whence is this deluge of sin on the earth but from the breaking of the fountains of the great deep, 'the heart of man', out of which 'proceed adulteries, fornications, murders, thefts, covetousness, wickedness'. Ye may, it may be, thank God that ye are not in these respects 'like other men'. And you have reason, for the corruption of nature is the very same in you as in them.

d. Cast your eye upon those terrible convulsions the world is thrown into by the wickedness of men. Lions prey not on lions, nor wolves on wolves; but men bite and devour one another. Upon how slight occasions will men sheathe their swords in one another's bowels! Since Cain shed Abel's blood, the world has been turned into a slaughter-house. And the chase has been continued, ever since Nimrod began his hunting—as on the earth, so in the seas, the greater still devouring the lesser. Now when we see the world in such a ferment, everyone stabbing another with words or swords, these violent heats among the sons of Adam speak the whole body to be distempered,[t] 'the whole head' to be 'sick, and the whole heart faint'.

e. Consider the necessity of human laws, fenced with terrors and severities. Man was made for society; and God himself said when he created him, it was not good for him to be alone. Yet the case is such now that in society he must be hedged in with thorns. And that from hence we may the better discern the corruption of man's nature, consider: 1) Every man naturally loves to be at full liberty himself; and were he to follow his inclination would vote himself out of the reach of all laws, divine and human. Yet 2) No man would willingly adventure to live in a lawless society, and therefore even pirates and robbers have laws among themselves. Thus men show they are conscious of the corruption of nature, not daring to trust

[s][p. 30.]
[t][p. 31.]

one another but upon security. 3) How dangerous soever it is to break through the hedge, yet many will do it daily. They will not only sacrifice their conscience and credit, but for the pleasure of a few moments lay themselves open to a violent death by the laws of the land wherein they live. 4) Laws are often made to yield to man's lusts. Sometimes whole societies break off the fetters and the voice of laws cannot be heard for the noise of arms. And seldom there is a time wherein there are not some persons so great and daring that the laws dare not look them in the face. 5) Observe[u] even the Israelites separated to God from all the nations of the earth. Yet what horrible confusions were among them when 'there was no king in Israel'! How hard was it to reform them when they had the best of magistrates! And how quickly did they turn aside again when they had wicked rulers! It seems one grand design of that sacred history was to discover the corruption of man's nature.

f. Consider the remains of natural corruption even in them that believe.[13] Though grace has entered, corruption is not expelled.[14] They find it with them at all times and in all places. If a man have an ill neighbour he may remove. But should he go into a wilderness, or pitch his tent on a remote rock in the sea, there it will be with him.[15] I[v] need not stand to prove so clear a point. But consider these few things on this head. 1) If it be thus in the green tree, how must it be in the dry! Does so much of the *old* remain even in those who have received a *new nature*! How great then must that corruption be in those where it is *unmixed* with renewing grace! 2) Though natural corruption is no burden to a natural man, is he therefore free from it? No, no. Only he is *dead*, and *feels* not the sinking weight. Many a groan is heard from a sickbed, but never one from a grave.[16] 3) The good man[17] resists the old nature. He strives to starve it, yet it remains. How must it spread then and strengthen itself in the soul where it is not starved, but fed, as in unbelievers! If the garden of the diligent find him full work in cutting off and rooting up, surely that of the sluggard must needs be 'all grown over with thorns'.

[u] [p. 32.]
[v] [p. 33.]

[13] Boston: 'the saints'. *Fourfold State*, 32.

[14] Wesley omits 'Though they have got the new creation, yet much of the old corrupt nature remains, and these struggle together within them . . .'. Ibid.

[15] Wesley omits 'It is especially active when he would do good'. Ibid., 33.

[16] Wesley omits 'In the saint as in the sick man, there is a mighty struggle'. Ibid.

[17] Boston: 'the godly man'. Ibid.

[g.] I[w] shall add but one observation more, that in every man naturally the image of fallen Adam appears; to evince which I appeal to the consciences of all, in the following particulars:

1) If God by his holy law or wise providence put a restraint upon us, to keep us back from anything, does not that restraint whet the edge of our natural inclinations, and make us so much the keener in our desires? The very heathen were convinced that there is this spirit of contradiction in us, though they knew not the spring of it. How often do men give themselves a loose in those things wherein if God had left them at liberty they would have bound up themselves! And is not this a repeating of our father's folly, that men will rather climb for forbidden fruit than gather what providence offers to them, when they have God's express allowance for it?

2) Is[x] it not natural to us to care for the body at the expense of the soul? This was one ingredient in the sin of our first parents (Gen. 3:6). O how happy might we be, if we were but at half the pains about our souls which we bestow upon our bodies! If that question, 'What must I do to be saved?' did but run near so oft through our minds as those, 'What shall we eat? What shall we drink? Wherewithal shall we be clothed?'

3) Is[y] not everyone by nature discontented with his present lot, or with some one thing or other in it? Some one thing is always missing; so that man is a creature given to change. If any doubt of this, let them look over all their enjoyments, and after a review of them, listen to their own hearts, and they will hear a secret murmuring, for want of something. Since the hearts of our first parents wandered from God, their posterity have a natural disease which Solomon calls 'the wandering of desire', literally, 'the walking of the soul' (Eccles. 6:9). This is a sort of diabolical trance, wherein the soul traverseth the world, feeds itself with a thousand airy nothings, snatcheth at this and the other imagined excellency, goes here and there and everywhere except where it should go. And the soul is never cured of this disease till it takes up its rest in God through Christ.[18]

[w] [p. 34.]
[x] [p. 35.]
[y] [p. 36.]

[18] Boston read: '. . . its everlasting rest in God through Christ. But till this be, if man were set again in paradise, the garden of the Lord, all the pleasures there would not keep him from looking, yea and leaping over the hedge a second time'. Ibid., 36.

4) Do[z] not Adam's children naturally follow his footsteps in 'hiding' themselves 'from the presence of the Lord' (Gen. 3:8)? We are just as blind in this matter as he was, who thought to 'hide himself from the presence of the Lord among the trees of the garden'. We promise ourselves more security in a secret sin than in one that is openly committed. 'The adulterer saith, no eye shall see me.' And men will freely do that in secret which they would be ashamed to do in the presence of a child, as if darkness could hide from an all-seeing God. Are we not naturally *careless* of *communion with God*? Nay, and *averse* to it? Never was there any communion between God and Adam's children where God himself had not the first word. If he would let them alone, they would never inquire after him.

5) How *loath* are men to *confess sin*, to take guilt and shame to themselves! And was it not thus in the case before us? Adam confesses his nakedness (which[a] indeed he could not deny), but not one word does he say about his sin. It is as natural for us to hide sin as to commit it. Many instances of this we see daily; but how many will there be in that day when 'God will judge the secrets of men'! Many a foul mouth will then be seen, which is now 'wiped and saith, I have done no wickedness'.

[6)] Lastly, is it not natural for us to *extenuate* our sin, and *transfer* the guilt to others? As Adam laid the blame of his sin on the woman. And did not the woman lay the blame on the serpent? Adam's children need not be taught this. For before they can well speak, if they can't deny, they lisp out something to lessen their fault, and lay the blame upon another. Nay, so natural is this to men that in the greatest of sins they will charge the fault on God himself, blaspheming his providence under the name of 'ill luck' or 'misfortune', and so laying the blame of their sin at heaven's door. Thus[b] does 'the foolishness of man pervert his ways', and his heart fretteth against the Lord. Let us then call Adam, father. Let us not deny the relation, seeing we bear his image.

[B.] I proceed to inquire into the *corruption of nature* in the several *parts* of it. But who can take the exact dimensions of it, in its breadth, length, height, and depth? 'The heart is deceitful above all things, and desperately wicked. Who can know it?' However, we may quickly perceive so much of it as may show the absolute necessity of

[z] [p. 37.]
[a] [p. 38.]
[b] [p. 39.]

regeneration. Man in his natural state is altogether corrupt, through all the faculties of his soul—corrupt in his understanding, his will, his affections, his conscience, and his memory.

1. The understanding[19] is despoiled of its primitive glory, and covered over with confusion. We[c] are fallen into the hands of our grand adversary, and are deprived of our two eyes. 'There is none that understandeth'. The 'very mind and conscience' of the natural man are 'defiled' or *spoiled*. But to point out this corruption of the understanding more particularly, let the following things be considered.

[a.] First, there is a natural *weakness* in the minds of men with respect to spiritual things. How hard is it to teach them the common principles of religion, to make truths so plain that they may understand them! Try the same persons in other things, speak of the things of this world, and they will understand quickly. But it is hard to make them know how their souls may be saved, or how their hearts may find rest in Christ. Consider even those who have many advantages above the common run of mankind. Yet[d] how small is their knowledge of divine things! What confusion still remains in their minds! How often are they mired, and 'speak as a child', even in the matter of practical truths! It is a *pitiable weakness* that we cannot perceive the things which God has revealed. And it must needs be a *sinful weakness*, since the law of God requires us to know and believe them.

[b.] Secondly, man's understanding is naturally overwhelmed with gross *darkness* in spiritual things. Man, at the instigation of the devil, attempting to break out a new light in his mind, instead of that broke up the doors of the bottomless pit, by the smoke whereof he was covered with darkness. When God at first made man his mind was a lamp of light, but sin has now turned it into darkness. Sin has closed the window of the soul. It is the land of darkness and the shadow of death, where 'the light is as darkness'. The 'prince of darkness' reigns therein, and nothing but the 'works of darkness' are framed there. That you may be the more fully convinced of this, take the following evidences of it.

1) The darkness that was upon the face of 'the world' before, and at the time that Christ came. When Adam by his sin[e] had lost his

[c] [p. 40.]
[d] [p. 41.]
[e] [p. 42.]

[19] Boston: 'The understanding, that leading faculty . . .'. Ibid., 39.

first light, it pleased God to reveal to him the way of salvation (Gen. 3:15). This was handed down by holy men before the flood. Yet the natural darkness of the mind of man so prevailed as to carry off all sense of true religion from the old world, except what remained in Noah's family. After the flood, as men increased, their natural darkness of mind prevailed again, and the light decayed, till it died out among the generality of mankind, and was preserved only among the posterity of Shem. And even with them it was near setting, when God called Abraham from 'serving other gods' (Josh. 24:15). God gave him a more full revelation, which he communicated to his family (Gen. 18:19). Yet the natural darkness wore it out at length, save that it was preserved among the posterity of Jacob. In Egypt that darkness so prevailed over them also that a new revelation was necessary. And many a dark cloud got above that during the time from Moses to Christ. When Christ came, nothing was to be seen in the Gentile world but 'darkness and cruel habitations'. They were drowned in superstition and idolatry. And whatever wisdom was among their philosophers, 'the[f] world by' that 'wisdom knew not God', but became more and more vain in their imaginations. Nor were the Jews much wiser. Except a few, gross darkness covered them also. Their traditions were multiplied, but the knowledge of those things wherein the life of religion lies was lost. They gloried in outward ordinances, but knew nothing of 'worshipping God in spirit and in truth'.

Now what but the natural darkness of men's minds could still thus wear out the light of external revelation? Men did not forget the way of preserving their lives. But how quickly did they forget the way of saving their souls! So that it was necessary for God himself to reveal it again and again. Yea, and a mere external revelation did not suffice to remove this darkness. No, not when it was made by Christ in person. There needed also the Holy Ghost sent down from heaven. Such[g] is the natural darkness of our minds that it only yields to the blood and spirit of Christ.

2) Every natural man's heart, how refined soever he appear, is full of darkness, disorder, and confusion. The unrenewed part of mankind are rambling through the world like so many blind men, who will neither take a guide, nor can guide themselves, and therefore fall over this and the other precipice into destruction. Some are

[f] [p. 43.]
[g] [p. 44.]

running after their covetousness, some sticking in the mire of sensuality, others dashing on the rock of pride—everyone stumbling on one stone of stumbling or other as their unmortified passions drive[h] them. And while some are lying along in the way, others are coming up and falling headlong over them. Errors swarm in the world. All the unregenerate are utterly mistaken in the point of true happiness. All desire to be happy, but touching the way to happiness there are almost as many opinions as there are men. They are like the blind Sodomites about Lot's house, all seeking to 'find the door', but in vain. Look into thine own heart (if thou art not born again), and thou wilt see all turned upside down, heaven lying under and earth a-top. Look into thy life, and see how thou art playing the madman, eagerly flying after 'that which is not', and slighting that which is, and will be for ever. Thus[i] is man's understanding naturally overwhelmed with gross *darkness* in spiritual things.

[c.] Thirdly, there is in the mind of man a natural *bias to evil*. Let us reflect a little, and[j] we shall find incontestable evidence of it.

1) Men's minds have a natural dexterity to do mischief. None are so simple as to want skill for this. None needs to be taught it. But as weeds without being sown grow up of their own accord, so does this 'earthly, sensual, devilish wisdom' naturally grow up in us.

2) We[k] naturally form *gross conceptions* of spiritual things, as if the soul were quite immersed in flesh and blood. Let men but look into themselves, and they will find this bias in their minds, whereof the idolatry which still prevails so far and wide is an incontestable evidence. For it plainly shows, men would have a *visible* deity. Therefore they change the 'glory of the incorruptible God into an image'. Indeed the reformation of these nations has banished gross idolatry out of our churches. But heart-reformation alone can banish mental idolatry, subtle and refined image-worship, out of our minds.

3) How difficult is it to 'detain' the carnal mind 'before the Lord'! To fix it in the meditation of spiritual things! When God is speaking to men by his Word, or they are speaking to him in prayer, the body remains before God, but the world steals away the heart. Though[l] the eyes be closed, the man sees a thousand vanities, and

[h] [p. 45.]
[i] [p. 46.]
[j] [p. 47.]
[k] [p. 48.]
[l] [p. 49.]

the mind roves hither and thither. And many times the man scarce 'comes to' himself till he is 'gone from the presence of the Lord'. The worldly man's mind does not wander when he is contriving business, casting up his accounts, or telling his money. If he answers you not at first, he tells you he did not hear you, he was busy, his mind was fixed. But the carnal mind, employed about spiritual things, is out of its element, and therefore cannot fix.

4) Consider how the carnal *imagination* supplies the want of real objects to the corrupt heart. The unclean person is filled with speculative impurities, 'having eyes full of adultery'. The covetous man fills his heart with the world, if he cannot get his hands full of it. The malicious person acts his revenge in his own breast. The envious, within his own[m] narrow soul, sees his neighbour laid low enough. And so every lust is fed by the imagination. These things may suffice to convince us of the natural *bias* of the mind *to evil*.

[d.] Fourthly, there is in the carnal mind an *opposition to spiritual truths*, and an aversion to the receiving them. God[n] has revealed to sinners the way of salvation. He has given his word. But do natural men believe it? Indeed they do not. They believe not the promises of the Word; for they who receive them are thereby made 'partakers of the divine nature'. They believe not the threatenings of the Word, otherwise they could not live as they do. I doubt not but most, if not all of you who are in a state of nature, will here plead, Not guilty. But the very difficulty you find in assenting to this truth proves the unbelief with which I charge you. Has it not proceeded so far with some that it has steeled their foreheads openly to reject all revealed religion? And though ye set not your mouths as they do against the heavens, yet the same bitter root of unbelief is in you, and reigns and will reign in you till overcoming grace captivate[o] your minds to the belief of the truth. To convince you of this,

Consider 1) How have you learned those truths which you think you believe? Is it not merely by the benefit of your education, and of external revelation? You are strangers to the inward work of the Holy Spirit, bearing witness by and with the Word in your hearts. And so you cannot have the *assurance of faith*, even with respect to the

[m] [p. 50.]
[n] [p. 51.]
[o] [p. 52.]

outward revelation.[20] And therefore ye are still unbelievers. 'It is written in the prophets, And they shall be all taught of God. Every-one therefore that hath heard and learned of the Father, saith our Lord, cometh unto me.' But ye have not 'come to Christ'. Therefore ye have not been 'taught of God'. Ye have not been so *taught*, and therefore ye have not *come*: ye believe not.

Consider,[p] 2) The utter inconsistency of most men's lives with the principles which they profess. They profess to believe the Scripture, but how little are they concerned about what is revealed therein! How unconcerned are ye even about that weighty point, whether ye be born again or not! Many live as they were born, and are like to die as they live, and yet live in peace. Do such believe the sinfulness of a natural state? Do they believe they are 'children of wrath'? Do they believe there is no salvation without regeneration? And no regeneration but what makes man 'a new creature'? O no! If ye did, ye could not live in your sins, live out of Christ, and yet hope for mercy.

[e.] Fifthly,[q] man is naturally high-minded. Lowliness is not a flower which grows in the field of nature. It[r] is natural to man to think highly of himself and what is his own. 'Vain man would be wise'—so he accounts himself, and so he would be accounted by others. His way is *right*, because it is *his own*; for 'every way of a man is right in his own eyes'. He is 'alive without the law' and therefore his hope is strong and his confidence firm. It is another tower of Babel. The Word batters it, yet it stands. One while breaches are made in it, but they are quickly repaired. At another time it is all made to shake, but it is still kept up—till God's Spirit raise an *heart-quake* within the man, which tumbles it down, and leaves not one stone upon another.

Thus much of the corruption of the understanding. Call the understanding Ichabod, for 'the glory is departed from it'. Consider this, ye that are yet in the state of nature, and groan ye out your[s] case before the Lord, that the sun of righteousness may arise upon you before ye be shut up in everlasting darkness. What avails your

[p] [p. 53.]
[q] [p. 54.]
[r] [p. 55.]
[s] [p. 56.]

[20] This sentence is omitted from *Works* (1773), perhaps because JW feared some would read it as denying that *believers* have assurance.

worldly wisdom? What do all your attainments in religion avail while your understanding lies wrapped up in darkness and confusion, utterly void of the light of life?

2. Nor is *the will* less corrupted than the understanding. It was at first faithful and ruled with God, but now it is turned traitor against God and rules with and for the devil. To open this plague of the heart, let the following things be considered.

[a.] First, there is in the unrenewed will an utter inability for what is truly good in the sight of God. Indeed a natural man has a power to choose and do what is *materially* good. But though he can will what is good and right, he can do nothing *aright* and *well*. 'Without me', that is, separate from me, 'ye can do nothing'—nothing truly and spiritually good. To[t] evidence this, consider,

1) How often do men see the good they should choose and the evil they should refuse; and yet their hearts have no more power to comply with their light than if they were arrested by some invisible hand! Their consciences tell them the right way; yet cannot their will be brought up to it. Else how is it that the clear arguments on the side of virtue do not bring men over to that side? Although heaven and hell were but a *maybe*, even this would determine the will to holiness, could it be determined by reason. Yet so far is it from this, that men, 'knowing the judgment of God, that they who do such things are worthy of death, not only do the same, but have pleasure in them that do them'.

2) Let[u] those who have been truly convinced of the *spirituality* of the law speak and tell if they then found themselves able to *incline* their hearts toward it. Nay, the more that light shone into their souls, did they not find their hearts more and *more unable* to comply with it? Yea, there are some who are yet in the devil's camp that can tell from their own experience, light let into the mind cannot give life to the will, or enable it to comply therewith.

[b.] Secondly, there is in the unrenewed will an *averseness to good*. Sin is the natural man's element, and he is as loath to part with it as the fishes are to come out of the water. He is sick, but utterly averse to the remedy. He loves his disease, so that he loathes the physician. He is a captive, a prisoner, and a slave; but he loves his conqueror, gaoler, and master. He is fond of his fetters, prison, and drudgery,

[t] [p. 57.]
[u] [p. 58.]

and has no liking to his liberty. For evidence of this averseness to good in the will of man,

Consider, 1) The *untowardness of children*. How[v] averse are they to restraint! Are they not 'as bullocks unaccustomed to the yoke'? Yea, it is far easier to tame young bullocks to the yoke than to bring young children under discipline. Every man may see in this, as in a glass, that man is naturally wild and wilful; that according to Zophar's observation, he 'is born a wild ass's colt'. What can be said more? He is like a *colt*, the colt of an *ass*, the colt of *a wild ass*; 'a wild ass used to the wilderness, that snuffeth up the wind at her pleasure. In her occasion who can turn her away?'

2) What pain and difficulty do men find in *bringing* their hearts to religious duties! And what a task is it to the natural man to *abide* at them! To leave the world but a little, and converse with God! When they are engaged in worldly business or company, time seems to fly, and is gone before they are aware. But how heavily does it drive while a prayer, a sermon, or a sabbath lasts! With many the Lord's day is the longest day in the week. And therefore they must sleep longer that morning, and go sooner to bed that night, than ordinarily they do, that the day may be made of a tolerable length. And still their hearts say, 'When will the sabbath be gone?'

3) Consider[w] how the will of the natural man 'rebels against the light'. Sometimes he is not able to keep it out, but he 'loves darkness rather than light'. The outer door of the understanding is broken open, but the inner door of the will remains shut. Corruption and conscience then encounter, till conscience is forced to give back. Convictions are murdered, and truth is made and *held* prisoner 'in unrighteousness'.

4) When the Spirit of the Lord is working a deeper work, yet what *resistance* does the soul make![21] When he comes, he finds the 'strong man keeping the house', while the soul is fast asleep in the devil's arms, till the Lord awakens the sinner, opens his eyes, and strikes him with terror, while the clouds are black above his head, and the sword of vengeance is held to his breast. But what pains is he at to

[v] [p. 59.]
[w] [p. 60.]

[21] Boston had said: 'Let us observe the resistance made by elect souls, where the Spirit of the Lord is at work, to bring them from the power of Satan to God'. *Fourfold State*, 60.

put a fair face on a black heart! To shake off his fears, or make head against them! Carnal[x] reason suggests if it be ill with him, it will be ill with many. When he is beat from this, and sees no advantage in going to hell with company, he resolves to leave his sins but cannot think of breaking off so soon—there is time enough, and he will do it afterwards. When at length he is constrained to part with some sins, others are kept as right hands or right eyes. Nay, when he is so pressed that he must needs say before the Lord he is willing to part with all his idols, yet how long will his heart give the lie to his tongue and prevent the execution of it!

[c.] Thirdly, there is in the will of man a natural proneness to evil. Men are naturally 'bent to backsliding from God'. They *hang* (as the word is) towards backsliding. Leave the unrenewed will to itself, it will choose sin and reject holiness, and that as certainly as water poured on the side of an hill will run downward and not upward.

1) Is not the way of evil the *first way* wherein the children of men go? Do not their inclinations plainly appear on the wrong side while they have not cunning to hide them? As soon as it appears[y] we are *reasonable* creatures, it appears we are *sinful* creatures. 'Foolishness is bound in the heart of a child, till the rod of correction drives it from him.' It is *bound* in the heart, woven into our very nature. Nor will the knots loose; they must be *broke* asunder by strokes. Words will not do. The rod must be taken to drive it away. Not that the rod of itself will do this, the sad experience of many parents testifies the contrary. And Solomon himself tells you, 'Though thou shouldst bray a fool in a mortar, yet will not his foolishness depart from him.' But the rod is an ordinance of God appointed for that end, which, like the Word, is made effectual by the Spirit's accompanying his own ordinance.

2) How easily men are led into sin! Persuaded to evil, though not to good. Those whom the Word cannot draw to holiness, Satan leads to wickedness at his pleasure. To learn doing ill is always easy to the unrenewed man. But to learn to do good is as difficult as for 'the Ethiopian to change his skin'. Were[z] the will evenly poised between good and evil, one might be embraced with as much ease as the other. But experience testifies it is not—yea, the experience of all ages. How often did the Israelites forsake the Almighty God and

[x] [p. 61.]
[y] [p. 62.]
[z] [p. 63.]

dote upon the idols of the nations! But did ever one of those nations forsake their idols and grow fond of the God of Israel? No, no. Though man is naturally given to change, it is but from evil to evil, not from evil to good. Surely then, the will of man stands not in equal balance but has a cast on the wrong side.

3) Consider how men go on still in the way of sin, till they meet with a stop from another hand than their own. 'I hid me, and he went on frowardly in the way of his own heart.' If God withdraws his restraining hand, man is in no doubt which way to choose. For the way of sin is 'the way of his heart'. His heart naturally lies that way. As long as God suffereth them, all nations 'walk in their own way'. The natural man is so fixed in evil that there needs no more to show he is off of God's way than to say he is upon his own.

[d.] Fourthly,[a] there is a natural contrariety, a direct opposition in the will of man to God himself. 'The carnal mind is enmity against God. It is not subject to the law of God, neither can be.'

I have a charge against every unregenerate man and woman, to be proved by the testimony of Scripture and their own conscience—namely, that whether they have the form of religion or no, they are *heart-enemies to God*; to the Son of God, to the Spirit of God, and to the law of God. Hear this, all ye careless souls that live at ease in your natural state.

1) Ye[b] are *enemies to God in your mind.* Ye are not as yet reconciled to him. The natural enmity is not slain, though perhaps it lies hid, and ye do not perceive it. Every[c] natural man is an enemy to God as he is revealed in his Word, to an infinitely *holy, just, powerful* and *true* Being. In effect men are naturally 'haters of God'. And if they could, they would certainly make him *another* than what he is.

To convince you of this, let me propose a few queries: a) How are your hearts affected to the infinite holiness of God? If ye are not 'partakers of his holiness', ye cannot be reconciled to it. The heathens, finding they were not like God in holiness, made their Gods like themselves in filthiness, and thereby discovered what sort of a God the natural man[d] would have. God is holy. Can an unholy creature love his unspotted holiness? Nay, it is 'the righteous' only that can 'give thanks at the remembrance of his holiness'. God is light.

[a] [p. 64.]
[b] [p. 65.]
[c] [p. 66.]
[d] [p. 67.]

Can creatures of darkness, and that walk in darkness, rejoice therein? Nay, 'everyone that doth evil hateth the light'. For what communion hath light with darkness? b) How are your hearts affected to the justice of God? There is not a man who is wedded to his sins but would be content with the blood of his body to blot that letter out of the name of God. Can the malefactor love his condemning judge? Or an unjustified sinner a just God? No, he cannot. And hence, since men cannot get the doctrine of his justice blotted out of the Bible, yet it is such an eyesore to them that they strive to blot it out of their minds. They ruin themselves by presuming on his mercy, 'saying in their heart, the Lord will not do good, neither will he do evil'. c) How are ye affected to the omniscience and omnipresence of God? Men naturally would rather have a blind idol than an all-seeing God, and therefore do what they can, as Adam did, to 'hide themselves from the presence of the Lord'. They no more love an omnipresent God than the thief loves to have the judge witness to his evil deeds. d) How are ye affected to the truth of God? How many hope that God will not be true to his word! There are thousands that hear the gospel, and hope to be saved, who never experienced the new birth, nor do at all concern themselves in that question whether they are born again or not. Our Lord's words are plain and peremptory:[e] 'Except a man be born again he cannot see the kingdom of God.' What then are such hopes but real hopes that God will *recall* his word, and that Christ will prove a false prophet? e) How are they affected to the power of God? None but new creatures can love him for it. Every natural man would contribute to the building another tower of Babel to hem it in. On these grounds I declare every unrenewed man 'an enemy to God'.

2) Ye are enemies to the Son of God, that enmity to Christ is in your hearts which would have made you join the 'husbandmen who killed the heir, and cast him out of the vineyard'. 'Am I a dog', ye will say, to have so treated my *dear* Saviour? So said Hazael in another case. Yet how did he act? Many call him 'dear' to whom their sins are ten times dearer than their Saviour. He is no otherwise 'dear' to them than as they abuse his death for the peaceable enjoyment of their sins, that they may live as they list in this world and when they die be kept out of hell. To convince you of this, I[f] will lay before you the enmity of your hearts against Christ in all his offices.

[e] [p. 68.]
[f] [p. 69.]

a) Every unregenerate man is an enemy to Christ in his prophetic office. For evidence of this consider, the entertainment he meets with when he comes to teach souls *inwardly* by his Spirit. Men do what they can to stop their ears, that they may not hear his voice. They 'always resist the Holy Ghost'. They 'desire not the knowledge of his ways'. The old calumny is thrown upon him again, 'He is mad', why hear ye him? 'The spirit of bondage' is accounted by many mere distraction and melancholy, men thus blaspheming God's work because they themselves are beside themselves and cannot judge of those matters.

Consider the entertainment he meets with when he comes to teach men *outwardly* by his Word. His *written* word, the Bible, is slighted. Many[g] lay by their Bibles with their Sunday clothes. Alas! The dust about your Bibles is a witness of the enmity of your hearts against Christ as a prophet. And of those who read them oftener, how few are there that read them as the Word of the Lord to *their* souls in particular, so as to keep up communion with God therein! Hence they are strangers to the solid 'comfort of the Scriptures'. And if at any time they are dejected it is something else, and not the Word of God, which revives their drooping spirits.

Christ's Word *preached* is despised. Men can without remorse make to themselves one silent sabbath after another. And alas, when they 'tread his courts', how[h] little reverence and awe of God appears on their spirits! Many stand like brazen walls before the Word, on whom it makes no breach at all. Nay, not a few are growing worse and worse, notwithstanding 'precept upon precept'. What tears of blood are sufficient to lament this? Remember, we are but the 'voice of one crying'. The speaker is in heaven. Yet ye refuse him that speaketh, and prefer the prince of darkness before the prince of peace. A dismal darkness overspread the world by Adam's fall, more terrible than if the sun and moon had been extinguished. And it must have covered us eternally had not 'the grace of God' *appeared* to dispel it. But we fly from it, and like the wild beasts, lay ourselves 'down in our dens'. Such is the enmity of the hearts of men against Christ in his prophetic office.

b) The natural man is an enemy to Christ in his priestly office. He is appointed of the Father 'a priest for ever', that by his sacrifice and intercession alone, sinners may have access to, and peace with

[g] [p. 70.]
[h] [p. 71.]

God. But 'Christ crucified' is ever a stumbling-block and foolishness to the unregenerate part of mankind.

None of Adam's children naturally incline to receive the blessing in borrowed robes, but would always climb up to heaven on a thread spun out of their own bowels. They[i] look on God as a great master and themselves as his servants, that must *work* and *win* heaven as their *wages*. Hence when conscience awakes they think that, to be saved, they must answer the demands of the law—*serve God as well as they can*, and pray for mercy wherein they come short. And thus many come to duties, that never come *out of them* to Christ.

Indeed the natural man, going to God in duties, will continually be found either to go *without* a mediator or with *more* mediators than one. Nature is blind and therefore venturous. It puts men on going immediately to God *without Christ*. Converse with many hearers of the gospel on their hopes of salvation and the name of Christ will scarce be heard from their mouth. Ask them how they think to find the pardon of sin. They say they look for *mercy*, because God is a merciful God—and this is all they have to *trust* in. Others look for mercy for Christ's sake. But how do they know Christ will take their plea in hand? Why, they 'pray, mourn, confess, and have great desires'. So they have something of their own to recommend them to him. They were never made 'poor in spirit', and brought empty-handed to God, to lay the stress of all on his atoning blood.

c) The natural man is an enemy to Christ in his kingly office.

How[j] unwilling are natural men to submit to the laws and discipline of his kingdom! However they may be brought to some outward submission to the king of saints, yet sin always retains its throne in their hearts, and they are 'serving diverse lusts and pleasures'. None but those in whom Christ is formed do really put the crown on his head. None[k] but these receive the kingdom of Christ within them, and let him set up and put down in their souls as he will. As for others, any Lord shall sooner have the rule over them than 'the Lord of glory'. They kindly entertain his enemies, and will never absolutely resign themselves to his government. Thus, you see, the natural man is an enemy to Jesus Christ in all his offices.[22]

[i] [p. 72.]
[j] [p. 73.]
[k] [p. 74.]

[22] JW omits a long digression on how hard it is to convince people that they reject Christ in all his offices. Boston, *Fourfold State*, 74-80.

3) Ye[l] are enemies to the Spirit of God. He is the spirit of holiness. The natural man is unholy, and loves to be so, and therefore 'resists the Holy Ghost'. The work of the Spirit is to 'convince the world of sin, righteousness, and judgment'. But O! how do men strive to[m] ward off these convictions, as they would a blow that threatened their life! If the Spirit dart them in so that they cannot avoid them, does not the heart say, 'Hast thou found me, O mine enemy?' And indeed they treat him as an enemy, doing their utmost to stifle their convictions, and to murder these harbingers that come to prepare the way of the Lord into the soul. Some fill their hands with *business* to put convictions out of their head, as Cain, who fell to building a city. Some put them off with fair *promises*, as Felix did. Some *sport* or *sleep* them away. And how can it be otherwise? For it is the work of the Holy Spirit to subdue lusts and burn up corruption. How then can he whose lusts are dear as his life fail of being an enemy to him?

[4)] Lastly, ye are enemies to the law of God. Though the natural man 'desires to be under the law', as a covenant of works, yet as it is a rule of life[23] he 'is not subject to' it, 'neither indeed can be'. For a) Every natural man is wedded to some sin which he cannot part with. And as he cannot bring up his inclinations to the law, he would fain bring down the law to his inclinations. And this is a plain, standing evidence of the enmity of his heart against it. b) The law set home on the awakened[24] conscience in its spirituality irritates corruption. It is as oil to the fire, which instead of quenching, makes it flame the more. 'When the commandment comes, sin revives.' What reason can be assigned for this but the natural enmity of the heart[n] against the holy law? We conclude, then, that the unregenerate are heart-enemies to God, his Son, his Spirit, and his law; that there is a natural contrariety, opposition, and enmity in the will of man to God himself and his holy will.

[l] [p. 80.]
[m] [p. 81.]
[n] [p. 82.]

[23] JW omits 'requiring universal holiness, and discharging all manner of impurity'. Ibid., 81.

[24] Boston: 'natural'. Ibid., 81. For Wesley, the 'natural' man is totally insensitive to God's law; if one is 'irritated' by the law, it is a sign of God's initial gracious work in 'awakening'. Cf. Sermon 9, 'The Spirit of Bondage and of Adoption', II, 3:255-60 in this edn.

[e.] Fifthly, the unrenewed will is wholly perverse in reference to the end of man. Man is a merely dependent being, having no existence or goodness originally from himself, but all he has is from God, as the first cause and spring of all perfection, natural and moral. Dependence is woven into his very nature, so that should God withdraw from him, he would sink into nothing. Since then whatever man is he is *of him*,[o] surely whatever he is he should be *to him*—as the waters which come out of the sea return thither again. And thus man was created, looking directly to God as his last end. But falling into sin, he fell off from God, and turned into himself. Now this infers a total apostasy and universal corruption in man. For where the last end is changed there can be no real goodness. And this is the case of all men in their natural state. They seek not God but themselves. Hence, though many fair shreds of morality are among them, yet 'there is none that doth good', no, not one. For though some of them *run well*, they are still *off the way*; they never aim at the right mark. Whithersoever they move, they cannot move beyond the circle of *self*. They seek *themselves*, they act for *themselves*; their natural, civil, and religious actions, from whatever spring they come, do all run into and meet in this dead sea.

Most men are so far from making God their end in their *natural* and *civil* actions that he 'is not in' all their thoughts. They eat and drink for no higher end than their own pleasure or necessity. Nor do the drops of sweetness God has put into the creatures raise their souls toward that ocean of delights that are in the Creator. And[p] what are the natural man's *civil* actions, such as buying, selling, working, but 'fruit to himself'? Yea, *self* is the highest end of unregenerate men, even in their *religious* actions. They perform duties for a name, for some worldly interest, or at best in order to escape from hell. They seek not God at all but for their own interest. So that God is only the means, and *self* their end.

Thus have I given a rude draught of man's will in his natural state, drawn from Scripture and our own experience. Now since all must be wrong where the understanding and will are so corrupt, I shall briefly dispatch what remains.[25]

[o] [p. 83.]
[p] [p. 84.]

[25] Wesley omits 'as following of course, on the corruption of these prime faculties of the soul'. Boston, *Fourfold State*, 84. He had become convinced that unholy affections corrupt reason as much as corrupt reason distorts the affections.

3. The *affections* are corrupted, wholly disordered and distempered. They are like an unruly horse, that either will not receive, or violently runs away with the rider. Man's heart is naturally a mother of abominations, 'for from within, out[q] of the heart of men, proceed evil thoughts, adulteries, fornications, murders, thefts, covetousness.' The natural man's affections are wholly misplaced. He is a *spiritual* monster. His *heart* is where his *feet* should be, fixed on earth. His heels are lifted up against heaven, which his heart should be set on. His face is toward hell, his back toward heaven. He *loves* what he should *hate*, and *hates* what he should *love*; *joys* in what he ought to *mourn* for, and *mourns* for what he should *rejoice* in; glories in his *shame*, and is *ashamed* of his glory; *abhors* what he should *desire*, and *desires* what he should *abhor*. If his affections are set on lawful objects, they are either *excessive* or *defective*. These objects have either too little of them or too much. But spiritual things have always too little.

Here is a threefold cord against heaven, not easily broken—a blind mind, a perverse will, disordered affections. The mind, swelled with pride, says the man *should not* stoop. The will, opposite to the will of God, says he *will not*. And the corrupt affections, rising against the Lord in defence of the corrupt will, say he *shall not*. And thus we stand out against God, till we are created anew by Christ Jesus.[26]

4. The conscience is corrupt and defiled. It cannot do its work but according to the light it hath to work by.[27] Wherefore, seeing 'the natural man discerneth not spiritual things', his conscience is[r] quite useless in that point. It may indeed check for grosser sins, but spiritual sins it discerns not. Thus it will fly in the face of many for drunkenness, who yet have a profound peace, though they live in *unbelief* and are utter strangers to *spiritual worship* and *the life of faith*. And the light[28] of his conscience being faint and languishing, even

[q] [p. 85.]
[r] [p. 86.]

---

[26] Boston reads: 'Thus the poor creature stands out against God and goodness; till a day of power come, in which he is made a new creation.' Ibid., 85. JW's revision avoids the possible equation of our entire renewal with the new birth.

[27] Boston reads: 'Being naturally unable to do its office til the Lord, by letting in a new light to the soul, awaken the conscience, it remains sleepy and inactive.' Ibid.

[28] Boston: 'natural light'. Ibid., 86. As JW stressed in a note added to the 2nd edn. of his *Survey of the Wisdom of God* (Bristol: Pine, 1770), 2:229, 'I believe all "the light of nature" so called, to flow from preventing grace.'

in the things which it does reach, its incitements to duty and struggles against sin are very remiss and easily got over. But there is also a false light in the dark mind, which often 'calls evil good, and good evil'.[29] And such a conscience is like a blind and furious horse, which violently runs down all that comes in his way. Indeed, whenever conscience is awakened by the spirit of conviction it will rage and roar, and put the whole man in a consternation. It makes the stiff heart to tremble and the knees to bow, sets the eyes a-weeping, the tongue a-confessing. But still it is an evil conscience, which naturally leads only to despair, and will do it effectually unless either sin prevails over it, to lull it asleep, as in the case of Felix, or the blood of Christ prevail over it, sprinkling and 'purging it from dead works'.

[C.] Thus[s] is man by nature wholly corrupted. But[t] whence came this total corruption of our nature? That man's nature was corrupt the very heathens perceived, but how 'sin entered' they could not tell. But the Scripture is very plain on the point. 'By one man sin entered into the world. By one man's disobedience many' (all) 'were made sinners.' Adam's sin corrupted man's nature, and leavened the whole lump of mankind. We putrified in Adam as our root. The root was poisoned, and so the branches were envenomed. The vine turned [into] 'the vine of Sodom', and so the grapes became 'grapes of gall'. Adam by his sin became not only *guilty* but *corrupt*, and so transmits guilt and corruption to his posterity. By his sin he stripped himself of his original righteousness and corrupted himself. We were in him *representatively*, as our moral head. We were in him seminally, as our natural head. Hence we fell 'in him' (as 'Levi paid tithes' when 'in the loins of Abraham'). 'By his disobedience' we 'were made sinners'. His first sin is imputed to us. And we are left without that original righteousness, which being given to him as a common person he cast off. And this is necessarily followed in him and us by the corruption of our whole nature, righteousness and corruption being two contraries, one of which must always be in man. And Adam our common father being corrupt, so are we, for 'who can bring a clean thing out of an unclean'?[30]

[s] [p. 87.]
[t] [p. 88.]

---

[29] Boston reads: 'But because there is a false light in the dark mind, and natural conscience following the same.' *Fourfold State*, 86. JW's addition of 'also' leaves room for the positive light of prevenient grace as well!

[30] JW omits a section arguing that if Adam had stayed obedient, we would have been saved by his obedience. Ibid., 88-90.

[D.] It[u] remains only to apply this doctrine. And first, [1.] for *information*. Is man's nature wholly corrupted? Then a. No wonder the grave opens its devouring mouth for us, as soon as the womb has cast us forth. For we are all in a spiritual sense dead-born, yea and *filthy* (Ps. 14:3), noisome, rank, and stinking, as a *corrupt* thing (so the word imports). Let us not complain of the *miseries* we are exposed to at our entrance or during our continuance in the world. Here is the venom that has poisoned all the springs of earthly enjoyments. It is the corruption of human nature, which brings forth all the miseries of life.

b. Behold here, as in a glass, the spring of all the *wickedness*, profaneness, and formality in the world. Everything acts agreeably to its own nature, and so corrupt man acts corruptly. You need not wonder at the sinfulness of your own heart and life, nor at the sinfulness and perverseness of others. If a man be crooked, he cannot but halt. And if the clock be set wrong, how can it point the hour right?

c. See here why sin is so *pleasant*, and religion such a *burden* to men. Sin is *natural*; holiness not so. Oxen cannot feed in the sea, nor fishes in the fruitful field. A swine brought into a palace would prefer the mire. And corrupt nature tends ever to impurity.

d. Learn from hence the nature and necessity of regeneration. First, the nature: it is not a *partial* but a *total* change.[31] Thy whole nature is corrupted. Therefore the whole must be renewed. 'All things' must 'become new.' If a man who had received many wounds were[v] cured of all but one, he might still bleed to death. It is not a change made by human industry, but by the Almighty Spirit of God. A man must be 'born of the Spirit'. Our nature is corrupt, and none but the God of nature can change it. Man may pin a new life to an old heart, but he can never change the heart. Secondly, the necessity: it is absolutely necessary in order to salvation. 'Except a man be born again, he cannot see the kingdom of God.' No unclean thing can enter the *new* Jerusalem, but thou art by nature wholly *unclean*. Deceive not thyself. No mercy of God, no blood of Christ, will bring an unregenerate sinner to heaven. For God will never open a fountain of mercy to wash away his own holiness and truth. Nor did Christ shed his precious blood to blot out the truths of God. Heaven!

[u] [p. 91.]
[v] [p. 92.]

[31] JW omits 'though imperfect in this life'. Ibid., 91.

What would you do there, who are not born again? An *holy* head, and *corrupt* members! An head full of treasures of grace, members filled with treasures of wickedness! Ye are noways adapted to the society above more than beasts to converse with men. Could[w] the unrenewed man go to heaven, he would go to it no otherwise than now he comes to the duties of holiness—that is, leaving his heart behind him.

[2.] We may apply this doctrine, secondly, for *lamentation*. Well may we lament thy case, O natural man, for it is the saddest case one can be in out of hell. It is time to lament for thee, for thou art dead already, dead while thou livest. Thou carriest about a dead soul in a living body, and because thou art dead, canst not lament thy own case. Thou 'hast no good in thee'. Thy soul is a mass of darkness, rebellion, and vileness before God. Thou 'canst do no good'. Thou canst do nothing but sin. For thou art 'the servant of sin', and therefore 'free from righteousness'. Thou dost not, canst not meddle with it. Thou art 'under the dominion of sin', a dominion where righteousness can have no place. Thou art a child and a servant of the devil as long as thou art in a state of nature. But to prevent any mistake, consider that Satan hath two kinds of servants. There are some employed, as it were, in coarser work. These bear the devil's mark in their *foreheads*, having no form of godliness, not so much as performing the external duties of religion, but living apparently as sons of earth, only minding earthly things. Whereas others are employed in more refined work, who carry his mark in their *right hand*, which they can and do hide by a form of religion from the view of the world. These sacrifice to the corrupt *mind*, as the other to *the flesh*. Pride, unbelief, self-pleasing, and the like spiritual sins, prey on their corrupted, wholly corrupted souls. Both are *servants* of the same house, equally void of righteousness.

Indeed,[x] how is it possible thou shouldst be able to do anything good, whose nature is wholly corrupt? 'Can an evil tree bring forth good fruit? Do men gather grapes of thorns?' If then thy nature be totally evil, all thou dost is certainly so too.

Hear, O sinner, what is thy case. Innumerable *sins* compass thee about. Floods of impurities overwhelm thee. Sins of all sorts roll up and down in the dead sea of thy soul, where no good can breathe because of the corruption there. Thy lips are unclean. The opening

[w] [p. 93.]
[x] [p. 94.]

of thy mouth is as the opening of a grave, full of stench and rottenness. Thy natural actions are sin, for 'when ye did eat, and when ye did drink, did not ye eat for yourselves and drink for yourselves'? (Zech. 7:6). Thy civil actions are sin—Prov. 21:4, 'The ploughing of the wicked is sin.' Thy religious actions are sin. 'The sacrifice of the wicked is an abomination to the Lord.' The thoughts and imaginations of thy heart are 'only evil continually'. A deed may be soon done, a word soon spoken, a thought pass; but each of these is an *item* in thy accounts. O sad reckoning! As many thoughts, words, actions, so many sins. And the longer thou livest, thy accounts swell the more. Should a tear be dropped for every sin, thine eyes must be 'fountains of tears', for nothing but sin comes from thee. Thy heart frames nothing but evil imaginations. There is nothing in thy life but what is framed by thy heart. Therefore there is nothing in thy heart or life but evil.

And all thy *religion*, if thou hast any, is lost labour, if thou art not born again. Truly then thy duties are sins.[32] Would not the best wine be loathsome in a foul vessel? So is the religion of an unregenerate man. Thy[y] duties cannot make thy corrupt soul holy, but thy corrupt heart makes them unclean. Thou wast wont to divide thy works into two sorts, to count some good and some *evil*. But thou must count again and put all under one head, for God writes on them all *only evil*.

And thou canst not help thyself. What canst thou do to take away thy sin, who art wholly corrupt? Will mud and filth wash out filthiness? And wilt thou purge out sin by sinning? Job took a potsherd to scrape himself, because his hands were as full of boils as his body. This is the case of thy corrupt soul, so long as thou art in a state of nature. Thou art *poor* indeed, extremely 'miserable and poor'. Thou hast no shelter but 'a refuge of lies', no garment for thy soul but 'filthy rags', nothing to nourish it but 'husks' that cannot satisfy. More than that, thou hast got such a bruise in the loins of Adam that thou art 'without strength', unable to *do* anything. Nay, more

[y] [p. 95.]

[32] Wesley came in later years to worry that this emphasis might discourage faithful seeking of regeneration; see the comment in the *Minutes* of the 1770 Conference that sparked debate with his Calvinist colleagues, 10:392–93 in this edn. When JW abridged the Anglican Articles of Religion to send to the Methodists in North America in 1784, he deleted Article XIII, which insisted that all works done before justification and regeneration have the nature of sin; see vol. 8 in this edn.

than all this, thou canst not so much as *seek* aright, but liest helpless as an infant exposed in the open field.

[3.] O that ye would believe this sad truth! How[z] little is it believed in the world! Few are concerned to have their evil lives reformed, but fewer far to have their evil nature changed. Most men know not what they are; as the eye, which, seeing many things, never sees itself. But until ye know every one 'the plague of his own heart', there is no hope of your recovery. Why will ye not believe the plain testimony of Scripture? Alas! That is the nature of your disease. 'Thou knowest not that thou art wretched, and miserable, and poor, and blind, and naked.' Lord, open their eyes, before they lift them up in hell, and see what they will not see now![33]

[4.] Meantime[a] let us have a special eye upon the corruption and sin of our nature. What avails it to take notice of other sins while this mother sin is unnoticed! This is a weighty point, in speaking to which I shall,

a. Point at some evidences of men's *overlooking* the sin of their nature. As 1) men's being so confident of themselves as if they were in no danger of *gross* sins. Many would take heinously such a caution as Christ gave his apostles, 'Take heed of surfeiting and drunkenness.' They would be ready to cry out, 'Am I a dog?' It would raise the pride of their heart, not their fear and trembling. And all this is a proof that they know not the corruption of their own nature. 2) Untenderness toward them that fall. Many in this case cast off all bowels of compassion, a plain proof that they do not know or 'consider themselves, lest they also be tempted'. Grace indeed does make men zealous against sin, in others as well as in themselves. But eyes turned inward to the corruption of nature clothe them with pity and compassion, and fill them with thankfulness that they were not the persons left to be such[b] spectacles of human frailty. 3) Men's venturing so boldly on temptation, in confidence of their coming off fairly. Were they sensible of the corruption of their nature, they would beware of entering on the devil's ground, as one girt about

[z] [p. 96.]
[a] [p. 97.]
[b] [p. 98.]

[33] JW omits the section (*Fourfold State*, 96-97) where Boston argues that children die because of their sinful nature, not actual sin; and that children of the elect will find God awakening them to their corruption when God is about to change their nature.

with bags of gunpowder would be loath to walk where sparks of fire were flying.

b. I[c] shall mention a few things in which ye should have a special eye to the sin of your nature. 1) In your application to Christ. When you are with the physician, O forget not this disease. They never yet knew their errand to Christ who went not to him for the sin of their nature, for his blood to take away the guilt and his spirit to break the power of it. Though ye should lay before him a catalogue of sins which might reach from earth to heaven, yet if you omit this you have forgot the best part of the errand a poor sinner has to the physician of souls. 2) Have a special eye to it in your repentance. If[d] you would repent indeed, let the streams lead you up to the fountain, and mourn over your corrupt nature as the cause of all sin, in heart, word, and work. 'Against thee, thee only have I sinned, and done this evil in thy sight. Behold I was shapen in iniquity, and in sin did my mother conceive me.' 3) Have a special eye to it in your mortification. 'Crucify the flesh with its affections and desires.' It is the root of bitterness which must be struck at, else we labour in vain. In vain do we go about to purge the streams, if we are at no pains about the muddy fountain. 4) Ye are to eye this in your daily walk. He that would walk uprightly must have one eye *upward* to Jesus Christ, another *inward* to the corruption of his own nature.

c. I shall offer some reasons why we should especially observe the sin of our nature.

1) Because of all sins it is the most *extensive* and *diffusive*. It goes through the whole man and spoils all. Other sins mar particular parts of the image of God, but this defaces the whole. It is the poison of the old serpent cast into the fountain, and so infects every action, every breathing of the soul.

2) It is the cause of all particular sins, both in our hearts and lives. 'Out of the heart of men proceed evil thoughts, adulteries', and all other abominations. It is the bitter fountain, and particular lusts are but rivulets running from it, which bring forth into the life a part only, not the whole of what is within.

3) It[e] is virtually *all* sins. For it is the seed of all, which want but the occasion to set up their heads. Hence it is called 'a body of death', as consisting of the several members which constitute that 'body of

[c] [p. 99.]
[d] [p. 100.]
[e] [p. 101.]

sins' (Col. 2:11) whose life lies in spiritual death. It is the cursed ground, fit to bring forth all manner of noxious weeds. Never did *every* sin appear in the conversation of the vilest wretch that ever lived. But look into thy nature, and thou mayst see *all* and *every* sin in the root thereof. There is a fullness of all unrighteousness there: atheism, idolatry, adultery, murder. Perhaps none of these *appear* to thee in thy heart, but there is more in that unfathomable depth of wickedness than thou knowest.

4) The sin of our nature is of all sins the most fixed and *abiding*.[34] Sinful actions are transient, though the guilt and strain of them may remain. But the corruption of nature passes not away. It remains in its full power, by night and by day, at all times, till nature is changed by converting grace.

You[f] may observe three things in the corrupt heart. a) There is the *corrupt nature*, the evil *bent* of the heart, whereby men are unapt for all good, and fitted for all evil. b) There are particular lusts or dispositions of that corrupt nature, such as pride, passion, covetousness. c) There is one of these stronger than all the rest, 'the sin which doth so easily beset us'. So that the river divides into many streams, whereof one is greater than the rest. The corruption of nature is the river-head, which has many particular lusts wherein it runs, but it mainly disburdens itself into that which we call the *predominant* sin. But as in some rivers the main stream runs not always in the same channel, so the besetting sin may change, as lust in youth may be succeeded by covetousness in old age. Now what does it avail to reform in other things while the reigning sin retains its full power? What if a particular sin be gone? If the sin of our nature keep the throne, it will set up another in its stead, as when a watercourse is stopped in one place it will break forth in another. Thus some cast off their prodigality, but covetousness comes in its stead. Some quit their profaneness, but the same stream runs in the other channel of self-righteousness.

[d.] That[g] you may have a full view of the sin of your nature, I would recommend to you three things. 1) Study to know the spirituality and extent of the law of God, for that is the glass wherein

[f] [p. 102.]
[g] [p. 103.]

[34] Wesley omits 'and the remains of it continue with the godly, until the death of the body'. Ibid., 101.

you may see yourselves. 2) Observe your hearts at all times, but especially under temptation. Temptation is a fire that brings up the scum of the unregenerate heart. 3) Go to God through Jesus Christ for illumination by his Spirit, saying unto him, 'What I know not, teach thou me.' And be willing to take in light from the Word. It is by the Word the Spirit teacheth. But unless he teach, all other teaching is to little purpose. You will never see yourself aright till he light his candle in your breast. Neither the fullness and glory of Christ, nor the corruption and vileness of our nature, ever were or can be rightly learned but where the spirit of Christ is the teacher.

[III.] To conclude: let the consideration of what has been said commend Christ to you all. Ye that are brought out of your natural state, be humble; still coming to Christ, still cleaving to him for the purging out what remains of your natural corruption. Ye that are yet in your natural state,[h] what will ye do? Ye must die. Ye must stand at the judgment seat of God. Will you lie down and sleep another night at ease in this case? See ye do it not. Before another day you may be set before his dreadful tribunal, in the *grave-clothes* of your corrupt state, and your vile souls cast into the pit of destruction, to be for ever buried out of God's sight. For I testify unto you, there is no peace with God, no pardon, no heaven for you in this state. There is but a step betwixt you and eternal destruction from the presence of the Lord. If the brittle thread of life, which may be broke with a touch, in a moment, or ever you are aware, be broken while you are in this state, you are ruined for ever, and without remedy. But come ye speedily to Jesus Christ. He hath cleansed as vile souls as yours. 'Confess your sins,' and he will both 'forgive your sins, and cleanse you from all unrighteousness'.[35]

Bristol, Aug. 17, 1757

[h] [p. 104.]

[35] Cf. 1 John 1:9—JW's closing addition.

APPENDIX

WESLEY'S TEXT: EDITIONS, TRANSMISSION, PRESENTATION, AND VARIANT READINGS

The introduction to Appendix A for the four volumes of *Sermons* (4:421-30) provides a detailed description of Wesley's publishing practices, the challenges these practices present for preparing a critical edition of his *Works*, and the guidelines adopted in this edition for selecting and presenting the main copy-text. As a general summary, the text of each of the treatises in this volume is that of the first edition, but incorporates as well all substantive revisions that certainly or almost certainly derive from Wesley.

The purpose of this appendix is to indicate the textual history of each treatise and provide a guide to textual variants among editions. Brief details are given for every edition of a treatise published during Wesley's life, including his collected *Works* of 1771–74. The relationship among these editions is then indicated graphically in a stemma. Finally, there is a list of variant readings with designation of the edition within which they appear. If the edition designation is followed by an arrow (e.g., B→), the variant reading listed occurs in that edition and in all editions connected from it downward in the stemma. If there is no arrow, the variant occurs only in the edition(s) listed. Using this list, it is possible to determine the substantive textual content of every edition (within the parameters of the guidelines used in this edition for handling abbreviations and the like; see 4:428-29).

Key to abbreviations:
e = errata in printed copy
m = Wesley's manuscript insertions in his personal printed copy
p = printer's proof for printed copy

The Doctrine of Salvation, Faith, and Good Works

A	Oxford: [s.n.], 1738	
B	London: [W. Strahan] for Hutton, 1739	
C	3rd	London: W. Strahan, 1740
D	4th	London: W. Strahan, 1741
E	5th	Bristol: F. Farley, 1742
F	6th	London: W. Strahan, 1744
G	[7th]	[Newcastle: J. Gooding, 1743; none extant]
H	8th	Newcastle: J. Gooding 17[46?]
I	9th	Dublin: S. Powell, 1747
J	9th	Bristol: S. & F. Farley, 1748
K	10th	Bristol: S. & F. Farley, 1748
L	10th	Cork: G. Harrison, n.d. [1750?]
M	9th	Newcastle: J. Gooding, 1749
N	10th	Limerick: A. Welsh, 1749
O	3rd	London: Foundery, 1755
P	11th	Bristol: W. Pine, 1762
Q	12th	Bristol: W. Pine, 1767
R	11th	Bristol: W. Pine, 1770
S	13th	Bristol: W. Pine, 1770
T	*Works*, 9:37-53, Bristol: W. Pine, 1772	
U	12th	London: R. Hawes, 1780

(For fuller details see *Bibliography*, No. 11.)

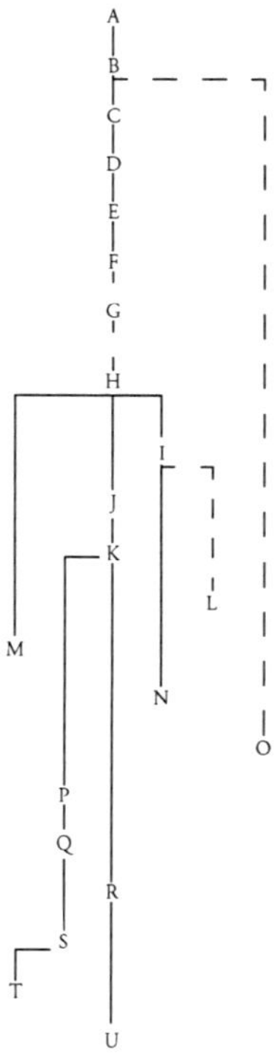

Variants

page	*line*	
33	2-3	T omits ‘or righteousness’.
	13-14	T omits ‘who . . . perfectly’.
	14	T omits ‘embraced’.
	15	E→ omit ‘and’.

34	4-5	T omits 'with fulfilling . . . throughly'.
34-35	29ff	T omits 'He for them paid . . . has supplied.'
37	24	T omits 'in outward profession'.
39	1-2	T omits 'of whom . . . benefit'.
	3-5	T omits 'For he . . . God's hand.'
	13-14	C→ omit 'called by St. Paul "the full assurance of faith" '.
40	24-26	T omits 'and that freely . . . reward'.
41	10	T omits 'for his own sake'.
42	25	T changes 'be naked, without' to 'be but naked, without'; then in T*e* calls to delete 'but naked', with resulting reading 'be without'.

An Extract of . . . Baxter's 'Aphorisms of Justification'

A		Newcastle: J. Gooding, 1745
B	2nd	London: W. Strahan, 1745
C	*Works*, 22:141-94, Bristol: W. Pine, 1773	
D	3rd	London: J. Paramore, 1784

(For fuller details see *Bibliography*, No. 99.)

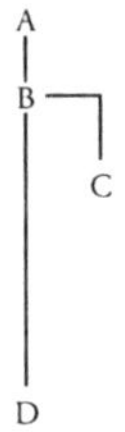

Variants

page	*line*	
56	8-9	C omits 'when it never . . . or desire it'.
57	17-18	C omits 'the doctrine of Scripture, much less with the phrase of'.
58	28	C omits 'to his violated law'.
	32	C replaces 'expressed in' with 'of'.
59	30	C changes 'manifest' to 'manifested'.

	36	C replaces 'a thousand places more' with 'in a thousand places'.
59-60	49ff	C omits these first two sentences of this paragraph.
60	13-14	C omits 'and of our corruption the case is plain'.
61	7-8	C omits 'or in reference . . . will bestow'.
	10	C changes 'they are' to 'they art'.
	22	C omits 'I know'.
	23	C omits 'null and'.
	24	C omits 'do'.
	26-27	C replaces 'which you find under the following position' with 'follow'.
	29	C changes 'as though' to 'as if'.
	34-35	C replaces 'the value and efficacy of his one offering and merits' with 'his works'.
62	1	C omits 'to you in what sense and'.
	25	C omits 'procured and'.
63	8	C omits 'or due to us'.
	13	C replaces 'any sin but the first' with 'sin'.
	14-16	C omits this last sentence.
	26-29	C omits these two sentences.
	34	C omits 'will'.
64	7	C omits the page references.
	9-14	C replaces 'a repealed law' with 'it', and omits the remainder of this paragraph.
	19	C replaces 'to the law' with 'for us'.
	22	C omits 'and glory'.
65	28	C changes 'offered' to 'offered it'.
66	12	C changes 'should have' to 'would have'.
	22	C omits 'to little purpose'.
67	6-8	C omits 'which, though . . . to Christ'.
	9-10	C omits this sentence.
	11	C changes 'another's' to 'another'.
	11	C omits 'so'.
	11-12	C omits 'we did not really'.
	21	C changes 'disobedience' to 'obedience' (likely a printer's mistake).
	32	C omits 'qualifications of our own persons or'.
	33	C omits 'fulfilled, nor'.
68	23-24	B→ change 'imperfect' to 'perfect'.
69	9	C replaces 'must needs be' with 'is'.

	14-15	C omits 'and as every . . . unsufferable.'
69-70	40ff	C deletes from 'What unsavoury' to end of paragraph.
71	7	C changes 'This rule, when' to 'When this rule'.
	18-19	C omits parenthetical remark.
	19-20	C omits 'or in anything he can do thereto, they'.
	31-32	C omits parenthetical remark.
72	24	C omits 'and'.
73	3	C changes 'It is an improper speech of some divines' to 'It is improper to say'.
	3	C changes 'justifieth' to 'justified'.
	10	C omits parenthetical remark.
	13	C changes 'seem' to 'seems'.
	14	C changes 'tend' to 'tends'.
	14-15	C replaces 'if it be understood in the worst sense, it will overthrow' with 'it overthrows'.
	16	C replaces 'will set' with 'sets'.
	17	C omits 'do'.
73	16	C omits 'then'.
	24-25	C omits 'or any benefit that God receiveth by it'.
74	10	C replaces 'have chosen to accept' with 'accept or not'.
	10	C omits 'yet'.
	21-31	C omits Proposition XXV, renumbers the next four, then skips the number XXIX so that numbering agrees again from XXX on. This omission was surely a printer's error.
75	1-2	C replaces 'unjust and unjustified, for all their conditional justification in Christ' with 'unjustified'.
	38	C omits 'and so having . . . here'.
	40	C changes footnote to read 'Baxter then held'.
76	8	C omits 'that this'.
	11-16	C deletes from 'The best' to end of paragraph.
	39	C changes 'Before it' to 'Before sin'.
	40	C omits 'properly'.
77	33	C replaces 'that he should, in' with 'had in'.
78	1	C omits 'have'.
	36	C omits 'and to will their absolution'.
	37	C omits 'of our divines'.
	39	C omits 'and pardoned'.
79	1	C omits 'pardon and'.

80	1-2	C omits Latin phrase.
	2	C omits 'and not as it is divided'.
	12	C omits 'or necessary . . . consequents'.
	29	C omits 'and so an essential part of it'.
	34-35	C omits 'for the attaining of its ends'.
	36	C omits 'painful'.
85	5-6	C omits 'which can be . . . justification'.
87	9	C changes 'easiness' to 'business' (likely a printer's mistake).

'An Extract of the Westminster Assembly's *Shorter Catechism*'

[There is no stemma or list of variants because the extract was never reprinted during Wesley's life after appearing in *Christian Library*, 31:109-50.]

The Doctrine of Original Sin

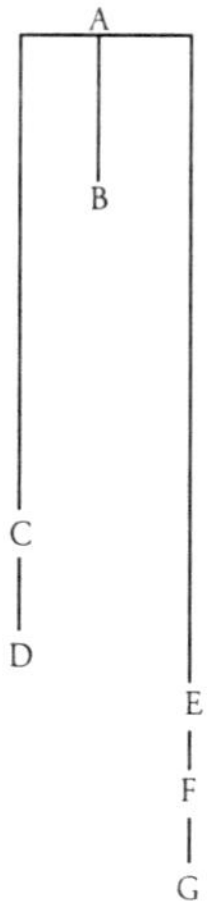

A*p* [Printer's proof for Parts I–II; held at Southern Methodist University]
A Bristol: Farley, 1757
B Works, 21, Bristol: W. Pine, 1773

Dignity of Human Nature
(separate reprint of Part I; *Bibliography*, No. 222.i)
C [n.p.: s.n.,] 1762
D London: J. Paramore, 1786

Doctrine of Original Sin
(separate reprint of Part VII [Boston]; *Bibliography*, No. 222.ii)
E London: J. Paramore, 1784
F Dublin: [s.n.], 1784
G London: Story for Whitfield, 1785
(For fuller details see *Bibliography*, No. 222.)

Variants

page	*line*	
156	7	B changes 'Mr. Taylor' to 'Dr. Taylor' here and throughout.
159	1	A: 'air of disdain'; corrected to 'disdain' in A*p*, A*e*, and B.
	6	A*p* inserts 'to', overlooked by printer.
160	5-8	C and D omit preface and revise first three sentences of this opening to read: 'In order to place this point in the clearest light, to the satisfaction of all impartial men, we have only to inquire . . .'.
	23	B omits 'only'.
169	30	A: 'the favourite'; corrected to 'this favourite' in A*p*, A*e*, B, C, D.
172	34	A: 'amiable men'; changed to 'amiable of men' in A*e* and B*m*.
176	18	A: 'after pray to'; changed to 'after prayed to' in B.
177	22	C→ change 'just' to 'justly'.
183	8-9	B*e* added closing phrase 'for calculating eclipses'; C→ add instead 'for foretelling eclipses'.
190	16	B changes 'we who are' to 'we are'.
	17	B changes 'We who' to 'We have'.
196	20	B adds note: 'By a late Act of Parliament there is an happy alteration made in this particular.'
208	33-34	B changes 'Roman heathen, tell the English heathens' to 'A Roman heathen tells the English heathen'.
209	19	B changes 'accounted not' to 'not accounted'.
211	11	C and D add closing sentence: 'Such (if we can believe our eyes, ears, or experience) is the present *dignity of human nature!*'
213	7	A reads 'your vice'; corrected to 'their vice' in A*p* (in Charles Wesley's hand), A*e*, and B.
269	13	A reads '18. "So as we . . ." '; corrected in A*p* (by Charles Wesley), and in B.

271	9	A misnumbers as '19'; corrected in A*p* (by Charles Wesley), and in B.
280	23	B adds at end of paragraph: 'I think we cannot deny it'.
309	28	B omits 'See B[axter]'s *Aph*[*orisms*]'.
402	1	B added designation as 'Part V'; only title appears in A.
424	1	B added 'Part VI', designating separately this longest Hebden extract.
448	1	B added designation as 'Part VII'; only title appears in A.
448	5-8	E, F, and G omit opening paragraph.
452	1-4	A and B read: 'Their beautiful bodies were', together with 'They were liable', 'And though they were . . . were not'—following Boston's original (p. 14) but omitting Boston's prior sentence about Adam and Eve, 'the happy pair'. E, F, and G correct to reflect singular subject.
462	36ff	B omits 'And so you cannot have the *assurance of faith*, even with respect to the outward revelation.'

CPSIA information can be obtained at www.ICGtesting.com
Printed in the USA
LVOW121351100912

298132LV00002B/3/P

9 781426 744303

DATE DUE
